SELF-
DECEPTION

An
Adaptive
Mechanism?

Joan S. Lockard
UNIVERSITY OF WASHINGTON

and

Delroy L. Paulhus
UNIVERSITY OF BRITISH COLUMBIA

Editors

PRENTICE HALL, Englewood Cliffs, New Jersey 07632

✓ 155.2
Se48l

Library of Congress Cataloging-in-Publication Data

Self-deception : an adaptive mechanism?
  (Century psychology series)
  Includes index.
  1. Self-deception.   2. Adaptability (Psychology)
I. Lockard, Joan S.   II. Paulhus, Delroy L., 1950–
III. Series: Century psychology series (Englewood Cliffs, N.J.)
BF697.5.S426S45   1988   155.2   88-4053
ISBN 0-13-803172-X

Editorial/production supervision and
  interior design: *Carole Brown*
Manufacturing buyer: *Raymond Keating*

century psychology series
James J. Jenkins
Walter Mischel
editors

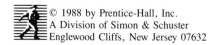
Quotation on page 9: Quirt, J. (1977, November 21). Taking the risk out of gambling. *Time*, p. 78.
Copyright 1977 Time Inc. All rights reserved. Reprinted by permission from TIME.

Quotation on page 189 taken from wire services report, October 8, 1987. Reprinted by permission of the
Associated Press.

Printed in the United States of America

10 9 8 7 6 5 4 3 2 1

ISBN 0-13-803172-X   01

Prentice-Hall International (UK) Limited, *London*
Prentice-Hall of Australia Pty. Limited, *Sydney*
Prentice-Hall Canada Inc., *Toronto*
Prentice-Hall Hispanoamericana, S.A., *Mexico*
Prentice-Hall of India Private Limited, *New Delhi*
Prentice-Hall of Japan, Inc., *Tokyo*
Simon & Schuster Asia Pte. Ltd., *Singapore*
Editora Prentice-Hall do Brasil, Ltda., *Rio de Janeiro*

CONTENTS

Susan M. Essock, Michael T. McGuire, and Barbara Hooper

FOREWORD

This is a very welcome book, both for the importance of the subject it treats as well as for the broad view it brings to the subject. Self-deception, loosely understood, is a tendency in ourselves to store contradictory information, with the true facts more often in the unconscious, leaving the conscious mind deceived. From observations of everyday life, there can be no doubt that self-deception, so understood, is a common feature of human mental life. But if this is true, a whole host of questions immediately arises. Is this a uniquely human trait, or do other creatures practice self-deception? In either case, what is the *function* of self-deception? In other words, did it evolve, and if so, what benefit does it give, and under what circumstances? Finally, according to what laws does it operate? What are the specific mechanisms by which we achieve the state of self-deception?

Biologists propose that the overriding function of self-deception is the more fluid deception of *others*. That is, hiding aspects of reality from the conscious mind also hides these aspects more deeply from others. An *unconscious* deceiver is not expected to show signs of the stress associated with consciously attempting to perpetrate deception. On the other hand, self-deception is an inherently dangerous game because the organism limits and distorts the information upon which conscious choices are based. The benefits of greater success at fooling others must be balanced by the costs of decreasing contact with reality.

At the same time, psychologists have recently made notable advances in the study of the mechanisms of self-deception. A brilliant experiment with voice recognition showed that a person's tendency to deny his or her own voice or to accept it can be manipulated by the experimenter. In addition, a wealth of studies in social psychology have demonstrated the ubiquity and variety of self-deception.

This book seeks to capture the emerging synthesis regarding self-deception, in the process treating the reader to a rich fare of facts and theories. Topics addressed include the evolutionary logic of self-deception, amnesias of various kinds, hypnosis and multiple personalities, the seductions of gambling, the growing competence of children in detecting deception, forms of self-deception during arousal, societal effects, "between point" behavior in tennis players, our inflated self-image as altruists, the dangers of deceiving down, and micromovements in the face as clues to deception.

Inevitably, some sections of this book are difficult. Self-deception as a concept is multifaceted, partly because it encompasses such a variety of phenomena and partly because we are, by definition, not very conscious of it in ourselves. Here the numerous introductions and summaries throughout the book are especially helpful, permitting a clear overview of the subject. There is, for example, quite some controversy over the actual internal mechanisms of self-deception (how it works) with competing alternatives being championed (as one would expect in a self-deceiving species) beyond their natural boundaries. But with his summary, Harold Sackeim puts us firmly back in touch with reality, often by showing that a more modest formulation of earlier conjectures greatly improves their chances of being correct.

Another welcome feature of this book is its attention to self-deception in everyday life. After all, ultimately the study of self-deception begins at home—as the scriptures say, only when the beam is removed from our own eye can we see the mote in our neighbor's. In one of my favorite examples, I wish to go from A to C, but cannot justify the expense in time and effort, given the self-indulgent purpose of the trip. Instead, I conjure up a reason to travel to B, three-quarters of the way to C. Hence, C is reached on a wave of self-deception. Moral: Our internal account of motivation is suspect; it may be produced for external consumption by others. How often we hear a defense of misbehavior consist of an account of what was being thought during the misbehavior but in all likelihood merely reflect a description of one's own system of self-deception.

One novel feature of this book deserves a comment. Self-deception is often treated in a favorable light. It may avert depression, it may help motivate positive action, and so on. Only rarely in this book does the ugly underbelly of the beast reveal itself. Barbara Tuchman has written an engrossing book of history entitled *The March of Folly.* It is a story of self-deception and its disastrous consequences on statecraft and warfare from the Greeks to the Vietnam War and is concerned with the reasoning of those who have condemned millions to die in foolish wars. "Woodenheadedness" is her term; self-deception is the language of this volume.* Or take another example: A colleague and I were very much struck by the cockpit conversation during takeoff and crash of Air Florida's Flight 90 in 1982, thinking we detected a clear pattern of self-deception and denial in the pilot and insufficient strength in the face of this by the copilot. Subsequent analysis of the thirty minutes of cockpit communication prior to the crash supported our thesis: The crash appeared partly to be caused by a pattern of self-deception in the pilot which allowed him to minimize and deny the many signs of danger around him.†

Reading the newspapers today must make us all wonder if self-deception will not be the death of us yet. Since the late 1950s, for example, the United States has detected a series of ominous Soviet military build-ups necessitating massive responses by the United States. Subsequent analysis invariably seems to reveal that the danger was greatly overrated and that the causation may often go in the other direction, the Soviets belatedly attempting to match massive United States military might. The extension of weaponry into space is justified on purely defensive grounds while it inevitably poses a serious offensive threat to others. Is it possible that we will eventually incinerate ourselves in a final paean to woodenheadedness? Let us hope not, and let us hope that this volume, in its own modest way, contributes to solving some of our problems by showing that processes of self-deception

---

*Tuchman, B. W. (1984). *The march of folly: From Troy to Vietnam.* New York: Alfred A. Knopf.

†Trivers, R., and Newton, H. P. (1982, November). The crash of Flight 90: Doomed by self-deception? *Science Digest*, pp. 66-67, 111.

can be defined and studied objectively, eventually to be understood as products of natural selection, the same process which has molded our abilities to comprehend reality objectively. Self-deception, in my opinion, all too often offers us a quick internal fix for our problems, while the problems themselves, left unattended, grow by the moment. At the same time, if the biological view is correct, then to minimize the costs of our self-deception we need to pay much more attention to our eagerness to lie to others.

Robert Trivers
University of California at Santa Cruz

The thoughts and writings of many colleagues have been instrumental in the completion of this volume. The late Daniel Krakauer is particularly remembered for the impact his ideas had on the initial chapters of the book. Great appreciation is also extended to Barbara Kirkevold, student and friend, for the numerous hours of proofreading she endured.

J. S. L.

Of the many colleagues who helped me with this book, none was more insightful than my student Gordon Murphy, who died tragically on April 2, 1988.

D. L. P.

GENERAL INTRODUCTION

The escape from the distress of seeing ourselves as we really are may in fact be a chronic need, since most of us live in societies in which we may well be wrong but cannot afford to know we are wrong. We certainly cannot afford to attend closely to the devices by which socially defined wrongness and rightness contend within us. (Murphy, 1975, p. 52)

The notion that people can lie to themselves is intuitively compelling—we can all bring to mind some instance in which we or someone we know appeared to perpetrate a self-deception. Allusions to the concept or its variants go at least as far back as Socrates in the third century B.C. (Hamilton & Cairns, 1971). Moreover, most extant societies have a comparable concept (Geertz, 1983). Nonetheless, many observers remain skeptical that such a phenomenon actually has a basis in reality (e.g., Haight, 1980; Elster, 1983; Gergen, 1985).

The skeptics notwithstanding, interest in the notion of self-deception has surged in recent years. This interest may be traced to a few seminal works. In philosophy, early commentaries by Sartre (1943), Demos (1960), Siegler (1962), Canfield and Gustafson (1962), and Penelhum (1966) led up to the first full-fledged treatise by Herbert Fingarette (1969). In sociobiology, a commentary by Trivers (1976) was followed quickly by more thorough treatments by Lockard (1978; 1980) and Alexander (1979). In psychology, earlier empirical work by Frenkel-Brunswik (1939) and Murphy (1970) preceded the first rigorous experiment by Gur and Sackeim (1979). Even a behaviorist account was soon available (Day, 1977).

The early 1980s saw a confirmation of this interest in the concept of self-deception with the convening of two symposia that focused, for the first time, on self-deception and its amenability to empirical analysis (Lockard, 1982; Paulhus, 1984a). Increasing belief in the scientific merit of this enterprise is evidenced by the recent spate of empirical reports on the subject (e.g., Monts, Zurcher, & Nydegger,

1

1977; Sackeim & Gur, 1978, 1979; Gur & Sackeim, 1979; Quattrone & Tversky, 1984; Paulhus, 1984b; Jamner & Schwartz, 1987; Tesser & Moore, 1987). Finally, books with "self-deception" in the title have begun to appear (Murphy, 1975; Haight, 1980; Martin, 1985, 1986; Goleman, 1986; Mele, 1987; Sloan, 1987).

The burgeoning interest in self-deception has emerged in human ethology, personality assessment, social psychology, clinical psychology, and psychiatry. The consensus emerging in all these areas is that self-deception is a normal (if not inevitable) process. This consensus seems to be part of a general zeitgeist favoring the view that human rationality is bounded (Elster, 1979; Greenwald, 1980; Nisbett & Ross, 1980; Kahneman, Slovic, & Tversky, 1982; Simon, 1986).

In human ethology, for example, the view that accurate information processing always benefits the organism is yielding to the view that limited awareness is adaptive (Lockard, 1978). Moreover, the evidence for self-deception in lower organisms implies an evolutionary basis for human self-deception (Alexander, 1979; Lockard, 1980; Campbell, 1983; Trivers, 1985). In social psychology, the rational man assumed by attribution theory has been disputed by evidence for motivated biases and distortions (e.g., Miller, 1976), including self-deception (Gur & Sackeim, 1979). In personality assessment, one component of socially desirable responding has been interpreted as a self-deceptive positivity (e.g., Weinberger, Schwartz, & Davidson, 1979; Paulhus, 1984b, 1986). Finally, in clinical psychology and psychiatry, the so-called rational therapies are under fire from evidence that depressed individuals are often more realistic than normal, well-adjusted individuals (e.g., Alloy & Abramson, 1979; Mischel, 1979). The positivistic distortion in normal individuals has been attributed to a self-deceptive bias (Sackeim & Gur, 1979; Sarbin, 1981; Sackeim & Wegner, 1986).

Given this zeitgeist, we feel that the time is propitious for an edited volume to present the major statements on self-deception in a thematic fashion. The format of the book represents the different intellectual roots of the two editors. Lockard, an animal behaviorist, was provoked by the sociobiological arguments of Robert Trivers. Paulhus, with a background in social cognition and personality, was most influenced by the information-processing implications of Sackeim and Gur's work. Accordingly, the first section presents biological and natural-history perspectives on self-deceit, discussing its origins, neural mechanisms, ontogeny, and exploitation by society. The second section presents specific psychological theories of self-deceit, including psychoanalytic, information-processing, and role-playing accounts. The third section provides behavioral and applied examples of self-deception as it is manifested in situations of subordination, gambling, social networks, sports, and the protection of lies.

The chapters within each of the three sections deal with self-deception at a common level of analysis. Accordingly, each section is previewed by its own introduction. Nevertheless, the three sections of the book all address the unifying theme—that self-deception is a normal and generally positive force in human behavior. For example, the chapters in the first section elucidate the selective advantage of self-deception in perpetuating the genetic structure of the organism and how experience and society direct the content of the self-deception. One theme here is that the ability to self-deceive contributes to an individual's ability to deceive others. More generally, the lack of awareness of one's motives may preclude their interfering with self-preserving behaviors. Chapters in the second section detail various ways in which self-deceptive biases may contribute to the psychological health, stability, and performance of the perpetrator. The last section provides analyses of specific behaviors, revealing the pervasiveness of, and the benefits conferred by, a certain degree of self-deception.

REFERENCES

ALEXANDER, R. D. (1979). *Darwinism and human affairs.* Seattle, WA: University of Washington Press.

ALLOY, L. B., & ABRAMSON, L. Y. (1979). Judgment of contingency in depressed and nondepressed students: Sadder but wiser? *Journal of Experimental Psychology: General, 108,* 441-485.

CAMPBELL, D. T. (1983). The two distinct routes beyond kin selection to ultrasociality: Implications for the humanities and social sciences. In D. Bridgeman (Ed.), *The nature of prosocial development: Theories and strategies.* New York: Academic Press.

CANFIELD, J. V., & GUSTAFSON, D. F. (1962). Self-deception. *Analysis, 23,* 32-36.

DAY, W. (1977). On the behavioral analysis of self-deception and self-development. In T. Mischel (Ed.), *The self: Philosophical and psychological issues* (pp. 224-229). Oxford: Basil Blackwell.

DEMOS, R. (1960). Lying to oneself. *Journal of Philosophy, 57,* 588-595.

LSTER, J. (1979). *Ulysses and the sirens.* New York: Cambridge University Press.

————. (1983). *Sour grapes.* New York: Cambridge University Press.

FINGARETTE, H. (1969). *Self-deception.* New York: Humanities Press.

FRENKEL-BRUNSWIK, E. (1939). Mechanisms of self-deception. *Journal of Social Psychology, 10,* 409-420.

GEERTZ, C. (1983). *Local knowledge.* New York: Basic Books.

GERGEN, K. J. (1985). The ethnopsychology of self-deception. In M. W. Martin (Ed.), *Self-deception and self-understanding* (pp. 228-243). Lawrence, KS: University Press of Kansas.

GOLEMAN, D. (1986). *Vital lies, simple truths: The psychology of self-deception.* New York: Simon & Schuster.

GREENWALD, A. G. (1980). The totalitarian ego: Fabrication and revision of personal history. *American Psychologist, 35,* 603-618.

GUR, R. C., & SACKEIM, H. A. (1979). Self-deception: A concept in search of a phenomenon. *Journal of Personality and Social Psychology, 37,* 147-169.

HAIGHT, M. R. (1980). *A study of self-deception.* Atlantic Highlands, NJ: Humanities Press.

HAMILTON, E., & CAIRNS, H. (Eds.). (1971). *The collected dialogues of Plato.* Princeton, NJ: Princeton University Press.

JAMNER, L. D., & SCHWARTZ, G. E. (1987). Self-deception predicts self-report and endurance of pain. *Psychosomatic Medicine, 48,* 211-223.

KAHNEMAN, D., SLOVIC, P., & TVERSKY, A. (Eds.). (1982). *Judgment under uncertainty: Heuristics and biases.* Cambridge: Cambridge University Press.

LOCKARD, J. S.   (1978). On the adaptive significance of self-deception. *Human Ethology Newsletter, 21,* 4-7.

―――.   (1980). Speculations on the adaptive significance of self-deception. In J. S. Lockard (Ed.), *The evolution of human social behavior* (pp. 257-276). New York: Elsevier.

―――.   (1982, August). Chair of symposium, *Self-deception.* Congress of the International Primatological Society, Atlanta.

MARTIN, M. W.,   (Ed.).   (1985). *Self-deception and self-understanding.* Lawrence, KS: University Press of Kansas.

―――.   (1986). *Self-deception and morality.* Lawrence, KS: University Press of Kansas.

MELE, A. R.   (1987). *Irrationality: An essay on acrasia, self-deception, and self-control.* Oxford: Oxford University Press.

MILLER, D. T.   (1976). Ego involvement and attributions for success and failure. *Journal of Personality and Social Psychology, 34,* 901-906.

MISCHEL, W.   (1979). On the interface of cognition and personality: Beyond the person-situation debate. *American Psychologist, 34,* 740-754.

MONTS, J. K., ZURCHER, L. A., & NYDEGGER, R. V.   (1977). Interpersonal self-deception and personality correlates. *The Journal of Social Psychology, 103,* 91–99.

MURPHY, G.   (1970). Experiments in overcoming self-deception. *Psychophysiology, 6,* 790-799.

―――.   (1975). *Outgrowing self-deception.* New York: Basic Books.

NISBETT, R. E., & ROSS, L.   (1980). *Human inference: Strategies and shortcomings of social judgment.* Englewood Cliffs, NJ: Prentice-Hall.

PAULHUS, D. L.   (1984a, August). Chair of symposium, *Self-deception.* American Psychological Association, Washington, DC.

―――.   (1984b). Two component models of socially desirable responding. *Journal of Personality and Social Psychology, 46,* 598-609.

―――.   (1986). Self-deception and impression management in test responses. In A. Angleitner & J. S. Wiggins (Eds.), *Personality assessment via questionnaire* (pp. 143-165). New York: Springer-Verlag.

PENELHUM, T.   (1966). Pleasure and falsity. In S. Hampshire (Ed.), *Philosophy of mind* (pp. 242-266). New York: Harper & Row.

QUATTRONE, G. A., & TVERSKY, A.   (1984). Causal versus diagnostic contingencies: On self-deception and the voter's illusion. *Journal of Personality and Social Psychology, 46,* 236-248.

SACKEIM, H. A., & GUR, R.   (1978). Self-deception, self-confrontation, and consciousness. In G. E. Schwartz & D. Shapiro (Eds.), *Consciousness and self-regulation: Advances in research* (Vol. 2, pp. 139-197). New York: Plenum.

―――.   (1979). Self-deception, other-deception, and self-reported psychopathology. *Journal of Consulting and Clinical Psychology, 47,* 213-215.

SACKEIM, H. A., & WEGNER, A. Z. (1986). Attributional patterns in depression and euthymia. *Archives of General Psychiatry, 43,* 553-560.

SARBIN, T. R. (1981). On self-deception. *Annals of the New York Academy of Sciences, 364,* 206-235.

SARTRE, J-P. (1956). *Being and nothingness* (H. Barnes, Trans.). New York: Washington Square Press. (Original work published 1943).

SIEGLER, F. A. (1962). Demos on lying to oneself. *Journal of Philosophy, 59,* 469-475.

SIMON, H. A. (1986). Alternative visions of rationality. In H. R. Arkes & K. R. Hammond (Eds.), *Judgment and decision making: An interdisciplinary reader* (pp. 97–113). New York: Cambridge University Press.

SLOAN, T. S. (1987). *Deciding: Self-deception in life choices.* London: Methuen.

TESSER, A., & MOORE, J. (1987). *The functioning of ambivalent self-beliefs.* Unpublished manuscript, University of Georgia.

TRIVERS, R. L. (1976). In R. Dawkins, *The selfish gene* (Foreword). New York and Oxford: Oxford University Press.

––––––. (1985). *Social evolution.* Menlo Park, CA: Benjamin/Cummings.

WEINBERGER, D. A., SCHWARTZ, G. E., & DAVIDSON, R. J. (1979). Low anxious, high anxious, and repressive coping styles: Psychometric patterns and behavioral and physiological responses to stress. *Journal of Abnormal Psychology, 88,* 369-380.

EVOLUTION,

ONTOGENY,

AND SOCIETY

As for you, let me advise you to care little about Socrates, far more about the truth; if you think I utter truth, agree with me; if not, assail my argument at every point. Watch out that in my eagerness I do not, with my self-deceit, deceive you also, and, like a honeybee, go off and leave my sting implanted in you!
Plato (translated by Cooper, 1941, p. 157)

One of the more salient biological inquiries of this decade is whether humans are unique among species in possessing self-knowledge, in being aware of their own existence, and in using such detachment to some survival advantage. Simultaneously, a related and even more difficult question to answer has surfaced regarding whether it is adaptive for humans, and possibly other social species (Lockard, 1978a), to ever deny self-knowledge (i.e., to self-deceive) and, if so, under what conditions and by what mechanisms.

This section on the adaptive significance of self-deception had its conceptual origins in an early preface by Trivers (1976; and more recently in greater detail: Trivers, 1985), in the writings of Alexander (1979), and in four speculative papers on self-deception by Lockard (1978b, 1980, 1982, 1984). These sociobiologists have regarded self-deception, at least in part, as a logical extension of the deception model in animal behavior (e.g., Wallace, 1973; Otte, 1975; Mitchell & Thompson, 1986). In their view, one major distinction between deception and self-deception, as the terms imply, is the matter of whether the masquerade is perpetrated by another or by oneself. Therefore, some understanding of the economics (risks versus returns) of deception in humans may, by analogy, illuminate some of the motivation involved in self-deception.

Lockard, Kirkevold, and Kalk (1980) conducted an analysis of the frequency of arrests in the United States (Department of Justice, 1978) for nonviolent crimes of interpersonal deception compared with those of stolen property. Several findings were revealed that were compatible with the hypothesis that deceit may be economically advantageous. In other words, interpersonal deception has allowed, with relatively low risk, the garnishing of unearned monetary resources that could be used to make one's own life, as well as the lives of family members, easier. Whereas there were several interesting differences among the categories of interpersonal deception such as fraud, embezzlement, and forgery-counterfeiting, their cost-to-benefit indexes were all considerably less than that for stolen property.

The following summarizes the salient information emerging from the analysis: (1) The rate of arrests for fraud far exceeded that for stolen property; (2) whereas crimes of stolen property were primarily committed by teenagers and young adults, crimes of deception (particularly fraud) peaked between 20 and 30 years of age but were also relatively frequent up to the age of 60 years; (3) fraud was prevalent in areas of both high (urban) and low (rural) population, whereas crimes of stolen property, embezzlement, and forgery-counterfeiting were restricted primarily to urban and suburban areas; (4) female offenders were relatively frequent in crimes of deception and far less involved than males in crimes of stolen property; (5) in cases of fraud there was a low risk of indictment, minimal penalty, and a relatively high potential gain; (6) even though the risk involved with embezzlement was considerably higher, so were the potential gains, but in the case of stolen property the likely benefit was far exceeded by the relatively high risk and greater punishment.

What these data suggest is that fraud may be committed by both men and women at almost any adult age, but particularly during maximal reproductive years; in locations of relative obscurity such as large cities or with inexperienced targets such as in rural areas; at low risk, with relatively high return. Embezzlement and forgery-counterfeiting are ploys on a similar theme, but for which opportunity and experience are important factors. All three categories of interpersonal deception are usually perpetrated in anonymity and among strangers, and in situations in which the likelihood of detection or the motivation for prosecution is relatively low.

If these cost-benefit indexes are indicative of a biological advantage as well as an economic one, it would seem that deception may be adaptive. It is relatively clear that crime in general does pay (e.g., Becker, 1968; Ehrlich, 1973) and that crimes of deception have a high monetary return at low risk. Nevertheless, the question still unanswered by these data is whether money and babies (i.e., reproductive success) can be equated, although it is a reasonable hypothesis that they can. The resources available to parents undoubtedly influence the number, health, and/or prosperity of their offspring or those of close relatives.[1] This leads us to consider in this section the adaptive advantage of self-

---

[1]One example of a crime of deception being perpetrated for the benefit of offspring was reported in the *Seattle Times* of Saturday, October 10, 1987, (Section A, p. 3) under the heading "Mom's an Embezzler, but Kids Support Her." An excerpt of the article is as follows: "Mom may be going to jail but she still means the world to her three children. She put them through college with $245,000 embezzled from the bank where she worked, but 'they are proud of her,' said her attorney. . . . Six years ago, while she was an officer of a Long Island bank, she began manipulating records to make withdrawals from the bank's administrative accounts and then used the funds to cover loans she had made to pay for her children's education. Last June she pleaded guilty to embezzlement."

deception, the topic of the present volume. Although interpersonal deception such as fraud, with its monetary gains versus imprisonment, may seem an extreme motivational model for self-deception, it may be a difference in degree rather than kind when mechanisms of self-deceit are addressed. Chapters 1 (Lockard) and 2 (Lockard and Mateer) provide evidence for the biological continuity of the concept by indicating nonhuman precursors (distal mechanisms) and neural bases of self-deception (proximal mechanisms), respectively. The first chapter makes explicit the notion that man is not the only species that "lies." Deception is prevalent between members of different species, as when certain American fireflies mimic the mating signals of other species for the purpose of preying upon them (Lloyd, 1986); similarly in the deceptive use of alarm calls by sentinel species in mixed-species flocks of neotropical birds (Munn, 1986); or when members of the shorebird family employ a variety of distraction displays as part of their antipredator strategies, particularly when their eggs or young are threatened (Sordahl, 1986).

Deceit may be evident even among members of the same species, as suggested by Morris (1986) for elephants or by de Waal (1986) for chimpanzees. As the nobler traits of culture, tool use and language (initially thought to characterize only humankind), fall within the domain of other animals, it is intriguing to speculate, as Lockard does in Chapter 1, whether there are evolutionary analogies even with respect to self-deception.

It was suggested by Trivers (1976) that if there is strong selection to detect deception in others, in turn there should be selection for anonymity of intent, even from oneself. Weaknesses and emotions that could interfere with the successful execution of a lie might be rendered impotent by relegating them to the unconscious. Carried to its limit, concealment of information from oneself that could interfere with biologically important objectives should lead to greater and greater self-deception. This may be the very condition that we find ourselves in today, possessed with a dual brain, lateralized functions, and a complicated interface between conscious and unconscious mechanisms.

A similar view was proposed by Fingarette (1969) in the appendix of his generally philosophical treatise on self-deception and by Lockard (1980) in a more biological treatment of the subject. Lockard and Mateer, in Chapter 2 of this volume, develop the idea further and present evidence for a neurological substrate that potentially allows or supports self-deception. Examples from clinical neurology are cited to demonstrate central nervous system compartmentalization. It is suggested that sensory information is processed by different centers of the nervous system that may be unaware of what information other brain areas have received. Further, it is hypothesized that cortical regions may know what they have perceived while subcortical regions may not possess the capacity for that kind of awareness.

Chapters 3 and 4 are concerned with the influence of learning and culture on self-deception. In Chapter 3, Feldman and Custrini present information relating to the question of how children develop the capability to be deceptive effectively and to recognize deception in others. Data are discussed that support the view that the manipulation and control of nonverbal behavior while being verbally deceptive should be considered skills that develop with age and with increases in social cognitive abilities. Studies are reported that show age-related changes in the nature of children's use of nonverbal behavioral cues in determining the veracity of others. Summarily, the view is presented that the use of nonverbal behavior represents impression management techniques.

Chapter 4 discusses the role of society in self-deceit. The author suggests that the reference group plays an insidious trick on its members by requiring them to deceive themselves as individuals. With respect to the processing of information, data confirming the prevailing cognitive schema may be invented while contradictory facts are ignored. Information about the normative behavior is embedded in a linguistic context so that the creed of a group is usually beyond members' capacity to question. This process is extended to an illogical conclusion when members of a reference group internalize the myths that mask their own behavior from themselves. This mismatch of the cognitive and the normative schemas is regarded by Welles as defining the condition of self-deception.

Taken together, the four chapters of this section reveal an interactive imperative of biology, ontogeny, and society in the manifestation of self-deception. They suggest that self-deceit may be preadapted (i.e., having some evolutionary propensity), facilitated in its execution by a multileveled brain, and subject in its expression to learning and the dictum of society. Certainly, by these criteria self-deception appears to be, if not carried to the extreme, a normal process of some benefit to the individual.

REFERENCES

ALEXANDER, R. D. (1979). *Darwinism and human affairs*. Seattle, WA: University of Washington Press.

BECKER, G. S. (1968). Crime and punishment: An economic approach. *Journal of Political Economy, 76,* 169-217.

DE WAAL, F. (1986). Deception in the natural communication of chimpanzees. In R. W. Mitchell & N. S. Thompson (Eds.), *Deception: Perspectives on human and nonhuman deceit* (pp. 221-244). New York: State University of New York Press.

EHRLICH, I. (1973). Participation in illegitimate activities: A theoretical and empirical investigation. *Journal of Political Economy, 81,* 521-565.

FINGARETTE, H. (1969). *Self-deception*. London: Routledge & Kegan Paul; New York: Humanities Press.

LLOYD, J. E. (1986). Firefly communication and deception: "Oh what a tangled web." In R. W. Mitchell & N. S. Thompson (Eds.), *Deception: Perspectives on human and nonhuman deceit* (pp. 113-128). New York: State University of New York Press.

LOCKARD, J. S. (1978a). Commentary: Speculations on the adaptive significance of cognition and consciousness. *The Behavioral and Brain Sciences, 4,* 583-584.

LOCKARD, J. S. (1978b). On the adaptive significance of self-deception. *Human Ethology Newsletter, 21,* 4-7.

LOCKARD, J. S. (1980). Speculations on the adaptive significance of self-deception. In J. S. Lockard (Ed.), *The evolution of human social behavior* (pp. 257-276). New York: Elsevier.

LOCKARD, J. S. (1982). Proximal mechanisms of self-deception. In J. S. Lockard (Coordinator), S. M. Essock-Vitale, J. Hartung, D. Krakauer, J. Welles, & S. Whittaker-Bleuler, *Self-deception: An adaptive strategy?* (symposium). *International Journal of Primatology, 3,* Abstract No. 3.

LOCKARD, J. S. (1984). Is lying to oneself uniquely human? In D. L. Paulhus (Coordinator), A. G. Greenwald, J. S. Lockard, T. R. Sarbin, & H. A. Sackeim, *Self-deception: Theoretical and empirical advances* (symposium). Annual Meeting of the American Psychological Society, Washington, DC.

LOCKARD, J. S., KIRKEVOLD, B. C., & KALK, D. F. (1980). Cost-benefit indexes of deception in nonviolent crime. *Bulletin of the Psychonomic Society, 16,* 303-306.

MITCHELL, R. W., & THOMPSON, N. S. (Eds.). (1986). *Deception: Perspectives on human and nonhuman deceit*. New York: State University of New York Press.

MORRIS, M. D. (1986). Large scale deceit: Deception by captive elephants? In R. W. Mitchell & N. S. Thompson (Eds.), *Deception: Perspectives on human and nonhuman deceit* (pp. 183-192). New York: State University of New York Press.

MUNN, C. A. (1986). The deceptive use of alarm calls by sentinel species in mixed-species flocks of neotropical birds. In R. W. Mitchell & N. S. Thompson (Eds.), *Deception: Perspectives on human and nonhuman deceit* (pp. 169-176). New York: State University of New York Press.

OTTE, D. (1975). On the role of intraspecific deception. *American Naturalist, 109*, 239-242.

PLATO. (1941). *On the trial and death of Socrates* (Lane Cooper, Trans.). Ithaca: Cornell University Press.

SORDAHL, T. A. (1986). Evolutionary aspects of avian distraction display: Variation in American avocet and black-necked stilt antipredator behavior. In R. W. Mitchell & N. S. Thompson (Eds.), *Deception: Perspectives on human and nonhuman deceit* (pp. 87-112). New York: State University of New York Press.

TRIVERS, R. L. (1976). In R. Dawkins, *The selfish gene* (Foreword). New York and Oxford: Oxford University Press.

———. (1985). Deceit and self-deception. In *Social evolution* (pp. 395-420). Menlo Park, CA: Benjamin/Cummings.

U. S. DEPARTMENT OF JUSTICE. (1978). *Sourcebook of criminal justice statistics*. Washington, DC: U. S. Government Printing Office.

WALLACE, B. (1973). Misinformation, fitness and selection. *American Naturalist, 107*, 1-7.

1

Origins

of Self-Deception

IS LYING TO ONESELF UNIQUELY HUMAN?

JOAN S. LOCKARD
University of Washington

IS DECEPTION OF OTHERS UNIQUELY HUMAN?

Many animal species have evolved a form of deception that is beneficial to their survival. For instance, some carnivores can be deceived by prey that pretend to be dead. In general, an aversion to eating carrion inundated with microorganisms that produce toxic byproducts is adaptive. However, this aversion is exploited by certain prey (e.g., some spiders, snakes, insects, and mammals) that fake death when approached by a predator.

On the other hand, some prey (e.g., wasps, bees, and rattlesnakes) protected by possessing toxins released through stings, bites, or sprays behave in conspicuous ways and may be brightly colored or emit warning noise before they strike. In this way, they do not have to be attacked to repel their enemies. Many nonnoxious species, however, manage through mimicry of these animals to differentially survive to reproduce more of their kind.

Deception is prevalent not only among members of different species, but also among animals of the same species. For example, cuckoldry in langur monkeys has been reported (Hrdy, 1974). Males of certain species of flies (Kessel, 1955) simulate ritualized feeding during courtship by offering the females empty food bags. In some fish (Assem, 1967), a nonresident male gains access to a nest defended by a resident male by mimicking the behavior of a receptive female, then releases his sperm in an attempt to fertilize some of the eggs. Hard-shell mantis shrimp (Caldwell, 1986) become particularly aggressive just prior to molting. They not only increase their claw displays but attack their opponent as if to establish a "reputation" just before the time they become vulnerable and, thus, unable to follow through on their threats.

Man, therefore, is not the only animal that "lies" to members of its own species. Wallace (1973) proposed a model of human deceit in which his basic assumption was that an accurate appraisal of one's environment is essential for high fitness. He hypothesized that an individual might increase his own relative fitness by causing a second individual to misinterpret the environment: "Thus, if two individuals are searching for food that is scarcely sufficient to support one of them alone, either one might raise his own fitness by convincing the other to search in barren places" (p. 2).

Wallace also intimated that the deceiver would achieve a greater increment in his genetic contribution to the next generation (inclusive fitness; see Hamilton, 1964) if the deceived were a nonrelative with whom fewer genes were held in common. He further theorized that the ease of deception should be a function of the relative frequency of individuals in a population perpetrating the deception and of the ability of other individuals in the population to detect the deception, until a point is reached at which either (1) a stable ratio of deceivers to potential recipients prevails (i.e., an evolutionarily stable strategy; see Maynard-Smith, 1976) or (2) it is no longer advantageous to continue the deception since those being deceived have, in turn, evolved to better detect (or detect more quickly) attempted ploys.

Wallace (1973) finally suggested that an individual who relies on lies for his survival should use large ones, since a big lie is not necessarily more difficult to contrive, or any greater risk than a small one. For instance, how much more advantageous is the deceit transmitted by a moth with eye spots if it conveys the message "Beware of the owl!" than "I'm not the moth you think I am" (p. 4)?

In essence, Wallace (1973) proposed that misinforming another individual may well be adaptive when:

1. vital resources are in demand (i.e., competition is high)
2. the recipients are nonrelatives
3. the deceivers are few and/or the ability to detect them is slight
4. the lie is a big one.

Otte (1975) has tempered such speculation by indicating that the lie, to be effective, must not exceed the degree of gullibility of the receiver. He further suggested that deceit among kin may in fact occur, and that it is:

1. not always disadvantageous
2. dependent on the degree of relatedness
3. contingent on the resources available
4. a function of the need to maintain cooperative alliances.

IS DECEPTION OF ONESELF UNIQUELY HUMAN?

Although we could reasonably conclude now that deception of others is *not* specific to humans, this does not answer the main question of this chapter: Does deception of oneself occur in other species? Trivers (1976) touched upon this issue in the foreword of Dawkins's book *The Selfish Gene*. He reasoned that since deceit is fundamental to animal communication (obviously including human communication), there must be strong selection to detect deception. He suggested that the probability of detection, in turn, ought to select for a degree of self-deception, rendering some facts and motives unconscious so as not to betray by subtle signs of self-awareness the deception being perpetrated.

Deception in Reproduction

The implications of this idea were evident in Trivers's paper on parental investment and sexual selection (1972), in which he emphasized that male and female reproductive strategies should never be identical even though they are ostensibly engaged in a joint task. Trivers suggested that the cost of sperm production and the copulatory act itself are relatively trivial to the male in comparison to the female's energy expenditure in the development of an egg and in the lengthy gestational process. By Trivers's reasoning one would expect males of monogamous species to retain some psychological traits consistent with promiscuity; that is, males should be selected to differentiate between females they will only impregnate and those with whom they will also raise young. It is quite likely that a male would be more successful in a mixed strategy if he could convince the two types of females of his intended fidelity. Moreover, if he is deceived regarding his own motives, his behavior might be even more convincing.

According to Trivers (1972), self-deception should also be adaptive in the event of desertion by males or cuckoldry by females. He suggested that an individual whose cumulative investment is exceeded by his partner's would theoretically be tempted to desert, especially if the disparity is large. The temptation would occur because the deserter loses less than his partner if no offspring survive. Therefore, the deserted partner would be more strongly selected to stay with the young to aid their survival. In other words, the reproductive success of the partner in this case would benefit the deserter.

Deception in Parenting

The benefit of self-deception is further implicated in another paper by Trivers (1974) on the topic of parent–offspring conflict. In the theory presented, socialization is regarded as a process by which parents attempt to mold each offspring in order to increase their own fitness. In turn, each offspring would be selected to resist some of the molding and attempt to shape the behavior of its parents and siblings in order to increase its own fitness. Again it seems reasonable that the less aware individuals are of their intent, the more convincing will be their behavior and the greater the likelihood of achieving their ends.

On the topic of parental manipulation, Alexander (1974) proposed that if parental pressures for altruism in offspring have led progeny to reproductive success, then such behavior represents a valuable social asset, even when it derives from an inability to recognize the reproductively selfish intent of the behavior. He went on to say that it is not difficult to be biologically selfish and still appear to be sincere if one is sufficiently ignorant of one's own motives. For example, in humans, an individual may be convinced that he is right (with moral and ethical "mandates from heaven") and may act in any way he feels is necessary to exist within the social group. He is then functioning in an adaptive manner, since his survival depends on his sociality. According to Alexander, "He will not see in himself what he does not wish to see, or what he does not wish his neighbors and fellows to see; and he is reluctant to see in other organisms what he will not see in himself. All of biology, all of science, all of human endeavors have been guided to some large extent by this circumstance" (p. 97).

Deception in Human Evolution

In a similar vein, I proposed (Lockard, 1977) that proximal and ultimate explanations of the same behavior may often be superficially inconsonant with one another. I suggested that it is likely that much of recent human evolution has entailed deceiving oneself into increasing one's fitness by providing proximal reasons (i.e., physiological, situational, or cultural) to champion why one behaves in certain ways. For example, global concepts such as "being in love with your spouse" or "caring for your children" help span the difficult moments of a quarrel with a lover or a defiant offspring.

In 1979, Alexander suggested that it may well be that we humans "doth protest too much" when it comes to our own evolution. He reiterated that the question of self-deception is not trivial, in that " . . . the genes and their mission before the advent of modern science and technology remained outside human knowledge. . . . we can be certain that our genes have not evolved to make the knowledge of their strategies conscious. . . . It is a remarkable fact that humans have not only failed throughout history to acquire an understanding that they have evolved to maximize reproduction, but that even today they deny the possibility vehemently. Even if the entire idea turns out to be wrong, which seems exceedingly unlikely at this point, we can still marvel at the hostility it engenders" (pp. 136–137).

Alexander (1979) suggested that the only way we can actually maximize our own evolutionary self-interest, and in so doing deceive others successfully, is by continually denying that we are doing such things. He proposed that our general cleverness at creating deceptions and detecting them has made it next to impossible for individuals to benefit from deliberate deception and, thus, we have evolved to deceive even ourselves about our true motives. The example he provided was concealment of ovulation by human females not only from others around them, but from themselves (Alexander & Noonan, 1979). It is hypothesized that continuous sexual receptivity in the female correlates evolutionarily with increased male parental care. Alexander (1979) stated: "At first, it seems that even if it were advantageous to the human female to conceal ovulation from all those around her, including her mate, she herself would still profit from knowing precisely when it occurred and being keenly aware of it. But this kind of knowledge would entail continual conscious and deliberate deception of her mate and others; perhaps such deception is contrary to our basic way of operating socially, and it would be too difficult and too discordant with the other aspects of sociality, for it to be maintained" (p. 139).

SELF-DECEPTION IN NONHUMAN SPECIES

With respect to the possibility of self-deception in nonhuman species, I proposed (Lockard, 1978) that in those fauna in which individual identification of conspecifics has been essential for survival, preadaptations for some degree of cognitive processing may also be manifested. I also suggested that in species that exhibit social deceit, the capacity for consciousness, or perhaps more importantly its possible antithesis, subconsciousness, is probable. Therefore, of those animals possessing cognition, species likely to have consciousness as well would be those in which the mating system was polygamous and the infancy period quite extensive. "In other words, animals which compete for mates, where the male and female mating strategies are dissimilar, and where the rearing of offspring may often have to be borne by one parent either by default (i.e., the death of the other parent) or by design (i.e., desertion by the other parent), are good candidates for possessing consciousness and by inference subconsciousness" (p. 584).

Self-Deception in Communication Systems

In 1985, Trivers reminded us that the most important thing to realize about systems of animal communication is that they are *not* systems for the dissemination of truth. He suggested that " . . . deception is a parasitism of the preexisting system for communicating correct information, and that a coevolutionary struggle emerges between deceiver and deceived that is frequency dependent: as deception increases in frequency, it intensifies selection for detection and as detection spreads, it intensifies selection on deceit. With powers to deceive and to spot deception being improved by natural selection, a new kind of deception may be favored: self deception" (p. 395).

Mechanisms of Self-Deception

Trivers (1985) was quick to point out that it must also be advantageous for the truth to be registered somewhere, so that mechanisms of self-deception are expected to reside side-by-side with mechanisms for the correct perception of reality (see Lockard, 1980, and Lockard & Mateer, in Chapter 2, on the neurology of self-deception). Trivers indicated that in human evolution, processes of deception and self-deception were greatly heightened by the advent of language, since it permits individuals to make statements about events distant in time and space. Having said that, however, he emphasized that " . . . self-deception is probably not limited to human beings. Other animals are often in situations of stress in which tight evaluations are being made. Self-confidence is a piece of information that may give useful information about the individual displaying it. . . . A certain amount of self-deception may give a convincing image of high self-esteem, thereby impressing others" (p. 416).

It was in a similar context that Trivers discussed five "mechanisms" of human self-deception: **beneffectance, exaggeration, the illusion of consistency, the perception of relationships,** and **perceptual defense and vigilance.** He proposed that we all have a tendency to represent ourselves as being beneficial and effective at the same time; to exaggerate our humanitarian accomplishments in the retelling; to rewrite past experiences to make them consistent with present conditions; to keep a self-fulfilling cumulative tally of favors and misdeeds of others close to ourselves; and to see what we wish to see and, in so doing, to remember such perceptions in a more positive light than reality would reveal.

Analogous mechanisms   Whereas on theoretical grounds we might conclude that self-deception is likely in social species other than our own, the preadaptations for such processes are still in question. It could be argued that self-deception is accomplished by means of biological processes originally selected to subserve other functions, and that, therefore, they are likely to be very different in origin in different species.

In a paper on the adaptive significance of self-deception (Lockard, 1980), I reiterated that many of the concepts routinely invoked to explain human behavior have little to say about the ultimate mechanisms mediating the behavior. The example given was the concept of parental love, in which I suggested that rarely do we (even the most avid of sociobiologists among us) view our daughters and sons as vehicles for our genes (Dawkins, 1976). However, if we were to evaluate such concepts in terms of Darwinian theory, for example, love of offspring becomes kin selection; a favor in kind, reciprocal altruism; hope or optimism, the will to survive; and exogamy, an incest taboo. Viewed in this light, such concepts are applicable (analogous in function) to many different species and/or different cultures, though they may not share a common origin. This may also be the case, to some extent, with the concept of self-deception. For example, parents of adopted offspring often care and provide for them as if they were their own.

Homologous mechanisms   In contrast, there is the possibility that certain mechanisms have evolved specifically to mediate the processes of self-deceit, and that these mechanisms may be similar (homologous) in different species sharing a common ancestry. The idea that self-deception is a "filtering process" whereby some information is admitted to consciousness (Lockard, 1980; Lockard & Mateer, Chapter 2) and that lateralized cerebral processes may have animal precursors is intriguing, but what is the evidence to substantiate the existence of such systems in nonhuman species? It would seem that studies are beginning to suggest the appearance of these systems in birds and mammals generally, and in primates particularly (Heestand, 1986; MacNeilage, Studdert-Kennedy, & Lindblom, in press). The stimulation studies of Mahut (1964) and Wilburn and Kesner (1972) suggest that an alerting system involved with motor memory may be present in the thalamus of a variety of animals. Dewson (1977) has identified a lateralized auditory short-term memory system in the temporal lobe of rhesus monkeys. Chimpanzees (Gardner & Gardner, 1969) as well as gorillas (Patterson, 1978) and orangutans (Miles, 1983) can be taught a manual and a symbolic communication system (Premack, 1976; Savage-Rumbaugh, 1981; see also review by Terrace, 1985), though it is currently unclear whether it is differentially mediated by one cerebral hemisphere more than the other.

A behavioral study that might suggest more directly the manifestation of self-deception in nonhuman primate species is one by Martenson, Sackett, and Erwin (1977). Their analysis of facial expressions as correlates of overt aggression in pigtail monkeys generally supports the commonly employed emotional interpretations of such behaviors. Threat faces and yawns were positively related to perpetration of aggression, and grimaces were exhibited by the recipients of aggression. However, grimaces did not occur during every instance of overt aggression, and lipsmacking was apparently manifested by both aggressors and aggressed animals. Of particular interest were the results with respect to the pucker face (called LEN). It was found to be unrelated to perpetrated or received aggression, but the incidence of received LEN was strongly related to incidence of received aggression. The capricousness of the grimace, lipsmack, and LEN as emotionality indicators in macaques may well indicate some attempt at deception of group members, if not frank self-deception. Similar observations have been reported in chimpanzees (de Waal, 1982) and suggest that primates (and perhaps social mammals generally) in aggressive situations have been selected to hide ambivalent motivation from conspecifics and possibly from themselves (Trivers, 1985).

CONCLUSIONS

Explicit examples of animal self-deceit that are most likely *not* mediated by higher brain functions are also available. The data emanate from studies on maternal or sexual imprinting. What more adaptive mechanism is there than to follow one's "mother" when young or to prefer to mate with conspecifics when older, at least until the processes go awry? Mayr (1974) suggested that opened genetic programs such as imprinting (in contrast to closed genetic strategies such as the species recognition signals of certain lizards) allow evolutionary flexibility and genetic efficiency. But how inverted is the self-deception of the goose that prefers Lorenz (1965) or the sheep that follows the collie away from the herd? From such data it would seem that self-deception at "some brain level" in other social species is no longer mere speculation. Therefore, we must conclude that lying to oneself is not uniquely human!

REFERENCES

ALEXANDER, R. D. (1974). The evolution of social behavior. *Annual Review of Ecology and Systematics, 5,* 325–383.

_____. (1979). *Darwinism and human affairs.* Seattle, WA: University of Washington Press.

ALEXANDER, R. D., & NOONAN, K. N. (1979). Concealment of ovulation, parental care, and human social evolution. In N. A. Chagon & W. Irons (Eds.), *Evolutionary biology and human social behavior* (pp. 436–453). North Scituate, MA: Duxbury Press.

ASSEM, J. VAN DEN. (1967). Territory in the three-spined stickleback, *Gasteroceus aculeatus. Behaviour Supplement, 16,* 1–164.

CALDWELL, R. L. (1986). The deceptive use of reputation by stomatopods. In R. W. Mitchell & N. S. Thompson (Eds.), *Deception: Perspectives on human and nonhuman deceit* (pp. 129–146). New York: SUNY Press.

DAWKINS, R. (1976). *The selfish gene.* New York and Oxford: University Press.

DE WAAL, F. (1982). *Chimpanzee politics: Power and sex among apes.* New York: Harper and Row.

DEWSON, J. H., III. (1977). Preliminary evidence of hemispheric asymmetry of auditory function in monkeys. In S. Harnard, R. Doty, L. Goldstein, J. Saynes, & G. Krauthamer (Eds.), *Lateralization in the nervous system* (pp. 63–71). New York: Academic Press.

GARDNER, B. T., & GARDNER, R. A. (1969). Teaching sign language to a chimpanzee. *Science, 165,* 664–672.

HAMILTON, W. D. (1964). The genetical evolution of social behaviour (I and II). *Journal of Theoretical Biology, 7,* 1–52.

HEESTAND, J. E. (1986). *Behavioral lateralization in four species of apes?* Unpublished dissertation, University of Washington, Seattle, WA.

HRDY, S. B. (1974). Male-male competition and infanticide among langurs (*Presbytis entellus*) of Abu, Rajasthan. *Folia Primatologica, 22,* 19–58.

KESSEL, E. L. (1955). Mating activities of balloon flies. *Systematic Zoology, 4,* 97–104.

LOCKARD, J. S. (1977). Panhandling as an example of the sharing of resources. *Science, 198,* 858.

_____. (1978). Commentary: Speculations on the adaptive significance of cognition and consciousness. *Behavioral and Brain Sciences, 4,* 583–584.

_____. (1980). Speculations on the adaptive significance of self-deception. In J. S. Lockard (Ed.), *The evolution of human social behavior* (pp. 257–275). New York: Elsevier.

LORENZ, K. (1965). *Evolution and modification of behavior.* Chicago: University Press.

MacNeilage, P. F., Studdert-Kennedy, M. G., & Lindblom, B.   (in press). Primate handedness reconsidered. *Behavioral and Brain Sciences.*

Mahr, E.   (1974). Behavior programs and evolutionary strategies. *American Scientist, 62,* 650–659.

Mahut, H.   (1964). Effect of subcortical electrical stimulation on discrimination learning in cats. *Journal of Comparative and Physiological Psychology, 58,* 390–395.

Martenson, J. A., Jr., Sackett, D. P., & Erwin, J.   (1977). Facial expressions as correlates of overt aggression in pigtail monkeys. *Journal of Behavioral Science, 2,* 239–242.

Maynard-Smith, J.   (1976). Evolution and the theory of games. *American Scientist, 64,* 41–45.

Miles, H. L.   (1983). Apes and language: The search for communicative competence. In J. de Luce & H. T. Wilder (Eds.), *Language in primates: Perspective and implications* (pp. 43–61). New York: Springer.

Otte, D.   (1975). On the role of intraspecific deception. *American Naturalist, 109,* 239–242.

Patterson, F.   (1978). The gestures of a gorilla: Language acquisition by another pongid species. *Brain and Language, 5,* 72–79.

Premack, D.   (1976). Mechanisms of intelligence: Preconditions for language. *Annals of the New York Academy of Sciences, 280,* 544–561.

Savage-Rumbaugh, E. S.   (1981). Can apes use symbols to represent their world? *Annals of the New York Academy of Sciences, 364,* 35–59.

Terrace, H. S.   (1985). In the beginning was the "Name." *American Psychologist, 40,* 1011–1028.

Trivers, R. L.   (1972). Parental investment and sexual selection. In B. Campbell (Ed.), *Sexual selection and the descent of man* (pp. 136–179). Chicago: Aldine.

———.   (1974). Parent-offspring conflict. *American Zoologist, 14,* 249–264.

———.   (1976). In R. Dawkins, *The selfish gene* (Foreword). New York and Oxford: Oxford University Press.

———.   (1985). Deceit and self-deception. In *Social evolution* (pp. 395–420). Menlo Park, CA: Benjamin/Cummings.

Wallace, B.   (1973). Misinformation, fitness and selection. *American Naturalist, 107,* 1–7.

Wilburn, M., & Kesner, R.   (1972). Differential amnestic effects produced by electrical stimulation of the caudate nucleus and nonspecific thalamic system. *Experimental Neurology, 34,* 45–50.

2

Neural Bases
of Self-Deception

JOAN S. LOCKARD
CATHERINE A. MATEER
University of Washington

The focus of this chapter is a discussion of evidence for a neurological substrate that might potentially allow or support either active self-deception (Lockard, 1980) or, as in most examples, more passive unawareness of information. There is a variety of naturally occurring phenomena related to neurological disease or dysfunction or to developmental phenomena in which there is evidence for a dissociation between knowledge and awareness. In some cases there is evidence that certain areas of the brain may "know" something or at least respond to information appropriately despite the individual's lack of awareness or consciousness of it.

IS SELF-DECEPTION A MULTILEVELED BRAIN PROCESS?

Before the processes of self-deception can be addressed from the perspective of neurology, some consensus must be reached regarding their brain pervasiveness. A reasonable progression would be to first define "perception" and to distinguish it from "deception," and subsequently from "self-deception." A dictionary definition of the term "perception" usually includes "consciousness" or "awareness" as synonyms. For example, perception is defined in one source as "the awareness of objects or other data through the medium of the senses" (Webster, 1964) and in another source as the "awareness of the elements of environment through physical sensation" (Webster, 1981). Implicit in such statements is a central nervous system

(CNS) "acknowledgement" of a specific physical reality by means of a receptor and cognitive registration. Phrased differently, perception could be regarded as the detection of an entity or event as it "really" is. In contrast, "de-ception" could be viewed as a distorted perception whereby the CNS acknowledges an entity or event (to some extent) as it really is not (Table 2–1).

TABLE 2–1

ENTITY OR EVENT	PERCEPTION	DECEPTION
	As It Is	As It Is Not

The distinction between deception and self-deception then is simply a matter of whether the masquerade is perpetrated by another or oneself. In the latter case, one believes or convinces oneself that an entity or event is not what it is; in the former case, the convincing is done by someone else (Table 2–2).

TABLE 2–2

TERM	DEFINITION
Perception	Aware of an entity or event as it "really" is
Deception	Convinced (without awareness of the "truth") by *another* of an entity or event as it is *not*
Self-Deception	Convinced by oneself (without awareness of the "truth") of an entity or event as it is *not*

The major complication with this simple approach to self-deception is that experientially there appear to be several "selves," not just one. For example, one could hypothesize a conscious self and a subconscious self, an emotional self and a cognitive self, a depressed self and an elated self, a confident self and a self-conscious self, and so forth. Moreover, each seeming dichotomy is more plausibly a multidimensional continuum of graded degrees of one self or the other (Table 2–3).

TABLE 2–3

Examples of Multiple Selves

Subconscious	————	Conscious
Emotional	————	Cognitive
Elated	————	Depressed
Confident	————	Self-Conscious

The problem of understanding processes of self-deception, then, becomes one of deciding which self or selves are relevant to a particular deception, and at what level of awareness, emotion, and/or confidence it or they function. It must also be determined at what stage of neural information processing—input, storage, retrieval, restorage, and/or output—the deception is occurring. To elaborate on this multifaceted approach, several dimensions of information processing will now be shown. This discourse will encompass peripheral versus central processes, memory processes, and left versus right brain processes.

PERIPHERAL VERSUS CENTRAL PROCESSES

Deceiving oneself (or for that matter, being deceived by another) could involve at least four sensory processes: habituation, selective perception, subliminal perception, and misperception. From the first to the last category of sensory input there is an apparent increase in CNS involvement (Table 2–4). **Habituation** is largely a peripheral mechanism for handling repetitive input at the receptor site. **Selective perception** requires at least subcortical processing that results in differential access of sensory information. **Subliminal perception** clearly involves cortical processes but is below the threshold of cognitive awareness. As for **misperception**, it is a CNS misclassification (i.e., misconception) of a sensory event.

TABLE 2–4

TYPE OF SENSORY PROCESS	LEVEL OF CNS INVOLVEMENT	
Habituation	+	(low)
Selective Perception	+ +	
Subliminal Perception	+ + +	
Misperception	+ + + +	(high)

For example, the likelihood of self-deceit in selective perception is illustrated by the study of Neisser and Becklen (1975). Individuals were shown two scenes superimposed (Figure 2–1) on a video screen. Each scene depicted a different game: In one scene several players were throwing a ball around; in the other, two people were slapping each other's hands. Each subject was asked to monitor one of the two games by pressing a key either when the ball was thrown (at about a rate of once per second) *or* when the hands were slapped. The results are analogous to those found for dichotic listening studies, namely, the unattended scene was essentially not seen. From such data it becomes obvious that the central organization of preception is affected by expectations (e.g., mental sets) and, therefore, subject to either deception and/or self-deception.

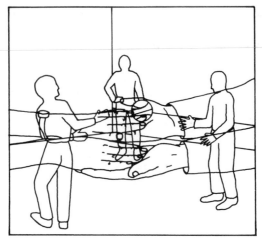

FIGURE 2–1   Selective looking (adapted from Neisser & Becklen, 1975)

MEMORY PROCESSES

Self-deception could occur as well during any of the many levels of memory processing, for example, working memory and long-term storage, retrieval, and restorage of information. After sensory input of an event, deceiving oneself could transpire at one or more of the transitional segments of the memory process, that is, from working to permanent storage; from storage to retrieval; from recall to restorage; and/or from retrieval to social conveyance. Also, analogous to the schematic of Table 2–4, the ease of possible distortion is likely to increase from the first to the fifth process (Table 2–5). Similar to the spread of a rumor from one person to another, the farther away from the original input the information is, the more amenable it is to reinterpretation.

TABLE 2–5

TYPE OF MEMORY PROCESS	EASE OF MISINTERPRETATION
Working memory	+
Encoding	+ +
Long-term storage	+ + +
Retrieval	+ + + +
Restorage	+ + + + +

For example, it has been shown that contrary to traditional belief, information stored in "long-term memory" may not be permanent (Loftus & Loftus, 1980). In a study to test the accuracy of eyewitness testimony, Loftus, Miller, and Burns (1978) had subjects view a series of thirty color slides depicting successive stages in an auto–pedestrian accident. The critical pair of slides consisted of one with a red Datsun at a stop sign, while the other nearly identical slide had the Datsun at a yield sign. The data revealed that misleading intervening questions hindered recognition performance. In one case, greater than 80% of the subjects indicated that they had seen the slide that corresponded to what they had been told rather than the slide that they had actually seen.

Similar results were obtained in a study by Robinson and Merav (1976) on patient recall of informed consent information. Despite meticulous attention to detail by the cardiac surgeon in a carefully conducted informed consent procedure, all twenty patients tested between four and six months postoperatively failed to recall accurately what had transpired at their interview. Even more interesting, however, from the point of view of self-deception, was the finding that the category most subject to recall error was the one concerning "potential complications." The accuracy of those items was only 10% primary recall and 23% secondary recall compared to an average in all six categories of 29% and 42%, respectively (Table 2–6). Especially noteworthy was a significant difference in the self-assurance with which patients responded to the questions in further interviews. The worst score of all patients reinterviewed was achieved by one who responded with no misgivings about his recollections. Two other patients who scored fifteenth and seventeenth also manifested similar confidence; in the words of the authors ". . . they were frequently in error but never in doubt" (Robinson & Merav, 1976, p. 212).

TABLE 2–6

Recall of Informed Consent Interview By Twenty Patients
Four to Six Months Postoperatively

CATEGORY OF INFORMED CONSENT INFORMATION	% PRIMARY RECALL	% SECONDARY RECALL
1. Diagnosis and nature of illness	33	46
2. Proposed operation	26	51
3. Risks of the operative procedure	35	42
4. Potential complications	10 ←——→ 23	
5. Benefits of the proposed operation	29	47
6. Alternative methods of management	43	43
Average	29	42

(Adapted from Robinson & Merav, 1976)

LEFT VERSUS RIGHT BRAIN PROCESSES

The asymmetry of function of the cerebral hemispheres has been well documented. This has been done in respect to such diverse phenomena as language, spatial organization, handedness, emotion, and cognition (see review, Springer & Deutsch, 1985). Moreover, lateralization of certain functions such as language manifest gender differences, too (McGlone, 1980; Mateer, Poler, & Ojemann, 1982; Kimura, 1987).

Hemispheric asymmetries exist at a subcortical (Ojemann, 1977) as well as a cortical level. Ojemann has provided evidence for lateralization of thalamic projections along a verbal–visual–spatial dichotomy but with left thalamic (verbal) alerting mechanisms dominant. The data (from surgical patients with Parkinsonism) indicated that stereotaxic stimulation during input to short-term verbal memory decreased later retrieval errors. The same current applied to the same sites blocked retrieval material already in short-term memory, whereas smaller currents at these same sites accelerated memory processes other than speech.

This apparent gating mechanism in the ventral lateral thalamus facilitates access of sensory input to memory and thereby modulates the likelihood of later retrieval. These effects are strongly lateralized, in that nondominant (right) thalamic stimulation had no effect on retrieval of verbal material, though it did facilitate recognition of visual spatial information. In contrast, dominant (left) thalamic stimulation both facilitated retrieval of verbal material and disrupted retrieval of visual spatial information. For instance, the effects of ventrolateral (VL) thalamic stimulation on short-term recognition memory of object names and shapes are shown in Figure 2–2.

FIGURE 2–2 Effects of ventrolateral thalamic stimulation on short-term recognition memory of object names and shapes (adapted from Ojemann, 1979). The bars indicate percent change in recognition errors from control levels during input, output, or input plus output stimulation on the same trial for six patients with left (solid bars) and eight patients with right (open bars) VL electrodes. Notice the decrease in errors (improved performance) with input stimulation, and the differential effects of right or left VL stimulation on verbal and nonverbal tasks (adapted from Ojemann, 1979).

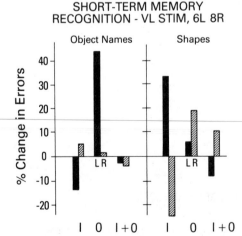

SHORT-TERM MEMORY
RECOGNITION - VL STIM, 6L 8R

In terms of self-deception, therefore, hemispheric asymmetries mean that the number of possible neurological processes involved may be many-fold more than would be hypothesized if the two hemispheres were in fact functional mirror-images of one another.

EXAMPLES OF SELF-DECEPTION FROM CLINICAL NEUROLOGY

Now that we have some appreciation for the complexity with which the normal brain may process self-deception, let us turn to clinical neurology. To illustrate processes of self-deception that might be operating with respect to multileveled and lateralized brain functions, several neurological syndromes and memory phenomena are described below.

Dissociation Between Sensory Input and Awareness/Recognition

Anosognosia   One of the most striking phenomena following neurological insult to the brain is that of **anosognosia**: the unawareness or denial of disease or dysfunction. Some of the first descriptions of this phenomenon were provided by Anton (1893). Occurring frequently, although not exclusively, after recovery from coma, a patient with paralysis of one half of his body refuses to admit the reality of his paralysis. Every attempt to show the patient that one side of his body is paralyzed is either met with indifference or grossly rebuffed. The patient may accuse the doctor of exaggeration or error. This has been termed **asomatognosia.**

A case of this sort was described by Olsen and Ruby (1941). The patient not only denied her left hemiplegia (paralysis) but declared that her left arm and leg belonged either to the doctor or to some other person sleeping in the same bed as she was. When she was asked to verify visually that her left arm was indeed the direct continuation of her left shoulder she replied, "My eyes and my feelings are not in agreement; and I must believe what I feel. I sense by looking that they are as if they are mine, but I feel that they are not; and I cannot believe my eyes." The common characteristic of this condition appears to be a failure to integrate one side of the body into the consciousness of the whole body. At times a patient may suffer from an acute and painful impression that one side of his body has disappeared, and despite evidence to the contrary presumably available to his sensory systems, he is uncertain of the integrity of his body.

It was Babinski (1914) who clearly demonstrated that these unilateral defects could result from a focal cortical lesion and that primary sensory deficiencies could not explain the disorder. Unilateral asomatognosia primarily affects the left side of the body in right-handed subjects with a right hemisphere lesion, although cases have been described that are exceptions to this rule (Table 2–7).

TABLE 2–7

HEMISPHERE DAMAGE	SOMATOGNOSIC DEFECT		
Right	Unilateral	39/136	(29%)
	Bilateral	4/136	(3%)
Left	Unilateral	7/172	(4%)
	Bilateral	34/172	(20%)

(Adapted from Hecaen, 1968)

Hemiagnosia for pain   More rarely observed is a **hemiagnosia**, a phenomenon in which painful stimuli applied to the impaired (hemiplegic) side of the body may produce unpleasant facial grimacing and even normal, pain-related verbal reactions, but the patient may make no effort with the healthy hand to drive away the painful stimulus. It seems as though neither the nature nor the location of the painful stimulus is identified by the patient. This syndrome is usually seen only in patients with significant reductions in the level of consciousness.

In some cases the failure to be normally aware of or to integrate one side of the body may persist unchanged for the life of the patient, while in others the disorder may be transient, appearing only during the acute stage of the illness. Usually, progressive readaption takes place and the patient eventually accepts the reality of his or her paralysis. Regression of the deficit parallels recovery of general motor and sensory functions. That is, the last parts of the body to recover from these deficits are the most distal portions of the limbs, the hands and feet (Bender & Teuber, 1949).

As for the anatomic basis of this kind of unilateral lack of awareness or denial, the bulk of the evidence from published studies supports the classical position that the right hemisphere of right-handers is responsible. In particular, the right interior parietal region has been implicated (Lhermitte, 1939). However, subcortical structures, including the thalamus, have also been implicated as regions that subserve specific features of the overall syndrome. Regions of the thalamus have been associated with alterations in pain perception, perceptual modifications of a phantom limb variety, and indifference to hemiplegia (Van Bogaert, 1934; Nielson, 1946). Hecaen and Goldblum (1972) insist, however, that lesions limited to the thalamus can produce only impressions of absence or loss of body parts, such as the feeling that a body segment does not really belong to the rest of the body. True disorders of recognition and knowledge of body scheme require involvement of cortical regions, particularly the parietal lobe. This would suggest that while a subcortical structure, the thalamus, may act as a gating mechanism for transmittal of sensory information to the cortex, the cortex itself may be necessary for true awareness and knowledge relative to sensory information.

Disorders of the Visual System

Still another example of dissociation between sensory input and awareness or recognition of sensory input is provided by disorders related to the visual system. It had traditionally been thought that bilateral destruction of the occipital lobes in humans caused total blindness because the cortex of the occipital lobe is a primary receiving area of visual information. However, research on residual vision in animals after ablation of occipital areas and observations of humans who have suffered extensive occipital injury have thrown this classical doctrine into doubt. Recent research on preserved visual capabilities in the blind with occipital lesions is compelling.

Visual anosognosia   A similiar syndrome to unilateral paralysis concerns patients who are cortically blind but who deny or refuse to recognize their loss of vision (von Monokow, 1897; Potzl, 1928; Hecaen & de Ajuriaguerra, 1954; de Angelergues, de Ajuriaguerra, & Hecaen, 1960; Hecaen & Albert, 1978). Patients with **visual anosognosia** refuse to admit their blindness, act as if they can see, and persist in this behavior despite all evidence to the contrary. They may obstinately refuse to learn to accept that they are blind, even though the incapacity disorients them, disrupts their pattern of living, and even injures them. They may stumble over objects or walk into walls. The clinical pattern may last hours or days, or it may be permanent. Sometimes it is manifest simply by an indifference to the blindness and a lack of complaints concerning the disability. Sometimes, in an apparent attempt to explain away the visual disorder, the patient invents excuses related to the environment: poor lighting, poor glasses, dust in the eye, and so forth. Sometimes patients even react angrily because someone suspects them of having a visual disorder. Although the symptom is sometimes seen in the context of a more general intellectual dysfunction, this can by no means account for all of the cases.

Visual field defects   A less extreme example of denial or unawareness is the unawareness of blindness in a particular part of the visual field. Any lesion of the visual cortex produces both a visual field defect and, in almost every case, the loss of awareness of the existence of this defective sector in the visual field. **Cortical blindness** may occur as a sudden reversible event, representing epileptic equivalents, migraine, or transient vascular disruptions. When associated with a significant vascular lesion or disruption of the blood supply causing tissue death, cortical blindness is generally longer lasting, extending to months or even years.

Another interesting phenomenon related to deficits in the visual system relates to the observation of residual visual function in cortically blind individuals. Often these residual capabilities are present without any "awareness" of their preservation by the individual. Weiskrantz, Warrington, Sanders, and Marshall (1974) studied the potential for vision in the blind half field of a 34-year-old man whose right occipital lobe had been surgically removed. Even though the patient had no awareness of "seeing" in his blind field, he was nonetheless able to respond to visual stimuli in a limited manner. He could reach for visual stimuli accurately, and he could differentiate the orientation of a vertical line from a horizontal and an X from an O, provided the stimuli exceeded a critical size. In another study, a 62-year-old man became cortically blind following disruption of the blood flow in the arteries serving both occipital lobes. He would deny his blindness inconsistently. Although he himself would occasionally state that he was "unable to see anything" and although he was considered totally blind by the attending physician and nurses, he was able to grasp an object in motion and to indicate the direction of motion (horizontal, vertical, or diagonal). He was, however, unable to see an object, even if it was larger than the moving objects he could see (Riddich, 1917; Hecaen & Albert, 1978).

Visual neglect   Another related deficit is the pattern of response to visual input, described as **visual neglect**. In this disorder, patients with a unilateral lesion involving visual pathways fail to respond to stimuli presented in the contralateral field, even though there may be documented "vision" in that field. This phenomenon is like the distribution of hemisensory deficits described in Table 2–7 and is seen more frequently with right hemisphere lesions. The reasons for this asymmetry are not well understood, but one proposed model is diagrammed in Figure 2–3. In this model the attention systems of the right brain respond to both ipsilateral and contralateral stimuli, while the left brain is generally responsive only to contralateral stimuli. Thus, information in the right field can be responded to by either the isolated left or right brain, but transmission of information in the left field requires right brain integrity. With a right visual system lesion, information in the left field is not attended to, resulting in a high incidence of left visual neglect after right lesions.

FIGURE 2–3   A model of visual neglect following right brain lesions. No awareness of X in the left field with a right hemisphere lesion. L = left; R = right.

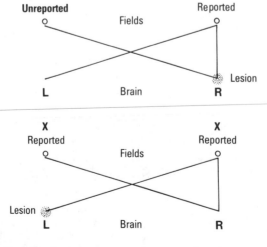

Significance of Visual System Deficits

These observations suggest that the visual capacity remaining after damage to the occipital or striate cortex may be greater than has been believed and, most importantly to this volume, far greater than patients themselves may realize. Both animal and human studies support that in certain clinical syndromes related to damage of the visual cortex, parts of the preserved, more primitive, subcortical visual systems may remain to compensate for the loss of visual perception (Weiskrantz, 1972). These subcortical systems are thought to be important for conveying information regarding the position and movement of objects in space. The subcortical region cannot, however, convey information about what it is that is in space. Thus the subcortical regions can convey information about where an object is but not what it is; they appear to be incapable of detailed pattern perception. This information, however, does not appear to be accessible to conscious awareness. The patient may vehemently deny that he has seen an object or knows where it is and yet point directly to it. The suggestion again is that cortical regions are important not only for the detailed analysis of perceptual information, but also for the awareness of receiving that information.

Disorders of the Auditory System

In turning our attention to the auditory system, at least one similar dissociation can be identified. In most right-handed individuals the left hemisphere of the brain subserves language functioning. If damage occurs in the posterior portion of the parasylvian region, in the temporal parietal cortex including portions of Wernicke's area, a fascinating form of aphasia, called **jargon aphasia**, often results (Wernicke, 1874; Head, 1926; Luria, 1966). In this expressive language disorder, spontaneous speech output is fluent, or in some cases hyperfluent with an increased rate of words per minute, but the patient is unable to bring a sentence to a close. Intonation patterns, the normal variability in pitch and rhythm, and facial and gestural expression remain normal, even while the content of the utterance is incomprehensible. This incomprehensibility is due not to impaired articulation of the word but rather to a substitution of incorrect words for correct ones. One of the most striking features of this kind of aphasia is that the patient often appears to be totally unaware of the errors or complete lack of meaning in his or her speech and will continue with gestural expressions and intonation patterns, apparently believing that the message being communicated is clear. In many if not most of these cases, understanding or comprehension of speech is similarily affected. The patient may not be able to respond to even the simplest of questions or instructions. In many such cases, however, he or she appears to understand what is being said through gestures, nods, and apparent surety of incomprehensible verbal responses. While the entire constellation of symptoms often clears, aspects of jargon aphasia such as severely impaired comprehension and dissociated awareness of the disorder often continue for a long time. Again the major region of the brain that appears essential to the self-deception is a cortical region, in this case areas surrounding the left auditory cortex.

Dissociation in Levels of Knowing

If we depart from primary sensory systems, additional dissociations characterized by response to information without any awareness of it are evident. One such area is that of **memory functioning**. Memory appears not to be served by any one area in the brain, or to be a single function, rather it is a byproduct of a complex information processing system in the brain.

Amnestic syndromes   A great deal of information about the neurological basis of memory has been provided by the study of individuals with **amnestic syndromes**. On standard measures of memory such as paragraph recall, list learning, paired-associate learning, or reproduction of visual forms, these individuals may show devastating impairments. They appear not to be able to record or store any new information. The anatomical basis of the disorder in these patients has been attributed to various systems within the brain, including the mesial temporal lobes, the limbic and hippocampal systems, and portions of the thalamus, particularly the nuclei which connect to the frontal lobes (Cermak, 1982; Squire & Butters, 1984). While for a long time many of these amnestic syndromes were thought to be equivalent, more recent analysis has strongly suggested that various amnestic syndromes resulting from different anatomical lesions may have strikingly different characteristics.

Procedural versus declarative memory   One very interesting phenomenon observed in many patients with amnesia is a dissociation between what is called **procedural memory**, memory for habits or rule-based learning, and **declarative memory**, the ability to verbally report or acknowledge information in memory (Huppert & Piercy, 1979; Cohen & Squire, 1980; Cohen, 1984). An example of this dissociation can often be seen in the neurologic clinic. For example, a patient with severe amnesia following a head injury utilized a particular computer program every day for several weeks. At the beginning of each session he professed that he had never been in the room before, had never used that particular computer before, and had no knowledge of having been in the environment previously. Despite his protestation, when asked to turn on the computer, he demonstrated a quick and facile ability to turn on, boot up, and initiate the program on which he had been working. Again, he professed no knowledge of experience with the computer.

This dissociation between *knowing that* and *knowing how* has been of great interest to memory researchers. In the context of this particular volume, the interest lies in the striking dissociation between knowledge at some level as demonstrated by behavior and awareness of that knowledge. In a similar phenomenon, patients are asked to solve a complex problem using blocks. It requires moving a stack of blocks from one peg to a third peg via a middle peg according to a series of specific rules. Although verbally professing that they have never seen the puzzle before, amnesic patients are nevertheless able to demonstrate improved performance in their acquisition and application of the rule base for solving the puzzle.

Yet another example of dissociation in levels of knowing is the sense of knowing that you know. Although the anatomic basis for these dissociations is not yet clear, several researchers have strongly supported a role of the frontal cortex in the phenomenon of "feelings of knowing." Patients with frontal lobe lesions appear to be less able to judge their knowledge base or accurately predict their performance on measures requiring memory (Nielson, 1946; Shimamura & Squire, 1986).

Childhood amnesia　Another interesting example relates to the phenomenon of memory in childhood and is termed **childhood amnesia**, that is, limited memory of large portions of early childhood. Clearly, during this early stage, for which there is no conscious awareness of memory, the child has many cortical functions. There is speech production and comprehension, visual–spatial analysis and perception, and some capacity for memory on a minute-to-minute or day-to-day basis. There appears to be, however, no permanent storage of these memories. Although at this point it might be termed wildly speculative, the importance of the frontal lobes in this phenomenon is becoming of interest because of their late evolutionary development.

Hemispheric dissociation　One final example of dissociation between responding and an awareness of knowing what one is responding to comes from the split brain literature. In some individuals who have had severe epileptic disorders, reduction of seizure frequency was attempted by hemispheric dissociation, the separation of the two hemispheres of the brain. Although on casual observation this procedure appears to have little if any behavioral effect, more detailed analysis and testing yield fascinating evidence of an apparent dissociation in awareness on the part of the two hemispheres (Gazzeniga & Le Doux, 1978). In testing these patients, specialized equipment projects information to one side of the brain or the other via very fast visual presentations. Thus, information can be presented in the left visual field which will go only to the right hemisphere and vice versa.

A split-brain patient sits in front of a screen with a small black dot in the center. She looks directly at the dot and when the experimenter is sure that she is doing so, a picture of a cup is flashed briefly to the right of the dot. The patient reports that she has seen a cup because this information has gone directly to her left (speaking) hemisphere. Again she is asked to fix her gaze on the dot, but this time a picture of a spoon is flashed to the left of the dot. She is asked what she saw and she replies, "No, nothing," because the information has gone only to her right (non-speaking) hemisphere. She is then asked to reach under the screen with her left hand and to select, by touch only, the item she has just seen. Her left hand, which is connected to her right hemisphere, palpates each object and then holds up the spoon. Thus there has been a match within the right hemisphere of the visual information and the tactile information. When asked what she is holding however, she says "pencil" because that tactile and visual information has not been accessible to the left (speaking) hemisphere.

Once again the patient is asked to fixate on the dot on the screen. A picture of a nude woman is flashed to the left of the dot, and she blushes a little and begins to giggle. She is asked what she saw and says, "Nothing, just a flash of light," and giggles again, covering her mouth with her hand. "Why are you laughing then?" the investigator inquires. "Oh, doctor, you have some machine," she replies. Thus, information presented to the right hemisphere has clearly been responded to in what might be considered an appropriate emotional fashion. Yet, not only is the patient unable to verbalize what she has seen, she is also unable to demonstrate any awareness of the nature of the stimuli. This again suggests dissociation between the nervous system response to sensory information and the individual's conscious awareness of that information. In this case the conscious, or at least explicit, verbalized awareness appears to require that the information be accessible to the left hemisphere of the brain.

CONCLUSIONS

The intent of these examples from clinical neurology has been to demonstrate a number of interesting features about nervous system organization. First, there appear to be degrees of compartmentalization. Different aspects of information are directed to different centers or systems and may or may not have access to portions of the brain important for awareness of that information. There appears to be a functional hierarchy related to phylogenetic development such that subcortical regions of the brain, including the thalamus and the midbrain visual system, do not have the capacity to provide certain kinds of awareness. Cortical regions, the most recently developed in the phylogenetic order, appear to be necessary for knowing that you know, or knowing that you have perceived.

Another emerging variable seems to be related to laterality. The integrity of the left hemisphere of the brain and its language systems appears to be necessary for several aspects of explicit knowing related to verbal mediation or specific description. Finally, while the major cortical sensory areas in the brain have all been implicated in dissociative syndromes, it may be that the frontal lobes of the brain are critical for the highest level of "knowing," the phenomenon of knowing that you know.

It may seem to the reader that these phenomena, while interesting, are quite distanced form a notion of self-deception, of a conscious or unconscious nature. Certainly we are not proposing them as examples of self-deception per se, in that they are not restricted to the criteria often regarded to typify self-deception. Rather, we believe that they set the stage within neurology and neuroanatomy for compartmentalization of an orderly but potentially restricted access to certain kinds of information. It thus supports a neurological substrate for possible "deception." The degree to which potentially adaptive self-deceptions may have simply grafted onto this system, or more actively directed the development or evolution of these dissociative symptoms, remains largely unknown.

REFERENCES

ANGELERGUES, R., DE AJURIAGUERRA, J., & HECAEN, H. (1960). La negation de la cecite a cours des lesions cerebrales. *Journal of Psychology, 4*, 381-404.

ANTON, G. (1893). Beitrage zur klinischen beurteilung zur localisation der muskelsinn-storungen im Grosshirn. *Zeitschrift für Heilkunde, 14*, 313-348.

BABINSKI, J. (1914). Contribution a l'étude des tronbles mentaux dans l'hémiplégie céré-brale (anosognosie). (Reprinted in *Revue Neurologique*, 1975, *46*, 315-332)

BENDER, M. B., & TEUBER, H. L. (1949). Disturbances of visual perception following cerebral lesions. *Journal of Psychology, 28*, 223-233.

CERMAK, L. S. (Ed.). (1982). *Human memory of amnesia*. Hillsdale, NJ: Erlbaum.

COHEN, N. (1984). Preserved learning capacity in amnesia: Evidence for multiple memory systems. In L. Squire & N. Butters (Eds.), *Neuropsychology of memory* (pp. 83-103). New York: Guilford Press.

COHEN, N., & SQUIRE, L. (1980). Preserved learning and retention of pattern-analyzing skill in amnesia: Dissociation of knowing how and of knowing that. *Science 210*, 201-202.

GAZZENIGA, M. S., & LE DOUX, J. E. (1978). *The integrated mind*. New York: Plenum.

HEAD, H. (1926). *Aphasia and kindred disorders of speech*. Cambridge, England: Cambridge University Press.

HECAEN, H. (1968). Essai d'interpretation des asomatognosics en pathologie caoticole. In M. M. Velasco-Suarey & F. Escobedo (Eds.), *Lobulo parietal* (pp. 141-156). Mexico City: Instituto National de Neurologia.

HECAEN, H., & ALBERT, M. L. (1978). *Human neuropsychology*. New York: Wiley.

HECAEN, H., & DE AJURIAGUERRA, J. (1954). Balent's syndrome (psychic paralysis of visual fixation and its minor forms). *Brain, 77*, 373-400.

HECAEN, H., & GOLDBLUM, M. (1972). Études neurolinguistigues sur l'aphasie sen-sorielle. In P. de Francisco (Ed.), *Dimensiones de la psiquiatria contemporanea*. Mexico City: S. A. Fournier.

HUPPERT, F., & PIERCY, M. (1979). Normal and abnormal forgetting in organic amnesia: Effect of locus of lesion. *Cortex, 18*, 358-390.

KIMURA, D. (1987). Are men's and women's brains really different? *Canadian Journal of Psychology, 28*, 133-147.

LHERMITTE, J. (1939). *L'image de votre corps*. Paris: Nouvelle Revue Critique.

LOCKARD, J. S. (1980). Speculations on the adaptive significance of self-deception. In J. S. Lockard (Ed.), *The evolution of human social behavior* (pp. 257-275). New York: Elsevier.

LOFTUS, E. F., & LOFTUS, G. R. (1980). On the permanence of stored information in the human brain. *American Psychologist, 35*, 409-420.

LOFTUS, E. F., MILLER, D. G., & BURNS, H. J. (1978). Semantic integration of verbal information into a visual memory. *Journal of Experimental Psychology, 4*, 19-31.

LURIA, A. R. (1966). *The higher cortical function in man.* New York: Basic Books.

MATEER, C. A., POLER, S. B., & OJEMANN, G. A. (1982). Sexual variation in cortical localization of naming as determined by stimulation mapping. *Behavioral and Brain Sciences, 5*, 310-311.

MCGLONE, J. (1980). Sex differences in human brain asymmetry: A critical survey. *Behavioral and Brain Sciences, 5*, 215-264.

NEISSER, U., & BECKLEN, R. (1975). Selective looking: Attending to visually specified events. *Cognitive Psychology, 7*, 480-494.

NIELSON, J. M. (1946). *Agnosia, aproxia, aphasia: Their value in cerebral localization* (2nd ed.). New York: Hoeber.

OJEMANN, G. A. (1977). Asymmetric function of the thalamus in man. *Annals of the New York Academy of Sciences, 299*, 380-396.

————. (1979). A review of the neurologic basis of human cognition, with special emphasis on language. *Allied Health and Behavioral Sciences, 1*, 341-384.

OLSEN, C. W., & RUBY, C. (1941). Anosognosia and autotopognosia. *Archives of Neurology and Psychiatry, 46*, 340-345.

POTZL, O. (1928). *Die optisch-agnostischen.* Deuticke, Leipzig-Wien: F. Storanger.

RIDDICH, G. (1917). Dissociation of visual perceptions due to occipital injuries, with special reference to appreciation of movement. *Brain, 40*, 15-47.

ROBINSON, G., & MERAV, A. (1976). Informed consent: Recall by patients tested postoperatively. *Annals of Thoracic Surgery, 22*, 209-212.

SHIMAMURA, A. P., & SQUIRE, L. R. (1986). Memory and metamemory: A study of the feeling-of-knowing phenomenon in amnesic patients. *Journal of Experimental Psychology, 12*, 452-460.

SPRINGER, S. P., & DEUTSCH, G. (1985). *Left brain, right brain* (2nd ed.). San Francisco: W. H. Freeman.

SQUIRE, L., & BUTTERS, N. (Eds.). (1984). *Neuropsychology of memory.* Hillsdale, NJ: Erlbaum.

VAN BOGAERT, L. (1934). Sur la pathologie de l'image de soi. *Annales Médico-Psychologiques, 92*, 519-555, 744-759.

VON MONOKOW, C. (1897). *Gehirn pathologie.* Wien: Nothnagel.

Websters's New World Dictionary of the American Language (college ed.). (1964). Cleveland and New York: World Publishing.

Webster's Third New International Dictionary. (1981). Springfield, MA: G. and C. Merriam.

WEISKRANTZ, L. (1972). Behavioral analysis of the monkey's visual nervous system. *Proceedings of the Royal Society of London* (Biological Sciences), *182*, 427-455.

WEISKRANTZ, L., WARRINGTON, E. K., SANDERS, M. D., & MARSHALL, J. (1974). Visual capacity in the hemianopic field following a restricted occipital ablation. *Brain, 97*, 709-728.

WERNICKE, C. (1874). *Der aphasische symptomenkomplex.* Breslau, Poland: M. Cahn and Weigert.

3

Learning to Lie
and Self-Deceive

CHILDREN'S NONVERBAL COMMUNICATION OF DECEPTION

ROBERT S. FELDMAN
ROBERT J. CUSTRINI
University of Massachusetts

Is lying bad? When the question is put in this most blunt form, most of us would readily agree that it is. So would most children; after all, we teach them that "honesty is the best policy," and George Washington's role in the early demise of his father's cherry tree is the subject of an oft-repeated tale. Yet, we also tell children that, given the appropriate circumstances, lying is quite acceptable—so acceptable, in fact, that at times we actually encourage them to be deceptive. What parents, for instance, have not informed their children that they should try to appear duly grateful and impressed upon the receipt of any gift, at least in the presence of the donor?

When we consider self-deception, the story is quite different. Aside from occasional comments to the effect of "don't fool yourself," not nearly the same explicit socialization effort is made. In fact, it is likely that most parents, teachers, and other socialization agents do not see self-deception as an issue to be addressed at all, or at least not with the same vigor that they attack the problem of other-deception.

Interestingly, this lack of interest has been mirrored in the research literature.

Much of the research discussed in this chapter was supported by grants from the National Institute of Mental Health, whose assistance is gratefully acknowledged.

Until the last decade, there has been little explicit attention given to self-deception. Moreover, when we consider the nonverbal behavioral correlates of self-deception, there is no research that can be identified on the topic.

In this chapter, we hope to spark some interest in self-deception, development, and nonverbal behavior by discussing a number of issues relating to both other- and self-deception. We will concentrate on research designed to show how children develop in their ability to manage nonverbal behavioral cues related to deception. Despite the fact that a dearth of experimental findings will force us to speculate shamelessly, we will try to demonstrate that research on deception toward others and on nonverbal skill has important implications for understanding how skill in self-deception changes during the course of development.

THEORETICAL BACKGROUND

Our perspective on self- and other-deception has been derived from theory and research on cognitive and social skills. We assume that the deliberate manipulation of nonverbal behavior that occurs when an individual is attempting to deceive reflects an ability that changes with age, experience, and socialization, and, as with other abilities, that there are individual differences in skill in the use of nonverbal behavior that occurs with verbal deception.

Experimental studies on deception and nonverbal behavior have repeatedly confirmed that nonverbal behavior can reveal when a person is being verbally deceptive (Zuckerman, De Paulo, & Rosenthal, 1981). For instance, Ekman and Friesen (1974) showed adult subjects both a pleasant and a stressful film, then the subjects were interviewed by a confederate. Subjects were told to inform the interviewer that the pleasant film was pleasant (honest condition) but that the stressful film was also pleasant (dishonest condition). Naive observers were able to distinguish, for the most part, which film (pleasant or stressful) the subjects had actually seen on the basis of the subjects' facial expressions and body movements. Moreover, voice tone (as measured by changes in pitch) was related to whether or not the subjects were being verbally deceptive (Ekman, Friesen, & Scherer, 1976). Similar results relating to pitch changes during deception were reported by Streeter, Krauss, Geller, Olson, and Apple (1977). Work by Feldman (1976) and Mehrabian (1971) also shows that a dissembling individual tends to disclose that he or she is being deceptive through nonverbal behavior.

Developmental Processes and the Management of Nonverbal Behavior

It seems reasonable that with increasing age children would show less spontaneous expressive nonverbal behavior as they gain increasing instrumental control over it. As children develop, they grow both in cognitive ability (e.g., Piaget & Inhelder, 1969) and fine muscular control (Charlesworth & Kreutzer, 1973). Furthermore, as children gain more awareness of social ecology and become less egocentric, they develop the ability to put themselves in the position of an observer and see the situation from the observer's point of view. Flavell and his associates have referred to this ability, in reference to verbal communication skill, as "taking the role of the other" (Flavell, Botkin, Fry, Wright, & Jarvis, 1968), or **role taking.**

With age, a child's ability to understand that there are differences between inner and outer states also increases. Selman (1980) has theorized that during middle childhood children come to understand that they can fool both themselves and other people. This is due to their growing realization that discrepancies can exist between their inner experience and their outer appearances. They come to see that they have greater access to their inner psychological experience and thoughts than do other people, and consequently are in a position to manipulate the appearance they present to others (Damon & Hart, 1982).

However, little research has looked directly at the development of the management of nonverbal behavior as a function of age. Some indirect evidence for the proposition that increasing age leads to more proficiency in the control and use of nonverbal behavior comes from a role-playing study by Odom and Lemond (1972). They asked children in kindergarten and fifth grade to encode poses representing eight emotions and found a clear developmental trend: the older subjects were more successful in producing the appropriate expressions (as determined by adult raters), suggesting that the older children had greater proficiency in the encoding and control of their nonverbal behavior. However, except for a few developmental studies comparing sighted with blind children in encoding ability (Dumas, 1932; Fulcher, 1942; Charlesworth, 1970), there appear to be no other studies that address the issue of what changes occur in the ability to produce nonverbal behavior.

DISCLOSURE OF DISSEMBLING FROM NONVERBAL BEHAVIOR

We began our own investigation into the development of the use and control of nonverbal behavior in children by experimentally examining how children disclose their verbal dissembling via their nonverbal behavior. Initially, our major goal was simply to demonstrate that children's nonverbal behavior would indeed reflect when they were being deceptive verbally.

In this first study (Feldman, Devin-Sheehan, & Allen, 1978), we used a tutoring situation in which grade-school-aged children acted as teachers to a confederate who was playing the role of student. The study investigated the teachers' nonverbal behavior when their positive verbal reinforcement was truthful or untruthful. The subjects (teachers) were instructed always to praise the responses of the student, regardless of whether or not the answers were correct. The confederate students answered most items correctly in one condition and incorrectly in another. Thus, the subject's response was veridical when the student performed well, and dissembled in the condition in which the student performed poorly. We hypothesized that the nonverbal behavior of the tutors would differ under the two conditions.

In order to test this hypothesis, short, silent samples of the subjects' behavior while they were being truthful or deceptive were shown to a group of judges. The judges were asked to rate how pleased the subjects actually were with their student. The judges' ratings showed that subjects appeared significantly happier when their praise was veridical than when it was nonveridical. Thus, the untrained third-grade observers could determine the truthfulness of the subjects' behavior simply through observation of their nonverbal behavior.

Results of an objective analysis of subjects' nonverbal behavior supported the observers' ratings. There were clear objective differences in the nonverbal behavior of truthful, compared with dissembling, subjects. Dissembling subjects smiled less, showed less pleasant mouth expressions and greater nervous hand movements, and paused more when speaking than did subjects who were being truthful. Thus, the major hypothesis of the experiment was confirmed: Genuine and dissembled praise resulted in differential nonverbal behavior. Not only was this difference apparent from objective measures of subjects' nonverbal behavior, but it could also be discerned by a group of untrained observers.

Still, our results did not show directly that children would be less proficient than adults in the ability to be deceptive toward others. To test this hypothesis more directly, our next study looked at the nonverbal disclosure of deception at three age levels.

DEVELOPMENTAL TRENDS IN THE NONVERBAL DISCLOSURE OF DECEPTION

In order to examine directly the assumption that children would be more obviously deceptive than adults, we carried out an experiment using three widely divergent age groups: first graders, seventh graders, and college students (Feldman, Jenkins, & Popoola, 1979). Our major hypothesis in the study was that due to age-related increases in cognitive ability, facial muscular control, and role-taking skills, success at avoiding the detection of verbal deception would increase with age.

We also examined the subjects' awareness of the possibility of nonverbal revelation of deception. It seems reasonable that the degree of publicness of a person's verbal deception (e.g., whether a person is under the scrutiny of the individual to whom he or she is lying) ought to affect the nonverbal disclosure of deception. If a person is cognizant that nonverbal behavior can reveal deception, then there ought to be manipulation of such nonverbal behavior—but only under public conditions. In contrast, private displays would not be censored, and thus the deception ought to be revealed more clearly in private than in public.

To test these hypotheses, we arranged for a group of first graders, seventh graders, and college-age students (with modal ages, respectively, of 6, 13, and 19 years) to be verbally truthful or deceptive while they were either alone or interacting with an adult interviewer. Our basic strategy was to devise a well-controlled situation in which the verbal behavior of the subjects was kept relatively constant. To do this, the subjects were told that the purpose of the experiment was to have them sample two drinks and to persuade an interviewer that both tasted good, regardless of the actual taste. According to the cover story, the purpose of the study was to determine how much ability people had in deceiving an observer, as actors in television commercials did.

Subjects were told to sample one of the drinks and then respond to a series of questions concerning how much they enjoyed the drink. They were encouraged by the experimenter to be as convincing as possible while describing both drinks in a favorable manner.

Each subject was actually responding truthfully with respect to one and deceptively when referring to the other. One drink was a sweetened grape beverage mixed according to directions, while the other was prepared without sugar. Because the subjects always evaluated both drinks positively, they were presumedly responding honestly after tasting the sweetened beverage and deceptively when discussing the bitter, unsweetened drink.

Subjects were assigned randomly to be interviewed in either a public or private situation. Those interviewed publicly were asked questions about the drinks in the presence of an interviewer and therefore realized that their facial expressions and body movements could be observed. Subjects interviewed privately received directions and questions from an audio tape recorder and believed that they could not be seen by the interviewer. In addition, they were told that only their verbal responses were being recorded.

A hidden videotape camera was used to record a frontal view of each subject's head and shoulders during the interview, and ten- to twenty-second silent samples from each subject were then shown to a group of adult observers, who rated subjects on how much they were actually enjoying the drink.

The results of the study provided clear support for the hypothesis under consideration: the age of the subject influenced observers' accuracy in detecting deception on the basis of facial expression. First graders were most accurately decoded by naive observers; observers could readily discern when they were being deceptive by analyzing their nonverbal behavior. In contrast, the seventh graders and college students were successful in avoiding detection of deception.

Interestingly, though, there appeared to be differences between the seventh graders and college students in the manner in which they avoided detection. Seventh graders were successful in deceiving naive observers by appearing to equally enjoy both drinks, while college students tended to exaggerate their nonverbal behavior so that they appeared to enjoy the unpleasant drink more than the pleasant drink.

These results suggest that successful deception using control of facial expressions may take at least two forms, as suggested by Ekman (1972) in his discussion of what he terms **display rules.** In one type of control, individuals may simply reproduce a facial expression that would be appropriate for a situation in which what they were saying was indeed true. In a second type of control, people may augment or exaggerate what would be their natural response if what was being verbalized were true. Applying these two categories of facial deception to the present results, it appears that the seventh graders were simply reproducing what their appropriate nonverbal reactions would be. The college-age group, on the other hand, was using the augmentative mode of control; they appeared to be actively exaggerating their nonverbal facial expression to convey the appropriate meaning. The data also show that at all three age levels subjects appeared to be more pleased in the public interview than in the private interview. This finding indicates that even the youngest subjects had some degree of control over their nonverbal behavior, since their facial expressions did appear more negative when they thought they could not be seen by the interviewer. The inability of the children to avoid detection, however, suggests that they may lack more subtle types of nonverbal skills.

The relationship between age and degree of nonverbal disclosure can be explained in terms of cognitive skills and degree of control over facial musculature. Older subjects are likely to have greater cognitive awareness regarding what is being displayed nonverbally and greater control over their facial musculature. They are also, presumably, more cognizant of the impact their nonverbal behavior has upon others. These abilities are assumed to increase with age as a result of experience in social interactions as well as physiological and cognitive development.

DETECTING DECEPTION FROM NONFACIAL CHANNELS

Our previous work confirmed quite clearly that there are developmental changes in the degree to which verbal deception toward others is disclosed from facial expressions. Obviously, however, the face is not the only nonverbal channel that potentially could be related to developmental changes in the disclosure of deception. Indeed, Ekman and Friesen (1969) have presented a comprehensive and systematic theoretical exposition of the relation between nonverbal behavior and deception in adults. They have suggested that nonfacial behaviors might be even more informative of verbal deception than facial nonverbal behavior, and their arguments have implications for developmental changes.

Ekman and Friesen's hypothesis rests on the assumption that an individual's ability to be nonverbally deceptive depends on three factors: (1) the **sending capacity** or amount of information a particular body location is capable of transmitting, (2) the **external feedback** or degree to which the behavior of others is perceived to be a reaction to one's own nonverbal behavior, and (3) the **internal feedback** or awareness of one's nonverbal behavior received from a particular body part. Variations in these factors result in the differential success in controlling and fabricating displays of nonverbal behavior.

According to Ekman and Friesen (1969), the face is considerably higher in sending capacity, external feedback, and internal feedback than the rest of the body. They suggest, further, that deception will be revealed differentially depending on body location in adults. Specifically, according to the theory, the face will show underlying feelings the least, since individuals will attempt to dissemble to the greatest degree by manipulating and using the face. It follows that, since individuals will be attending primarily to the face, the rest of the body will tend to reveal what is being felt more clearly.

It should be noted that Ekman and Friesen's theory was meant to apply to adult behavior. However, the theory's developmental implications are clear: Young children, who are relatively insensitive to the need to control their nonverbal behavior and who lack cognitive and muscular sophistication, might be expected to be more revealing in their facial nonverbal behavior than in their bodily nonverbal behavior. As their age increases, children's deception might be increasingly revealed by body movements rather than facial expressions.

To test this hypothesis, we carried out an experiment in which we examined the ability of adult observers to detect verbal dissembling from the nonverbal cues transmitted by the faces and bodies of children (Feldman & White, 1980). We reasoned that the degree to which untrained adults could detect deception would differ according to the age of the child and according to whether the face or the body was being viewed.

The study concentrated on a sample of children ranging in age from 5 through 12. The procedure employed to elicit verbal deception was similar to that used in the previous study. The subjects were told that the purpose of the experiment was to sample two drinks and convince an interviewer that both drinks tasted good or that both tasted bad. Again, since in one case the drink actually tasted good and in the other it tasted bad, the children were being truthful half of the time and deceptive half of the time. Two cameras simultaneously recorded each child. One was focused on the subject's face, and the other provided a view of the child's body from the neck down. Judges then rated samples of the children, indicating the degree to which they appeared deceptive.

The results of the study revealed distinctly differing developmental trends for boys and girls, depending on whether the face or body was being rated. Looking first at the girls' data, it appeared that our hypothesis of a decrease with age in how much the face revealed was confirmed. There was a clear (and statistically significant) linear trend in the decline with age. Unexpectedly, however, ratings of body disclosure tended to *increase* with age. Thus, the females showed a decrease in their facial revelation and an increase in their body revelation with age.

The males' data represented a surprising contrast to that of the females. Male disclosure of deception, using facial cues, tended to increase with age, producing a significant linear trend. In contrast, there was a slight (although nonsignificant) decrease in revelation of deception in the boys' movements. Although we do not have a definite explanation for the discrepancy between male and female ratings, one likely explanation rests on the differential socialization accorded boys and girls. Buck's work on the encoding of emotional experience facially has shown an increase in female expressivity and a concomitant decrease in male expressivity in preschool children (Buck, Savin, Miller, & Caul, 1972; Buck, Miller, & Caul, 1974). Buck suggests that women may be rewarded for being more emotionally expressive than men. Because females may have greater opportunity to experience and learn about their own nonverbal displays of emotion, they may become increasingly proficient in the control of their nonverbal behavior. In comparison, males, who may be discouraged from displays of nonverbal behavior, may become less adept at its manipulation. Such an argument is highly speculative, however, and until the finding of increasing male revelation is replicated, these results should be regarded as tentative.

Perhaps the most intriguing finding to emerge from this study is that decreases in facial disclosure are related to increases in body disclosure. Such a finding is reminiscent of the equilibrium processes described by Argyle and Dean (1965). They suggest that individuals try to maintain an equilibrium between various nonverbal and verbal signals of intimacy. When one manifestation of intimacy increases (such as a closer interpersonal distance), an individual will compensate by decreasing the intimacy of some other signal (such as decreased eye contact). We can apply this notion to our findings by suggesting that verbal deception produces an internal state of arousal. If nonverbal cues relating to arousal are not discharged through one channel (e.g., the face), they may occur in some other channel (e.g., the body).

DECEPTION AND ROLE TAKING

We suggested earlier in this chapter that there were a number of factors related to success at deception, including cognitive ability, muscular control, and role-taking skill. Although the research reported here provides evidence for a number of age differences in nonverbal disclosure of deception, it does not provide information regarding the mechanisms that underlie our findings. In the following experiment, however, we directly examined the effect of children's role-taking ability on their skill at manipulating their nonverbal behavior while being verbally deceptive (Feldman, White, & Lobato, 1982).

Role-taking skills would seem to be particularly critical in developing control over nonverbal behavior during social interaction. Role-taking theory assumes that the skill to be an effective interactant in social situations rests upon the ability to take the "other" (the interactant) into account. The individual must not only possess a set of attributes or performance skills in a given situation, but he or she must also be aware of the nature of the impact that various alternative behaviors will have upon the other. Thus, an individual must have a sensitivity toward the presence of an interactant.

To test the hypothesis that role-taking skill is related to the ability to avoid detection of verbal deception via nonverbal behavior, we administered an objective measure of role taking to a group of children and then led them to be either verbally deceptive or truthful. Untrained adult judges then rated whether they thought the children were being truthful or deceptive.

The results of the study provided support for the hypothesized relationship between role-taking ability and skill at avoiding detection while being deceptive. There was a significant positive relationship between the ability to take the perspective of others and success at avoiding detection. The awareness that one's nonverbal behavior during social interactions has an impact on the perception of others appears to be an important factor influencing the ability to control nonverbal cues. Children who are better able to take the perspective of others in the role-taking task are also more effective at controlling their nonverbal behavior.

SPECULATIONS ON DEVELOPMENT, NONVERBAL BEHAVIOR, AND SELF-DECEPTION

The studies we have discussed provide clear support for the position that the ability to control and manipulate one's nonverbal behavior is a developmental skill. We suggested that due to differences in cognitive ability, muscular control, and role-taking skills children would vary in how well they are able to make their nonverbal behavior congruent with their verbal behavior. Each of the studies reported here lends support to these propositions. In the first two experiments, we found evidence that children are not as adept as adults in the ability to avoid detection of verbal deception. For instance, while first graders were decoded with relative accuracy, seventh graders and college students were able to manipulate their nonverbal behavior sufficiently well to avoid detection.

Results of our third and fourth experiments provide evidence that changes in the ability to use and control nonverbal behavior are not just a function of age per se. Rather, the data suggest that differential socialization processes in males and females may result in different patterns of changes in the use of nonverbal behavior. Moreover, the data indicate that proficiency in manipulating one's nonverbal behavior may be tied to role-taking skill. We found that, quite apart from age-related trends, better roletakers were less able to be detected from their nonverbal behavior while being verbally deceptive than were poorer roletakers.

These later results are particularly important from a theoretical point of view because they allow us to relate deception toward others (what we will call other-deception) to self-deception, and speculate on the relationship between nonverbal behavior and self-deception.

Before considering self-deception it is necessary to delineate some of the differences between self- and other-deception. One major point regards the inherent antagonism between a deceiver and audience in other-directed deception. When a child attempts to deceive another person, it is generally an adversarial relationship; the deceiver is trying to "put something over" on the audience and not reveal his or her deception. Likewise, the research paradigms that we and other researchers have employed to investigate deception assume that the audience is trying to uncover the deception.

In contrast, the same degree of antagonism inherent in other-deception does not exist in self-deception, or at least the nature of the antagonism is qualitatively different. For instance, guilt over lying to another is absent from self-deception. Moreover, the consequences for failing to successfully carry out the deception are different for self- and other-deception. When a child is caught in a deception, the act may have *external* consequences: a spanking or some other form of punishment. In contrast, failures of *self*-deception may result in unwanted knowledge or revelations about oneself, which may produce *internal* consequences.

On the other hand, there are general similarities between other- and self-deception. We saw how younger children, lacking the ability to take the role of the other, are unlikely to try to modify their nonverbal behavior in reaction to the presence of an audience. They simply lack the cognitive ability to know that others may have a different perspective from their own and therefore do not attend to their nonverbal behavior.

Analogously, we may assume that one's emotional responses are associated with a labeling process that becomes increasingly sophisticated and accurate with age (Buck, 1984). If this assumption is correct, we could speculate that young children involved in self-deception, being unable to hold or consider more than a single perspective at a time, would show a relative lack of introspective tendencies. They would accept their initial understanding and labeling of an emotion as correct and not question that the label they have used, or their perception, might be inaccurate. If this were true, the increasing sophistication of the older child might make self-deception more difficult. The same processes that make older children and adults better at deceiving others might operate to make them *less* adept at deceiving themselves.

There are other reasons to assume that, as children get older, their increasing cognitive and nonverbal skills allow them to become less effective self-deceivers. Specifically, there is evidence that not only do children increase in the ability to present themselves effectively towards others, they also grow in their decoding abilities regarding the detection of deception through the use of *others'* nonverbal behavior (e.g, DePaulo & Jordan, 1982). Since the facial musculature of the developing child becomes increasingly more sophisticated, as do presumably the neural links between the muscles and brain, we might likewise expect that older children would be more adept at understanding their own facial expressions. If the facial expressions reflect self-deception, and the older children are able to better decode and understand the meaning of these expressions, then we could again argue that older children would be less adept at self-deception.

Arguments Suggesting that Children Develop Greater Skill at Self-Deception

While the evidence at first seems to point directly towards the view that children show less skill in self-deception with increasing age, in fact one could argue just the opposite. For one thing, it is reasonable to assume that with increasing age there not only is greater decoding skill generally, but there is also greater awareness that the nonverbal behavior of others represents a significant channel of communication which requires attention and monitoring (Feldman, White, & Lobato, 1982). It is possible that as children learn to attend more to the nonverbal behavior of others their attention is focused away from their own nonverbal behavior. Ultimately, this could result in their being better at deceiving themselves, since they might be less attentive to and may overlook self-generated nonverbal deception cues.

Increased Sophistication in the Use of Defense Mechanisms

Another possibility is that children, as they mature and become better able to detect their own attempts at self-deception, employ **defense mechanisms** which show an increasing level of sophistication in their capacity to distort reality and thereby alleviate feelings of anxiety. Primitive defense mechanisms such as **denial** or **repression** are, of course, not eliminated entirely; as Vaillant (1971) suggests, it is probably more useful to think of these lower-level defenses as evolving into more mature mechanisms rather than being abandoned or replaced. The more highly evolved the defenses become, the more effective they are in allowing the individual to distort reality.

Such evolutionary changes in the employment of defense mechanisms are postulated in a work by Cramer (1983), who suggests that mature forms of a given defense are preceded by a series of substages which may be directly linked to the individual's level of physical and cognitive development. According to the author, the earliest precursor to the denial defense, for example, is illustrated by a young child's ability to "tune out" his or her environment by sleeping through a loud party or fireworks display. As children begin to develop physically, they begin engaging in "denial in act," in which the eyes or ears might be covered in an attempt to block out an aversive stimulus. Finally, with the development of language, verbal statements designed to distort reality and thereby make it more pleasant become common.

We have seen how a single type of defense—in this case, denial—may evolve and become more effective as the young child matures. It has also been suggested that certain forms of defensive strategies predominate at different stages of development: Primitive forms such as denial or repression are common in early childhood, and more complex forms such as **intellectualization** or **sublimation** predominate in adolescence and adulthood. There is some empirical evidence to suggest that this may be the case.

Cramer (1983) examined the relative frequencies of occurrence of three increasingly complex defense mechanisms—**denial, projection**, and **identification**—among four groups of children with mean ages of 6, 10, 14½, and 16 years. Using subject responses to a series of TAT cards, she found that the use of denial was highest among the youngest group, projection was highest among the two middle groups, and identification was highest among the oldest group. The results from this study suggest the possibility of a positive relationship between an individual's age and the level of sophistication of his or her most frequently used defenses.

We could speculate that it is the individual's growing ability to detect his or her own self-deception which ultimately motivates the development of increasingly more advanced defenses. Consider a five-year-old girl whose mother is killed in an automobile crash. Unable to cope with this sudden loss, the child may attempt to shield herself by pretending that the accident never occurred. Ten years later, when the girl must face the death of a close friend, the denial defense may no longer be effective in alleviating her pain; so she resorts to the use of the more advanced mechanism of intellectualization, in which she distances herself from her true emotions by telling herself that death is a natural phenomenon which we must all eventually face.

In another example, a ten-year-old boy caught leafing through the pages of a hard-core sex magazine may convince himself that he only looked at the pictures because a friend "made him," thereby projecting his own undesirable urges onto his friend. At the age of twenty, though, projection is no longer an adequate mode of defense against these urges. He must now employ a more sophisticated mechanism to avoid feeling anxious, perhaps by working as an undercover detective in a police department vice squad where his undesirable urges may be transformed into a more socially acceptable form through sublimation.

It is important to note that the more "mature" defenses are also relatively *more* effective at alleviating anxiety than are the age-appropriate defense mechanisms used by younger children. Projecting the blame for the initial instance of magazine viewing onto a friend may have been effective at first, but future desires to repeat the act in the friend's absence are liable to bring about new pangs of guilt in our ten-year-old. With continued use, the projection defense is likely to lose its palliative effect quite rapidly. However, sublimation of these urges through a socially accepted occupation which allows for the partial fulfillment of such desires has the potential for long-lasting effectiveness in the alleviation of such guilt. Thus it is possible that as we mature from children to adults, we become more adept at self-deception not only in technique, but also in the overall effectiveness and generalizability of our defenses to various types of anxiety-producing situations.

CONCLUSIONS

In sum, there is a cogent argument to be made for the position that self-deception will become more pronounced with increasing age. The research on other-deception shows quite clearly that children become increasingly successful in being deceptive nonverbally toward others and in identifying, through the use of nonverbal behavioral cues, when others are being deceptive. As children's understanding of other-deception grows, however, they are more likely to understand their own instances of self-deception. If this is the case, they are forced to use increasingly sophisticated defense mechanisms to protect themselves. Ability in self-deception, then, is likely to increase with age. It is ironic indeed that the increased skill in understanding others may act to decrease one's awareness of oneself.

REFERENCES

ARGYLE, M., & DEAN, J. (1965). Eye-contact, distance, and affiliation. *Sociometry, 28,* 289-304.

BUCK, R. (1984). *Nonverbal behavior and the communication of affect.* New York: Guilford.

BUCK, R., MILLER, R. E., & CAUL, W. F. (1974). Sex, personality, and physiological variables in the communication of emotion via facial expression. *Journal of Personality and Social Psychology, 30,* 587-596.

BUCK, R., SAVIN, V. J., MILLER, R. E., & CAUL, W. F. (1972). Communication of affect through facial expressions. *Journal of Personality and Social Psychology, 23,* 362-371.

CHARLESWORTH, W. R. (1970). *Surprise reactions in congenitally blind and sighted children.* National Institute of Mental Health Progress Report.

CHARLESWORTH, W. R., & KREUTZER, M. A. (1973). Facial expressions of infants and children. In P. Ekman (Ed.), *Darwin and facial expression* (pp. 91-168). New York: Academic Press.

CRAMER, P. (1983, August). *Defense mechanisms: A developmental study.* Paper presented at the 91st Annual Convention of the American Psychological Association, Anaheim, CA.

DAMON, W., & HART, D. (1982). The development of self-understanding from infancy through adolescence. *Child Development, 53,* 841-864.

DEPAULO, B. M., & JORDAN, A. (1982). Age changes in deceiving and detecting deception. In R. S. Feldman (Ed.), *Development of nonverbal behavior in children* (pp. 151-180). New York: Springer-Verlag.

DUMAS, G. (1932). La mimique des aveugles. *Bulletin de l'Academie de Medicine, 107,* 607-610.

EKMAN, P. (1972). Universals and cultural differences in facial expressions of emotions. In J. Cole (Ed.), *Nebraska Symposium on Motivation, 1971* (Vol. 19, pp. 207-283) Lincoln, NB: University of Nebraska Press.

EKMAN, P., & FRIESEN, W. V. (1969). Nonverbal leakage and clues to deception. *Psychiatry, 32,* 88-106.

———. (1974). Detecting deception from the body or face. *Journal of Personality and Social Psychology, 29,* 288-298.

EKMAN, P., FRIESEN, W. V., & SCHERER, K. (1976). Body movements and voice pitch in deceptive interaction. *Semiatica, 17,* 23-27.

FELDMAN, R. S. (1976). Nonverbal disclosure of deception and interpersonal affect. *Journal of Educational Psychology, 68,* 807-816.

FELDMAN, R. S., DEVIN-SHEEHAN, L., & ALLEN, V. L. (1978). Nonverbal cues as indicators of verbal dissembling. *American Educational Research Journal, 15,* 217-231.

FELDMAN, R. S., JENKINS, L., & POPOOLA, L. (1979). Detection of deception in adults and children via facial expressions. *Child Development, 50,* 350-355.

FELDMAN, R. S., & WHITE, J. B. (1980). Detecting deception in children. *Journal of Communication, 30,* 121-128.

FELDMAN, R. S., WHITE, J. B., & LOBATO, D. (1982). Social skills and nonverbal behavior. In R. S. Feldman (Ed.), *Development of nonverbal behavior in children* (pp. 259-277). New York: Springer-Verlag.

FLAVELL, J. H., WITH BOTKIN, P. T., FRY, C. K., WRIGHT, J. D., & JARVIS, P. T. (1968). *The development of role-taking and communication skills in children.* New York: Wiley.

FULCHER, J. S. (1942). "Voluntary" facial expressions in blind and seeing children. *Archives of Psychology, 27,* 5-49.

MEHRABIAN, A. (1971). Nonverbal betrayal of feeling. *Journal of Experimental Research in Personality, 5,* 64-73.

ODOM, R. D., & LEMOND, C. M. (1972). Developmental differences in the perception and production of facial expressions. *Child Development, 43,* 359-369.

PIAGET, J., & INHELDER, B. (1969). *The psychology of the child.* New York: Basic Books.

SELMAN, R. (1980). *The growth of interpersonal understanding.* New York: Acadmic Press.

STREETER, L. A., KRAUSS, R. M., GELLER, V., OLSON, C., & APPLE, W. (1977). Pitch changes during attempted deception. *Journal of Personality and Social Psychology, 35,* 345-350.

VAILLANT, G. E. (1971). Theoretical hierarchy of adaptive ego mechanisms. *Archives of General Psychiatry, 24,* 107-117.

ZUCKERMAN, M., DEPAULO, B., & ROSENTHAL, R. (1981). Verbal and nonverbal communication of deception. In L. Berkowitz (Ed.), *Advances in experimental social psychology* (Vol. 14, pp. 1-59). New York: Academic Press.

4

Societal Roles
in Self-Deception

James F. Welles
Box 821, Orient, New York

Know Thyself! For over two thousand years Western civilization has developed and flourished without ever quite coming to grips with this most basic challenge of Greek philosophy. The general trend in Western culture has been to replace belief with knowledge, but we seem to excel at gathering knowledge about everything while understanding too little about ourselves. Recent history has played like a spectacular Hollywood extravaganza gone berserk, with lavish technical effects but no character development. One is tempted to suggest that perhaps we just do not want to know who we really are.

One of the primary problems in learning about ourselves is that we are emotionally involved in the process. Our emotions affect our judgment, and even the scientists responsible for replacing belief with knowledge have been much too emotional about who we are. Objectivity fades when scientists accommodate their thinking to the moral implications of their theories about human behavior. However, respect for knowledge has led to a trend away from theories preadapted to some particular view of human nature (e.g., people are good, bad, intrinsically moral, or whatever) toward conceptualizations grounded on functional analysis.

One of the more flattering scientific theories of humanity views people as rational beings who process information logically; its corollary is that human behavior is under conscious control. Another more sophisticated theory sees humans in terms of learning through social interaction. The control mechanism in this model comes in the form of social norms. A third theory, which is really an extreme extension of the learning model, views people as inner directed, with control internalized through the superego. For each of these theories there is a corresponding form of self-deception based on the formation and interaction of psychic schemas—patterns or templates for thought and behavior.

The thesis presented here is both simple and profound: Self-deception is a fundamental principle of life in human social groups. Any particular social group is defined by the sharing of cognitive and normative schemas. Self-deception is the systematic discrepancy between these schemas—that is, between the expressed set of beliefs and the relevant behavioral acts. Groups members characteristically persuade themselves that they are something more than they are or do. This basic disposition has been the leading edge of cultural advancement in that it allows imagination to transcend reality and alter everything but our dependence on self-deception.

This chapter concerns itself primarily with the interaction of self-deception and group identity. Although theorists have roundly ignored this relationship, reference will be made to relevant work in the field of personality psychology that deals with the function of self-deception at the level of the individual psyche.

Allport (1937) provided a brief account of the human capacity for self-deception. He pointed out that at first sight, the ability to fool oneself would seem to be a fatal invention of nature, for living would seem to require an accurate evaluation of one's own motives and capacities. He considered the survival advantage of self-deception to be the delay it permits a person in coping with unpleasant truths.

Trivers (1976) suggested that the selective advantage of self-deception is due to its role in deceiving others. A person who is unconscious of his own motives is not likely to betray them to someone else.

Krakauer (1978) perceived an even more profound role of self-deception in the individual. He reasoned that egos that are separated from their unconscious have less emotional involvement and therefore can think better. Although this may be a primary survival advantage of self-deception, there is also a drawback in that perception is skewed away from an accurate appraisal of events; the assessment of reality becomes a compromise between rational objectivity and emotional commitment to existing schemas.

Experimental evidence that self-deception occurs was provided by investigations of Gur and Sackeim (1979) into the processes of subconscious perception and rejection of information. They had subjects listen to taped voices, some of which were their own. The subjects were to identify their own voices when they heard them. At the same time, the Galvanic Skin Response was measured. As the reaction to one's own voice registers differently on the GSR than does the reaction to someone else's, a subconscious measure of voice identification was available. This demonstrated that information is indeed sifted out at the subconscious level, for a subject was often not consciously aware of the identity of a voice which he had correctly recognized and reacted to at the subconscious level. Of course, this implies a more complex psychic organization than the simple, conscious level of functioning recognized within the limitations of the rational model.

THE RATIONAL MODEL

Richard Leakey (1977) provided a classic statement of the evolution of humanity as viewed by supporters of the rational model. He stated that the trend has been toward monitoring more accurately what is happening in the real world and assembling the incoming information to form an even clearer *Gestaltwelt*, artificial but representative, in the brain. This is fine as far as it goes. Our perception of the world is becoming both more extensive and progressively refined, but it is still hampered by our desires and expectations.

A description of the ideal rational personality has been provided by Hall and Lindzey (1970). According to them, when the symbolized experiences that constitute the self faithfully mirror the experiences of the person, the individual is adjusted, mature, and fully functioning. Such a person can accept the entire range of organismic experience without threat or anxiety and is able to think realistically. One can only hypothesize an ideal society for such an ideal personality.

The ideal mental state appropriate for the rational model is one of **cognitive consistency**. Although the principle of consistency relates here primarily to cognitions, it presumably applies not only to an individual's cognitions but also to the relations between those and various forms of behavior (Shaver, 1981). There is a need for *Gestalt*, a need to know, with discrepancies in the cognitions of the perceiver creating ''dissonance'' or ''strain,'' which motivates the person to think and behave in ways which will result in greater cognitive consistency (Proshansky & Seidenberg, 1965).

Cognitive dissonance is, according to the rational model, the common motivating factor for human behavior. It occurs when an individual simultaneously holds two inconsistent cognitions. The existence of dissonance, being psychologically uncomfortable, motivates a person to reduce the dissonance and achieve consonance (Festinger, 1957).

However, the theory of cognitive dissonance does not explain the human disposition to act in an *irrational but unemotional* pattern of behavior contradictory to expressed beliefs. Nor does it explain why emotional distress rather than relief results from revelation of such a contradictory state. Nor, finally, does it explain why group members get emotionaly disturbed when someone presumes to behave according to beliefs officially sanctioned and unofficially ignored.

Beliefs

Beliefs are the fundamental building blocks of the rational conceptual structure. On the basis of direct observation or information received from outside sources, a person forms or learns a number of beliefs about an object. The totality of a person's beliefs serves as the informational basis that ultimately determines attitudes, intentions, and behaviors (Fishbein & Ajzen, 1975).

Beliefs are descriptive or inferential. **Descriptive beliefs** are formed on the basis of direct observation and tend to be fairly veridical. There is little evidence that personal factors such as desires, attitudes, or personality characteristics have any systematic effects on the formation of descriptive beliefs (Fishbein & Ajzen, 1975). (Inferential beliefs will be considered later in this chapter.)

Within the framework of the rational model, beliefs formed are thought to reflect accurately what occurred. Festinger (1954) suggested that people strive to hold correct opinions or beliefs about the world. He posited the existence of a drive to determine whether or not one's opinions were ''correct.'' The ultimate in the rationality of belief formation is Bayes's theorem, which is concerned with the formation or revision of beliefs in light of new information. This theorem is a model that describes optimal revision in probabilities; that is, it describes how probabilities should change if the available information is properly utilized (Fishbein & Ajzen, 1975).

Fishbein and Ajzen explicitly view the human as an essentially rational organism who uses the information at his disposal to make judgments, form evaluations, and arrive at decisions. They cite abundant evidence to indicate that an individual's belief structure in a carefully controlled experimental situation is internally consistent and tends to be compatible with Bayes's theorem. Thus, although a person may misperceive objective probabilities (this is a crucial qualification), when his subjective probabilities are considered, Bayes's theorem allows quite accurate predictions of belief information, if not behavior. The human may be accordingly viewed as a fairly rational processor of information. Belief formation is not capricious, nor is there any systematic distortion by motivational or emotional biases.

All in all, Fishbein and Ajzen appear to be describing the ideal human mind in splendid isolation—a mathematical, rational computer. This is the last scene of a divine act—the behavioral scientist creating man in his own image.

The Schema

Looking outward from the rational model, the search for information is guided by a **cognitive schema** which affects perception by leading one to emphasize or ignore particular cues from the external world. From the time a schema is constructed, the individual will attend to incoming information that agrees with elements of the schema and ignore much of the information that is discrepant. Further, the schema affects memory by limiting recall of stored information and even fills in for missing information should experience be limited (Hamilton, 1979). Also, it affects social perception through the self-perpetuating act of stereotyping (Snyder & Uranowitz, 1978).

The vital role of the schema cannot be overemphasized. This was made dramatically clear by the disintegration of the nonpolitical middle-class prisoners in German concentration camps (Bettelheim, 1943). These people were least able to withstand the shock of internment and found themselves utterly unable to comprehend what had happened to them. They had no consistent philosophy to protect their integrity as human beings, so they turned to antisocial behavior and suicide.

While it may seem odd to suggest that people died in such places for lack of a functional schema, that is apparently exactly what happened. Other groups of prisoners coped with the same physical circumstances and survived in greater proportion and with their self-respect intact because they were psychologically capable of coping with their plight.

An existing schema may be not merely vital but sacred to the point of irrational resistance to revision. A tragic demonstration of such a commitment was made by members of the medical profession in 1847, when Dr. Ignaz Semmelweis attempted to introduce sanitary measures in a maternity ward of the Allgemein Krankenhaus in Vienna. Mortality rates stood at 18% in such wards before Dr. Semmelweis insisted that physicians wash their hands between performing autopsies and examining patients. Within a month, mortality plummeted to below 3% and in the next month below 2%.

His professional colleagues, all of whom had taken a sacred oath to relieve pain and suffering, relieved Dr. Semmelweis instead. His contract was not renewed at the end of the year. Out went the basins, along with the time-wasting nuisance of hand washing. Mortality returned to a comfortable 18%. The schema, not the patients, had been saved.

This story would be sad enough if it stopped there, but it repeated itself the next year in Budapest. The only change was that Dr. Semmelweis stayed on the staff of the hospital in Hungary, enduring the disdain and sarcasm of his colleagues, until his mind snapped. He died in a mental institution (McMillen, 1968).

Another example from the history of medicine adds an amusing twist to the basic theme of the rejection of information which threatens the schema. This occurred in the seventeenth century, when the University of Paris was the international Supreme Court of Medicine. The standard treatment for fever was bleeding when, in 1638, the Jesuits in Peru discovered quinine. The cures accomplished by the use of this drug were nothing short of miraculous, due in part to its own merit and in part to the fact that patients escaped the prevailing medical practice of the day. It is hardly surprising to learn that the University of Paris banned the drug as "unconstitutional" and dangerous—meaning, presumably, to the patients.

Enter a quack named Talbot. He mixed Peruvian bark with other ingredients, such as honey, and put the result out as a secret panacea. He gave it a new name and sold it under a theory which did not conflict with the rational ideas of the time about the cure of fever. After curing the Dauphin, he refused a princely sum to disclose the secret. Instead, he accepted a large annuity and a patent of nobility in return for his promise to disclose the contents of his remedy after his death. Ten years after Talbot died, the learned men of the time found it was the despised Peruvian bark which had been the foundation of the career of this distinguished medical statesman. By this time, thanks largely to their own efforts, his reputation was unassailable, so the drug had to be accepted (Arnold, 1937).

The schema may be protected not only by rejecting information which is incompatible with it but also by inventing information which is supportive. An unfortunate example of this phenomenon comes from the annals of science around the turn of this century. In 1903, Rene Blodlot, a distinguished French physicist at the University of Nancy, discovered a new type of radiation called N rays. This would have been remarkable under most circumstances, but it is even more remarkable when one considers that they did not even exist. It was not a hoax—just an honest mistake. Even more remarkable, however, were the confirming reports which poured in from around the world. Once N rays became a part of the cognitive schema of science, the affair truly became a case of believing is seeing. In fact, some scientists vied for the honors of prior discovery. Eventually, the self-corrective mechanism of science caught up with the more imaginative practitioners, and the matter was quietly deflated (Klotz, 1980).

The rational model in and of itself is too self-contained and sterile to be of much value to anyone hoping to understand human behavior. It leaves one with an image of elemental beliefs and ideas banging around the barren spaces of the mind, combining to form the most probable intellectual compounds that conditions of time, space, and pressure permit. Even in its shortcomings, however, the rational model points the way to a more engrossing and complex problem—how does the mind interact with the environment to obtain the information it uses to construct the sustaining schema?

THE LEARNING MODEL

The learning model assumes that successive revisions of hypotheses occur according to the effects of social influence. This influence takes two forms—informational and normative. Both affect the cognitive schema.

Inferential Beliefs

Informational social influence leads to the formation of **inferential beliefs** through a person's acceptance of data obtained from another as evidence about reality (Deutsch & Gerard, 1955). In contrast to the independent formation of descriptive beliefs by an individual, personality factors play a major role in the formation of inferential beliefs, as these are based on data gathered through interactions with other people (Fishbein & Ajzen, 1975). These inferential beliefs are crucial to the modification of the cognitive schema by social experience, and they make the cognitive schema of an individual a party to a system of beliefs—the creed—of a group.

Norms

Along with the creed composed of mutual beliefs, group members also hold a **common normative schema** that provides a set of behavioral expectations based on similar experiences of normative social influences. As the achievement of a group's objectives may depend on the extent to which the activities of its members are coordinated, the learning of norms is vital in determining who does what, when, and how, and is thus crucial for promoting group success (Proshansky & Seidenberg, 1965).

Indirectly, the norms of a group influence and contribute to the creed, or "social reality," of the members. Some inferential beliefs of a person cannot be validated by objective means or by logical criteria. The truth of these beliefs is considered established by consensual agreement; the fact that other people who behave in similar ways hold similar beliefs attests to their validity (Proshansky & Seidenberg, 1965). It is important to note that the cognitive and normative schemas are not necessarily mutually consistent. In fact, the discrepancy is systematic and defines the condition of self-deception.

An indication of how this condition can be learned is provided by the double-bind hypotheses of the origin of childhood schizophrenia. The basic situation is one of a conflict between verbal and nonverbal messages. An example would be of a parent saying, "I love you" while holding a child stiffly away, implying "you disgust me" (Bateson, Jackson, Haley, & Weakland, 1956). One way to cope with the inherent confusion of such an experience is for the child to deal with the verbal and nonverbal stimuli on separate tracks. One leads to a cognitive schema of verbal information, the other to a normative schema of behavioral expectation. As we shall see, the two are interrelated to a degree inversely proportional to emotional involvement.

Attitudes

The double-bind experience is, of course, an extreme and dramatic example of the more general phenomenon of learning adaptive responses to a social world. The learning model is based on the assumption that a person's schemas and attitudes all develop in response to the reinforcing influences of the surrounding culture. The attitudes formed are evaluative; that is, they determine if an event is construed as good or bad. Members of a culture may entertain logically incompatible attitudes toward objects in their culture (e.g., ancestor worship and fear of the dead) without any stress, so long as such incompatible attitudes are not brought into association (Osgood & Tannenbaum, 1955). One of the prime functions of self-deception is to keep such incompatible elements independent, thus protecting the psyche from potential stress.

Although some attitudes may be contradictory and separate, there is a tendency for them to cluster and to be related to each other in terms of a generalized abstraction regarding all classes of events. Each set of attitudes reflects the operation of an underlying value, and all these attitudes and values, contradictory or not, define the person's religious system (Proshansky & Seidenberg, 1965).

For a group, the religious creed must be verbal to permit expression of a fundamental basis of agreement. In the Christian religion, it is the Bible. In the secular religion of justice, it is the law. The general behavior of the majority of people is controlled by the religious aura of the creed (for one can believe in much more than can be known and understood) and the commonly accepted, unspoken norms of expected behavior. Any logical incompatibility between these two is usually unrecognized, for the cognitive schema sustains itself by systematically revising incoming information. The mechanism for this revision of information is, of course, language.

Language

Human society rests on the capacity to use words. This ability makes possible the communication of meaning and the sharing of experience. Although language is excellent for these purposes, it has a subjective influence on the faculty of perception. This effect follows from the intrinsic nature of symbolic labels (words).

The elevation of sounds to names lifted communication above an immediate emotional context. However, the categories created by labeling made language a fifth dimension—the context in which all events are construed by humans. Linguistic categories are not mere abstractions but have concrete consequences for perception. People think, feel, and understand by means of, and within the limits imposed by, the content and structure of their language (Proshansky & Seidenberg, 1965). Whorf (1940) was extreme in stating that language defined the human ability to peceive reality. Brown and Lenneberg (1958) were more restrained in attributing to language the schematic capacity to direct attention to certain aspects of the environment and away from others.

Further, some of these categories evolved their own emotional impact as they came to convey the superego values of the group. The emotional valance of labels for these categories compounds the subjective effect of language on perception.

Until now, there have been two dominant schools of philosophy of language (Durbin, 1973). Ordinary-Language Analysis views language as a form of social behavior that should be studied through a detailed analysis of the individual words and expressions. Logical Positivism avers that language functions primarily in the statement of truths. To these, I would like to suggest a third—Logical Negativism. This philosophy recognizes that, along with its other functions, language plays a role in obscuring the truth by adversely affecting perception.

Perception

Impulses transmitted from the sense organs to the brain are there subjected to the selective process of linguistic categorization. A given comment or gesture is thus subject to various interpretations, since the category in which an act is construed varies with the general circumstances and specific identity of the agent.

It is important to note here that perceptions of one's own actions tend to find their way into emotionally acceptable categories and thus receive favorable if misleading interpretations and evaluations according to the creed of the group. (This is half of the mechanism of self-deception; the other half is the nonverbal, normative schema which really mediates between the behavior of the individual and his social world, the superego notwithstanding.) When an act is subjectively ambiguous, the structuring of the psyche leads to a simple meaning which has adaptive value in terms of past experience and present interests. This is accomplished by a process which is best described by analogy with the social processing of rumors.

Rumors

It may seem odd that people would process information about their own behavior in a manner similar to the way in which a group processes a rumor, but this analogy appears more plausible when one recognizes that **ambiguity** is a basic element common to both phenomena. When evaluating one's own behavior, there is little doubt as to what was done, but there may be considerable ambiguity regarding the appropriate context for assessing the meaning of the particular acts. With rumors, one is dealing with, at best, secondhand information, so there is ambiguity as to exactly what happened. Thus, the description of the embedding of rumors provided by Allport and Postman (1945) provides a model for appreciating the manner in which one's own behavior is assessed so as to maximize both emotional economy and the integrity of the cognitive schema.

As rumors circulate, they undergo **embedding**—the result of the concurrent processes of leveling, sharpening, and assimilation. Leveling refers to the shortening of rumors as they travel. With passage through society, a rumor will become more concise, more easily told, and more easily understood. In successive versions, fewer words are used and fewer details are mentioned. Society accomplishes as much leveling within a few tellings of a rumor as individual memory does after weeks of having first heard a story.

Sharpening is the selective perception, retention, and reporting of a limited number of details from a larger context. Sharpening is the retention of odd or attention-getting words which catch the attention of each successive listener and are passed on in preference to other details intrinsically more important to the story. The tendency for labels to persist is a direct parallel to the categorization which determines the emotional impact of one's own behavior on the schema.

Assimilation refers to the powerful attractive force exerted upon rumors by the listener's existing habits, interests, and sentiments. These lead to the obliteration of some details and the emphasis of others; it accounts for all transpositions, importations, and other falsifications that mark the course of rumors. Rumors are really a form of social-deception.

In the construction of a rumor, what was outer becomes inner; what was objective becomes subjective. The kernel of objective information (in self-deception, the behavioral information) becomes so embedded in the society's own dynamic mental life that the result is chiefly a compound of social values projected onto an event. A rumor is created when, in an effort to construct meaning, a group projects the deficiencies of its retentive processes and the biases of its attitudes onto an ambiguous field. The product reveals as much about the group's emotional state as it does about the reported incident.

This process of embedding (leveling, sharpening, and assimilating) appears to be a characteristic feature of the human mind, defining not only the handling of rumors and the structuring of self-deception, but also the functioning of the memory process as well. It has been uncovered and described in the experiments on individual retention conducted by Wulf, Gibson, and Allport[1] and in Bartlett's (1932) memory experiments carried out on both individuals and groups. Embedding occurs when a subject finds the outer stimulus-world far too hard to grasp and retain in its objective character. It must be recast not only to fit his span of comprehension and his span of retention but also his personal needs and interests, just as a person's own behavior must be construed by him—through this same process of embedding—to be consistent with his creed.

Roles

Between the two extremes of mobs and lovers, people spend most of their social lives playing roles of varying intensity in groups of various sizes. The behavioral standard for any given group is the norm, as mentioned above. A group functions as a **normative reference group** for a person to the extent that its evaluations of him are based upon the degree of his conformity to certain standards of behavior and to the extent that the delivery of rewards or punishments is conditional upon these evaluations (Kelley, 1952). It is self-deception that saves the creed when the informal, behavioral norms of a group conflict with its own formal, stated standards.

The social basis for self-deception lies in the fact that when group members interact they are not usually trying to be honest or learn about themselves. They are trying to prolong a relationship through maintenance of group face. This is not the goal of interaction but is a necessary condition for its continuation. If any incident threatens the face of a participant, a cosmetic process of face-work is initiated to preserve the interaction (Shaver, 1981). Any attempt to introduce objectivity into such a situation must be discreet.

The social reality of a group must have some basis in fact, but no one in the group will be too critical on this point. Subversion by dissenting voices could lead to immediate collapse. To preserve its view of reality, a group tends toward uniformity of opinion, particularly on issues which define group identity (Festinger, 1950).

The more important the issue, the less tolerance there is for disagreement. As the cohesion of a group increases, the pressure toward uniformity of opinion intensifies, thus setting up a positive feedback loop. Attempts to induce uniformity of opinion are followed, if they fail, with rejection of the deviant member (Schachter, 1951). The irony of this arrangement is that the more crucial a matter becomes, the less objective a group will be.

Detective Third Grade Frank Serpico, shield number 761 of the New York Police Department, learned this the hard way. He dared the unheard-of, the unpardonable in police circles. Having solemnly sworn to uphold the law, he proceeded to do just that—to enforce it against everybody, including dishonest cops. He had

---

[1]Summarized in K. Koffka. (1935). *Principles of gestalt psychology. New York: Harcourt, Brace & World.*

either too much or too little imagination. He structured his behavior not to the informal norms of the group but to the official oath, the formal verbal creed. He would not go along with the graft, the bribes, the shakedowns; and he refused to look the other way. That made him unique. He was the first officer in the history of the police department who not only reported corruption in its ranks but voluntarily testified about it in court (Maas, 1973).

For four years he was repeatedly rebuffed in his efforts to get action from high police and political officials. Finally, he went to the newspapers with his story. As a result, a Commission to Investigate Alleged Police Corruption was formed; the police commissioner resigned; departmental organization and procedure underwent drastic revision; criminal indictments were announced; police officials at last admitted under oath that, despite the specific allegations brought to their attention by Serpico, they had done nothing (Maas, 1973). All this made Serpico much less than a hero in the eyes of his colleagues. After being wounded in action, he retired to obscurity. Of course, he would have always been obscure had he simply learned the schemas of his reference group to the extreme of internalization.

THE INTERNAL MODEL

The ultimate state resulting from the learning of norms is the internalization of the behavioral schema to the point that the person is what he does. As the creed is concurrently internalized to the point of mythology, norms become safe from effective critique by group members. Behavioral compliance according to the rational model is superficial, with conformity occurring because the person thinks he must. With the private identification with norms that accompany learning, conformity occurs because certain behavior is expected. Internalization produces conformity because specific behavior is perceived as right (Shaver, 1981).

Personality theorists and clinicians emphasize the internal dynamics underlying attitudes in which the individual's need to preserve his self-image and self-integrity becomes more important than external rewards and punishments (Proshansky & Seidenberg, 1965). For this point to be reached, external influences must have become internalized through learning. The superego takes over, and contrary behavior notwithstanding, the narcissistic satisfaction provided by the cultural ideal becomes a major force within the cultural unit (Freud, 1927/1961).

Myths

One great source of satisfaction for a group is the myth that its creed is a valid description of its actual behavior. At best, the **creed** (cognitive schema) might describe how people should behave and serve as an ideal toward which group members could strive, but it corresponds to the normative schema only with respect to behavior that will cause no great emotional stress when judged by standards of the superego. The function of self-deception is to make behavior that is contradictory to the creed (and that would be emotionally disturbing if correctly perceived) appear to the performer in an emotionally acceptable context. The creed becomes a myth when it is internalized, not as a belief but as a story distracting people from perceiving what they are actually doing. Norms are then forever protected from self-revelation because analysis is limited by the same language people employ to construct their myths.

In such a self-contained, internally consistent system, myths furnish the limit beyond which controversy cannot extend. Arguments may occur within the terms of the myths, but to attack a myth itself is literally unthinkable. The historic mavericks like Serpico, who have failed to internalize the conventional cognitive and normative schemas in their respective tracks, have paid penalties varying from ostracism to execution.

Scholars are often such victims, because devotion to philosophical principles can lead to an exposé of what people should find shameful (i.e,, when the behavior of a group contradicts its own expressed creed). After the heretic is punished for nonconformity, society adjusts to his valid criticism by creating subrosa institutions which are practically necessary, but hidden so as to violate the myth as discreetly as possible. Scholars thus fulfill a superego role for a culture which believes it should know itself, commits some energy toward that goal, and then fends off results which conflict with immediate prevailing interests.

The myth (cognitive schema) is a fantasy—a false fantasy, if you will—but it defines the basis for rational discussion of issues. This is a direct result of the superego function of language, the role that language plays in binding a group with common goals and values. The knowledge that one's behavior may be contradictory to a myth is eased psychologically by the embedding process, so that both the cognitive and normative schemas may survive. It is important to note that the individuals involved are *not* lying to themselves. They are simply functioning according to a basic psychic principle by which members identify themselves with reference groups.

With the dominance of the superego, most people are obliged to use devious means of gratifying their impulses. In an attempt to resolve inner conflict, they minimize or obliterate certain aspects of their emotional life. Deflected impulses attain partial expression by means of **symptom formation**, a device that, however incapacitating, serves a dual and paradoxical function: (1) it permits expression of the unconscious impulse, and (2) it prevents the individual from becoming aware of the existence of this impulse (Proshansky & Seidenberg, 1965). One may hypothesize that the same phenomenon occurs at the social level, with a group thrashing around expressing tension it cannot define, acknowledge, or resolve.

Attitudes may thus be viewed as both ego defense mechanisms and symptoms of social problems. The amount of gross distortion of the referent of an attitude is related to the degree of defensiveness of the individual. Since distortion has the function of protecting the person from facing his internal conflicts, attitudes are not referred to the external world for reality testing. This is the psychological basis for resistance to change, because novelty could produce a confrontation between modified behavioral norms and established internal values. When a group finds itself forced into novel circumstances, it derives considerable confidence from the retention of familiar expressions and rhetoric.

Modern American Mythology

There are two situations that lead to the learning and internalization of schemas: a person (1) is born into a particular culture, and (2) subsequently joins groups according to his circumstances and desires. Americans who lived through the 1930's were born into one myth and circumstances, then created another. It was a collective experience that vividly exemplifies the role of self-deception in human affairs.

In the first third of the twentieth century, government was conducted according to a political myth and an economic creed. The political myth of democracy was based on the great moral values of freedom and individualism, which were to combine in action to produce the best for the moment, and the future be damned. The economic creed of capitalism was to supply the principles that were to make incoherent legislative bodies act with unity. No one knew what these principles were, but, nevertheless, that is what they were supposed to do (Arnold, 1937).

In the crusade against communism and fascism to make the world safe for capitalism, there was very little conflict about the principles of democracy. This is because, by the 1930's, democracy had no principles. It had become a myth. The democratic tradition had become unrecognizable and had ceased to be regarded as a set of guiding principles. Government of, by, and for the people had been sacrificed to the more pragmatic notion that popular majorities were necessary for a successful government, whatever the creed happened to be (Arnold, 1937).

Ironically, democracy as a myth triumphed most noticeably in the totalitarian states of Russia and Germany, where the governments went to great lengths to arouse the intense enthusiasm of the people and keep it at a high pitch (Arnold, 1937). Where voting was essentially meaningless in terms of selecting between or among candidates, parties, or programs, the governments were most insistent that the people take part in the travesty.

In these dictatorships, as well as in the republics of the West, democracy had changed from a creed defining how the political process should function to a myth obscuring how it, in fact, does function—from a set of symbols which could be accepted on faith and conveniently ignored to a storybook institution that must retain the loyalty of its members or perish. Democracy works because it carries its people along emotionally—not because the people make decisions, but because they are the objects of intense attention from the state.

In American thinking about democracy, we have dropped the medieval approach. We do not argue about it any more as we argue about a creed. We have ceased to write books describing how sacred it is. We realize that in its essence it means that an effective leader must maintain the morale as well as the discipline of the followers. It has become for us a myth which is neither intellectually questioned nor emotionally revered; it is just used (Arnold, 1937).

As a creed, democracy never even remotely resembled political realities in this country. As a myth, it produced a spiritual government in Washington to embody its ideals and a temporal government in our industrial centers that gave scope to the productive energy of the people. All this was done to the people without losing their support, violating their normative taboos, or being perceived as contradicting their mythology (Arnold, 1937).

A basic tenet of America's favorite myth is the inherent malevolence of governmental interference with business (Arnold, 1937). The 1930's thus presented the country with a dilemma that really could not be faced. Forbidden governmental interference clearly had become a necessity. As it turned out, the American psyche neatly accommodated both reality and mythology by the normal process of constitutional government.

The Constitution, along with court decisions, might just as well have been written in Sanskrit, as far as the people were concerned. The United States by the 1940's had become a fascist state, complete with its very own concentration camps for a persecuted racial minority (the Japanese-Americans), and was built on myths that were based on long-vanished social conditions. Those myths postulated an individualistic economy and law predicated on the bedrock principles of private enterprise and freedom of contract (Lundberg, 1980). That these notions did not encompass reality was the essential lesson Americans had not learned during the era of corporate America.

From 1871 to 1933, capitalism was truly a religious creed. Its priests were lawyers and economists. In the 1930's, the systems over which we had our theological disputes were no longer Christianity and Islam, nor monarchy and democracy, but capitalism and the modern heresies of communism and fascism. We literally believed in capitalism as we once believed in democracy—not as a tool to be used, but as a set of abstract principles to be followed. Of course, by the early 1930's, laissez faire capitalism was no more descriptive of the American economy than the theology of the monarchy was descriptive of France before the deluge (Arnold, 1937), but the schema of capitalism still had a future. After it failed as a creed, capitalism was promoted to the rank of myth.

The Depression tried faith and found it wanting. The prayers that went up demonstrated a fundamental distrust of governmental organizational controls. No one in this self-styled democracy could admit that the people should indeed govern themselves. Leaders tried to escape the hard necessity of making practical judgments and sought the comfort and certainty of appeals to priests. In the early 1930's, the entire priesthood of law and economics directed its reactionary influence against governmental interference with corporate management of temporal affairs. When this influence was overcome with the election of Franklin Roosevelt, we clearly became a fascist republic.

As governmental interference and control were phased in, the label "fascism" was not. Fascism is the appropriate term for a system characterized by governmental control of private enterprise (Webster, 1970), but Americans never use it when referring to their own economy. It simply would not have done for FDR to have admitted, "We are fascists." It would have been true but not particularly astute politically. So, the myth of capitalism survived, quietly at odds with the normative behavioral schema of a fascistic economic regime. We kept the labels of the old order—freedom, individuals, and so forth. The New Deal was simply construed as increasing personal freedom by extending economic independence to the multitudes. It did not really matter that the people were not independent; they depended on the government, not themselves.

The priests of the 1930's were replaced by a new brand of wizards in the 1940's. These were the younger economists (like John Kenneth Galbraith), political scientists, and lawyers. Their mythology omitted the American businessman (Arnold, 1937). The story became one of the big government helping the poor little people. We are just now coming to grips with the effects of this myth on our national life and character.

The Challenge

We are currently faced with a number of soul-searching problems. First and foremost, we must create an environment in which we can thrive. To do this, we must control our technology by controlling ourselves. We must use our intellect for analysis of reality and not let imagination run rampant to the point of hiding the real world in myths. Myths serve a purpose in maintaining group identity, but they are dangerously misleading if anyone really wants to solve social problems. If solutions to such problems as inflation, unemployment, and racism are to be found, our current myths must be set aside and we must see and say who we are so that we may become who we want to be.

CONCLUSIONS

The reference group plays an insidious trick on its members: It forces them to deceive themselves as individuals. With respect to the processing of information, data confirming the prevailing cognitive schema may be invented while contradictory facts are ignored. Information about normative behavior is compartmentalized by being embedded in a linguistic context so that the creed (set of beliefs) of a group is beyond its members' capacity to question. This process is extended to an illogical conclusion when members internalize the myths (stories) that mask their own behavior from themselves.

In spite of the drawbacks imposed on the human condition by the inherent limitations of language, people can reach a clearer understanding of their role in the universe. A transcendent advance in understanding behavior will be effected when we acknowledge that self-deception defines the distinctive way the human mind functions by shaping the way we perceive reality, gather information, process data, code and decode messages, and create and solve problems.

When we understand this, we will know ourselves.

REFERENCES

ALLPORT, G. (1937). *Personality*. London: Constable.

ALLPORT, G., & POSTMAN, L. (1945). The basic psychology of rumor. *Transactions of the New York Academy of Sciences* (Series II), *8*, 61-81.

ARNOLD, T. (1937). *The folklore of capitalism*. New Haven: Yale University Press.

BARTLETT, F. C. (1932). *Remembering: A study in experimental and social psychology*. New York: Macmillan.

BATESON, G., JACKSON, D., HALEY, J., & WEAKLAND, J. (1956). Toward a theory of schizophrenia. *Behavioral Sciences*, *1*, 251-264.

BETTELHEIM, B. (1943). Individual and mass behavior in extreme situations. *Journal of Abnormal and Social Psychology*, *38*, 417-452.

BROWN, R., & LENNEBERG, E. (1958). Studies in linguistic relativity. In E. Maccoby, T. Newcomb, & E. Hartley (Eds.), *Readings in social psychology* (3rd ed., pp. 9-18). New York: Holt Rinehart and Winston.

DEUTSCH, M., & GERARD, H. (1955). Study of normative and informational social influences upon individual judgment. *Journal of Abnormal and Social Psychology*, *51*, 629-636.

DURBIN, M. (1973). Cognitive anthropology. In J. Honigmann (Ed.), *The handbook of social and cultural anthropology* (pp. 447-478). Chicago: Rand McNally.

FESTINGER, L. (1950). Informal social communication. *Psychological Review*, *57*, 271-282.

———. (1954). A theory of social comparison processes. *Human Relations*, *7*, 117-140.

———. (1957). *A theory of cognitive dissonance*. Stanford, CA: Stanford University Press.

FISHBEIN, M., & AJZEN, I. (1975). *Belief, attitude, intention, and behavior*. Reading, MA: Addison-Wesley.

FREUD, S. (1961). The future of an illusion. In J. Strachey (Ed. and Trans.), *The standard edition of the complete psychological works of Sigmund Freud* (Vol. 21, pp. 3-56). London: Hogarth Press. (Original work published 1927.)

GUR, R., & SACKEIM, H. (1979). Self-deception: A concept in search of a phenomenon. *Journal of Personality and Social Psychology*, *37*, 147-170.

HALL, C., & LINDZEY, G. (1970). *Theories of personality*. New York: Wiley.

HAMILTON, D. (1979). A cognitive-attributional analysis of stereotyping. In L. Berkowitz (Ed.), *Advances in experimental social psychology* (Vol. 12, pp. 53-84). New York: Academic Press.

KELLEY, H. (1952). Two functions of reference groups. In G. Swanson, T. Newcomb, & E. Hartley (Eds.), *Readings in psychology* (2nd ed., pp. 410-414). New York: Holt Rinehart and Winston.

KLOTZ, I.   (1980). The N-Ray affair. *Scientific American, 242*, 168-175.

KRAKAUER, D.   (1978). The adaptive significance of self-deception. Personal communication to Dr. J. Lockard. Cited in J. Lockard (Ed.), *The evolution of human social behavior* (p. 260). New York: Elsevier.

LEAKEY, R.   (1977). *Origins.* New York: Dutton.

LUNDBERG, F.   (1980). *Cracks in the constitution.* Secaucus, NJ: Lyle Stuart.

MAAS, P.   (1973). *Serpico.* New York: Viking.

McMILLEN, S.   (1968). *None of these diseases.* Old Tappan, NJ: Fleming H. Revell.

OSGOOD, C., & TANNENBAUM, P.   (1955). The principle of congruity in the prediction of attitude change. *Psychological Review, 62*, 42-55.

PROSHANSKY, H., & SEIDENBERG, B. (Eds.).   (1965). *Basic studies in social psychology.* New York: Holt Rinehart and Winston.

SCHACHTER, S.   (1951). Deviation, rejection, and communication. *Journal of Abnormal and Social Psychology, 46*, 190-207.

SHAVER, K.   (1981). *Principles of social psychology* (2nd Ed.). Cambridge, MA: Winthrop.

SNYDER, M., & URANOWITZ, S.   (1978). Reconstructing the past: Some cognitive consequences of person perception. *Journal of Personality and Social Psychology, 36*, 941-950.

TRIVERS, R.   (1976). In R. Dawkins, *The selfish gene* (Foreword). Oxford: Oxford University Press.

WEBSTER.   (1970). *New world dictionary.* New York: World.

WHORF, B.   (1940). Science and linguistics. *Technology Review, 44*, 229-231.

*P*SYCHOLOGICAL *T*HEORIES

If it is true, as claimed by Sartre, that we all fundamentally want to be simultaneously en-soi and pour-soi, resting in ourselves like a thing and yet at a distance from ourselves that allows us to enjoy this, then we are indeed striving for an end that is logically or conceptually incoherent. Acting on this desire will be as self-defeating as the attempt to turn around, very swiftly, to catch one's own shadow. (Elster, 1983, p. 11)

Elster's observation is apropos for two reasons. First, the dualistic nature of the self required for self-deception may have an essential incoherence. Second, theoretical analyses of self-deception in the past have often exemplified the futility of trying to "catch one's shadow." Thus, the quotation doubly portends the formidable nature of the task taken on by the writers of the five theoretical papers in this section.

The contributors represent rather diverse perspectives in contemporary psychology: psychoanalysis (Eagle), social psychology (Greenwald), environmental psychology (Suedfeld), role theory (Sarbin), personality (Paulhus), and biopsychiatry (Sackeim). What these writers have in common is an empirical orientation toward psychological issues. All are concerned with integrating the available research evidence into their theories. Indeed, all except Eagle are currently engaged in research bearing on their theories of self-deception.

The interest of these writers was triggered by two seminal pieces, namely Herbert Fingarette's (1969) book, entitled *Self-deception,* and a research report, "Self-deception: A concept in search of a phenomenon," by Ruben Gur and Harold Sackeim (1979). The Fingarette book was the first in-depth philosophical treatment of self-deception and provided, in particular, a clear definition to which subsequent theorists could anchor their own positions. The impact of the Gur and Sackeim (1979) article is attributable to its ostensible empirical demonstration of an instance of self-deception. It was not that Fingarette's definition and Gur and Sackeim's experiments were widely accepted; rather, these reports were milestones because they demonstrated that self-deception was susceptible to rational analysis.

The stumbling block for most previous attempts was the so-called "paradox of self-deception"—how can an individual know something and not know it at the same time? The paradox has been alluded to at least as far back as Kant (1765/1964): "intentionally to deceive oneself seems to contain a contradiction" (p. 93). One reaction has been to agree that such a situation is paradoxical and therefore logically impossible (e.g., Haight, 1980; Elster, 1983; Gergen, 1985). Many writers, however, are convinced that the phenomenon exists, and the five contributors to this section promise in various ways to unravel the paradox.

Both of the seminal works directly confronted this apparent paradox. These two accounts of the paradox are, in fact, cited by all the contributors to this section of the book. Before we continue, then, some details of these analyses are warranted.

Fingarette's Analysis

One of Herbert Fingarette's important contributions was his thorough review of previous analyses (e.g., Sartre, 1943/1956; Demos, 1960). He judged previous accounts to be inadequate in reconciling the paradox. In their stead, Fingarette proposed a new language for characterizing the problem, a language designed to undo the confusion wrought by standard terminology. In brief, he argued that self-deception occurs when an individual disavows responsibility for a personal engagement.

For example, an individual may have an emotional engagement of hating his boss. This hate, however, is inconsistent with his current identity as a tolerant person and a loyal worker. Because psychological distress would ensue if the hatred were spelled out, the individual chooses to disavow the engagement as his own. This self-deception permits the individual to continue with his current engagements without compromising his identity. More recently, Fingarette (1985) has applied his theory to the alcoholic personality. He criticizes the medical community's designation of alcoholism as a disease because it underemphasizes volition, thereby encouraging the individual to deny responsibility. Thus, the self-deception inherent in alcoholism is actually promoted.

Fingarette's (1969) book has elicited a series of reactions in the philosophical literature (e.g., Szabados, 1973; Haight, 1980; Martin, 1986). The most thorough of these is the book by Pears (1984). Of the contributors to the present book, Fingarette's view has had the most impact on Sarbin and Eagle.

Sackeim and Gur

Apart from the 1979 paper mentioned above, Sackeim and Gur have written a number of other chapters and experimental reports on self-deception (Sackeim & Gur, 1978, 1979; Sackeim, 1983, 1986; Sackeim & Wegner, 1986). Their contribution has been threefold: They provided a clear definition in terms of four criteria for ascribing self-deception; they developed an experimental paradigm; and they developed a personality measure of self-deception. Their four necessary and sufficient criteria for ascribing self-deception are:

1. The individual holds two contradictory beliefs.
2. The two beliefs are held simultaneously.
3. The individual is not aware of one of the beliefs.
4. The act that determines which belief is not subject to awareness is a motivated act.

In their 1979 article, Gur and Sackeim described an experiment designed to illustrate the four criteria for self-deception. They first identified a private experience that people with low self-esteem feel a particular aversion toward, namely, recognizing their own voice on a tape recording. Like looking in a mirror, recognizing oneself on a tape recording seems to be a form of self-confrontation and is therefore threatening if one's current self-view is negative. To set up the voice recognition task, the experimenters recorded each subject reading the same statement. During the playback session, subjects had to say ''me'' or ''not me'' to each of the voices on the tape.

Given the ambiguity of recognizing one's own voice, Gur and Sackeim conjectured that subjects' claims and denials were good candidates for satisfying self-deceptive needs. For instance, if self-esteem were threatened by putting subjects through a contrived failure experience, they would be more sensitive to the painful confrontation of acknowledging their voice. That is exactly what the data showed. After a failure, subjects were more likely to deny that their recorded voice was actually their own. Polygraph records, however, verified that accurate recognition of the voice did occur.

Here, then, is a split in awareness. At one level (reflected in the autonomic nervous system) the subject knows the voice belongs to him or her; at another level (reflected in conscious awareness) the subject honestly denies this knowledge. Moreover, this split is motivated. That is, subjects showed more denial when they were most sensitive to their inadequacies—right after a failure.

For the first time, then, self-deception had been demonstrated in the laboratory. Although the results have been replicated (Sackeim, 1983), the experiment has not been without its critics (Douglas & Gibbins, 1983; cf. Sackeim & Gur, 1985). An obvious limitation is the artificial and rather esoteric nature of the demonstration. Nevertheless, the authors' objective was to show one instance of self-deception to demonstrate that people are indeed capable of such a feat. Their demonstration certainly dispels the accusation that the concept is paradoxical. (At least one other demonstration has since been conducted: Quattrone & Tversky, 1984.) Whether self-deception is the mechanism underlying such significant phenomena as alcoholism or love is, of course, another matter.

The third contribution of Gur and Sackeim was their development of a measure of individual differences in self-deception. The measure, dubbed the Self-Deception Questionnaire (SDQ), was first described in Sackeim and Gur's (1978) chapter. The SDQ is a self-report instrument containing 20 questions about undesirable thoughts and feelings. The items have a psychoanalytic flavor (e.g., Do you enjoy your bowel movements? Have you ever hated one or both of your parents? Do you have sexual fantasies?). The construct validity of the SDQ has been supported in a number of studies (Gur & Sackeim, 1979; Sackeim & Gur, 1979; Paulhus, 1982, 1984; Sackeim 1983; Winters & Neale, 1985; Linden, Paulhus, & Dobson, 1986; Paulhus & Levitt, 1987). Even after all reference to psychopathology has been removed from the items, the denial of undesirable thoughts is predictive of hindsight bias, beneffectance, and psychological health (Paulhus, 1986). Finally, in the Gur and Sackeim (1979) study detailed earlier, the SDQ predicted which subjects would tend to make errors in recognizing their own voice after a failure experience.

This background will, I hope, prepare the reader for the five contributions on theories of self-deception. The contributors, all familiar with the seminal works, generally agree that self-deception involves the masking of some painful belief about the self. As you will see, however, they disagree greatly about the processes involved.

FIVE CONTRIBUTIONS

Morris Eagle examines in detail the relation between self-deception and psychoanalytic defenses; he concludes that there is little overlap. Psychoanalytic defenses are said to be mechanistic operations, whereas self-deception is a goal-directed, deliberate act. Being deliberate, self-deception also has moral implications for the perpetrator. Moreover, self-deception, unlike repression, is held to be reversible through direct confrontation with the undesirable belief. Self-deception and psychoanalytic defenses are both shown to have adaptive as well as maladaptive consequences. Therapists are advised to take note of this delicate balance between inducing insight and successful psychotherapy.

Theodore Sarbin's contribution is an elaboration of his semiotic theory of self-deception (Sarbin, 1981). The style that some people use to present self-related information to the world parallels the style of good literature: In both cases the narrative has clarity, coherence, and unity. Thus, additions, deletions, and distortions of the self-narrative operate in the service of effective dialogue with other people. The Fingarettian idea of disavowing engagements is used to explain how some dialogue engagements can become self-deceptive.

Sarbin details how the hypnotic induction can be seen as an induction of self-deception. The client must interpret such counterfactual communications as "Your arm will rise by itself," along with the implication that such an event would be desirable and remarkable. Thus, some subjects (those who are "hypnotizable") are led genuinely to disclaim agency. According to Sarbin, this sincere denial of agency for one's own behavior constitutes self-deception.

The next two contributions, one from Anthony Greenwald and the other from Delroy Paulhus and Peter Suedfeld, are couched in modern information-processing language. Greenwald develops his view of self-deception in the context of a levels of representation (LOR) theory of social knowledge. Incoming information passes through a maximum of four stages of processing. Passage from any one stage to the next may be inhibited by a habitualized "stop-thinking" response. Thus, four types of knowledge avoidance can occur. One of these, the inhibition of unpleasant inferences, is closest to traditional self-deception but without the paradoxical flavor. A number of examples, including the Gur and Sackeim (1979) experiment, are analyzed in terms of LOR theory. Greenwald also lays out the necessary and sufficient conditions to demonstrate knowledge avoidance.

Paulhus and Suedfeld postulate a temporary form of self-deception that they term "transient self-deception." This phenomenon is described in the context of a model of dynamic complexity (Paulhus, 1984, 1987). The central proposition is that arousal reduces cognitive complexity and polarizes evaluation in social judgments, including those regarding the self. Self-deception may occur when old information about the self is being reprocessed. Under conditions of arousal, two representations of a domain may exist simultaneously—one in active memory and one in long-term memory. This situation appears to satisfy the Sackeim-Gur criteria for self-deception. Thus, the judgment made under arousal may differ from that made before and after the arousal state. This model is designed to explain the apparent self-deception in the judgments of individuals who are emotionally aroused.

In the final chapter, Harold Sackeim provides a critical analysis of all four theory chapters. This seems to be an appropriate role for Sackeim given that his work with Gur triggered the interest of all the contributors. Moreover, they all address his work in their present contributions. In light of developments since the Sackeim and Gur (1978) paper, particularly the contributions of the current contributors, Sackeim presents a revised set of criteria for ascribing self-deception.

REFERENCES

DEMOS, R. (1960). Lying to oneself. *Journal of Philosophy, 57*, 588-595.

DOUGLAS, W., & GIBBONS, K. (1983). Inadequacy of voice recognition as a demonstration of self-deception. *Journal of Personality and Social Psychology, 44*, 589-592.

ELSTER, J. (1983). *Sour grapes.* New York: Cambridge University Press.

FINGARETTE, H. (1969). *Self-deception.* New York: Humanities Press.

―――. (1985). Alcoholism and self-deception. In M. W. Martin (Ed.), *Self-deception and self-understanding* (pp. 52-67). Lawrence, KS: University Press of Kansas.

GERGEN, K. J. (1985). The ethnopsychology of self-deception. In M. W. Martin (Ed.), *Self-deception and self-understanding* (pp. 228-243). Lawrence, KS: University Press of Kansas.

GUR, R. C., & SACKEIM, H. A. (1979). Self-deception: A concept in search of a phenomenon. *Journal of Personality and Social Psychology, 37*, 147-169.

HAIGHT, M. R. (1980). *A study of self-deception.* Atlantic Highlands, NJ: Humanities Press.

KANT, I. (1964). *The doctrine of virtue* (Mary J. Gregor, Trans.). Philadelphia: University of Pennsylvania Press. (Original work published 1765)

LINDEN, W., PAULHUS, D. L., & DOBSON, K. S. (1986). The effects of response styles on the report of psychological and somatic distress. *Journal of Consulting and Clinical Psychology, 54*, 309-313.

MARTIN, M. W. (1986). *Self-deception and morality.* Lawrence, KS: University Press of Kansas.

PAULHUS, D. L. (1982). Individual differences, self-presentation, and cognitive dissonance: Their concurrent operation in forced compliance. *Journal of Personality and Social Psychology, 43*, 838-852.

―――. (1984, August). *Self-deception: An information processing approach.* Paper presented at the meeting of the American Psychological Association, Toronto.

―――. (1986). Self-deception and impression management in test responses. In A. Angleitner & J. S. Wiggins (Eds.), *Personality assessment via questionnaire* (pp. 143-165). New York: Springer.

―――. (1987). *A dynamic complexity theory of personality processes.* Manuscript submitted for publication.

PAULHUS, D. L., & LEVITT, K. (1987). Socially desirable responding triggered by affect: Automatic egotism? *Journal of Personality and Social Psychology, 52*, 245-259.

PEARS, D. (1984). *Motivated irrationality.* New York: Oxford University Press.

QUATTRONE, G. A., & TVERSKY, A. (1984). Causal versus diagnostic contingencies: On self-deception and the voter's illusion. *Journal of Personality and Social Psychology, 46*, 236-248.

SACKEIM, H. A. (1983). Self-deception, self-esteem, and depression: The adaptive value of lying to oneself. In J. Masling (Ed.), *Empirical studies of psychoanalytic theories* (pp. 101-157). Hillsdale, NJ: Erlbaum.

_____. (1986). A neuropsychodynamic perspective on the self: Brain, thought, and emotion. In L. M. Hartman & K. R. Blankstein (Eds.), *Perception of self in emotional disorders and psychotherapy*. New York: Plenum.

SACKEIM, H. A., & GUR, R. C. (1978). Self-deception, self-confrontation and consciousness. In G. E. Schwartz & D. Shapiro (Eds.), *Consciousness and self-regulation: Advances in research* (Vol. 2, pp. 139-197). New York: Plenum.

_____. (1979). Self-deception, other deception, and self-reported psychopathology. *Journal of Consulting and Clinical Psychology, 47,* 213-215.

_____. (1985). Voice recognition and the ontological status of self-deception. *Journal of Personality and Social Psychology, 48,* 1369-1372.

SACKEIM, H. A., & WEGNER, A. Z. (1986). Attributional patterns in depression and euthymia. *Archives of General Psychiatry, 43,* 553-560.

SARBIN, T. R. (1981). On self-deception. *Annals of the New York Academy of Sciences, 364,* 206-235.

SARTRE, J-P. (1956). *Being and nothingness* (H. Barnes, Trans.). New York: Washington Square Press. (Original work published 1943.)

SZABADOS, B. (1973). Wishful thinking and self-deception. *Analysis, 33,* 201-205.

WINTERS, K. C., & NEALE, J. M. (1985). Mania and low self-esteem. *Journal of Abnormal Behavior, 94,* 282-290.

5

Psychoanalysis
and Self-Deception

MORRIS EAGLE

York University

One would expect that of all the theoretical approaches to personality and behavior psychoanalytic theory would be the most preoccupied with self-deception and would have the most to say about it. After all, psychoanalysis and psychoanalytic theory are concerned with the very stuff of which self-deception seems to be made—unconscious wishes and aims; defenses such as repression, projection, rationalization, and denial; and manifest contents that are disguised representations of underlying latent contents. Indeed, some writers on self-deception view it as a superordinate category subsuming psychoanalytic defenses (Sackeim, 1983). Others have equated psychoanalytic defenses with self-deception (e.g., Dilman, 1972). And still others have attempted essentially to translate psychoanalytic concepts (e.g., defenses, the unconscious) into the language of self-deception. This can be seen, for example, in the work of Fingarette (1969) and perhaps Sartre (1943/1956). And yet, as far as I know, one finds in the entire corpus of Freud's writings only three brief and trivial references to the term self-deception (see Guttman, Jones, & Parrish, 1980). Nor does one find any reference to self-deception either in LaPlanche and Pontalis's (1973) *The Language of Psychoanalysis* or in Eidelberg's (1968) *Encyclopedia of Psychoanalysis*. This would not necessarily be of any great significance if the logic of Freud's concepts and formulations suggested that, in fact, they dealt with self-deception, even if the term itself was not employed. Do basic psychoanalytic concepts such as repression and defense entail some idea of self-deception? This is one of the questions that will be examined in this chapter. The other is the place of denial in psychoanalytic theory.

DIFFERENT CONCEPTIONS OF SELF-DECEPTION

Before one can answer the first question above, one ought to be clear regarding what is meant by self-deception. However, this leads to a number of difficulties from the start. A variety of different, sometimes even incompatible, definitions of self-deception have been proposed over the years. It would be useful to consider a few—hopefully representative. A recent definition offered by Sackeim (1983) sets four criteria for self-deception: (1) the individual must hold two contradictory beliefs, (2) these beliefs must be held simultaneously, (3) one of these beliefs must not be subject to awareness, and (4) the act that determines which belief is subject to awareness and which belief is not must be a motivated act. An example provided by Sackeim that purportedly illustrates these criteria is the case of a woman who believes fervently that her delinquent son is a "good boy" and denies that he is delinquent but runs to the phone with trepidation every time it rings (suggesting the contradictory belief or expectation that he is in trouble again). Further, according to Sackeim, one can reasonably assume that her denial of his delinquency is a motivated "act," motivated by such factors as anxiety, threat to self-image, and so on.[1]

Fingarette's Definition

Another definition of self-deception is provided by Fingarette (1969), who, obviously influenced by Sartre (1943/1956), stresses the failure to "spell out" particular features of the "projects" in which one is engaged. According to Fingarette, the self-deceiver engages in a "project" and purposely avoids spelling out some feature of his engagement in order to escape guilt, anxiety, and responsibility, and in order to maintain a particular personal identity. The self-deceiver rejects both the option of forgoing an engagement that is inconsistent with his governing principles and the option of accepting the engagement as his and bearing the consequences that follow. Instead, he takes a third course in which he enters the engagement but neither spells it out nor accepts it as part of himself. According to Fingarette, the first option obviously requires self-discipline, the second requires the spiritual courage to accept sin and responsibility, and the third reflects a "lack of spiritual courage" and a moral limbo in which one is neither saved nor damned. It should be apparent from this brief description of Fingarette's position that his stance toward self-deception is a thoroughly moral one. Indeed, Fingarette contrasts the teleological and moral language of choice, integrity, and responsibility charac-

---

[1]Strictly speaking, these two beliefs are not necessarily contradictory. The mother can simultaneously believe, without contradiction, both that her son is, basically, a "good boy" and that he is very likely to get into trouble because, say, he has bad companions, because the authorities are picking on him, or some other reason.

teristic of Sartre's position (which is close to his own) with Freud's nonteleological and nonmoral language of mechanisms and energy. To a large extent, Fingarette's efforts are directed to translating the latter into the former. Finally, it should be noted that, almost in direct contradiction to Sackeim's conceptualization, Fingarette argues that self-deception turns upon the personal identity one accepts *rather than the beliefs one has.*

Sartre's Definition

Sartre's (1943/1956) view of self-deception rests ultimately on his attitude toward freedom and choice and on his conception of the human being as both, in his words, "a facticity and a transcendence." In this context, one kind of self-deception (originally translated as "bad faith") can derive from denying one's freedom to be other than one is—that is, by reducing oneself to facticity and denying one's transcendent potential. Another related kind of bad faith rests on Sartre's distinction between prereflective consciousness ("nonthetic" knowledge) and reflective consciousness ("thetic" knowledge). Put generally and perhaps too simply, good faith consists in the two coinciding and bad faith in the disjunction between the two. As Fingarette puts it, "In Sartrian terms . . . the core of self-deception is the disavowal of responsibility for, and the consequent refusal to reflect upon, some project of Consciousness" (Fingarette, 1969, p. 99).

The above can be illustrated by Sartre's own example of bad faith in which a man takes a girl's hand, but she does not notice that she is leaving her hand in his because she is busy talking about lofty, intellectual matters. According to Sartre, allowing her hand to remain in his and thereby encouraging further sexual advance is a voluntary action for prereflective consciousness even though it is not noticed by reflective consciousness. The bad faith consists not simply in not noticing or not reflecting upon her prereflective project—for as Stevenson points out, in that case bad faith would be commonplace—but in reflectively *denying* what she is prereflectively doing and prereflectively aware of doing. Thus, the girl does not simply fail to reflect upon her prereflective "project," but reflectively *denies* that "project." (See Stevenson, 1983, for a recent and clear attempt to explicate Sartre's concept of "bad faith.")

Dilman's Definition

As a final example of different conceptions of self-deception, I refer to Dilman's (1972) description of people who "may be unaware of their own mental states, be reluctant to recognize them, even fight such recognition, thus deceiving themselves about their own desires, motives, and emotions" (p. 316). According to Dilman, Freud wanted to talk of the unconscious "only where a person actively avoids recognizing his own feelings, desires, and intentions, that is, where a person is in the grips of self-deception about himself. Hence, he [Freud] talked of what is unconscious as being repressed. . . ." (p. 336). It is obvious that for Dilman self-deception and repression are equated and the key feature of both is the active avoidance of recognizing one's own feelings, desires, and motives.

PSYCHOANALYTIC DEFENSES AND SELF-DECEPTION

If one is to discuss the relation between psychoanalysis and self-deception, one ought to employ a conception of the latter that is at least compatible with psychoanalytic ideas. If self-deception is involved in psychoanalytic defenses, it could only rest on the motivated failure to recognize one's unconscious aims and the consequent pursuit of substitute aims that constitute disguised and compromised versions of the denied aims. Hence, without attempting a detailed and precise definition of self-deception, the general idea is as follows: In order for one to conclude that self-deception is operating, three conditions must be met: (1) one denies or avoids acknowledging some mental content X, which can be a thought, reason, motive, desire, goal, belief, or internal representation of a state of affairs; (2) there is evidence that at some level one has processed or "knows" mental content X; (3) the denial or disavowal of mental content X is a motivated "act," the usual motives including the need to avoid anxiety and maintain a particular kind of personal identity and a level of self-esteem. Certain problems and questions are raised by this definition, such as the ambiguity of the phrase "at some level" and the danger of an infinite regress whereby one denies that one is denying, and so on. Not all of these issues will be dealt with here. For the present, suffice it to say that the definition is compatible not only with psychoanalytic ideas but also with Dilman's conception and with Fingarette's emphasis on the failure to "spell out" and the motives to escape guilt, anxiety, and responsibility and maintain a particular personal identity. It is also partially compatible with Sackeim's (1983) conception outlined above.

Repression

Having formulated a working definition of self-deception, let us take a look at particular psychoanalytic concepts to determine the ways in which they lend themselves to understanding self-deception. An obvious place to begin is with the concept of repression, the basic psychoanalytic defense and, according to Freud (1914/1957), the "cornerstone" hypothesis of psychoanalysis. Is repression simply a psychoanalytic term for self-deception as, for example, Dilman (1972) suggests?

There is no simple answer to this question. In order to approach an answer, one must take up other issues and questions. One such issue has to do with what Rubinstein (1977) has broadly referred to as the distinction between person and organism or, in the present context, the distinction between **personal action** and **subpersonal mechanism**. In the philosophical literature, self-deception has often been discussed in a moral context because the implicit or explicit assumption has been that it is something a *person does*, an "act" he or she carries out. Just as a person lies to others, so he or she lies to himself or herself.

If self-deception is an "act" a person carries out, then we must determine whether repression too is such an "act" before deciding whether the two are identical (as Dilman would have it) or whether repression is a subcategory of self-deception (as Sackeim would have it). Although Freud's (1893–1895/1955) clinical descriptions of repression, particularly in the early case histories, are cast in the language of persons intentionally doing things, the theoretical concepts of formulations that emerge from the clinical material are presented in the language of *mechanisms* and *processes*.

Freud's "Project"   There has always been a tension in Freud's writings between, on the one hand, the clinical descriptions cast in the language of persons doing things and, on the other hand, theoretical formulations cast in the language of subpersonal, or at least impersonal, mechanisms and processes. Holt (1972) refers to this duality as Freud's humanistic and scientific images of man. I believe it can be shown that many, perhaps most, of Freud's core concepts and ideas, presented in protoneurological terms in the "Project" (Freud, 1895), found expression in Freud's later writings, but cast in psychological language. Freud had little choice. There simply was not enough neurophysiology and anatomy known to get very far in descriptions and accounts of the mental process (this, of course, continues to be true). However, while Freud was now writing in the clinical psychological language of persons, he continued to pursue the mechanical model of the mind begun and pursued in the "Project." Nowhere is this more apparent than in his conception of repression. For one not entirely absorbed in the clinical language, it is clear that the essential logic or structure of repression is that it is a feedback mechanism that includes the components of anxiety cue and automatic shut-off, which are followed by reduction of anxiety. More specifically, when a prohibited wish or idea threatens to reach conscious experience, "signal anxiety" (i.e., a signal or warning of "situations of danger") is elicited which, in turn, through the operation of the **pleasure principle**, serves to prevent the wish or idea from reaching consciousness and thereby functions to avoid and/or reduce anxiety. This is essentially a description of a negative feedback system in which a particular cue (i.e., an incipient wish or thought) triggers anxiety which then, in turn, shuts off whatever further processing normally leads to conscious experience. Although one can describe these events as if a person were directing them, they can be considered to occur at a subpersonal "automatic" level.

Self-deceptive mechanisms   If the events involved in repression are "automatic" and subpersonal, can they be said to constitute self-deception in the normal sense of the term? Perhaps repression can be thought of as a **self-deceptive mechanism** insofar as it entails the failure to recognize a wish or impulse that, at some level, one does entertain. But it does not appear to be an instance of self-deception as classically defined. Whatever one thinks of Sartre's (1943/1956) discussion of "bad faith" and self-deception, one is, I believe, quite right in understanding Freud's concept of repression as mechanical and subpersonal and in contrasting, therefore, this mechanical view with Sartre's own personal, moral, and teleological conception of "bad faith." He wanted to argue that the phenomena with which Freud was concerned were not the outcome of subpersonal mechanical processes, but of personal moral choices, as reflected in the very term "bad faith." Indeed, for Sartre, the very claim that repression is a subpersonal mechanism rather than a personal choice is itself an act of bad faith! Whether or not one accepts Sartre's concept of bad faith, he was correct in his characterization of the Freudian interpretation of repression as a subpersonal mechanism.

I would suggest, not only for repression, but also for many of the processes psychological literature deals with in this area, that the term self-deceptive mechanisms be used to distinguish them from self-deception as classically defined in the philosophical literature. In the case of the latter, the focus is on *persons* doing things out of particular motives (e.g., avoidance of responsibility, maintenance of a particular self-image) and, as noted earlier, on such issues as spiritual failure and moral weakness (Sartre, 1943/1956; Kierkegaard, 1956; Fingarette, 1969). It seems to me that although Freud's clinical descriptions often employ the language of persons doing things, repression as an explanatory theoretical concept is best understood as a self-deceptive mechanism occurring at a *subpersonal* level.

Another way to approach the question is to determine whether or not repression fulfills the three criteria for self-deception outlined earlier: (1) Is there avoidance of acknowledging a mental content, such as a wish or desire? Yes, this would seem to be a central aspect of what one means by repression. (2) Is there evidence that at some level one has processed or "knows" the repressed mental content? There is no clear-cut answer to this question. For, as noted, one can conceptualize repression as a "shut-off" mechanism in which some anxiety cue encountered relatively early in the stages of processing would essentially "flip" a switch, triggering the mechanism (see Anscombe, in press). Also, if repression can be thought of as a subpersonal mechanism, it is not clear that one can say, except in a metaphoric sense, that at some level "one knows" the repressed content (more on this below). (3) If one's failure to acknowledge a mental content is the outcome of a subpersonal mechanism, it is difficult to think of it as a motivated act or an act of any kind. Although a subpersonal mechanism may be *functional* (its function is to avoid anxiety), it cannot be motivated in any standard sense of the term. Thus, while it is reasonable to say that a *function* of the heart is to circulate blood to the body, it would not make too much sense to say that the heart's *motive* is to circulate blood or that the heart is *motivated* by the goal, desire, or wish to circulate blood. Persons, not mechanisms or organs, have motives (see Hempel, 1965, and Moore, 1984, for a discussion of functional explanation). Hence, once again, I conclude that repression should be viewed as a *self-deceptive mechanism* rather than as self-deception proper.

What Is "Knowing"?

The typical sort of reasoning that goes into the judgment that a set of behaviors represents self-deception is that, while at the level of conscious awareness one denies *having* or *knowing* mental content *X* (e.g., a belief, desire, or wish), at some level, he or she *has* or *knows X*. A typical example would be that one denies having a particular wish (or belief) that, at some level, one has. It then seems natural to think of self-deception. After all, the reasoning goes, if a mental content (e.g. a wish or desire) one disowns is nevertheless one's own, some kind of lying to oneself or "bad faith" or "moral trickery" (Penelhum, 1971) must be occurring. Almost always, however, "knows" is meant in some approximate or perhaps even metaphoric sense. Something similar goes on with "at some level" and "has" or "having." When one says that at some level A has a mental content he denies having, it is not clear at what level A has the mental content and it is also not clear in what sense A "has" the denied mental content. I would suggest that at least in some cases the sense of elusiveness and even of mystery that accompanies discussions of self-deception trades on the vagueness of the terms "know," "at some level," and "has" or "having."

Let us begin with such locutions as "having a desire." As noted above, if one denies having a desire that, at some level, one has and is therefore one's own, it appears that some kind of self-deception or "bad faith" or "moral trickery" is operating. A good deal, however, hinges on the meaning of such terms as "having a desire," "at some level," and "one's own." It seems to me that much of this paradox is resolved if one distinguishes between the narrower concept of self or personal identity and the broader concept of **personality**. A desire can be part of one's personality and at the same time, if it is disowned, *not* part of one's personal identity and self-system. This distinction, as I have argued elsewhere (Eagle, 1984, 1985), is the essence of Freud's id-ego model as well as Sullivan's (1953) distinction between "bad me" and "good me" on the one hand and "not me" on the other.

The id and the ego   A denied or unconscious wish or desire is part of one's overall personality and, in that sense, "one's own." But, insofar as it is not part of one's acknowledged self and personal identity, it is not "one's own." The apparent paradox is created by using "having a desire" and "one's own" in two different contexts or frames of reference. If our reference was A's personal identity and self-system, we could not properly say of a repressed unconscious wish that he *has* it or that it is *his*. It would be more accurate to say of repressed unconscious wishes, at least in the context of psychoanalytic theory, that they exist within the personality and are causally relevant to the generation of certain behaviors (e.g., slips, neurotic symptoms, interpersonal patterns of behavior—see Shope, 1970). Our ordinary language, however, leaves little room for such locutions, and we speak of unconscious repressed wishes in the same manner as we do of ordinary conscious wishes. The more specialized psychoanalytic language attempts to capture the above distinctions. Thus, when Freud distinguishes between id and ego, he is contrasting "it" and "it happens" with "I" and "I wish" experiences (this is more apparent in the literal rather than the Latinized translations of the original German terms *das Es* and *das Ich* into "*the It*" and "*the I*"—Brandt, 1966; Bettelheim, 1983; Eagle, 1984). And when he states the therapeutic goal of psychoanalysis as "where id was, there should ego be," he is suggesting that in successful treatment the "it" and "it happens" experiences more and more become "I" and "I wish" experiences.

What follows from the above discussion is that while one may not have access to and therefore be mistaken regarding the identification or even existence of disowned desires, it would not necessarily follow that one was engaging in self-deception when one denied having these desires. In order to even begin to consider the possibility that self-deception is at work, one would have to show that the denial was the result of, in Sackeim's (1983) words, a "motivated act"—the motives including the avoidance of anxiety, the maintenance of a particular self-image, and the enhancement of pleasure and gain. I shall come back to this issue of motivated act. But first, let us turn to another typical case attributed to self-deception in order to determine whether the above analysis of "having a desire" applies equally to "knowing" a particular mental content.

"Knowing" and "acting"   The same argument as the one above can be made with regard to "knowing" a mental content that, at the level of conscious awareness, one denies knowing. Sartre accuses the woman in the cafe of bad faith because he believes that, although at the conscious level (the level of reflexive consciousness and "thetic" knowledge) she does not know and denies cooperating with the ongoing seduction, at another level (at the level of prereflexive consciousness and "nonthetic" knowledge) she "knows" that she is being complicit in the project of seduction.

One reasonable way of interpreting the claim that at some level B "knows" mental content X is that there is evidence that X has been processed despite the fact that it has not gained access to conscious awareness. But this state of affairs by itself would hardly warrant the conclusion that B is deceiving herself. For a great deal of information is processed that does not gain access to conscious awareness (e.g., Marcel, 1983a, b; Cheesman & Merikle, 1985). We also tacitly know a great deal that we do not know we know and therefore cannot make explicit. In speaking and writing grammatically correct English sentences, for example, we obviously "know" grammatical rules even though we do not always know we know them and often cannot spell them out. Would anyone want to claim that these are all instances of self-deception? What else, then, is required to give serious consideration to the claim that self-deception is at work? Again, one would have to show that the failure to know at the level of conscious awareness that one has, in fact, processed a particular set of information is the result of an avoidant motivated "act."[2]

But note that, as with the word "know" earlier, I have used quotation marks around word "act." When this occurs, as you've learned, I am employing the word in an approximate or metaphoric sense because the process by which mental content (e.g., a belief or desire) is kept from awareness is not at all clear. While this process

[2]This is a particularly important point because there is a tendency in the recent literature to interpret somewhat indiscriminately a variety of cognitive constructions, biases, and distortions as instances of self-deception (e.g., Gilbert & Cooper, 1985). Cognitive mechanisms and processes that select and even distort information do not necessarily entail self-deception—particularly if the mechanism does not require (1) that the information filtered out has been fully or near fully processed at some level, and (2) that if the information has been fully processed, its failure to gain access to conscious awareness is not the result of an avoidant motivated "act." Paulhus (1986) suggests the term "auto-illusion" to represent these cognitive and informational biases that appear to be based on nonmotivational mechanisms (see Nisbett & Ross, 1980, for a description of a variety of such mechanisms).

may be similar to an intentional action in its apparent purposiveness, it may, as I have argued, operate at an involuntary subpersonal level. In the latter case, which includes repression, I believe it makes more sense to speak of a functional mechanism rather than a motivated "act." In part, this suggestion is a matter of semantics, but in part it is not simply that and involves a more substantive issue. As noted earlier, in the traditional view self-deception is accommodated to the category of action and quasi action, with all the implications for moral responsibility and moral and spiritual failure that that accommodation implies. In speaking of self-deceptive mechanisms rather than self-deception proper, one is freer to focus on and attempt to elucidate the processes through which certain contents are kept from conscious awareness rather than on the moral implications of deceitful maneuvers.

It seems to me that when one represses certain wishes (e.g. hostile or incestuous wishes), one is not merely deceiving oneself or avoiding recognition of these wishes (as Dilman, 1972, would have it). If it were merely a matter of avoidance or reluctance to recognize certain wishes, then being forced (by oneself or another) to attend to them would be sufficient to become aware of them. But this is not the case with repression. In contrast to ordinary avoidance, no amount of ordinary effort, self-confrontation, and self-honesty will make repressed wishes available. There may be **approximations of repression** or related processes in which one *does* avoid recognizing one's wishes and motives and in which, therefore, confrontation, attentive effort, and self-reflection may be sufficient to bring them into conscious awareness. But these do not represent instances of repression, as it is defined in psychoanalytic theory. It is even possible that repression does not occur in reality and that only self-deception does (or vice versa). However, the conceptual differences between them that I have outlined would nevertheless remain.

NEUROTIC SYMPTOMS AND SELF-DECEPTION

According to Freud, neurotic symptoms, as is the case with slips and dreams, are the consequence of a compromise between repressed wishes and censoring and controlling forces. Thus they constitute disguised gratifications of unconscious forbidden wishes. Again, all this seems to be the very essence of self-deception. And yet, can one say that according to psychoanalytic theory the development of a symptom constitutes self-deception?

Two Clinical Examples

Consider first a patient, A, I treated whose presenting symptom was obsessive homosexual thoughts, an experience he found distressing and frightening. In the course of treatment, it became apparent that one of the situations in which A's symptom was more likely to appear and become exacerbated was when the issue of emotional commitment to his girlfriend became salient. Furthermore, he stated clearly that he really couldn't seriously consider getting engaged, let alone married, as long as his troubling symptom persisted. On one occasion, when his girlfriend said she loved him, A had a dream in which he was being smothered and was "slipping into black nothingness." This and other related evidence indicated that to A heterosexual emotional closeness and commitment were quite dangerous, equivalent to being smothered and engulfed. My formulation was that the symptom of obsessive homosexual thoughts protected him from the "black nothingness" that emotional closeness and commitment obviously represented to him. One can characterize this pattern in the form of Aristotle's practical syllogism whereby A's unconscious goal was to avoid the danger of engulfment (of "slipping into black nothingness"); his unconscious belief was that if he were homosexual, or at least preoccupied about being homosexual, he would accomplish that goal (more specifically, he would avoid emotional commitment and in that way accomplish the goal of escaping the danger of engulfment); and he in fact accomplishes his goal by developing his symptom.[3]

Although, as this example suggests, symptoms can appear to show central characteristics of ordinary intentional action, there are important differences between them. In ordinary purposive behavior, one accomplishes one's goals through **voluntary action,** while in the case of symptoms, one does not *do* anything. Instead, *things just happen.* Herein lies the puzzling, even paradoxical, nature of Freud's account of neurotic symptoms. In that account, symptoms are *both* purposive and involuntary, thereby challenging our normal categories in which purposive is linked with voluntary behavior (Flew, 1949). Or to state the point in another way, while in voluntary behavior the practical syllogism is characterized by conscious goals, conscious beliefs, and implementing *action*, in the case of neurosis, *unconscious goals are implemented through the development of particular symptoms.* How the development of those symptoms that accomplish a particular goal (in compromised and disguised fashion) takes place is a mystery. It is tempting to try to "solve" this mystery by assimilating the development of symptoms to the categories of voluntary action and moral culpability by reference to such accounts as malingering, "moral trickery" (Penelhum, 1971), "bad faith" (Sartre, 1943/ 1956), and self-deception. If however purposive they may be or seem to be, symptoms are phenomena that *just happen* to one, how meaningful is it to view them as instances of self-deception? In self-deception, one is *doing something,* even if it is lying or deceiving.

Consider another clinical example: B's obsessive thought is that harm will come to her infant. There is evidence that what is involved in this symptom is the unconscious wish to hurt, even kill, her baby. This wish is too horrible, too anxiety provoking, and too sharply at variance with her self-image for her to experience it consciously. One can, I suppose, say that B avoids recognizing her wish to harm her baby and that this avoidance is motivated by the need to ward off anxiety and

---

[3]Other goals may have also been "served" by his symptoms. However, a consideration of these goals is not necessary for the present discussion.

maintain a particular self-image. From this point of view, one can perhaps say that B is deceiving herself. But something doesn't seem quite right. What is going on does not seem to be captured simply by saying that B is deceiving herself. This example seems so different in flavor and tone from Sartre's example of the woman in the cafe who shows "bad faith" by allowing her hand to remain in her male companion's hand all the while talking of lofty intellectual matters. The stakes are so different. For the woman with the infant, the thought of harming her baby is so horrible, so anxiety provoking, and so inimical to her sense of who she is that automatic anxiety-avoiding and self-preserving mechanisms come into play. While Sartre's woman in the cafe may be showing the kind of "bad faith" and moral weakness that is perhaps corrected by confrontation and moral suasion, the woman with the infant is engaged in a life and death struggle. Furthermore, and this seems to me critical, while all that is going on with Sartre's woman in the cafe remains at the level of voluntary action (as Stevenson, 1983, points out "allowing her hand to remain in his . . . is a voluntary action even though it consists in immobility, for her hand is not paralyzed" p. 256), in the case of the woman with the infant, the wish to harm her baby gets transformed into the symptomatic obsessive thought such that there is no longer "I desire" or "I wish," but "it happens" (see Eagle, 1985, for a further discussion of this issue). Similarly with patient A, discussed earlier: His conflicts surrounding heterosexual emotional commitment were transformed into obsessive symptoms.

Having a desire that one denies (and yet behaving as if one knew one had that desire) or failing to resist a desire that one says one wants to resist belong to the world of experience in which, perhaps, it makes good sense to talk about self-deception. But, as I have noted elsewhere (Eagle, 1985), "the kinds of phenomena . . . that are of central concern to psychoanalysis and to the psychoanalyst are the largely pathological *transformations* of disowned desires such that they no longer appear in consciousness as desire but rather as obsessive thoughts, compulsive rituals, phobias, and other symptomatic expressions" (p. 19). That is, these transformations no longer have the form of "I desire" but rather of "it happens." Self-deception implies that a person is deceiving or lying to himself. This language pertains to the world of persons. However, in the pathological transformations of desire into symptomatic expressions, one is not engaged in the act of self-deception or, for that matter, any other act. Rather, one is the victim of certain events or happenings (mechanisms) which, though poorly understood, clearly are not a matter of one *doing* anything. It is precisely the fact that one is a victim that Sartre, for example, wants to deny with his substitution of "bad faith" for repression. The former is meant to convey the idea that the individual as agent is somehow choosing to deceive himself rather than, as he claims, being victimized by impersonal forces. While perhaps certain things that one does, including deceiving oneself, may make one more susceptible to developing symptoms, the development of a symptom (e.g., a phobia or a compulsive ritual) is not simply a matter of self-deception. It involves other transformational processes that are not at all well understood. (See Mullhane, 1983, for a discussion of symptom-formation in psychoanalytic theory.)

THE ADAPTIVE FUNCTION OF PSYCHOANALYTIC DEFENSES

Although, as I have tried to show, psychoanalytic defenses (as well as other psychoanalytic concepts) cannot be subsumed under the logic of self-deception, they may nevertheless have certain functional properties in common. In particular, I want to address the question of their adaptiveness.

Recently, there has been an increased interest in the adaptive function of illusion, denial, and self-deception (for example, see Greenwald, 1980; Breznitz, 1983). And Sackeim (1983) has challenged the psychoanalytic insistence that the functions of self-deceptive defenses are limited to warding off anxiety and other disastrous consequences by attempting to show that such defenses can also serve the function of promoting self-enhancement and positive gain. The very title of this volume reflects an interest in and emphasis on the adaptive aspects of self-deceptive mechanisms.

Recognition of the adaptive function of these truth-denying and truth-distorting tendencies has been contrasted with the apparent psychoanalytic assumption that these tendencies are generally pathological and the corollary assumption that "the truth shall set ye free," that insight is conducive to health. Sackeim (1983), for example, asks whether as psychologists and clinicians, we ought to be more concerned with dispensing truth or increasing comfort, and clearly opts for the latter. It seems to me that this recent perspective on denial and self-deception *does* serve as a corrective to the Freudian emphasis on the clinical value of insight. And it is, of course, also the case that in Freudian theory repression is the primary causal pathogen in neurosis (as well as the primary causal factor in slips and dreams). However, a full understanding of the concept of repression in psychoanalytic theory will indicate that it is both a primary pathogenic agent and that it serves clear adaptive functions as well.

Repression

When Freud's topographical model predominated in psychoanalytic theory, the therapeutic goal of psychoanalysis was to make the unconscious conscious, and the essential logic of repression consisted in keeping unacceptable, anxiety-provoking impulses, wishes, and ideas from consciousness. When the topographical model was replaced by the structural model (of the psychic structures of id, ego, and superego), the therapeutic goal became "where id was, there should ego be," and the logic of repression now centered on disowning unacceptable anxiety-provoking impulses, wishes, and ideas—that is, rendering and experiencing them as an ego-alien "it" rather than as an "I." Obviously, the two models are related insofar as one way of disowning a mental content is to banish it from consciousness. What does all this have to do with the adaptive function of repression? The point is that in either model repression serves the highly adaptive functions of protecting the individual from unbearable, ego-threatening anxiety and from catastrophic threats to the integrity and unity of the self. As Klein (1976) makes clear, repression is a way of dealing with extreme incompatibilities of aims that threaten the integrity of the self. In repression, one banishes or, to use Klein's term, "fractionates" one set of aims with the adaptive result that what remains as part of the self is experienced as a unity. Although repression exacts a certain cost (e.g., a certain degree of ego restriction, failure to give expression to and gratify certain aims and needs), the benefits it bestows, when it operates effectively, are that one experiences oneself as a unity and avoids overwhelming anxiety.

The adaptive aspects of repression also become clear when one considers the consequences of (1) the inability to employ repression and the need, therefore, to resort to more primitive dissociative defenses and coping methods, and (2) the failure of repression once it has been employed. With regard to the first point, there is at least clinical evidence that more primitive defenses, exacting greater costs on the personality, are employed when the capacity to employ repression has not been sufficiently developed. Perhaps the most dramatic example of more primitive dissociative defenses is the development of multiple personalities. Bahnson (1984), who has studied multiple personalities for many years, believes that in these cases the more primitive personality represents ego-alien, repressed material and that "the multiple personality patient has no capacity for repression of dangerous emotions or impulses *other than* through the shift from one personality nucleus to another . . ." (pp. 6-7).

With regard to the failure of defense, it is important to point out that in psychoanalytic theory it is not repression per se that is a direct causal agent of neurosis but rather the partial *failure of repression* and the consequent "return of the repressed." As already noted, when repression is effective, whatever the other costs, anxiety is avoided and the integrity of the personality is maintained. When, for whatever reasons, repressive defenses fail, the unacceptable and anxiety-provoking wishes and impulses that have hitherto been excluded from consciousness threaten to "return." The result is distressing anxiety and/or the outbreak of other symptoms that represent compromises between the unacceptable wishes and ego defensive forces. As Freud (1917/1963, pp. 410-411) pointed out, symptoms are a kind of second line of defense against anxiety when repressive defenses fail. For example, as distressing as, say, a phobic symptom might be, insofar as it contains and localizes anxiety to a specific set of circumstances it is preferable to continual "free-floating" anxiety. However, in the present context, the basic point to note is that anxiety and symptoms erupt only when repression fails and there is a consequent "return of the repressed."

At least in moderate degrees, repression, as we have seen, serves an important adaptive function. Of course, a massive degree of repression is likely to be pathological for at least two related reasons. First as noted earlier, repression exacts the cost of ego restriction and the failure of certain vital needs to be gratified. When repression is massive, these costs became pathological. Second, the more massive and rigid the repression, the greater the likelihood of eventual failure and the consequent outbreak of anxiety and symptoms. But the dangers and costs of repression should not blind one to the adaptive role it plays in personality functioning.

Up to this point, I have been speaking of the adaptive role of repression in regard to **intrapsychic** functioning. In psychoanalytic theory, repression also plays an adaptive role in regard to the relationship between the individual and society. Particularly in *Civilization and its Discontents*, Freud (1930/1961d) makes clear his belief that the individual could not function in society without some degree of repression. He also emphasizes that the repressive demands of civilization make neurosis just about inevitable. One can escape neurosis and adapt to society's demands through **sublimation**, but most people are not capable of extensive sublimation and, under the pressure of society's repressive demands, succumb to neurosis of some kind. Does this contradict the claim that repression serves an adaptive function? I think not. What Freud had in mind when he spoke of the individual succumbing to neurosis under repressive social pressures is that because society demands an *excessive* degree of repression, greater than the individual can meet, repression inevitably fails and neurosis follows.

In demonstrating the adaptive aspect of repression, I am not suggesting that there are not more ideally adaptive alternatives. I have already indicated that according to psychoanalytic theory, sublimation is a more adaptive alternative to repression. It would also seem that a more adaptive alternative to repression would be a less condemning and less anxiety-ridden response to one's own instinctual impulses, so that repression would not be as necessary and more direct gratification would be possible. But here the psychoanalytic literature is somewhat ambiguous and the story does not seem quite that simple. On the one hand, the logic of psychoanalytic theory is such that for at least some of one's instinctual impulses, direct gratification would appear to be the healthiest option. On the other hand, it is also part of the logic of psychoanalytic theory that certain more primitive and infantile wishes would seem to *require* repression in order for adaptive adult functioning to take place. Furthermore, Anna Freud (1966) observes that there is a "primary antagonism" between instinct and ego, strongly suggesting that a certain degree of repression of instinctual impulses is necessary for intact ego functioning. This "primary antagonism" obviously derives from Freud's view that insofar as they carry the potential threat of ego-damaging excessive excitation, instinctual impulses are the natural enemy of the ego, and some kind of repressive forces are necessary to deal with that threat. So, once again, from still another vantage point, we see the near inevitability and adaptive role of some degree of repression.

Denial

Before concluding this chapter, some comments should be made regarding the psychoanalytic conception of denial. In some of his writings, Freud (1924/1961a, 1924/1961b) contrasted repression, which was seen as both a defense against *inner* impulses and wishes and a characteristic of neurosis, with denial or disavowal, which was taken to be a primitive defense against *external* reality and thought to indicate a weak ego and more severe pathology. However, what is often overlooked is that in his later writings, Freud noted that this view needed to be revised on the basis of his clinical findings of nonpsychotic instances of denial. One such example cited by Freud (1940/1964a) is the child's disavowal of what is to him or her the reality of "intolerable real danger" (i.e., castration threats) in order to satisfy instinctual wishes through masturbation. Other clinical examples are cited in the context of discussing fetishism and the simultaneous denial and recognition of the reality of a close one's death (Freud, 1927/1961c). With regard to this last example, Freud makes the point that what distinguishes nonpsychotic from psychotic denial is that in the latter case the reality aspect is completely denied and the recognition (of reality) aspect is completely absent (see also Freud, 1940/1964b).

Despite, Freud's recognition of the possibility of nonpsychotic and adaptive denial, however, psychoanalytic theory has relatively little to say regarding the adaptive potential of denial, and instead places greatest stress on the value of such factors as insight and self-knowledge. It is also apparent that Freud assumed that in optimal therapeutic circumstances knowing the truth about oneself—that is, insight—was curative. He believed firmly that only interpretations that "tally with what is real" were therapeutically effective (see Grunbaum, 1984). Perhaps the firmness of this belief was, at least partly, based on his failure to distinguish between truth as a personal value and truth as an effective therapeutic agent.

The necessity of illusion   Only recently has there been much discussion of the possibly healthy, adaptive nature of denial (and of related processes, such as illusion and self-deception), at least in certain circumstances (e.g., Breznitz, 1983; Sackeim, 1983). Some have argued that in certain core areas (e.g., denial of death, see Becker, 1973), denial and related mechanisms are necessary in order for one to live a healthy and normal life. Central themes in such classic works of literature as O'Neill's *The Iceman Cometh* and Ibsen's *The Wild Duck* include the necessity of illusion (in *The Iceman Cometh*, they are called "pipe-dreams") and the destructive, soul-destroying power of zealously bringing "the truth" into people's lives without regard for consequences and the psychological state of the individuals to whom "the truth" is being presented.

Reality testing   Freud was concerned with inner conflict and did not concern himself in his clinical work with extreme situations (e.g., life-threatening illness or circumstances), in which the adaptive use of denial is most apparent. As Eitinger (1983) points out, in extreme, life-threatening situations denial is more likely to be adaptive insofar as it prevents reactions such as panic, which would preclude the possibility of adaptive behavior. There are certain situations (e.g., concentration camps), he points out, in which the problems one faces cannot be solved, and in fact may be hindered, by full awareness of the reality one confronts. However—this is a critical point—even in the extreme situation of the concentration camp, if it were to further survival, denial had to be selective. As Eitinger puts it, "Denying death could be life-saving under certain circumstances, while denying the small seemingly unimportant factors of daily life and struggle would result in certain and premature death" (p. 211). In other words, simultaneous with the denial of death, one's **reality-testing functions** about the details of one's everyday life had to be reasonably intact if one were to avoid early and certain death. One had to know, for example, that using medical excuses to avoid work or retreating into daydreaming were death warrants.

Similar factors seem to operate in other life-threatening situations. For example, denying the seriousness of his or her illness may be adaptive for the cardiac patient who is in the intensive care unit following a heart attack. But, in order for the denial to be adaptive it must be selective and must not obliterate reality-testing functions and behaviors. If the denial is sufficiently massive and total such that it results in, say, the patient refusing his medication, checking out of the hospital, or deciding to go jogging immediately upon leaving the hospital, he will certainly put his life at great risk. With all the stress on the adaptive function of denial, it is worth noting that whatever the patient may say explicitly, he is, implicitly at least, *not* denying when he *does* take his medication, does *not* check out of the hospital, and does *not* go jogging. The fact is that he is denying in certain areas and not denying in others. As Freud (1927/1961c, 1940/1964b) notes, in nonpsychotic denial one finds existing side by side *both* "psychical attitudes"—one that denies reality and the other that takes account of reality.

The general point is that the adaptive or maladaptive nature of denial is a matter of the context in which and the degree to which it occurs. Although it has been shown that denial can have adaptive value in certain circumstances, it does not mean that the suspension of reality-testing functions is also adaptive. The evidence indicates that it is not. The available evidence also strongly suggests that denial is likely to be adaptive when it is brought into play mainly in relation to those aspects of situations about which one can do little or nothing (or in response to which one is likely to experience total despair, panic, or intense anxiety) and is not directed to those elements of situations in which problem-solving and reality-oriented responses are both possible and even necessary for survival.

The Adaptive Value of Self-Deception

I suspect something very similar is also true regarding the adaptive value of self-deception. When awareness and insight about oneself lead mainly to despair, panic, and a sense of helplessness, self-deception would seem to be a more adaptive alternative. For the residents of Harry Hope's Cafe of Last Resort in *The Iceman Cometh*, the insight brought by Hickey, the Iceman, to the effect that all their plans and hopes are illusions and "pipe-dreams" that will never be implemented is soul-shattering and death-dealing. They are all certainly better off with their "pipe-dreams" than without them. But this is because they cannot and will never carry out the plans (to cross the street, to get a job, etc.) they keep putting off each day. They are too shattered and hopeless. The lesson to be learned from *The Iceman Cometh* is not, I believe, that "pipe-dreams" and self-deception are superior to self-knowledge or even that they are necessary for survival. The insights to be gained are more complex ones. They are that unless self-knowledge and truth can be used constructively and unless such knowledge and understanding can lead to alternatives that are more satisfying and meaningful than one's current way of life, one may be better off with one's "pipe-dreams" and self-deceptions.

The sheer abrupt presentation of "the truth" to another (particularly if it is a painful truth), without preparation and without further involvement and help, is generally destructive and may often involve destructive motives on the part of the truth-dispenser. In Hickey's case, this is clear. His truth is death-dealing; it is intended to be so. Hickey's life is over and he wants everyone else's life to be over also. I have always felt that every psychotherapist should read and absorb the lessons of this play in order to better understand and dampen whatever zealous impulses they have to reveal and dispense "the truth."

Despite O'Neill's insistence on the necessity of "pipe-dreams" and the psychoanalytic emphasis on insight, I do not believe that the two are necessarily contradictory. For in psychoanalysis there is a healthy respect for the necessity of repression (the psychoanalytic analogue of "pipe-dreams") to preserve the integrity of the personality. In agreement with O'Neill, most psychoanalysts would argue that to attempt to undo repressions in an abrupt, Hickey-like manner, without regard for the individual's general psychic state and without ongoing support, *would* be countertherapeutic and destructive. The psychoanalytic emphasis on insight must be understood properly and must be placed in proper context. For example, merely hearing or being forced to hear distressing truths about oneself is not insight. At least in a therapeutic context, insight implies some degree of integration of material and an active and central role for oneself in achieving such integration. This implies that people achieve insight when they are ready for it, not when it is thrust upon them. Hence, it is simplistic as well as mistaken to assume that a concern with insight and self-understanding necessarily prevents one from appreciating the possible value of and need for "pipe-dreams" and self-deception.

CONCLUSIONS

One final point regarding *The Iceman Cometh*. Although O'Neill undoubtedly presents the plight of the denizens of the Cafe of Last Resort as representative of the human condition, for most of us the reality of our lives and of ourselves may not be as grim. Given their shattered state and the desperation of their lives, it is difficult to imagine that anything but "pipe-dreams" (and a perpetual state of drunkenness) could sustain Harry Hope and his crew. What kind of insight could one imagine being useful to them?

In a certain sense, the residents of the Cafe of Last Resort are similar to concentration camp inmates. In most areas of their lives they can do little or nothing, or can only experience total despair and panic. Hence, there is no adaptive reason to give up their denial and "pipe-dreams" and become aware of their hopeless plight. That way lies certain and quick death. Also like the concentration camp inmates, if they are to survive, they cannot suspend all reality-testing functions. They must be certain, for example, that their supply of whiskey is not stopped.

For most of us, at least in some areas of our lives, more constructive alternatives are available and certain insights could help us achieve these alternatives, become less self-condemning, and experience greater satisfaction. This does not mean, however, that avoidance, denial, and self-deception may not be adaptive in other areas of our lives.[4] If Becker (1973) is right, perhaps some degree of denial of death is an example of a near universal and adaptive kind of denial. In any case, in the present context an emphasis on the critical importance of insight and self-understanding need not be incompatible with a recognition of the possible adaptive value of such responses as avoidance, denial, and self-deception. In fact, one can only fully understand the value of insight and help oneself and others achieve it by appreciating the psychological necessity and adaptive functions served by such processes as repression, avoidance, denial, and self-deception. It does not do justice to the complexity or subtlety of psychoanalytic theory—and further, it is simplistic—to simply pit insight against self-deception without taking adequate account of such factors as situational context, degree of self-deception, ego strength, motives, and psychological and reality consequences—the domains of life in which self-deception and insight operate.

---

[4]Lazarus (1983) makes a useful distinction between avoidance and denial. For example, to avoid thinking about something stressful is not necessarily the same as denying the reality of the stressful situation.

REFERENCES

ANSCOMBE, R. (in press). The ego and the will. *Psychoanalysis and Contemporary Thought.*

BAHNSON, C. B. (1984, August). *Integration and disintegration of personality: Multiple personality and altered ego states.* Paper presented at Annual Convention of the American Psychological Association, Toronto.

BECKER, E. (1973). *The denial of death.* New York: Free Press.

BETTELHEIM, B. (1983). *Freud and man's soul.* New York: Knopf.

BRANDT, L. W. (1966). Process or structure? *The Psychoanalytic Review, 53,* 50-54.

BREZNITZ, S. (1983). *The denial of stress.* New York: International Universities Press.

CHEESMAN, J., & MERIKLE, P. M. (1985). Word recognition and consciousness. In D. Beaner, T. G. Waller, & G. E. McKinnon (Eds.), *Reading research advances in theory and practice* (Vol. 5). New York: Academic Press.

DILMAN, I. (1972). Is the unconscious a theoretical construct? *Monist, 56,* 313-342.

EAGLE, M. N. (1984). *Recent developments in psychoanalysis: A critical evaluation.* New York: McGraw-Hill.

————. (1985, March). *Psychoanalysis and the personal.* Paper presented at Conference on Psychoanalysis and the Philosophy of Mind, The University of St. Andrews, Fife, Scotland.

EIDELBERG, L. (1968). *Encyclopedia of psychoanalysis.* New York: Free Press.

EITINGER, L. (1983). Denial in concentration camps: Some personal observations on the positive and negative functions of denial in extreme life situations. In S. Breznitz (Ed.), *The denial of stress* (pp. 199-212). New York: International Universities Press.

FINGARETTE, H. (1969). *Self-deception.* New York: Academic Press.

FLEW, A. (1949). Psychoanalytic explanation. *Analysis, 10,* 8-15.

FREUD, A. (1966). *The ego and the mechanisms of defense.* New York: International Universities Press.

FREUD, S. (1954). *The origins of psychoanalysis: Letters to Wilhelm Fliess, drafts and notes: 1887–1902 by Sigmund Freud.* (M. Bonaparte, A. Freud, & E. Knis, Eds., E. Mosbacher & J. Strachey, Trans.). New York: Basic Books.

————. (1955). Studies on hysteria. In J. Strachey (Ed. and Trans.), *The standard edition of the complete psychological works of Sigmund Freud* (Vol. 2). London: Hogarth Press. (Original work published 1893–1895.)

————. (1957). On narcissism: An introduction. In J. Strachey (Ed. and Trans.), *The standard edition of the complete psychological works of Sigmund Freud* (Vol. 14, pp. 67-102). London: Hogarth Press. (Original work published 1914.)

_____. (1961a). Neurosis and psychosis. In J. Strachey (Ed. and Trans.), *The standard edition of the complete psychological works of Sigmund Freud* (Vol. 19, pp. 148-153). London: Hogarth Press. (Original work published 1924.)

_____. (1961b). The loss of reality in neurosis and psychosis. In J. Strachey (Ed. and Trans.), *The standard edition of the complete psychological works of Sigmund Freud* (Vol. 19, pp. 182-187). London: Hogarth Press. (Original work published 1924.)

_____. (1961c). Fetishism. In J. Strachey (Ed. and Trans.), *The standard edition of the complete psychological works of Sigmund Freud* (Vol. 21, pp. 149-157). London: Hogarth Press. (Original work published 1927.)

_____. (1961d). Civilization and its discontents. In J. Strachey (Ed. and Trans.), *The standard edition of the complete psychological works of Sigmund Freud* (Vol. 21, pp. 59-145). London: Hogarth Press. (Original work published 1930.)

_____. (1963). Introductory lectures on psychoanalysis (Part III). In J. Strachey (Ed. and Trans.), *The standard edition of the complete psychological works of Sigmund Freud* (Vol. 16). London: Hogarth Press. (Original work published 1917.)

_____. (1964a). Splitting of the ego in the process of defence. In J. Strachey (Ed. and Trans.), *The standard edition of the complete psychological works of Sigmund Freud* (Vol. 23, pp. 273-278). London: Hogarth Press. (Original work published 1940.)

_____. (1964b). An outline of psychoanalysis. In J. Strachey (Ed. and Trans.), *The standard edition of the complete psychological works of Sigmund Freud* (Vol. 23, pp. 141-207). London: Hogarth Press. (Original work published 1940.)

GILBERT, D. T., & COOPER, J. (1985). Social psychological strategies of self-deception. In M. Martin (Ed.), *Self-deception and self-understanding* (pp. 75-94). Lawrence, KS: University Press of Kansas.

GREENWALD, A. G. (1980). The totalitarian ego: Fabrication and revision of personal history. *American Psychologist, 35*, 603-618.

GRUNBAUM, A. (1984). *The logical foundations of psychoanalysis: A philosophical critique.* Berkeley: University of California Press.

GUTTMAN, S. A., JONES, R. L., & PARRISH, S. M. (1980). *The concordance to the standard edition of the complete psychological works of Sigmund Freud.* Boston: G. K. Hall.

HEMPEL, C. (1965). *Aspects of scientific explanation.* New York: Free Press.

HOLT, R. R. (1972). Freud's mechanistic and humanistic images of man. *Psychoanalysis and Contemporary Science, 1*, 3-24.

KIERKEGAARD, S. (1956). *Purity of heart.* New York: Harper Torch Books.

KLEIN, G. S. (1976). *Psychoanalytic theory: An exploration of essentials.* New York: International Universities Press.

LAPLANCHE, J., & PONTALIS, J. B. (1973). *The language of psychoanalysis.* New York: Hogarth Press.

LAZARUS, R. S. (1983). The costs and benefits of denial. In S. Breznitz (Ed.), *The denial of stress* (pp. 1-30). New York: International Universities Press.

MARCEL, A. J. (1983a). Conscious and unconscious perception: Experiments on visual masking and word recognition. *Cognitive Psychology, 15,* 197-237.

————. (1983b). Conscious and unconscious perception: An approach to the relations between phenomenal experience and perceptual processes. *Cognitive Psychology, 15,* 238-300.

MOORE, M. (1984). *Law and psychiatry.* Cambridge: Cambridge University Press.

MULLHANE, H. (1983). Defense, dreams and rationality. *Synthese, 57,* 187-204.

NISBETT, R., & ROSS, L. (1980). *Human inference: Strategies and shortcomings.* Englewood Cliffs, NJ: Prentice-Hall.

PAULHUS, D. L. (1986). Self-deception and impression management in test responses. In A. Angleiter & J. S. Wiggins (Eds.), *Personality assessment via questionnaire* (pp. 143-165). New York: Springer.

PENELHUM, T. (1971). The importance of self-identity. *Journal of Philosophy, 68,* 667-678.

RUBINSTEIN, B. B. (1977). On the concept of a person and of an organism. In R. Stern, L. S. Horowitz, & J. Lynes (Eds.), *Science and psychotherapy* (pp. 1-17). New York: Haven Publishing.

SACKEIM, H. A. (1983). Self-deception, self-esteem, and depression: The adaptive value of lying to oneself. In J. Masling (Ed.), *Empirical studies of psychoanalytical theories* (Vol. 1, pp. 101-157). Hillsdale, NJ: The Analytic Press.

SARTRE, J. P. (1956). *Being and nothingness* (Hazel Barnes, Trans.). New York: Washington University Press. (Original work published 1943.)

SHOPE, R. (1970). Freud on conscious and unconscious intentions. *Inquiry, 13,* 149-159.

STEVENSON, L. (1983). Sartre on bad faith. *Philosophy, 58,* 253-258.

SULLIVAN, H. S. (1953). *The interpersonal theory of psychiatry.* New York: Norton.

Self-Deception
in the Claims
of Hypnosis Subjects

Theodore R. Sarbin
University of California, Santa Cruz

Scientists' concern with uncovering the causes of hypnotic conduct has distracted investigators and theorists from examining the phenomena as instances of self-deception. When hypnosis subjects deny agency for their actions in the face of evidence to the contrary, causality seekers have leaned on speculative neurology as a source of explanatory metaphors. In this chapter I argue that the claims of hypnosis subjects are better conceptualized as self-deception. The hypnosis encounter, I believe, may serve as a model for clarifying some of the obscurities of self-deception.

THE MYSTERY OF HYPNOSIS

In reviewing the history and present status of hypnosis, we are compelled to conclude that the defining criterion for the curious mixture of behaviors called hypnosis is ''conduct that is contrary to expectations.'' To explain such counterexpectational conduct, psychologists and other scientists have turned to both science and theology

This chapter is adapted from Sarbin (1984). Permission to reproduce selected passages granted by the editors of The Psychological Record.

(and sometimes folklore) for their descriptive and explanatory metaphors. For the most part, the choice of metaphors has been influenced by assuming a causal connection between the benign monologue[1] of the hypnotist and the often dramatic behavior of the subject. Some of the metaphors adopted to describe or explain the phenomena have communicated an air of mystery. Most were chosen to give body to the apparent mysteries of catalepsy, hallucination, amnesia, posthypnotic compulsive actions, and so on. "Trance" has been a popular descriptive and explanatory metaphor. It has often been employed to connote a causal entity. The poetic imagery stimulated by the trance metaphor has helped sustain the atmosphere of mystery.

Abundant arguments have been advanced to show the futility of building a viable theory on the notion of trance (Spanos & Chaves, 1970; Sarbin & Coe, 1972). These arguments notwithstanding, the underlying subtext in many current writings—the doctrine of mental states—bears a strong family resemblance to trance. The substitution of "mental states" or "unconscious processes" for "trance" has not reduced the coefficient of mystery.

The current candidate for supplying the atmosphere of mystery is "**the classic suggestion effect.**" Weitzenhoffer (1978) complained that scales to assess hypnotic responsiveness fail to take into account the classic suggestion effect, that is, the apparent absence of agency in the subject's performances. Weitzenhoffer's complaint has spurred a number of experimenters to explore the possibility of capturing this effect through various types of phenomenological reports (see, for example, Bowers, K. W., 1981; Wedemeyer & Coe, 1981; Bowers, P., 1982; Farthing, Brown, & Venturino, 1983; Lynn, Nash, Rhue, Frauman, & Stanley, 1983).

The language of the experimenter's monologue and inquiry sets the stage for the subject to disclaim volition and effort. Terms such as "degree of effort," "voluntariness," and "automatic" direct the subject to assign causal attributions to his or her conduct. The classic suggestion effect is said to occur when the subject asserts that he or she is not the author of certain actions. Either free verbal responses or structured rating scales provide the experimental data from which the classic suggestion effect is inferred.

It is important to emphasize that both the experimenter and the subject are members of a language community who recognize the distinction between intentional acts performed by an agent and events that just happen. An **act**, such as throwing a ball, writing a letter, driving a car, or raising one's arm, is categorically different from a **happening**, such as a toothache, a pateller reflex, an itch, or a gastric growl. The linguistic form for describing an act is "I did it"; the linguistic form for describing a happening is "It happened to me." The first form implies that the speaker, the I, is the active agent; the second implies that the speaker is not the

---

[1]"Monologue" may not be the best label for the hypnotist's communication. Other writers employ "induction," "recital," or "spiel." Strictly speaking, the hypnotist's communicative acts are part of a dialogue. The reciprocal part of the dialogue is the subject's (usually) nonverbal responses, such as body language, facial expressions, and gestures. My usage of "monologue" in the present context implies the presence of a responding other.

agent of the action, but a passive recipient, an object acted upon by physical, chemical, biological, or other forces.[2]

The typical hypnosis monologue contains sentences that imply a nonagentic formula, such as "your eyelids are heavy," "your body feels warm," "you are drifting away." As a result, the subject faces the task of assigning his acts to the category of happenings. More specifically, the content of the monologue invites the subject to regard certain of his or her acts, such as finger interlock and eyelid closure, as if they belonged to the category of happenings—the category that includes kneejerks and sneezes.

A TYPICAL PHENOMENON

To simplify my presentation, I take arm levitation as a typical phenomenon about which agency can be acknowledged or denied. (It is interesting to note that we still use the opaque word "levitation," rather than the more transparent "raising the arm." "Levitation" contributes to the aura of mystery.) Assume a panel of scientific observers in an exercise in which a volunteer subject, Fred Jones, slowly raises his left arm in response to a suggestion contained in the hypnotist's monologue. The communication conveys the manifest message "your arm will rise of itself." The hypnotist's communication does not meet the usual criteria for an order, a command, or even a request. Rather, the hypnotist asserts that the arm will rise, implying that Jones will not be the agent of his act. Jones's inference, then, is that the arm is to rise as if some unspecified causal entity were at work.

At the conclusion of the exercise, the hypnotist asks Jones to render a phenomenological report about the source of the arm movement. Usually, the request is for an appraisal of the degree of volition, effort, or automaticity experienced.

The observers would quickly lose interest in the scene if Jones matter-of-factly said, "I just raised my arm." In other than hypnotic settings, the observers would hold the ordinary expectation that Jones would make the claim of agency for his actions. There would be no riddle to solve, no mystery to explore, if Jones were to raise his arm and then meet ordinary expectations with the acknowledgment, "I raised my arm."

When Jones retrospectively reports that his arm moved by itself, without effort, he disclaims being the agent. The observers' interest in the scene is quickened when confronted by such a contradictory state of affairs. The observers saw Jones raise his arm; he was clearly the agent of his act. There is no reason to believe that Jones's arm was pulled by strings, electronic gadgets, or "Star Wars" technology. A lifetime of experience created the expectation that Jones would acknowl-

[2]The sharp distinction between acts and happenings is something of an oversimplification. Happenings may be instigated by intentional acts. Running up the stairs to fetch a book is an intentional act. The increased heart-rate, respiration, and perspiration induced by the act are happenings. Although triggered by my acts, they are no longer under my agency. An observer might well ask for the *reasons* for my running upstairs and for the *causes* of the physiological changes.

edge authorship of his act and say, ''I did it.'' His disclaimer, ''I didn't do it,'' is contrary to expectation. We are faced with a paradox.

Three resolutions of the paradox are possible:

> *Resolution 1*: To assign credibility to Jones's disclaimer of agency. The implication of this resolution is that Jones's arm levitation must be accounted for by invoking mysterious agencies such as spirits, magnets, or magic. Although such explanations are no longer taken seriously, the use of certain mentalistic concepts such as dissociation and trance keeps alive the notion of mysterious agency.

> *Resolution 2*: To assign credibility to the observation that Jones was the agent of the act, and for various reasons, attempted to deceive the experimenter, claiming that he was not the agent. We can neutralize the possible moral connotations of deception by describing Jones's compliance in the language of dramaturgic role taking. That is to say, Jones sustained the dramatic interaction through the artful employment of histrionic and rhetorical skills.

> *Resolution 3*: To assign credibility to the observation that Jones was the agent of the act, and for various reasons, attempted to deceive the experimenter *and* himself, claiming that he was not the agent. If Jones were not the agent of his act (when they know that he was the agent), then a diagnosis of self-deception must be entertained.

Resolutions 2 and 3 require more extended treatment. To deceive another is no small achievement, requiring rhetorical and histrionic skills. But to deceive oneself requires special skills—skills more complex than those of the subject who tries only to deceive an experimenter.

RESOLUTION 2: A DRAMATURGICAL ACCOUNT

Before sketching the dramaturgical process of Resolution 2 and the process of self-deception of Resolution 3, I want to touch upon a few background notions. I have made the argument before that the prevailing paradigm for studying hypnosis encourages the practice of perceiving the experimental subject or client as an object or laboratory specimen irreversibly partitioned from the hypnotist.

I advocate the use of a different paradigm. I regard the interaction between hypnotist and subject as a *discourse*, a set of interactive communications whereby both parties perform their respective roles. The partition between hypnotist and subject is illusory. By looking upon hypnosis as a discourse, our attention is directed to overt verbal and nonverbal communications as well as to the implications and entailments hidden in the discourse. Conversational discourse is an appropriate model for the study of hypnosis; in the monologue, the hypnotist employs predominantly verbal stimuli addressed to the subject. The subject responds with predominantly motoric actions except when a verbal report is requested.

As in any discourse, the two actors in the hypnosis situation are faced with the task of communicating their intentions. Inasmuch as the actions subsumed under the label "hypnosis" presumably follow from the hypnotist's monologue, a semiotic analysis of the monologue should illuminate the flow of the discourse, including that part of the discourse in which the subject assigns agency to mysterious or unknown forces.

Hypnosis As Metaphoric Encounter

In another work, I have argued that hypnosis might be viewed as a metaphoric encounter of the fourth class (Sarbin, 1980). Because all metaphors have two terms—the literal and the figurative—and each term may be expressed *or* implied, four classes may be generated. The first type (both terms are expressed) is the one most frequently encountered in academic discussions of metaphor. Such metaphors are easy to identify since both terms are expressed, for example, Lincoln was a giant or the poet is a nightingale.

In the second type of metaphor the literal term is expressed; the figurative term is silent and must be construed from the context or invented. An example is Lady Macbeth's declaration, "Out, out, damned spot" accompanied by handwashing motions. She is speaking literally, the figurative "cleansing of guilt" is silent and must be inferred from the context.

The third class of metaphor (the literal term is silent, the figurative term is expressed) is readily illustrated by the use of a proverb. The speaker utters a statement that, given the appropriate context, is figurative. The job for the listener is to construct a literal meaning. For example, a child is telling his mother about his detailed plans for next summer's camping trip, and his mother interrupts the telling with the apparently irrelevant remark, "Don't count your chickens before they are hatched." None of the terms in the remark has anything to do with the child's discussion of his summer plans. If the child is familiar with the proverb, he will translate metaphorically expressed folk wisdom into a literal statement of counsel.

In the fourth class of metaphor both terms are hidden, implied, or suppressed. The listener must engage in more epistemic work to create an acceptable meaning than in the other classes, in which not more than one term is silent. Perrine (1972) gives several poetic examples, among them, "Let us eat and drink, for tomorrow we shall die." The verb "shall die" connotes the literal component, "tomorrow" connotes the figurative component. The suppressed literal term is a lifetime; and its figurative equivalent is one day. The general meaning is that life is very short (Perrine, 1971). Neither the literal nor the figurative appears directly in the quotation—both must be construed.

Needless to say, metaphoric analysis is applicable to actions other than the reading or composing of poetry. In the following paragraphs, I demonstrate that hypnosis may be understood as metaphoric discourse in which the figurative and literal terms are both silent.

The focus of attention for students of hypnosis is the subject's contrary-to-expectations conduct, such as "age regression" (acting according to childlike standards), "hallucination" (perceptual responses that are not veridical or consensual), amnesia (not remembering when intact memory is expected), and claiming nonvolition (attributing causality to mysterious forces rather than the self), and so on. The explanatory task is that of showing how the hypnotist's part of the discourse is interpreted by the subject, and how the subject fashions his or her part of the discourse—both verbal and motoric—to establish and maintain a collaborative interaction.

The Hypnotic Situation

The episode of behavior begins when the hypnotist talks to the subject. (Parenthetically, the distinction between the benign quality of the hypnotist's talk and the often dramatic quality of the subject's responses has encouraged many writers to invoke causal explanations that maintain the aura of mystery.) The hypnotist's monologue is recognizably different from ordinary conversation in style. Changes in tempo are common: The hypnotist usually speaks slower than in preliminary conversation. Many—if not all—hypnotists reduce ordinary variations in pitch to a monotone. Some words and phrases are repeated, even chanted, for example, "sleepy and drowsy . . . sleepy and drowsy . . . heavier and heavier."

These stylistic variations possess no intrinsic power to direct the subject's actions. Whatever the effect on the subject, it is the meanings attributed to the stylistic shifts that influence the subject's conduct. This aspect of the monologue must be examined from a semiotic standpoint—to inquire into the *meanings* of communications. Most writers fail to ask the question: What is being communicated by changes in the hypnotist's tempo, pitch, and rhythm?

In addition to stylistic changes, a semiotic examination of the content of the monologue is needed. The specific words and phrases will vary from person to person and even from one time to another. Most hypnotists will employ a recital similar to the one prepared by Friedlander and Sarbin (1938). Beginning with assurances that there is nothing fearful about hypnosis, the hypnotist describes hypnosis as a state of mind that is similar to the absorbed attention experienced while reading an intriguing novel or seeing a good movie or play. The subject is told to relax and that he or she will experience something akin to, but not identical with, sleep. In the course of the induction, the hypnotist includes a number of problematic or contrary-to-fact statements: "your arm is getting lighter," "your eyes want to close," "you are drifting away," "you are surrendering your normal state of consciousness." Some monologues fashion epistemological frames for the subject, such as "your subconscious mind is being activated."

These problematic or contrary-to-fact communications impose a condition of epistemic strain on the subject, who tries to make sense of the contradictions introduced by the problematic utterances. He or she might reflect on the hypnotist's sentence, "your arm is rising of its own accord," against the background of experience that supports the contrary proposition: "my arm does not move unless I move it." If the subject joins his observation that the hypnotist is uttering contrary-to-fact statements with his or her observation of the shift in pitch, tempo, and rhythm, then the subject might well entertain the question: "What is the meaning of the hypnotist's talk?"

One answer might be "The hypnotist's utterances are nonsense. My arm is not rising, I am not drifting." If the subject assigns the hypnotist's problematic sentences to the category "nonsense," then there is no basis for continuing the interaction. Such subjects are classified by hypnosis investigators as "not hypnotizable."

An alternative answer to the semiotic question might be formulated as follows: "Since the hypnotist is *dramatizing* his talk, and is telling me things that are fictional, perhaps he is inviting me to participate in an adult version of the game of 'let's pretend' and also to pretend that this is serious business." The subject might then consider that "the hypnotist is casting me in a role for a theatrical enterprise, which demands that I engage in 'as if' behavior." Such an implication would follow from instantiating the monologue as an extended metaphor. The hypnotist's talk does not openly direct the subject to enter into a dramatic action— *the subject must construe the metaphor from the context.*

Within the context as predefined by both interactants, the contrary-to-fact utterances of the hypnotist metaphorically serve the same function as a stage director's more literal instruction: "Larry, you play the part of Lear." Children at play also use literal language when assigning roles and the conduct expected from each player. One child will agree to act the role of doctor, his or her playmate, the role of patient (see Feldman & Custrini, Chapter 3).

Through the use of metaphors and the avoidance of literal language, both interactants proceed by indirection. The monologue is an extended metaphor; the sentences contain various combinations of expressed and implied terms. The overall metaphor is of the fourth type, in which the literal and the figurative terms are unexpressed. The subject could formulate the metaphoric transformation somewhat as follows: "The interaction between the hypnotist and me is a miniature dramatic enterprise. While it is play, it is serious play. The setting and the hypnotist's demeanor call for seriousness and sincerity." Both participants enact their roles, neither overtly describing the action as theater, neither overtly expressing the literal and figurative terms that make the enterprise a theatrical one. The hidden metaphor in the hypnosis situation is a special case of a widely used metaphysical postulate "Life is theater." It is hidden in the monologue in the same way that Shakespeare concealed the same life-is-theater metaphor in the oft-quoted "All the world's a stage and all the men and women merely players. . . ."

The employment of implicit metaphors is not unique to the hypnosis situation. For example, courtship behavior frequently demands indirection. The man and the woman engage in speech and nonverbal communications that advance the courtship, at the same time pretending that the actions have no ulterior motives. Their speech and nonverbal actions, on analysis, also constitute metaphors of the fourth type. In hospital wards that serve terminally ill patients, a tacit agreement is frequently arranged by the patient and the staff to pretend that the patient is not dying. The agreement is not spelled out literally, but is contained in the metaphoric and rhetorical acts of the participants (Glaser & Strauss, 1965).

RESOLUTION 3: SELF-DECEPTION

These notes on hypnosis as a form of metaphorical discourse serve as a backdrop for an analysis of the claim of nonvolition made by some hypnosis subjects. Earlier I proposed three resolutions to the paradox created by the observation that some subjects claim nonvolition for acts that are volitional. Resolution 1 calls for the intervention of mysterious forces, a resolution not to be taken seriously. Resolution 2 and Resolution 3 are more complex.

In Resolution 2, the subject accepts the theatrical casting and to the best of his or her ability creates the illusion that the hypnotic conduct was caused by an agent other than the self. Under various kinds of demands, pressures for honesty, and detailed inquiry, the subject admits to participating in the dramaturgical enterprise. The subject interprets the ambiguities and contradictions contained in the mono-logue to mean "join in the game." Little more need be said about Resolution 2, the dramaturgic solution, save to mention the work on compliance summarized by Wagstaff (1981). His detailed analysis supports the notion that most subjects in hypnosis experiments are docile in the face of role demands, expectations, and metaphoric instructions.

Resolution 3, self-deception, is a complex, albeit fairly common phe-nomenon. To deceive oneself is to construct an unwarranted belief, that is, unwar-ranted from the perspective of a critical observer. The belief serves as a guide to action. The self-deceiver supports his belief by claiming "ignorance" of contradic-tory propositions that are presumably supported by appropriate evidence. Further, the self-deceiver characteristically rejects, distorts, or reinterprets information that would challenge the claim of ignorance. The self-deceiver, in effect, convincingly says "I don't know" when the evidential context calls for the contradictory state-ment, "I know."

A popular, although not very helpful, way of explaining this perplexing state of affairs is to invoke "knowing" at different "levels of consciousness." However, consciousness and cognate mentalistic terms are opaque and abstract and tend to confound the mystery. "Levels of consciousness" does not take us very far in understanding how people in general, and hypnosis subjects in particular, organize their overt conduct and their covert actions so that others may assign the label: self-deception.

The concept of self-deception is most often employed as a generic category for conduct that is tagged as rationalization, denial, repression, selective inatten-tion, subception, hysteria, paranoia, delusion, and so on. The usual formulation regards these actions as *happenings mechanically activated by unconscious forces.*

Active or Passive Responses?

Another way of looking at the process of self-deception describes human action without recourse to mechanistic or mentalistic conceptions. We begin with the assertion that the contradictory state of affairs (knowing and not knowing) is the product of the agent's intentional actions, not passive reactions to mechanical or other forces. The basis for a definition has been offered by the philosopher Herbert Fingarette:

> . . . the self-deceiver is one whose life situation is such that, on the basis of his/ her tacit assessment of the situation, finds there is overriding reason for adopting a policy of not spelling out some engagement in his or her world. (1969, p. 62)

Characteristically, the self-deceiver goes beyond not spelling out his recognition of events as they are. To make his story whole, he invents and distorts the world of occurrences so as to produce an apparent correspondence between his account and that of a critical observer. He does not "spell out that he is doing this. . . . the fabrication he tells us he also tells himself" (Fingarette, p. 62).

Spelling-out is the central metaphor; it conveys the imagery of an agent articulating, elaborating, detailing, describing causal relations, recognizing intentions and reasons, and so on. Equally important in constructing a plausible account of a person's life situation is a complementary skill, the skill in **not-spelling-out**, not articulating, not recognizing causal relations, not elaborating, and so on.

Earlier attempts to construct a systematic account of self-deception leaned heavily on hypothetical mental machinery and allegorical figures, as in Freud's use of the ego besieged by the id and the superego. The rise of phenomenology influenced the unmasking of the allegorical figures and the recognition that instances of self-deception, like instances of deception, were actions of human beings trying to make their way in problematic, uncertain, and imperfect worlds. The skills of spelling-out and not-spelling-out belong to such an action framework.

THE SELF-NARRATIVE

In the remainder of this chapter, I will show how the skills of spelling-out and not-spelling-out serve the more general purpose of **storytelling**. My arguments follow from a postulate, defended elsewhere (Sarbin, 1981), that the flow of experience is made intelligible through the use of narrative structure. The postulate seems reasonable when we are reminded that our dreams, our fantasies, the rituals of daily life, and the pageantry of special occasions are organized as if to tell stories. Our rememberings and our plannings are guided by narrative. Even films of geometrical figures in random motion are spontaneously emplotted into coherent stories containing common human sentiments and purposes (Heider & Simmel, 1944; Michotte, 1946/1963).

To tell a story is to organize bits and pieces of unorganized experience into a coherent account with a beginning, a middle, and an end. Of the various forms of storytelling, the self-narrative—a story about oneself—is relevant to our present concerns. We are interested here in exploring how a person creates a coherent self-narrative out of the contradictory propositions, "I did it" and "it happened to me."

More firmly to impart the notion of self-narrative, I remind the reader of the organized fantasy life of Thurber's unforgettable character Walter Mitty, or George

Washington's supposed silent rehearsal of the story he prepared to tell his father about the cherry tree incident. These silent narratives have the self as the central figure. From fragments of fact and fancy, a person selects some items for elaboration and justification, and ignores other items, the inclusion of which would render the story implausible, unconvincing, or absurd. It is the skillful use of "spelling-out" and "not-spelling-out" that facilitates the telling of a proper story, whether about others or about oneself.

It is now a commonplace among hypnosis researchers that the attribution of nonvolition is not sustained by a large proportion of experimental subjects. Under prodding, incentive conditions, and demands for honesty, such subjects admit being the agents of their acts. As noted above, these subjects fit the description of those who employ Resolution 2 to resolve the contradiction between action and attribution. The remainder of the subjects continue to claim involuntariness: These subjects employ Resolution 3, the resolution that depends on successful self-deception.

"I" or "Me"

Both kinds of subjects construct self-narratives, taking into account the language of the experimenter, the setting, and so on. Their self-narratives are different, however, and depend on the differential use of grammatical forms.

Our grammar is such that the self can at one time be the *author* of action, as represented by the pronoun "I," or the *object* of happenings, as represented by the pronoun "me." The focus of an episode in a self-narrative, then, may be on the "I" or on the "me." "I" stands for author, "me" stands for roles or parts played in a life drama.

The Resolution 2 subjects tell their stories from the perspective of "I" as author. They might summarize the episode with the statement: "Yes, I raised my arm, and, for various reasons, I said I did not raise my arm." Dramaturgy is an apt metaphor for the creative storytelling of these subjects.

For the subjects who claim nonvolition, even under conditions designed to breach the claim (Resolution 3 subjects), the self-narrative is different. The silent story calls for a focus on the referents for the pronoun "me." That is, the self is the *object* in the story, the narrative figure imaginatively created by the self as author. To maintain the plausibility of the narrative, the person must be very skillful in not-spelling-out those actions that would render the story unconvincing.

In the same way that a person can become deeply involved in the actions of fictional characters such as Jonathan Livingston Seagull, Luke Skywalker, or Don Quixote, so can the Resolution 3 subject become deeply involved in the role of narrative figure in his or her own life story. In declaring "I did not raise my arm," the hypnosis subject utters a communication that elides the ongoing social interaction into the plot of the self-narrative: a plot in which he or she is the central character. The self-reports as well as the motoric acts are public performances directed to the hypnotist and to others as spectators. The self-reports ratify his or her public role as a special performer, as the star of the show. In demonstrating what appears to be a transcendence of normal behavior, the subject shows that he or she is a remarkable character indeed. Further, the self-report of nonvolition validates the story in which the subject has become an important feature of the magical kingdom of entrancement and enchantment.

JUSTIFYING THE SELF-DECEPTION

I employ the "magical kingdom" metaphor advisedly. To create a self-narrative in which certain engagements are not spelled out, as in the claim of nonvolition for intentional acts, is to strain one's commitment to conventional logic.

We must backtrack for a moment to the discussion of metaphors of the fourth kind before we can answer the question: How does the self-deceiver convince himself that he is not the agent of his actions? As noted before, the task for the subject is to make sense out of the communications intended by the hypnotist but not overtly expressed.

The Question of Belief

I asserted earlier that three types of response were possible to resolve the epistemic strain induced by the problematic and contrary-to-fact utterances. In the first, the agent decides on the credibility of the implied proposition that occult or mysterious forces are operative. The assignment of credibility to a metaphor is the same as not recognizing or denying the "as if" quality of the utterance. In short, the metaphor is reified and may serve as the starting point for the unfolding of a myth. Not unique to hypnosis, literalizing the metaphor also occurs under less dramatic conditions, for example, when scientists treat the metaphor *mind* as if it were a literal entity. Elsewhere (Sarbin, 1982), I have referred to this transformation of metaphor as the "credo" (I believe) solution. Instead of reading the hypnotist's intentions as figurative, the subject reads the intentions as literal. The problematic utterances are taken to be literal assertions to be incorporated into one's self-narrative. From the credo stance, the subject arrives at one of two conclusions, either "I believe" or "I don't believe." In the latter case, there is no basis for continuing the discourse.

Most subjects in hypnosis experiments do not adopt the credo stance, rather they interpret the problematic utterances as "as if" statements, or obliquely expressed figures of speech. Because they "figure" or fashion "as if" meanings, I call this solution the **figural strategy**. As noted before, a typical subject interprets the suppressed metaphor as an invitation to participate in a theatrical enterprise. Unlike the credo resolution to the veiled intentions in the hypnotist's monologue, the figural solution is accepted if it fits the interactant's criteria for *aptness*. The subject might silently raise the query: Given the context, is the theatrical interpretation an apt one?

The subject may decline or accept the implied invitation to join in the game of "let's pretend." If playing the game is consistent with the subject's unfolding self-narrative, the quality of the performance will depend upon personal attributes, such as skill in rhetorical expression (verbal and nonverbal), and personal reasons for joining in the dramaturgical action. The subject then performs to convince the hypnotist that he or she was not the agent for certain acts. Such an interactant may be compared to a Shakespearian actor who, although playing the role to the hilt, never loses sight of the fact that he is not Richard III, but an actor in a theatre, a skillful dissimulator.

Assertion or Metaphor?

The just-preceding remarks are appropriate to understanding the semiotic process through which Resolution 2 is generated. It remains to apply this semiotic analysis to Resolution 3, which I have labeled self-deception. Our target is the subset of subjects who appear to believe genuinely that they are not the agents of certain acts, the subjects who, in their self-reports, disclaim agency for such acts as arm levitation. Self-reports are usually assumed to reflect the silent epistemic actions used to make sense out of potential nonsense. When we hear a problematic, contrary-to-fact, or ambiguous utterance, we employ a disjunctive query: Is the utterance to be taken as an assertion (*literally*) *or* as a metaphor (*figuratively*). The *or* is required if we are to follow the implications of the axiom of noncontradiction (that something cannot be and not be at the same time). This axiom is indispensable in everyday affairs involving such dimensions as time, space, and ponderability.

The subject who adopts Resolution 3, in the interest of sustaining the story in which the narrative figure (''me'') is the star in a show, puts aside (temporarily) the axiom of noncontradiction. He or she exercises *choice* in epistemological assumptions. Like the child who is involved in the tale of Cinderella or Sleeping Beauty, mundane epistemology is bypassed. The effect on the interpretation of contrary-to-fact utterances is to assume a *conjunctive* rather than a *disjunctive* posture. Instead of forcing a choice between the interpretation, ''the hypnotist's statements are literal'' and the interpretation ''the hypnotist's statements are figurative,'' the subject says the problematic statements are *both* literal and figurative. The credo solution and the aptness solution are employed simultaneously. The subject does more than ''figure'' the problematic utterance; he or she ''transfigures'' it, thereby making a metaphoric translation and then—putting aside the axiom of noncontradiction—adopting the credo solution. Instead of looking upon the hypnotist's sentences as either literal or figurative, the subject attempts to accomplish the difficult epistemic feat of construing the sentences as both apt figures of speech and truths. **''Believed-in imaginings''** is an alternate descriptive phrase.

The claim of nonvolition by some subjects follows from the meanings that the subject assigns to the hypnotist's contrary-to-fact, problematic statements. The subject is in a problem-solving situation and the solution chosen and its sequelae are not divorced from the person's self-narrative. The relatively small proportion of subjects who convincingly disclaim agency for their acts fits the criteria of self-deception. In order to justify the self-deception (not spelling-out certain features of personal experience) the subject sets aside everyday rules of logic and transfigures the metaphor implicit in the hypnotist's monologue. The epistemic actions are not different in principle from those of the worshipper praying before an icon. He *knows* that it is a painted ceramic statuette (an icon, a copy, a likeness, a figure, a metaphor) yet he *believes* that it has noumenous powers. He has fused the credo and the figural interpretations, *transfiguring* the object.

Disclaiming agency for one's acts, then, is not inconsistent with the epistemological requirements of a special, extraordinary metaphysical orientation. What the critical observer perceives as self-deception is regarded as ''truth'' by the subject.

CONCLUSIONS

I have avoided the mechanistic path taken by traditional analysts of hypnosis. Instead, I have adopted a contextualist perspective. I began with the recognition that in hypnosis a special discourse is taking place and that the participants are enacting social roles. Then I applied a semiotic analysis to the observation that some subjects disclaim being the agents of their acts.

The hypnosis monologue is a grand metaphor, the literal and figurative terms of which are tacit and open to interpretation by the subject. Three kinds of interpretations are indentified, one of which makes possible the disclaiming of agency. The subjects who disclaim agency fit the criteria for self-deception. How a person accomplishes the complex task of deceiving oneself is analyzed with the aid of two conceptions: (1) the motivational features of the self-narrative and (2) the adoption of a metaphysical stance such that the disclaiming of agency does not appear irrational to oneself.

REFERENCES

BOWERS, K. W. (1981). Do the Stanford Scales tap the "classic suggestion effect?" *International Journal of Clinical and Experimental Hypnosis, 29*, 42-53.

BOWERS, P. (1982). The classic suggestion effect: Relationship with scales of hypnotizability, effortless experiencing, and imagery vividness. *International Journal of Clinical and Experimental Hypnosis, 30*, 270-279.

FARTHING, G. W., BROWN, S. W., & VENTURINO, M. (1983). Involuntariness of response on the Harvard Group Scale of Hypnotic Susceptibility. *International Journal of Clinical and Experimental Hypnosis, 31*, 170-181.

FINGARETTE, H. (1969). *Self-deception*. London: Routledge and Kegan Paul.

FRIEDLANDER, J.W., & SARBIN, T.R. (1938). The depth of hypnosis. *Journal of Abnormal and Social Psychology, 33*, 457-475.

GLASER, B., & STRAUSS, A. L. (1965). *Awareness of dying*. Chicago: Aldine.

HEIDER, F., & SIMMEL, E. (1944). A study of apparent behavior. *American Journal of Psychology, 57*, 243-249.

LYNN, S. J., NASH, M. R., RHUE, J. W., FRAUMAN, D., & STANLEY, S. (1983). Hypnosis and the experience of non-volition. *International Journal of Clinical and Experimental Hypnosis, 31*, 293-308.

MICHOTTE, A. E. (1963). *La perception de la causalité* [The perception of causality]. (T. R. Miles & E. Miles, Trans.). London: Methuen. (Original work published 1946.)

PERRINE, L. (1971). Four forms of metaphor. *College English, 33*, 125-138.

SARBIN, T. R. (1980). Hypnosis: Metaphorical encounters of the fourth kind. *Semiotica, 30*, 195-209.

––––––. (1981). On self-deception. *Sciences, 364*, 220-235.

––––––. (1982). A preface to a psychological theory of metaphor. In V. L. Allen & K. E. Scheibe (Eds.), *The social context of conduct: Psychological writings of Theodore Sarbin* (pp. 233-249). New York: Praeger.

––––––. (1984). Nonvolition in hypnosis: A semiotic analysis. *Psychological Record, 34*, 537-549.

SARBIN, T. R., & COE, W. C. (1972). *Hypnotism: The social psychology of influence communication*. New York: Holt Rinehart and Winston.

SPANOS, N. P., & CHAVES, J. F. (1970). Hypnosis research: A methodological critique of experiments generated by two alternative paradigms. *American Journal of Clinical Hypnosis, 13*, 108-127.

WAGSTAFF, G. F. (1981). *Hypnosis, compliance, and belief*. New York: St. Martin's Press.

WEDEMEYER, C., & COE, W. C. (1981). Hypnotic state reports: Contextual variation and phenomenological criteria. *Journal of Mental Imagery, 5*, 107-118.

WEITZENHOFFER, A. M. (1978). Hypnotism and altered states of consciousness. In A. Sugarman & R. E. Tarter (Eds.), *Expanding dimensions of consciousness* (pp. 183-225). New York: Springer.

Self-Knowledge
and Self-Deception

ANTHONY G. GREENWALD
University of Washington

The term *self-deception* describes the puzzling situation in which a person appears both to know and not to know one and the same thing. Consider as an example a cancer patient who maintains the expectation of recovery even while surrounded by the signs of an incurable malignancy. Presumably this patient knows unconsciously that the disease is incurable, but manages to defend against that knowledge becoming conscious. Interestingly, one of the reasons for concluding that the patient *un*consciously knows of the incurable malignancy is the very success of the defense. How could that defense be maintained so skillfully *without* using knowledge of the unwelcome fact to anticipate the forms in which it might try to intrude itself on consciousness?

Another example is one that received much publicity. Jim Fixx, a well-known advocate of recreational running, died suddenly of a heart attack while running. Fixx was apparently unaware of his heart trouble, even though he had reason to be

This chapter is expanded from a presentation at the American Psychological Association meeting in Toronto (August, 1984), in the symposium, "Self-deception: Theoretical and empirical advances," chaired by Delroy L. Paulhus. Preparation was aided by a grant from The National Science Foundation, BNS 82-17006.

aware of both a familial predisposition to heart trouble (his father had died of heart disease at age 43) and the possibility of an imminent crisis (he had noted excessive fatigue and tightness in his throat when running). However, he had also avoided several opportunities to undergo a stress test, which could have revealed his condition. Perhaps this was a case of self-deception. Perhaps, that is, Fixx knew unconsciously of his life-threatening condition, and used that unconscious knowledge to prevent the threat from becoming conscious. (For a detailed report, see Higdon, 1984.)

THE PARADOX OF SELF-DECEPTION

The sense in which these examples are puzzling, or paradoxical, is shown in Figure 7–1. Some encountered situation, or stimulus, is assumed to receive both unconscious and conscious analyses. The unconscious analysis, which is assumed to be prior, identifies a threatening, or anxiety-evoking, aspect of the stimulus, which is represented in Figure 7–1 as some proposition, p, such as, "My heart is about to fail" or "I have a terminal malignancy." Conscious analysis, however, fails to produce the same conclusion.

There are three puzzling aspects of this situation. First, how can the person manage unconsciously to reach the conclusion that proposition p is true, while not also reaching that conclusion consciously? Second, what good does it do for the person not to know consciously that p is true: shouldn't it produce anxiety just to know unconsciously that p is true? And, third, why is it that the unconscious system gives both a faster and a more thorough analysis: wouldn't it be sensible to have one's most acute cognitive abilities available to consciousness?

FIGURE 7–1   The paradox (or puzzle) of self-deception

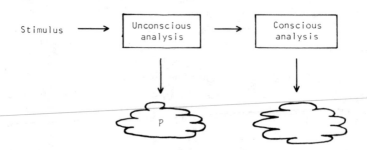

QUESTIONS

1. How does the person both know p and not know it?
2. What good does it do not to know p consciously?
3. Why is the faster, more accurate system unconscious?

Interest in Self-Deception

Self-deception has attracted the interest of scholars of several different disciplines, and for several different reasons. For clinical psychologists and psychiatrists self-deception is seen as a means of protection from painful knowledge (Murphy, 1975; Schafer, 1976; Sackeim & Gur, 1978). But, at the same time, it seems a strangely cumbersome method of defense. That is, it appears to create more problems for the psyche than it can possibly solve. How, therefore, can it protect? From this clinical perspective, understanding self-deception has implications for the conduct of psychotherapy.

For cognitive psychologists and philosophers (e.g., Fingarette, 1969), self-deception is seen as a paradoxical condition of knowledge. How does a knowledge system accommodate an apparent internal contradiction? From this epistemological perspective, achieving an understanding of self-deception should shed light on the organization of human knowledge.

For ethologists, self-deception is seen as a strategy that could provide an advantage in animal social interaction (e.g., Lockard, 1980; Trivers, 1985). By unconsciously deceiving itself, an animal might become a more effective deceiver of others. From this perspective, the investigation of self-deception might justify placing the psychological concept of the unconscious under the explanatory umbrella of sociobiology.

The intellectual perspectives of clinical psychology, psychiatry, cognitive psychology, epistemology, and sociobiology collectively yield a set of questions that must be answered by a complete analysis of self-deception. Most fundamentally, how is self-deception to be conceived in terms of knowledge organization: if it requires unconscious processing, how does that unconscious processing relate to conscious processing? Second, what is the function of self-deception: what psychic gain results from the combination of knowing something unconsciously, while not knowing it consciously? Third, how common is self-deception: is it an ordinary phenomenon of everyday life, or is it perhaps an exotic, even pathological phenomenon? And fourth, what empirical criteria can be used to identify self-deception: how can it be studied in the laboratory?

The theoretical analysis used in this chapter provides answers to these four questions and, in doing so, introduces an alternative to existing accounts of defenses against cognitive threat. This analysis—which also suggests the use of **knowledge avoidance** as a more accurate label for many phenomena that have previously been identified as "self-deception"—borrows from cognitive psychology the concept of an ordered series of **stages**, or **levels**, of cognitive processes. The levels idea, as will be shown, provides an effective alternative to assuming autonomous unconscious processes that regulate access to awareness.

Previous Analyses

The most thorough previous analysis of self-deception is by philosopher Herbert Fingarette in his 1969 book titled *Self-Deception*. Fingarette sought to develop a paradox-free account of self-deception. Ultimately, his attempt to avoid paradox must be judged as unsuccessful. Nevertheless, his review and analysis advanced the topic considerably, and provided a stimulating entry point for researchers. Notable among subsequent researchers are Gur and Sackeim (1979; see also Sackeim & Gur, 1978) who provided a careful statement of the self-deception paradox and suggested a laboratory procedure for its investigation.

Fingarette's (1969) analysis   Fingarette started his review by criticizing the previous attempts of philosophers to analyze self-deception. His critique concluded that previous attempts to resolve the paradox of self-deception either (1) had not addressed themselves to the proper phenomena of self-deception, or (2) rather than resolving the paradox, had merely portrayed it in a "variant form." Fingarette's own analysis went part of the way toward a solution. However, he too managed to reintroduce the paradox before completing his account. This reintroduction occurred in the form of an unnamed mechanism that analyzes the true (threatening) import of circumstances and, on the basis of the knowledge so obtained, purposefully prevents the emergence into consciousness of both the threatening information and the defense against it. Fingarette's unnamed mechanism is capable of inference and intention in a way that requires sophisticated symbolic representation, yet Fingarette assumed that this mechanism operates *outside* of the ordinary machinery of inference and symbolic representation—that is, outside of consciousness. The paradox that remains in Fingarette's analysis is reminiscent of the frequently observed paradoxical aspects of Freud's censor (the agency of repression), which operates from a base within the conscious ego, and, although it appears to have ego's reasoning powers, nevertheless is assumed to operate without ego's consciousness (Freud, 1923/1961).

Gur and Sackeim's (1979) analysis   In seeking to demonstrate the paradoxical character of self-deception, Gur and Sackeim used a voice recognition task that had been developed about a half-century earlier by Wolff (1932; see also Huntley, 1940). In this task, after making recordings of samples of their own voice, subjects were asked to judge whether each of a series of played-back samples was or was not their own voice. The critical evidence comes from a comparison of skin conductance responses (SCRs) with overt verbal identifications of the voice stimuli. The SCR is assumed to indicate unconscious own-voice recognition, whereas verbal identification indicates conscious recognition. Self-deception is judged to occur when SCR disagrees with verbal identification, for example, when an SCR occurs on an own-voice trial, yet the subject fails to say that the voice is his or her own.

Why are such trials paradoxical? It is not simply that the SCR and verbal response appear to disagree. That disagreement could be explained nonparadoxically (and not very interestingly) by assuming, for example, that the skin conductance system is more prone to error (perhaps by influence from stray events), or that it is susceptible to sources of error that differ from those that disrupt verbal identification. The response disagreement becomes interestingly paradoxical, however, when one concludes that the SCR reflects an unconscious own-voice identification that plays a role in the purposeful blocking of conscious identification. It is therefore relevant that Gur and Sackeim demonstrated a correlation between individual differences in voice identification accuracy and scores on a Self-Deception Questionnaire measure, suggesting a motivated blocking of conscious voice recognition that is initiated by a knowing observer operating outside of consciousness.

Resolving the Paradox by Changing Assumptions

Paradoxes stimulate theoretical advance by making it apparent that there is a troublemaker lurking somewhere among one's theoretical assumptions. One candidate troublemaker, in the case of the self-deception paradox, is the assumption of **personal unity** that implicitly underlies much psychological theory (cf. Greenwald, 1982). This is the assumption that each person's knowledge is organized into a single, unified system. As an alternative, it can be assumed that there are dissociations within personal knowledge systems (Hilgard, 1977). For example, in the case of the voice-recognition task, one might assume that the right hemisphere (or some other modular brain subsystem—see Gazzaniga, 1985) controls the SCR independently of the left hemisphere's control of verbal identification responses. By thus abandoning the assumption of unity within the knowledge system, discrepancies between SCR and verbal identification of own-voice stimuli are not paradoxical— no more than it would be paradoxical for two people to disagree in identifying a voice.

However, abandoning the assumption of personal unity is quite a drastic step. Although one gains a ready ability to explain findings of discrepancy between response systems, one simultaneously sacrifices the ability to explain *relationships* between response systems—relationships of the sort that are heavily appealed to in psychological theory, for example, in the influential mediationist behaviorisms of Spence (1956), Mowrer (1960), or Osgood (1953), and in cognitive interpretations of emotion such as those of Schachter and Singer (1962) or Lazarus (1984). Fortunately, there is another possible troublemaking assumption that is more easily sacrificed. This is one that can be called the assumption of a **coordinate unconscious**: the assumption that unconscious and conscious systems are coordinate, or equivalent in power, and therefore capable of the same mental operations. When the assumption of a coordinate unconscious is abandoned, it becomes possible to set unconscious processes into a multilevel conception of mental representations—a conception that is readily able to explain self-deception phenomena without paradox. The alternative to the coordinate unconscious is an unconscious system that is decidedly weaker in analytic power than conscious systems: a **subordinate unconscious**. The subordinate unconscious assumption will be described below after introducing a multilevel conception of human representational abilities. It will develop that the role of unconscious processes in cognitive defense becomes much less central in the cognitive, multilevel analysis than it has been in previous psychoanalytically inspired analyses.

THE NONPARADOX OF KNOWLEDGE AVOIDANCE

Levels of Representation

The familiar cognitive psychological concept of an ordered set of information processing stages provides the basis for a multilevel analysis of mental representations. Figure 7–2 shows a minimal levels-of-representation analysis, containing just two stages or levels. The first stage produces a relatively crude representation of an experienced event, which serves both to control some response directly and to provide input for a second, higher, level of analysis. The second level, in turn, produces its own representation, which may control a different response to the event.

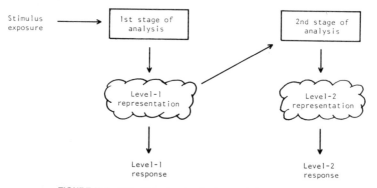

FIGURE 7–2   **Two-stage levels of representation scheme**

The simple device of assuming that cognitive analyses occur in series or stages, illustrated minimally in Figure 7–2, provides the basis for replacing the paradoxical concept of self-deception with the nonparadoxical concept of knowledge avoidance. The manner in which a levels-of-representation analysis avoids paradox can be seen clearly with the aid of a two-stage behavioral analog for the mundane problem of dealing with junk mail.

The Junk-Mail Model of Knowledge Avoidance

Many people find it annoying to deal with unsolicited broadcast mailings of material such as advertisements and charity appeals (''junk'' mail). Fortunately, there are usable cues that warn addressees of the likely worthlessness of an envelope's contents. In particular, the postage may be lower than the rate for personal letters, the address may be machine printed and impersonally targeted (to ''occupant''), and the envelope may be made of low-quality paper. The organizational identification on a return address sometimes provides more specific cues to worthless content. Certainly many people have the habit of discarding, without opening, envelopes that provide such warnings. This is a useful avoidance response: one

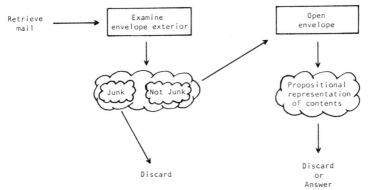

FIGURE 7-3   Junk-mail version of the two-stage model

avoids wasting the time required to open and read the contents of the junk-mail and can put the saved time to a more valuable use.

The two stages of the junk-mail model (see Figure 7–3) are, first, examining the exterior of the envelope and, second, reading the contents. It is clear that the second stage's processing can be avoided on the basis of cues that are available to the first stage. In other words, one needn't know specifically what is inside the envelope in order to discard it.

To relate the junk-mail model to phenomena of self-deception, let us return to the example of the terminally ill cancer patient. Perhaps the patient is able to pick up cues indicating that *some* unwelcome knowledge may be available (like seeing the outside of the envelope) and then avoids learning precisely what the unwelcome knowledge is (like discarding the letter). There is no more paradox in the cancer patient's avoiding certain knowledge of terminal illness than there is in the junk-mail recipient's avoiding certain knowledge of the contents of an unopened envelope. This analysis, which proposes that an avoidance response can be based on partial analysis of a stimulus, is a close relative of ones offered previously by Allport (1955), Eriksen and Browne (1956), and Kempler and Wiener (1963) in reviews of research on perceptual defense.

Nonparadoxical Account of the Voice-Recognition Experiment

Figure 7–4 analyzes Gur and Sackeim's (1979) voice-recognition procedure in terms of levels of representation. In the two-level model of Figure 7–4, the SCR is controlled by the first level, which analyzes the acoustic features of a voice sample. The SCR may be elicited by voice-spectrum features that are similar to those of one's own voice. Importantly, this sensory-feature-based SCR is *not* equivalent to voice identification any more than examining the outside of an envelope is equivalent to reading its contents. Voice identification occurs only at the second stage of analysis, presumably based on paralinguistic cues such as accent, speech rate, and inflection. As was the case for the two levels of the junk-mail model, the two levels of the voice analysis model involve different types of analysis. The

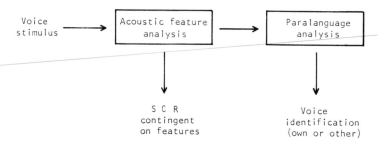

FIGURE 7–4   Two-stage model of the voice-recognition experiment

second stage requires greater analysis than the first, and it produces a more abstract representation. Because the first-stage SCR and the second-stage identification are responsive to different stimulus information, there is *no* paradox when a first-stage SCR is unaccompanied by own-voice identification at the second stage.

Levels of Representation Elaborated

Figure 7–5 expands the two-level model of Figure 7–2 into a four-level structure that is rich enough to account for a broad variety of human cognitive capabilities (based on Greenwald & Leavitt, 1984; elaborated further in Greenwald, 1987). At the lowest level is sensory feature analysis, a process that is assumed to operate automatically and without leaving memory traces—that is, unconsciously. In the model in Figure 7–5, unconscious processes are confined to this first (lowest) level, which is capable only of detecting sensory features, not of more abstract representational processes. (This assumption makes the model one of a subordinate, rather than coordinate, unconscious.) The second level identifies objects and accesses word meanings. The third level encodes verbal information into propositional representations (i.e., sentence meanings). The fourth and highest level uses stored conceptual knowledge to generate inferences from the third level's propositional representations.[1]

"Self-Deception" as Avoidance of Inference

The levels-of-representation framework can be used to analyze the previously introduced examples of unawareness of terminal illness. In those examples, critical processing occurred at the third level—the level at which events are analyzed in terms of propositions such as "The doctor said they got all the tumor" or "I have a tight feeling in my throat." After that processing occurs, it is still necessary to use the fourth level—the level of reasoning from conceptual knowledge—to draw inferences such as "The doctor didn't tell me to expect complete recovery: that means my chances aren't so good" or "The tightness in my throat is angina pain:

---

[1]In a further development of this analysis (Greenwald, 1987), the second level is split into two functions—object identification and categorization—which are treated as separate levels.

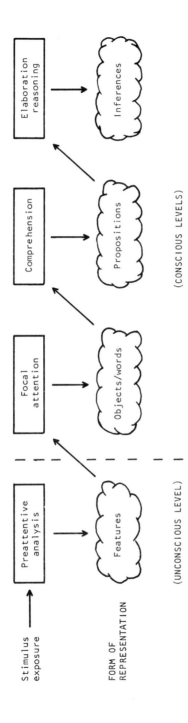

FIGURE 7–5 Four-level model of human cognitive abilities

my coronary arteries must be obstructed.'' By not going beyond the third level, by not drawing inferences, one *avoids* an unwelcome conclusion. That is, cognition does not proceed to the level of identifying the threat specifically; the unwelcome news remains unknown. This analysis, in which a painful conclusion is avoided, differs from the analysis of Figure 7–1, in which the painful conclusion is simultaneously known (unconsciously) and not known (consciously).

In the two examples being considered, it may seem unlikely that either the hypothetical cancer patient or Jim Fixx could have totally avoided interpreting the available indications of malignancy or heart trouble. Let us assume, alternatively, that some interpretation did occur: that each suspected the *possibility* of unwelcome news. If, however, their suspicions were not followed up—that is, by not asking the doctor directly or by not taking a stress test—then knowledge of death's imminence was still successfully avoided. In the case of Jim Fixx, it appears that he indeed did have knowledge of possibility, which he avoided converting into certainty. Apparently, that is, Fixx was aware of symptoms that he knew were possibly (but not certainly) predictive of heart failure. Nevertheless, he clearly avoided a series of opportunities to obtain the sure confirmation that a stress test would have provided (Higdon, 1984).

In addition to providing an account of the apparent self-deceptions associated with terminal illness, this analysis applies to daily acts of avoidance that almost everyone routinely engages in. For example, every time we hear news of nuclear weapons development or of no progress in arms reduction talks, we could conclude that our lives are in imminent danger. However, most of us routinely avoid drawing that conclusion. This is a case of a possible terminal illness of worldwide proportions that most of us habitually avoid contemplating. The analysis is quite similar to that of the terminally ill cancer patient. That is, we all have reason to believe that an unwelcome outcome is possible, but most of us avoid treating that possibility as a realistic one. Our not treating nuclear war in this way may be a consequence of our developing the habit of interrupting trains of thought that lead to an unpleasant conclusion (see the discussion below of automating knowledge avoidance). Of course, not all people avoid drawing frightening conclusions about their personal vulnerability to nuclear weapons. But, then, neither do all terminally ill patients avoid drawing the conclusion that they are dying.

OTHER TYPES OF KNOWLEDGE AVOIDANCE

In terms of the four-level model of Figure 7–5, the examples of avoiding knowledge of terminal illness and avoiding anxiety about nuclear warfare are conceived as avoidance responses located between the third and fourth levels. Experienced events are analyzed to the level of propositions (such as ''Arms reduction talks are making little progress''), but anxiety-producing inferences are avoided. Failure to draw such inferences may be the phenomenon that is most frequently identified, in previous analyses, as involving (paradoxical) self-deception. Those previous analyses have assumed, unlike the present one, that the inference must be made at an unconscious level at the same time that it is avoided consciously. The model in Figure 7–5, however, provides no mechanism for achieving any unconscious inferences and does not require that such inferences be made in order for successful avoidance to occur.

The four-level model of Figure 7–5 allows for the occurrence of knowledge avoidance not only at the junction between its third and fourth levels, but also in the transitions between the first and second, and second and third levels. The following consideration of these possibilities suggests that *knowledge avoidance is a pervasively ordinary phenomenon.*

Avoidance of Comprehension

Avoidance of third-level processing would occur if the words in a message were perceived individually (second-level processing), but the perceiver avoided comprehending their sentence-level meaning. Such avoidance of comprehension may occur commonly in dealing with the content of mass media. Television and radio programs are frequently interrupted by short commercial announcements in which one is uninterested; newspapers and magazines contain advertisements and uninteresting articles interspersed between interesting news or articles. In these situations, the perceiver may be consciously aware of the individual words of a message but not bother to comprehend their sentence-level meaning. Hearing or seeing a brand name may act as a cue to avoid comprehension of the message in which it occurs. Similarly, the title of a magazine article or the headline of a newspaper story may contain a name or topic word that is sufficient to forestall further analysis. (These cognitive avoidance responses can be recognized as analogs of the behavioral avoidance response of discarding junk mail.) Avoidance of comprehension may be what has happened when one at first reacts to someone else's remark by asking for it to be repeated but then is nevertheless able to retrieve the individual words and comprehend the remark.

Avoidance of Attention

Treisman and Gelade (1980) suggested that the process of attention be understood as the integration of sensory features into perceived objects. On this basis, the avoidance process that occurs when first-level analysis of sensory features is not followed by further perceptual analysis may be identified as avoidance of attention. The well known cocktail party effect—being able to focus on a single one of several simultaneously heard voices—is an example of avoiding attention. The listener successfully avoids perceiving the component words of extraneous conversations on the basis of analyzing sensory features such as voice pitch and spatial location (Broadbent, 1958; Moray, 1970). A second example is provided by an experience familiar to most skilled automobile drivers, called "driving on automatic pilot." This occurs when, shortly after driving some portion of a familiar route, one is unable to recall stimuli that must have been processed, such as whether the last traffic light was red or green. In this case, it is not so much that object perception is undesired as that it is not necessary: driving is so well learned that it can be performed automatically, with habitual responses occurring to important stimulus features, even when those features are not integrated into object perceptions. It is tempting to interpret the process of avoidance of attention as an *unconscious* avoidance of knowledge. Whether or not one finds that label agreeable will depend on what criteria one accepts as indicative of unconscious processing. (This question is considered further, below, in discussing empirical criteria for knowledge avoidance.)

Avoidance of Exposure

Perhaps the most common type of knowledge avoidance is one that cannot be located between stages of the levels-of-representation model because it involves complete nonexposure to stimuli that might lead to useless or otherwise unwelcome cognitive analyses. As an example, consider the consequence of a heavy smoker's not engaging in physical exercise. The smoker can thus avoid encounters with stimuli (excessive fatigue, difficulty breathing, etc.) that could indicate adverse physical effects of smoking. In a similar fashion, by soliciting no student evaluations, a professor can avoid negative feedback that could threaten self-esteem. And, to take an almost trivial example, many recreational tennis players effectively avoid discovering that they routinely commit the error of foot-faulting (stepping into the playing area before hitting a serve) because—consistent with good tennis form—they simply don't look at their feet while serving. Because there is no exposure to events that could lead to unwelcome knowledge, this strategy can be very effective; the avoider has no basis for suspecting that anything is being avoided. In terms of the four-level model, such behavioral avoidance of exposure to unwelcome stimuli preempts the first level of analysis; it is located off the left side of the model.

Automating Knowledge Avoidance

The following (fabricated) example is intended to illustrate that habitual forms of knowledge avoidance can develop through dealing repeatedly with a given type of anxiety-evoking situation.

Imagine a young and hard-working career woman (CW). She enjoys friendships with women and is attractive to men. Also, she enjoys children very much and has always wanted to have a family. At the same time, the demands of CW's work make it difficult for her to find time for satisfying personal relationships with either men or women. And, because advancement in her career is highly competitive, no let-up of these demands is in sight. In attempting to deal with these conflicting forces, she has already turned down an offer of marriage, choosing instead to pursue her career. But the decision was not easy, and she questions it frequently. The conflict between career and traditional female roles resurfaces daily, and her momentary inclinations shift now in one direction, now in another. CW has considered the possibility of a compromise solution of having both a career and a marriage, but concluded that this mixture would do justice to neither. It might be ideal for CW simply to forget that she enjoys children, forget that she misses a stable sexual relationship, and forget that she envies the family lives of the wives of some of her male colleagues. Unfortunately, she is continually reminded of these renounced alternatives each time she sees children, visits her own family, or attends social functions at which wives of her male colleagues are present.

One option for CW is avoidance of exposure to stimuli that might trigger anxiety-producing thoughts of marriage and family. She can, for example, decline all social invitations, work late hours, become reclusive, socialize only at places frequented by unmarried adults, and establish friendships exclusively with people who are single or have failed marriages.

It is plausible that such a behavioral (avoidance-of-exposure) strategy could be successful. The possibility of equivalently successful strategies that are purely cognitive is, perhaps, less intuitively compelling. Nevertheless, such a cognitive strategy has been well analyzed by Dollard and Miller (1950) in their analysis of "stopping thinking." **Thought-stopping** is a cognitive strategy that can be understood by analogy to a behavioral avoidance response. For example, a fear of heights can be controlled behaviorally by not visiting high places. Similarly, the anxiety produced by thinking about high places should be controllable cognitively by not thinking such thoughts.

In CW's case, a cognitive avoidance strategy could enable her to avoid confronting the thoughts of desirability of marriage and family that conflict with her career-pursuit decision. This avoidance strategy may initially be aided by use of behavioral strategies such as working late, and so forth. But CW may become skillful at interrupting trains of thought that lead to marriage and family, and may eventually be capable of such virtuoso performances as encountering colleagues' children and wives socially without noticing fondness for the former or envy of the latter. She may, after practice, come to assert that children should be seen and not heard, and she may urge colleagues' wives to develop their own career aspirations.

For CW, the cognitive avoidance solution—that is, the habitual (and increasingly anticipatory) stopping of trains of thoughts that lead to contemplation of attractive, renounced alternatives—should be a far more effective solution than is the action-restricting strategy of avoiding situations that contain reminder cues. Thought-stopping is an attractive solution in part because it can be used in the situations that contain those reminder cues.

There is no need to interpret CW's successful cognitive avoidance as self-deceptive (in the paradoxical sense). Although CW's thought-stopping had its origin in an initial phase of conscious contemplation of the pleasures that were absent from her life, it evolved to a phase in which she had no need to be aware, consciously or unconsciously, of avoided thoughts (any more than the junk-mail recipient needs to know the content of discarded mail). The evolution of CW's thought-stopping habit can be understood as a progression from a knowledge-avoidance response that was initially located between the third and fourth stages of the model in Figure 7–5 to one located progressively further to the left in the model—occurring in response to lower levels of analysis, and therefore becoming increasingly less accessible to self-report.[2]

EMPIRICAL CRITERIA FOR KNOWLEDGE AVOIDANCE

Of the several procedures that have been used in attempted laboratory demonstrations of self-deception and other psychoanalytically conceived defense mechanisms, none has escaped criticism that the resulting evidence is inconclusive. For every sympathetic review of findings on topics such as perceptual defense (Erdelyi, 1974; Dixon, 1981) or repression (Erdelyi & Goldberg, 1979; Shevrin & Dickman, 1980), one can point to opposing reviews (e.g., Eriksen, 1958; Holmes, 1974; Loftus & Loftus, 1980). Sackeim and Gur's (1978) presentation of criteria for an empirical demonstration of (paradoxical) self-deception makes clear that such a demonstration is difficult to achieve. Their criteria are the following:

1. The individual holds two contradictory beliefs (*p* and not-*p*).
2. These beliefs are held simultaneously.
3. The individual is not aware of holding one of the beliefs (*p* or not-*p*).
4. The act that determines which belief is and which belief is not subject to awareness is a motivated act (p. 150).

In drawing conclusions from his review of the research literature, Erdelyi (1985) observed that a consistent shortcoming of laboratory models of cognitive defenses is their failure to demonstrate that "the perceiver can intentionally and selectively reject perceptual inputs [of emotional stimuli]" (p. 256).

The levels-of-representation analysis of knowledge avoidance provides a sharply different perspective on laboratory attempts to demonstrate cognitive defenses. Because cognitive avoidance does not require specific knowledge of what is being avoided, the first two of Sackeim and Gur's criteria become irrelevant. Similarly unnecessary is Erdelyi's assumption that a demonstration of motivated ("tendentious") cognitive avoidance requires demonstrating the availability of the avoided content somewhere in the psyche—"perceiv[ing] at one level without perceiving at another level" (p. 254), as he puts it.[3]

---

[2]In addition to its relation to Dollard and Miller's (1950) behaviorist account of cognitive defense mechanisms, the example of CW also fits well with Festinger's (1964) dissonance theory analysis of the cognitive aftermath of difficult decisions. In Festinger's analysis, cognitive dissonance is reduced by cognitive diminution of the attractiveness of rejected alternatives. Stopping thinking about the attractive features of rejected alternatives can be an effective means of thus reducing dissonance, particularly when cues that are likely to initiate thoughts about the rejected alternatives will be encountered repeatedly.

[3]A modification of the junk-mail model in Figure 7–3 makes clear why it is perhaps impossibly difficult to meet the empirical criteria proposed by Sackeim and Gur (1978) or Erdelyi (1985). These authors assume that the agency responsible for cognitive defense is cognizant of what is being avoided, and is also dissociated from conscious mechanisms that control verbal report. It is as if one's mail were screened by a secretary who reads everything in full and discards the uninteresting items. Naturally, it will be frustrating to try to discover evidence that the discarded mail's content has been examined by directing inquiries to the addressee! (But such evidence is, in effect, being demanded of laboratory demonstrations of cognitive defenses.)

The question naturally follows: In the context of the levels-of-representation analysis, what are the required criteria for demonstrating purposive cognitive defense? These may be described in a way that makes clear their difference from those stated by Sackeim and Gur:

1. The person fails to perceive an object, comprehend a proposition, or infer a conclusion.

2. The stimulus that could be cognized as object, proposition, or inference is analyzed at a lower level than the one avoided.

3. The lower-level analysis detects content that is predictive of the unwelcomeness of further processing.

The particularly interesting case of unconsciously based knowledge avoidance requires additionally showing that

4. The analysis that detects content sufficient to control an avoidance response is one of which the subject is not conscious.

These four criteria have been stated in conceptual terms, which importantly leaves to be specified the empirical operations that should be accepted as fulfilling them. Some suggestion of these operations will be offered here and illustrated by considering how they are met in the well-known procedures of selective listening experiments.

1. Failure of perception, comprehension, or inference will typically be indicated by the absence of indicators of these cognitions from a verbal report. (In the selective listening experiment, responses to questions about the ignored message typically indicate failure to remember either its meaning or the specific words contained in it.)

2. Verbal reports can also be used to verify the occurrence of analysis at a lower level than the one avoided. (In selective listening, the subject is able to report sensory features of the ignored message, such as its position in space, whether it was in a male or female voice, or whether it was loud or soft.)

3. The detected content should be demonstrably predictive of unwelcome results of a higher-level analysis. (This is achieved by the stimuli and instructions used for the selective listening task; the message that is to be ignored is defined in terms of a discriminative sensory feature such as spatial position.)

4. Two types of procedures can be suggested as bases for concluding that a stimulus has been analyzed unconsciously. One is that, although some aspect of a stimulus is shown to affect the subject's performance, that aspect cannot be recalled or recognized on a later test. A more stringent procedure is that the response-affecting stimulus cannot be detected at the time it is presented.[4] (In selective listening experiments, the features that guide avoidance of verbal analysis are certainly detected, and are presumably recallable, although they may be recallable more because of the subject's memory of instructions than because of memory of their occurrence during performance of the task.)

[4]Empirical problems associated with these procedures have been discussed by Cheesman and Merikle (1985), and Holender (1986)—but see Greenwald, Klinger, & Liu (1987) for an apparently successful demonstration of processing of undetected stimuli.

In experiments that meet the first three suggested criteria for demonstrating cognitive defense, the processing that is defended against is typically of a sort that would interfere with the subject's performance of an assigned task, such as selective listening or selective vision (e.g., Rock & Gutman, 1981). Whether there are any replicable demonstrations that meet the first three criteria in situations for which the avoided cognition is an anxiety-evoking one is uncertain (see review by Erdelyi, 1985). Further laboratory attempts to demonstrate defenses against anxiety-evoking cognitions might be more likely to achieve success if they (1) use the presently suggested criteria (rather than the more stringent ones of Sackeim & Gur, 1978), and (2) seek to demonstrate defenses against stimuli that the subject has had practice defending against.

CONCLUSIONS

The levels-of-representation analysis in this chapter allows an account of purposeful cognitive avoidance without having to make the paradoxical assumption that one must know unconsciously what it is that is being avoided consciously. The levels-of-representation model rejects the idea of a coordinate unconscious—that is, of an unconscious that is capable of the same powerful mental operations that can be performed consciously. The alternative assumption of a subordinate unconscious— the unconscious as a primitive front-end processor for a much more powerful set of conscious systems—is well rooted in contemporary cognitive psychological theory.

There are some exotic knowledge avoidance phenomena that have not been considered in this chapter and that are also not readily accounted for by the levels-of-representation analysis. For example, amnesias and multiple personalities almost certainly require interpretation in terms of dissociative processes. These phenomena may be nonparadoxically interpretable only by suspending the assumption of personal unity, and thereby allowing for coordinate, dissociated knowledge systems within the person. Nevertheless, the levels-of-representation analysis can be used successfully for most of the phenomena that have been classified (misleadingly, it is here suggested) as paradoxical self-deceptions.

REFERENCES

ALLPORT, F. H. (1955). *Theories of perception and the concept of structure.* New York: Wiley.

BROADBENT, D. E. (1958). *Perception and communication.* London: Pergamon Press.

CHEESMAN, J., & MERIKLE, P. M. (1985). Word recognition and consciousness. In D. Beaner, T. G. Waller, & G. E. MacKinnon (Eds.), *Reading research: Advances in theory and practice* (Vol. 5). New York: Academic Press.

DIXON, N. F. (1981). *Preconscious processing.* London: Wiley.

DOLLARD, J., & MILLER, N. E. (1950). *Personality and psychotherapy.* New York: McGraw-Hill.

ERDELYI, M. H. (1974). A new look at the new look: Perceptual defense and vigilance. *Psychological Review, 81,* 1-25.

———. (1985). *Psychoanalysis: Freud's cognitive psychology.* New York: Freeman.

ERDELYI, M. H., & GOLDBERG, B. (1979). Let's not sweep repression under the rug: Toward a cognitive psychology of repression. In J. F. Kihlstrom & F. J. Evans (Eds.), *Functional disorders of memory* (pp. 355-402). Hillsdale, NJ: Erlbaum.

ERIKSEN, C. W. (1958). Unconscious processes. In M. R. Jones (Ed.), *Nebraska symposium on motivation: 1958* (pp. 169-227). Lincoln, NB: University of Nebraska Press.

ERIKSEN, C. W., & BROWNE, C. T. (1956). An experimental and theoretical analysis of perceptual defense. *Journal of Abnormal and Social Psychology, 52,* 224-230.

FESTINGER, L. (1964). *Conflict, decision, and dissonance.* Stanford, CA: Stanford University Press.

FINGARETTE, H. (1969). *Self-deception.* London: Routledge & Kegan Paul.

FREUD, S. (1961). The ego and the id. In J. Strachey (Ed. & Trans.), *The standard edition of the complete psychological works of Sigmund Freud* (Vol. 19, pp. 3-66). London: Hogarth Press. (Original work published 1923.)

GAZZANIGA, M. S. (1985). *The social brain: Discovering the networks of the mind.* New York: Basic Books.

GREENWALD, A. G. (1982). Is anyone in charge? Personalysis versus the principle of personal unity. In J. Suls (Ed.), *Psychological perspectives on the self* (Vol. 1, pp. 151-181). Hillsdale, NJ: Erlbaum.

———. (1987). *Levels of representation.* Unpublished manuscript. University of Washington, Department of Psychology, Seattle.

GREENWALD, A. G., & LEAVITT, C. (1984). Audience involvement in advertising: Four levels. *Journal of Consumer Research, 11,* 581-592.

———. (1985). Cognitive theory and audience involvement. In L. Alwitt & A. A. Mitchell (Eds.), *Psychological processes and advertising effects: Theory, research, and application* (pp. 221-240). Hillsdale, NJ: Erlbaum.

GREENWALD, A. G., KLINGER, M. R., & LIU, T. J.   (1987). *Limited unconscious processing of meaning.* Unpublished manuscript. University of Washington, Seattle.

GUR, R. C., & SACKEIM, H. A.   (1979). Self-deception: A concept in search of a phenomenon. *Journal of Personality and Social Psychology, 37,* 147-169.

HIGDON, H.   (1984, November). Jim Fixx: How he lived, why he died. *The Runner,* pp. 33-38.

HILGARD, E. R.   (1977). *Divided consciousness: Multiple controls in human thought and action.* New York: Wiley.

HOLENDER, D.   (1986). Semantic activation without conscious identification in dichotic listening, parafoveal vision, and visual masking: A survey and appraisal. *Behavior and Brain Sciences, 9,* 1-66.

HOLMES, D. S.   (1974). Investigations of repression: Differential recall of material experimentally or naturally associated with ego threat. *Psychological Bulletin, 81,* 632-653.

HUNTLEY, C. W.   (1940). Judgments of self based upon records of expressive behavior. *Journal of Abnormal and Social Psychology, 35,* 398-427.

KEMPLER, B., & WIENER, M.   (1963). Personality and perception in the recognition threshold paradigm. *Psychological Review, 70,* 349-356.

LAZARUS, R. S.   (1984). On the primacy of cognition. *American Psychologist, 39,* 124-129.

LOCKARD, J. S.   (1980). Speculations on the adaptive significance of self-deception. In J. S. Lockard (Ed.), *The evolution of social behavior* (pp. 257-275). New York: Elsevier.

LOFTUS, E. F., & LOFTUS, G. R.   (1980). On the permanence of stored information in the human brain. *American Psychologist, 35,* 409-420.

MORAY, N.   (1970). *Attention: Selective processes in vision and hearing.* New York: Academic Press.

MOWRER, O. H.   (1960). *Learning theory and behavior.* New York: Wiley.

MURPHY, G.   (1975). *Outgrowing self-deception.* New York: Basic Books.

OSGOOD, C. E.   (1953). *Method and theory in experimental psychology.* New York: Oxford University Press.

ROCK, I., & GUTMAN, D.   (1981). The effect of inattention on form perception. *Journal of Experimental Psychology: Human Perception and Performance, 7,* 275-285.

SACKEIM, H. A., & GUR, R. C.   (1978). Self-deception, self-confrontation, and consciousness. In G. E. Schwartz & D. Shapiro (Eds.), *Consciousness and self-regulation, Advances in research* (Vol. 2, pp. 139-197). New York: Plenum.

SCHACHTER, S., & SINGER, J. E.   (1962). Cognitive, social, and physiological determinants of emotional state. *Psychological Review, 65,* 379-399.

SCHAFER, R.   (1976). *A new language for psychoanalysis.* New York: Yale University Press.

SHEVRIN, H., & DICKMAN, S.   (1980). The psychological unconscious: A necessary assumption for all psychological theory? *American Psychologist, 35,* 421-434.

SPENCE, K. W.   (1956). *Behavior theory and conditioning.* New Haven: Yale University Press.

TREISMAN, A. M., & GELADE, G.   (1980). A feature-integration theory of attention. *Cognitive Psychology, 12,* 97-136.

TRIVERS, R.   (1985). *Social evolution.* Menlo Park, CA: Benjamin/Cummings.

WOLFF, W.   (1932). Selbstbeurteilung and fremdbeurteilung im wissentlichen und unwissentlichen versuch. *Psychologische Forschung, 16,* 251-329.

8

A Dynamic Complexity Model of Self-Deception

Delroy L. Paulhus
Peter Suedfeld
University of British Columbia

Sackeim and Gur (1978) defined self-deception as the motivated unawareness of a belief that contradicts some other belief that the individual is aware of. The contradictory belief must be represented somehow in the individual's belief system and is therefore potentially accessible. While Sackeim and Gur have applied this conception to a variety of theoretical and empirical issues, they have not provided details of specific cognitive mechanisms.

This chapter is an attempt to characterize self-deception in terms of an elementary cognitive attribute—**cognitive complexity**. Self-deception may then be subsumed under a more general information processing theory of psychological defenses. The main thesis is that psychological stress reduces cognitive complexity, resulting in polarized evaluative judgments. The model has been described to varying degrees in a number of articles and paper presentations (Paulhus, 1984a, 1987; Paulhus & Levitt, 1987); however, it is expanded somewhat here.

To best develop our perspective, we have divided this chapter into three sections. In the first section we will lay out the general model of dynamic cognitive complexity. In the second we will apply the model to psychological defenses in general and self-deception in particular. In the third we will address the relation between self-deception and cognitive complexity in terms of individual differences.

THE DYNAMIC COMPLEXITY MODEL

The model owes much to the long tradition of work on information processing and cognitive complexity conducted at Princeton, Purdue, and Syracuse. For purposes of discussion, these researchers will be called the PPS group. The tradition was anchored by Harold Schroder but also included Harvey, Hunt, Driver, Streufert, Suedfeld, and Halverson. This group defined cognitive complexity (CC) most generally as the degree of elaboration in an individual's cognitive structures. The **differentiation** component of CC refers to the number of separate viewpoints or dimensions considered by the individual. The **integration** component of CC refers to the degree of reconciliation of the various points of view. The model presented below focuses primarily on the differentiation aspect.

The model has five central propositions. First, emotional arousal tends to reduce the complexity of information processing. Second, these reductions in complexity tend to amplify the role of evaluation in making judgments. Third, psychological threat triggers a fast-rising arousal, which reduces complexity before other information is processed. Fourth, this dynamic complexity is adaptive and defends the individual from threats. Fifth, individual differences in trait complexity moderate the changes in complexity and, therefore, the effectiveness of defense. These five propositions constitute a powerful framework for explaining a wide range of human behavior, including psychological defenses. For example, we will argue that such a sequence operating during the reception of information explains denial, whereas such a sequence during retrieval explains certain forms of self-deception.

Proposition I: Arousal Reduces Complexity

Most domains of human judgment can be considered to be multidimensional. For instance, many domains are configured in terms of the three dimensions of the semantic differential: evaluation, potency, and activity (Osgood, Suci, & Tannenbaum, 1957). However, there is substantial evidence from diverse types of research that, under emotional arousal, dimensionality is reduced. For instance, using archival materials, Suedfeld and Tetlock have shown in several studies that sophisticated judgments by political leaders decrease in complexity just before conflict (Suedfeld & Tetlock, 1977; Tetlock, 1979; Porter & Suedfeld, 1981; Suedfeld, 1981). In a simulation study by Guetzkow (1959), the dimensionality just before war erupted decreased to two dimensions: evaluation and dominance. Presumably, during war one needs to know two facts about other countries: how friendly they are and how powerful they are. In more controlled studies, Driver (1962) showed that simulated threats in war games reduced complexity in the same fashion. Other experimental studies (e.g., Wallsten & Barton, 1982) have shown that, under urgent conditions, the dimensionality of judgments gradually decreases from many dimensions to the most salient dimension. All these findings are generally consistent with the so-called Easterbrook hypothesis (Easterbrook, 1959) that emotional arousal reduces the number of cues utilized in decision making.

The most direct evidence that arousal reduces complexity is found in a series of studies by Paulhus and Lim (1985). Subjects were asked to make similarity ratings under high-arousal conditions (loud noise) and low-arousal conditions (low noise). Multidimensional scaling of the similarity ratings showed lower dimensionality under high arousal. This effect was obtained in all three domains tested: self-roles, acquaintances, and university courses. Again, dimensions dropped out in reverse order of importance. Thus the process is one of "graceful degradation"—a phrase borrowed from computerese. Similar results were obtained when the arousal agent was physical exercise (Paulhus, Lim, Reid, & Murphy, 1986) or an impending examination (Paulhus, 1987).

This proposition requires a statement of limitation. The relation between stress and complexity is probably an inverted-U (Easterbrook, 1959; Harvey, Hunt, & Schroder, 1961). The rising portion of the curve, however, addresses the increase from zero to optimal levels. This portion is always more difficult to investigate in laboratory studies or, indeed, in any interpersonal situation, because arousal levels are usually moderate or above. In any case, the dynamic complexity model expressly focuses on complexity reductions beyond optimal levels of stress.

Proposition II: Complexity and Evaluative Extremity

The second proposition is that lowering complexity increases the predominance of evaluation as the basis for judgments. Consider a domain which is normally perceived in Osgood's (Osgood, Suci, & Tannenbaum, 1957) three dimensions (evaluation, potency, and activity), for example, social judgments. As complexity is reduced, evaluation plays a larger and larger role until supreme urgency commands that *only* evaluation be used. This evaluative focus is functional in emergencies, when the organism needs only to decide whether the stimulus is good or bad. The good is approached, the bad is avoided. In short, the most well-adapted organism will exhibit complex judgments in cool, reflective situations, and fast, evaluative judgments when threatened.

Already there is substantial empirical evidence that low complexity is associated with a predominance of evaluation in social judgments. In research on individual differences in complexity, Halverson (1970), and more recently, Linville (1982a), have demonstrated that low-complexity individuals show more extrem evaluative judgments. Tetlock (1983, 1984) found that complexity was associate with moderate political positions and simplicity with more extreme positions, bo in the U.S. Senate and the British House of Commons. In the most recent findin de Vries and Walker (1986) found that same curvilinear relation between comple ity and extremity of attitude toward capital punishment. In the most comprehensi analysis, Scott, Osgood, and Peterson (1979) showed that low-dimensional reas ing is linked to a wide variety of measures of evaluative dominance (for qualifi tions, see Judd & Lusk, 1984, and Millar & Tesser, 1986).

More importantly for Proposition II, the link also holds for situational mar ulations of complexity (Linville, 1982a). Driver (1962) showed that when comp' ity is forced lower by stress, judgments become more highly correlated with evaluation. Again, the most direct demonstrations come from the studies by Paulhus and Lim (1985). In three different domains, they found that, as white noise reduced the complexity of social judgments, the importance of evaluation increased. Similar results were found when arousal was induced through physical exercise (Paulhus, Lim, Reid, & Murphy, 1986) or through threat of an examination (Paulhus, 1987).

Proposition III: Threat Triggers a Fast-Rising Arousal

A number of years ago, Erdelyi (1974) pointed out that psychological defenses were explicable in information processing terms, given constrictions at vital points in the processing sequence. A missing step in such models is how threat could constrain the processing of information. The proposition here is that threat triggers a **fast-rising arousal**, which then alters the complexity of processing. In other words, information is processed differently during a threat. A recent study by Paulhus and Levitt (1987) has provided some evidence for the operation of this fast-rising arousal in response to threat. Traits were presented on a microcomputer screen; subjects had to respond "me" or "not me" as the computer recorded their responses and reaction times. We tried to influence the responses by presenting a distractor word near the trait although subjects were told to ignore the distractors. Sometimes the distractor word was threatening—a word associated with sex or violence. When the subject responded, the trait and distractor disappeared from the screen. Results showed that the presence of a threat did influence responses: subjects claimed more positive traits and fewer negative traits. The reaction time results seemed to implicate a fast-rising arousal. One way of demonstrating arousal is to show a facilitation of dominant responses and a debilitation of nondominant responses. That is indeed what happened. Dominant responses, that is, "me" responses to positive traits and "not-me" responses to negative traits, were speeded up under threat. Other responses, including responses to neutral traits, were slowed down under threat.

The onset of arousal must be very fast given that it channeled the trait decisions, which took only 1.4 seconds on the average. Moreover, it appeared to subside in less than 10 seconds. Thus it resembles **cortical**, rather than **autonomic arousal** (Lacey, 1967; Paulhus, 1987). We believe such a fast-rising arousal is a key to the operation of psychological defenses. The arousal is fast enough to precede the processing of other information about the stimulus. Paulhus and Levitt (1987) went further, arguing that the sequence is automatic (see Bargh, 1984), for a view of automaticity). They speculated that many cases of self-enhancement are automatic, not deliberate, impression management.

In sum, there is evidence for the first three stages of the defensive sequence: (1) threat triggers arousal, (2) arousal reduces complexity, and (3) reduced complexity exaggerates the weighting of evaluation in judgments. In fact, several investigations mentioned above showed more than one stage of the sequence (e.g., Paulhus & Lim, 1985; Paulhus & Levitt, 1987), and two showed all three (Driver,

1962; Paulhus, 1987). Given the variety of domains implicated, it appears that dynamic complexity involves a general system change influencing any target domain.

Proposition IV: Dynamic Complexity is Adaptive

Sometimes complexity is advantageous, and other times simplicity is advantageous. Dynamic complexity is behaviorally adaptive because it negotiates the changing demands of the environment (Streufert & Streufert, 1978). A high degree of complexity is preferable when a safe, calm environment permits time for detailed planning and subtle analysis. Lower complexity is preferable when fast decisions are required. Often, in emergencies, any decision is better than none—better yet is a decision based on the best available summary of the cost-benefit ratio. Affective responses provide such a summary. We concur with Zajonc (1980) that global evaluations are available independent of the informational details. Consequently, even when fast decisions are made, they are more often right than wrong.

An optimal processing system would also have a fast-acting switch that decides when the complex or simple mode is appropriate. We propose that emotional reactions constitute the switch: If a stimulus provokes emotion, then simplicity ensues. While not invariably adaptive, the emotion-complexity link is a good approximation. For example, the most potent source of arousal is danger, which typically calls for fast decisions, for example, fight or flight.

The adaptive value is lost to some extent in the transfer from jungle to social interactions. Under social stress, inappropriate reductions in complexity are common: Public speakers go blank, athletes choke, and ardent suitors fumble for words. Intrapsychic functioning, however, generally benefits from emotion-derived simplicity. Greenwald (1980) has detailed how, under psychological threat, the self acts to maintain itself by denial, distortion, and revision of history. Other writers have shown how threats to self-esteem are nullified by various cognitive mechanisms (e.g., Carver & Scheier, 1981; Tesser & Campbell, 1983). We will show in the second section of this chapter how many of these defense mechanisms are explicable with the dynamic complexity model.

Proposition V: Individual Differences Moderate Effects of Threat

It is likely that the above effects are more true for some people than for others. The most obvious moderator variable to consider is **trait complexity**, that is, chronic individual differences in cognitive complexity. The first issue of interest is whether high- or low-complexity individuals are more susceptible to dynamic changes in complexity. This issue is currently controversial. Work by Linville (1982b, 1985) suggests that low-complexity individuals are most susceptible to psychological threats. Using Scott's H-statistic as an index of trait complexity, Linville found that cognitively simple subjects showed (1) more negative affect in response to failure, and (2) more extreme mood swings in longitudinal self-report data than did more complex subjects.

However, earlier work by the PPS group suggests a more complicated relationship (Schroder, Driver, & Streufert, 1967). In general, low-complexity individuals resist change demanded by new information. Hence they should be *less* likely to show mood swings. However, when pushed far enough, low-complexity types eventually snap and suffer severe negative affect. Thus any failure manipulation in the laboratory might be strong enough to snap some low-complexity individuals but not others. In contrast, high-complexity subjects accept new information, but change slowly. Moreover, they are said to tolerate conflict without negative affect, and therefore show little tendency to distort information.

Summary

Any one of a variety of psychological threats (e.g., sex, violence, or threats to self-esteem) can trigger a fast-rising arousal. This arousal reduces the normal complexity of judgments such that evaluation becomes predominant. The system then responds to protect the organism, both physically and psychologically. Such a system provides an automatic mechanism for governing a speed-accuracy trade-off in processing social information.

SPECIFIC DEFENSES

Let us return at this point to Sackeim and Gur's (1978) specification of self-deception: Two contradictory beliefs are simultaneously represented in the belief system, but motivation inhibits accessibility of one belief. They claim that this state of affairs obtains during the successful operation of all defense mechanisms (cf. Eagle, Chapter 5). In the language of dynamic complexity we would say that defense mechanisms entail a less than complete representation of available information. The representation is incomplete in a specifiable way: Dimensions are dropped according to the principle of graceful degradation and evaluation is amplified.

Self-Relevance

What happens when the information is relevant to the self? In some aspects information about the self may be processed differently from information about others (Greenwald & Pratkanis, 1984). One similarity is that both domains are anchored by a central evaluative dimension. Thus any factor that reduces the complexity of the self-concept should yield an increased focus on self-evaluation. For instance, we know that increased arousal leads to (1) an increased self-focus (Wegner & Giuliano, 1981), and (2) an increased focus on the evaluative dimension of self-roles (Paulhus & Lim, 1985).

When one's self-concept is reduced to pure evaluation (positive for most people), then the validity of self-relevant information is judged purely on that basis—does it match one's current self-evaluation? A number of tendencies should ensue: New negative information should be rejected and old negative information distorted. No new negative information can slip in because it happens to satisfy some other criterion for truth. In short, the dynamic complexity model predicts that arousal can help protect self-esteem.

Transient Self-Deception

Recall that Erdelyi (1974) showed how different defenses could be accounted for by placing filtering mechanisms at critical stages of the information flow. Now that we have specified such a filtering mechanism, namely, cognitive complexity, we can consider the more specific effects of altering CC at various steps of the process: encoding, retrieval, and so forth.

Consider first the reduction of complexity due to emotional arousal during retrieval. This is the form of self-deception we have called **transient self-deception** (Paulhus, 1984a). The distortion is only transient because the stored information is retained in the original complex form. Thus, the individual can later see a truth which was hidden to him under conditions of threat. When the threat subsides, a more realistic judgment can be made. Because the individual can later see the truth, the necessary information must have been available at the time of threat. Thus, the label self-deception seems appropriate.

Consider some everyday examples. During a family dispute, you claim ''I *always* take out the garbage.'' The claim is made honestly during the argument; you later recognize in a cooler moment that you were entirely wrong. Or consider the situation in which you hand your cigarettes to a friend and say, ''Don't give me one even if I beg you for it.'' Sure enough, when withdrawal time comes you beg for a cigarette and argue honestly that one more won't hurt. Later, in a cool moment you realize that one cigarette would have effectively ruined your chances of quitting smoking. In all of these cases the deception withers along with the threat, and insight becomes possible. Thus, the complexity model presented above can be applied: Threat triggers a fast-rising arousal which reduces complexity until the threat subsides. During the self-deceptive episode, judgments are made primarily on the basis of their affective significance. The individual is thus temporarily protected from information that may threaten self-esteem.

In transient self-deception, then, normally well-differentiated judgments about stored information become temporarily engulfed by their evaluative implications. In most cases the bias should vanish when the threat vanishes. Note that this recoverability does not apply to processes like cognitive dissonance wherein the cognitive changes are permanent. Paulhus (1982), for example, tried to undo such attitude change using the bogus pipeline (a pseudo lie-detection procedure). Approximately half of the attitude change was not reversible.

Repression

What happens if a strong affective association is automatically triggered whenever a certain idea arises (Clark, 1982)? Let's say that, due to a traumatic event, a strongly conditioned emotional response is evoked. According to the dynamic complexity model, analysis of this idea would always be performed under low complexity. For most purposes, the information is functionally simple and largely evaluative. Thus, the mechanism of repression may be viewed as a functionally permanent form of self-deception. This situation would obtain when any attempt to process information about, say, one's father, triggers massive anxiety, which then reduces complexity, thereby precluding an accurate perception of him.

Often, classical repression is described as the complete inaccessibility of a fact or even a complete set of facts surrounding a belief (e.g., Eagle, Chapter 5). If so, the present model cannot easily provide an account. Not much different, however, are cases in which affect so greatly distorts the recall that relevant facts are, in effect, ignored. If all cases of repression can be couched in these terms, then the dynamic complexity model may be all that is needed.

Note the sanguine implications. Repressed information is potentially accessible, at least in principle. The key is to find some way to access the information without triggering the affect.

Other Defenses

Consider the effect of arousal during the encoding of new information. As a general principle, new information is accepted to the extent that it matches current knowledge structures. Under arousal, however, the knowledge structure will appear simple and dominated by evaluation. If the new information does not match this exaggerated evaluation, it will be rejected. This is the case in denial when negative or inconsistent information is rejected outright. Although it has few contemporary supporters, perceptual defense represents a similar principle applied to perception. Emotion may constrain the perceptual representation of stimuli such that some information is lost or degraded.

INDIVIDUAL DIFFERENCES

The dynamic complexity model has implications for individual differences in self-deception. The assessment of self-deception as a personality variable was first proposed by Sackeim and Gur (1978). They developed the Self-Deception Questionnaire (SDQ) to assess the denial of thoughts about psychologically threatening ideas: hating one's parents, enjoying one's bowel movements, fear of homosexuality. Paulhus (1984b) later refined the scale by balancing the keying direction and replacing some items. The construct validity of the scale has been supported in a number of studies (Sackeim & Gur, 1978, 1979; Gur & Sackeim, 1979; Paulhus, 1982; Sackeim, 1983; Winters & Neale, 1985; Paulhus & Levitt, 1987). In particular, the SDQ has been shown to anchor the unconscious dimension of socially desirable responding (Paulhus, 1984b). In factor analyses, the SDQ appears at the center of a cluster of measures of defensive style (Linden, Paulhus, & Dobson, 1986; Paulhus, 1986).

By applying the dynamic complexity model to self-deception, we can make a number of predictions about the relation of the SDQ to other individual difference measures. For example, self-deceptive individuals should show more evaluative extremity. This prediction was confirmed in a series of studies reported by Lim and Paulhus (1986). The SDQ showed significant positive correlations with evaluative extremity across a number of target domains. Another prediction suggested by the model is that self-deceptive individuals should be low in trait complexity. In fact, the reverse appears to be true: The SDQ is positively correlated with a variety of measures of trait complexity, including the Paragraph Completion Test (Schroder, Driver, & Streufert, 1967). This relation will be more understandable after our discussion of the relation of trait complexity with adjustment.

Trait Complexity and Adjustment

Recall that Proposition IV of the dynamic complexity model states that reductions in complexity protect self-esteem. One might conclude, therefore, that individuals with chronically low cognitive complexity should be better adjusted. The available evidence suggests otherwise. Individuals low in trait complexity seem to be less well-adjusted. For instance, Lim and Paulhus (1986) found low-complexity individuals to be lower in self-esteem and higher in anxiety. Using Scott's H-statistic as a measure of trait complexity, Linville's (1982b, 1985) research also suggests poor adjustment among low-complexity individuals. For instance, individuals low in trait complexity rated themselves as more depressed and responded more severely to a failure experience. They also reported more mood fluctuation over a four-week period.

On the surface, these individual difference data appear to conflict with Proposition IV of the dynamic complexity model. Let us consider several possible resolutions to this apparent paradox. To begin, one must distinguish between the effects of trait complexity and the effects of situational changes in complexity. It is not paradoxical that temporarily reducing complexity is adaptive while chronic low complexity tends to be maladaptive. One resolution follows from noting that low-complexity individuals have fewer dimensions to discard and therefore less flexibility in dealing with threats. Thus, the defensive advantages of lowering complexity may be chronically less available to these individuals and low self-esteem may be inevitable.

Another resolution follows from assuming that some individuals are chronically prone to negative affect for temperamental reasons (Bell & Byrne, 1978; Watson & Clark, 1984) or because of continuing situational stressors. Such individuals are constantly trying to defend themselves and thus show low complexity in many domains. The defense is only partially successful. Nonetheless, at any given moment, even these individuals are better off than if they had retained their maximal complexity. Because the defense is not completely effective, low trait complexity will continue to show an association with maladjustment.

A third resolution requires a clarification of Proposition IV. Reduced complexity protects self-esteem only for those originally high in self-esteem. This follows from the corollary that arousal magnifies current self-evaluation: Individuals with high self-esteem will feel better about themselves, but those initially low in self-esteem will feel worse. Thus, threats or other sources of arousal actually worsen the plight of the maladjusted. This does not explain why high self-esteem is positively associated with high trait complexity. It may be that the damage done to low-complexity individuals during the stressful periods encountered by all social beings brings about chronic deficits in self-esteem.

The available evidence leads us to favor the third resolution. The most recent work from our laboratories (Paulhus & Reid, 1987) has supported the view that arousal has differential effects on high and low self-esteem people. Moreover, the exaggeration of negative affect in trait-simple persons outweighs the exaggeration of positive affect (Linville, 1985). In short, the costs of simplicity outweigh the benefits.

CONCLUSIONS

We have outlined an information-processing model of psychological defenses (Paulhus, 1987) and applied it to self-deception. Following the principles of Erdelyi (1974), we have specified a filter mechanism, namely, cognitive complexity, to govern the flow of information. Under conditions of emotional arousal, processing is reduced in complexity and the importance of evaluation inflated. When evaluation is amplified, negative information about the self tends to be rejected. These effects occur on representation in working memory, leaving untouched the long-term representation.

If the source of the arousal (e.g., anger) is extraneous to the domain being judged (e.g., taking out the garbage), the self-deception will be transient. If, however, the arousal is triggered by merely thinking about that domain, reduced complexity cannot be avoided, and the self-deception is chronic, as in repression. If arousal occurs during the encoding of new self-relevant information, negative information tends to be rejected outright as in classical denial.

Defense mechanisms have traditionally had a magical, ineffable aura that has deterred research. By couching them in modern information-processing terms, we hope to move defense mechanisms into the pale of testable phenomena.

REFERENCES

BARGH, J. A. (1984). Automatic and conscious processing of social information. In R. S. Wyer & T. K. Srull (Eds.), *Handbook of social cognition* (Vol. 3, pp. 1-43). Hillsdale, NJ: Erlbaum.

BYRNE, D., & BELL, P. (1978). Repression-sensitization. In H. London & J. Exner (Eds.), *Dimensions of personality* (pp. 449-486). New York: Academic Press.

CARVER, C. S., & SCHEIER, M. F. (1981). *Attention and self-regulation: A control theory approach to human behavior.* New York: Springer-Verlag.

CLARK, M. S. (1982). A role for arousal in the link between feeling states, judgments, and behavior. In M. S. Clark & S. T. Fiske (Eds.), *Affect and cognition* (pp. 263-289). Hillsdale, NJ: Erlbaum.

DE VRIES, B., & WALKER, L. (1986). Cognitive complexity and attitude toward capital punishment. *Developmental Psychology, 100,* 99-109.

DRIVER, M. J. (1962). Conceptual structure and group processes in an inter-nation simulation. Part One: The perception of simulated nations. *ETS Research Bulletin, RB,* 62-15.

EASTERBROOK, J. A. (1959). The effect of emotion on cue utilization and the organization of behavior. *Psychological Review, 66,* 183-201.

ERDELYI, M. (1974). A new look at the new look: Perceptual defense and vigilance. *Psychological Review, 81,* 1-25.

GREENWALD, A. G. (1980). The totalitarian ego: Fabrication and revision of personal history. *American Psychologist, 55,* 603-618.

GREENWALD, A. G., & PRATKANIS, A. R. (1984). The self. In R. S. Wyer & T. K. Srull (Eds.), *Handbook of social cognition* (Vol. 3, pp. 129-178). Hillsdale, NJ: Erlbaum.

GUETZKOW, H. S. (1959). A use of simulation in the study of inter-nation relations. *Behavioral Sciences, 4,* 183-190.

GUR, R. C., & SACKEIM, H. A. (1979). Self-deception: A concept in search of a phenomenon. *Journal of Personality and Social Psychology, 37,* 147-169.

HALVERSON, C. F. (1970). Interpersonal perception: Cognitive complexity and trait implication. *Journal of Clinical and Consulting Psychology, 34,* 86-90.

HARVEY, O. J., HUNT, D. E., & SCHRODER, H. M. (1961). *Conceptual systems and personality organization.* New York: Wiley.

JUDD, C. M., & LUSK, C. M. (1984). Knowledge structures and evaluative judgments: Effects of structural variables on judgment extremity. *Journal of Personality and Social Psychology, 46,* 1193-1207.

LACEY, J. I. (1967). Somatic response patterning and stress. In M. H. Appley & R. Turnball (Eds.), *Psychological stress* (pp. 67-80). New York: Appleton-Century-Crofts.

LIM, D. T. K., & PAULHUS, D. L. (1986, August). *Complexity and extremity.* Paper presented at the meeting of the Canadian Psychological Association, Toronto.

LINDEN, W., PAULHUS, D. L., & DOBSON, K. (1986). Effects of response styles on the report of psychological and somatic distress. *Journal of Consulting and Clinical Psychology, 54,* 309-313.

LINVILLE, P. W. (1982a). The complexity-extremity effect and age-based stereotyping. *Journal of Personality and Social Psychology, 42,* 193-211.

————. (1982b). Affective consequences of complexity regarding the self and others. In M. S. Clark & S. T. Fiske (Eds.), *Affect and cognition: The seventeenth annual Carnegie symposium on cognition* (pp. 79-105). Hillsdale, NJ: Erlbaum.

————. (1985). Self-complexity and affective extremity: Don't put all of your eggs in one cognitive basket. *Social Cognition, 3,* 94-120.

MILLAR, M. G., & TESSER, A. (1986). Thought-induced attitude change: The effects of schema structure and commitment. *Journal of Personality and Social Psychology, 51,* 259-269.

OSGOOD, C. E., SUCI, G. J., & TANNENBAUM, P. H. (1957). *The measurement of meaning.* Urbana, IL: University of Illinois Press.

PALLAK, M. S., & PITTMAN, T. S. (1972). General motivational effects of dissonance arousal. *Journal of Personality and Social Psychology, 21,* 349-358.

PAULHUS, D. L. (1982). Individual differences, cognitive dissonance, and self-presentation: Their concurrent operation in forced compliance. *Journal of Personality and Social Psychology, 43,* 838-852.

————. (1984a, August). *Self-deception: An information processing approach.* Paper presented at the meeting of the American Psychological Association, Toronto.

————. (1984b). Two-component models of socially desirable responding. *Journal of Personality and Social Psychology, 46,* 598-609.

————. (1986). Self-deception and impression management in test responses. In A. Angleitner & J. S. Wiggins (Eds.), *Personality assessment via questionnaire* (pp. 143-165). New York: Springer-Verlag.

————. (1987). *A dynamic complexity model of personality processes.* Manuscript submitted for publication.

PAULHUS, D. L., & LEVITT, K. (1987). Socially desirable responding triggered by affect: Automatic egotism? *Journal of Personality and Social Psychology, 52,* 245-259.

PAULHUS, D. L., & LIM, D. T. K. (1985, August). *The effects of arousal on cognitive complexity and evaluation.* Paper presented at the meeting of the American Psychological Association, Los Angeles.

PAULHUS, D. L., LIM, D. T. K., REID, D. B., & MURPHY, G. (1986, August). *Exercise and cognitive complexity.* Paper presented at the meeting of the American Psychological Association, Washington, DC.

PAULHUS, D. L. & REID, D. B.   (1987). *Dynamic complexity and self-esteem.* Unpublished study, University of British Columbia.

PORTER, C. A., & SUEDFELD, P.   (1981). Integrative complexity in the correspondence of literary figures: Effects of personal and societal stress. *Journal of Personality and Social Psychology, 40,* 321-330.

SACKEIM, H. A.   (1983). The adaptive value of lying to oneself. In J. Masling (Ed.), *Empirical studies of psychoanalytic theories* (pp. 101-157). Hillsdale, NJ: Erlbaum.

SACKEIM, H. A., & GUR, R. C.   (1978). Self-deception, self-confrontation, and consciousness. In G. E. Schwartz & D. Shapiro (Eds.), *Consciousness and self-regulation: Advances in research* (Vol. 2, pp. 139-197). New York: Plenum.

————.   (1979). Self-deception, other-deception, and self-reported psychopathology. *Journal of Consulting and Clinical Psychology, 47,* 213-215.

SCHRODER, H. M., DRIVER, M. J., & STREUFERT, S.   (1967). *Human information processing: Individuals and groups in complex social situations.* New York: Holt Rinehart & Winston.

SCOTT, W. A., OSGOOD, D. W., & PETERSON, C.   (1979). *Cognitive structure: Theory and measurement of individual differences.* Washington, DC: Winston/Wiley.

STREUFERT, S., & STREUFERT, S. C.   (1978). *Behavior in the complex environment.* Toronto, Ontario, Canada: Wiley.

SUEDFELD, P.   (1981). Indices of world tension in the Bulletin of the Atomic Scientists. *Political Psychology, 2,* 114-123.

SUEDFELD, P., & TETLOCK, P. E.   (1977). Integrative complexity of communications in international crises. *Journal of Conflict Resolution, 21,* 169-184.

TESSER, A., & CAMPBELL, J. D.   (1983). Seif-definition and self-evaluation maintenance. In J. Suls & A. G. Greenwald (Eds.), *Psychological perspectives on the self* (Vol. 2, pp. 101-129). Hillsdale, NJ: Erlbaum.

TETLOCK, P. E.   (1979). Identifying victims of groupthink from public statements of decision makers. *Journal of Personality and Social Psychology, 37,* 1314-1324.

————.   (1983). Cognitive style and political ideology. *Journal of Personality and Social Psychology, 45,* 118-126.

————.   (1984). Cognitive style and political belief systems in the British House of Commons. *Journal of Personality and Social Psychology, 46,* 365-375.

WALLSTEN, T. S., & BARTON, C.   (1982). Processing probabilistic multidimensional information for decisions. *Journal of Experimental Psychology: Human Learning and Memory, 8,* 361-384.

WATSON, D., & CLARK, L. A.   (1984). Negative affectivity: The disposition to experience aversive emotional states. *Psychological Bulletin, 96,* 465-490.

WEGNER, D. M., & GIULIANO, T.   (1981). Arousal-induced attention to the self. *Journal of Personality and Social Psychology, 38,* 719-726.

WINTERS, K. C., & NEALE, J. M.   (1985). Mania and low self-esteem. *Journal of Abnormal Behavior*, *94*, 282-290.

ZAJONC, R. B.   (1980). Preferences need no inferences. *American Psychologist*, *35*, 151-175.

9

Self-Deception

A SYNTHESIS

Harold A. Sackeim
New York University
and
New York State Psychiatric Institute

As evidenced by this volume and other recent work, there has been an extraordinary increase of interest among philosophers, clinicians, and scientists in the topic of self-deception. The term *self-deception* has been applied by ethologists to explain the deceptive behavior of lower organisms (e.g., Lockard, 1980; Trivers, 1985), by social psychologists to account for the seemingly motivated shifts in beliefs of subjects in laboratory and quasi-experimental circumstances (e.g., Paulhus, 1982; Quattrone & Tversky, 1984), and also by personality psychologists to account for nonveridical questionnaire responses (e.g., Paulhus, 1984, 1986). The concept has been used to describe the behavior of hypnotic subjects (Sackeim, Nordlie, & Gur, 1979; Sarbin, 1984), certain manifestations of brain damage (Sackeim, 1983, in press), and differences in attributional patterns between depressed and non-depressed individuals (Abramson & Martin, 1981; Sackeim, 1983; Roth & Ingram, 1985; Sackeim & Wegner, in press).

The growing popularity of self-deception as a descriptive or explanatory concept has also created divergence. The contributions of Eagle, Sarbin, Green-wald, and Paulhus and Suedfeld in this volume also demonstrate that the meaning of the term *self-deception* varies considerably from theorist to theorist. The aim of this

Preparation of this chapter was supported in part by grant MH 35636 from the National Institute of Mental Health and grant AG 05433 from the National Institute of Aging.

146

chapter is to outline the nature of some of these differences and to suggest some avenues for conceptual resolution.

THE PARADOX OF SELF-DECEPTION

What is meant by self-deception has long been debated in the philosophy of mind literature (e.g., Plato, 386 B.C./1953; Sartre, 1943/1958; Canfield & Gustafson, 1962; Penelhum, 1966; Fingarette, 1969; Gardiner, 1970). At the heart of the controversy has been the issue of whether or not the logic of self-deception conforms to the logic of other deception, that is, lying to others. When we lie to someone else we usually communicate a proposition *p* that we believe not to be true. In essence, we state that we believe that *p* is true, but in reality we believe that *not-p* is true.

The assimilation of the logic of other-deception to that of self-deception is often viewed as paradoxical largely because it entails the same individual having contradictory beliefs. Perhaps Sartre best expressed the nature of this paradox:

> The one to whom the lie is told and the one who lies are one and the same person, which means that I must know in my capacity as deceiver the truth which is hidden from me in my capacity as the one deceived. Better yet, I must know the truth very exactly in order to conceal it more carefully—and this not at two different moments, which at a pinch would allow us to re-establish a semblance of duality—but in the unitary structure of a single project. How can the lie subsist if the duality which conditions it is suppressed? (1943/1958, p. 49)

If we accept the Lockean view that mental contents (beliefs, wishes, feelings) are necessarily subject to awareness, there are obvious problems in assimilating the logic of other-deception to that of self-deception. Beliefs cannot be "hidden" from ourselves if one presumes that consciousness is transparent (see Sackeim & Gur, 1978).

In this respect, the problem of self-deception touches on fundamental issues concerning the nature of consciousness. In the next section, I examine various solutions that have been offered to this problem in the philosophy literature. As we shall see later, some of the solutions, entailing somewhat different meanings of the term self-deception, have been adopted by the psychologists who have contributed to this volume.

RESOLUTIONS OF THE PARADOX

Timing of Beliefs

One way out of the problem of contradictory beliefs is to assume that the beliefs are not held simultaneously. At *t*1, John believes that he is an excellent writer, and at *t*2 John believes that he is a poor writer. At *t*2 John has forgotten that he held the original belief. This type of position allows us, as Sartre indicated, "to re-establish a semblance of duality'' and still maintain the view that consciousness is transparent.

This position was also embodied in Nisbett and Wilson's (1977) influential paper on the inaccuracies in people's accounts of the causes of their behavior. In providing an explanation of the phenomenon of subliminal perception, they wrote:

> It is now generally recognized that many more stimuli are apprehended than can be stored in short-term memory or transferred to long-term memory. Thus, subliminal perception, once widely regarded as a logical paradox (''How can we perceive without perceiving''), may be derived as a logical consequence of the principle of selective filtering. *We cannot perceive without perceiving, but we can perceive without remembering.* The subliminal perception hypothesis then becomes theoretically quite innocuous. . . . (p. 240, italics added)

Nisbett and Wilson appear to mean that subliminal perception involves a brief awareness of a stimulus that is rapidly forgotten. The perceptual experience, although forgotten, may still influence behavior. Likewise, a similar account may be offered for self-deception.

As an explanation of self-deception, there are two main problems with this type of ''sequential'' resolution. First, it does not conform to how the term self-deception is used in ordinary language. Second, were a set of criteria developed to ascribe self-deception based on the ''sequential'' resolution, many instances of behavior would fit the criteria that are patently not instances of self-deception. With regard to the ordinary language use of the term, the ''sequential'' resolution thereby violates both conditions of necessity and sufficiency. For example, we often take a defense of amnesia as contradicting a charge of self-deception. We mean something different in stating that John now acts friendly towards his boss and has forgotten his original hatred towards him, and in stating that despite the fact that John believes he likes his boss, ''deep inside'' he hates him. Further, were self-deception only a matter of forgetting, we would have to apply the construct to any occasion in which we come to different beliefs on an issue and do not have access to our original belief.

Of note, the solution that Nisbett and Wilson suggested for the problem of subliminal perception also violates what investigators of the phenomenon have typically meant by their use of the term (e.g., Dixon, 1971). Whether or not satisfactorily realized, the aim in studies of subliminal perception has been to demonstrate that perceptual stimuli can influence behavior simultaneous with lack of representation in awareness of the stimuli (e.g., Marcel, 1983; Mathews & Macleod, 1986).

Self-Deception and False Beliefs

In providing an account of self-deception that was in accord with behavioral approaches in psychology, Canfield and Gustafson (1962) proposed that to be self-deceived, a person must hold a belief in adverse circumstances. In other words, the evidence available to the individual does not support the belief. In this volume,

Sarbin partially adopts this position. He argues that the hypnotic subject, placed in a bind between his or her knowledge of the world and the "magical" context provided by the hypnotist, opts to join in a dialogue that violates his or her knowledge of reality. A major difficulty with this view is that the beliefs about which people lie to themselves may be veridical. For example, John may accurately profess to be a good writer, although "deep inside" he believes otherwise. John may assert that superstitions are foolish, but somehow never leaves the house on Fridays that fall on the thirteenth day of the month.

From a logico-linguistic perspective (Sackeim & Gur, 1978), the relation of beliefs to evidence is irrelevant in determining whether or not the term self-deception should be ascribed. When Sarbin (Chapter 6) states that the self-deceiver "invents and distorts the world of occurrences" he is not providing a generic or comprehensive view of what is entailed by self-deception. The relation of beliefs to evidence is not irrelevant, however, from an epistemological or psychological vantage point. The way we find out that others are lying to themselves may typically be in circumstances in which the belief being espoused contradicts the available evidence. What must be distinguished here is (1) what is meant when we say someone is lying to himself or herself and (2) how we come to infer self-deception.

Sarbin, in adopting the position of Fingarette (1969), also accepts the position taken by Canfield and Gustafson (1962). As Penelhum (1966) noted, an additional problem with the Canfield and Gustafson criteria is that instances of ignorance cannot be separated from instances of self-deception. Undoubtedly, all of us hold beliefs that are in contradiction of the available evidence. This hardly means that all instances in which it turns out that we were wrong in our thinking are instances of self-deception.

Blind Faith

In going beyond the formulation of Canfield and Gustafson (1962), Penelhum (1966) suggested a more stringent set of criteria which he claimed to be necessary and sufficient for the ascription of self-deception. In essence, Penelhum argued that the self-deceiver maintains a belief in the face of strong evidence to the contrary, knows of the evidence, and recognizes its import. The prototypic example here would be the individual who knows that results of a biopsy are positive, is aware that a positive biopsy of this type indicates a malignancy, but staunchly believes, nonetheless, that there is no cancer.

This formulation can likewise be criticized for only requiring that the espoused belief be nonveridical. Gardiner (1970) raised two other problems, one of which is germane at this point. He noted that Penelhum's criteria do not allow us to distinguish between self-deception and blind faith.

Accepting the existence of blind faith allows that individuals may maintain strong beliefs that run counter to all available evidence, be aware of the evidence and its import, and yet not be lying to themselves. The example Gardiner (1970) used was that of Hitler at the close of the Second World War. Apparently, despite the reports that his armies were being overwhelmed and retreating, Hitler maintained an unshaken belief in eventual victory. The point originally raised by Gardiner is that individuals exist who are so rigid in adopting a belief that no evidence to the contrary will dissuade them. It is not the case that "deep in their hearts" they believe the opposite, or that they are "half-believing" or ambivalent in their convictions.

The possibility of blind faith offers an alternative characterization of some phenomena that might be conceived of as instances of self-deception. The characterization by Sarbin of the behavior of hypnotic subjects may be an example. One interpretation of his position is that the hypnotic subject understands that the nature of dialogue with the hypnotist requires suspension of ordinary rules of evidence. The objective grounds for forming beliefs are not relevant to the hypnotic context. The hypnotic subject sincerely adopts another reality on "blind faith." The reasons for doing so may relate to the demand characteristics of the hypnotic situation.

This formulation departs from that offered by Sarbin (Chapter 6) in that it does not require an **active avoidance**, or an inhibition of the spelling out of beliefs. It suggests that the hypnotic subject does not fight against an evidence-based approach to belief generation, but is capable of establishing beliefs independent of the usual rules concerning "objective" evidence, if the situation calls for it. My own view is that this is not a fully acceptable account of hypnotic phenomena (cf., Sackeim, Nordlie, & Gur, 1979). However, I am arguing that it is a plausible account and may have explanatory power for other circumstances, such as accounting for religious convictions that fly in the face of objective evidence.

Information streams   Let us now consider a more subtle formulation of phenomena that may be related to blind faith. Elsewhere (Sackeim, 1983), I have suggested that psychodynamically oriented accounts of self-deception and defensive processes posit splits in consciousness such that incompatible beliefs may be simultaneously maintained in two separate streams of information processing, with only the products of one stream subject to awareness. I suggested that this psychodynamic view was in some respects distinctly optimistic regarding the correspondence between "reality" and beliefs. It assumes that there is frequently a greater correspondence between unconscious information processing and what is real than between representations in awareness and reality.

In contrast, one can entertain the notion that many of our beliefs are the outcome of a unitary stream of information processing. Indeed, this is the type of formulation offered in this volume by Greenwald. Using signal detection terminology, we can further posit that like any decision process, the outcome of belief generation is a function of current sensitivity and response criteria for evaluating available evidence. Individuals may adopt a response criterion so extreme that, regardless of their sensitivity to the evidence, an unshaken belief is maintained.

This type of formulation may well apply to many instances of distorted cognition. The social psychology literature is now replete with studies demonstrating that normal functioning is often characterized by self-serving, egocentric biases (Greenwald, 1980; Sackeim, 1986; Sackeim & Wegner, 1986). For example, most individuals believe that there is a greater probability of positive events happening to them than to their peers, with the probabilities reversed in direction for future negative outcomes (e.g., Weinstein, 1980). It is not necessary to interpret such phenomena as instances of self-deception. Indeed, such interpretations may be wrong. It is quite conceivable that the response criteria often adopted in belief generation are such that *the beliefs will serve to protect or enhance self-esteem* (Sackeim, 1983; Tesser & Paulhus, 1983). At no point in the process does the individual harbor a contradictory belief at any level, or avoid spelling out the implications of the evidence, or more generally avoid knowledge.

Thus some, if not many, forms of distorted cognition may reflect a "blind faith" process—a single stream of information processing with reduced sensitivity or an extreme response criterion. This possibility should stand as a corrective to attempts to view all such distortions as examples of self-deception. Virtually all theorists in the area of self-deception take the stand that this phenomenon (or set of phenomena) involves the inhibition or avoidance of belief generation (e.g., Fingarette, 1969—failing to spell out) or the adoption of partially (e.g., Greenwald, Chapter 7) or fully incompatible beliefs (e.g., Sackeim & Gur, 1978). Put another way, we may frequently be wrong when we assume that "deep inside" individuals must know the truth when they espouse beliefs so contrary to the evidence. Such a position may fail to acknowledge that *evidence at times is not a primary foundation for belief* and that, even when evidence is contributory, thresholds may be so high that the usual grounds for changing convictions or establishing them in the first place do not apply.

I noted earlier that psychodynamic theory may take an unusually "optimistic" view of the nature of human information processing. This is because a traditional version of this theory posits a dual stream of processing in which one of the streams, typically not subject to awareness, is more accurate in its appraisals than the other. Notice that this implies a circumstance in which, at some level of consciousness, veridical processing is maintained. The "blind faith" or single-biased processing model suggests that this need not be the case. At no level of consciousness is there more veridical representation.

The Spelling Out of Beliefs: The Problem of Agency

Sarbin (Chapter 6) bridles against accounts of self-deception in terms of mentalistic conceptions of levels of consciousness and, in particular, "as *happenings mechanically activated by unconscious forces* (italics in the original). Rather, he appeals to Fingarette's (1969) formulation that self-deception involves a deliberate act of not spelling out some engagement in the world. On the other hand, Eagle (Chapter 5) questions the suggestion I had offered that self-deception be considered a superordinate category subsuming the traditional psychoanalytic formulations of defense mechanisms. Surprisingly, his grounds for doing so reflect a belief that self-deception is an "act" that people carry out, whereas repression is a "subpersonal mechanism." He indicates that since self-deception is a personal action, it is often discussed in a moral context, with respect to issues of motive and responsibility. He claims that it is inappropriate to use the language of motives for subpersonal mechanisms, such as repression, despite the fact that such mechanisms may be functional.

Sarbin's preference for viewing self-deception in "nonmentalistic" terms goes unjustified and appears to be a matter of personal theoretic preference. The difficulty we face here, of course, is attempting to understand the psychological processes that underlie self-deception. For example, as Greenwald (Chapter 7) points out, when we try to translate Fingarette's characterization into the language of psychology, we run into difficulties. What does it mean to "fail to spell out" one's engagement in the world? Is one aware of such avoidance? What processes are involved in spelling out and failing to spell out? What processes in consciousness determine such decisions? Appropriately, Greenwald suggests that this formulation, at the surface, may appear to provide a satisfactory resolution to the problem of defining self-deception and determining whether its logic is similar to that of other-deception. It is superficially satisfactory, precisely because the issues of contradictory beliefs, their relations to awareness, and so on, are side-stepped by use of other metaphors.

The problem of "choice"   This may become clearer when Sartre's (1943/1958) position on the issue is reexamined. His theoretical framework entailed the view that *consciousness is both unitary and transparent.* He adopted the position that all mental content can be subject to awareness. He viewed resolution of the problem of self-deception, or "bad faith," as central to the difference between his existentialist position and the philosophy of mind reflected in psychoanalytic theory. Nevertheless, in accounting for self-deception he appealed not just to mentalistic conceptions, but suggested specifically that the warded-off mental contents reside, so to speak, in "pre-reflective consciousness" and epitomize what he called "nonthetic" knowledge. While Sartre, like Fingarette (1969), used the language of choice, responsibility, and morality to discuss self-deception, and while Freud often used the language of mechanisms, forces, and energy, in strictly logical terms Sartre's resolution is actually quite Freudian. It would seem to make little difference in an absolute sense whether we speak of unconscious ideas or nonthetic knowledge. We are still stuck with the problem of accounting for individuals believing and not believing at the same time.

Fingarette asserted that he avoided the restatement of the paradox that is inherent in both Sartre and Freud. If he has done so, it may be because of the inherent vagueness of what is meant by failing to spell out some engagement in the world. At minimum, one can inquire whether avoiding such "spelling out" requires, at times, foreknowledge of the beliefs that would be generated.

Eagle (Chapter 5) accepts the view that the language of choice, responsibility, and morality applies to this concept of self-deception but claims that this is not the case for psychoanalytic defense mechanisms. If I understand him correctly he has presented two arguments to support this distinction. Both may be questioned.

Eagle indicates that repression and other defense mechanisms result in symptoms. He claims that in developing symptoms one does not act, ". . . one does not *do* anything. Instead, *they just happen''* (Chapter 5, italics in the original). In contrast, Eagle views self-deception as an act. Indeed, he contrasts the development of symptoms with ordinary purposive behavior, that is, voluntary action.

The difficulty here seems to be in the reification of the phenomenological experience of some patients. Patients indeed may report at times that they experience their symptoms as unwanted behaviors that seem to "just happen" to them. Obsessions, fears, and fetishes are commonly reported to be ego-alien and ego-dystonic. Yet, it would seem that such a characterization hardly applies to all symptomatic behavior. Further, it would seem that the phenomenological experience that accompanies behavior is hardly relevant to determining what is meant by self-deception.

With regard to the issue of extension, symptoms expressed in disorders of mood are frequently not ego-alien. The depressed patient, who feels worthless and is self-critical and riddled with guilt, may likely claim that he or she has come to an accurate self-appraisal. The symptoms are not experienced as imposed from without, or an outcome of a mechanism outside of personal identity.

The more critical issue here is that the phenomenological experience of individuals regarding the "voluntariness" of their own behavior has no bearing on determining whether or not the behavior is an outcome of self-deception. Our beliefs are frequently the subject of our self-deceit. One would be hard pressed to characterize the "voluntariness" in our phenomenological experience when we establish beliefs. Is it a matter of voluntary or involuntary behavior that I believe I will have dinner tonight? Granted, at times, we may make ourselves believe something and expose ourselves selectively only to confirmatory evidence or refuse to listen to opposing views. It is highly questionable that such occurrences are prototypic of our instances of belief generation, in general, or of self-deception, in particular.

In my view, the distinction Eagle is raising here between repression and self-deception is untenable because he is not contrasting repression with self-deception. Rather, he is contrasting the language of action as applied to self-deception with reports of the phenomenological experience of individuals concerning the hypothetical *outcomes* of repression. It could well be argued that excessive utilization of self-deceptive strategies also results in symptomatic behavior, whose symptoms may or may not be experienced as ego-alien.

Motivation Versus Reflex

The second argument raised by Eagle is more difficult. He wishes to distinguish between **purposive behavior** and **motivated behavior**. He views repression as purposive, but not motivated, whereas self-deception reflects a motivated act. The major goal of repression is the avoidance of pain. However, this purpose is viewed much like a physiological function. Eagle views the goal-oriented aspect of repression as akin to stating that the function of the heart is to pump blood or that the function of gamma aminobutyric acid (GABA), a neurotransmitter, is to inhibit neuronal excitation. In contrast, he accepts the view that self-deception reflects motivated behavior (Sackeim & Gur, 1978).

There seems to be a fundamental problem with this argument. He appears to be stating that because self-deception reflects motivated behavior, self-deception is voluntary. Further, to Eagle voluntary behavior "is characterized by conscious goals, conscious beliefs, and implementing *action*" (Chapter 5, italics in the original). In contrast, he claims repression must be viewed as an involuntary mechanism, involving the pursuit of unconscious goals.

One must object strongly to the equating of motivated behavior with the awareness of goals and the establishment of conscious beliefs. One would think that one of the most significant contributions of Freud was raising the theoretical possibility that motives can determine behavior and yet that those motives may not be subject to awareness. Essentially, Eagle is curtailing the Freudian position to argue that repression does not extend to motivated behavior, but is reflexive in nature.

This problem can be highlighted by contrasting extreme positions on the nature of purpose and motives in self-deception. At one extreme, the formulations by Demos (1960) and Penelhum (1966) failed to attribute any form of purposefulness to self-deception. The insufficiency of their criteria was well described by Gardiner (1970):

> The role of motives in self-deception has been to some extent ignored or played down in recent discussions of the topic, yet it is surely crucial. It is, for example, not clear what could be meant by, or what justification there could be for, speaking of somebody as deceiving himself if it were at the same time contended that what he was said to be deceiving himself about was a matter of total indifference to him, in no way related to his wants, fears, hopes, and so forth: could we, e.g., intelligibly talk about "disinterested" or "gratuitous" self-deception? (p. 242)

The problem of the assimilation of self- and other-deception rears its head here, too. One can hardly speak of deceiving or lying to others as a matter of happenstance, as instances of reflexive or unmotivated behavior.

At the other extreme is the position taken by Fingarette (1969). He appeared to attribute full-blown intentionality to the act of self-deception. For instance, he stated that Demos, Siegler, Canfield, and Gustafson, and also Penelhum all failed to appreciate that the "deep paradox of self-deception lies in . . . intentional ignorance" (p. 29). He claimed that in self-deception "there is an over-riding reason *not* to spell-out some engagement, where we skillfully take account of this and systematically avoid spelling-out the engagement, and where, in turn, we refrain from spelling-out this exercise of our skill in spelling-out. In other words, we avoid becoming explicitly conscious that we are avoiding it" (p. 43). Fingarette, following Kierkegaard (1954) and Murphy (1965), called this "willful ignorance" (p. 47) and suggested that the act of self-deception reflects the exercise of a skill.

Eagle has adopted Fingarette's (1969) view of the "willful" nature of self-deception and has gone further by incorporating conscious intent as part of the motivational fabric. The phenomena in life that would fit Eagle's formulation are rather restricted. An example may be the following: Many of us set our watches or alarm clocks ahead with the deliberate intent of fooling ourselves about the real time. When we later consult our clocks, we may actively avoid spelling out our prior actions. Is this the essence of *motivated*, selective awareness?

Awareness It seems to me that we have little difficulty conceptualizing behavior as motivated in the absence of awareness of the motives. There is a long history in psychology of investigating the motivational determinants of the behavior of lower organisms (e.g., Irwin, 1971). When we observe a rat learning to run left or right in a T-maze as a function of the location of food and its history of food deprivation, we infer that the behavior was under motivational control. If the rat always runs to the left regardless of food location and history of food deprivation, we do not infer motive. The issue of awareness is independent of the attribution of motivation. We demonstrate that behavior is motivated by manipulating the hedonic value of outcomes and by showing that the occurrence of the behavior is dependent on the contingencies between behavior and outcomes.

In this light, we can intelligibly state that *when we lie to ourselves we are often not aware of our motives for doing so*, or for that matter, that we are engaging in self-deceit. Likewise, there appears to be no necessity in Eagle's restricting the operation of Freudian defense mechanisms to reflexive processes. This restriction in fact contradicts Freud's own formulation. Freud (1915/1957) claimed that repression was highly selective and that its operation was a function of the degree to which an idea (or wish) was distorted and of the prevailing hedonic circumstances. "The same result as follows from an increase or a decrease in degree of distortion may also be achieved at the other end of the apparatus, so to speak, by a modification in the condition for the production of pleasure and unpleasure" (pp. 150-151). In essence, Freud was adopting a similar framework for arguing that repression is driven by motivational factors. The critical determinants of whether or not a mental content would be repressed were the contingency between awareness of the mental content and the ensuing affective state and hedonic needs of the individual. The aim of repression, according to Freud, was the warding off of anxiety. Whether or not a mental content is to be repressed is determined by the extent to which awareness of the content would precipitate anxiety (i.e., the contingency) and the individual's capacity to tolerate anxiety. Indeed, a primary goal of much of psychoanalytically oriented psychotherapy is to lift repression by altering the contingencies between awareness or nonawareness of the mental content and the ensuing affective state. Likewise, Eagle's position runs against the psychoanalytic tradition of explicitly detailing what are termed the "motives for defense," which generally are said to be "governed by striving to avoid objects" (Fenichel, 1945, p. 140).

If one accepts the view that there is nothing inherently distinct about the motivational bases of self-deception, on the one hand, and repression on the other, then much of the rest of Eagle's formulation loses its force. He argues that repression is a subpersonal mechanism, a behavior of the organism, not the person. He states that self-deception is an act, with implications for moral responsibility and spiritual failure. He claims that no amount of effort or self-confrontation will undo repression, but that it may undo self-deception. These claims rest largely on the assumption that repression is a psychological reflex, whereas the motivated aspects of self-deception involve a conscious, deliberate intention to avoid self-knowledge. The analogy in learning theory terms is that repression operates through principles of classical conditioning, whereas self-deception is operant in nature. The view I suggest is that self-deception (and its instantiation as repression) must be viewed as "operant," otherwise, the selectivity of repression, its flexibility in extending to aspects of mental contents, and the theoretically claimed reversibility of repression in the context of psychoanalysis cannot be explained. By Eagle's formulation, psychoanalysis becomes a sophisticated form of systematic desensitization.

The Motivational Basis of Self-Deception

One of Eagle's contributions is the notion that, at times, self-deception may indeed contain a deliberate, conscious element. In the first statement Gur and I made about the meaning of self-deception, we suggested that the act that determined which belief was subject to awareness was motivated. We went further, in line with Sartre and Fingarette, and claimed that this act was itself not reflected upon. "Just as one cannot go to sleep while reflecting upon going to sleep, one cannot determine between beliefs to be denied while reflecting upon the determination" (Sackeim & Gur, 1978, pp. 150-151). This statement was in error. For example, setting our watches ahead to fool ourselves about the time is a likely exception to the statement. It may be that at times we are conscious of the act of determining what we will lie to ourselves about. I suggest, however, that while such an example may point to psychologically interesting variants of self-deception, the example is not prototypic. It may well be that *our success in creating and maintaining self-deception often depends on our lack of awareness of the process*. Particularly when what we lie to ourselves about are issues that are highly affectively-charged and critical to our self-esteem, it is improbable that we can establish sincere conviction in the self-deceits with conscious foreknowledge of the lie. Likewise, it would be a rather exceptional circumstance if we could successfully deceive others and share with them our explicit intention to do so.

The possibility that self-deception may at times permit awareness of the act of belief rejection makes the concept broader than the psychoanalytic notions of defense. By definition, defensive processes occur outside of awareness. This is an additional ground for considering self-deception superordinate to the classical concepts of defense. (For other grounds see Sackeim & Gur, 1978.)

The discussion of the position taken by Eagle raises problems with the exemplification of self-deception offered by Paulhus and Suedfeld (Chapter 8). They argue for a general psychological principle that the complexity of cognitive processing is reduced under conditions of emotional arousal. The evidence weighed in generating a belief may be evaluated on a restricted set of dimensions when individuals are highly aroused. In such circumstances, people will espouse beliefs that differ from what they would espouse otherwise. At issue is whether this information-processing model characterizes self-deception or an alternative set of phenomena.

Paulhus and Suedfeld's experiments   The main problem here also centers on the issue of motivation. Paulhus and Suedfeld describe experiments in which cognitive complexity is reduced by enhancing arousal through exposure to noise. Likewise, one would think that fatigue, psychoactive substances, and hunger would alter the complexity of cognitive judgment. Certainly, if an individual espouses a belief under these circumstances that contradicts a long-held belief, we would not readily assume self-deception. Inconsistency in our expression of beliefs, in itself, is insufficient. Indeed, in the framework developed by Paulhus and Suedfeld it is likely for an individual to be aware of the inconsistency or change in beliefs. The highly aroused individual may state, "I know I told you *p* yesterday, but I was wrong."

The contribution of Paulhus and Suedfeld is relevant to considerations of self-deception in three ways. First, they point to a set of phenomena that may be incorrectly interpreted as instances of self-deception. The characterization of self-deception Gur and I had offered (Sackeim & Gur, 1978; Sackeim, 1983) posits that the individual simultaneously holds contradictory beliefs. The person believes that *p* and *not-p* are true. One can adopt the position, however, that beliefs are not "held" like money in a vault. Rather, following a constructionist view of cognitive processes, beliefs are newly arrived at when espoused. Recall of evidence, memory for previous expressions of belief, current affective state, and a variety of other factors determine the content of a presently expressed belief. Following this formulation, there is no empirical reality to the concept of self-deception as we had defined it. Paulhus and Suedfeld have described an important set of factors that determine the nature of belief generation and that may well apply to phenomena that would appear on the surface to be instances of self-deception. They point out that apparently inconsistent and, at times, contradictory beliefs are expressed when arousal conditions are altered. Here it would be a mistake to assume that the individual simultaneously holds contradictory beliefs.

This formulation is compatible with models of a single stream of information processing. In many respects, it entails a less complicated view of psychological functioning and may be more in accord with evidence concerning the constructionist nature of perception and memory. The weakness in this view is that it does not deal adequately with conditions in which there are grounds to infer simultaneously held contradictory beliefs. For example, it does appear at times that individuals deny having a desire ("I have no homosexual inclinations"), but simultaneously act in ways that strongly suggest that they do have that desire ("but I prefer being with members of my own sex").

The second issue raised by Paulhus and Suedfeld is the suggestion of a set of phenomena that appear to more closely mimic self-deception in our original sense (Sackeim & Gur, 1978), but in which the holding of contradictory beliefs is, in fact, a matter of happenstance. Let us presume that John believes *p*. Under conditions of high arousal, there is a failure of recall or belief accessibility, as perhaps, when individuals state "I do not know what I believe anymore." Further, due to reduced cognitive complexity, the belief that is generated contradicts the long-held view, and John espouses *not-p*. This model might be termed **simultaneous inconsistency**, whereas the prior formulation might be termed **serial inconsistency**. The simultaneous inconsistency model fails to instantiate notions of self-deception in relation to the issue of motivation. It is not the affective consequences of believing *p* that lead John to espouse *not-p* or fail to recall his long-held belief, *p*. Rather, there has been a cognitive breakdown due to extrinsic factors, such as fatigue. Again this model may also provide an alternative formulation of some phenomena that are mislabeled as instances of self-deception.

The third possibility to emerge from Paulhus and Suedfeld involves considering whether they have provided a characterization of cognitive processes that may contribute to some instances of true self-deception. The central issue here is whether the purposeful, motivated character of self-deception is sufficiently addressed in their model. The most difficult case is when the holding of a belief itself generates arousal—thereby restricting cognitive complexity and belief accessibility—and results in the espousal of a contradictory belief.

I would tend to argue that in principle this is a fair formulation of psychological processes that may be involved in some instances of self-deception. Some writers might resist considering this model as adequate because of the temptation to view motivated behavior as directed by a "homunculus." In stating that the selective awareness of beliefs reflects a motivated act, there is a tendency to presume that whether conscious or unconscious, the act is "willful" in the sense of Fingarette (1969), Kierkegaard (1954), or Murphy (1965). Undoubtedly it is this tendency that brings issues of responsibility and morality into discussions of self-deception. At the same time, when we attempt to translate phenomena like self-deception into psychological processes, it is patently naive to insist on a homunculus.

Paulhus and Suedfeld's model   As indicated above, it would seem that in establishing whether or not behavior is under motivational control, it is critical to determine whether the frequency of the behavior is **contingency-dependent**. The basic issue here is whether awareness or unawareness of the belief is a function of whether the belief results in arousal. The model advanced by Paulhus and Suedfeld assumes precisely this. There is no reduction in cognitive complexity or interference with accessibility if the belief does not elicit arousal. Were we capable of changing the intrapsychic contingencies, we could manipulate which beliefs would and would not be subject to awareness. In this respect, the model would meet minimal criteria regarding the issue of motivation.

A second area of resistance concerns the effects of reduction in cognitive complexity on establishing an espoused inconsistent or contradictory belief. In the model, the espoused belief is a function of a simplification in cognitive processing. Ordinarily, when considering the nature of self-deception, we presume that not only is there a psychic gain in failing to espouse a belief, but that the expressed belief may also serve the individual. One could argue that by positing a reduction in cognitive complexity as the process responsible for the espoused belief generation,

Paulhus and Suedfeld have introduced a randomness that violates the purposefulness of self-deception. However, the response here is that the breakdown in cognitive processes is not random. Cognitive complexity is reduced so that the evaluative dimension is particularly salient. Indeed, based on this dimension, beliefs may be established in relation to their capacity to maintain or enhance self-esteem. By this analysis, therefore, Paulhus and Suedfeld have given a plausible account of the psychological processes involved in some instances of self-deception.

Lying to inflate self-esteem This model outlines only one possible set of processes that may be involved in some instances of self-deception. It may have particular difficulty with circumstances in which individuals lie to themselves in order to achieve a positive end, not to avoid anxiety. Elsewhere (Sackeim, 1983), I have argued that a central weakness in psychoanalytic formulations of the motives for defense is the presumption that we distort our beliefs only to avoid negative affect. It is quite likely that we are capable of establishing false beliefs to inflate our self-esteem. For example, do we not at times believe our own exaggerations of our accomplishments? These mood-enhancing, self-deceptive acts are not necessarily motivated by negative affect aroused by accurate appraisal. Just as we may lie to others not only to avoid loss but also to achieve a positive end, so we may deceive ourselves. The Paulhus and Suedfeld position may have difficulty in accounting for this type of self-deception in the sense that the belief not subject to awareness does not produce arousal. The motivational components are tied in to the fact that the espoused belief produces a greater ''good'' than does the unexpressed belief.

In summary, Paulhus and Suedfeld have described a set of psychological processes that may or may not be involved in instances of self-deception. The impact of arousal on cognition may extend to a far broader set of phenomena than self-deception. Interestingly, the simultaneous inconsistency formulation, in which externally elicited arousal leads to the generation of contradictory beliefs, may mimic self-deception in several details and provide for more practical experimental investigation.

The Content of Self-Deception: Beliefs Only?

Alternative formulations of the nature of self-deception differ in their accounts of what people lie to themselves about. In the original formulation offered by Gur and myself (Sackeim & Gur, 1978), we argued that to be self-deceived, the individual must hold simultaneously two contradictory beliefs: *p* and *not-p*. Much of the discussion in this chapter has centered on beliefs as the subject of self-deceit.

An objection may be raised to the claim that self-deception is a superordinate category subsuming psychoanalytic defense mechanisms because many defensive processes do not involve direct espousal of contradictory beliefs. The mechanism of **projection** may serve as an example. John is unable to admit to himself his hostile impulses towards Bill. Rather, he believes that Bill hates him. Clearly the proposition ''John hates Bill'' and ''Bill hates John'' are not contradictory. Therefore, projection cannot be a form of self-deception and perhaps only mechanisms of repression and denial are instances of self-deception as defined by Sackeim and Gur (1978).

In my view this is not a major difficulty. Psychoanalytic theory presumes that all defensive processes involve rejection of a mental content and, at times, the disguised expression of that content. In believing that Bill hates him, John actively avoids the knowledge that he hates Bill. In essence the avowed belief serves psychologically to express the belief that John does not hate Bill. Put another way, psychoanalytic theorists must assume that if John were confronted with the statement "You hate Bill," he would deny it. In this respect, self-deception is intrinsic to the operation of all defensive processes.

A more difficult problem arises when we consider whether the content of self-deception is restricted to **beliefs**. As we have seen, much of the philosophy of mind literature discusses self-deception in relation to the avowal or disavowal of beliefs and the avoidance of knowledge, and in terms of motivated ignorance. This is a serious restriction of perspective.

To illustrate this problem, take the example of the hypnotic "virtuoso" who is given the suggestion of complete blindness. My colleagues and I reported on two such subjects (Sackeim, Nordlie, & Gur, 1979) and I have recent experience with a third. Two of the three subjects performed at 100% accuracy in a variety of visual discrimination tasks while simultaneously claiming total blindness and receiving no performance feedback. The subjects were tested over several occasions, and one of them was administered several thousand trials. This subject reported complete absence of visual stimulation ("Everything was pitch black") and yet failed to make a single error on any trial. The subject did report having "hunches" or feelings as to the correct choices and typically estimated his performance accuracy over a series of trials as approximately 60%. When confronted at the end of the study with the data of perfect performance, the subject expressed dismay and shock.

Presuming that he truly believed that he was not experiencing visual stimulation, that he was indeed blind, could we fairly attribute contradictory beliefs? Certainly, at a superficial level, his performance data indicated that he was "seeing." However, to claim that the subject believed both that he could not see and that he could see may be trading in on the ambiguity of what we mean by "seeing." It is quite possible that the hypnotically blind subject was not aware of visual images and yet gave veridical reports that he experienced total darkness. We impute that he could "see" from the data that extensive processing of visual information took place and that the products of the processing were available to the subject. However, as in cases of blind-sight secondary to brain damage (Weiskrantz, Warrington, Sanders, & Marshall, 1974), the products of such processing may be experienced as hunches or feelings about the nature of what is out there in the visual environment without there being visual representation in awareness. The phenomenological report of blindness and the accurate judgment behavior reflect different aspects of the stream of information processing. It would not be appropriate to infer that the subject believed at some level that he was not momentarily blind. Therefore, he was not characterized by contradictory beliefs. This example illustrates, I believe, the important contribution offered by Greenwald. When we attempt to be more precise in examining the content of self-deception, we are in danger of opening a Pandora's box with respect to identifying the mental contents about which we lie to ourselves.

Transforming mental content   This problem can be illustrated from another direction. As Eagle (Chapter 5) pointed out, in psychoanalytic theory the usual objects of repression are not beliefs but rather wishes, impulses, and affects. In the projection example, while it may be the case that John believes Bill hates him, it is not the case that he unconsciously believes that he hates Bill. He does unconsciously hate him, but has no belief regarding this. The aggressive impulses, not an inference or a belief, are being denied.

In essence, we must deal with a situation in which the self-reports of individuals frequently express propositions that would contradict other mental contents were those mental contents *transformed* into propositional form. Alice may believe she does not hate Joan. Her behavior and other signs indicate that she does hate Joan. It involves a leap to suggest that Alice both hates Joan and at some level *believes* that she hates Joan. It is only when this last step is justified that we are entitled to attribute simultaneous contradictory beliefs and consider the ascription of self-deception in the strong form suggested by Sackeim and Gur (1978).

The difficulty in empirical investigation of the ontological status of this strong form of self-deception centers on identifying the conditions that justify ascription of a belief. If we permit a distinction between hating someone and believing that one does so, then it should be evident that somewhat different criteria are involved in establishing that either is the case. We have particular problems in providing operational criteria for beliefs that are not subject to awareness. Our usual grounds for establishing that individuals do hold a belief is to determine whether or not they report such a belief under circumstances in which we accept the sincerity or honesty of the report. The strong form of self-deception posits that individuals are capable of the levels of symbolic representation involved in belief generation with both the information processing and the products of the processing occurring outside of awareness.

The problem in determining whether a mental content merits consideration as a belief is perhaps less difficult when the mental content does not pertain to an affective state or impulse, or to features of a stimulus in the present perceptual environment. If there is evidence that individuals have derived an evaluation of an external object (e.g., John is evil; walking under ladders is dangerous), we may be on safer ground in inferring that the mental content reflects belief. It is precisely when the mental content is specific to the affective state of the individual (''I am angry'') or to an impulse (''I want to help you'') that there are greater difficulties in determining whether the mental content merits status as belief. Furthermore, the prototypic experimental investigations of self-deception (e.g., Gur & Sackeim, 1979) rely on paradigms in which subjects report on perceptual experiences, and contradictory "beliefs" are inferred from stimulus-dependent changes in other response systems. In this circumstance, it is extremely difficult to determine whether the unconscious mental content merits status as a belief.

Varieties of self-deception   The essence of this discussion is agreement with Greenwald that there may be varieties of self-deception. To use his terminology, the strong form of self-deception would require a "coordinate unconscious" in the sense that full symbolic representation and belief generation is said to occur without awareness. This presumably is what is meant when in everyday language we are told "You *know* in your heart that I am right" or "Deep inside you *know* the truth." Such colloquial usage posits not just that early stages of information processing are not subject to awareness, but also that full-blown inferences are not subject to awareness. Further, to extend Greenwald's ideas, the problem for the strong form of self-deception is not just with the distinction among stages of information processing, but also with affective states, wishes, and impulses. The common use of self-deception suggests reflection upon or knowledge of such mental contents without awareness.

We must face the possibility that frequently the mental contents that are out of our awareness are not the subject of our beliefs. I may truly dislike Joe, be unaware of my feelings towards him, and never generate the belief that I dislike him. Indeed, following Greenwald, the failure to generate this belief may be triggered by the consequences of my feelings towards Joe. I may be uncomfortable around him and restrict further processing of Joe-related cognition. I am left with the consciously held belief that I have no feelings towards Joe, one way or the other. In a strict logical sense, my belief of absence of feelings is not incompatible with the mental content of dislike. The domains of beliefs and feelings are logically distinct. Nonetheless, we would commonly consider this to be an instance of self-deception.

My suggestion here is that we broaden the conceptualization of self-deception to include weaker varieties. These weaker forms may involve incompatibility between an avowed belief and the propositional translations of mental contents of any variety. In essence, I suggest that we consider mental contents as if they had reached the status of beliefs. (In some respects this is akin to Fingarette's notion of failure to spell out.) By including weaker forms of self-deception, the concept is extended well beyond the realm of belief. The four criteria for ascribing self-deception originally proposed by Gur and myself (Sackeim & Gur, 1978) still apply with incorporation of this modification. Formally, the revised criteria would be as follows:

1. The individual has two mental contents, which if expressed as propositions are contradictory (p and *not-p*).
2. These two mental contents occur simultaneously.
3. The individual is not aware of one of the mental contents.
4. The operation that determines which mental content is and which is not subject to awareness is motivated.

CONCLUSIONS

This critical review of the theoretical contributions to this volume has highlighted some of the conceptual problems that surround the topic of self-deception. It has been emphasized that there are probably a variety of ways in which mental experience is distorted that are not necessarily instances of self-deception. Furthermore, within the domain of self-deception there is variability. One of the possibilities raised here is that at times people may initiate a process of self-deceit and be aware of doing so (the watch-setting example). Perhaps more critically, the issue of the content of self-deception raises unique problems. The tendency to restrict discussion of the topic to incompatible beliefs is now viewed as overly simplistic and pertinent to what might be termed the strong version of self-deception. Weaker versions may allow for incompatibility between different domains of mental experience. The introduction of different varieties of self-deception allows for new approaches to alternative information-processing models of the phenomena and for new investigations of the psychological conditions that predispose to strong and weak self-deception.

REFERENCES

ABRAMSON, L. Y., & MARTIN, D. (1981). Depression and the causal inference processes. In J. Harvey, W. Ickes, & R. Kidd (Eds.), *New directions in attribution research* (Vol. 3, pp. 117-168). Hillsdale, NJ: Erlbaum.

CANFIELD, J. W., & GUSTAFSON, D. F. (1962). Self-deception. *Analysis, 23*, 32-36.

DEMOS, R. (1960). Lying to oneself. *Journal of Philosophy, 57*, 588-595.

DIXON, N. F. (1971). *Subliminal perception: The nature of a controversy.* London: McGraw-Hill.

FENICHEL, O. (1945). *The psychoanalytic theory of neurosis.* New York: W. W. Norton.

FINGARETTE, H. (1969). *Self-deception.* London: Routledge & Kegan Paul.

FREUD, S. (1957). Repression. In J. Strachey (Ed. and Trans.), *The standard edition of the complete psychological works of Sigmund Freud* (Vol. 14, pp. 143-158). London: Hogarth Press. (Original work published 1915.)

GARDINER, P. L. (1970). Error, faith, and self-deception. *Proceedings of the Aristolelian Society, 50*, 221-243.

GREENWALD, A. G. (1980). The totalitarian ego: Fabrication and revision of personal history. *American Psychologist, 35*, 603-618.

GUR, R. C., & SACKEIM, H. A. (1979). Self-deception: A concept in search of a phenomenon. *Journal of Personality and Social Psychology, 37*, 147-169.

IRWIN, F. W. (1971). *Intentional behavior and motivation: A cognitive theory.* Philadelphia: Lippincott.

KIERKEGAARD, S. (1954). *The sickness unto death* (W. Lowrie, Trans.). New York: Anchor.

LOCKARD, J. S. (1980). Speculations on the adaptive significance of self-deception. In J. S. Lockard (Ed.), *The evolution of social behavior* (pp. 257-275). New York: Elsevier.

MARCEL, A. J. (1983). Conscious and unconscious perception: An approach to the relations between phenomenal experience and perceptual processes. *Cognitive Psychology, 15*, 238-300.

MATHEWS, A., & MACLEOD, C. (1986). Discrimination of threat cues without awareness in anxiety states. *Journal of Abnormal Psychology, 95*, 131-138.

MURPHY, A. E. (1965). *The theory of practical reason.* Chicago: Open Court.

NISBETT, R. E., & WILSON, T. D. (1977). Telling more than we can know: Verbal reports on mental processes. *Psychological Review, 84*, 231-259.

PAULHUS, D. L. (1982). Individual differences, cognitive dissonance, and self-presentation: Their concurrent operation in forced compliance. *Journal of Personality and Social Psychology, 43*, 838-852.

————. (1984). Two-component models of socially desirable responding. *Journal of Personality and Social Psychology, 46*, 598-609.

————. (1986). Self-deception and impression management in test responses. In A. Angleitner & J. S. Wiggins (Eds.), *Personality assessment via questionnaire* (pp. 143-165). New York: Springer-Verlag.

PENELHUM, T. (1966). Pleasure and falsity. In S. Hampshire (Ed.), *Philosophy of mind* (pp. 242-266). New York: Harper & Row.

PLATO. (1953). Cratylus. In R. Jowett (Ed. and Trans.), *The dialogues of Plato* (Vol. 3). Oxford: Clarendon Press. (Original work published circa 386 B.C.).

QUATTRONE, G. A., & TVERSKY, A. (1984). Causal versus diagnostic contingencies: On self-deception and on the voter's illusion. *Journal of Personality and Social Psychology, 46*, 237-248.

ROTH, D. L., & INGRAM, E. R. (1985). Factors in the Self-Deception Questionnaire: Associations with depression. *Journal of Personality and Social Psychology, 47*, 243-251.

SACKEIM, H. A. (1983). Self-deception, self-esteem, and depression: The adaptive value of lying to oneself. In J. Masling (Ed.), *Empirical studies of psychoanalytical theory*. (Vol. 1, pp. 101-157). Hillsdale, NJ: The Analytic Press.

————. (1986). A psychoneurodynamic perspective on the self: Brain, thought, emotion. In L. M. Hartman & R. Blankstein (Eds.), *Perception of self in emotional disorder and psychotherapy* (pp. 51-83). New York: Plenum.

SACKEIM, H. A., & GUR, R. C. (1978). Self-deception, self-confrontation, and consciousness. In G. E. Schwartz & D. Shapiro (Eds.), *Consciousness and self-regulation: Advances in research* (Vol. 2, pp. 139-197). New York: Plenum.

SACKEIM, H. A., NORDLIE, J. W., & GUR, R. C. (1979). A model of hysterical and hypnotic blindness: Cognition, motivation, and awareness. *Journal of Abnormal Psychology, 88*, 474-489.

SACKEIM, H. A., & WEGNER, A. (1986). Attributional patterns in depression and euthymia. *Archives of General Psychiatry, 43*, 553-560.

SARBIN, T. R. (1984). Nonvolition in hypnosis: A semiotic analysis. *Psychological Record, 334*, 537-549.

SARTRE, J. P. (1958). *Being and nothingness: An essay on phenomenological ontology* (H. Barnes, Trans.). London: Methuen. (Original work published 1943.)

TESSER, A., & PAULHUS, D. (1983). The definition of self: Private and public self-evaluation management strategies. *Journal of Personality and Social Psychology, 4*, 672-682.

TRIVERS, R. (1985). *Social evolution*. Menlo Park, CA: Benjamin/Cummings.

WEINSTEIN, N. D. (1980). Unrealistic optimism about future life events. *Journal of Personality and Social Psychology, 39*, 806-820.

WEISKRANTZ, L., WARRINGTON, E. K., SANDERS, M. D., & MARSHALL, J. (1974). Visual capacity in the hemianopic field following a restricted occipital ablation. *Brain, 97*, 709-728.

BEHAVIOR

AND APPLICATIONS

No understanding of self-deception as an adaptive mechanism would be complete without coverage of the application of self-deceit to daily life. Therefore, this segment of the book is charged with providing evidence for the utility of self-deception in the "market place." The impetus to seek data on the applied significance of self-deception emanated, in part, from a symposium by Lockard et al. (1982), where it was suggested that the test bed for a suspected adaptation is in the quantification of the behavior of individuals. The data to be presented provide some measure of the merit in considering self-deception as a common phenomenon, detectable in the interactions of others.

Chapters 10 (Hartung), 11 (Hayano), 12 (Essock, McGuire, and Hooper), and 13 (Whittaker-Bleuler) provide behavioral applications of self-deception in situations of subordination, gambling, social-support networks, and sports. Fittingly, the last chapter (Ekman) is concerned with the detection of misinformation and the role of self-deceit in the successful deception of others.

Hartung's hypothesis is that people use self-deception to lower their self-esteem when it is to their advantage to occupy a position for which they are initially overqualified. (Self-deceiving down is regarded as the opposite process of self-deceiving up, Goffman, 1959, 1971.) Consider a man whose job is lower ranking than he deserves—if he has no hope of advancement he may eventually, through self-deception, convince himself that he is commensurate with his status. This downward adjustment of self-esteem enables psychological, social, and economic security that would otherwise be in jeopardy. The disparity between his perceived and actual status would be reconciled, allowing him to accept bureaucratic superiors as actual superiors. In turn, such reconciliation would enhance his ability to behave submissively toward them, make everyone more comfortable with his presence, and increase his likelihood of remaining employed. This theme of deceiving down is developed within the framework of general self-deception, and the prediction is made that females tend to self-deceive down more than males. Thus, it follows (as the pertinent data suggest, Amenson & Lewinsohn, 1981) that more females than males suffer from "down" psychopathologies.

Hayano begins his chapter by enumerating several stereotypic views of gamblers: The accepted wisdom suggests that most gamblers indulge themselves in much more self-deception and fantasy than do nongamblers. Indeed, the testimonials from gamblers themselves tend repeatedly to emphasize these traits (Hayano, 1982). Furthermore, self-deception and fantasy are usually seen to be highly maladaptive and ultimately destructive (Moran, 1970; Custer, 1978). The approach taken by Hayano is not to challenge such claims immediately, but rather to examine the social conditions under which self-deception and fantasy are most likely to occur and be supported. It is argued that wide expressive variation in these states can be found among both gamblers and nongamblers as common adaptational responses to uncertainty. The ways by which gamblers "deal with life" in their chance activities are intended to illuminate more general problems of social organization and styles of coping with an unpredictable world.

Essock, McGuire, and Hooper propose that altruism, being ultimately selfish, may rely critically on self-deception. To test this thesis, self-report data were gathered from a random sample of 300 white, middle-class women, ages 35–45 (Essock-Vitale & McGuire, 1985). Detailed questioning (including reliability measures from local siblings) established each subject's pattern of giving and receiving help from family and friends. Measures included the availability of potential helping partners and their actual patterns of helping. The analyses concentrated on differences between the subjects' perceptions of potential sources of help (e.g., kin, friends) and the actual sources reported, noting those factors that appear to influence one's likelihood of helping (e.g., kinship, age, wealth, reproductive history). The authors also address the subjects' ability to assess accurately the amount of assistance forthcoming from non-kin, examining, in particular, deviations from subjects' expectations of reciprocity and actual practice. The data suggest that some subjects appear to be able to assess more accurately (i.e., to self-deceive less) than others regarding who will be good exchange partners; hence, characteristics predictive of self-deception seem to be specifiable.

Whittaker-Bleuler focuses on deception and self-deception as a dominance strategy in competitive sport. She attempts to model the conditions under which deception and self-deception are likely to be manifested in tennis by drawing on data from a study designed to investigate the use of nonverbal behavior to detect whether players are winning or losing (Whittaker-Bleuler, 1980). One hundred sixty experienced adult tennis players and an equal number of adults who were not experienced players participated in the study. Videotaped episodes of championship players were viewed without knowledge of point or match outcome. The subjects made a judgment of point won or lost on each episode and also expressed their degree of confidence in their judgment. Experienced subjects were significantly better than inexperienced subjects at detecting won and lost points and expressed more confidence in their judgments. The author speculates that awareness of such nonverbal messages may optimize success by increasing confidence against an opponent who is displaying losing behavior and by allowing a player to exhibit a winning message even after losing a point. Such behavior could be very disconcerting to the opponent, leading ultimately to the sender's success. It follows, therefore, that the need to be convincing is greatest when one's behavior is antithetic to both the total number of previous points won and the immediate outcome, and when the opponent is skilled rather than average. With some exceptions, the data supported the model.

In Chapter 14, Ekman distinguishes self-deceit from deceit and suggests that self-deception is *not* a form of lying. Although self-deception may be successful in the transmission of misinformation, it is the intentional, deliberate misleading of another person which the author regards as a lie (Ekman, 1985). The main focus of the discourse is the question of why lies fail, that is, why people sometimes make mistakes when they lie. Several reasons having to do with the preparation of the liar and the emotions involved in the lie are elucidated. Types of social situations when lies would be most and least likely to succeed are also discussed. The chapter ends, as does the book, on the note that although self-deception is not lying in the usual sense, it does hinder the detection of untruths, the discovery of which would lay bare many interpersonal relationships. As such, self-deception should be regarded as a positive and more frequent process then heretofore recognized.

REFERENCES

AMENSON, C. S., & LEWINSOHN, P. M. (1981). An investigation into the observed sex difference in prevalence of unipolar depression. *Journal of Abnormal Psychology, 90*, 1-13.

CUSTER, R. L. (1978). Pathological gambling. In *Diagnostic and Statistical Manual of Mental Disorders* (3rd ed.). Washington DC: American Psychiatric Association.

EKMAN, P. (1985). *Telling lies: Clues to deceit in the marketplace, politics, and marriage.* New York and London: W. W. Norton.

ESSOCK-VITALE, S., & MCGUIRE, M. (1985a). Women's lives viewed from an evolutionary perspective. I. Sexual histories, reproductive success, and demographic characteristics of a random sample of American women. *Ethology and Sociobiology, 6*, 137-154.

———. (1985b). Women's lives viewed from an evolutionary perspective. II. Patterns of helping. *Ethology and Sociobiology, 6*, 155-173.

GOFFMAN, E. (1959). *The presentation of self in everyday life.* New York: Doubleday.

———. (1971). *Strategic interaction.* Philadelphia: University of Pennsylvania Press.

HAYANO, D. M. (1982). *Poker faces: The life and work of professional card players.* Berkeley: University of California Press.

LOCKARD, J. S. (COORDINATOR), ESSOCK-VITALE, S. M., HARTUNG, J., KRAKAUER, D., WELLES, J., & WHITTAKER-BLEULER, S. (1982). Self-deception: An adaptive strategy? (symposium). *International Journal of Primatology, 3*, Abstract No. 3.

MORAN, E. (1970). Gambling as a form of dependence. *British Journal of Addiction, 64*, 419-428.

WHITTAKER-BLEULER, S. A. (1980). Detection of nonverbal winning and losing behavior in sport. *Research Quarterly, 51*, 437-440.

10

Deceiving Down

CONJECTURES ON THE MANAGEMENT OF SUBORDINATE STATUS

JOHN HARTUNG

State University of New York,
Health Science Center at Brooklyn

MAKING THE FOOT FIT THE SHOE

The hypothesis here is that people use self-deception to lower their self-esteem when it is to their advantage to be satisfied with a position which they would otherwise perceive as unfair. Consider a man whose job is lower ranking than he knows he deserves. If he has no hope of advancement he may eventually, through self-deception, convince himself that he is commensurate with his job's status. Instead of seeing himself as too good for his job, this form of self-deception will enable him to reconcile the disparity between his self-image and his reality. That will allow him to see his bureaucratic superiors as actual superiors and enhance his ability to behave subordinately toward them. In turn, everyone will become more comfortable with his presence, and he will increase his likelihood of remaining employed. Accordingly, downward adjustment of self-esteem can facilitate psychological, social, and economic security that would otherwise be in jeopardy (see Rosman & Burke, 1980, for the relationship among work satisfaction, self-esteem, and competence).

I am grateful to the late Erving Goffman for encouragement, advice, and inspiration. I thank Felix Barroso and John Pfeiffer for constructive criticism and patience; James E. Cottrell and the Department of Anesthesiology, SUNY Health Science Center at Brooklyn, for support; and Gloria J. Evans and Vena R. Crichlow for processing these words.

For example, this man could be a bookkeeper who knows more about accounting than his boss knows. In order to lower his self-esteem and consequently his self-image, he might recall his school days and dwell upon a section of an accounting textbook that he never understood. Without going back to the book, he can reconstruct his conundrum, causing himself to feel the same sense of insecurity that he felt so keenly on the night before the final exam. Without being explicitly cognizant (without actually saying so to himself), he imagines that all *real* accountants understand that section of that textbook. If he recollects this insecurity often enough, eventually it will not need to be rehearsed. It will come to him out of context, but it will come at appropriate times. It will come when his boss insists that he use an inappropriate debiting procedure. It will come when he gets only half of the raise that he expected. It will come when someone else is complimented for work that he did. It will come when the boss's son is rude to him, and so forth.

Up and Down

Self-deceiving *down* is the mirror image of self-deceiving *up*—a process described through example in works by Goffman (e.g., 1959, 1971) and discussed in the abstract by literary figures, philosophers, and psychologists (e.g., Gide, 1926/1955; Sartre, 1943/1958; Camus, 1956/1957; Fingarette, 1969). Self-deceiving up means raising one's self-esteem in order to occupy a position for which one is initially underqualified. Whether self-deceit is up or down, manipulation of self-esteem can be a self-fulfilling prophecy. That is, if one has not lowered or raised one's self-esteem too much, anxiety over the disparity between self-image (consciously perceived) and reality (subconsciously perceived) may motivate one to work toward an adjustment of actual competence (or incompetence).

Deceiving down is distinct from affects like "playing dumb" to gain short-term social facility with people who are anxious about their own relative worth. That is, pretending to be less than you are requires self-confidence, but actually becoming less than you were, or otherwise would have been, requires a reduction of confidence. Self-deceiving down is required in long-term situations, like being an employee or a spouse, in which compatibility through subordination is required over so many years of close interaction that ploys would be found out (see Gove, Huges, & Geerken, 1980, on playing dumb and men's propensity to do so more frequently than women).

Other-Deceit → Detection → Self-Deceit → Effective Other-Deceit

Trivers put self-deceiving up in an evolutionary framework (1971, 1976, 1985). His reasoning followed from the observation that many animals have evolved an ability to deceive others in a social context. A concrete example would be a blowfish "lying" about his size by literally inflating himself. Trivers's logic extends to subtle interactions between higher vertebrates (in which animals often figuratively inflate themselves) and to the speculation that strong selection pressures have acted upon individual abilities to deceive and detect deception, especially in organisms capable of engaging in "reciprocal altruism" (see also Axelrod & Hamilton, 1981). Alexander (1975) has applied the same logic to people's perceptions of their own motivations, concluding that individuals can be more effectively selfish if they perceive themselves as altruistic.

The evolution of self-deceit follows from an escalating spiral of selection for ability to deceive and ability to detect deception. That is, if an individual can deceive himself or herself (by virtue of having a dual system of awareness— conscious and subconscious—see Lockard, Chapters 1 and 2), he or she will be able to deceive others while maintaining the behavioral cues that go along with telling the truth (see Ekman, Chapter 14). So deception through self-deception is less detectable than "straight" deception, and the escalating interplay between ability-to-deceive and ability-to-detect-deception has become so internalized that people have a conscious ability to interpret their perceptions in a manner that enables them to behave in their own self-interest while subconsciously perceiving enough of the truth to know where their advantage lies. In this sense humans may be the only organism in which the self can be considered a social unit; that is, the self has social interaction with itself, controlling information transfer between the conscious and subconscious in order to manipulate its own behavior, in much the way that an individual in an aggregate of individuals controls information in order to manipulate the perceived image, self-image, and behavior of others (see Jones, 1986, for a review of the latter phenomenon).

Self-Control

Self-deceit for the purpose of manipulating one's dealings with one's self has been empirically demonstrated by Alloy and Abramson (1979; Abramson & Alloy, 1981). They found that normal people (as distinct from depressed people) consistently delude themselves about the amount of control they have over outcomes. In a series of games in which the players' actual amount of control was secretly influenced by the experimenter, if things turned out well (the experimental subject won money), normal subjects overestimated their responsibility for the result. If things turned out poorly, normals assessed their degree of control as much less than it actually was. Depressed subjects, on the other hand, made consistently accurate assessments of their degree of control. In the authors' words:

> One adaptive consequence of being biased to view the self as the cause of successes but not failures may be the maintenance or enhancement of self-esteem. A second adaptive consequence of the nondepressive style of causal inference may be invulnerability to depressive reactions in the face of failure. . . . Greenwald (1980) speculated that the bias to view the self as the cause of positive but not negative outcomes may increase behavioral persistence. . . .

> It is tempting to further speculate that contrary to the cognitive theories of depression, the depressive's problem is not that he or she suffers from the presence of depressogenic cognitive biases, but rather that he or she suffers from an absence of nondepressive cognitive biases. (1981, p. 445)

In plainer English, the speculation is that some self-deceit is essential for mental health and an insufficient amount (too accurate a perception of self) causes, and is caused by, depression. If this is the case, its generalization contradicts the underlying assumption of psychoanalysis: that leading a patient to an accurate perception of self, through self-insight, is the key to mental health.

Deceiving Down

The permutation to be added here is that self-deceiving down, like self-deceiving up, can also be an adaptive behavior, as opposed to a noise-in-the-system byproduct or maladaptation. The logic is that situations have commonly existed, over evolutionary time, in which it is to an individual's reproductive advantage (in gaining material, social, and sexual security) to convincingly occupy a subordinate position and/or engage a dependency which confers benefits that recoup more than the manipulated loss.

An important contemporary example might be the position of being the wife of a man whose success in self-deceiving up has significant impact on family income. That is, if a man makes a living in a manner that is affected by other people's assessments of his ability to do his job, the impression he gives regarding his competence may be subject to enhancement by self-deceiving up. If the person he spends much of his off-the-job time with can enhance his ability to self-deceive up, they can both profit from his resulting success. Unfortunately, that latter enhancement may often require his wife to self-deceive *down*—building her husband's self-confidence by providing a standard of lower competence (see Lundgren, Jergens, & Gibson, 1980, for the importance of marital solidarity to wives and self-evaluation to husbands). If, in addition, this woman works at a job in which subordinate behavior is required, her ability to self-deceive down may make the difference between having a home and family or losing both.

The implications of self-deceiving down are as multifarious and nefarious as one's imagination compels, but I would like to focus on just three aspects: (1) sex bias in the direction of self-deceit, (2) the relationship between self-deceit and psychopathology, and (3) deceiving down as a link between psychopathology and disparity in economic opportunity.

SEX BIAS

The expected bias is that females self-deceive down more easily and more frequently, and males self-deceive up more easily and more frequently. This prediction follows, at a distal level of causation, from the across-sex difference in within-sex variance for reproductive success (with males having much higher variance potential). That is, since a man with ten wives can have more children than could a woman with ten husbands, male success has been more dependent on direct competition with other males for possession of females, with the quantity of mates having more effect than the duration and stability of each relationship (see Trivers, 1972; Hartung, 1976, 1981a). Given the variance constraints inherent to bearing, nursing, and rearing children, female success has probably more frequently depended on an ability to attract and remain compatible with successful (especially economically successful) males (Hartung, 1981b, 1982, 1985, and references therein). It follows that men have more often been in a position in which self-deceiving up has been to their reproductive advantage (as a strategy when competing with other males and when advertising ability to invest in females), and self-deceiving down has more frequently been to the advantage of females (as a strategy for being nonthreatening, supportive, dependent, and assuring of fidelity). Accordingly, there may be some inherent difference in propensity to self-deceive in each direction (e.g., Hogan's 1978 review of female and male estimates of other's intelligence).

A growing literature indicates that there is a positive relationship between high self-esteem and a tendency to positively deceive one's self about one's attributes (e.g., Monts, Zurcher, & Nydegger, 1977; Ickes & Layden, 1978), and there is evidence that a positive relationship exists between low self-esteem and a tendency to negatively deceive one's self about one's attributes (Korabik & Pitt, 1981). Sackeim and Gur (1979) have found a negative relationship between self-reported psychopathology scores and the tendency to self-deceive (see also Gur & Sackeim, 1979). They conclude that since "there is no evidence to date indicating that actual psychopathology is inversely associated with degree of self-deceptive behavior, the most plausible interpretation of the findings is that the more likely individuals are to engage in self-deception, the less likely they are to report psychopathology" (p. 215). Leaving plausibility to the eye of the beholder, a more straightforward interpretation of Sackeim and Gur's finding is that the data mean just what they say: that self-deceit, as employed in a population of normal college students, is a mechanism for maintaining mental health and that those who self-deceive effectively are mentally healthier (as suggested by Abramson & Alloy, 1981; see also Lewinsohn, Mischel, Chaplain & Barton, 1980). Indeed, the Self-Deception Questionnaire devised by Sackeim and Gur is directed only toward detecting propensity to self-deceive up (as distinguished here), and they found that the negative relationship between self-deceit and self-reported psychopathology is significantly stronger for males. This accords with the predicted sex bias.

If it is true that self-esteem is manipulated by self-deceit, evidence from Hinrichsen, Follansbee, and Ganellen (1981) also supports the predicted sex bias. Males and females were rated for masculinity and femininity (BEM Sex-Role Inventory) and divided into sex-typed individuals (masculine males, feminine females), and cross sex-typed individuals (feminine males, masculine females). Masculine females tended to rate their physical, social, and overall self-satisfaction higher than did feminine females. The opposite held for males: cross sex-typed males (feminine males) rated themselves lower than did sex-typed males.

Evidence bearing more directly on the element of self-deceit comes again from the elegant experiments of Alloy and Abramson (1979; see also Alloy & Abramson, 1982; Tabachnik, Crocker, & Alloy, 1983; and Crocker, Tabachnik-Kayne, & Alloy, 1985). When nondepressed subjects were asked to explain their judgments about the degree to which they controlled outcomes, they used "invalid heuristics" (like the absolute number of times that a favorable outcome occurred, regardless of the number of times they tried to obtain that outcome) and tended to justify their fallacious reasoning by noting overall success (e.g., in the face of obviously illogical "reasoning," they would point to winning $5 as evidence that they controlled outcomes). A revealing sex difference in this result is that males' "illusions of control" were "larger and, in fact, quite pronounced" (Alloy & Abramson, 1979, p. 468) when there was little emphasis put on rationality. That is, when males realized that they would have to explain their assessment, they tended to judge their degree of control more accurately, but when there was no explanation required, their tendency to delude themselves greatly increased. There was no apparent difference for nondepressed females in this regard (again, depressed persons of both sexes tended to make accurate judgments about their degree of control and used rational logic to explain their judgments, so being required to make explanations had no effect on their accuracy). The inference I draw here is that those who habitually self-deceive up to maintain their self-esteem must be careful in situations in which they will be held immediately accountable to a rational or objective standard. That is, just as people do not lie to others when they know that the truth will soon be apparent, so they do not lie to themselves under that condition. This holds for "up" lies more than "down" lies, because it is much easier to get away with falsely failing than with falsely succeeding. That is, under conditions in which it is adaptive to lie "down" (in order to secure subordinate or dependent status), one is not likely to be challenged by superiors who are being accommodated. Conversely, lying "up" is often to someone else's disadvantage, and thus is more subject to challenge. Accordingly, the sex difference in sensitivity to anticipated accountability is in the predicted direction.

Psychopathology

Though self-deceit up or down, when functioning properly, is conjectured here to be a mechanism for maintaining mental/emotional equilibrium, it can only do so as long as the discrepancy between self-image and reality is manageable. If that discrepancy becomes too large, if one's conscious perception and subconscious perception are untenably disparate, mental dysfunction and/or malfunction are likely results (see Mischel, 1974; Miller & Norman, 1981; Schafer & Keith, 1981; Gotlib, 1982). Three general outcomes of too large a discrepancy are: (1) the individual reduces the discrepancy by adjusting his or her conscious perception, that is, reduces the amount of self-deception by facing reality (whether that reality is that the individual is *not* worthy of a position obtained or aspired to, or that the individual *is* worthy of a position that cannot be obtained and so should not be aspired to); (2) the individual reduces the discrepancy by adjusting subconscious perception, that is, loses touch with reality and/or maintains multiple accommodating delusional realities (schizophrenia); or (3) the individual does not adjust conscious or subconscious perception (does not reduce the amount of discrepancy) but puts his or her mind into a sort of holding pattern regarding affective behavior and motivation, that is, becomes depressed in the clinical sense (as distinct from being sad, dismayed, and disillusioned while maintaining affective behavior and motivation, as accompanies outcome 1—see Lewinsohn, Steinmetz, Larson, & Franklin, 1981; Raps, Peterson, Reinhard, Abramson, & Seligman, 1982).

Sex Bias and Psychopathology: DSM III

Too much up self-deceit may lead to different sorts of syndromes than too much down self-deceit. The hypothesis put forth here suggests a sex difference in psychopathologies: females have more down disorders (straight depression) and males have more up and up-to-down disorders (euphoria and manic depression).

The Diagnostic and Statistical Manual of Mental Disorders (American Psychiatric Assn., 1980), subclassifies "Major Affective Disorders" into "Major Depression" and "Bipolar Disorder." Major depression (or unipolar depression) entails "dysphoric mood, usually depression, or loss of interest or pleasure in almost all usual activities and pastimes . . . and a sense of worthlessness that varies from feelings of inadequacy to completely unrealistic negative evaluations of one's worth. The individual may reproach himself or herself for minor failings that are exaggerated and search the environment for clues confirming the negative self-evaluation. Guilt may be expressed as an excessive reaction to either current or past failings or as exaggerated responsibility for some untoward or tragic event. The sense of worthlessness or guilt may be of delusional proportions" (pp. 210-211).

Bipolar disorder (often called manic depression and usually followed by major depression) entails a mood which "may be described as euphoric, unusually good, cheerful, or high; often has an infectious quality for the uninvolved observer, but is recognized as excessive by those who know the individual well. . . . Characteristically, there is inflated self-esteem, ranging from uncritical self-confidence to marked grandiosity, which may be delusional. For instance, advice may be given on matters which the individual has no special knowledge of, such as how to run a mental hospital or the United Nations. . . . God's voice may be heard explaining that the individual has a special mission. Persecutory delusions may be based on the idea that the individual is being persecuted because of some special relationship or attribute. . . . A common associated feature is lability of mood, with rapid shifts to anger or depression. The depression, expressed by tearfulness, suicidal threats, or other depressive symptoms, may last moments, hours, or more rarely, days" (p. 215-217).

With regard to the sex ratio estimated from the patient population for major depression, "Studies in Europe and in the United States indicate that in the adult population, approximately 18% to 23% of the females and 8% to 11% of the males have at some time had a major depressive episode sufficiently severe to require hospitalization" (p. 211). For bipolar disorder, "It is estimated that from 0.4% to 1.2% of the adult population have had Bipolar Disorder. In contrast to Major Depression, Bipolar Disorder is apparently equally common in women and in men" (p. 217). (See Amenson & Lewinsohn, 1981, for details on the strength and tenacity of the sex difference in prevalence of major depression.)

It has been conjectured that the high percentage of females with reported affective disorders is partially due to a skew in the propensity of women to seek help or otherwise be reported. However, manic depression has been shown to be highly heritable, with the implicated genes being dominant x-linked (Baron et al., 1987) and autosomal (Egeland et al., 1987; Hodgkinson et al., 1987). It follows that the actual incidence of manic depression should show a substantial skew toward females. Since the reported incidence of manic depression distributes equally, or nearly equally (Angst, 1978), across the sexes, this implies that there is not a female-weighted sex bias in reporting. Independent of the purported lack of substantive sex bias in incidence of bipolar disorder, Angst (1978) has shown from a large survey that bipolar men experience more manic episodes than depressive episodes while bipolar women experience more than three depressive episodes for each manic episode (see also Taschev, 1974). This accords well with the predicted sex bias, as does the 2:1 sex bias for major depression, which is far more prevalent than manic depression, far less heritable, and more likely to be engendered by initially adaptive downward self-deceit.

So What?

Recall the woman whose employment and marriage depended upon her ability to deceive down. Add the condition that she must submit to sexual abuse under threat of physical violence—violence which erratically erupts anyway, despite the consistency and intensity of her submissions. If leaving is not an economically viable option and suicide is unacceptable, adaptation may require an extremely low level of self-esteem—a level low enough to suppress the expression of any attitude that might increase her risk of being beaten. Just as Alloy and Abramson's (1979) gamblers deceived themselves up into thinking that they were responsible for what was actually good fortune, so this woman will deceive herself down into believing that she deserves her misfortune. Such a level of self-esteem might not be maintainable if based upon imagination alone. Accordingly, independent empirical evidence may be required to convince her that she is sufficiently unworthy to deserve her plight. If so, she may arrange to fail at tasks that she previously knew herself to be capable of accomplishing. She may seek out challenges that she is incapable of meeting, and she may arrange prospects that are likely to bring disappointment. All of this requires effort. In lieu of continuing to make that effort, she may eventually come to depend upon her husband's abuse as the evidence that she deserves to be abused. At this point she will manifest the most severe symptoms of a self-defeating personality.

Sex Bias, Psychopathology, and Economic Opportunity: DSM III-R

A revised version of the DSM III was recently under debate (American Psychiatric Assn., 1987). One focus of controversy was the proposal to include a category for ''self-defeating personality.'' This categorization was objected to on the grounds that the majority of people so categorized would be female, and "elevating" this syndrome to the status of a discrete mental disorder would gratuitously stigmatize women (see Holden, 1986, for review). The same logic allows the argument that most of our criminal codes gratuitously stigmatize men. That is, since the vast majority of prisoners are male, and since prisons seldom rehabilitate prisoners, criminal codes stigmatize men without offering them substantial help. Unfortunately, the rate at which psychoanalysis cures personality disorders is not an improvement over the rate at which prisons rehabilitate prisoners (nor, for that matter, is the success rate of psychoanalysis distinguishable from the rate of spontaneous remission or cure by placebo effect (see Eysenck, 1952, 1985; Rachman & Wilson, 1980; and Prioleau, Murdock, & Brody, 1983; see also Grunbaum, 1984, 1986). The difference between prison and psychoanalysis, in this regard, is that prisons serve a useful function independent of their ability to rehabilitate. The upshot of these realizations is that if psychoanalysis were the best we could offer to people with a self-defeating personality disorder, then this categorization, like all other such categorizations, *would be* a gratuitous stigmatization. Fortunately, there is more to psychiatry than psychoanalysis, but the point here is that the primary cause of self-defeating personality is not psychological.

Specifically, although self-defeating personality, like criminality, may have a genetic component (Mednick, Gabrielli, & Hutchings, 1984), both have a fundamentally economic etiology. When people of either sex are chronically required to subordinate themselves in order to secure economic survival, they may need to self-deceive down. If chronic circumstances require extremely subordinate behavior, this normal adaptation to subordination can be pushed beyond its psychodynamically manageable limits. If economic circumstances cause women to be maneuvered into positions of chronic extreme subordination more frequently than men (see Fuchs, 1986), we should not pretend that this is not the case.

WHAT IS TO BE DONE?

> The top two percent of the population receive 14 percent of total income and have 28 percent of total net worth. Similarly, the top ten percent's share of income (33 percent) almost doubles to a 57 percent share of net worth. In contrast, the bottom 50 percent of the population have 4.5 percent of total net worth. About half of the country's top wealth holders got there by inheriting their holdings. (Thurow, 1987, p. 30)

In other words, approximately 5% of the United States' population possesses, by virtue of inheritance, six times the amount of wealth that is distributed across 50% of the population. Accordingly, our average modern-day aristocrat possesses, independent of contribution to the economy, more than 63 times the amount of wealth possessed by the average person who is not on the top half of the economic ladder. More infuriating than this fact is the realization that things are getting worse instead of better (Thurow, 1987; see also Batra, 1985).

When men lose control they are more likely than women to do something that will land them in prison. When women lose control they are more likely than men to behave in a manner that will land them in psychotherapy. But this is not fallout from a battle between the sexes. In the vast majority of cases both the man who beats his wife and the woman who is beaten are economic victims. They are fallout from a battle between those who do not have economic opportunity and those who have an unearned abundance of opportunity. If we had an economic system that combined genuine *equality of opportunity to contribute* with real *reward according to contribution* very few people would be forced into positions that require chronic, extreme subordination. Unfortunately, in the United States the effort to obtain true capitalism has focused on giving economic aid to those who are born into poverty. What is needed is a radical reorientation of focus.

Because economic opportunity is a zero-sum game, inequality of opportunity is necessarily perpetrated, wittingly or unwittingly, by those who are born into wealth. Just as lack of economic opportunity may necessitate an unmanageable amount of downward self-deceit, so overprivilege may encourage an unmanageable amount of upward self-deceit. . . . but the mental problems of the rich are not the subject at hand. Of far more importance is the realization that cross-generational congestion at the top of the economic scale necessarily causes chronic congestion at the bottom. It is the people who start the ten-lap race on lap four, or five . . . or nine who ultimately cause our penal and mental institutions to be overcrowded. Even a modest inheritance can critically improve an individual's economic trajectory. That is, even those who start the race on lap two have a significant advantage over those who start at the starting line (Kohn & Schooler, 1983, and references therein; Hartung, 1984). This fact has been somewhat obscured by the passable amount of economic mobility available to people in the lower middle classes. A few can become middle class. This often leaves observers with the impression that there is real economic mobility for the lower classes. Unfortunately, as long as people in upper-middle or higher classes inherit enough capital to significantly increase the probability that they and their children and their children's children *ad infinitum* will remain in those classes (see Modigliani, 1986, p. 710), even the best self-help programs for the poor can only produce false hope. To put a point on that, it is not steep hierarchies and disparity in the distribution of wealth *per se* that make our system moribund, it is the *heritability* of those hierarchies that saps the life out of what would otherwise be an invigorating and motivating force (whether inheritance is millions of dollars or membership in a closed plumber's union).

What we need is real capitalism. Only then will winners be genuine winners, and so only then will losers be genuine losers. With that accomplished, there would be far fewer extreme winners, and so far fewer extreme losers. Most important, those who lose would not be required to play demeaning games with their self-esteem in order to lower their self-image and eventually destroy their original potential.

CONCLUSIONS

Natural selection has given us a powerful ability to generate a refined array of self-deceptions, most of which are adaptations to everyday life. These deceits are mechanisms for the presentation of self to self in a manner that maximizes marketability to others while maintaining internal acceptability. A primary conjecture of this essay is that just as upward self-deceit is a requirement of mental health under normal circumstances, so downward self-deceit is a natural adaptation to oppressive circumstances. It follows that psychotherapists (talk therapists) should not endeavor to bring their depressed patients to the most accurate possible perception of themselves, but should, instead, foster *manageable* increments of positive self-deceit (amounts which will engender goals that can be feasibly aspired to—goals toward which enough progress can be made to have encouragement outweigh discouragement).

For the most severe cases, a manageable increment in self-esteem may only bring the patient to a less down position (as distinct from being up relative to the accurate self-perception that characterizes mildly depressed persons). Many such cases may require a practical change in circumstances, like a better way to make a living (or *any* way to make a living), in order to successfully manage the amount of positive self-deceit that will restore mental health. For such cases, psychotherapists should help change the conditions which make deceiving down the most viable accommodation (for example, by referral to a job counselor). In no case should therapists accommodate unfortunate circumstances by lowering a depressed patient's self-image through adaptive downward self-deceit because accommodating injustice that has been inflicted upon one's self is acceptable, but manipulating such an accommodation for others would be both insidious and invidious.

Unfortunately, some downward self-deceptions are adaptations to such extraordinarily oppressive economic circumstances that even modest worthwhile goals cannot be feasibly aspired to. The extended conjecture of this essay is that such circumstances, promulgated and promoted by the disparities in economic opportunity that necessarily result from inherited wealth, can engender a pathological degree of downward self-deceit that is fundamentally intractable. It is difficult to know how to treat the symptoms of such disorders, but doing so is a worthwhile endeavor and is always rewarded and encouraged. Unfortunately, efforts to effectively treat the cause of economically rooted mental disorder are seldom rewarded and are frequently discouraged. Indeed, recent U.S. administrations have pursued both foreign and domestic policies that are designed to assure that the rich will stay rich, not the least of those efforts having more than doubled the amount of wealth that can be transferred in the form of gifts and inheritance without being taxed (cf. Chomsky, 1982, p. 17 and subsequent discussion; see also Chomsky, 1986).

Too many of us focus so narrowly on underprivilege that we fail to perceive its relationship to overprivilege. Too few of us focus on the realization that unearned wealth is not available to be earned, just as bequeathed rungs on the top half of the economic ladder are not available for occupation. The connection between mental disorder and lack of economic opportunity is indirect, but ultimately it is only more subtle than the connection between mental disarray and a gunshot wound to the head.

Far fetched as it may seem, legislation against inherited wealth, whether that wealth is in the form of money, position, or unearned access to same, would do more to reduce mental disorder than will all of the psychologizing that will undoubtedly be funded by all of the well-meaning inheritors of wealth who sit in the board rooms of our philanthropic and governmental institutions.

REFERENCES

ABRAMSON, L. Y., & ALLOY, L. B. (1981). Depression, nondepression, and cognitive illusions: Reply to Schwartz. *Journal of Experimental Psychology: General, 110* (3), 436-447.

ALEXANDER, R. D. (1975). The search for a general theory of behavior. *Behavior Science, 20,* 77-100.

ALLOY, L. B., & ABRAMSON, L. Y. (1979). Judgment of contingency in depressed and nondepressed students: Sadder but wiser? *Journal of Experimental Psychology: General, 108* (4), 441-485.

————. (1982). Learned helplessness, depression, and the illusion of control. *Journal of Personality and Social Psychology, 6,* 1114-1126.

AMENSON, C. S., & LEWINSOHN, P. M. (1981). An investigation into the observed sex differences in prevalence of unipolar depression. *Journal of Abnormal Psychology, 90* (1), 1-13.

AMERICAN PSYCHIATRIC ASSOCIATION. (1980). *Diagnostic and statistical manual of mental disorders* (3rd ed.). Washington, DC: Author.

————. (1987). *Diagnostic and statistical manual of mental disorders* (rev. ed.). London: Routledge & Kegan Paul.

ANGST, J. (1978). The course of affective disorders: II. Typology of bipolar manic-depressive illness. *Arch Psychiatr Nervenkr, 226,* 65-73.

AXELROD, R., & HAMILTON, W. D. (1981). The evolution of cooperation. *Science, 211,* 1390-1396.

BARON, M., RISCH, N., HAMBURGER, R., MANDEL, B., KUSHNER, S., NEWMAN, M., DRUMER, D., & BELMAKER, R. H. (1987). Genetic linkage between X-chromosome markers and bipolar affective illness. *Nature, 326,* 289-292.

BATRA, R. (1985). *The great depression of nineteen ninety.* Dallas, TX: Venus.

CAMUS, A. (1957). *The fall.* New York: Vintage. (Original work published 1956).

CHOMSKY, N. (1982). *Towards a new cold war: Essays on the current crisis and how we got there.* New York: Pantheon.

————. (1986). *Pirates and emperors: International terrorism in the real world.* New York: Claremont Research & Publications.

CROCKER, J., TABACHNIK-KAYNE, N., & ALLOY, L. B. (1985). Comparing the self with others in depressed and nondepressed college students: Reply to McCauley. *Journal of Personality and Social Psychology, 48* (6), 1579-1583.

EGELAND, J. A., GERHARD, D. S., PAULS, D. L., SUSSEX, J. N., KIDD, K. K., ALLEN, C. R., HOSTETTER, A. M., & HOUSMAN, D. E. (1987). Bipolar affective disorders linked to DNA markers on chromosome 11. *Nature, 327,* 783-787.

EYSENCK, H. (1952). The effects of psychotherapy: An evaluation. *Journal of Consulting Psychology, 16,* 319-324.

_____. (1985). *The decline and fall of the Freudian empire.* New York: Viking.

FINGARETTE, H. (1969). *Self-deception.* London: Routledge & Kegan Paul.

FUCHS, V. R. (1986). Sex differences in economic well-being. *Science, 232,* 459-464.

GIDE, A. (1955). *The counterfeiters.* New York: Modern Library. (Original work published 1926).

GOFFMAN, E. (1959). *The presentation of self in everyday life.* New York: Doubleday.

_____. (1971). *Strategic interaction.* Philadelphia: University of Pennsylvania Press.

GOTLIB, I. H. (1982). Self-reinforcement and depression in interpersonal interaction: The role of performance level. *Journal of Abnormal Psychology, 91* (1), 3-13.

GOVE, W. R., HUGES, M., & GEERKEN, M. R. (1980). Playing dumb: A form of impression management with undesirable side effects. *Social Psychology Quarterly, 43,* 1.

GREENWALD, A. G. (1980). The totalitarian ego: Fabrication and revision of personal history. *American Psychologist, 35,* 603-618.

GRUNBAUM, A. (1984). *The foundations of psychoanalysis: A philosophical critique.* Berkeley, CA: University of California Press.

_____. (1986). The foundations of psychoanalysis: A philosophical critique. *Behavioral and Brain Science, 9* (2), 217-284.

GUR, R. C., & SACKEIM, H. A. (1979). Self-deception: A concept in search of a phenomenon. *Personality and Social Psychology, 37* (2) 147-169.

HARTUNG, J. (1976). On natural selection and the inheritance of wealth. *Current Anthropology, 17* (4), 607-622.

_____. (1981a). Genome parliaments and sex with the red queen. In R. D. Alexander & D. W. Tinkle (Eds.), *Natural selection and social behavior: Recent research and new theory* (pp. 382-402). New York: Chiron Press.

_____. (1981b). Paternity and inheritance of wealth. *Nature, 291* (5817) 652-654.

_____. (1982). Polygyny and inheritance of wealth. *Current Anthropology, 23,* 1-12.

_____. (1984). Commentary: Blood group and socio-economic class. *Nature, 309,* 398.

_____. (1985). Matrilineal inheritance: New theory and analysis. *Brain and Behavioral Sciences, 8* (4), 661-688.

HINRICHSEN, J. J., FOLLANSBEE, D. J., & GANELLEN, R. (1981). Sex-role-related differences in self-concept and mental health. *Journal of Personality Assessment, 45* (6), 584-592.

HODGKINSON, S., SHERRINGTON, R., GURLINE, G., MARCHBANKS, R., REEDERS, S., MALLET, J., MCINNIS, M., PETURSSON, H., & BRYNJOLFSSON, J. (1987). Molecular genetic evidence for heterogeneity in manic depression. *Nature, 327,* 805-806.

HOGAN, H. W. (1978). I.Q. self-estimates of males and females. *Journal of Social Psychology, 106,* 137-138.

HOLDEN, C. (1986). Proposed new psychiatric diagnoses raise charge of gender bias. *Science, 231*, 327-328.

ICKES, W., & LAYDEN, M. A. (1978). Attributional styles. In J. Harvey, W. Ickes, & R. Kidd (Eds.), *New directions in attribution research* (Vol. 2, pp. 119-152). Hillsdale, NJ: Erlbaum.

JONES, E. E. (1986). Interpreting interpersonal behavior: The effects of expectancies. *Science, 234*, 41-46.

KOHN, M. L., & SCHOOLER, C. L. (1983). *Work and personality*. Norwood, NJ: Ablex.

KORABIK, K., & PITT, E. J. (1981). Self concept, objective appearance, and profile self-perception. *Journal of Applied Social Psychology, 10* (6), 482-489.

LEWINSOHN, P. M., MISCHEL, W., CHAPLAIN, W., & BARTON, R. (1980). Social competence and depression: The role of illusory self-perceptions? *Journal of Abnormal Psychology, 89* (2), 203-212.

LEWINSOHN, P. M., STEINMETZ, J. L., LARSON, D. W., & FRANKLIN, J. (1981). Depression-related cognitions: Antecedent or consequence? *Journal of Abnormal Psychology, 90* (3), 213-219.

LUNDGREN, D. C., JERGENS, V. H., & GIBSON, J. L. (1980). Marital relationships, evaluations of spouse and self and anxiety. *Journal of Psychology, 106*, 227-240.

MEDNICK, S. A., GABRIELLI, W. F., & HUTCHINGS, B. (1984). Genetic influences in criminal convictions: Evidence from adoption cohort. *Science, 224*, 891-894.

MILLER, I. W., & NORMAN, W. H. (1981). Effects of attributions for success on the alleviation of learned helplessness and depression. *Journal of Abnormal Psychology, 90* (2), 113-124.

MISCHEL, T. (1974). Understanding neurotic behavior: From mechanism to intentionality. In T. Mischel (Ed.), *Understanding other persons*. Totowa, NJ: Rowman & Littlefield.

MODIGLIANI, F. (1986). Life cycle, individual thrift, and the wealth of nations. *Science, 234*, 704-712.

MONTS, J. K., ZURCHER, L. A., & NYDEGGER, R.V. (1977). Interpersonal self-deception and personality correlates. *Journal of Social Psychology, 103*, 91-99.

PRIOLEAU, L., MURDOCK, M., & BRODY, N. (1983). An analysis of psychotherapy versus placebo. *Behavioral and Brain Sciences, 6*, 275-285.

RACHMAN, S. J., & WILSON, G. T. (1980). *The effects of psychological therapy*. New York: Pergamon.

RAPS, C. S., PETERSON, C., REINHARD, K. E., ABRAMSON, L. Y., & SELIGMAN, M. E. P. (1982). Attributional style among depressed patients. *Journal of Abnormal Psychology, 91* (2), 102-108.

ROSMAN, P., & BURKE, R. J. (1980). Job satisfaction, self-esteem, and the fit between perceived self and job on valued competencies. *Journal of Psychology, 105*, 159-169.

SACKEIM, H. A., & GUR, R. C.   (1979). Self-deception, other perception, and self-reported psychopathology. *Journal of Consulting and Clinical Psychology, 47* (1), 213-215.

SARTRE, J. P.   (1958). *Being and nothingness: An essay on phenomenological ontology* (H. Harnes, Trans.). London: Methuen. (Original work published 1943).

SCHAFER, R. B., & KEITH, P. M.   (1981). Self-esteem discrepancies and depression. *Journal of Psychology, 109,* 43-49.

TABACHNIK, N., CROCKER, J., & ALLOY, L. B.   (1983). Depression, social comparison, and the false-consensus effect. *Journal of Personality and Social Psychology, 45* (3), 688-699.

TASCHEV, T.   (1974). The course and prognosis of depression on the basis of 652 patients decreased. In T. K. Schattauer (Ed.), *Symposia medica* (Vol. 8, pp. 157-172). New York: Hoechst; Stuttgart: Schattauer Verlag.

THUROW, L. C.   (1987). A surge in inequality. *Scientific American, 256* (5), 30-37.

TRIVERS, R. L.   (1971). The evolution of reciprocal altruism. *Quarterly Review of Biology, 46* (4), 35-57.

_____. (1972). Parental investment and sexual selection. In B. Campbell (Ed.), *Sexual selection and the descent of man* (pp. 136-179). Chicago: Aldine.

_____. (1976). Introduction to the selfish gene. In R. Dawkins, *The selfish gene* (Foreword). Oxford: Oxford University Press.

_____. (1985). Deceit and self-deception, In *Social evolution* (pp. 395-420). Menlo Park, CA: Benjamin/Cummings.

11

Dealing with Chance

SELF-DECEPTION AND FANTASY AMONG GAMBLERS

DAVID M. HAYANO
California State University at Northridge

You cannot depend upon your eyes when your imagination is out of focus.

—Mark Twain

GAMBLING TRENDS

The voluminous report of the Presidential Commission on Gambling (1976) finds that gamblers are drawn from every socioeconomic, religious, ethnic, educational, and geographic grouping in the country. They are included in the majority of Americans who either endorse or tacitly engage in some kind of legal or illegal gambling, amounting to over $22 billion per year. Furthermore, the dollar amounts wagered are growing annually as more and more states pass measures approving state-run lotteries. Following Nevada and New Jersey, some states are even considering the legalization of Las Vegas-style gambling casinos to increase their revenues. If sums from private, recreational forms of gambling such as home poker and bingo games are included, this would push the monetary figure for gambling even higher. It is sufficient to say that the legitimate gambling industry—casinos, race tracks, off-track betting parlors, lotteries, bookmaking offices, and cardrooms—is a significant and powerful industry in the United States today; its influential tentacles reach into virtually every corner of society.

My concern in this chapter, however, is not to evaluate the trends of gambling or its broad economic effects but to address a narrower set of questions: How does an industry that thrives on its customers' losses and misfortunes continue to flourish? And what role do self-deception and fantasy play in this process?

INTERPRETATIONS OF GAMBLING BEHAVIOR

We know very little about gamblers and gambling behavior in natural settings. It has only been within the last few decades that the social sciences have even considered gambling to be a subject worthy of academic scrutiny in its own right (Frey & Eadington, 1984). Most early studies of gamblers were conducted by clinicians or psychologists whose focus was the compulsive gambler. Their scholarly attention was limited in scope and primarily directed towards Freudian interpretations of gambling. Between 1914 and 1957 less than twenty studies were published on compulsive gamblers (Harris, 1964, p. 513); this was, in fact, the extent of gambling research. To this day these initial findings, which were developed apart from the actual observation of gamblers in their natural environment, have geared the public's attitude toward the notions that all gamblers, and compulsive gamblers in particular, subconsciously desire to lose, possess low self-esteem, and harbor masochistic or anal personalities (e.g., Bergler, 1958). Indeed, the "popular image" of gamblers (Oldham, 1978) portrays them living in a dream world, loving to lose, and in perpetual torment because of their self-delusions and unfulfilled fantasies.

Since the 1960's, several new attempts have been made to define and outline the characteristics of compulsive gambling as a special subtype of gambling behavior in general (Kusyszyn, 1978). The American Psychiatric Association has now officially classified "pathological gambling" as a "disorder of impulse control" (Custer, 1978). Expanding upon this description, the most recent consensus seems to be that compulsive gambling should be treated as a kind of *psychophysiological dependence or illness* which can be likened to alcohol or drug addiction (Moran, 1970). In this instance an individual develops a tolerance for a "substance," for example, gambling, and subsequently requires larger and more frequent doses. Herman (1976) has termed this the "heroin model" of addiction.

Milkman and Sunderwirth (1983) outline three styles of coping with an addiction: **arousal**, **satiation**, and **fantasy**. Gambling compulsion in its extreme state ordinarily involves the constant search for arousal. Players of this sort "seek to feel active and potent in the face of an environment that they view as overwhelmingly dehumanizing" (Milkman & Sunderwirth, 1983, p. 38). Satiation and fantasy are also equally important aspects of the gambler's experience. The first, satiation, manifests itself as a habitual form of responding to a limited set of stimuli; and the second, fantasy, is important in motivating behavior and organizing discordant beliefs.

This current "medical" definition of compulsive gambling draws attention away, I think correctly, from many of the earlier, dubious psychoanalytic interpretations. Instead, it places the onus of blame on the blemishes of the individual, but that, too, is unfortunate because gambling can be distinguished from both alcohol and drug abuse in several significant ways. First, one can conceivably make a legitimate living and even win consistently at certain kinds of gambling games like poker (Hayano, 1982) or blackjack (Uston, 1977); one is not likely to find a "professional" alcoholic or heroin addict. Secondly, gambling normally requires a supporting social organization: other players, equipment, an operator, rules, a bank, and a physical setting which establishes how play is organized, when it occurs, and how payoffs are made. In short, gambling is never a solitary activity, but requires an accessible social system—even if only linked by a telephone—and the cooperation of other individuals to sustain, define, and encourage it. This is where self-deception and fantasy as social constructions are involved.

SELF-DECEPTION AND GAMBLING

As a type of illusive mental state, the phenomenon of self-deception has usually been investigated through methods of indirect inquiry, by attempting to infer what people do and do not believe. Recently, however, more direct methods of observation have been implemented in several novel experimental studies (Sackeim & Gur, 1978; Gur & Sackeim, 1979). Yet the expression of self-deception in natural settings has been almost completely neglected. The point is that self-deception is more than an individual mental state; it can be found in interpersonal, group, and societal levels, and it can be shared. The linkages between individual self-deception and its aggregate form have yet to be studied thoroughly, but *the institutionalization of self-deception is probably a common and cross-culturally universal phenomenon* involving social institutions of varying kinds—educational, religious, political, entertainment, and business—all of which play a supporting and creative role.

Back to the gamblers. It would appear from both lay and scholarly opinion that gamblers would be a "classic case" for any discussion of self-deception. As alluded to above, central to the majority of studies is the notion that most gamblers really prefer to lose and that their misguided thoughts contribute significantly to their fallen states (Bergler, 1958; Livingston, 1974, p. 54; Martinez, 1976; Lesieur, 1977, pp. 49-50, 94-95; Oldham, 1978). We can offer some specific examples:

> During the conscious mood of fantasy, the mind [of the gambler] dreams *luxurious dreams* not usually generated by the routine of everyday life. . . . In the mind of the deeply involved subject, control over destiny becomes possible through fantasy. (Martinez, 1976, p. 357, italics in original)

> What the gambler wants are winnings that will free him from debt, pay off everyone owed, and have some left over to fulfill fantasies. (Lesieur, 1977, pp. 49-50)

The chief problem for the gambler is to present an image of success which will allow him to fool himself into thinking others believe it—to minimize the contradictory data which he cannot avoid. To the community he displays the proper goods or else reduces his visibility. (Livingston, 1974, p. 58)

In their most extreme state these derangements of self-deception and fantasy are usually taken to be one of the primary factors in the etiology of compulsive gambling. It would be fruitless to deny that these subjective states are found in much of the gambler's world, but I do not wish to be sidetracked by trying to ascertain their varying proportions in normal, as opposed to compulsive, gamblers, or in gamblers versus nongamblers.

The emphasis here is that self-deception and fantasy among gamblers can be profitably analyzed as a *dependent variable*, its presence and severity conditioned by the social organization of gambling settings which serve both to support and replenish individual fabrications (Goffman, 1974). My thrust, then, is not to question whether or not ordinary gamblers or compulsive gamblers regularly deceive themselves through their fantasies while losing (although this would certainly be worthy of study) but rather to understand how beliefs, even contrary ones, are sustained. More succinctly: What are the social organizational influences on the production of self-deception and fantasy?

THE SOCIAL ORGANIZATION OF GAMBLING

Gambling is a pastime with a lengthy and indeterminate past, and has always seemed to create feelings of ambivalence in the general public. Even today it is sometimes considered to be immoral or illegal, operated and controlled by thieves and cheats, or an extension of organized crime. But recently, legitimate gambling enterprises have attempted to combat these stereotypes and portray themselves in a brighter light, as respectable businesses and a successful growth industry. Note the following from a 1977 *Time* (Vol. 110, p. 78) magazine article (cited in Mandel, 1982, p. 174):

Harrah's is literally run by the book. More than 50 operations manuals, written by executives over the past quarter of a century, spell out everything from window-washing policy to the importance of maintaining a businesslike decorum. The company's pit bosses are referred to as administrators, and cocktail waitresses taking orders at the craps tables are instructed to call out, to the bartender, say, "Two double Scotches for C" instead of shouting the word craps. Every effort is made to dispel the rowdy, green eyeshade image of gambling. . . .

This meticulous attention to self-presentation has in no small way contributed to the immense profits generated by the legitimate casinos, while at the same time assuaging the public's fear of being duped and cheated in a "gambling joint." What should be obvious is that casino profits are derived from the predictable losses of the millions of customers who gamble regularly. Why, in the face of this apparent reality, do people persist in gambling? I must first dismiss (perhaps too perfunctorily) the idea that gamblers, even compulsive ones, actually desire to lose, since my observations suggest quite the opposite: Most gamblers would prefer to win. But they fail to do so not necessarily because they deceive themselves, dream fantasies, or act compulsively, but rather because of the laws of probability which are reformulated by the social organization of gambling environments.

At the heart of all gambling games is a monetary wager which is made on the occurrence of an indeterminate event; this may be the outcome of a football game, a horse race, a roll of the dice, the fall of a roulette ball, the selection of a series of lottery numbers, or the fall of a card. Casino gambling games operate on the principle that when a player bets on an event, the house automatically charges a fee, known as the vigorish (or "vig"), for each bet. Bettors are paid off at less than the statistically expected odds for a specific future event. Therefore, in every game of chance, the house or casino which banks the game and supplies the paraphernalia for action builds for itself an intractable probabilistic advantage.

Table 11–1 lists a comparison of the most common types of gambling games on a luck/skill continuum. The important point to consider in this excursion into chance-dominated gambling games (excluding games of skill and strategy like poker and blackjack) is that winning in the long run, over a series of many bets, is highly unlikely, if not impossible. One might, of course, win big once and then run with the money as do some grand lottery and slot machine winners, but the faithful, regular, daily gambler has little hope to succeed. Although many believe that perseverance will eventually lead to success, thus imbuing their fantasies with a kind of secular work ethic, such views are misguided. Lerner's (1975) claim is that the belief in a "just world" where good things happen to good people is a fundamental delusion. Gamblers are notoriously susceptible to these "just world" fallacies.

TABLE 11–1

A Luck/Skill Continuum in Gambling Games

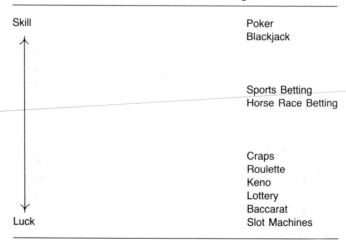

Skill	Poker
	Blackjack
	Sports Betting
	Horse Race Betting
	Craps
	Roulette
	Keno
	Lottery
	Baccarat
Luck	Slot Machines

TECHNIQUES OF DEFLECTION

For the serious or professional gambler, how much he loses—whether for a single playing-session or a month—is always subject to immediate self-inspection, and therefore, self-deception. He may convince himself that he has not lost at all, and account for expeditures of money in meals, gasoline, household bills, money loaned out, or a variety of other nongambling reasons. Inaccurate bookkeeping, at least among perpetual gambling losers, adds to the conviction that one is not really losing that much, and that other legitimate expenses are actually responsible for the disappearing fund of money.

Gamblers dwell mostly not on why they win but rather on why they lose. Losing requires an explanation or excuse, while subjecting winning to analysis would be anticlimatic. Much of the gambler's daily conversation and folklore is coded in commonly told and retold "bad beat" stories and a regular stock of excuses. The gambler's accounts of losing usually take the form of verbal denials or blame, such as having "a bad day" or running into "bad luck." One can also point to specific reasons for failure: the team that blew a big lead or the quarterback who injured his arm in the first half. Among gamblers, most attributions of failure and loss are blamed on external causes beyond the control of the individual (Hayano, 1982, pp. 109-110). Their verbal explanations usually take the form of abrupt, standardized cliches. These might be called "scripts" or forms of "emplotment" (Sarbin, 1981, pp. 228-229). This procedure involves creating a "story line" that mixes fact with fiction, or what is thought to be fact or fiction. Order is created out of chaos, and a sense of linearity out of randomness. Sarbin (1981, p. 230) adds that we are all "guided by the search for a coherent story." This is, of course, crucial in the gambler's world of chance, where, lacking real prescient knowledge, he must apply ad hoc situational explanations to give meaning to his experiences.

The gambler's store of formulaic utterances offers a way out of situations of stress or uncertainty. They provide him with a world view that is "reasonable" and shows his challenges as surmountable. Hiding or denying reasons for loss allows the gambler to cope and therefore continue in his quest for gain. By doing so, he cannot prove himself wrong: There is always a "good" reason for loss, for failure, and for returning the next day.

Sustaining belief systems in any culture or subculture requires a supportive network of social institutions and physical settings. In most legal public cardrooms and casinos there are four main processes which contribute to self-deception and heightened modes of fantasy: (1) neutralization, (2) masking, (3) ritual, and (4) glorification. All of these are methods by which institutions sanctify belief.

It has been observed that gambling, for the majority of participants, is an "irrational" economic activity because losing is statistically a foregone conclusion (Hess & Diller, 1969), especially as the luck or chance factor takes on greater weight in particular games. Many more gamblers lose than win; hence a major part of the advertising that is related to the promotion of gambling appeals to the notion that playing in luxurious hotel-casinos will enhance one's worldliness and self-image, and that winning is highly possible as long as one holds a certain level of confidence. Indeed, the art of casino management is in providing attractive feelings to the clientele (Skolnick, 1978, p. 40). But in the face of the insurmountable odds, self-deception always serves as a handy buffer of reality.

The **neutralization of stimuli** contributes to the belief that the pleasures of gambling far exceed the painful costs, that the enjoyment of playing in comfortable settings is worth the time and money. Soft carpeting, dim lights, lavish hotel rooms, and availability of action day and night aid in accomplishing this purpose. Neutralization techniques are directed toward creating an ambiance of propriety and decorum in architecture, interior decorating, and more subtle forms of advertising. They blunt the effect of the potentially damaging side of gambling.

The physical layout of gambling casinos is thus organized towards encouraging customers to gamble, even if they are simply browsing. Clanging slot machines are visible from the entrance, noisy crap tables are bunched around the center of the floor, and to reach the restrooms, restaurants, or cashier's windows one must walk by the gaming tables. Normally, wall clocks are not visible, making day and night unimportant to the customers. The invention of luxury and taste in modern gambling casinos is meant to be aesthetically appealing. Self-containment and timelessness characterize most casinos. These are insulated fortresses, whose primary concern is providing continuous service, entertainment, and action. They are, in a sense, twenty-four-hour shopping centers (Skolnick, 1978, p. 36). As such, gambling casinos are constructed with a different set of rules or "frame" for conduct than that normally found in everyday life; that life, in fact, is meant to be of secondary importance or held in suspension (Goffman, 1961, 1967, 1974).

Masking is another way of diverting the gambler's attention away from loss. For example, complimentary drinks are routinely offered to gamblers involved in betting action. Free meals, show tickets, rooms, and other complimentary expenditures add up to millions of dollars per year for every casino (Sternlieb & Hughes, 1983, pp. 146-147). But the most prominent method is the quick conversion of money into chips, which are much easier bought and lost. As a player begins to win he is paid off in chips of higher denominations than those with which he started. This encourages him to increase the size of his bets. Gamblers who are marked as "high rollers" and willing to risk thousands of dollars per day are usually accorded first-class treatment in gambling casinos throughout the world. Often, they use credit markers instead of cash so that debts are recorded only on paper slips. While appearing to be a convenient method of accounting, these can also be interpreted as "pretense episodes" (Glaser & Straus, 1975, p. 361).

Masking is a method, then, of changing labels: referring to gambling as "entertainment" or "recreation"; advertising a gambling trip as a "vacation"; or converting cash to "checks," "chips," or "credit lines." Gambling casinos have become professional merchants of metaphor.

The **ritualization of interpersonal behavior** between casino personnel and customers is organized to provide easy, trouble-free interaction. Note this brief description of a high-stakes baccarat game in London:

> The event is ritualized, rather like a dance with commentary spoken in French, and highlighted by the dealer's exquisite skill in employing a palette to separate and dispense oversized chips. (Skolnick, 1978, p. 4)

In Las Vegas casinos, dealers must follow strict rules about how much they talk to customers and what they are to say. This interaction is directed to be perfunctory and polite (Solkey, 1980). The fundamental concern for the casino management is that the speed and amount of betting should not be allowed to slacken. Ritual interaction in the manner of a predictable routine for both the dealers and customers fulfills this aim. Players can slip from one game to the next exhibiting none of the expected ritual routines of everyday life. No words of greeting, leave-taking, nor comments need be spoken. The nonverbal placement of a wager defines the interaction. Ritual and prediction help mollify the anxiety resulting from play. Bok (1978, p. 137) has called this a game of "mutual deceits":

> . . . where both parties know the rules and play by them. It represents, then, a pact of sorts, whereby what each can do, what each gains by the arrangement, is clearly understood. A game of poker is such a pact. It mingles trust and distrust, bargaining and gambling. Mutual deceits can be short-lived, like a poker game, or they can last indefinitely. The stakes can be insignificant or very high. At best, the practice is voluntarily and openly undertaken, and terminated at will.

Overlaying the techniques of neutralization, masking, and ritual in the subculture of gamblers is **glorification:** stories of fame and fortune circulated on billboards, television, and in every specialized gambling publication (Hayano, 1984). The glorification of gambling and winning seeks to remind the average losing player that he is potentially a winner who might achieve the "American dream" through a shortcut. Faith and hope are byproducts of the process of glorification. They maintain the organization of self-deception and captivate the participants; faith and hope offer reasons to continue in the face of overwhelming odds.

Many gamblers adopt the practice of appearing like big winners, adorning themselves with expensive clothes and jewelry, flashing large bankrolls, or bragging about recent wins and monthly profits. Although these presentations of self are clearly deceptive as well as self-deceptive, they are important to the gambler, especially the professional one, because they provide him or her with a sense of confidence. The mere masquerade of winning provides a kind of socio-psychological comfort. If it were not for this form of positive denial it seems less likely that so many "rational" individuals would regularly pursue their "irrational" pursuits.

Whereas neutralization, masking, and ritual are socially situated, glorification is not. But it is perhaps the most important source of the gambler's self-deception and fantasy: glorification is portable and can be taken wherever he or she goes, whether inside the casino or outside. Glorification to a large extent drives all gamblers—professional, compulsive, social, novice—to seek out the action (see also Goffman, 1967). Once found, it is the characteristic most likely to be eventually extinguished as the other deflection techniques acquire a more influential role. How and when these thoughts of glory and hope are reignited, whether in one hour or in one month, is plainly a complex issue which will not be considered in depth here. But these hopes in themselves are not sufficient conditions to explain gambling failure, nor is their presence a critical typological feature that separates compulsive gamblers from "normal" ones.

Gambling environments present an illusory version of chance. They invent scenarios of success and the physical location where these fantasies may be played out. A current television commercial, for example, describes a popular downtown Las Vegas hotel-casino as ''a magical place.'' To the mass of losers and compulsive gamblers there is always the hope that they might someday beat the odds. Gambling settings deal in the culturally approved organization of fabrication, and they represent a symbiotic arrangement of need and offering. And, except for cheats and thieves, the casinos will accept everybody, even ''helping'' the blind to make their bets. The casino

> is the most democratic, or perhaps simply undiscriminating, of social organizations. A player can enjoy a whole new world of social acceptance within its confines. Outside, he may be a bookmaker or a pimp, a banker or a physician. Inside, the only question is: ''How's his action.'' (Skolnick, 1978, p. 46)

In short, the marketing methods of the legitimate gambling industry do not deal with guilt, aggression, or the competitive and negative aspects of gambling. They focus instead on good reasons for people to gamble. These include a rational-economic motive, the idea that one can win and should gamble in a particular casino; a motive that gambling is fun and enjoyable as a kind of entertainment; and an appeal to the motives of prestige, to be seen wagering money and being relatively carefree about it in luxurious surroundings (Hess & Diller, 1969).

Technically, the gambling industry's methods of self-promotion are neither lies nor deceptions. Although some observers have referred to casinos as a ''gigantic confidence game'' (Skolnick, 1978, p. 50), they are more like deflections, which are intended to draw attention away from everyday experience to those experiences which can be actively invented and nurtured.

My intention is not to view the gambler simply as a ''judgmental dope'' (Garfinkel, 1967, pp. 66-68), as one who blindly follows standardized expectancies, although it is a fact that the lure of the casinos is strongest for those who are the least knowledgeable about the real odds. In Atlantic City these include the numerous underage gamblers and the elderly, many of whom are known as the ''bus people'' (Sternlieb & Hughes, 1983, p. 167). Experienced gamblers are inveterate strategists and decisionmakers, trying to work around the regular outcome of loss; most can see beyond the neon and advertising promotions. But what is operating here is a ''rapture effect'': an attraction to risky, challenging situations that only occasionally do offer rewards of fulfilled fantasy.

DEALING WITH CHANCE

Our limited perceptual and intellectual capacity to comprehend the world-as-it-is results in a certain amount of delusion (Murphy, 1975; Devereaux, 1979, p. 29). It would probably be reasonable to assume that the world as we experience it is frequently unjust, chaotic, unpredictable, and chancy. Yet numerous studies have shown that *there is an urgent need for individuals to believe that some degree of control in most situations is possible*, even when subjects are given random stimuli (Langer, 1975). And in cases of extreme misfortune, such as a severe accident, most people deny the reality of what has happened to them, instead relying on the belief that the world is orderly and meaningful, rather than punitive and whimsical (Bulman & Wortman, 1977).

It can be argued then that human belief systems, whether they are erroneous, inconsistent, misguided, or self-deceptive, nevertheless act as formulae for behavior and explain to the holder the reasons for fortune and misfortune. Many belief systems are self-regulating in the cybernetic sense, that is, they can be corrected with new information. Experimental science falls into this category. The vast majority of folk belief systems, however—gambling beliefs included—are not self-corrective. This routine distortion of information may lead to socially acceptable states of self-deception and fantasy. The effects of an untested and imperfect knowledge of the environment may have wide-ranging effects, from tragedy (Bouissac, 1981) to euphoria and success. Nevertheless, gambling belief systems function as controls and methods of adaptation in chance situations; being so, they "work," on at least one level, for those who hold these ideas.

The view of the **positive adaptations of self-deception** has been more fully articulated by Lazarus (1979) and Lockard (1980, Chapters 1 and 2). Both draw attention to the importance of self-deception as a coping mechanism of great aid in human evolutionary adaptation. Lazarus (1979, p. 44) goes so far as to remark that denials and illusions may be "the healthiest strategies in certain situations." Thus, where chance and unpredictability are involved, as in most forms of gambling, other features such as magical thinking, ritual control, and fantasy seem to come into play. Shweder (1977) in fact believes that adults often choose not to use correlational or contingency thinking, and that we are all subject to "magical thinking" to one degree or another. Moreover, anthropologists have shown that there are numerous cross-cultural elaborations both in the content and tolerance of magical beliefs and fantasies (e.g., Obeyesekere, 1981, p. 167).

This line of argument opens the way to the thought that there may be specialized institutions or subcultures in most societies which make a practice of denying everyday, conventional definitions of reality. Game-playing and gambling environments are the primary examples. Following their own rules, these environments create "membranes" (Goffman, 1961) between their world and the world outside. Also present is an undeniable pleasure principle, in which self-deception, other-deception, fantasy, and fun are accepted, even codified into rules or tactics for successful play (Hayano, 1980). One is not usually admonished to "face reality" during games; these are culturally defined areas in which individuals can indulge themselves in the pleasurable transformations of everyday life. Gambling environments then manipulate both behavior and thought into limited patterns and routines. Attention is drawn to the action at hand rather than inwards towards self-awareness. These lowered states of self-awareness seem to follow as a defensive reaction to the large number of persuasive stimuli emanating from the environment (Roloff, 1980, p. 60).

I do not mean to imply that all forms of self-deception and fantasy and their social modes of production are necessarily adaptive or unproblematic. But at this point we do not quite know the limits of their abuse.

CONCLUSIONS

Goffman (1974, p. 112) has argued that delusion or self-deception is a "fundamental defect" of "normal actors." But as I have argued here, the production of self-deception and fantasy, whether deliberate or inadvertent, seems to be a fairly routine procedure, constructed of routine techniques in most social institutions, indeed, in cultures in general. Promotional fables and techniques of deflection from self-awareness are not limited to the gambling industry; neither are self-deception and fantasies unique byproducts of the gambler's psychological make-up. Lazarus (1979, pp. 47-48), for example, sees a general process at work:

> The fabric of our lives is woven in part from illusions and unexamined beliefs. There is, for example, the collective illusion that our society is free, moral, and just, which, of course, isn't always true. Then there are the countless idiosyncratic beliefs people hold about themselves and the world in which they live. . . . [these] illusions can be a sign of pathology, or they can make life worth living.

Self-deception and fantasy in themselves are not necessarily the main cause of loss or compulsion in gamblers. They only appear to be of more significance in gamblers because of the casino's endowments in creating an appropriate image and stage for gamesmanship. Thus it seems likely that self-deception and fantasy are much more universal than might be admitted, and especially as adaptive processes which are linked to situations of chance, risk-taking, and adversity.

In poker, the best kind of bluff is an unintentional one, in which one does not know the value of one's hand in relation to the others (Goffman, 1974, p. 123). We might take a lesson from professional gamblers who frequently use intentional and unintentional bluffs to struggle through situations of imperfect knowledge. Tactics which allow us to rely on "irrational" beliefs and illusions might, after all, not always be bad ones in dealing with everyday life.

REFERENCES

BERGLER, E. (1958). *The psychology of gambling*. London: Hanison.

BOK, S. (1978). *Lying: Moral choice in public and private life*. New York: Vintage.

BOUISSAC, P. (1981). Behavior in context: In what sense is a circus animal performing? In T. A. Sebeok and R. Rosenthal (Eds.), *The clever Hans phenomenon: Communication with horses, whales, apes, and people. Annals of the New York Academy of Sciences* (Vol. 364, pp. 18–25). New York: The New York Academy of Sciences.

BULMAN, R. J., & WORTMAN, C. B. (1977). Attributions of blame and coping in the "real world": Severe accident victims react to their lot. *Journal of Personality and Social Psychology, 35*(5), 351-363.

CUSTER, R. L. (1978). Pathological gambling. In *Diagnostic and Statistical Manual of Mental Disorders* (3rd ed.). Washington, DC: American Psychiatric Association.

DEVEREAUX, G. (1979). Fantasy and symbol as dimensions of reality. In R. H. Hook (Ed.), *Fantasy and symbol* (pp. 19-31). New York: Academic Press.

FREY, J. H., & EADINGTON, W. R. (EDS.). (1984). Gambling: Views from the social sciences. *The Annals of the American Academy of Political and Social Science* (Vol. 474). Beverly Hills, CA: Sage.

GARFINKEL, H. (1967). *Studies in ethnomethodology*. Englewood Cliffs, NJ: Prentice-Hall.

GLASER, B., & STRAUS, A. (1975). The ritual drama of mutual pretense. In D. Brissett & C. Edgley (Eds.), *Life as theatre* (pp. 358-364). Chicago: Aldine.

GOFFMAN, E. (1961). *Encounters: Two studies in the sociology of interaction*. Indianapolis: Bobbs-Merrill.

———. (1967). *Interaction ritual*. New York: Anchor.

———. (1974). *Frame analysis*. New York: Harper and Row.

GUR, R. C., & SACKEIM, H. A. (1979). Self-deception: A concept in search of a phenomenon. *Journal of Personality and Social Psychology, 37*(2), 147-169.

HARRIS, H. I. (1964). Gambling addiction in an adolescent male. *Psychoanalytic Quarterly, 33*, 513-525.

HAYANO, D. M. (1980). Communicative competency among poker players. *Journal of Communication, 30*, 113-120.

———. (1982). *Poker faces: The life and work of professional card players*. Berkeley, CA: University of California Press.

———. (1984). The professional gambler: Fame, fortune, and failure. In J. Frey & W. R. Eadington (Eds.), Gambling: Views from the social sciences, *The Annals of the New York Academy of Sciences* (Vol. 474, pp. 157-167). Beverly Hills, CA: Sage.

HERMAN, R. (1976). *Gamblers and gambling*. Lexington, MA: D. C. Heath.

HESS, H. F., & DILLER, J. V. (1969). Motivation for gambling as revealed in the marketing methods of the legitimate gambling industry. *Psychological Reports, 25,* 19-27.

KUSYSZYN, I. (1978). "Compulsive" gambling: The problem of definition. *International Journal of the Addictions, 13,* 1095-1101.

LANGER, E. (1975). The illusion of control. *Journal of Personality and Social Psychology, 32,* 311-328.

LAZARUS, R. S. (1979). Positive denial: The case for not facing reality. *Psychology Today, 13*(6), 44-60.

LERNER, M. J. (1975). The justice motive in social behavior. *Journal of Social Issues, 31,* 1-19.

LESIEUR, H. R. (1977). *The chase: Career of the compulsive gambler.* Garden City, NY: Anchor.

LIVINGSTON, J. (1974). *Compulsive gamblers.* New York: Harper and Row.

LOCKARD, J. S. (1980). Speculations on the adaptive significance of self-deception. In J. Lockard (Ed.), *The evolution of human social behavior* (pp. 257-275). New York: Elsevier.

MANDEL, L. (1982). *William Fisk Harrah: The life and times of a gambling magnate.* Garden City, NY: Doubleday.

MARTINEZ, T. (1976). Compulsive gambling and the conscious mood perspective. In W. R. Eadington (Ed.), *Gambling and society* (pp. 347-370). Springfield, IL: Charles Thomas.

MILKMAN, H., & SUNDERWIRTH, S. (1983). The chemistry of craving. *Psychology Today, 17*(10), 36-44.

MORAN, E. (1970). Gambling as a form of dependence. *British Journal of Addiction, 64,* 419-428.

MURPHY, G. (1975). *Outgrowing self-deception.* New York: Basic Books.

OBEYESEKERE, G. (1981). *Medusa's hair.* Chicago: University of Chicago Press.

OLDHAM, D. (1978). Compulsive gamblers. *Sociological Review, 26,* 349-371.

PRESIDENTIAL COMMISSION ON THE REVIEW OF THE NATIONAL POLICY TOWARD GAMBLING. (1976). *Gambling in America: Appendix 2. Survey of American gambling attitudes and behavior.* Washington, DC: Government Printing Office.

ROLOFF, M. E. (1980). Self-awareness and the persuasion process. In M. E. Roloff & G. R. Miller (Eds.), *Persuasion: New directions in theory and research* (pp. 29-66). Beverly Hills, CA: Sage.

SACKEIM, H. A., & GUR, R. C. (1978). Self-deception, self-confrontation, and consciousness. In G. E. Schwartz & D. Shapiro (Eds.), *Consciousness and self-regulation* (Vol. 2, pp. 139-197). New York: Plenum.

SARBIN, T. (1981). On self-deception. In T. A. Sebeok & R. Rosenthal (Eds.), *The clever Hans phenomenon: Communication with horses, whales, apes, and people. Annals of the New York Academy of Sciences* (Vol. 364, pp. 220-235). New York: The New York Academy of Sciences.

SHWEDER, R. A. (1977). Likeness and likelihood in everyday thought: Magical thinking in judgments about personality. *Current Anthropology, 18*(4), 637-658.

SKOLNICK, J. H. (1978). *House of cards: The legalization and control of casino gambling.* Boston: Little Brown.

SOLKEY, L. (1980). *Dummy up and deal.* Las Vegas, NV: Gambler's Book Club.

STERNLIEB, G., & HUGHES, J. W. (1983). *The Atlantic City gamble.* Cambridge, MA: Harvard University Press.

USTON, K., & RAPPAPORT, R. (1977). *The big player.* New York: Holt Rinehart and Winston.

12

Self-Deception
in Social-Support
Networks

SUSAN M. ESSOCK
MICHAEL T. MCGUIRE
BARBARA HOOPER
University of California at Los Angeles

DECEIT AND ALTRUISM

According to evolutionary theory, humans have evolved to behave in ways which maximize their inclusive fitness. In this sense, all behavior is "selfishly" motivated to enhance the probability of an individual perpetuating his or her genes into the future—either directly, by producing offspring, or collaterally, by helping kin to reproduce. Nonetheless, as Alexander (1979) points out, humans throughout history have not expressed any conscious understanding of the selfish genetic interests which motivate their everyday acts. In fact, the contrary is true: Individuals tend to see themselves as altruistic and beneficent rather than as actors in their own behalf.

This tendency was demonstrated clearly in a study of the patterns of helping of 300 Los Angeles women (Essock-Vitale & McGuire, 1985a, 1985b). Data revealed that the women distributed help "selfishly"—that is, in ways which maximized their inclusive fitness. Yet these women reported themselves as altruists, giving help more often than they received it and paying back more often than they

The original research reported here was funded by a grant to Susan M. Essock and Michael T. McGuire from the Harry F. Guggenheim Foundation. Computing funds were made available from the office of Academic Computing at UCLA.

were paid back. Were they unique and truly altruistic? Were they consciously deceiving the interviewer, painting a prettier-than-reality self-portrait? Or, were these women self-deceived, consciously unaware of their true motives? Using the helping data from the earlier study, this chapter investigates these questions, exploring how deceit and self-deception might operate in the ways individuals give and receive help.

METHODS

The original study collected data via a lengthy, structured interview and was designed to control for age, race, ethnicity, and socioeconomic status so that a culturally homogenous group would be achieved. Steps were also taken to gather a random sample so that incidence figures would be representative of the larger population (Essock-Vitale & McGuire, 1985a, 1985b).

The interview method of data collection took advantage of the subjects' ability to give reliable verbal self-reports on a host of relevant variables. Although data gained in this manner has the disadvantages inherent in all retrospective reporting (e.g., correlational but not causal statements may be inferred from such data), the relative expediency and low cost when compared to a prospective study, and the existence of multiple means of assessing the accuracy of self-reported data make the interview methodology attractive.

Subjects   Participants were 300 white, non-Hispanic, middle-class women aged 35–45 living in greater Los Angeles. All were native born and raised by at least one of their natural parents. The subjects were contacted by telephone to solicit their participation. Target telephone numbers were generated using a modified random-digit dialing procedure (thereby assuring that a listed and unlisted number had an equal likelihood of being dialed). Subjects were paid $25 plus babysitting expenses, when needed.

The interview   The interview was lengthy (average duration 4-3/4 hours), but pilot interviews indicated that the subjects found recalling the requested information an enjoyable, if time-consuming, task. There was not a problem with subjects electing to terminate the interview early, although all were free to do so. The interview took place either in the subject's home or at UCLA, whichever the subject preferred, at a time selected by the subject. The interview consisted of the administration of a questionnaire plus brief break periods. The interviews were given by professional interviewers who were each female, white, non-Hispanic, and blind to the hypotheses being tested.

The questionnaire   The questionnaire consisted entirely of questions with brief, easily coded answers. Although the questionnaire covered a wide range of topics (e.g., assistance from paternal versus maternal kin, proximity of kin and friends, reproduction), only those questions relating to the giving and receiving of various types of help are discussed here. Specifically, for each of five different types of investment (financial help, help during illness, help with housing, emotional support, and help with everyday living) the subject was asked (1) when she most needed that kind of help, (2) who helped her at that time, and (3) as of the present, who has done most of the helping, herself or the individual she named. The subject also was asked a parallel set of questions concerning instances when investment flowed in the opposite direction, that is, times when she gave each of the types of assistance just listed. The people named in these major helping instances are referred to as **major helping partners**.

Reliability measures   Reliability of the interview data was assessed in two ways. To check the consistency of the subjects' subjective interpretations of events, each subject was requestioned by telephone between two weeks and twelve months after the original interview. Subjects were requestioned using one of the seven subsets of questions randomly selected from the original questionnaire. The duration of the requestioning period was approximately ten minutes.

A second procedure for assessing reliability involved questioning a sample of the subjects' full siblings. Thirty sisters who lived locally and were closest in age to the subjects (mean age difference = 3.5 years, standard deviation = 1.8) were questioned using those sections of the questionnaires covering the years the sisters lived together, plus questions about relatives alive at the time of the interview. These two procedures allowed the removal from analysis of unreliable questions (which were defined as having less than 60% shared variance between original and comparison responses) and allowed the demonstration of the high degree of consistency in the subjects' responses.

SUMMARY OF PREVIOUS FINDINGS

The original study utilized the evolutionary theories of kin selection and reciprocal altruism to investigate whether or not the collected survey data revealed patterns of helping that served to maximize the subjects' inclusive fitness.

Kin selection   As put forth by Hamilton (1964), **kin selection** refers to the natural selection of genes that increase the fitness of genetic relatives (hereafter referred to as "kin"), even at some cost to the individual. Kin selection will operate when, on the average, the loss in individual fitness is more than offset by an increase in inclusive fitness. (**Individual fitness** refers to one's genetic representation in future generations via direct descendants, whereas **inclusive fitness** refers to one's genetic representation in future generations via direct and collateral descendants.) This model provides an evolutionary explanation for the existence of cooperative and altruistic behaviors toward kin, and makes possible specific predictions pertaining to the form and direction that behaviors among kin should take. For example, the amount of altruistic behavior that an individual should be willing to confer on another should be directly related to the degree of genetic relatedness between them. No potential for payback need exist for such altruistic behavior to be adaptive. Rather, *kin selection requires only that an individual's potential decrease in individual fitness for having engaged in the behavior is more than compensated for by the probable increase in inclusive fitness.*

Reciprocal altruism   In contrast to kin selection, **reciprocal altruism** (Trivers, 1971) implies the trading of acts, which, if they occurred only in one direction (e.g., A gives to B, but B does not reciprocate), would increase the inclusive fitness of one individual at another's expense. In their simplest form, reciprocal altruism systems may be thought of as collections of dutiful bonds between individuals in which individual A gives to B because, at some future time, A may be in need and B will give to A. The potential for payback is inherent in all such assistance; the emphasis is on "reciprocal."

Findings

Data revealed that the subjects gave and received help in accord with predictions derived from the theories of kin selection and reciprocal altruism. Helping was distributed with respect to biologically relevant variables; hence, the patterns of the subjects' helping behaviors were revealed to work toward maximizing inclusive fitness. These patterns, which emphasize the direction of the helping behavior rather than absolute amounts of help distributed, are as follows:

1. Helping among non-kin was more likely to be reciprocal than helping among kin. Evolutionary theory would predict that kin would be more likely to tolerate the lack of reciprocity because when help goes unreciprocated they still derive some inclusive fitness benefit, whereas non-kin do not. Subjects typically reported reciprocal helping with approximately 35% of kin, in contrast to approximately 54% of non-kin (Figure 12–1).
2. Among kin, investment increased as kinship distance decreased. Figure 12–2 illustrates that while help exchanges with kin comprised only about one-third of all helping exchanges, within the kin category help was most likely to come from close kin.
3. Among kin, helping was an increasing function of the recipient's expected reproductive potential (Figure 12–3).

Table 12–1 shows the relative distribution of current primary helping partners across various classes of individuals. Subjects were asked to list the three individuals who helped them most and the three whom they had helped most during the past year. As seen in Table 12–1 and Figure 12–3, investment tended to flow from older to younger kin. For equally close kin of the same generation (e.g., full siblings), exchange relationships were more reciprocal. Table 12–1 shows that age and kinship taken together are better predictors of helping than either taken alone.

How help to and from kin varied with specific reproductively relevant characteristics of the kin was also addressed. Each subject was asked to rate separately, for each of her close kin, how likely it was that the relative in question would have

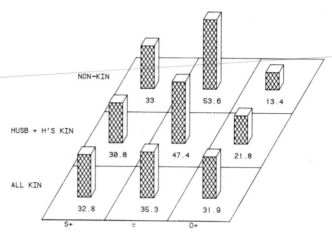

FIGURE 12–1 Reciprocity balance for three classes of relationships: all kin, husband plus husband's kin, and non-kin (friends). Within each category, for each subject the percentage of individuals falling in each of three categories: *S+* (S helped more), = (S and other helped about equally), *0+* (other helped more) was computed. These scores were then averaged across subjects and plotted. (*Source*: Essock-Vitale & McGuire, 1985b.)

FIGURE 12–2 Percentage of major helping by closeness of kinship, where *r* = coefficient of relationship (e.g., *r* of ½ = parents, full siblings, children; *r* of ¼ = half siblings, grandparents, aunts, uncles, grandchildren, nieces, nephews; *r* greater than zero but less than ¼ = cousins, children of half-siblings, etc.). (*Source*: Essock-Vitale & McGuire, 1985b.)

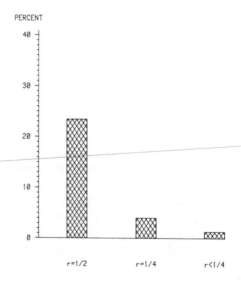

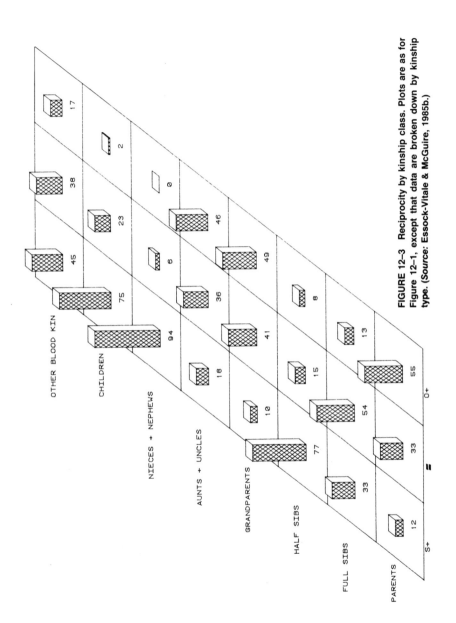

FIGURE 12–3 Reciprocity by kinship class. Plots are as for Figure 12–1, except that data are broken down by kinship type. (Source: Essock-Vitale & McGuire, 1985b.)

TABLE 12–1

RELATIONSHIP	HELP DIRECTION			
	FROM *S*		TO *S*	
Parent	289	(10.9)	663	(26.3)
Full-Sibling	222	(8.4)	133	(5.3)
Half-Sibling	29	(1.1)	2	(0.1)
Grandparent	30	(1.1)	25	(1.0)
Aunt or Uncle	20	(0.7)	35	(1.4)
Niece or Nephew	32	(1.2)	3	(0.1)
Child	171	(6.5)	49	(1.9)
Other blood kin	28	(1.1)	15	(0.6)
Husband	99	(3.7)	251	(10.0)
Husband's Kin	236	(8.9)	235	(9.3)
In-law (no blood relation to *S* or husband)	43	(1.6)	33	(1.3)
Step or adopted individual	23	(0.9)	16	(0.6)
Other non-kin (friends)	1429	(53.9)	1060	(42.1)
TOTAL	2651	(100)	2520	(100)

Frequency with which individuals of different relationships to the subjects were reported as helping partners, by direction of help. Numbers in parentheses give the percentage of total helping instances for that direction of help. (Source: Essock-Vitale & McGuire, 1985b.)

additional children, the relative's financial situation, how much help the subject had been to that relative, how much help that relative gave to the subject, how much the subject would be willing to help that relative in the future, and how much help to the subject that relative would be willing to provide. Subjects were also asked how many children each close relative was supporting and the age of the youngest child being supported. These questions were asked for each parent, grandparent, sibling, half-sibling, aunt, uncle, niece, nephew, and grandchild the subject had. Subjects' ratings on questions such as "How likely is it that *X* will have another child?" on a 1 to 5 scale were highly reliable. For example, for the question just mentioned, the test-retest reliability measure was 0.79.

Analyses were performed to determine if, among equally close kin, certain characteristics of the kin would predict helping (see Essock-Vitale & McGuire, 1985b). Results revealed that, in general, subjects reported being more likely to receive help from kin who were wealthy, female, and supporting children of their own. Help from the subjects was most likely to be given to kin who were wealthy, female, supporting children, and likely to have more children.

These data are sufficient to indicate how simplistic it is to speak of relationships among "kin" without also examining how these relationships might vary as a function of other biologically and culturally relevant factors such as age, health, proximity, and familiarity.

The patterns of helping among the sample of Los Angeles women appeared to have underlying regularities which biased their behavior toward maximizing inclusive fitness. Help was distributed neither randomly nor altruistically, but in a strategic manner which, however (un)consciously, favored the biological goals of survival and reproduction.

Were the women aware of the selfish nature of this behavior? Were they cognizant of the fact that even as they were "giving" they were receiving by making the helping decisions which increased their chances of perpetuating their genes into future generations? When examining the data, it became clear that the subjects were not reporting themselves to be selfish in their helping exchanges. In fact, the contrary was true: the majority reported themselves as givers much more frequently than receivers. It was this discovery that prompted an examination of the survey data in terms of deceit and self-deception.

DECEIT AND SELF-DECEPTION

Since Freud, at least, it has been a common view that the conscious reasons individuals create to explain their behavior are often not the true reasons. In recent years, investigators concerned with the evolution of social behavior have applied evolutionary theory to this idea and developed suggestions for why it might be so. If there are genetically induced behavioral biases which continuously nudge behavior into conformance with ultimate goals of survival and reproduction, and if we have evolved to have no conscious knowledge of these biases or to deny them, then the critical question is: "Why?" Of what value is it to the individual to deceive and/or be self-deceived about behaviors which operate so potently throughout life?

Alexander (1979) suggests that, in a social environment, the only way individuals can advance their separate, frequently conflicting goals is to practice deception: to deny to themselves and others that they are acting to maximize their own individual interests. By presenting themselves as altruists, as people concerned with the welfare of others, they become desirable associates—a necessary condition if they are to survive in a social context of mating, friend making, and resource sharing. Self-deception, which allows one to deceive others more consistently and effectively, likely evolved to further the goal of deceit.

Trivers (1985) elaborated upon these ideas, positing that natural selection for deception is expected to generate self-deception: an "active, organized process" which employs various psychological mechanisms such as "beneffectance" to improve the potency of one's deception. One becomes a more creditable liar if one believes the lie to be truth.

This evolutionary view of deceit and self-deception has a clear application in reference to human patterns of helping. In order to survive in a social context of resource sharing it is likely to be adaptive to be able to *present* oneself as a good helping partner. Though their ultimate goals may be the same—that is, those selfishly attuned to maximizing genetic representation in future generations—all else being equal, the individual who successfully masquerades as an altruistic, beneficent person would be more likely to attract a mate and friends than one who displays his or her selfishness unmasked. Likewise, the individual convinced of his or her own beneficence has a greater chance of convincing others than the individual who, with false conviction, attempts to deceive. Hence, *deceit and self-deception work hand-in-hand in helping individuals accomplish the critical task of becoming socially acceptable, thereby enhancing the likelihood of reproduction.*

Assessment of Findings on Deceit and Self-Deception

As demonstrated above, the survey data clearly indicated that the subjects helped in specific ways which worked toward maximizing their own inclusive fitness. The data also revealed that the subjects reported occupying the role of giver more frequently than receiver and paying back more frequently than they were paid back, hence indicating that deceit and/or self-deception might be at work.

Evidence of the subjects believing their behavior to be altruistic emerged in three prime places. First, analyses examining relationships among help type, direction of help, and whether an instance of helping was reported indicated that subjects were significantly more likely to report that they had given help than that they had received help (Essock-Vitale & McGuire, 1985b).

Second, subjects were questioned directly about their "balance of payments" with the various major helping partners they identified. For each partner mentioned, they were asked to answer the following question: "Considering all of the times you helped X and X helped you throughout your life, who usually did more of the helping between you and X: Was it almost always you, more often you, you and X about equally, more often X, or almost always X?" Analyses of these data concerning 3,166 major helping partners indicated that nearly half (49%) of these relationships were reported to be reciprocal. Of those in which one party was reported to owe the other, the subjects were much more likely to report that they had helped more than to report that the other person had helped more (63.5% versus 36.5%, respectively).

Third, in response to questions concerning the likelihood of paying back help in those instances in which the balance of payments was not equal, subjects reported perceiving themselves as significantly more likely to pay back than to be paid back.

Several interpretations of these findings are possible. One is that the subjects were telling the truth; that is, they were altruists who gave more help than they received. While a random draw of subjects would make this unlikely, such a biased draw would not be impossible. Perhaps selecting exclusively women for the study biased the results in this direction. It could be that women do give more than men; also, given the subjects' ages and the high instance of children in the home, it may be that for this period of their lives the women more frequently helped others than they were helped. Perhaps over a lifetime giving and receiving do balance out, but there are particular periods—the child rearing years—wherein either the giver or the receiver role predominates.

A second interpretation is that the subjects were consciously and purposely deceiving the interviewer in order to appear more altruistic than they actually were. In this case, even if they did not believe themselves to be as beneficent as they reported, they would still be acting in accord with evolutionarily sound motives by attempting to conform to the more socially acceptable model.

An alternative interpretation is that the subjects honestly believed themselves to be the altruists they reported and were deceived in their beliefs. Several lines of reasoning support this interpretation:

1. High reliability of the data. Consistent presentation of the data by the subjects, as confirmed by the reliability measures outlined in the "Methods" section, suggest that the subjects were reporting the "truth" as they saw it. It would be much more difficult to lie consistently; if the subjects had been lying, they would have produced low test-retest reliability scores. Instead, only one of the helping questions proved unreliable (this being when the subject was asked whether she felt a sense of obligation to continue the relationship with a helping partner).

2. Subjects believed that they gave more than they received. Perhaps there is no way of objectively assessing the equality of helping between individuals because the internal mechanisms which calculate cost/benefit ratios are inherently too subjective to have general application. Even two exchanges of something so apparently quantifiable as $50 loans cannot be assumed to be equal. One individual may overvalue and another undervalue the act in accordance with his or her perception of the act's value to the recipient; one may be loaning a greater or lesser proportion of his or her income; one may be acting casually while another acts against a lifetime credo of believing "Neither a borrower nor a lender be." All of this is to say that helping exchanges may not sum to zero; the giver's costs may not equal the receiver's benefits. Nonetheless, the majority of subjects, when asked to perform these calculations, readily, unequivocably, and consistently calculated to their own advantage, weighting more heavily the help they gave than the help they received.

3. Subjects were more likely to give help to wealthier relatives than to poor ones. Here the subjects were not acting beneficently—giving to those with greater need—but in accord with self-interest, as wealthier helping partners would be more likely to have resources to invest in the subjects than poorer ones.

4. The subjects usually did not seek help from people they had helped in the past and who thus "owed" them in return. More often, help was sought from individuals who had proved to be already good sources of assistance and to whom they were already "in debt." Here again, the subjects were acting to their own advantage rather than in the interest of keeping things "fair."

Subject-Sibling Exchanges

Perhaps the most dramatic support for the operation of self-deception is found in the sibling data. Because the subjects and their siblings were of the same generation, biases present when comparing subjects to kin of other generations were not present. The tendency for helping to flow from older to younger was neutralized by a random draw of subjects, and one would expect to see equal giving and receiving. Table 12–1 and Figure 12–3 both indicate that this was not the case. While the subjects' exchange relationships with their full siblings were more reciprocal than those with any other kinship class, the subjects still believed themselves to occupy the role of giver more than receiver (33% versus 13%). When considering only the major helping instances described above, the subjects also were 1.7 times more likely to report helping siblings than they were to report siblings helping them (222 versus 133 helping instances, respectively).

As data reported earlier indicated, there are subcategories to which either the subjects or their siblings might belong which could bias the giving and receiving of help in either direction. Being married, having children, sex of helping partner, age, and wealth all were shown to influence the nature of one's helping exchanges. However, because the sample was random, insurance was provided that, with one exception, a predominate number of subjects or siblings would not belong to any one subcategory. The exception, of course, is the subcategory of sex. While one might argue that brothers are less likely to give help to sisters than receive it, thus skewing the direction of the help in alignment with the subjects' reporting, this cannot be the case in the other instances. In short, it appears clear that either deceit or self-deception was operating in the helping exchanges between the subjects and their siblings.

CONCLUSIONS

The data presented here support the suggestion that deceit and self-deception operate frequently in our social relationships. The role they play in helping behaviors, as evolutionary interpretations suggest, is probably critical in that it facilitates our exchanges with others by masking and making more palatable the self-interest which actually guides us. Because we would not survive and reproduce without these exchanges, it is clear that an individual's fitness would benefit by behaviors which promote him or her as a good exchange partner.

In a culture which promotes selflessness as a virtue, it clearly would not serve one's interests to be viewed as selfish. Hence we must deceive. Self-deception, the blissful rose-tinted unawareness which unburdens individuals of the truth and allows them to believe that they truly are those generous, beneficent, altruistic creatures whose masks they publicly wear, is a means of accomplishing the deceit. By this trick of unconsciousness of motive we are allowed to think positively of ourselves and to enter into helping relationships free of the uncomfortable burden of deliberate deceit, thus more successfully convincing our partners of our desirability. In this paradoxical manner, by denying to ourselves and to others that we are selfishly motivated, the selfish ends of evolution are achieved.

REFERENCES

ALEXANDER, D. (1979). *Darwinism and human affairs*. Seattle, WA: University of Washington Press.

ESSOCK-VITALE, S., & MCGUIRE, M. (1985a). Women's lives viewed from an evolutionary perspective: I. Sexual histories, reproductive success, and demographic characteristics of a random sample of American women. *Ethology and Sociobiology, 6,* 137-154.

————. (1985b). Women's lives viewed from an evolutionary perspective: II. Patterns of helping. *Ethology and sociobiology, 6,* 155-173.

HAMILTON, W. D. (1964). The genetic theory of social behavior: I and II. *Journal of Theoretical Biology, 7,* 1-52.

TRIVERS, R. L. (1971). The evolution of reciprocal altruism. *Quarterly Review of Biology, 46,* 35-57.

————. (1985). *Social evolution*. Menlo Park, CA: Benjamin/Cummings.

13

Deception
and Self-Deception

A DOMINANCE STRATEGY
IN COMPETITIVE SPORT

SHARON A. WHITTAKER-BLEULER
University of British Columbia

The intent of this chapter is to discuss the establishment and maintenance of social dominance hierarchies in competitive sport. Two particularly interesting and possibly adaptive strategies—deception and self-deception—are considered in the realization of sport success. For the purpose of this chapter, a **deceptive strategy** in sport is defined as player behavior antithetic to point outcome, and an **adaptive strategy** is said to be evident when a consistent game approach leads to sport success.

Sports differ in factors such as the number of persons involved, rule structure, and social distance of competitors. Brown (1975) suggests that even a slight increase in group size alters both the complexity and nature of dominance relationships. Therefore, an individual sport, tennis (singles), has been considered here instead of a team sport. Dyadic interactions would seem to be more readily analyzed and interpreted than more complex social relationships.

Sport activities as a whole are considered by many to constitute a social institution. Competitive sport, in particular, provides an excellent opportunity to study human dominance and deception in a field setting. Displays of dominance and submission are present in athletics in a variety of forms. It is reasonable to assume that the degree of dominance or submission displayed will co-vary with an athlete's winning or losing performance.

A critical distinction in this chapter is that winning or losing may refer either to a specific point in a game or to the outcome of a match. For example, a player who has won at least two-thirds of the previous points in a tennis match might be considered to be winning the match, although he or she may win or lose a specific point at any given moment. The central thesis of this chapter is that *the behavior an athlete exhibits at critical times in the game is likely to reflect the probable match outcome as well as that of the last point.*

SPORT DOMINANCE MODEL

Although the opponent can see the outcome of specific points, the game and/or match outcome is not known for certain until the last point is played. The behavior of the players at particular times may be important in providing some indication of the global outcome. The behavior of interest here is that seen after points have been won or lost. Most probably there will be little difficulty in predicting overall outcome if there is agreement between the point outcomes and the behavior exhibited. However, if a player wishes to provide the opponent with misinformation to optimize his or her chances of success or to delay the realization of failure, a strategy of deception could be employed (see Figure 13–1). For example, deception may be particularly crucial in the later stages of a match.

    Neutral behavior might also be advantageous and, therefore, substituted for frank winning or losing behavior in some situations. For example, displaying a "poker face" could have an effect similar to the display of a contradictory message. In fact, such calmness could be particularly distracting to the opponent in situations in which the player is clearly winning or losing the match.

    Although the display of dominant, submissive, or neutral behavior is more accurately regarded as a graded message that exhibits varying degrees of subtlety and not as a discrete "on-off" signal, it may be beneficial for a player to be obvious at specific points during a contest. Indeed, if a player wants to be sure that a particular message is being conveyed, he or she may wish to exhibit a higher frequency of behavior clearly associated with winning or losing. On the other hand, deception might be enhanced at times by employing neutral behavior. Such

FIGURE 13–1 All possible combinations of point outcome (first letter) and behavior (second letter)

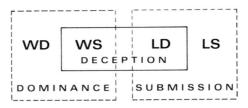

W = point won
L = point lost
D = dominant behavior
S = submissive behavior

behavior may be easier to convey successfully to an opponent than either of the more extreme postures of winning or losing.

DEGREES OF DECEPTION AND SELF-DECEPTION

For purposes of analysis and discussion of the possible degrees of deception being perpetrated, Table 13–1 presents all combinations of tennis outcome (previous points and specific point) with respect to dominant, submissive, or neutral behavior. **High deception** is defined as behavior antithetic to both the most immediate point outcome and the probable match outcome based on the number of previous points won or lost. For example, it is likely that high deception is being attempted if the

TABLE 13–1

Assumed Degree of Deception and Self-Deception in Tennis Singles (as a function of majority of previous points and current point won or lost)

MAJORITY OF PREVIOUS POINTS	CURRENT POINT	BEHAVIOR	DEGREE OF DECEPTION
W	W	D	None
L	W	D	Moderate
W	L	D	Low
** L	L	D	High
** W	W	S	High
L	W	S	Low
W	L	S	Moderate
L	L	S	None
* W	W	N	High
L	W	N	Low
W	L	N	Low
* L	L	N	High

KEY

W = win   * = low self-deception
L = loss   ** = high self-deception
D = dominant
S = submissive
N = neutral

player continues to display dominant behavior after losing two-thirds of the previous points as well as the current point. **Moderate deception** is regarded as behavior agreeing with the current point outcome but not with the probable match outcome at the time. **Low deception** is defined as behavior consistent with the most likely match outcome but not with the immediate point outcome. Similar reasoning determines the degree of deception assigned in the case of neutral behavior. Therefore, one must be most convincing in sending a message to an opponent when both the total number of previous points and the current point outcome are contradictory to the behavior one wishes to display. When the outcome of the total number of previous points is consistent with current behavior, though the present point is not, one need not have to be as convincing.

Self-deception is also likely to be advantageous in conveying misinformation to one's opponent, especially when the total number of previous points and the current point outcome are both inconsistent with the behavior to be displayed. **High self-deception** would be beneficial when the behavior is inconsistent with both outcomes. **Low self-deception** is more likely if the behavior exhibited is not at odds with probable success, as when neutral behavior is displayed under conditions of consistent point and match outcomes (Table 13–1). In any deception, however, success may hinge upon an ability to effectively deceive oneself, since self-deception may enhance one's own performance as well as affect the opponent's attitude about the encoder's dominance.

ABILITY LEVEL AND DOMINANCE IN SPORT

For some players, competitive sport provides a social mobility that may not otherwise exist (Blalock, 1962). The zero-sum (winner takes all or nearly all) reward system has contributed to intensified displays of dominance and an attitude of "win at all cost." Such resultant social recognition and achievement in athletics has become quite important in many cultures (Moss & Kagan, 1961), to the extent that it is a goal for which children also strive.

Experienced individuals in specific social contexts have been found to be more accurate in decoding nonverbal messages than inexperienced persons (Dittman, Parloff, & Boomer, 1965; Ekman & Friesen, 1974; Whittaker-Bleuler, 1980). Recognition of particular behavioral displays is most probably acquired through involvement in the relevant activities. Therefore, elite athletes are likely to be those who are not only highly skilled in a sport but also have become both successful encoders and decoders of specific dominant sport behavior. In contrast, submissive displays do not seem to be prevalent in the behavioral repertoire of successful athletes. Such athletes may have internalized (through some self-deception) a role of winning, often providing a posture of success even when losing.

Although ideas of "fair play" are often associated with competitive sport, individual sport survival may require the adoption of "gamesmanship" strategies such as those humorously written about by Potter (1978). These strategies may not necessarily be sportsmanlike but, nevertheless, they enjoy widespread adoption. In adopting such a strategy in the context of sports, one may not feel the same guilt as might occur in other environments. For example, a former tennis champion, Owen Davidson, when speaking of today's better tennis players, was quoted as saying ". . . Europeans aren't any better—not the big names, but the lesser ones. Boy! Do they cheat. Intimidating linesmen into such disarray that they'll give you points is just as much cheating as anything else, and they're masters at it" (Cobb, 1982, p. 24).

Regardless of the conventional value judgments that downplay dominant and particularly deceptive behavior in sport, player superiority is often conveyed by both verbal and nonverbal dominance displays. For example, champion athletes are sometimes accused of an "aloofness" or a detachment from other competitors that was not characteristic of them prior to success. The **nonverbal channel** is more frequently utilized as most athletes are discouraged from verbal pretentiousness.

Walker (1977) found that the nonverbal channel was better for conveying confidence, inferiority, superiority, and empathy. Such displays usually involve body and head movements in addition to facial expressions. Nonverbal behavior in particular provides affective information that may influence performance and, therefore, game success. This may be especially so for competitors closely matched in skill and fitness, since they may be relying on subtle cues. At the beginning of a contest both displays of dominance and submission may occur as a function of point outcome. However, their frequency and intensity are likely to change during the competition with one of the two displays eventually assuming a more prominent role based on the game strategy that the player adopts.

Wilson (1975, p. 176) has defined biological communication as "the action on the part of one organism . . . that alters the probability pattern of behavior in another organism . . . in a fashion adaptive to either one or both of the participants." Although nonverbal displays may be beneficial to both sender and receiver, the focus here is on those situations in which the display is advantageous to the sender but not to the receiver. Any time there is room for only one person (or team) to succeed, such as in competitive sports, one might expect "false" or deceptive messages. Moreover, in order to survive for long periods of time at the top of a chosen sport, it may be necessary not only to be deceptive but to be superior in both sending and interpreting the verbal and particularly nonverbal behaviors (deceptive or otherwise) of others. Indeed, Ekman and Friesen (1974) found that highly trained observers were better at judging deceptive facial behavior than were those with less training.

DETECTION OF DECEPTIVE NONVERBAL MESSAGES

Studies of human nonverbal deception in everyday life have been few. However, there has been some research that utilized posed or spontaneous deception in a laboratory environment (Mehrabian, 1971; DePaulo, Rosenthal, Eisenstat, Rogers, & Finkelstein, 1978; DePaulo & Rosenthal, 1979). The literature on nonverbal deception has found that persons generally rely upon the face rather than the body when interpreting information conveyed nonverbally. Ekman and Friesen (1969, 1974) have found that "leakage" of deceptive information may be more likely to occur in the legs and feet, that is, in the parts of the body that are farthest from the face.

Distance Between Players

Since the face tends to mask undesired emotion more readily than the body, and since we attend first to the face (Ekman, 1985, and Chapter 14), a deceptive strategy may be more successful in sports when the participants are close enough to one another to see each other clearly. However, athletes may have to be more cognizant of body movement than nonathletes since the distance between competitors in some sports may not allow a clear view of facial cues. Therefore, depending on how far away the players are from one another, specific sports may differ in the parts of the body that provide the greatest leakage of deceptive information.

Ability Level of Players

Whittaker (1980) found that experienced tennis players, regardless of sex, were significantly better than inexperienced players at detecting winning and especially losing behavior. The subjects viewed selected total body "between-point" episodes (from the end of one point to the beginning of the next) of selected championship male and female tennis players. The experienced players were also consistent in their decoding of nonverbal behavior over time. When asked to indicate which components of the behavioral episode determined their responses, both experienced and inexperienced players were frequently aware of gross body movement of the lower extremities even though they indicated that their initial attention focused on the head region. However, in other sports (e.g., table tennis) the results may also depend upon the extent to which the body is visible.

Age of Players

Since skilled male and female adult tennis players are superior to less-skilled players in the detection of dominant or submissive behavior, the amount of tennis experience appears to be an important consideration in decoding accuracy. Therefore, it is likely that children would not be as astute as adults in correctly interpreting deceptive messages (Feldman & Custrini, Chapter 3). Developmental studies in nonsport environments (Feldman & White, 1980; Zuckerman, Blank, DePaulo, & Rosenthal, 1980) have found some evidence of deceptive ability in children, concluding that older children are more accurate than younger children in decoding deceptive messages, particularly of dominance and submission. Similarly, since experienced individuals are better than inexperienced persons at decoding specific nonverbal winning and losing information, it may follow that their keen awareness may also cause them to be better encoders of such information than are less experienced competitors. In other words, knowing which behavioral cues to select may allow the experienced player to successfully encode such information more accurately than a less-experienced player.

Detection and Self-Deception

Wallace (1973) suggested that whereas the difference in risk of detection in large versus small lies is negligible, the potential benefit to the perpetrator of a large lie is appreciable. In applying this strategy to sport, conveying dominance even when losing may increase the possibility of success or delay the outcome of failure. However, Otte (1975) indicated that detection is also a function of gullibility and it is unlikely that too obvious a masquerade would deceive an experienced opponent.

In order to be completely successful when deceiving another, it may be important to also deceive oneself (Lockard, 1980, and Chapters 1 and 2). Being aware of "cheating" an opponent may affect a competitor's performance and ultimately the outcome of the contest, particularly if feelings of guilt accompany this awareness (Ekman, 1985, and Chapter 14). A person who calls "out" in a tennis match at a crucial point when the ball is obviously "in" may actually be seeing the ball as out (self-deception) or employing a strategy that will optimize his or her success by arousing anger and decreasing concentration in the opponent. Such calls might be most advantageous at crucial points in the match. For example, when two competitors are tied or close in score, "cheating" might serve to provide the advantage for the individual performing the act.

Subtle Versus Overt Displays

Since actual confrontation in most sports is not sanctioned, subtle displays that accomplish the same end should benefit the sender. One example of low-keyed interaction is the stare that is often seen between opponents meeting at the net when changing ends in a tennis match. The dominant or winning player of the moment generally attempts to make eye contact with the opponent. The less successful player may respond by either looking down or may cross the net at the opposite side to avoid returning the stare. Obviously it would not be prudent for the players to engage in a physical encounter. First, penalty or eviction from the game would be a likely consequence, but more importantly, an altercation may serve to reduce concentration upon the task and thus affect success. The latter may be especially true when the athletes are close in skill. For example, in his Wimbledon victory over Borg, McEnroe was reported to comment that he had controlled himself because he needed all his concentration to realize victory against this opponent. Also, an intense emotional display would have expended considerable energy.

A sport such as tennis requires a competitor to participate continuously for long periods of time. Therefore, subtlety of behavioral expression would be, all else equal, more advantageous as the length of individual participation increased. Subtlety of expression may be more important when playing against an experienced as compared to a less-experienced opponent, since energy conservation might be essential to success in this case. Moreover, a skilled opponent may be more difficult to deceive than a less-skilled player and less-overt deceits may be more successful.

Alternative Strategies

Although subtle displays may be energy efficient, there are at least three alternative strategies that could be employed. First, the sender may overemphasize messages of dominance while suppressing those indicating submission. Second, submissive behavior may be stressed to give the opponent a false sense of well-being. Finally, a sender may choose a neutral posture, revealing little or no emotion. The preferred strategy may vary during a contest, depending upon variables such as points won or lost, personality, skill, fitness, sex, and/or the particular sport.

Whittaker (1980) found that championship male and female tennis players suppress losing behavior. Although some players initially expressed losing behavior after loss of a point, they subsequently changed to a more dominant display. The inexperienced player, on the other hand, may be a less effective and/or less subtle encoder due to infrequent practice in identifying cues associated with winning and losing. As a result, such players may not be as good at masking winning and especially losing behaviors, and their behavior may be easier to decode than that of an experienced athlete. Therefore, it is hypothesized that as experience increases so does one's ability to be successful in deception. Since experienced players are better than less-experienced ones at decoding, self-deception may also increase as experience increases. Indeed, it may be possible to even predict when deception, and particularly self-deception, are most likely to occur in tennis.

TENNIS VARIABLES AND DECEPTION

Some aspects of a tennis match may be particularly important when attempting to maintain a dominant status: position in the match (beginning, middle, end), the point score, the game score, and service or receipt of service. A tennis match consists of many points and games (also divided into sets) of which a player serves and receives an equivalent portion. The extent of the contest precludes a continuous display of dominant behavior, and such displays are likely to be especially crucial at specific times.

Match Time

Since a player has a maximum of three or five sets (the first to reach six games, provided the individual is ahead by two games, wins a set) to complete a tennis match, certain times during the match may be more important for a display of dominance than other times. The early games of a match are important in "setting the stage for winning" while the later games are essential in maintaining an advantage. Losing behavior exhibited in the middle of a match may have less impact on match outcome than at other times. However, closeness in skill level (shown by the set score of 5-4 as opposed to 5-2) may dictate the utilization of every opportunity to influence match outcome. Applying similar logic to a specific game, deceptive behavior (including self-deception) may be more important when the score is close and/or as the end of the game approaches.

Game Scores

Specific game scores in a set of tennis may also dictate more deception than do others. A close score of 2-2 may not be as important to a tennis player as the game following the score of 3-3. The latter score is the "middle" of the set and, as known to a skilled player, the seventh game in a set is critical. The outcome of the seventh game will either cause one player to move well ahead (from 4-2 to 5-2) or provide a player with the opportunity to remain a viable opponent (from 3-3 to 4-3). A convincing display of dominance even when losing may be more important during the seventh game than at any other time.

Whenever the score is close it may be advantageous for a player to give an opponent a false sense of security by displaying losing behavior. It seems likely that such behavior would occur at crucial times during the match.

Service Advantage

Finally, service and receipt of service are different situations in a tennis contest. Equally matched opponents often emphasize both "holding service" as well as "breaking the opponent's service." In such a match, the former may actually be more important than the latter. If this is the case, it is likely that deception would be more important during service. For example, a set can be won if a player consistently holds service and breaks the opponent's service only once.

A TEST OF THE SPORT DOMINANCE MODEL

Table 13–2 shows 6 deceptive "between-point" episodes (of a total of 76 episodes originally viewed) extracted from a study by Whittaker (1980, Study C) and the corresponding behaviors identified with them. The purpose of the study was to ascertain the behavioral components of "between-point" (from the end of one point to the beginning of the next) episodes that were consistently identified as either winning or losing. Some 80 (40 male and 40 female) experienced and 80 inexperienced (40 male and 40 female) tennis players viewed a videotape of 21 (11 male and 10 female) "between-point" behavioral sequences of 6 (3 male and 3 female) championship tennis players. Only those episodes were used that were identified correctly or incorrectly (as indicative of winning or losing the previous point) by at least 84% of 240 experienced subjects (equal number of males and females) in a previous study (Whittaker, 1980, Study B). The subjects were given a list of

TABLE 13–2

Episodes Identified Incorrectly by 65% or More (usually 90%) Male and Female Subjects

EPISODE	SUBJECT	CORRECT RESPONSE	BEHAVIORS IDENTIFIED (EXPERIENCED)		BEHAVIORS IDENTIFIED (INEXPERIENCED)	
			Males	*Females*	*Males*	*Females*
1	F2	Loss	20,26	None – Divided	1	1
3	F3	Win	None – Divided	None – Divided	20	14
9	M1	Win	1,4,28	1,4,28	1,4,28	1,4,25,28
17	F2	Win	4,6,24,30	1,4,6,24,30	1,4,6,24,30	1,4,6,24,25,30
20	F3	Loss	20	5,20	2,5,20	2,5,20
6	F1	Win	–	–	3	1,3

(*Source*: Whittaker, 1980, Study C)

TABLE 13–3

**An Identification of Salient Winning and Losing Behaviors Selected By Male
and Female Experienced Tennis Players
(selected by at least 50% of subjects)**

LOSING BEHAVIORS	DESCRIPTION
1	head down (i.e., face down)
2	looking around
4	shaking the head horizontally
6	looking at the racquet
10	circling in the corner behind the court
14	kicking the foot and leg forward and up
18	throwing the racquet
21	making quick, jerky movements with body extremities
23	letting the arm and racquet drop, bent-arm position to racquet pointing at the ground with arm straight
24	walking more slowly
27	hitting or throwing ball to back of player's own court
28	hand on hip
30	going through the stroke motion without a ball
WINNING BEHAVIORS	
3	fixing the hair
5	head up
16	putting the racquet behind the head and resting it on the shoulder
20	walking more quickly
26	strutting (i.e., walking with a lift)
AMBIGUOUS BEHAVIORS	(occurs in both of the above categories)
7	wiping the face with arm or hand
BEHAVIORS NOT CHOSEN	(by 50% or more of the subjects)
8	shoulders hunched forward
9	turning the back on the net slowly
11	shoulders back (i.e., standing tall)
12	moving constantly on the spot
13	shoulder shrug and then lowering of shoulders
15	bouncing the ball very quickly
17	arm(s) drop to straight and palm faces forward
19	kicking the foot and leg backwards
22	throwing the arms out (bent to straight)
25	throwing the ball to the opponent while facing him or her
29	self-abuse (i.e., hitting self with racquet or extremity)

(*Source:* Whittaker, 1980, Study C)

TABLE 13–4

An Identification of Salient Winning and Losing Behaviors Selected By Male
and Female Inexperienced Tennis Players
(selected by at least 50% of subjects)

LOSING BEHAVIORS	DESCRIPTION
2	looking around
10	circling in the corner behind the court
18	throwing the racquet
21	making quick, jerky movements with the body extremities (i.e., arms and/ or legs)
23	letting the arm and racquet drop from bent-arm position to racquet pointing at the ground with the arm straight
27	hitting or throwing the ball to the back of the player's own court
WINNING BEHAVIORS	
6	looking at the racquet
15	bouncing the ball very quickly
16	putting the racquet behind the head and resting it on the shoulder
30	going through the stroke motion without the ball
AMBIGUOUS BEHAVIORS	
1	head down (i.e., face down)
3	fixing the hair
4	shaking the head horizontally (i.e., from side to side)
5	head up (i.e., held high)
7	wiping the face with arm or hand
14	kicking the foot and leg forward and up
20	walking more quickly
24	walking more slowly
25	throwing the arms out (bent to straight)
28	hand on hip
BEHAVIORS NOT CHOSEN	
8	shoulders hunched forward
9	turning the back on the net slowly
11	shoulders back (i.e., standing tall)
12	moving constantly on the spot
13	shoulder shrug and then lowering of shoulders
17	arm(s) drop to straight and palm faces forward
19	kicking the foot and leg backwards
22	throwing the arms out (bent to straight)
26	strutting (i.e., walking with a lift)
29	self-abuse (i.e., hitting self with racquet or extremity)

(*Source:* Whittaker, 1980, Study C)

behaviors (an exhaustive list from observations of the taped players compiled by the author) and, after viewing each of the 21 episodes, were asked to indicate if the person in the taped episode had won or lost the previous point and to identify the behaviors on the list that allowed them to come to that decision (Table 13–3, experienced players; Table 13–4, inexperienced players).

Ability of Players

Of the six deceptive episodes in Table 13–2, five were identified incorrectly by at least 65% (and more usually 90%) of both experienced and inexperienced players (episode #6 was identified only by inexperienced players). Table 13–1 also shows that behaviors associated with high deceptive episodes for experienced players were winning (dominant) behaviors when the current point was lost, and losing (submissive) behaviors when the point was won. Inexperienced players (Table 13–4) for the most part identified behaviors that were ambiguous (a behavior that had elements of both winning and losing). However, with correctly identified episodes, inexperienced players responded similarly to experienced players by associating winning behaviors with the previous point won and losing behaviors with a lost point. These results support the definition of deception presented earlier (see Figure 13–1).

Tennis Variables

Table 13–5 shows a breakdown of each deceptive episode in relation to its position of occurrence in a specific tennis match. It was suggested earlier that position in the match (beginning, middle, end), service or receipt of service, point score, and game score may be important in predicting when deception and self-deception are likely to occur. However, the data only partially supported the hypotheses. The deceptive episodes did occur at either the beginning or end of a match, as predicted, and not in the middle, but the specific game score was not able

TABLE 13–5

The Position of Occurrence of Deceptive Episodes in Selected Tennis Matches

Episode	Subject Sex and Identity	Correct Response	Subject Response	Point Score	Position During Match	Serving (S) or Receiving (R)
1	F2	Loss	Win	30–40	End	R
3	F3	Win	Loss	15–30	End	R
9	M1	Win	Loss	30–40	End	R
17	F2	Win	Loss	0–30	Beginning	R
20	F3	Loss	Win	30–15	End	R

(*Source:* Whittaker, 1980)

to be determined from the original data as the 76 episodes did not represent all points and games in the match. The prediction that there would be more deceptive behavior when the point score was close and when the game was almost over was not upheld. A score of 30-40 is close, but scores of 15-30, 30-15, and 0-30 (Table 13–5) are not close or near the end of the game. However, it should be noted that for each of these scores the person was receiving service and in four of the five deceptive episodes the receiver was ahead in the game. Nevertheless, if the variable of service or receipt of service by itself is considered, the five deceptive episodes all occurred when the players were receiving and not during service, as predicted. Perhaps it is more important to be deceptive when the other player is serving, as serving is generally considered to be a position of control in skilled tennis.

Gender in Decoding Deceptive Messages

Some literature (e.g., Hall, 1978) has suggested that females may be both better encoders and decoders of affect than males, particularly in the case of facial messages. The tennis data did not show sex differences in ability to decode winning and losing behavior of male or female players. However, four of the five deceptive episodes for experienced subjects and five of the six deceptive episodes for inexperienced subjects were of taped segments of female championship players. Female players, and particularly skilled ones, may indeed be better at encoding deceptive affect (see Feldman & Custrini, Chapter 3). It would then follow that the amount of detail perceived by a female decoder might favor detection of deception since more intuitive information would be available to help uncover the ploy. However, the tennis data did not specifically address this question.

Winning Versus Losing Displays

In the five deceptive episodes common to both groups, there were more losing than winning episodes identified correctly. Players may be more cognizant of losing than winning behavior. Also, losing behavior may be more obvious than winning behavior, as suggested by both experienced and inexperienced subjects in the original studies (Whittaker, 1980). If this is the case, a sender may be more successful in deceit when displaying winning behavior, given that a winning display is a potentially more appropriate strategy (see Ekman, Chapter 14, regarding positive versus negative affect). However, regardless of the nature of the behavior conveyed, an average player may not be as proficient in deceit as a skilled player, especially when playing a skilled opponent.

Finally, championship players appeared to employ one of two strategies: either emphasizing winning behavior when losing or losing behavior when winning. The data suggested that the second strategy, although seemingly more difficult to execute, might be successful under some circumstances. Displaying losing behavior when winning in a particularly close match may place the opponent at a disadvantage by giving him or her a false sense of security.

CONCLUSIONS

Deception, particularly in the form of masking losing behavior, may be an important strategy for the championship athlete playing against a skilled opponent. By masking losing affect, submissive behavior is suppressed and the sender displays an aura of confidence. Such behavior could be very disconcerting to the opponent, leading ultimately to the sender's success. Since experienced players are better at detecting both winning and losing behavior than inexperienced players, the former may need to be more convincing when playing individuals of equivalent skill. Therefore, in order to optimize their chances of success, skilled opponents may have a greater need to self-deceive than the average player. It also follows that the need to be convincing may be greatest when one's behavior is antithetic to both the total number of previous points and the immediate outcome. As a result, the likelihood of self-deception may also be maximal under these circumstances.

Behaviors exhibited in the deceptive tennis episodes were either at variance with those normally associated with the point outcome or ambiguous. These data are consistent with the definition of deception in sport presented in Figure 13–1. However, the findings only partially support the predicted times in the match when deceptive behaviors were more likely to occur (see Table 13–1). This does not detract from the utility of the model since in this study it was impossible to test all combinations of the four variables of interest: position during the match, point outcome, game outcome, and service or receipt of service. Future studies should include all combinations of variables as well as investigate sex differences in the amount of detail decoded and the ability to mask behavior that might detract from sport success. The ability to subtly convey a sense of dominance to a sport opponent appears to be beneficial to the experienced competitor especially when the skill and fitness levels of the participants are equivalent.

REFERENCES

BLALOCK, H. M., JR. (1962). Occupational discrimination: Some theoretical propositions. *Social Problems, 9*, 240-247.

BROWN, J. L. (1975). *The evolution of behavior.* New York: Norton.

COBB, D. (1982, August/September). Legends in their own times. *Racquets Canada*, 16-27.

DEPAULO, B. M., & ROSENTHAL, R. (1979). Telling lies. *Journal of Personality and Social Psychology, 37*, 1713-1722.

DEPAULO, B. M., ROSENTHAL, R., EISENSTAT, R. A., ROGERS, P. L., & FINKELSTEIN, S. (1978). Decoding discrepant nonverbal cues. *Journal of Personality and Social Psychology, 36*, 313-323.

DITTMAN, A. T., PARLOFF, M. B., & BOOMER, D. S. (1965). Facial and bodily expression: A study of receptivity of emotional cues. *Psychiatry, 28*, 239-244.

EKMAN, P. (1985). *Telling lies: Clues to deceit in the marketplace, politics, and marriage.* New York: Norton.

EKMAN, P., & FRIESEN, W. V. (1969). Nonverbal leakage and clues to deception. *Psychiatry, 32*, 88-106.

————. (1974). Detecting deception from the body or face. *Journal of Personality and Social Psychology, 29*, 288-298.

FELDMAN, R. S., & WHITE, J. B. (1980). Detecting deception in children. *Journal of Communication, 30*, 121-128.

HALL, J. A. (1978). Gender effects in decoding nonverbal cues. *Psychological Bulletin, 85*, 845-857.

LOCKARD, J. S. (1980). Speculation on the adaptive significance of self-deception. In J. S. Lockard (Ed.), *The evolution of human social behavior* (pp. 257–275). New York: Elsevier.

MEHRABIAN, A. (1971). Nonverbal betrayal of feeling. *Journal of Experimental Research in Personality, 5*, 64-73.

MOSS, H. A., & KAGAN, J. (1961). Stability of achievement and recognition seeking behaviors from early childhood through adulthood. *Journal of Abnormal Social Psychology, 62*, 504-513.

OTTE, D. (1975). On the role of intraspecific deception. *American Naturalist, 109*, 239-242.

POTTER, S. (1978). *The complete upmanship.* New York: New American Library.

WALKER, M. B. (1977). The relative importance of verbal and nonverbal cues in the expression of confidence. *Australian Journal of Psychology, 29*, 45-57.

WALLACE, B. (1973). Misinformation, fitness, and selection. *American Naturalist, 107*, 1-7.

228   *Deception and Self-Deception: A Dominance Strategy in Competitive Sport*

WHITTAKER, S. A.   (1980). *Nonverbal communication of winning and losing tennis.* Unpublished doctoral dissertation, University of Washington, Seattle.

WHITTAKER-BLEULER, S. A.   (1980). Detection of nonverbal winning and losing behavior in sport. *Research Quarterly, 51*, 437-440.

WILSON, E. O.   (1975). *Sociobiology: The new synthesis.* Cambridge, MA: Belknap Press of Harvard University Press.

ZUCKERMAN, M., BLANCK, P. D., DEPAULO, B. M., & ROSENTHAL, R.   (1980). Developmental changes in decoding discrepant and nondiscrepant nonverbal cues. *Developmental Psychology, 16*, 220-228.

14

Self-Deception
and Detection
of Misinformation

PAUL EKMAN

University of California at San Francisco

DECEIT IS PART OF LIFE

Lying is such a central characteristic of life that its understanding is relevant to almost all human affairs. Some might shudder at this statement because they view lying as reprehensible. I do not share this view nor prescribe to the dictum that every lie be unmasked. It is too simple to hold that no one in any relationship must ever lie. As Goffman (1959, p. 64) has indicated " . . . there is hardly a legitimate everyday vocation or relationship whose performers do not engage in concealed practices which are incompatible with fostered impressions."

Lies can be cruel, but all lies are not in this category. Some lies are harmless, even humane. Some lies, many fewer than liars will claim, are altruistic. Some social relationships are enjoyed because of the myths they preserve. But no liar should presume too easily that a victim desires to be misled. And no lie catcher should too easily presume the right to expose every lie. Unmasking certain lies may

Although the emphasis on self-deception is new, most of this chapter is excerpted from my book (Ekman, 1985) Telling lies: Clues to deceit in the marketplace, politics, and marriage. *The title of this chapter uses the term "misinformation" rather than "lying" as I assume the latter is always a deliberate act. In other words, an individual who misinforms another but is unaware of his or her falsification is not a "liar" by my definition of the term.*

humiliate the recipient or a third party. Wohlstetter (1981) suggested in her analysis of cheating in arms races that the cheater and the side cheated have a stake in allowing the error to persist and that they both need to preserve the illusion that the agreement has not been violated.

Thus, in some situations *self-deception by either the conveyor of misinformation and/or the recipient may be beneficial to one or both* (Lockard, 1980, and Chapters 1 and 2). Only fabricators who are aware of their lies are likely to be caught. Also, in many deceits the victim overlooks the liar's mistakes to avoid the terrible consequences of uncovering the lie. For example, by overlooking the signs of his wife's affairs, a husband may at least postpone the humiliation of being exposed as a cuckold or, alternatively, may be able to believe, no matter how unlikely, that the affair did not take place.

The intent of this chapter is to explore the impact of self-deception on the detection of misinformation, that is, its success in preventing leakage and/or deception clues. However, before a meaningful discussion of this issue can take place, some understanding must first be reached regarding a definition of lying, the forms lying takes, the major clues to deceit, and how deceit is detected.

A DEFINITION OF LYING

Lying is defined as a deliberate choice to mislead a target without giving any notification of the intent to do so. The focus here is on what Goffman (1959, p. 59) called barefaced lies, ones ''. . . for which there can be unquestionable evidence that the teller knew he lied and willfully did so.'' The lie may or may not be justified, in the opinion of the liar or the community. The liar may be a good or a bad person, liked or disliked. But the person who fabricates could choose not to and knows the difference between lying and being truthful. Therefore, pathological liars who know they are being untruthful but cannot control their behavior do not meet this requirement. Nor would people who do not even know they are lying, those said to be victims of self-deceit. Also, a liar may over time come to believe in his or her lie. If that happens, that person would no longer be a liar; untruths, then for reasons to be explained later, would be much harder to detect.

It is not just the liar that must be considered in defining a lie but the liar's target as well. In a lie the target has not asked to be misled, nor does the liar give any prior notification of an intention to do so. It would be bizarre to call actors liars. Their audience agrees to be misled; that is why they are there. Actors do not impersonate, as does the con man, without giving notice that it is a pose put on for a time. A customer would not knowingly follow the advice of a broker who said he would be providing convincing but false information. Also, untruths in poker (Hayano, 1979, Chapter 11)—concealment or bluffing—are *not* examples of lying. No one expects poker players to reveal the cards they have drawn. Similarly, in collective bargaining (Horowitz, 1981) no one is expected to put all of his or her cards on the table at the outset; the declaration ''that is my final offer'' often signifies just the beginning in a series of compromises. Therefore, in this definition of a lie or deceit, one person intends to mislead another, doing so deliberately, without prior notification of such a purpose, and without having been explicitly asked to do so by the target.

CONCEALMENT AND FALSIFICATION

There are two major forms of lying: **concealment** and **falsification** (Handel, 1982; Whaley, 1982). In concealing, the liar withholds some information without actually saying anything untrue. In falsifying, an additional step is taken. Not only does the liar withhold true information but presents false information as if it were true. Often it is necessary to combine concealing and falsifying to pull off the deceit, but sometimes a liar can get away just with concealment. If there is a choice about how to lie, liars usually prefer to conceal rather than to falsify. There are several advantages to concealment alone. It is easier than falsifying; nothing has to be made up. Concealment lies are also much easier to cover if discovered afterwards. There are many available excuses, such as memory failure or ignorance. Concealment may also be preferred because it seems less reprehensible than falsifying. It is passive, not active. Even though the target may be equally victimized, liars may feel less guilt when they conceal than when they falsify.

Although concealing and falsifying are the predominant ways to lie, they are not the only ones. Other ways to lie include misdirecting (acknowledging an emotion but misidentifying what caused it), telling the truth falsely (admitting the truth but with such exaggeration or humor that the target remains uninformed or misled), half-concealing (admitting only part of what is true so as to deflect the target's interest in what remains concealed), and incorrect-inference dodging (telling the truth but in a way that implies the opposite of what is said). Any of these lies can be betrayed by some aspect of the deceiver's behavior.

LEAKAGE AND DECEPTION CLUES

Once challenged by the victim, the liar loses the choice of whether to continue to conceal only or to compound the lie. Falsification now becomes necessary, even though the original lie did not directly require it, to help the liar cover evidence of what is being concealed. This use of falsification to *mask* what is being concealed is especially required when emotions must be concealed. It is easy to conceal an emotion no longer felt but much harder to conceal an emotion felt at the moment, especially if the feeling is strong. Terror is harder to conceal than worry, just as rage is harder to conceal than annoyance. *The stronger the emotion, the more likely it is that some sign of it will leak* despite the liar's best attempt to conceal it. Putting on another emotion, one that is not felt, can help disguise the felt emotion. Falsifying an emotion can cover the leakage of a concealed emotion.

Any emotion can be falsified to help conceal any other emotion; the smile is the mask most frequently employed. It serves as the opposite of all the negative emotions: fear, anger, distress, and disgust. It is selected often because some variation on happiness is the message required to pull off many deceits. The disappointed employee must smile if the boss is to think she is not hurt or angry about being passed over for promotion. The cruel friend should pose as well meaning as he delivers his cutting criticism with a concerned smile.

There are two kinds of clues to deceit. A mistake may reveal the truth, or it may only suggest that what was said or shown is untrue without revealing the truth. When a liar mistakenly reveals the truth, it is called **leakage**. When the liar's behavior suggests he or she is lying without revealing the truth, it is called a **deception clue**. A deception clue answers the question of whether or not the person is lying, although it does not reveal what is being concealed. Only leakage does that. Often in everyday life it does not matter. When the question is whether or not a person is lying, rather than what is being concealed, a deception clue is good enough. Leakage is not needed. What information is being held back can be figured out or is irrelevant. For example, if an employer senses through a deception clue that an applicant is lying, that may be sufficient, and no leakage of what is being concealed may be needed to make the decision not to hire the applicant.

WHY LIES FAIL

Both leakage and deception clues are mistakes. They do not always happen. Not all lies fail. Lies fail for many reasons, such as discovery by the victim or the betrayal of the liar by someone else. What is of concern here are those mistakes made during the act of lying, mistakes the deceiver makes despite himself, lies that fail because of the liar's behavior. Not anticipating the need to lie, guilt from having lied, fear in discovery, or delight in deceiving others can all be shown in facial expression, vocal expression, or body movement, even when the liar is trying to conceal them. Just the struggle to prevent nonverbal leakage may produce deception clues.

A failure to think ahead, plan fully, and rehearse a false line may furnish clues to deceit. Even when there are no inconsistencies in what is said, lack of preparation or a failure to remember the line one had adopted may produce clues to the spoken deception. The need to think about each word before it is uttered—weighing possibilities, searching for a word or idea—may be obvious in pauses during speech or, more subtly, in slight changes in gestures or facial expressions such as a tightening of the lower eyelid or eyebrow.

Mistakes are also made because of difficulty in concealing or falsely portraying emotion. Not every lie involves emotions, but those that do cause special problems for the liar. People do not actively select when they will feel an emotion. When emotions are aroused, changes occur automatically without choice or deliberation. While concealing an emotion is not easy, neither is falsifying the appearance of an unfelt emotion. Trying to look angry is not simple, but if fear of discovery is also felt, the person is caught between two antagonistic facial expressions. The brows, for example, are involuntarily pulled upward in fear. But to falsify anger the person must pull them down. Often the signs of this internal struggle between the felt and the false emotion betray the deceit.

Even when the lie is about something other than emotion, emotions may become involved. A vain man might be embarrassed about his vanity, and to succeed in lying about his age he would have to conceal his embarrassment as well. The plagiarist might feel contempt toward those she misleads, and to pretend to have ability that is not hers she would have to conceal her contempt. Once involved, the emotions must be concealed if the lie is not to be betrayed. Any emotion may be the culprit, but three emotions are often inexorably intertwined with deceit: fear of being caught, guilt about lying, and delight in having duped someone.

Deception apprehension is greatest when the target has a reputation for being difficult to fool; the target starts out being suspicious; the liar has had little practice and no record of success; the liar is especially vulnerable to the fear of being caught; the stakes are high; both rewards and punishments are at stake, or, if it is only one or the other, punishment is at stake; the punishment for being caught is great, or the punishment for what the lie is about is so great that there is no incentive to confess; or the target in no way benefits from the lie.

Deception guilt will be greatest when the target is unwilling; the deceit is totally selfish in that the target derives no benefit from being misled and loses as much as or more than the liar gains; the deceit is unauthorized, and the situation is one in which honesty is authorized; the liar has not been practicing the deceit for a long time; the liar and target share social values; the liar is personally acquainted with the target; the target cannot easily be faulted as mean or gullible; or there is reason for the target to expect to be misled, or, just the opposite, the liar has acted to win confidence in his or her trustworthiness.

Duping delight will be greatest when the target poses a challenge, having a reputation for being difficult to fool; the lie is a challenge, because of the nature of what must be concealed or fabricated; or others are watching or know about the lie and appreciate the liar's skillful performance.

DETECTING DECEIT

There is no one certain sign of lying; if there were, people would most assuredly lie less. It is not a simple matter to catch lies. One problem is the barrage of information. There is too much to consider at once, too many sources—words, pauses, sound of the voice, expressions, head movements, gestures, posture, respiration, flushing, blanching, and sweating. However, not every source of information during a conversation is equally reliable. Strangely enough, the least trustworthy sources—words and facial expressions—are attended to the most.

Word Clues

Liars are unable to monitor, control, and disguise all of their behavior. They tend to be most careful about their choice of words because they know they will be more accountable for their words than for the sound of their voice, facial expressions, or most body movements. An angry expression or a harsh tone of voice can always be denied; it is much harder to deny having said an angry word. Words are also the chief target for disguise because they are easy to falsify. In addition, the speaker has continual feedback—hearing what he says—and thus is able to fine-tune his message or rehearse it. Only a highly trained actor could precisely plan each facial expression, gesture, and voice inflection.

Surprisingly, many liars are betrayed by their words because of *carelessness*: they neglect to fabricate carefully or cannot remember and are inconsistent in the telling from one time to another. A few are betrayed by a **slip-of-the-tongue** (Freud, 1901/1976, p. 86), ". . . something one did not wish to say: it becomes a mode of self-betrayal." It is tempting to speculate that slips occur when the liar "wants" to be caught, although there are no studies on this issue. **Tirades** are a third way liars may betray by word leakage. The information does not slip out, it pours out as the liar is carried away by emotion and does not realize until afterward the consequence of what is revealed. Often, if the liar had remained cool, he or she would not have been discovered. A fourth source of word leakage is the convoluted answer or sophisticated **evasion**, though some studies (see review by Zuckerman, DePaulo, & Rosenthal, 1981) have not found it to be a reliable deception clue. When they lie, some people give indirect replies, are circumlocutious, and give more information than requested. A few people always speak this way, and for them it is not a sign of lying but a personality trait.

Voice Clues

The voice refers to everything involved in speech other than the words themselves. The most common vocal deception clues are **pauses**. Hesitating at the start of a speaking turn, pauses that may be too long or too frequent, or speech errors such as stammering, repetitions, or partial words may arouse suspicion. These vocal clues can occur for two related reasons: not being prepared to lie or high detection apprehension.

Deceit may also be revealed by the sound of the voice. The best-documented vocal sign of emotion is **pitch** (Scherer, 1982). For about 70% of the people studied, pitch becomes higher when the subject is upset, particularly if the feeling is anger or fear. There is some evidence that pitch drops with sadness or sorrow. Research has not been conducted regarding how pitch changes with excitement, distress, disgust, or contempt. Other promising signs of emotion, though not as well established, are louder, faster speech, as during anger or fear, and softer, slower speech, as in manifestations of sadness. Other aspects of voice quality such as timbre, different frequency bands of the energy spectrum, and changes related to respiration are also likely to be fruitful clues to deception.

In the strictest sense, voice intonation, such as raised pitch, is not itself a sign of deceit; it is a sign of fear or anger, perhaps also of excitement. The sound of the voice can also betray lies that were not undertaken to conceal emotion, if emotion has become involved. Detection apprehension will produce the voice sound of fear, and it is likely that deception guilt, if it were to be studied, might produce the same changes in the sound of the voice as sadness does. The problem for the lie catcher is that apprehensive, innocent people, not just liars, are also emotionally aroused. Also, the failure to show a sign of emotion in the voice is not necessarily evidence of truthfulness; some people never or rarely show emotion in their voice. Thus, there is no voice sign of lying *per se*, only of negative emotions. Machines designed to measure voice stress do no better than chance in detecting lies; they also don't do well at the easier task of telling whether or not someone is upset (Lykken, 1981).

Body Clues from Skeletal Muscles

Research from 1914 to 1954 (see review, Ekman & Friesen, 1969) has failed to find support for the claim that nonverbal behavior provides accurate information about emotion and personality. More recent studies on emblems (Johnson, Ekman, & Friesen, 1975), illustrators (Efron, 1972), manipulators (Ekman & Friesen, 1974a), certain postures (Mandler, 1984), and autonomically controlled behaviors (Ekman, Levenson, & Friesen, 1983) have been more productive.

Emblems   The shrug and the "finger" are two examples of actions that are called **emblems**, to distinguish them from all of the other gestures that people make. Emblems have a very precise meaning, known to everyone within a cultural group. They can be used in place of a word or when words cannot be used. Most other gestures do not have such a specific meaning. Examples of other well-known emblems are the head-nod "yes," head-shake "no," come-here beckon, wave hello/goodbye, finger-on-finger "shame on you," hand-to-ear louder request, and hitchhiker's thumb.

Although emblems are almost always performed deliberately, they sometimes leak information a person is trying to conceal. There are two ways to tell if an emblem is a slip and not a deliberate message: if only a fragment of the emblem is performed or if the emblem is performed in an area other than between the waist and the neck. When an emblem is a slip, only one element will be shown and/or it will be performed out of the usual presentation location. For instance, in a shrug, raising one shoulder and then only barely, or giving the "finger" out of view, say, in your lap while seated at a table are leakage emblems. While not every liar shows an emblematic slip or does so in plain sight, when emblematic slips are detected they are quite reliable as a clue to a message the person does not want to reveal. Moreover, a lie catcher does not need previous acquaintance with a suspect to interpret an emblematic slip.

Illustrators   Another type of body movement that can provide deception clues during conversation is a **speech illustrator**. People from different cultures not only use different illustrators, but some illustrate very little while others illustrate a lot. It is the hands that usually carry out this function, although brow and upper-eyelid movements may emphasize speech, and the entire body or upper trunk can do so also. In contrast to emblematic slips that may increase in deceit, illustrators usually decrease.

Illustrators are used to help explain ideas that are difficult to put into words. Snapping the fingers or reaching in the air seems to help the person "find" the words. Such word-search illustrations may have a self-priming function, helping people put words together into reasonable, coherent speech. Speech illustrators increase with emotional involvement and, thus, decrease whenever a person carefully considers or censors the words being spoken, or when a person is emotionally uninvolved with the topic of conversation.

The lie catcher must be more cautious in interpreting illustrators than in interpreting emblematic slips. The crucial differences between emblems and illustrators are in the precision of movement and message. For the emblem, both are highly prescribed: not any movement will do; only a highly defined movement will convey a precise message. On the other hand, illustrators may involve a wide variety of movements and convey a vague rather than a specific message, and their absence is less reliable as a indication of deceit than the presence of an emblematic slip.

Manipulators   A third category of body movement, **manipulators**, is the least reliable sign of deceit. Manipulators include all those movements in which one part of the body grooms, massages, rubs, holds, pinches, picks, scratches, or otherwise manipulates another body part. Such activity may either be of very short duration or go on for many minutes. The brief episodes seem to be purposive: the hair is rearranged, matter is removed from the ear canal, or a part of the body is scratched. Manipulators that last a long time seem to be purposeless: hair is twisted and untwisted, fingers rubbed, or a foot tapped incessantly.

While most people were brought up not to perform these "bathroom behaviors" in public, they have not learned to stop doing them, only to sometimes stop noticing that they do them. Manipulators are on the edge of consciousness and may occur in spite of efforts to inhibit their manifestation. Others look away when a manipulator is performed. Such polite inattention to manipulators is also a strong habit, often operating without thought.

Manipulators are unreliable signs of deceit because they may indicate opposite states: discomfort or relaxation. They occur either when one is restless and ill at ease or when one is quite relaxed and very much at ease, that is, "letting one's hair down." Also, liars know that they should try to squelch manipulators since the common folklore is that restlessness and fidgeting are valid deception clues, when in fact they may not be. Liars may succeed in inhibiting manipulators, at least part of the time, particularly if the stakes are high.

Postures   Another aspect of the body—**posture**—has been examined by a number of investigators (e.g., Kraut & Poe, 1980), but little evidence of deception leakage has been found. Posture seems well under control and successfully managed when someone is deceiving. There is the tendency to move forward with interest or anger and backward with fear or disgust, but a motivated liar should be able to inhibit all but the most subtle signs of postural clues to these emotions.

Body Clues Under Autonomic Nervous System Control

In addition to body actions involving skeletal muscles, the autonomic nervous system (ANS) also produces some noticeable changes in the body with emotional arousal: the pattern of breathing, the frequency of swallowing, and the amount of sweating. (Facial changes are also ANS-mediated, such as blushing, blanching, and the dilating of pupils discussed in the next section.) These changes occur involuntarily when emotion is aroused, are very hard to inhibit, and for that reason can be very reliable clues to deceit.

General versus specific ANS changes   Until very recently, most investigators (see review by Mandler, 1984) were of the opinion that breathing rapidly, sweating, and swallowing were general characteristics of any emotion. In other words, it was thought that ANS changes marked how strong an emotion was, not which emotion it was. This view contradicts the experiences of most people: they report feeling different bodily sensations when they are afraid, for example, as compared to when they are angry. This has been explained in the past by the assumption that people interpret the same set of bodily sensations differently if they are afraid than if they are angry.

My research (e.g., Ekman, Levenson, & Friesen, 1983) challenges the view of general ANS changes and suggests that there are particular combinations specific to each emotion. If correct, such information would be important in detecting lies. It would mean that a lie catcher could discover not just whether a suspect is emotionally aroused but which emotion is being felt, that is, whether the suspect is afraid or angry, disgusted or sad. While similar information is conveyed in the face (as discussed below), people are able to inhibit many of the facial signs. Bodily changes under ANS control are much harder to censor.

Facial Clues to Deceit

With the exception of words, the face receives the greatest amount of attention from others. It is the mark and symbol of the self, the chief way we distinguish one person from another. It is also the primary site for the display of emotions. But most important for the present discourse is that the face can both lie and tell the truth, often at the same time.

The true, felt expressions of emotion occur because facial actions can be produced involuntarily, without thought or intention. The false ones happen because there is voluntary control over the face, allowing people to interfere with the felt emotion and assume a false one. Therefore, the face is a **dual system**, including expressions that are deliberately chosen and those that occur spontaneously, sometimes without the person even being aware of the facial expression that emerges. Studies of patients with different kinds of brain damage dramatically show that the voluntary and the involuntary expressions involve different parts of the brain (Tschiassny, 1953). For example, patients who have damage to the pyramidal neural systems are unable to smile if asked to do so but will smile when they hear a joke or otherwise enjoy themselves. The pattern is reversed for patients who have suffered damage to another part of the brain, involving the nonpyramidal systems: they can produce a voluntary smile but are blank-faced when enjoying themselves.

The involuntary facial expressions of emotion are the product of evolution (Ekman, 1973). Those facial expressions indicating happiness, fear, anger, disgust, sadness, and distress are universal—the same for all people regardless of age, sex, race, or culture. However, the face can show not only which emotion is felt but also whether or not two emotions are blended together and the strength of the felt emotion, say, from annoyance to rage or apprehension to terror. Also, as people grow up they learn **cultural display rules** of emotions and, thus, of facial expressions. After a time, many display rules for the management of emotional expression come to operate automatically, modulating facial changes without choice or even awareness.

In addition to automatic habitual controls of facial expressions, people can and do choose deliberately, quite consciously, to censor the expression of their true feelings or falsify the expression of an emotion not felt. Most people succeed in some of their facial deceits. However, most are not facile in detecting false expressions of others even though they believe they are. When individuals lie, their most evident, easy-to-see expressions are the ones to which people pay attention, and these are often false ones. The subtle sign that these expressions are not felt and the fleeting hints of the concealed emotions are usually missed. The problem is that there are thousands of facial expressions, each one different from another, many having nothing to do with emotion. A considerable number of facial expressions are **conversational signals** (analogous to body-movement illustrators that emphasize speech or provide syntax) such as facial question marks or exclamation points. There are also many **facial emblems,** such as the one-eye closure wink; the raised-eyebrows, droopy-upper-eyelid, horseshoe-mouth shrug; and the one-eyebrow-raised skeptical look. There are **facial manipulators**, such as lip biting, lip sucking, lip wiping, and cheek puffing. And then there are the emotional expressions, the true ones and the false.

There is not one expression for each emotion but dozens, and for some emotions, hundreds. In fact, there are more facial expressions than there are words for any emotion. Every emotion has a family of expressions, all visibly different from one another. Consider the members of the anger family: Anger varies in (1) intensity, from annoyance to rage; (2) how controlled it is, from explosive to fuming; (3) how long it takes to begin (onset time), from short-fused to smoldering; (4) how long it takes to end (offset time), from rapid to lingering; (5) temperature, from hot to cold; and (6) genuineness, from real anger to the phony anger an amused parent shows a naughty, charming child.

The face may contain many different clues to deceit: micro elements, squelched expressions, leakage through facial musculature, blinking, pupil dilation, tearing, blushing, blanching, facial asymmetry, mistakes in timing, mistakes in location, and false smiles. Some of these clues provide leakage, betraying concealed information; others provide deception clues indicating that something is being concealed but not what; and still others mark an expression as false. Like the clues to deceit in words, voice, and body, facial signs of deceit vary in the precision of the information they convey. Some clues reveal exactly which emotion is felt, even though the liar tries to conceal that feeling. Other clues reveal only whether the emotion being concealed is positive or negative, not which emotion the liar feels. Still other clues are even more undifferentiated, betraying only that the liar feels some emotion, but not revealing whether the concealed feeling is positive or negative.

Micro facial elements   These expressions are full-face emotional expressions that last only a fraction of their usual duration (approximately ¼ second)—so quick they are usually not seen—and are followed immediately by an opposite false facial expression. For example, in a psychiatric patient who was falsely trying to convince her psychiatrist that she was no longer suicidal, the filmed interview (Ekman & Friesen, 1984), shown in slow motion, revealed a very brief sad face followed by a longer-duration false smile. Although micros provide reliable leakage of a concealed emotion, they occur very infrequently. Much more common are masked expressions.

Squelched facial expressions   If as an expression emerges the person seems to become aware of what is beginning to show and interrupts the expression, sometimes also covering it with another expression, this is an example of a squelched facial expression. The smile is the most common cover or mask. When an expression is squelched, it does not always reach a full display (but lasts longer than a micro), and the interruption itself may be noticeable. However, not all liars show a micro, a squelched facial expression, and/or a mask, so the absence of these expressions is not necessarily evidence of truth. Also, some truthful individuals become emotional when suspected of lying and may reveal micros, squelches, or masks that do not indicate deceit.

Reliable facial muscles and leakage   Not all muscles that produce facial expressions are equally easy to control. Some muscle actions are more reliable indicators of true emotions than others, in that very few people can make them deliberately. For example, only a small percentage of individuals can voluntarily pull the corners of their lips downward without moving their chin muscle. However, these same people will show the downward lips without chin involvement when they feel true sadness, sorrow, or grief. The **chin muscles** are reliable because individuals do not know how to deploy them in false expressions. It follows that there would be difficulty in squelching a true facial message involving the chin muscles.

The chief locus for reliable muscle movements is the **forehead**. Figure 14–1a

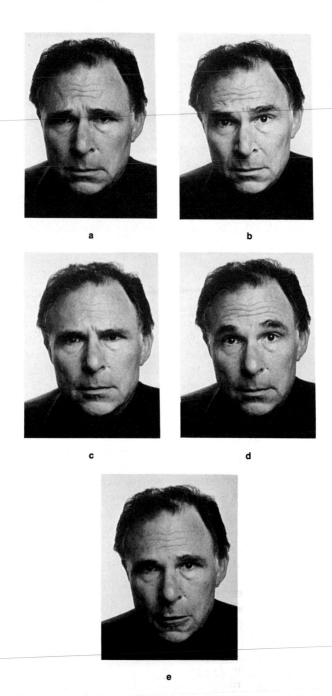

FIGURE 14–1   Facial cues of emotions: a—inner corners of the eyebrows are pulled upward: occurs reliably with sadness, grief, distress, or probably guilt; b—eyebrows are raised and pulled together: occurs reliably with fear, worry, apprehension, or terror; c—lowered eyebrows: occurs with anger, and as a conversational signal to emphasize speech; d—raised eyebrows: occurs with surprise, and as a conversational signal to emphasize speech; e—reliable mouth clue to anger: red area of lips becomes less visible. (See text for description of each.)

shows the reliable muscle movements that occur with sadness, grief, distress, and probably also with guilt. Note that the inner corners of the eyebrows are pulled upward. Usually this will also triangulate the upper eyelid and produce some wrinkling in the center of the forehead. Again, very few individuals (fewer than 15%; Ekman, Hager, & Friesen, 1981) can produce this movement deliberately. Therefore, it would not be expected to be present in a false display of these emotions and should be present when individuals truly feel them.

Figure 14–1b shows the reliable muscle movements that occur with fear, worry, apprehension, or terror. Notice that the eyebrows are raised and pulled together. This combination of action is extremely difficult to make deliberately (fewer than 10% of those tested could do so; Ekman, Hager, & Friesen, 1981). The illustration also shows the raised upper eyelid and tensed lower eyelid that typically mark fear. These eyelid actions may drop out when a person attempts to conceal fear, for these are not difficult actions to control. The eyebrow position is more likely to remain.

Figures 14–1c and 14–1d show the eyebrow and eyelid actions that occur with anger and surprise, respectively. These eyebrow actions—lowering or raising—are the most frequent facial expressions. However, the muscle movements are not reliable, in that everyone can make them deliberately. Therefore, they would be expected to appear in false expressions or to be easily concealed. These actions are also often used as conversational signals to accent or emphasize speech. Brow raises are deployed as exclamations, questioning expressions of disbelief, or emblems of skepticism. Darwin called the muscle that pulls the brows down and together the muscle of difficulty (Ekman, 1973). He was correct in asserting that this action occurs with difficult tasks of any kind, from lifting something heavy to solving complex arithmetic problems. Lowering and drawing the brows together is also common with expressions of perplexity and concentration.

There are no other distinctive eyebrow and eyelid actions that mark other emotions, although it is commonly believed, sometimes incorrectly, that the eyes can convery concealed emotions. Muscles surrounding the eyeballs do not provide reliable clues to deceit, nor does the direction of gaze, as gaze aversion is easily inhibited and common to several emotions: downward with sadness, down or away with shame or guilt, and away with disgust. Whereas involuntary blinking and pupil dilation indicate emotional arousal, they do not reveal which emotion it is. Similarly, tears as a source of information from the eye area are also common to several emotions: distress, sadness, relief, certain forms of enjoyment, and uncontrolled laughter.

There is a reliable **mouth clue to anger**. Figure 14–1e shows how in this expression the red area of the lips becomes less visible, although the lips are not sucked in or necessarily pressed. This muscle action is very difficult for most people to make. It often appears when someone starts to become angry, even before the person is aware of the feeling. It is a subtle movement and one easily concealed by smiling. Much of the face also turns red with anger, but no one knows how this reddening might differ from the blush of embarrassment, shame, or guilt. In more controlled anger, the face may whiten or blanch as it does with fear. However, there has been very little study of tears, blushing, reddening, or blanching in relation to the expression or concealment of specific emotions.

Facial leakage by asymmetry, timing, or location   Facial deception clues may also be revealed by asymmetry, timing, or location of expression. In **asymmetrical facial expressions** the same actions appear on both sides of the face, but the actions are stronger on one side than on the other. They should not be confused with **unilateral expressions,** those that appear on only one side of the face. Such one-sided facial actions are not signs of emotion, with the exception of the contempt expressions in which the lip corner is tightened on one side. Instead, unilateral expressions are used in emblems such as the wink or the skeptical raise of one eyebrow.

Crooked expressions, in which the actions are slightly stronger on one side of the face than the other, are a clue that the feeling shown is not felt, although some studies have indicated otherwise. Sackeim, Gur, and Saucy (1978), under the assumption that the right cerebral hemisphere is more involved than the left in the control of emotional expression, cut facial pictures I had supplied in half and created double-left or double-right photographs. Each reconstructed picture was a full-face, mirror image of one or the other side of the face. People rated emotion as more intense when they saw the double-left (mediated by the right hemisphere) than the double-right pictures. I noticed that there was one exception: there was no difference in the judgments of the happy pictures. Being the photographer, I knew that the happy pictures were the only nonposed emotional expressions because the rest had been made by asking models to move particular facial muscles deliberately; the happy pictures were of models in off-guard moments while they were enjoying themselves.

Ekman, Hager, and Friesen (1981) had a different assumption, namely that the cerebral hemispheres direct voluntary facial movements while the lower brain areas mediate involuntary movements. They found a much lower incidence of asymmetrical expressions (slightly stronger on the left side of the face if the person was right-handed) with genuine, felt (not staged) smiles than did Sackeim, Gur, and Saucy (1978). When people were asked to smile deliberately or pose happiness, more asymmetry emerged (Ekman, 1980). In addition to the smile, Hager and Ekman (1985) found that the brow-lowering action, often part of the anger display, was stronger on the left side of the face when the action was made deliberately. Also, the nose-wrinkling action involved in disgust and the stretching of the lips back toward the ears found in fear were usually stronger on the right side of the face if the actions were deliberate.

Although many asymmetrical facial expressions are unfelt, asymmetry is not certain proof that an expression is unfelt. Similarly, the absence of asymmetry does not prove that the expression is felt; asymmetry is not leakage but a category of deception clues that includes facial timing and location as well.

Timing encompasses the duration of a facial expression and its onset and offset latencies. Most felt expressions are of short duration (less than five seconds). Therefore, expressions of long duration (greater than five seconds) are likely to be false. Long expressions are usually emblems or mock expressions. For onset and offset latencies there is no hard and fast rule governing when they are likely to be deception clues, except in the case of surprise. Onset, offset, and duration all must be short—less then a second—if surprise is genuine. If it is longer it is mock surprise (the person is playing at being surprised), a surprise emblem (the person is referring to being surprised), or false surprise (the person is trying to seem surprised when not). For all other emotional expressions the onset and offset may be abrupt or more gradual, depending upon the context in which the expression occurs. For example, in a joke-telling situation, the time it takes for the smiling actions to appear depends upon the build-up to the punch line, and the length of time for the smile to disappear is a function of the type of joke.

The **location** of an expression in relation to the flow of speech, voice changes, and body movements is the third source of deception clue in the facial category. For instance, if someone is falsifying anger and says so before the angry expression appears, the expression is more likely to be false than if it appeared at the start, or even a little before the verbal statement. There seems to be less latitude about where to position facial expression in relation to body movement. Suppose during the verbal statement of anger an individual banged a fist on the table. If the angry facial expression followed the bang it is more likely to be false. Facial expressions that are not synchronized with body movement are most probably deception clues.

Smiles as signs of deceit   No discussion of deception clues would be comprehensive without considering smiles, the most frequent of all facial expressions. They are unique among facial displays of emotion because it takes but one facial muscle to express happiness while most other emotions require the action of three to five muscles. The common element in most members of the smile family is the change in appearance produced by the zygomatic major muscle. This muscle reaches from the cheekbones down and across the face, attaching to the corners of the lips. When contracted, the zygomatic major pulls the lip corners up at an angle toward the cheekbones. With a strong action this muscle also stretches the lips, pulls the cheeks upward, bags the skin below the eyes, and produces crow's-feet wrinkles beyond the eye corners. (In some individuals this muscle also pulls the tip of the nose down slightly; in still others there will be a slight tug at the skin near the ears.) Other muscles merge with the zygomatic major to form different members of the smile family; and a few smiling appearances are produced not by the zygomatic but by other muscles.

The **simple smile**,[1] Figure 14–2a, produced by singular action of the zygomatic major muscle is a genuine, uncontrolled, positive expression. The simple

---

[1]In Ekman, 1985, the simple smile is called the **felt smile**.

FIGURE 14–2 Genuine smile: a—simple smile (called *felt smile*, Ekman, 1985). Smiles as signs of deceit: b—fear smile; c—contempt smile; d—dampened smile; e—miserable smile; f—Chaplin smile; g—false smile. (See text for description of each.)

smile is the easiest facial expression to recognize and can be seen from further away (300 feet) and with a briefer exposure than other emotional expressions (Hager & Ekman, 1979). No other muscles in the lower part of the face enter into this felt smile. The only action that may also appear in the upper face is the tightening of the muscle that circles the eyes. This change in the upper face can also be produced by a strong action of the zygomatic major—raised cheeks, bagged skin below the eyes, and crow's-feet wrinkles. Felt smiles last longer and are more intense when positive feelings are more extreme (Ekman, Friesen, & Ancoli, 1980; Ekman & Friesen, 1982).

The **fear smile** (Figure 14–2b) has nothing to do with positive emotions but is sometimes mistakenly classified as such. It is produced by the risorious muscle pulling the lip corners horizontally toward the ears so that the lips are stretched to form a rectangular shape. As the risorious pulls the lips horizontally, the lip corners will sometimes tilt upward to cause confusion in smile classification. In a fearful expression the rectangular-shaped mouth (with or without an upward lip-corner tilt) will be accompanied by the brows and eyes shown in Figure 14–2b.

The **contempt smile** (Figure 14–2c) is another misnomer since it, too, has little to do with positive emotions, although it is often so construed. It involves a tightening of the muscle in the lip corners, often a dimple, and a slight angling up of the lip corners. (Contempt can also be shown by a unilateral version of this expression in which one lip corner is tightened and slightly raised.) Again, it is the angling up of the lip corners as well as the dimple—shared characteristics with the simple smile—that cause the confusion. The chief difference between the two expressions is the tightened lip corners, which are present in contempt and absent in the simple smile.

The **dampened smile** (Figure 14–2d) expresses a positive emotion but with an attempt to display less intense feelings than are actually being felt. The aim s to dampen, to keep within bounds, but not to suppress the emotional experience. The lips may be pressed, the lip corners tightened, the lower lip pushed up, or the lip corners pulled down, or any combination of these actions may merge with the simple smile.

The **miserable smile** (Figure 14–2e) acknowledges the experience of negative emotions. It is not an attempt to conceal but a facial comment on being miserable. The appearance of the expression also means that, at the moment, the person is not going to protest the misery—he is going to grin and bear it. The key difference between the versions of the miserable and the dampened smiles shown in Figure 14–2 is the absence in the former of any evidence of the muscle tightening around the eyes. The crow's-feet wrinkles and the pulling in of the skin around the eyes are part of the dampened smile because enjoyment is felt; they are absent from the miserable smile because enjoyment is not felt. The miserable smile may also show in the eyebrows and forehead, the felt negative emotions being acknowledged.

The **smile blend** (not shown) is the simultaneous expression of a combination of two or more emotions experienced at once. Any emotion can blend with any other emotion. The examples described here are blends with the simple smile. In the enjoyable-contempt expression the simple smile merges with the tightening of one or both lip corners. In the enjoyable-sadness blend the lip corners may be pulled down in addition to the upward pull of the simple smile, or the simple smile may merge with the upper portion of the sad face. In the enjoyable-surprise face the brow is raised, the upper lid is raised, and the simple smile is evident from the dropped jaw.

The flirtation smile and the embarrassment smile (not shown) are two other examples of blends, but ones in which the simple smile is combined with a particular gaze. The Chaplin smile (Figure 14–2f) is an unusual expression, produced by a muscle that most people cannot move deliberately. It is a supercilious smile that smiles at smiling: the lips angle upward much more sharply than they do in the simple smile. And, finally, there are four other smiles (not shown) that are made deliberately and share the same appearance but serve quite different social functions, as their names suggest: the qualifier smile, the compliance smile, the coordination smile, and the listener-response smile (Ekman, 1985, pp. 156-157). These unfelt smile blends can be replaced at any time by the simple smile if the individual is truly enjoying the social situation.

The false smile   Now let us consider the only smile that lies. The **false smile** (Figure 14–2g) is intended to convince another person that positive emotion is felt when it is not. Nothing much may be felt, or negative emotions may be felt that the liar may try to conceal by using the false smile as a mask. Unlike the miserable smile that acknowledges that pleasure is not felt, the false smile tries to mislead the other person into thinking that the smiler is having positive feelings.

There are a number of clues for distinguishing false smiles from the felt smiles they pretend to be. False smiles: (1) are more asymmetrical than felt smiles, (2) are not accompanied by the involvement of the muscles around the eyes, (3) have noticeably inappropriate offset times, and (4) act as masks, covering only the actions of the lower face and lower eyelid and not the reliable muscles of the forehead.

A test of facial deceit   In an initial study (unpublished) of felt versus unfelt smiles involving student nurses, two clues to detection of unfelt smiles were tested. We measured the absence of movement of the muscle around the eyes and the presence of signs of disgust (nose wrinkling) or contempt (tightening of the lip corners). It was hypothesized that the nurses would show felt smiles in an "honest" interview (when they had watched a pleasant film and described their feelings frankly), and conversely, that they would show false smiles in the "deceptive" interview (when they had watched a very unpleasant film but tried to appear as if they were seeing another pleasant film). The results were exactly as predicted, and very strong: in the honest interview there were more felt than false smiles and no smiles that leaked either disgust or contempt; in the deceptive interview the leakage smiles appeared and there were more false than felt smiles. The strength of the findings was surprising in that most people seemed not to use these clues when judging others. In earlier studies (Ekman & Friesen, 1974b), the very same videotapes of facial expression were shown to subjects who were asked to judge when the nurses were lying. They did no better than chance.

SELF-DECEPTION IN THE PERPETRATION OF MISINFORMATION

Whereas no special talent is required to understand how to spot clues to deceit, it is apparent that practice is necessary to become skilled in doing so. But anyone who spends the time, looking and listening carefully, watching for the clues described above, can improve in detecting misinformation. While there could be a school for lie catchers, a school for liars would make little sense. Lying cannot be improved appreciably by merely knowing what to do and what not to do. And for two reasons, I seriously doubt that practice alone could make one an exceptional liar. First, a self-conscious liar, who planned each move as he made it, would be like a skier who thought about each stride as he went down the slope. Second, it is very difficult, even if you are skilled at lying, to make no mistakes. Most people escape detection only because the targets of their deceits do not care enough to work at catching them. It is very hard to prevent any leakage or deception clues, although the degree of success would be dependent in part on the difficulty of the lie.

Degree of Lie Difficulty

An easy lie for a liar should produce few mistakes and, therefore, be hard to detect, while a hard lie should be easy to detect. An easy lie would not require concealing or falsifying emotions because there would have been ample opportunity to practice the specific lie, the liar would be experienced in lying, and the target would not be suspicious. The hardest lies are those about emotions felt at the time of the lie; the stronger the emotions and the greater the number of different emotions to conceal, the harder the lie will be to execute.

Emotional Reexperience

A technique that might allow difficult lies to be more successfully perpetrated involves **method acting** (also called the Stanislavski acting technique; Stanislavski, 1936). This theatrical technique can be used to bring reliable facial muscles into play because it teaches the actor how to accurately show emotion by learning how to remember and reexperience it. This was the method utilized in the ANS research mentioned earlier. In those studies, when a subject used the technique, his or her facial expressions were not made deliberately but were the product of the reexperienced emotion. As the research findings suggested, the physiology of emotion was similar to felt emotion.

Self-Deception Minimizes Leakage or Detection Clues

The line between false and felt becomes fuzzy when emotions are produced by the Stanislavski technique. A situation that should prove even more successful would be one in which the deceiver came to believe that the lie was true. Such deception would be virtually undetectable and "bested" only by the deceiver who believed the lie was true from the very beginning. Under such circumstances, the emotions of the perpetrator would not be those of a liar who inadvertently might leak or reveal the deception. Rather, the deceiver would believe the information to be accurate and, therefore, not a lie. *Self-deception avoids the apprehension and guilt of deceit.*

Sociality Breeds Self-Deception

Finally, let us return, armed with more information, to the idea stated at the beginning of this chapter—that deceit is a way of life—and consider what it would be like if false information were always conveyed or, alternatively, the truth never manifested. Suppose treachery was as easy with emotions as with ideas. If expressions and gestures could be disguised and falsified as readily as words, our emotional lives would be impoverished and more guarded than they are. If, on the other hand, we could never deceive, if a smile was always reliable and never present without pleasure, life would be rougher than it is, many relationships would be harder to maintain. Politeness, attempts to smooth matters over, to conceal feelings one wished one did not feel—all that would be gone. There would be no way not to be known, no opportunity to sulk or lick one's wounds except alone.

CONCLUSIONS

It does seem that our sociality requires, if not demands, a middle ground (some degree of deception), be it concealment, falsification, or self-deception. And, only with self-deception can we escape many of the potential problems of deceit, for it is the "truth" as the perpetrator sees it that is used to deceive. What better way to convince others of that which is false than to believe that your argument is true?

REFERENCES

EFRON, D. (1972). *Gesture, race, and culture.* The Hague: Mouton Press.

EKMAN, P. (1973). *Darwin and facial expression: A century of research in review.* New York: Academic Press.

———. (1980). Asymmetry in facial expression. *Science, 209,* 833-836.

———. (1985). *Telling lies: Clues to deceit in the marketplace, politics and marriage.* New York: Norton.

EKMAN, P., & FRIESEN, W. V. (1969). The repertoire of nonverbal behavior: Categories, origins, usage, and coding. *Semiotica, 1,* 49-98.

———. (1974a). Noverbal behavior and psychopathology. In R. J. Friedman & M. N. Katz (Eds.), *The psychology of depression* (pp. 203-232). Washington, DC: J. Winston.

———. (1974b). Detecting deception from body or face. *Journal of Personality and Social Psychology, 29,* 288-298.

———. (1982). Felt, false, and miserable smiles. *Journal of Nonverbal Behavior, 6,* 238-252.

———. (1984). *Unmasking the face.* Palo Alto, CA: Consulting Psychologists Press.

EKMAN, P., FRIESEN, W. V., & ANCOLI, S. (1980). Facial signs of emotional experience. *Journal of Personality and Social Psychology, 39,* 1125-1134.

EKMAN, P., HAGER, J. C., & FRIESEN, W. V. (1981). The symmetry of emotional and deliberate facial actions. *Psychophysiology, 18,* 101-106.

EKMAN, P., LEVENSON, R. W., & FRIESEN, W. V. (1983). Autonomic nervous system activity distinguishes between emotions. *Science, 221,* 1208-1210.

FREUD, S. (1976). The psychopathology of everyday life. In J. Strachey (Ed. & Trans.), *The standard edition of the complete psychological works of Sigmund Freud* (Vol. 6). London: Hogarth Press. (Original work published 1901.)

GOFFMAN, E. (1959). *The presentation of self in everyday life.* New York: Anchor.

HAGER, J. C., & EKMAN, P. (1979). Long distance transmission of facial affect signals. *Ethology and Sociobiology, 1,* 77-82.

———. (1985). The asymmetry of facial actions is inconsistent with models of hemispheric specialization. *Psychophysiology, 22,* 307-318.

HANDEL, M. I. (1982). Intelligence and deception. *Journal of Strategic Studies, 5,* 122-154.

HAYANO, D. M. (1979, March). Poker lies and truth. *Human Behavior,* p. 20.

HOROWITZ, B. (1981, November 16). When should an executive lie? *Industry Week,* pp. 81-83.

JOHNSON, H. G., EKMAN, P., & FRIESEN, W. V. (1975). Communicative body movements: American emblems. *Semiotica, 15,* 335-353.

KRAUT, R. E., & POE, D.   (1980). Behavioral roots of person perception: The deception judgments of custom inspectors and laymen. *Journal of Personality and Social Psychology, 39*, 784-798.

LOCKARD, J. S.   (1980). Speculations on the adaptive significance of self-deception. In J. S. Lockard (Ed.), *The evolution of human social behavior* (pp. 257–275). New York: Elsevier.

LYKKEN, D. T.   (1981). *A tremor in the blood.* New York: McGraw-Hill.

MANDLER, G.   (1984). *Mind and body: Psychology of emotion and stress.* New York: Norton.

SACKEIM, H. A., GUR, R. C., & SAUCY, M. C.   (1978). Emotions are expressed more intensely on the left side of the face. *Science, 202*, 434.

SCHERER, K.   (1982). Methods of research on vocal communication: Paradigms and parameters. In K. Scherer and P. Ekman (eds.) *Handbook of methods in nonverbal behavior research.* (pp. 136–198). New York: Cambridge University Press.

STANISLAVSKI, G.   (1936). *An actor prepares.* New York: Theater Arts Books.

TSCHIASSNY, K.   (1953). Eight syndromes of facial paralysis and their significance in locating the lesion. *Annals of Otolaryngology, Rhinolaryngology, and Laryngology, 62*, 677-691.

WHALEY, B.   (1982). Toward a general theory of deception. *Journal of Strategic Studies, 5*, 179-192.

WOHLSTETTER, R.   (1981). Slow Pearl Harbors and the pleasures of deception. In R. L. Pfaltzgraff, Jr., U. Ra'anan, & W. Milberg (Eds.), *Intelligence policy and national security* (pp. 23-34). Hamden, CT: Archon.

ZUCKERMAN, M., DePAULO, B. M., & ROSENTHAL, R.   (1981). Verbal and nonverbal communication of deception. In L. Berkowitz (Ed.), *Advances in experimental social psychology* (Vol. 14, pp. 1–59). New York: Academic Press.

SELF-DECEPTION

WHERE DO WE
STAND?

This book has exemplified the rampant diversity of positions on self-deception. This diversity is understandable given the contrasting backgrounds of the contributors. Philosophers, psychologists, anthropologists, sociologists, and animal behaviorists are unlikely to see eye-to-eye on any topic. The broadest statement of agreement is that self-deception involves the masking of one possible representation of self-related information, one that would be painful to acknowledge. This definition, however, risks being overinclusive; certain related phenomena must be distinguished from self-deception.

It is not passive ignorance: Information about ourselves may be biased for any number of nonmotivational reasons (e.g., Demos, 1960; Nisbett & Ross, 1980; Paulhus & Suedfeld, Chapter 8). Indeed, lack of awareness of our mental processes seems to be the rule rather than the exception (Nisbett & Wilson, 1977; Wilson, 1985). Self-deception is also distinguishable from a variety of differences in the processing of self-related versus other-related information (Greenwald & Pratkanis, 1984; Greenwald, Chapter 7).

Another related phenomenon, blind faith, involves setting impossibly high criteria for rejecting a belief; it differs from self-deception in that no threatening representation is being masked (Sackeim, Chapter 9).

Wishful thinking is another distinguishable phenomenon wherein one's hope that something is true strengthens one's belief that it is true (Szabados, 1973; Sackeim & Gur, 1978). Self-deception should not be equated with denial, the refusal to accept an overwhelming external reality. Nevertheless, there is an overlap between the two concepts, as is evident in the work of Breznitz (1983), Goldberger (1983), Spence (1983), and Lazarus (1983). Finally, self-deception is not weakness of will: In this kin concept, the individual is only too aware of his or her best interest and that he or she is acting against it (Elster, 1979; Pears, 1984).

A number of writers outside this volume (e.g., Schafer, 1976; Lazarus, 1983; Gilbert & Cooper, 1985; Goleman, 1985) have subsumed several of these phenomena under the rubric of self-deception. We would argue that the present volume is more useful because of its narrowed definition. Least useful of all is the common definition of self-deception as the state of being mistaken about oneself (e.g., Webster's New Collegiate Dictionary, 1970).

The disagreements among the contributors to this book are most evident in the theoretical chapters. Let us look in detail at a number of contentious issues that continue to recur in the theoretical contributions.

Persons and mechanisms   Eagle describes in some detail how Freud presented psychoanalytic theory, including defenses, at two levels of analysis. At one level, the language of persons, defenses were described as if autonomous entities were communicating, much like separate individuals would. The other level, the language of mechanisms, dealt with cognitive structures responding automatically to stimulus conditions. Eagle concludes that Freud's "person" level was strictly metaphorical, developed for didactic purposes only. Nevertheless, psychoanalysis has left us with a dualistic legacy that continues to divide theorists, even within this volume. Sarbin and Eagle, for instance, argue that self-deception should be discussed in the language of persons, not mechanisms. Greenwald, Paulhus and Suedfeld, and Sackeim eschew the "person" language, arguing that the mechanistic language is most compatible with an empirical approach.

Motivation   All the theoretical contributors except Greenwald cite motivation as a necessary component of self-deception. Greenwald's model of habitualized knowledge avoidance seems to obviate motivation during self-deception, although motivation is presumably active during the development of the habit for repeated avoidance. Sarbin does not dwell on the role of motivation but simply uses Fingarette's statement that an individual may sometimes have an overriding reason for not spelling out an engagement. He does cite the motivational qualities of (1) trying to maintain a dialogue with another individual, and (2) wanting to be the remarkable character whose arm can rise by itself during hypnosis. For Welles, the motivation is a striving to share group identity and avoid the group sanctions against contrary beliefs. The most direct disagreement about motivation is between Eagle and Sackeim: Eagle sees motivation behind self-deception as being goal-oriented and conscious, whereas Sackeim sees motivation as being automatic, as in the conditioning of an operant.

Note that at least one motivational position is not well represented in this volume. Several writers have emphasized the development of self-deception from other-deception (e.g., Schlenker, 1980; Gilbert & Cooper, 1985; Snyder, 1985). For purposes of impression management, people will present themselves positively to an audience. If the audience does not reject the presentation the actor will tend to internalize it. Thus, people come to believe positively biased self-images (Baumeister, 1986).

The unconscious   The unconscious appears to play the most central role in Sackeim's concept of self-deception, albeit without the autonomy of Freud's unconscious. It remains in the nontransparent partitioning of awareness. For Welles, the embedding of myths in language effectively makes their impact unconscious.

Eagle, however, sees the unconscious as unnecessary in classical self-deception because events remain at a voluntary level. Sarbin's view, like that of Fingarette, finds the unconscious superfluous, because engagement–disavowal has properties of both consciousness and unconsciousness. Greenwald, too, sees consciousness as a secondary issue: Although habitualized knowledge avoidance can become unconscious, self-deception *per se* is not necessarily unconscious. In the Paulhus and Suedfeld model, one belief is temporarily unattended because of a transient change in the structure of decision making. Here again, the unconscious is unnecessary. In general, however, theories without an unconscious cannot explain "unfinished business," that is, the continuing influence of a masked belief on behavior.

ADAPTIVE?

The title of this volume proffers the question of whether or not self-deception is an adaptive mechanism. Now is the time to consider how well this question has been answered. Given the diversity of opinions on the essence of the concept, the question of adaptiveness may seem gratuitous. To the contrary—the multiplicity of positions serves to highlight the necessity of narrowing the question to specify for whom self-deception is adaptive (the individual? the genes? society?) and over what time period (short-term? long-term?).

The question in the title was originally phrased to have a dual meaning, a duality reflecting the different intellectual roots of the two editors. To the sociobiologist the book title poses the question of whether self-deception is evolutionarily adaptive. That is, do self-deceptive mechanisms help perpetuate the genes of organisms that engage in them? In Chapter 1, Lockard sets the stage for this point: Cogent arguments are provided for the procreative benefits to advanced organisms of incomplete knowledge of their motivation. This thesis is complemented by that of Lockard and Mateer, who indicate that the neurological substructure required for self-deception is in place. In short, both distal and proximal causes of self-deception are in evidence.

From the perspective of social cognition, the title has a different interpretation: Does self-deception provide some behavioral and/or psychological benefit to the perpetrator? Sackeim's chapter seems most sanguine: Self-deception is not only useful for defense, but it may be used to promote self-esteem above current levels. Eagle agrees that self-deception is adaptive when nothing can be done about the threat. He warns, however, that where corrective action is possible, self-deception may be maladaptive. Even where corrective activities are impossible (e.g., in a prisoner-of-war camp) some awareness of the threat is necessary to avoid serious punishment. Sarbin's view is that self-deception may provide short-term psychological comfort, but may promote long-term psychological problems.

Paulhus and Suedfeld claim both behavioral and cognitive adaptiveness. In calm conditions it is adaptive to use all relevant information in making decisions; in emergencies it is adaptive to respond quickly and simplify one's decision making. The degree of threat (as indicated by one's emotional arousal) determines the complexity of the processing. Thus, the organism benefits behaviorally by making decisions that are tailored to the fluctuating demands of the environment. In addition, the individual benefits cognitively from a simplistic view of the world that protects self-esteem during threat. In their chapters, Welles and Hartung describe the benefits of self-deception to the stability of the society while noting the maladaptive consequences to individual members of the society. A major casualty is the society's flexibility to undergo social change.

Only a Pollyanna would claim any consensus here. Nonetheless, an overall pattern emerges: *An organism may be advantaged by having dual (or even multiple) representations of the same stimulus.* The notion of separate systems for the cognitive and affective representations has been championed by Zajonc (1980). Others have postulated separate representations for the true and available causes of behavior (Nisbett & Wilson, 1977). Fodor (1984) has argued the most general case for the advantages of cognitive modularity. The critical requirement for self-deception, however, is a mechanism by which the affective representation regulates the cognitive processing (Epstein, 1983; Erdelyi, 1985).

The mixed blessings of such a system have been detailed by the contributors. Self-deception promotes short-run psychological health and adaptive decisions. It also helps maintain the societal status quo, thus promoting political stability. Long-run psychological health and beneficial social change, however, are thereby constrained. Together these propositions suggest that genetic selection favors the trade-off of short-term happiness (which promotes reproduction) over self-insight that might save *Homo sapiens* from ultimately self-destructive enterprises.

NEW DIRECTIONS

The mainstream positions in psychological thought are well represented in this volume. There are, however, several promising lines of investigation deriving from ostensibly unrelated literatures. These include the work of economists and memory theorists.

Several writers on economic behavior have developed sophisticated models addressing the issues of self-deception, although they do not necessarily use that label. Thomas Schelling (1984), for example, has argued for the notion of multiple selves. To explain economic behavior, a mental model with multiple and dynamic preferences is required (see also Chanowitz & Langer, 1985). Ainslie (1982, 1984) specifies particular preference functions that lead to counterrational decisions. Thaler and Shefrin (1981) distinguish two cognitive agents, the "planner" and the "consumer." The former acts in the long-term interest of the individual, but the consumers have myopic vision. The discrepancy leads at times to apparently irrational behavior. Jon Elster's two books (1979, 1983) are lucid, cogent, and the most comprehensive of all current treatments of bounded rationality. He concludes that man has imperfect rationality, but that he may anticipate his weak moments and bind himself against temptation. All these writers exemplify the widespread dissatisfaction among economists with the traditional view of the economic man as rational. The new *Homo economicus* has a propensity for illusions, wishful thinking, and self-deception.

The work of Endel Tulving (1972) on semantic versus episodic memory also has possibilities for understanding self-deception. Semantic memory is characterized by knowledge that, although firmly held, is not accompanied by a record of events upon which the knowledge is based. The actual record of events is stored primarily in episodic memory. This memory, however, is subject to gaps and distortions. If the true explanation is not clear, then the episodic record can be drawn on to provide one. If the explanation is disturbing, the episodic record may with time be rewritten to conform to the semantic knowledge. This rewriting mechanism is consistent with Greenwald's (1980) conception of the ego as a self-perpetuating system. Not unrelated is Anderson's (1981) distinction between procedural and declarative memory (see Cantor & Kihlstrom, 1987).

A third promising perspective on self-deception comes from the distinction between automatic and controlled processing (e.g., Posner & Snyder, 1975; Schneider & Shiffrin, 1977). When cognitive responses become automatized through practice, the motivation behind them is hidden; indeed, in many cases the original motivation is long since gone. It is not until controlled processing is invoked that issues of discrepancy arise. Only recently has this automatic/controlled distinction been applied to self-related phenomena (Bargh, 1984; Paulhus, 1988; Paulhus & Levitt, 1987).

Finally, Quattrone and Tversky (1984) have operationalized self-deception as the tendency to select actions that are diagnostic of favorable outcomes even though the actions do not cause those outcomes. For example, when subjects were told that a short life-expectancy is predicted for those who experience a cold-press test as painful, they tended to rate the cold-pressor as less painful. I have used a similar approach to develop an individual-differences measure (Paulhus & Murphy, 1987).

Such promising avenues lead us to believe that a multiperspective view of self-deception will continue in the near future (e.g., Krebs, Denton, & Higgins, 1988). These new avenues make salient the many-faceted nature of the topic. At the same time, the interest converging from so many disciplines speaks for the central importance of self-deception in human affairs. The present volume has made only modest progress in linking biology to psychology. The accelerating progress of neuropsychology, however, leads us to be optimistic about the possibility of mapping the psychological concepts directly onto the physiological substrate.

REFERENCES

AINSLIE, G. (1982). A behavioral economic approach to the defense mechanism: Freud's energy theory revisited. *Social Science Information, 21,* 1-14.

————. (1984). Behavioral economics II: Motivated involuntary behavior. *Social Science Information, 23,* 247-274.

ANDERSON, J. R. (1981). *Cognitive psychology and its implications.* San Francisco, CA: Freeman.

BARGH, J. A. (1984). Automatic and conscious processing. In R. S. Wyer & T. K. Srull (Eds.), *Handbook of social cognition* (Vol. 3, pp. 1-43). Hillsdale, NJ: Erlbaum.

BAUMEISTER, R. F. (ED.). (1986). *Public self and private self.* New York. Springer-Verlag.

BREZNITZ, S. (ED.). (1983). *The denial of stress.* New York: International Universities Press.

CANTOR, N., & KIHLSTROM, J. F. (1987). *Personality and social intelligence.* Englewood Cliffs, NJ: Prentice-Hall.

CHANOWITZ, B., & LANGER, E. J. (1985). Self-protection and self-inception. In M. W. Martin (Ed.), *Self-deception and self-understanding* (pp. 117-135). Lawrence, KS: University Press of Kansas.

DEMOS, R. (1960). Lying to oneself. *Journal of Philosophy, 57,* 588-595.

ELSTER, J. (1979). *Ulysses and the sirens.* New York: Cambridge University Press.

————. (1983). *Sour grapes: Studies in the subversion of rationality.* New York: Cambridge University Press.

EPSTEIN, S. (1983). The self-concept and levels of awareness. In J. Suls & A. G. Greenwald (Eds.), *Psychological perspectives on the self.* Hillsdale, NJ: Erlbaum.

ERDELYI, M. H. (1985). *Psychoanalysis: Freud's cognitive psychology.* New York: Freeman.

FODOR, J. A. (1984). *Modularity of mind.* Boston: MIT Press.

GILBERT, D. T., & COOPER, J. (1985). Social psychological strategies of self-deception. In M. W. Martin (Ed.), *Self-deception and self-understanding* (pp. 75-94). Lawrence, KS: University Press of Kansas.

GOLDBERGER, L. (1983). The concept and mechanisms of denial: A selective overview. In S. Breznitz (Ed.), *The denial of stress* (pp. 83-96). New York: International Universities Press.

GOLEMAN, D. (1985). *Vital lies, simple truths: The psychology of self-deception.* New York: Simon & Schuster.

GREENWALD, A. G. (1980). The totalitarian ego: Fabrication and revision of personal history. *American Psychologist, 35,* 603-618.

GREENWALD, A. G., & PRATKANIS, A. R. (1984). The self. In R. S. Wyer & T. K. Srull (Eds.), *Handbook of social cognition* (Vol. 3, pp. 129-178). Hillsdale, NJ: Erlbaum.

KREBS, D., DENTON, K., & HIGGINS, N. C. (1988). On the evolution of self-knowledge and self-deception. In K. MacDonald (Ed.), *Sociobiological perspectives on human development* (pp. 105-139). New York: Springer-Verlag.

LAZARUS, R. S. (1983). The costs and benefits of denial. In S. Breznitz (Ed.), *The denial of stress* (pp. 1-30). New York: International Universities Press.

NISBETT, R. E., & ROSS, L. (1980). *Human inference: Strategies and shortcomings.* Englewood Cliffs, NJ: Prentice-Hall.

NISBETT, R. E., & WILSON, T. D. (1977). Telling more than we can know: Verbal reports on mental processes. *Psychological Review, 84,* 231-259.

PAULHUS, D. L. (1988). *Automatic and controlled self-presentation.* Paper presented at the annual meeting of the American Psychological Association, Atlanta, GA.

PAULHUS, D. L., & LEVITT, K. (1987). Desirable responding triggered by affect: Automatic egotism? *Journal of Personality and Social Psychology, 52,* 245-259.

PAULHUS, D. L., & MURPHY, G. (1987). *Individual differences in motivated bias.* Unpublished manuscript, University of British Columbia, Vancouver.

PEARS, D. (1984). *Motivated irrationality.* New York: Oxford University Press.

POSNER, M. I., & SNYDER, C. R. R. (1975). Attention and cognitive control. In R. L. Solso (Ed.), *Information processing and cognition: The Loyola symposium.* Hillsdale, NJ: Erlbaum.

QUATTRONE, G. A., & TVERSKY, A. (1984). Casual versus diagnostic contingencies: On self-deception and on the voter's illusion. *Journal of Personality and Social Psychology, 46,* 237-248.

SACKEIM, H. A., & GUR, R. C. (1978). Self-deception, self-confrontation, and consciousness. In G. E. Schwartz & D. Shapiro (Eds.), *Consciousness and self-regulation: Advances in research* (Vol. 2, pp. 139-197). New York: Plenum.

SCHAFER, R. (1976). *A new language for psychoanalysis.* New Haven, CT: Yale University Press.

SCHELLING, T. C. (1984). Self-command in practice, in policy, and in a theory of rational choice. *American Economic Review, 74,* 1-11.

SCHLENKER, B. R. (1980). *Impression management.* Monterey, CA: Brooks-Cole.

SCHNEIDER, W., & SHIFFRIN, R. M. (1977). Controlled and automatic human information processing: I. Detection, search, and attention. *Psychological Review, 84,* 1-66.

SNYDER, C. R. (1985). Collaborative companions: The relationship of self-deception and excuse-making. In M. W. Martin (Ed.), *Self-deception and self-understanding* (pp. 35-51). Lawrence, KS: University Press of Kansas.

SPENCE, D. P. (1983). The paradox of denial. In S. Breznitz (Ed.), *The denial of stress* (pp. 103-124). New York: International Universities Press.

SZABADOS, B. (1973). Wishful thinking and self-deception. *Analysis, 33,* 201-205.

THALER, R. H., & SHEFRIN, H. M. (1981). An economic theory of self-control. *Journal of Political Economy, 89,* 392-406.

TULVING, E. (1972). Episodic and semantic memory. In E. Tulving & W. Donaldson (Eds.), *Organization of memory.* New York: Academic Press.

Webster's Seventh New Collegiate Dictionary. (1970). Springfield, MA: G. and C. Merriam.

WILSON, T. D. (1985). Self-deception without repression: Limits on access to mental states. In M. W. Martin (Ed.), *Self-deception and self-understanding* (pp. 95-116). Lawrence, KS: University Press of Kansas.

ZAJONC, R. B. (1980). Feeling and thinking: Preferences need no inferences. *American Psychologist, 35,* 151-175.

INDEX

DIRTY SEXY MONEY

DIRTY SEXY MONEY

THE UNAUTHORIZED BIOGRAPHY OF KRIS JENNER

CATHY GRIFFIN
and DYLAN HOWARD

Skyhorse Publishing

Visit our website at www.skyhorsepublishing.com.

10 9 8 7 6 5 4 3 2 1

Library of Congress Cataloging-in-Publication Data is available on file.

Cover design by 5mediadesign
Cover photo credit: Getty Images

Print ISBN: 978-1-5107-6199-5
eBook ISBN: 978-1-5107-6207-7

Printed in the United States of America

CONTENTS

"There's a lot of people that have great ideas and dreams and whatnot, but unless you're willing to work really, really hard and work for what you want, it's never going to happen."

—Kris Jenner

AUTHORS' NOTE

Dirty Sexy Money: The Unauthorized Biography of Kris Jenner is the definitive account of how a Beverly Hills socialite with little formal education built herself a global empire.

This tell-all tome unravels the family's meteoric rise to fame and the dark secrets they've struggled to hide . . . until now. Together, we have delved behind the headlines and social media hype to tell the true story of Kris's life—rather than the rosy picture she likes to paint.

Dirty Sexy Money is an unflinching look at Kris's triumphs and losses, her crises and celebrations, her famous friendships and family conflicts. It examines in unprecedented detail Kris's troubled two decades with Bruce Jenner and the end of their marriage as Bruce transitioned to Caitlyn; it exposes the truth about her current affair with a much younger man . . . and it reveals what she really thinks of her daughter's very public marriage to Kanye West.

Inside are a wealth of previously untold stories, including intimate details of how Kim's sex tape jump-started her career and the true story of how Kris sold her long-running television reality series—as well as shocking, never-before-heard revelations about her friendships with O. J. Simpson and his murdered wife Nicole.

To gain access to the most private aspects of Kris's life, we conducted extensive interviews with multiple first-person sources closest to Kris, including family members, business associates, and other intimates—some of whom are speaking on the record for the first time. In some instances, we have employed the technique of recreated dialogue.

The result is a dramatic narrative account of Kris's real story as you've never heard it before . . . in all its dirty, sexy glory.

INTRODUCTION

It's the greatest paradox when it comes to the Kardashians, one of the world's most scandalous dynasties: Just how low—and how high—can this family go?

For Kris Jenner and her controversial Kardashian-Jenner clan, it seems there is no end in sight. From sanctioning incestuous comments on the family's sixteen-season flagship reality series *Keeping Up With the Kardashians*, to Kris being publicly outed as a "little whore" by her own daughter, Kourtney, the high-profile "momager" has said and done nearly everything to make her family millions and even billions—including allegedly selling her second eldest daughter Kim's sex tape. In fact, the sixty-five-year-old matriarch has been suspected of having been the driving force behind the February 2007 public release of Kim's X-rated home video, filmed three years earlier when Kim was twenty-three.

While Kris continues to profess her innocence, there's little room for doubt that "Kris was there every step of the way as a middleman was brought in to market it to an adult entertainment company," an insider claimed. "I saw Kris Jenner's signature on the contract."

Inspired by Kim's close pal and fellow Hollywood socialite Paris Hilton, who earned a whirlwind of publicity when her sex tape *1 Night in Paris* was released shortly before the debut of Paris's reality series *The Simple Life*, Kris reportedly sold the rights to Kim's sex tape to Vivid Entertainment for a reputed half-million dollars. The salacious footage was titled *Kim Kardashian Superstar* and put Kim's face—and other body parts—on the world stage.

At the time of the video's release, Kim called it "humiliating" and added, "I feel very betrayed, but I'm not pointing any fingers." It has always been assumed she was referring to her on-screen partner as the driving force behind the sale.

The Kardashians initially refuted the "disgusting and disturbing" claim that Kris sold her daughter out. Kim then sued Vivid for violating her right to privacy, which raised questions as to whether Kim actually knew that the tape was being released, whether the lawsuit itself was part of a grand publicity scheme by Kris, or whether someone other than Kris was responsible for selling Kim's video. However, Kim dropped the lawsuit in April 2007 and agreed to a lump-sum financial settlement with Vivid. "We've always known we had the legal right to distribute this video," a Vivid executive said at the time. "We've always wanted to work something out with Kim so she could share in the profits."

The Kardashians eventually conceded that Kim's sex tape was the invaluable asset that introduced their family to the world. Kris slyly stated, "We wouldn't be the Kardashians if we censored ourselves. The camera loves drama!" Nudity and sex, to the Kardashian-Jenner clan, are commodities to be revered, not reviled. It has nothing to do with morals or values in their eyes. Their perception is not every person's cup of reality.

Having groomed her two youngest daughters—twenty-three-year-old Kendall and twenty-one-year-old Kylie—for the global spotlight, it seems there will be no shortage of ways for Kris to keep herself in the news in the future—and rake in the dough by exposing her family to public scrutiny.

To those who know her best, Kris's never-ending drive to embellish the family name is based not on stability and happiness, but on a never-enough attitude and an unquenchable thirst for publicity. Whether the TV drama is real or totally manufactured—as most people believe—it's clear that Kris has been pulling the strings behind the scenes, giving her stamp of approval as her family's antics seem to continually sink deeper into her pile of *dirty sexy money*. But the sex tape is not the beginning of the Kardashian-Jenner empire. She did not just fall into a vat of luck. The role of a ruthless business entrepreneur was one she had been preparing for all of her life.

PROLOGUE

On April 19, 2017, the Manhattan sky was lit up by *Harper's BAZAAR* and Tiffany & Co. in honor of the magazine's 150th anniversary. Projected on the Empire State Building was a larger-than-life display that covered forty-two of the building's 102-story frontage and memorialized fifteen decades of the most celebrated images from *BAZAAR's* archives.

As the cover girl for the commemorative issue, supermodel Kendall Jenner—daughter of Kris and Caitlyn Jenner—was the star of this prestigious anniversary celebration being held at the Rainbow Room atop Rockefeller Center. It was her third time on a *BAZAAR* cover in the past three years. The other stars attending the elegant soiree included Christie Brinkley, Demi Moore, Iman, and Tory Burch, all of whom gravitated toward the stacks of copies of the magazine. It was sure to be a collector's item. Twenty-one-year-old Kendall looked every bit the composed and confident icon in her thigh-high slit Redemption gown, which had a barely-there, plunging neckline. Her long dark brown hair was pulled back. Pearl drop earrings gave Kendall's sexy evening wear a classic look.

Mother-of-the-model Kris was dressed Upper East Side New York in a floor-length black wool coat and black, high-waisted tuxedo pants. As Kendall's "co-star," Kris was welcome on the press line, where she posed for photographers alongside her daughter. No matter how long the day, or how tired Kris Jenner felt, she never bailed on a photo op. Even after almost ten years of constant media attention, Kris thoroughly looked forward to walking the VIP carpets as the star and mastermind of the hit reality series *Keeping Up With the Kardashians.*

Kris took a seat on a couch as the lights dimmed while the guest-of-honor made her way over to the nearby wall where she pulled on a lever that controlled the lighting for the *Harper's BAZAAR* exhibit. Kendall rushed over to sit next to her mom. Kris reached for Kendall's hand and squeezed it tightly as they looked out the floor-to-ceiling windows across the city's skyline to behold Kendall's gigantic image lighting up the side of the Empire State Building. Kris's jaw almost dropped at the sight.

Against the black backdrop of skyscrapers, the red dress Kris suggested Kendall wear just popped. Here Kris was, watching her kid featured alongside Kris's own movie star favorites, Elizabeth Taylor and Audrey Hepburn, as well as supermodels Kate Moss and pop icons Beyoncé and Lady Gaga. As the cell phones came out of evening bags and coat pockets around the room, the guests would find no weather obstacles to get in the way of capturing the perfect shot. It was a crystal clear, beautiful spring night. Of course, the queens of social media, Kris and Kendall, wasted no time posting their pictures to their individual Snapchat accounts.

Kris's gushing caption read, "The moment when I looked out across the city and saw my daughter's image on the Empire State Building . . . so breathtaking. I am so proud of you!"

Kendall's dad was nowhere in sight as Kris made sure to shout out to *Harper's* "for having Kendall on 3 different covers for this special month!" She also thanked Tiffany & Co. for the undoubtedly swell swag she would find when she opened the gift bag. Kris deserved a present. It had been a trying day in the media for her, thanks to her ex-husband, who skipped out on what had to be the most memorable night of Kendall's life. While disappointed for Kendall, Kris couldn't help but be relieved that Caitlyn wasn't there.

During their twenty-three-year marriage, Caitlyn was always a supportive dad to her two children with Kris, and her four Kardashian children, but on this night, she was a no-show. Instead of playing the proud papa and posting Kendall's snapshot onto her social media pages, Caitlyn was at home in Malibu, working her own angles on the West Coast. She tweeted with wild enthusiasm, reminding her fans and friends to tune in the next night to *PrimeTime Live* on ABC. Caitlyn was excited about her big hit as part of her publicity tour for her memoir, *The Secrets of My Life*. There was a history with the network. Caitlyn had shared her lifelong desire to become a woman with Diane Sawyer's worldwide audience in 2015. The two had even become frequent phone pals. Caitlyn was counting on big book sales from the upcoming Sawyer interview. Since it had been pre-taped, there was no need for Caitlyn to be at the studio, so she could have easily flown her private plane into New York to share in her child's special night.

The Kardashian and Jenner children had endured Caitlyn's shameless self-promotion all week long, which included Caitlyn's incessant chatter alerting news media to share with the world that she no longer had a penis. Earlier in the day, Caitlyn's news bulletin sniped her ex-wife, as Caitlyn confessed she found sex with Kris "uncomfortable."

The weekly trailer for the upcoming episode of *Keeping Up With the Kardashians* showed a pissed off Kris telling her kids she was "done" with her ex-spouse after reading Caitlyn's autobiography, which she basically considered a work of fiction. "I've never been so angry and disappointed in somebody in my whole life," Kris confessed to the cameras.

The episode had been shot months prior to Caitlyn's book tour, but for those less savvy about the TV production schedule, it looked as if Kris was instantly responding to Caitlyn's remarks about their sex life.

While Caitlyn's autobiography was not fiction, it certainly had some credibility issues when held up to stories she told about Kris in her 1999 memoir, *Finding the Champion Within*. Throughout that book, Jenner (then Bruce) painted an entirely different portrait of intimacy with Kris, as he described his feelings for her during their whirlwind courtship in 1990. "There was incredible chemistry between us, that perfect union that's like two bodies of water merging and becoming one. We were soul mates, each filling up the empty spaces in the other." They had been married almost ten years by this point and Jenner still seemed smitten with Kris.

When Kris returned to her hotel room after the *Harper's* party, she could not crawl between the luxury sheets on the bed in her hotel room fast enough. She was dead on her feet, drained from the events of the bittersweet day. Yet, as tired as she was, she couldn't help but think back and say a prayer of gratitude to God about how blessed she was to have such a beautiful, darling daughter as Kendall. So much grace and style.

It was Caitlyn's loss. She missed the memory of a lifetime.

It was well after midnight as Kris began drifting off to sleep. Suddenly her mind flashed to April 22, her wedding anniversary, just a few days away. She mused over whether Caitlyn would remember this would have been their twenty-sixth year of marriage. Caitlyn would be sore finding out she forgot their anniversary, for it would be a missed opportunity for additional press coverage. Kris chuckled at the ironies.

CHAPTER ONE
THE FIRST MOMAGERS

Mother Nurtures

Many people—most people—marginalize Kris Jenner's thirteen-year stronghold on pop culture and television as a "phenomenon." Her financial domination as the matriarch of one of the richest families in Hollywood is commonly discounted. It's skewed as the fruits of an overly ambitious, shameless fame whore who greedily built an empire on her daughters' backs. Even if these theories and opinions are accurate, it is unlikely that the television superstar and international businesswoman could have maintained and increased her personal and family's wealth exponentially. In addition, the fact that Kris has sustained personal closeness with all six of her children after making them multimillionaires (and some billionaires) denotes an unparalleled family dynasty.

As the heiress apparent to a dynasty, Kris is neither a freak of nature nor a fluke. But the Kristen Houghton-Kardashian-Jenner brand didn't just happen all by itself. Kris's "no holds barred" approach to family and fame has its roots in two extraordinary country girls from Arkansas: her mother, Mary Jo, and her maternal grandmother, Lou Ethel. Their achievements, values, and philosophies are stitched into the fabric of Kris's empire. Her birthright stems from these two entrepreneurial women, who cultivated Kris's work discipline, business acumen, and perfectionism. They passed their appreciation of beauty, fashion, and design down to Kris. She was groomed in the importance of keeping up with traditions as an essential component of bonding a family. Kris learned the value of surrounding herself with like-minded and accomplished role models. Supreme self-confidence and resilience are perhaps Kris Jenner's greatest assets, and she comes by them honestly as a descendant of these formidable women.

To fully understand Kris's rise to her enviable pinnacle of fortune and fame, it is crucial to understand her original influencers.

Lou Ethel Campbell was born on October 20, 1913, in Hope, Arkansas. As was typical for the times, Lou married young. She gave birth to one child, daughter Mary Jo Campbell, on July 26, 1934. Kris knew her grandmother to be "strong-willed and stubborn." When Lou's husband cheated on her with another woman, she did the unthinkable for a small-town girl in Arkansas—she picked up and moved, without any help or support, to Southern California. Since she was good with numbers, she found work as an accountant on a naval base in San Diego, where she met a quiet, handsome man named Jim Fairbanks.

Fairbanks was five years younger than Lou. He was immediately smitten with the spunky gal from Arkansas. The two married and settled in La Mesa, a small city outside San Diego.

Lou Ethel Fairbanks made a lovely home for Jim. He earned a good income at San Diego Glass and Paint. Every payday he handed his check to his wife, who managed the family finances. She was careful with their coins, but by no means stingy. Her blonde hair was coiffed to perfection and she wore the essential shades of foundation and blush to complement her fair skin tone and green eyes. Lou had a flair for fashion. She chose timeless, practical pieces as opposed to trendy garments, which would soon go out of style. Kris later recalled her grandmother's attention to detail: "She always wore beautiful slacks with a matching blazer and the perfect blouse and shoes. Fashion and grooming were very important to her. Even if we were going to Disneyland, she made sure to take us shopping a few days beforehand to buy us new outfits for the outing."

Kris said if she or her younger sister Karen had a friend along with them, her grandmother bought the child a new outfit as well. The present-day

Kardashian-Jenner tribe's opulent gift-giving and penchant for grand celebrations of birthdays, anniversaries, and holidays such as Christmas, Thanksgiving, and even their over-the-top Halloween observances were established by Lou Ethel. "We celebrated everything endlessly," Kris said.

Lou Ethel exhibited equal excitement and enthusiasm for milestones in each family member's life, no matter how minor the accomplishment. There was no defeat in failures, only lessons learned. The matriarchal mantra of "dream big and never give up" and the words of her stepfather helped Kris define her own code: "If somebody tells you no, you're talking to the wrong person."

In the 1940s, Lou Ethel Fairbanks knew that if her daughter Mary Jo wanted to catch the perfect "Mr. Right," she would have to cultivate a certain class to evoke images of glamorous movie stars like Grace Kelly and Audrey Hepburn. Mary Jo was every bit as fetching as her mother, only with darker hair. They shared the same slender build, and Mary Jo enjoyed wearing the latest styles of dress suitable for conveying the image of a proper young lady. Lou Ethel enrolled Mary Jo in Fashionality, a charm school in a nearby community. Public schools were adequate for learning to read, write, and do arithmetic, but an education in class and style was something sorely missing from an educational institution's curriculum. Mary Jo learned about fashion, travel, beauty, grooming, and etiquette, and at the center of all of this knowledge was good posture. One charm school alumna explained, "Spines were to be thought of as a string of pearls that ladies were to keep pulled straight but not taut."

Mary Jo was only fifteen at the time, and it seemed she had a bright and promising career ahead of her as a fashion model or actress. But she would not be able to access those fantasies for a few more years because she was still three years away from graduation. Upon graduating from high school, before she was able to chase her dreams in Los Angeles, New York City, London, Paris, or Milan, Mary Jo fell in love with a young man four years her senior, Robert Clee Toovey, a regular guy who appreciated her as the finest thing in life. They wed in San Diego on September 21, 1952.

Unfortunately, their union was brief, and they divorced a mere two months later.

Cut from Different Cloth

Not long after the ink was dry on the divorce papers, the dashing young executive Mary Jo had envisioned appeared on the scene to woo her. Robert True Houghton—Bob, as he was called—was an aircraft engineer at Convair, an airline manufacturing company in San Diego that had been a principal producer of military aircraft during World War II.

Bob was charming and intelligent, and he earned an excellent income. He was tall, dark-eyed, handsome, clean-cut, and suave. In high school, he had competed in track meets and was a member of the Lettermen's Club and prom committee. He was an enthusiastic outdoorsman who enjoyed fishing and hunting.

Mary Jo married Bob in a small private ceremony. Soon after, they welcomed Kristen "Kris" Mary Houghton into the world at Scripps Hospital in San Diego on November 5, 1955. Four years later, they had another daughter, Karen Lee.

"We were spoiled with love, not money," Karen recalled of her humble upbringing.

Born of British, Scottish, Irish, German, and Dutch descent, the Houghton girls inherited both parents' striking looks. But the sisters' similarities ended there. Kris had raven black hair, while Karen's was light brown. From an early age, Kris proved to be the more outgoing of the two.

Perhaps Kris had a sense she had more to prove than her sibling. "The whole world knows Kris is vain," Karen admitted, claiming that her sister's lifelong body insecurities and love of plastic surgery stemmed from her being "kind of chubby when she was little."

Their passions were also dissimilar. "She came out of the womb saying, 'Where's my Ferrari?'" Karen said. "It's called wanting power. It's Gucci purses, Bentleys, all the things I don't care about that she does."

Despite their differences, the girls were extremely close growing up. Mary Jo made a beautiful home for them in Point Loma, an upscale seaside community in San Diego County where many of Robert's colleagues resided. Robert was proud of Mary Jo's love for interior design and he took pride in showing off all that his wife had done to make their grand white home his castle. Guests were so impressed with the Houghtons' home that it was dubbed the "White Palace."

When the young Mr. and Mrs. Houghton walked into a room, heads turned to take a second look at the well-heeled couple. "My mom was drop-dead gorgeous and my dad looked just like Elvis," Karen recalled. "They had class and they always dressed to kill."

From the outside, the Houghtons enjoyed a life of privilege. Mary Jo was a stunning and attentive wife of a successful husband. But even with all that going for them, Bob was hard pressed, years later, to explain what went wrong between him and Mary Jo. He would scratch his head in bewilderment over why they fought so much when they had been so much in love.

He never said a bad word about his wife, shrugging their incompatibility off as two people who were just too young. It's doubtful Mary Jo understood then why her husband had such terrible outbursts when they were alone. Ultimately, he was an undiagnosed alcoholic who continued down a path of drunken self-destruction until it killed him. In the end, it robbed him of the joys of being a father, giving away his daughters in marriage, and becoming a grandfather to their children. The marriage ended in divorce.

Mary Jo Goes to Town

Mary Jo was devastated over her marriage ending, but she was miserable and the children were being negatively affected. Karen said years later her father was abusive, though that is all she ever said about the matter.

Kris was only seven years old when her parents moved forward with their divorce in 1963. Kris fantasized that her parents would one day get back together. Despite Bob not being there to tuck his children in and read a bedtime story, or to wake them up in the morning, he continued to have a consistent presence in their lives for the remainder of the year. Yet Kris could not shake the idea that she was somehow responsible for her dad leaving them.

With two young daughters to raise, Mary Jo moved closer to her parents, who lived in the neighboring city of Clairemont. She started working in the family store, Candelabra. Lou Ethel had taken her passion for candles and turned it into a business. She had started making them in her home's garage, but became so successful she leased a retail space in the trendy oceanfront community of La Jolla. Lou Ethel thought of Candelabra as the family business. Several years later, Mary Jo opened a shop of her own a few streets over from her mother's.

Kris has vivid and fond memories of visiting Candelabra, and at age ten she started helping out at her grandma's store. In her 2011 autobiography *Kris Jenner . . . And All Things Kardashian*, Kris noted that Lou Ethel taught her "the value of hard work." She recalled that her favorite candle was also the most popular one with customers, the fittingly named Gloomchasers. Whenever the vivacious little girl found herself having a case of the blues over her broken home life, she would escape into the scents and magic properties she believed the candles possessed. However, Kris never fully eradicated the insecurities she faced as a result of her parents' divorce, which greatly influenced her need for attention, control, and financial security.

Cancer Scare Scars Kris

As the Houghtons settled into their "new normal" lives, Kris faced a shocking health crisis. She was rushed into surgery to remove a potentially cancerous tumor in her left knee. She had banged her shin against a wall and the swelling and pain was enough for her to require X-rays. This was Kris's first lesson in learning that no matter how bad things get, they can always get worse. She had only just discovered the meaning of the grown-up word *divorce* when she was faced with a new scary addition to her vocabulary: *amputate.* Her worried mom and dad set aside any lingering negative feelings from their divorce. Everyone had to face the unthinkable—that in order to save her life she might lose her leg all the way up to the hip.

Privately, Mary Jo contemplated how Kris would deal with the catastrophic consequences of having only one leg. Up until that point, Mary Jo had taken comfort in how Kris's exquisite beauty would take her anywhere she wanted to go in life. While she knew looks were not everything, being a pretty woman certainly had its rewards and made life a whole lot easier in a male-dominated world. Mary Jo wept at the thought of her baby girl's potentially dire forecast.

Several hours later, Kris's surgeon exited the operating room doors. Mary Lou and her family stood grasping each other as they waited for his report. The doctor looked at Mary Jo and Bob and announced, "I'm pleased the surgery was a success, but—"

"But what?!" Lou Ethel blurted, cutting the doctor off in mid-sentence.

"But," he continued, "Kris will need to stay a few extra days to ensure her body doesn't develop an infection."

He looked as relieved as Mary Jo when he announced: "There was no need to amputate. Your daughter will make a full recovery."

Cries of gratitude filled the room that night, and for many nights thereafter. Mary Jo and Bob were at the hospital day and night during Kris's stay. They couldn't stop kissing, cuddling, and squeezing her as if they would never let her go. Kris's mom and dad filled her room with presents. Her mom gave her a stuffed monkey, which Kris christened "Anabelle," and Bob treated her to a transistor radio in a black case. Karen gave her sister a crayon stick-figure drawing, showing the two of them in front of a big house.

It was the last time her family would be together and dote on her. Kris saved these gifts all the way up to her own motherhood.

Drawing on her strength to overcome adversity, Lou Ethel instilled a confidence and fearlessness in young Kris at a critical time in her growth and development. Kris took the scars of the emotional displacement of her parents' divorce with her into adulthood, but she triumphed in spite of them and refused to let "product of a broken home" be more than a chapter in her history. In many ways these residual insecurities fueled her ambitions. Were it not for her grandmother's guidance, and bearing witness to Lou Ethel's strength, determination, and the importance she assigned to putting family first, Kris's story might be an entirely different one today. Lou Ethel's life choices inspired Kris to refuse to let her circumstances define her.

Keeping Up with Lou Ethel

As a single mother of two young girls in the sixties, Mary Jo had to go to work full time. The only downside was that she couldn't be there for Kris and Karen as much as she had been when she was a 24/7 homemaker. She also couldn't afford a live-in nanny. Mary Jo and Lou Ethel's houses were only a couple of blocks from Longfellow Elementary, so Kris could walk home from school every day. The grandparents were thrilled to step in and have a more active role in the Houghton girls' lives, and they did their absolute best to ensure stability and make life enjoyable. Jim built an adorable playhouse for Kris and Karen in the front yard of their new home, and Kris was enrolled in a Girl Scout Brownie troop. Their life was starting to shape up.

No matter how tired she was from working all week, Mary Jo found time create special outings on the weekends for her girls, such as picnics on the beach. Mary Jo's friends would join her for an ocean view lunch. Kris recalled the thrill of riding in the backseat with the top down in her mom's 1956 T-Bird convertible.

"She did so many fun things on the weekend with us, and it was clear we were going to persevere," Karen remembered.

Lou Ethel bought her granddaughters two toy poodles, Toulouse and Bridgette, but Mary Jo insisted they stay with her mother, as she had little time to care for them with her work schedule. Kris and Karen never wanted to miss watching Lou Ethel bathe the puppies and trim their nails. They looked for any opportunity to wedge their way into helping with the grooming process. She made life fun for the girls.

Domestic disciplines were stressed. From an early age Kris was taught the value of nesting and the importance of keeping up a beautiful home and maintaining order and cleanliness. She and Karen had lovely clothes and shoes and a plethora of toys, but they were not spoiled. They learned how to care for their personal items and to pick up after themselves. They were taught how to put away their things neatly and efficiently. Everything had its place and was arranged just so. There was no clutter. They hung up their clothes, and immediately after eating they took their dishes to the sink and washed them.

Kris listened and nodded in agreement as Lou Ethel would say, "Clean the sink and polish it." Kris and Karen followed their grandmother around the house learning the discipline of daily chores. Beds were made, floors were swept, and carpets and rugs were vacuumed. Every inch of the Houghton and Fairbanks homes was dust free. Mary Jo was known to dust in a bikini and an apron. Mirrors and windows adorned with lovely drapes were gleaming and streak free. Their homes had the prettiest lawns. Kris and Karen would sit on their knees and watch their grandmother tend to her rosebushes out front and hold the baskets for Mary Jo's bounty of avocados she plucked from the tree next to the birdbath in her backyard.

Kris never minded rolling up her sleeves to work alongside her grandmother. It was more important to Kris to bask in the five-star smile of her grandmother's approval than to get straight A's on her report card from school. She was too young to know then that these moments with her grandmother were bonding them, not only as blood relatives, but as females. She loved the satisfaction of completing each task. Nesting practices provided Kris with a sense of peace and serenity that replaced the churning anxiety in her stomach. All of these life lessons were steps toward her life's purpose. Her young imagination conceived how she would one day have children and teach them everything Lou Ethel had taught her. They, too, would learn how to control and manipulate their environment to appear perfect at all times.

When Harry Met Mary Jo

Mary Jo was consistently employed but moved around in the job market. She was always on the lookout for a position that paid better and had potential for advancement. Catering to a large number of male customers also became an important factor in her job searches. Despite two failed marriages, Mary Jo was still very young and she knew she would marry again. She wanted to be prepared should Mr. Right come along.

Working under her mother's maiden name after her divorces, Mary Jo Campbell found a good fit as a salesclerk in the pro shop on a golf course at the La Costa Country Club, where there were plenty of successful and polished men. Kris recalled that her mother was just as fashion conscious as her grandmother: "She went to work every day dressed like Jacqueline Kennedy. She was the mom doing the housework and making dinner, but at the same time she was wearing these gorgeous dresses cinched at the waist. . . . She always looked like she had on some fabulous Chanel ensemble—and her hair was perfect."

Many guys wanted to take her out, but Mary Jo dated few. And then along came Harry Shannon. Dapper and debonair with wavy, sandy hair, Harry was charming and dressed with elegant sophistication. He resembled the Austrian-born Hollywood film idol of the 1930s and '40s, Paul Henreid. Harry's smile radiated from his full lips set against a backdrop of olive skin. Once he laid his cool blue eyes on the stunning Mary Jo, he was convinced that she was the girl for him. Mary Jo did not play "hard to get" for long. Almost immediately, she fell madly in love with Harry. He had the talk and Mary Jo had the charm school walk. Both were gregarious and fun-loving. She had not felt this excited about any man since she met Robert Houghton.

Harry Shannon was a colorful character with a lively past. Other than listing his credits as a "businessman" and "yacht" broker, very little has been reported in biographical information pertaining to Kris. This is surprising since he came into her life when she was a preteen and remained a constant presence in her life until his death when Kris was forty-eight.

With her biological dad now moving all over the country searching for work, and his inconsistent calls and letters making it impossible to nurture and maintain a relationship with him, Kris found Harry to be reliable in word and deed during her formative years. Harry became Kris's go-to guy for fatherly love and emotional and financial security, as well as advice that extended beyond her childhood. As a shrewd entrepreneur, Harry was her first male role model in the art of deal-making.

Like Mary Jo, Harry had been married twice. Both times he married strong women who were heiresses to magnificent fortunes. Named after his father, Harry was born on April 28, 1926, in San Diego, California. He was the youngest of his mother May's three children. His father died when Harry was a young boy. Harry excelled in school and was popular. He was voted senior class president of Point Loma High School. After graduation he joined the military, where he served in the Navy during World War II.

Harry was an asset to all of his employers, but he was also a wandering soul in his youth. He loved liquor. During a stint in the Texas Panhandle, he fell in love with a wealthy and attractive young divorcee, Dixie Lee Hedgecoke, who was the second-generation owner of the multi-thousand-acre Hedgecoke Ranch. Other investments on her father's side of the family included oilfields and mercantile stores. Due to her family's financial and social standing in the community, Dixie Lee was a prominent Texas socialite in Amarillo. By the time she met Harry, Dixie Lee was twenty-five, with two failed marriages and two children. Harry adopted the kids after he and Dixie Lee married in the spring of 1950. The following year, the couple had a daughter.

Harry not only helped Dixie Lee raise her kids but assisted in overseeing her ranch and a major shopping center.

Harry and Dixie Lee's marriage lasted less than a decade. After their divorce, Harry moved back to the San Diego area. There, he won the heart of Carol Smith, the only daughter of banking tycoon C. Arnholt Smith, who was known as "Mr. San Diego." In addition to the largest bank in the city, the self-made millionaire owned hotels, an airline, silver mines, seafood canneries, a fleet of yellow cabs, and the San Diego Padres baseball team. Carol's stepmother, Maria Helen Alavarez, was the first female CEO in television and a millionaire in her own right. Carol and Harry married on September 18, 1959. Carol had a son from a prior marriage. As before, Harry adopted his wife's child. Harry and Carol also became parents to their own son, Stephen. Harry was primed to become his father-in-law's right-hand man and Smith thought highly of his talents, but he didn't care much for his son-in-law's excessive drinking.

"Harry would come blazing up to the valet stand in a white Mercedes, with tags that read 'San Diego Open,'" remembered a bellman at the La Costa Resort and Spa, where Harry's father-in-law was one of the financial investors. "Harry was often sloshed out of his mind when he stayed here and would get belligerent and mouth off. He got into a pretty gnarly fight with one of our guys once. The cops were called after the man decked Harry, but it was all settled without anybody going to jail."

Harry's drunkenness contributed to the demise of their marriage. After their divorce, Harry frequently resided at La Costa, where he continued to network with the heavy hitters and business connections.

In the mid-1960s, La Costa was the new luxury playground for the super-rich. Las Vegas and Chicago mobsters allegedly pumped teamsters' pensions into building the luxury hot spot, located less than a half hour from the ponies racing at the Del Mar Thoroughbred Club. The property provided ultra-privacy in a restricted neighborhood of mostly undeveloped land in Carlsbad, just north of San Diego. It was a breathtakingly beautiful resort that catered to jetsetters. It offered world-class lodging, entertainment and cuisine, sparkling swimming pools, therapeutic mineral waters, tennis courts, and horseback riding. Nestled in the beautiful coastal foothills, it was a picturesque setting for the eighteen-hole golf course, which hosted the famous golfers on the professional circuit. The Rat Pack and other Hollywood movie stars flocked to La Costa for the action, as sun-drenched San Diego was the fastest-growing city in the country.

Mary Jo had chosen the perfect place to work. La Costa was a gorgeous environment and the clientele was stimulating, especially since it was chock full of eye candy with handsome and wealthy men. Outside of country clubs, meeting a proper beau from the upper echelons of society in those days meant attending parties in private homes or going out to nightclubs with girlfriends. Mary Jo rarely spent entire evenings away from Kris and Karen. When she visited with girlfriends, she preferred outings that were suitable for bringing her girls along, like picnics or seeing the latest movies at the local cinema.

Top-notch Las Vegas headliners performed at La Costa, so Mary Jo could stop in at the restaurant bar and watch a superstar like Frank Sinatra perform. She could enjoy a cocktail as she caught a set of songs from one of her favorite music artists, and still make it home in time to read her kids a bedtime story. Since she was an employee of the resort, she was on a first-name basis with the staff, so she felt comfortable sitting at the bar without a chaperone. It was a more conservative time, when any woman on her own in a drinking establishment could be perceived as a lush, or a floozy, or a gold digger. In addition, Mary Jo was a stunning woman who wore exquisite clothes, so she was even more likely to attract attention and unwelcome advances from men. She could always count on the guys behind the bar to fend off the wolves, and hotel security saw her safely to her car.

La Costa employee Rudy Hutagalung has undoubtedly seen a million faces since his first day of work in 1965, yet he instantly recalled Mary Jo and her distinctive style. "She was a real lady," he said. "I saw her a couple of times having a drink with a well-to-do guy before she got with Harry Shannon. If memory serves me, I saw Tony Bennett sitting with her a couple of times. She was a real beauty."

Harry was a high roller, always carrying a wad of $100 bills, which were tucked away in a money clip in his pocket. He was generous to a fault, almost to the point of being a little too flashy for Mary Jo's more conservative tastes. He blew cash on caviar, champagne, and pricey steak and lobster dinners at fancy restaurants. If Mary Jo thought he was a little too much, he could justify his spending on cocktails and parties as business expenses he wrote off as entertainment. As a yacht broker, it was the required shtick to court his high-end prospective clients.

Even as a child, Kris was impressed with Harry's panache. "He walked around in fabulous white linen slacks, jackets, and fabulous loafers," she remembered. "He was the coolest, most beautiful dresser. He always looked like a Ralph Lauren ad."

He introduced Mary Jo to an exciting set of new couples who became their friends. He was a salesman's salesman, even occasionally seducing Lou and Jim to join them when he and Mary Jo hosted parties. He won them over as they saw how he treated their daughter and the splendid way he cared for Kris and Karen. Harry Shannon knew how to make any female, no matter how old or young, feel special. When he walked in the door of Mary Jo's house, he often pulled a bouquet of flowers out from behind his back for Mary Jo, as well as thoughtful little gifts for Kris and Karen. He could make all three of his Houghton girls scream with laughter with his funny stories. He was the ultimate raconteur. He was an accomplished sailor and taught Mary Jo how to sail during their frequent weekend adventures. Mary Jo wanted to spend the rest of her life with him, as she knew they would make great partners.

Mary Jo appreciated Harry's luxury lifestyle, and she certainly enjoyed the attentions of this magical man. They were compatible on all levels. She loved being intimate with him emotionally and physically. But he simply drank too much, and she suspected he, like her ex-husband Bob, was an alcoholic. She would have given anything to be wrong, but her instincts had never let her down before. She inherited a spirit of discernment from Lou Ethel. Still, Mary Jo went through a small period of confusion, because Harry's behavior when he was drunk was the polar opposite of her ex-husband Bob's. Whereas Bob was angry, verbally abusive, and resentful, Harry was a happy drunk—the sloppy but affectionate kind. It took her a while to be sure. Once she was certain, she began distancing herself from him and limited his visits around Kris and Karen.

Of course, the girls noticed—everyone did, including Harry. He would sober up long enough to give Mary Jo hope that he could limit his drinks to one or two, but Harry could not drink like a normal person. He was an alcoholic. One drink wasn't enough and two were too many. She would date him, and they would be almost back to the way things were, but she would ultimately break up with him again when his demons showed up. The situation with Harry was getting worse.

Harry was crazy about Mary Jo, and he knew he risked losing her if he didn't quit drinking, but the addiction owned him. He thought he could handle it until his drunkenness resulted in him crossing a line with Mary Jo. One night Mary Jo and the girls were awakened by a loud banging on the front door. It was a drunk and belligerent Harry.

"Mary Jo! Open this door! Let me in!" he screamed.

Kris, who was twelve at the time, described how she and her eight-year-old sister peeked through the curtains of the window by the door to see Harry swaying and stumbling, yelling at the top of his lungs.

Mary Jo was furious. She screamed back at him through the door. "Go home, Harry, and come back when you sober up! You're in no shape to be here."

Harry was unfazed and continued acting like a fool. "Let me in!" he screamed, but Mary Jo just ignored him, hoping he would go away before the neighbors called the police.

She calmly took the girls to her bedroom, where she closed the door and locked them in for safety. She put them in her bed and held them as they shook from fear. She rocked them back and forth in her arms.

As the banging got louder, the Houghton girls grew more alarmed. Mary Jo remained calm for them.

Harry eventually left. It was difficult for anyone to get back to sleep, so Mary Jo had a family meeting right there in her bed. She turned her bedside table lamp on and promised they would never have to be subjected to such a terrifying ordeal. Harry was out of her life for good . . . or so they thought.

The next morning Harry was frantically ringing Mary Jo. She didn't answer the phone, and he didn't come to her home. Finally, after a few days of incessant phone calls, Mary Jo talked to him. She told him she never wanted to see him again. She would not put up with his drunken behavior, and she certainly was not going to continue to expose her daughters to this kind of melodrama.

Harry did what all drunks do when they're dealing with the damage they've caused under the influence of alcohol. He promised Mary Jo he would never drink again. He begged her to forgive him. He declared his love for her and the girls and asked her to marry him.

"Show me. Don't tell me," she declared. "Quit drinking and we'll get married."

Harry never had another drink for the rest of his life. He soon proved to Mary Jo's satisfaction that he was sincere about staying sober. He promised to always be a good provider, both as a husband and as a stepfather. Harry and Mary Jo wed in a private ceremony in Puerto Vallarta in June 1968, with only a few friends as witnesses. None of his biological or adopted children from his previous marriages were in attendance. Even Kris and Karen stayed behind at their grandparents' house.

It had been five years since Kris and Karen had a father figure living in their home. They were eager for their mom and new stepdad to return from Mexico so they could be a real family.

Welcome to Tuna Town

When he and his new bride came back from Puerto Vallarta, Harry was on fire. Full of vitality and drive. He was eager to provide a brilliant income for his new family. He had been successful flipping everything from luxury yachts to used cars, and the profits from those sales would more than cover their overhead, but Harry dreamed bigger. He was grateful for a second chance with a good woman.

One day, not long after their wedding, Harry excitedly told the girls they were moving to Oxnard, California, to operate a new business harvesting abalone. Harry had hit on the idea as a result of his ex-father-in-law's lucrative tuna fleet canneries and ownership in fishing bait vessels in San Diego.

Thanks to C. Arnholt Smith, it was the city's third largest industry. Japan's dominance of the tuna industry was cutting into America's sales, and there was a shortage of fresh tuna in the waters around Southern California. Smith became a major player after purchasing freezing plants in Peru and freighter ships built for the purpose of carrying frozen tuna to the port of San Diego, where they were delivered to his processing plants. Harry knew the next part of his plan was to distribute the product directly to grocery stores. He wanted in on that action, but Smith would not have taken kindly to Harry attempting to lay claim to a portion of his industry in the San Diego area. Harry found a business partner who understood the trade and secured the money to invest in the Abalone Processing Plant in Oxnard. At 155 miles from San Diego, Harry felt the plant was far enough from Smith's stronghold.

By this time, Kris was in junior high and was distressed at leaving her hometown of San Diego. She felt her mother was unapproachable about the move. Mary Jo and Harry were united in thinking that the tuna industry was their family's future. They agreed to move to Oxnard, the land of strawberries and lima beans. Kris said they went from a house in San Diego to an apartment in Oxnard. To her, the thought of fishermen harvesting slimy snails was dreary and not at all glamorous. According to Kris, as soon as the fishing boats came back, Harry had people "pounding and preparing the abalone for sale."

When Kris and her family dined out at local restaurants, they were expected to eat burgers made from abalone.

"The whole move was just a big hot mess," Kris later proclaimed. "I hated abalone."

"I could have said, 'Oh, I'm getting the next train to La Jolla,'" Kris later explained. "I guess I could have lived with my grandmother. But that was my mother's first year of marriage, and I was part of a family unit. Still, all I could think about was getting out."

This miserable feeling of being helpless over her fate instilled a need for control and independence that would become a distinctive trademark in how she lived her adult life, both personally and professionally.

After three months of hell, Kris learned they were moving back to San Diego. Harry's partner had bankrupted the company when he took off with all the cash, approximately $15,000. They were back in Clairemont in no time and moved into a house directly across the street from Lou Ethel, just in time for Kris and Karen to go back to their schools.

For Kris, life was grand again, but Mary Jo and Harry were devastated. Harry had lost every dime he had rustled up. And the cracks of Mary Jo's perfect man began to show. Some of their family troubles might have been avoided if Harry had sought help for his alcoholism instead of stopping cold turkey and jumping into a new business venture. He and Mary Jo were unaware of the pitfalls of doing too much in early sobriety. It's suggested in alcoholic support groups that major changes—which include new romantic relationships, changes of employment, and moves—are to be avoided for the first year to give the brain time to heal and avoid additional stressors that might lead to a relapse. Newly sober, Harry Shannon had done all three.

To his credit, Harry did not pick up the bottle despite the chaos swirling around him. He just kept busy. He was lucky to have such versatile talents. Harry went to work for his brother Jim, who owned a car dealership. He also bought into the Ugly Duckling Rent-A-Car franchise. Mary Jo joined him in that venture. The pair also operated an antenna installation company. Harry did most of the installations until they could afford to hire help. Then he learned car striping and sold his services to car dealerships all over the county. Kris was fascinated with Harry's business moxie, and all of his wheeling and dealing had a major impact on her. Once again, she learned from another adult that all she needed to succeed and have whatever she wanted was the willingness to work hard and turn adversity into an opportunity.

Kris credits Harry for giving her many lessons about life.

Almost fifty years later, Stephanie Shepherd, an executive assistant to the Kardashians, has witnessed Kris's powerful tenacity and persistence. "If someone tells her no, she has no problem standing her ground and saying, 'We're not accepting that, get someone on the phone and make it happen,'" Stephanie said. "That woman can literally get on the phone and change the world."

CHAPTER TWO
KRIS TEES OFF

Going for the Green

The first celebrities Kris Houghton met were sports stars. Harry and his brother, Jim, frequently played golf together. They were members of the swanky country clubs in the resort beach communities around San Diego that catered to the professional golfers. Mary Jo shared Harry's enthusiasm for golf, so they spent a lot of their time traveling the golfing circuit. Jim ran a golf tournament at Torrey Pines Golf Course. Harry and Mary Jo ran the scoreboard.

During her teenage years, Kris would have lunches and dinners at the La Costa Country Club with Harry and Mary Jo. Kris absorbed the sophistication of the country clubs. Wealth and social status were intoxicating to her. She observed how the socialite wives of these rich men dressed and behaved. She studied every detail of club life, analyzing the many courses of fine cuisine and how meals were presented. While she was too young to drink alcohol, she pored over the wine list and noted how patrons sniffed the glasses of the elegant brandies they imbibed. It was an education she found much more interesting and exciting than her high school courses. Socially, her status as a cheerleader at Clairemont High ensured she was popular, but she wasn't interested in silly teenage chatter. She was mature beyond her years. She always felt comfortable with adults. Mary Jo and Lou Ethel always treated her like a peer.

Kris soaked up adult conversations at her mom's table. She tuned into the talk between the women in the powder rooms. Kris eavesdropped as she checked her hair in the mirror and reapplied her lip gloss. She listened to how they gossiped about other women, how they talked about their husbands while they primped and preened. She made mental notes of how they wore their hair and the shades of their makeup as they patted powder and blush on their faces. She would compliment them on their clothes or hair as she asked them to reveal the shades of their lipsticks and nail polishes.

And, of course, Kris was aware of the men, and they couldn't help but notice her. Most of the men were much older than Kris, and they were married. It did wonders for her self-confidence whenever these successful men glanced her way and let her know by how they looked at her that they found her attractive and desirable. When Kris caught a guy checking her out, it gave her a high like a drug. She was not only a stunning brunette, but also charming and fun. Her smile was warming, and she knew how to use her mouth muscles to evoke expressions for dramatic affect: starting at the halfway mark, turning up the corners slowly until she reached a full smile, while her big kohl-rimmed eyes twinkled in delight and amusement. She instinctively knew men loved being heard. She could tilt her head in a certain way and nod in agreement. Men felt she heard and understood them.

Most of the men spoke to her with motives for a quick thrill. Almost always, the conversational interludes were merely a fast flirtation with a pretty young thing while their wife wasn't looking. It became an experiment of sorts for Kris to see how long she could maintain their initial advances. She found men took a real interest in her because she feigned such genuine interest in *them*. It was all research for learning how men operate. It was an education for Kris to discover that wealth and prestige could be easily obtained.

Many of the guys at the golf clubs were senior citizens, but there were a few who were only a decade older than Kris, some of whom she fancied, especially the superstars of the pro golf set. She was meeting some of these men through her friend Debbie Mungle's mother, who managed professional golfer Phil Rodgers. The superstar had garnered a best-of-the-best reputation in the 1960s. Kris had heard Harry animatedly recount Rodgers's five PGA tournament wins. She also had heard stories about Rodgers's competitors Jack Nicklaus and Arnold Palmer. The men were known as the "Big Three."

In 1973, as an early high school graduation present, Debbie's mother treated the girls to a trip to Honolulu to watch the Hawaiian Open golf tournament. Rodgers was playing that weekend and seventeen-year-old Kris was thrilled with the invite.

Because Kris had already accompanied Debbie and her mom to several of Rodgers's tournaments, Mary Jo let her teenage daughter go on the trip. But she was well aware that Hawaii was a whole different ball game. She knew the high schooler would be seen as a tantalizing young woman.

Excited by the adventure, Kris spent days assembling the perfect wardrobe for visiting the tropical paradise. She was sure she had come up with the right clothes, shoes, hats, and bags to look the part and create the desirable image she wanted to convey. She was equally confident that she had saved enough money working her part-time jobs to invest in sorely needed spring accessories to freshen up her closet picks for Hawaii.

Donuts before Diamonds

Kris never complained about the 5:00 a.m. call time for her shift at the neighborhood donut shop. Like a ray of sunshine before the morning light, she was wide awake and smiling brightly for her regular customers.

After a few hours of donut duty, which included scraping glaze off the shop floor, Kris changed into her school clothes and crossed the street to catch the bus for Clairemont High. After school, Kris walked to Candelabra for her other part-time job, gift wrapping and stocking the display table. Kris needed no direction. She prided herself on being a self-starter. She learned by living with her mom and grandma that there was always some task that required attention. Kris cleaned the entire back room and organized what was already organized in the little area assigned to gift wrapping. She practiced making gift bows from the jewel-toned ribbons.

Lou Ethel was impressed with how Kris instantly saw what needed to be done and did it. When she was promoted to gift wrapper, she continued to clean despite her elevated position with the family business. The two businesses—donuts at dawn and candles at sunset—couldn't have been more different, but Kris enjoyed the variety and the satisfaction of doing two jobs well.

Kris was always comfortable with working hard. In her home, she saw the rewards that came from crafting a plan and implementing her ideas. She witnessed her mom, stepdad, and grandparents making businesses out of whatever they chose. They were all doers. It was the path to the luxurious lifestyle she craved.

On Fridays, Kris had a third job. Her mother had assigned Kris and her sister weekly chores. Kris hummed Disney tunes while she raked and fluffed the red shag carpeting in the living room. She always completed her household assignments to Mary's Jo's satisfaction. Despite her heavy workload, Kris always found time to grab the keys to the shiny red Mazda RX-2 that Harry had given her for her sixteenth birthday and go to the movies or for a drive with friends.

Kris's only afternoons off were when she had cheerleading practice. Naturally, the football jocks and other sports stars in her class fancied the spunky, dark-haired beauty. She was a head-turner, different from the rest of the popular teenage girls who lived in the small beachside community towns surrounding San Diego in the 1970s. Kris was social, and feminine, and could surf the ocean waves with ease, but she had no interest in the guys from her school. Although she would smile and laugh at their stories, she felt the boys were missing substance. They were just not her type. They lacked the direction and maturity she was looking for in a husband. These kids could teach her nothing. She needed a man with worldly sophistication. Kris had no desire to slave away at a job to put her guy through medical or law school while she attended to the children. The thought of spending four years attending college was akin to a prison sentence for a free spirit like Kris. She had no aspirations to reign as a sorority sister, pinned to the football captain. These were the dreams of children. Small-time goals were not on Kris Houghton's bucket list.

"Kris dated the least attractive guy in school because he drove a Ferrari," a family friend revealed.

Kris couldn't wait to get out of high school so she could move to Los Angeles, where she would meet all kinds of rich and famous people. That's where she would find a great guy, get married, and have six children. She already had a plan.

Aloha, Cesar!

From the moment she stepped off the plane in Honolulu and had a lei placed around her neck, to her discovery of the gift baskets at the gorgeous Royal Hawaiian Hotel suite, everything spelled VIP to Kris.

On a perfect Sunday in February, Kris and Debbie attended the Hawaiian Open. They sat in the private area reserved for golfers, management, and Sony corporate executives who were sponsoring the tournament. While Mrs. Mungle tended to her client, Debbie and Kris were free to roam. The girls were infatuated with the golfers. The men were older, wealthy, and sophisticated. Later, as they dressed for a night out in Honolulu, they fantasized about landing two professional golfers as husbands. Since most of the pros were married, netting a single guy who was free of attachments was problematic. However, Kris soon scored a prospect: Cesar Sanudo, a professional golfer and friend of Phil Rodgers.

Cesar was popular on the professional golf circuit. The twenty-nine-year-old had won a PGA event at the 1970 Azalea Open Invitational at Cape Fear Country Club in Wilmington, North Carolina. He was a hot-blooded, charismatic Hispanic and had all the qualities Kris sought in a man. Twelve years older than Kris, Cesar was worldly and, most importantly, an eligible bachelor. In fact, he had never married. Kris was ready to have a meaningful relationship with a real man. Cesar fit the bill, and he didn't live far from her in San Diego County.

At first, Kris only wanted to hear about the celebrities Cesar knew. She was wildly impressed by Cesar's famous pals. As they got to know each other, he shared how he had played and socialized with major film stars, even US presidents. Cesar wasn't prone to name-dropping; he was just describing his life. He told Kris stories about his times with famous people such as Clint Eastwood, Bob Hope, Richard Nixon, Gerald Ford, and George Bush Sr.

"Everyone liked to hang around Cesar," recalled his good buddy and fellow golfer, Jack Spradlin. "He had a winning personality."

Cesar was five feet nine inches and slightly stocky, with sandy hair. He might have been self-conscious about the inch-long scar on his left cheek— the result of walking through a plate glass window—but he didn't show it.

Born in Mexico in 1954 to a family of meager means, Cesar was raised in the dust-filled streets of Tijuana. His father had deserted him and his four siblings. Raised by his mother, Cesar found himself drawn to the Tijuana Country Club. He dreamed about opportunities where he could better his life and help his mother financially. One day he walked into the club and talked his way into a job caddying for the golfers. When he wasn't working, he taught himself to play. Cesar befriended his golf hero "Super Mex" Lee Trevino, who became his mentor. Trevino taught the young man the finer points of how to land endorsement deals, as Lee had raked in a fortune in commercials as the spokesman for aspirin, automobiles, and soft drinks. Lee introduced Cesar to all the right people to help further his career beyond golf. He told Cesar, "This good life we are living, like all things, will one day come to an end, and you need to be ready with a game plan for living out the rest of your days."

During the Hawaiian Open in 1973, Cesar literally charmed the pants off Kris after their first meeting at the Waialae Country Club. He was absolutely smitten with the seventeen-year-old, and Kris found Cesar a worthy beau. They were inseparable after returning to San Diego.

"He made all the boys I'd hung out with in high school seem like, well, boys," Kris later admitted. "Maybe I was just a golf groupie, but I liked him immediately."

Kris made life with Cesar her full-time project. It was her first grown-up affair and she was completely devoted to him, and to being his mature girlfriend. Cesar proudly showed off his new younger girlfriend to his buddies.

"Kris was a looker," recalled Spradlin. "She wasn't like a ten, but Kris was a very attractive girl. Extremely nice, very social, and she had a great personality."

Kris had told both her grandmothers and Mary Jo all about Cesar and his famous friends during their phone chats while she was in Hawaii. Mary Jo heard more about Cesar as Kris unpacked her clothes upon her return from Honolulu. Mary Jo said little. She was reserving judgment until after she met Kris's older love interest. She and Harry were cautiously optimistic about Kris's new romance.

For Mary Jo, it seemed like the perfect time to talk to Kris about whether she planned to go to college. Kris's response, in a word: "No."

"I'm not interested in college," she informed her mother. "It's not for me."

And that was that. Mary Jo said no more, and she and Harry accepted Cesar into their lives. The Shannons were avid fans of golf, so they had an instant rapport with him. All in all, Mary Jo and Harry came to believe Cesar was a good match for their daughter, even though he was ten years older and she was seventeen and still in high school.

Harry thought Cesar was a good catch. What was good for Kris was also beneficial to Harry. He developed his own relationship with Cesar. The two could easily sit and talk for hours on end about golf, but Kris was always there to keep Cesar in motion.

"Come on, Cesar," she'd politely but firmly interrupt when she was done hearing the men prattle on. "You need your rest. Tomorrow's a big day."

Cesar never put up any fuss. He loved Kris's devotion to him, and Kris loved being in charge. Over the next few months Kris was Cesar's constant companion. He took her with him to his golf games, where she would move alongside him from hole to hole. Kris didn't care if she looked like a golf groupie. She was helping Cesar. She claimed his game always seemed to improve when she was within eyeshot of him. She carried a small folding chair with a round cushioned seat so she could watch and listen to the golfers as they played. She lit up her megawatt smile to ensure Cesar's competitors took notice of her.

Quit Playing Games

One spring afternoon between weekend tournaments, Kris inadvertently "went public" with her grand plans for Cesar. As she sat on the bed in her grandmother's guest room painting her toenails "passion pink," fashion magazines and tabloids sprawled around her, Kris was talking on the phone to Debbie. Lou Ethel walked by just in time to hear Kris say, "Fuck the prom! I want to get married and have six children. That's right. I'm dead serious."

When her nails were dry, Kris walked in the kitchen for a glass of iced tea. She sat down at the table across from Lou Ethel, who had a stack of vendor invoices from Candelabra.

"Do you need any help?" Kris asked. Her grandmother declined.

"Kris, are you not going to your high school prom?" Lou Ethel inquired.

"What?" Kris said, slowly realizing that her grandmother must have heard her talking on the phone. "Why do you ask?"

Kris retraced her previous conversation as she listened to Lou Ethel.

"Well, dear. Are you really going to miss your high school prom? That would be tragic. You want those memories, don't you? You can never repeat high school again, you know?"

The thought of ditching high school pleased Kris, but she remained silent.

"Does your mother know, dear?" her grandmother asked. "Because she hasn't mentioned it to me."

"Well, Grandma," Kris answered, "I'm not sure yet. But it's looking like I'm not going. Here's the deal. I met Cesar in February, it's already late spring, and he and I go almost everywhere together."

Lou Ethel gave Kris a knowing smile. Kris sat up in the chair to make sure Lou Ethel saw her posture was that of a grown woman. It was sweet, but Lou Ethel was still concerned. When Lou Ethel talked to Mary Jo about this guy Kris was dating, her daughter assured her it was nothing serious. Now she feared Kris was changing her plans for this man.

Kris continued, "I mean, really, I'm going to get out of school very soon. Should I just draft some guy at school to escort me to the prom so I can have my picture taken to say that I was there? And how is that going to make my real boyfriend feel? I'm sure Cesar, as a professional golfer, would not want to pin a corsage on me and escort me to the prom."

"I am not suggesting you take your fellow, that golfer, to your prom," Lou Ethel said. "That would not be appropriate given he's much older than you. Kris." She paused for effect. "That would not be wise."

"Great! It's settled then, Grandma!" Kris said, walking around the table to give Lou Ethel a kiss on the cheek. "I'm so glad we had this little talk. I love you."

Full-Time Commitment

After her high school graduation, Kris traipsed all over the world with Cesar, staying in the finest hotels and resorts. From his native Mexico City, where she met his mother, to London, Scotland, and Japan, Kris Houghton was now officially part of the jet set. Mary Jo was aware that people gossiped about how, as a mother, she could let her daughter, who was not even eighteen, fly all around the world with an older man. Mary Jo kept her own counsel. She never paid attention to what other people thought about her business.

Kris wasn't going to college. She made that clear. She might as well find a good husband. It might be Cesar, it might not. But she was meeting many successful men on the road with him. She might not be in a position to meet these kinds of men any other way. Who knew what wonderful husband material was awaiting her beautiful daughter at the next port of call? And Kris always brought Mary Jo expensive gifts from every city she visited.

For the next year, Cesar was Kris's career. She might as well have been his manager. She looked after him like one. Kris met all the big names in golf that she had watched on television with Harry, including Tom Watson and Ben Crenshaw. Famous golfers always had movie star friends hanging around them. Crooners and film stars Dean Martin and Bing Crosby were frequent companions of Cesar's. Granted, since Cesar was a decade ahead of her in age, the stars were more her mother's generation, but they were still relevant in Kris's eyes, and she could meet other famous people through them. Kris absorbed every minute of being in their company.

Cesar and Kris became a popular couple on the local golf scene. Besides hitting all the oceanfront golf clubs in Pebble Beach, the golfers and football players relaxed at Bully's, a sports bar in San Diego. It was the hot spot for celebrity athletes.

"Kris wanted to be a part of it all," Spradlin remembered. "She was no wallflower, content on sitting in the corner while the men talked. She liked to have her glass of wine and be really with us."

Kris's ears always perked up when the talk turned to endorsements. It was a fascinating world and Kris was smack dab in the middle of it, taking it all in.

For Kris, life on the road with Cesar was the next best thing to living her dream in Los Angeles. In a way, Hollywood was coming to *her*.

"Cesar introduced her to a lot of showbiz big shots," said Cesar's brother, Carlos Sanudo. "He'd take her to big parties at mansions and on yachts."

The couple enjoyed pretending they were wealthy while socializing, drinking, and playing with the millionaire amenities.

Kris's Big House

Soon after she turned eighteen, Kris persuaded the lovestruck Cesar to let her move into his two-bedroom, two-bath condominium in Mission Beach, an oceanfront community in San Diego County. She also convinced Cesar to allow Debbie to move in. Kris admitted later that she and Debbie were "little con artists."

While still a teenager, Kris proved she was already a great closer. Debbie followed Kris's lead as they did what all great salespeople do—they made it all about Cesar. How they could help him by living there for free. The girls convinced Cesar he needed to focus on his game because he was just entering some pivotal moments in his career and would soon be a mega-successful golfer. The acceleration of his golf commitments was imminent. It made so much sense for Cesar to have the convenience of Kris and Debbie looking after his affairs while he concentrated on his game. When she suggested the three of them try it temporarily, with no commitment if it didn't work out, Cesar agreed. Kris had negotiated terms brilliantly to strike her deal. He left money for her to pay for groceries and household needs, as well as additional cash for her personal use.

Cesar never wanted Kris to work. He liked for her to remain available to travel with him. Debbie had a full-time job, which kept her busy most of the time. It was a sweet situation for Kris. She had a base of operation.

Cesar's condo was his castle, and Kris was definitely the queen. She organized every inch of it, throwing out unnecessary clutter. Cesar was neat and orderly, but Kris enhanced his bachelor pad. She color-coordinated his wardrobe and laid his clothes out on the bed for him most days. Cesar's maid came in regularly, but Kris usually cleaned up behind her. She bought fresh flowers for the living room, patio, and bedroom. Lou Ethel let Kris go wild on a shopping spree at Candelabra. Kris bought plump new decorative pillows for the couch in the living room. The macho side of Cesar appreciated how his girl was taking care of him. Her efforts symbolized love and respect for her man.

But the matriarchs of Kris's family consistently reminded her that it was critical she maintain her independence. Many girls Kris's age would have lounged around their boyfriend's house and basked in being a lady of leisure: sunbathing all day, hair appointments, manicures, shopping, and fancy oceanfront lunches. Kris did her share of these things, but she also continued to help out her grandmother at the store and work part-time at a boutique dress shop in La Jolla. As she put it, "I was already multitasking."

Double Dating with Dad

As Kris adjusted to living with a man, she was also reconnecting with her father. Bob's involvement in Kris's and Karen's lives had been irregular. Kris called Harry Shannon "Dad." He was the perfect stepfather. Yet barely a day went by that Kris didn't feel the sting of Bob's abandonment. She longed for his attention and love. There were broken promises of trips to see her and Karen, and a few missed phone calls, and even fewer letters. It hurt her that he missed out on time together over the years: the empty seat he should have filled at football games when she was a cheerleader, the birthdays and holidays when he didn't reach out. It was not acceptable to Kris. Like most kids from a broken home, Kris had to fend off feelings that she wasn't worthy or had done something wrong. But she wouldn't indulge herself in the sadness for very long. When these awful thoughts flashed across her mind, she would busy herself with a project—anything productive to chase away the negative chatter in her head.

The truth was that Bob felt just as bad about it as Kris, if not more so. After his job transfer from Convair took him to Los Angeles, he eventually left his engineering career and drifted in and out of freelance jobs. His alcoholism had progressed to the point that he could no longer hold down steady employment. He called out sick often and frequently quit before he was fired.

Self-employment fit better into his drinking lifestyle, but it was also fraught with insecurity from not having a steady paycheck. He always managed to pay his rent and maintain a car, but there was little extra cash for treating his daughters to presents and outings, so he stayed away. Although Mary Jo never asked him for money, he paid child support when he was working. On holidays and birthdays, Bob looked forward to calling the girls, but after he had knocked back a couple of cocktails, the day always got away from him. Full of remorse, he couldn't face apologizing only to hear the hurt in his little girls' voices. The disappointments stacked one on top of the other until many years were lost.

He would console himself with how the girls were better off without him, and he was sure their stepdad was a good substitute father. He had no way of knowing how many times young Kris had cried herself to sleep wondering why he stayed away.

Just as he had gone from job to job, Bob went from woman to woman, never able to maintain a solid relationship for any length of time because of his excessive drinking. All that changed in 1972, when Robert met a vivacious, pert blonde while working as a recruiter at a business college in downtown Los Angeles.

Leslie Johnson was new to LA, having just moved there from San Diego. They had an instant connection. While she looked for a house with a yard for her two dogs, Leslie accepted Robert's offer to move into his downtown apartment temporarily. Before long, Bob and Leslie's friendship had blossomed into a romance.

"I found a lovely two-bedroom house, on a tree-lined street in Culver City, close to the Santa Monica freeway," Leslie remembered of their impulsive decision to live together. "As I showed my new place to Robert, we just said, 'Hey! Why don't we live here together?'"

Leslie found Bob handy around the house. Living together saved them both a ton of money. "It was a darling little cottage, but it had been trashed by the prior tenants," Leslie said. "Robert could fix anything. We had it all painted and fixed up in no time at all."

On the weekends, Bob and Leslie would browse antique stores and visit flea markets. She was impressed with how much knowledge he had about the objects. He explained how his parents were avid collectors-turned-sellers. Bob frequently fantasized about having a relationship like his parents, where he and a woman were partners in a similar business. He found the dream partner in Leslie.

"Robert was so good at knowing how to pick antiques, so we started working the area swap meets," Leslie said. "We were buying out estates and refurbishing furniture to sell at our booth. It was so much fun. I had never done anything like that before. We were passionate about our little side business."

She added, "Bob had this amazing entrepreneurial spirit. He always had ideas. 'We can make a lot of money if we do this!' His 'we can do anything' kept our lives exciting and interesting. We were always on the go."

They found so much joy in making extra money from their creative pursuits that Bob and Leslie, both educated people, soon found themselves dissatisfied with their jobs at the college. It was a strictly commission-paying position, with no room for advancement. They also missed San Diego. Bob often told Leslie how he longed to see his daughters on a regular basis. Finally, for the first time since he and Mary Jo had lived together in their big house in Point Loma so many years ago, Bob felt like he could be a family man again. He had a good woman in his life, which provided him with a sense of stability. He was ready to reclaim his fatherhood.

Bob reapplied at a company where he had previously worked, General Dynamics, and Leslie landed a job as a teacher at a community college. They rented a house a few blocks from Bob's parents, True and Mary Lee, and eventually bought a home together. He wasted no time reestablishing a bond of communication with his daughters once he was settled. He was thrilled to have a home for them. Leslie was happy he reunited with his daughters.

"He was doing an okay job of it, after having missed so much of their lives," she said. "There had to be some hostility and hurt that Robert wasn't in their lives growing up. But they were willing to give him a chance."

Bob found his girls to be completely different in their passions. Karen was quieter, and into horses and nature, so he would go and watch her ride. Leslie found Karen to be the more "normal" and down-to-earth of the two sisters.

Kris was more gregarious. She fancied *human* pets. "Kris was very much into social climbing," Leslie revealed. "That was her thing. Robert and I adapted to her world, in order for him to spend time with her."

Bob and Leslie double-dated with Kris and Cesar. They took turns entertaining at each other's homes. Kris would invite her dad and Leslie over when she was hosting parties at the condo she shared with Cesar. Kris and Debbie would cook everything from steaks to tacos and serve peach margaritas to their guests. Robert was happy Kris included him, and Kris enjoyed introducing him.

"This is my dad," she would say.

During their dinners, Bob and Leslie observed Kris and Cesar as a couple. Leslie later confided, "Bob was concerned that Cesar was too old for Kris, but having been an absentee father, he didn't feel he had any right to butt his nose into her affairs. We both thought Cesar was a really good guy, who cared deeply for Kris. He wasn't the golfer with the most wins, so I don't think Kris was real thrilled about that. Instead of citing *his* accomplishments, she would name drop about famous people she had met while on tour with him. He was a humble and modest guy. He was always fine with Kris taking center stage during our conversations. I think he was proud to have been able to introduce her to the perks that came from living in his world."

Leslie said Kris made no attempt to disguise her ambitions to move up in the world. It was obvious that Cesar was not her forever guy. "She wanted to be at the top. I think that everybody along the way were stepping-stones . . . I had never known anybody, especially at that age, who was so driven."

Kris would often drop by her dad's house on her way to join Cesar at a tournament or his favorite hangout spots.

"Kris and Debbie were dressed to the nines," recalled Leslie of their outings. "Whether it was day or night, they got themselves all dolled up. Debbie had a crush on another golfer, and so they would plot over how she was going to seduce him."

As they bounced out the door, swimming in lip gloss and perfume, Leslie would watch them give each other an approving last-minute fashion appraisal, before Leslie heard Kris say, "Let's see who we can drum up today."

A Change of Greenery

As Kris reached the six-month mark of living with Cesar, following him around to his golf spots became redundant and stale. She had met everybody who was anybody in the golfing world. With Cesar's connections conquered, Kris needed to step up her game if she was going to move beyond golfing greats and lower-tier celebrities. She was curious what opportunities awaited her beyond the city limits of San Diego. She suspected the grass might be greener. Kris set her sights on Los Angeles, where she would make a life for herself in Beverly Hills and socialize with Hollywood producers and movie stars. She and Debbie would have a whole lot more fun seeking out their own adventures.

Kris decided to invite some girlfriends to the Del Mar Thoroughbred Racetrack, only twenty miles from San Diego. While she and Debbie lived on their own, some of their other friends still lived at home, under the supervision of their parents. Kris assuaged their fears. She promised that they would be home by nightfall.

"There will be lots of guys there," Kris excitedly told her posse of gal pals, enticing them further with promise of movie and television stars that usually showed up during the summer months. Having been there many times, Kris was an authority. Mary Jo took Kris and Karen to the racetrack every year on opening day, so she knew her way around the venue just enough to be at ease with her surroundings. Harry Shannon was well versed in horse racing, after living with his second wife, Carol. He, of course, didn't bring up his other family to his stepdaughters, but he was an encyclopedia of knowledge.

Kris rarely deviated from her formula for attracting the opposite sex. She wore white dresses and white pant suits, with big hats and "Jackie O" sunglasses. Kris would have looked every bit the elegant and chic movie starlet, but there was one small incongruity that gave her away. She was still a teenager who wore her favorite gold necklace, which read: "OH SHIT."

Cesar called Kris every night from wherever he was in the world. There had been talk about marriage between them, but Kris had her doubts about spending the rest of her life with Cesar. While he was away, she knew she had to behave at all of his haunts, lest he get reports of her dalliances. She was too high profile as his girlfriend to fly under the radar, which was all the more reason to travel in some other circles. Some distance from all things Cesar also gave her a clear head to sort out her feelings concerning the golf pro.

* * *

On a beautiful July day in Southern California, Robert Kardashian, a thirty-year-old Beverly Hills attorney and music executive, decided that he and his brother Tommy deserved to take an afternoon off from their jobs. Del Mar was a hundred miles south of Los Angeles—just far enough from Robert's law offices to unwind. They would bet on the horses, have lunch and a few cocktails, and bask in the sunshine and ocean view. There was also the prospect of meeting gorgeous women.

That afternoon, Kris and her girlfriends were having a raucous time as they lunched at Del Mar's members-only Turf Club. Her parents allowed her to charge the bill to their account.

"My treat," Kris told the girls. "Order whatever you like!"

Kris and Debbie excused themselves from the table to make $2 bets on the next horse race and to visit the ladies' room. After placing her bet, Kris was people-watching while waiting for Debbie to place hers at another window. As she stared, she fancied herself Audrey Hepburn from the film *Breakfast at Tiffany's*. Kris loved old movies, especially the glamour of the Golden Age of Hollywood. She idolized Jean Harlow, Carole Lombard, Paulette Goddard, and Clara Bow. All of these women were class acts. Kris felt like she was part of the historic Hollywood hangout just by standing there. Gary Cooper and other legendary stars like Laurel and Hardy had pitched in to finance the racecourse. Cesar told her that Bing Crosby was there in 1937 on opening day. Kris swooned at the thought of elegantly dressed leading men like Cary Grant and Rock Hudson, or Paul Newman and Robert Redford, passing by her as they stepped up to a window. *It could happen*, she thought.

Kris interrupted her own fantasy when she spotted a man who, at first glance, looked like crooner Tony Orlando. The stranger had a bushy moustache and coal-black hair. With his platform shoes, the look was disco-meets-porn-star, except he wore an expensive tailored blazer and slacks. The man approached the young lady. Kris recalled in her autobiography the first words he said to her.

"Hi, is your name Janet?"

"That is the worst pickup line I have ever heard," Kris responded.

The gentleman didn't flinch. He continued to engage Kris in his banter, eventually introducing himself.

"I'm Robert Kardashian," he said.

"Okay, my name is Kris."

When Robert pressed for her last name, Kris coyly asked why he wanted to know. He was smitten by the beautiful, feisty brunette, who reminded him of movie star Natalie Wood. Her eyelashes curled upward, resembling a long-legged spider, which was a popular look in those days. Robert reckoned the girl could not have been more than eighteen, yet she handled herself like a seasoned woman. She was a saucy, sexy dame who was reminiscent of a bygone era. This was no teenybopper. As Robert sized Kris up, she was making her own assessments—wealthy, successful, but too old for her.

Tired of the back and forth, Kris gave up her last name, and even spelled it for him, then she readied to make her exit from the apparent pickup artist. She motioned to Debbie, who was silently watching Kris in action. Sensing his time was running out, Robert stepped up his game.

"Where do you live?" he inquired.

"San Diego," she answered.

Anticipating his next question, she said "no," that she would not consider going out with him. His only play left was to give her a compliment.

"Nice necklace," he remarked.

With that, Kris politely thanked him and turned on her toes and walked away. As she and Debbie headed back to the Turf Club, Robert called out to her and asked for her phone number. Without stopping, Kris said "no."

Robert couldn't believe that this pretty young thing had rejected him. He was intrigued and attracted to her moxie. He trolled around Kris for the rest of the afternoon, watching and smiling. He made sure she knew he only had eyes for her. As the day wore on, he was concerned she might get away, so he brought his brother Tommy into the mix and introduced him to Kris, but to no avail.

Robert stayed until Kris and her friends left. Despite all of his charm, Robert was unable to coax a phone number out of the girl, a first for the swarthy stud.

The Love Plot Thickens

Joni Migdal and Robert Kardashian had been best friends since junior high school. She had been privy to all of his secrets and his many girlfriends, and had giggled with him as he shared stories about his pranks and other escapades. Sometimes, she even participated as a coconspirator in his fun-loving antics. Joni was Robert's first call after he got home from the racetrack.

"I just saw the most beautiful girl that I've ever met," he told her.

His friend listened as Robert gushed over Kris Houghton's physical attributes and personality. She didn't give much credence to Robert's prattling on about the latest object of his desire. Her boyhood chum was an unmarried man in his thirties who deserved his reputation as a playboy.

"Yes, well, add her to the list," Joni said in an all-knowing tone.

Robert explained his frustration with striking out with Kris. Joni didn't hesitate when he asked for her help in nailing Kris's phone information.

"How do you want to do this?" Joni asked.

Robert had done some sleuthing while at the racetrack and got the skinny on Kris's love life. "Her boyfriend is a golf pro, and I think that she may be living with him," he said. "He's going to be playing at Riviera. I'm pretty sure she will be with him."

It just so happened that Robert and Tommy were members of the Riviera Country Club in Los Angeles. In fact, Robert already knew Cesar, having played golf with him.

Joni's assignment was clear. She was to join Robert at the golf tournament, cozy up to Kris, and get her phone number.

Rumor Has It It's Complicated

A crisp ocean breeze was in the air in mid-February 1974, as Joni and Robert trolled the Los Angeles Open at the Riviera Country Club in the Pacific Palisades. They had no trouble spotting Kris on the fairway. She was positioned on her black folding chair. Robert stood back and observed, studying her posture, her expressions, what she was really like with people. He smiled privately at Kris's animated gestures as she chatted with her girlfriend, unaware of his impending descent into her secret world. He was impressed with her girlfriend-of-a-golfer outfit: a tight-fitting cashmere sweater that covered her curvy figure. She even had on a pair of brand-new golf shoes.

The legendary Arnold Palmer was playing that day. Palmer had golf groupies who followed him everywhere—"Arnie's Army," as they were called. Kris had been shopping for weeks for this tournament because she knew there would be all kinds of reporters covering Palmer's game.

Glen Campbell, the multiple Grammy-winning singer and television star, was hosting the event, and his presence alone assured a good media turnout. Kris wanted to be ready for her close-up. She wore a new pair of "movie star" sunglasses and carried an elegant wood-handled purse. She and Debbie had turned their room at the nearby Holiday Inn into a walk-in closet for the event.

As she folded up her seat to walk to the next tee, Robert and Joni were in motion to catch up with her. Robert tapped her on the shoulder.

"Remember me?"

At first, Kris assumed Robert and Joni were an item and felt comfortable chatting with them. Cesar wouldn't have an issue with Robert with a woman at his side. Kris was open, and Joni seized the opportunity to retrieve the pertinent details Robert requested. When she shared information about activities around her home in Mission Hills, Joni heard her cue.

"If you come down to LA, why don't you give me a call?" Joni said.

With that, they exchanged phone numbers. Cesar approached, curious about these people vying for Kris's attention. He didn't recognize them, though Robert looked vaguely familiar. He thought he knew all of Kris's friends. She didn't care to have many. She was content with adopting Cesar's friends as her own. Before Kris turned around to introduce them, Robert and Joni shared a conspiratorial wink. Then Robert brazenly made a flirtatious overture to Kris, which Cesar couldn't help but see.

"Cute glasses," the attorney said.

The compliment instantly pleased her. Kris didn't know what a prankster Robert was, so she was stunned with his follow-up.

"They're filthy," Robert smiled, hoping to momentarily flummox her. "You better clean them." Kris cleaned them on the spot, and everyone had a good laugh. All the laughter bred an intimacy between Kris and Robert. He was growing on her.

Robert started calling her twice a week on her private phone line at Cesar's condo. The pair embarked on an emotional affair over the telephone until Kris gave in to his persistent pursuit and went out on a date.

In addition to an extensive collection of stories about his close friend O. J. Simpson, Robert frequently peppered his conversations with Kris to include all the other big-name celebrities that hung out with him.

Thanks to Robert, Kris never ran out of celebrity gossip when speaking with her friends and family. She loved being in the know about all things Hollywood. It made her the special one in the group. Just having the inside information made Kris a celebrity of sorts. Whenever Leslie would share a cup of tea at Mary Lee Houghton's dining room table, she would hear the latest rundown on Kris's complicated love life. Bob's mother was thrilled to have Kris confiding in her.

"I heard all about the celebrities Kris talked about to Mary Lee," Leslie recalled. "She was proud of her granddaughter."

CHAPTER THREE
ROBERT KARDASHIAN

Getting to Know Him

Kris was not surprised to discover Robert Kardashian was born into privilege—comfort and wealth steeped in old-world Eastern European traditions. He was schooled in the sacrifices made by his Armenian ancestors. He knew the difficulties they endured to ensure his birth in a free land. But his life of luxury had its limitations. Confidence and a marginal sense of entitlement were instilled in young Robert. Humility and gratitude were also emphasized. These values saved him from being swallowed up by self-absorption and narcissism. He abided by the creed of familial loyalty, but he inherited a strong sense of protectiveness, which at times could be smothering and border on possessiveness. What was his was his.

Strong family bonds were equally important in Kris's upbringing. All of her major life events demonstrated the importance of being there for one another in good times and bad. Like Robert, her family believed in upholding family traditions. However, there was a major difference between Robert's and Kris's families. Robert's parents were still in love with each other after almost forty years of marriage.

Kris occasionally sensed the societal shame attached to coming from a broken home. While she adored her stepfather, she still missed out on the perfect "Ozzie and Harriet" family upbringing that Robert had experienced. She dwelled on those few years when there was no dad in her home. She realized this hole was mended by her mother and grandmother, both of whom bounced back from failed marriages and rebounded as independent women. They inspiringly found true love while they were still young. Kris's strong matriarchs taught her that it was the women who held the small family together.

When talk turned to religion, which was very important to Robert, Kris could only tell him she was raised Presbyterian. The religious denomination served mostly as a form of identification. Her church life, prayer, and biblical teachings were limited. Mary Jo only took them to services on national religious holidays, like Easter Sunday, and for other special occasions, such as weddings and funerals.

The Armenian Connection

"Tell me more about your people," Kris said, wanting Robert to explain his Armenian heritage.

On the other end of the phone line, Robert began telling his life story. Kris pulled a cashmere throw over her long legs and tucked it underneath her hips as she lay on the living room couch in Cesar's condo. She brought a crystal wine goblet up to her lips and sipped. She glanced at a Tiffany's-framed photo of her and Cesar wrapped in each other's arms. It was taken on the greens of a golf course at a tournament. She didn't want to think about that day, or anything else that would distract her from Robert. But guilt began to creep into her thoughts. She rationalized that her phone conversations with Robert weren't cheating. However, they were becoming more frequent. She turned her eyes to the ceiling, took another sip of wine, then closed them again to listen to Robert.

He told her a fascinating story about an ancient world, one completely foreign to her and mired in centuries of traditions, rituals, culture, and spiritual responsibility. There was much more to this family dynasty than eating Armenian food and celebrating Armenian holidays.

The Republic of Armenia is located west of Turkey. This mountainous region is positioned between the Caspian Sea and the Black Sea. To the north is Georgia, Azerbaijan to the east, and Iran to the south. Armenia is touted as the birthplace of the oldest Christian nation on earth. Following the death of Jesus Christ, the early apostles brought Christianity to the people of Armenia. Scores of Armenians' ancestors hailed from ancient Israel. As such, they were knowledgeable about the coming of the Messiah. The majority of Armenians embraced the faith-based Christian doctrine. Legend has it that Armenia is the final resting place of Noah's Ark.

Ordinarily, Kris was bored by geography and history lessons, but she found Robert's narration fascinating.

In the nineteenth century, Armenia was conquered by the Russian Empire. There was a faction of Protestant Armenians in the mid-nineteenth century who rebelled against the Eastern Orthodox faith. They became known as the Molokans, which loosely translates to "milk lovers." They were infamous for refusing to abide by the sacred laws of fasting on holy days and were treated as heretic lepers by their countrymen. The villagers harassed this religious sect by digging up the corpses of their friends and relatives and hanging their remains on trees. They petitioned Russian Czar Nicholas II for protection from the religious persecution. The czar granted clemency to the Molokans, providing them with relocation to a safe haven.

Nestled squarely against the foothills of Mount Ararat, the rocky province of Karakala became the new home of the Molokans. Having settled in Karakala, two villagers—Saghatel "Sam" Kardaschoff and his wife, Hrepsema, "Horom"—continued growing their family. In 1896, they gave birth to a son named Tatos. He was Robert Kardashian's grandfather.

Tatos and his five brothers and sisters grew up hearing the fascinating story of Efim Klubiniken. In 1850, the eleven-year-old mystic had shaken up the village with his fatalistic prophecies. Known throughout the province as the "Boy Prophet," Efim was a devout Pentecostal. He was an old soul, vigilant in his devotion to praying and fasting for lengthy periods in his tiny stone cottage. His primary education was limited to spiritual teachings. Though he could not read or write, he had psychic visions enabling him to understand elaborate handwriting and messaging on charts.

During a stringent seven-day binge of images, Efim sat at the family's modest wooden table and reproduced distinctive symbols and characters on shreds of paper. Following this spiritual sabbatical, a weary Efim delivered his modest manuscript to villagers who could read. To their astonishment, this illiterate boy had managed to flesh out Russian letters. They spelled out a horrific forewarning of a holocaust, where the majority of their people, practically their entire village, would be mercilessly wiped off the face of the planet.

This impending doomsday prediction even had skeptics rattled. They all wondered "when?" But Efim's previsions did not stipulate a definitive time and date. The catastrophic warning was not entirely fatalistic. Young Efim provided a specific set of directives on how to prepare in advance to avoid the massacre. Despite never viewing anything resembling a geography book, the Boy Prophet pinpointed where his fleeing elders should take their families. The warning was specific: *Those who believe in this will go on a journey to a far land, while the unbelievers will remain in place. Our people will go on a long journey over the great and deep waters. People from all countries will go there. There will be great war. All kings will shed blood like great rivers. Two steamships will leave to cross the impassable ocean.*

There was no room for speculation as to what large body of water Efim was describing to them. It was the Atlantic Ocean, and the "far land" was the eastern cities of the United States. The citizens of Karakala who found this prophetic advisory incomprehensible could also scarcely fathom the second half of Efim's navigational guide. The boy told them that once they landed in the land of the free, they were to keep moving across the country until they reached the west coast, where they would put down roots. He sealed the prophecy with a bright promise from God. Blessings and prosperity would be showered upon them and their heirs for this supreme sacrifice.

As the days, months, and years passed without any sign of trouble, the luster of Efim's futuristic news flash faded from the community's consciousness. His warning became a distant, legendary yarn of almost trivial importance.

Four decades later, Efim's prophecy was met with cynicism by many Molokans, who dismissed it as merely the tall tales of a young boy. But at age fifty-five, Efim still stood by his original warnings. However, there was renewed urgency to his words as he declared, "We must flee to America. All who remain here will perish."

Efim and his family were among the first townsfolk to depart. Over the next ten years, thousands of Armenians braved the voyage to the other side of the world, where they forged new lives. Before leaving their country, many dissolved their property assets and left behind possessions which had been passed down from generations of ancestors.

In April 1915, as World War I raged across Europe, the government of the Ottoman Empire turned against its Armenian people. A million and a half Armenians, mostly Christians, were murdered by Muslim Turks between 1915 and 1917. Armenian men, women, and children were abducted from their homes, tortured, and sent single file to die at the hands of their tormentors. Tens of thousands of bodies were heaped on top of each other in mass graves. The slaughter of Armenia's citizens continued until 1923. Robbing them of their worldly wealth, members of Turkey's ultranationalist party, the Young Turks, raped Armenian women, sold young girls into slavery, and either deported or executed the survivors.

Almost all of the nonbelievers who didn't budge were annihilated in what came to be known as the "Great Calamity." The savage, hate-mongering Turks murdered millions of Armenians. Adolph Hitler is said to have carefully studied the Armenian genocide. He then copied the blueprint of unspeakable crimes against humanity with even more precision during his persecution and extermination of Jews during World War II.

As a third-generation American, Robert never had to witness the heinous bloodshed, or endure the hardships his grandfather's father and mother had encountered three decades earlier. But he was raised as if the experiences were his own.

The Kardashians of Los Angeles didn't face the fear of financial insecurity many other Americans grappled with. Robert's grandfather was a self-made entrepreneur. He was a classic example of how an immigrant in the early 1920s, having fled earlier persecution from governmental powers in his native land, could find solace and opportunities upon arriving in America. He laid his claim to the American dream: work hard and accumulate wealth.

"I'm glad they made it out of there, or we wouldn't have you," Kris purred.

Cash for Trash

In 1913, Tatos's parents were among the last of the Armenians to leave Karakala.

A few weeks later, seventeen-year-old Tatos followed his family on the SS *Koln*, sailing from Bremen, Germany, to Boston, Massachusetts, in the first leg of his long relocation. As steerage passengers, the Kardaschoffs were squeezed together like human cargo in the bottom rungs of the ships.

As he sailed toward this unfamiliar land, Tatos kept company with another Karakala refugee, an alluring girl named Hamas Shakarian. Like Tatos, her parents had lived in Erzurum. They fell in love on the ship and made plans to marry.

To seem more American, Tatos Kardaschoff changed his name to Tom Kardashian.

Tom bought a patch of land and took up farming. He also opened a trash collection service, which quickly grew into a lucrative enterprise.

In 1917, Tom and Hamas gave birth to a son they named Arthur. He was the first American-born member of the Kardashian dynasty.

Saint Helen

Arthur's future wife was born that same year, on July 15, 1917, in Oakland, California, to Armenian refugees Vartanoosh Miroyan and Arakel Mgrditchian.

In stark contrast to her three dark-haired sisters and younger brother, Helen had light blonde hair. Her bright blue eyes were set wide apart and she had a slight gap between her two upper front teeth. Helen's closest friend growing up was her maternal cousin Charlotte Minasian.

Helen married Arthur in February 1938. Photos from their wedding day reveal an opulent celebration. The bride wore an ornate long-train wedding gown. A veil of lace trailed all the way down past her waist. With her wavy chin-length hairstyle and finely tweezed eyebrows, Helen resembled the silent movie star Clara Bow. Arthur had his own movie star look, displaying a noble posture in his perfectly tailored tuxedo. Slightly taller than Helen, Arthur had coal-black eyes, thick dark hair with a distinctive widow's peak in the center of his long forehead, and full lips. His olive skin was more in the ethnic realm of Armenian, but he could easily have passed for a suave Italian.

Arthur and his younger brother Bob were partners in a meatpacking plant in Vernon, an industrial city a few miles southeast of downtown Los Angeles.

With his rubbish collection company running smoothly, Tom Kardashian sought out other investments to diversify his financial portfolio. The fast growth of two animal stockyards in Vernon signaled a golden opportunity to Tom. It made sense that having a slaughterhouse nearby for processing the livestock would be of great convenience to the stockyards' owners. The timing was perfect. The California meat industry—especially the Los Angeles factories—were being awarded lucrative World War II government contracts for sending meat overseas to feed the troops.

Arthur's keen business instincts were apparent. His Great Western Meat Packing Company became a major financial success. It wasn't long before meat processing became a hive of industry in Vernon and served as the city's most prized source of economic activity.

Growing Up Kardashian

In 1939, just a few days before the Kardashians' first wedding anniversary, Helen gave birth to a baby girl, Barbara Helene. Their son, Thomas Arthur, was born a year later. A third child, Robert George Kardashian, named after Arthur's brother Bob, was born on February 22, 1944.

While they were not flashy show-offs, Helen and Arthur did not pretend to live modestly or apologize for their abundant wealth. To look at him, one would never know Arthur Kardashian's business was chopping off the heads and limbs of cows and pigs. He was always immaculately groomed, dressed like an elite corporate executive. Everything about his looks portrayed the image of first-class luxury. His accessories included ornate cufflinks, an expensive gold watch, and a gold pinky ring on his left hand.

Helen wore timeless, classic pieces, and her hair was always beautifully coiffed. She enjoyed entertaining guests in their two-story home in the Windsor Hills suburbs of LA. Her furnishings and other décor were elegant but comfortable. Robert and his brother Tommy shared a bedroom upstairs, with their initials—"R" and "T"—inscribed in the green leather headboards of their beds. The children were dressed in clothes befitting a high-end boarding school. As a boy, Robert's go-to wardrobe included preppy pull-over sweaters and crisp cotton shirts.

"Robert, Tommy, and Barbara were known as our 'rich cousins,'" recalled Ralph Saroyan, a member of the extended family. "Robert and I played many a game on their pool table, and there was even a slot machine, which Robert had the key [to]."

Business interests in Bakersfield, which was a two-hour drive from LA, often resulted in Arthur spending several days a month away from home. He could rest assured that Helen could flawlessly hold down the home front.

Saroyan explained, "Helen was the disciplinarian. She was in charge. We weren't afraid of her. She was always a lot of fun to be around. We were entertained, but at the same time you did exactly as she said. When she walked into a room, you knew it. She had such a presence and charisma. She and Arthur both loved to laugh and have fun with their kids. They were very attentive, treating all of us as little adults, never talking down to us just because we were children, as so many parents tend to do. It was just the proper balance of relaxation and disciplines. They felt secure in their mom and dad's love, which is why I believe Robert had such strong self-confidence as an adult."

Helen and Arthur were fluent in Armenian and English, but they typically spoke English around the house, likely to spare their children the rampant discrimination against Armenians in California during the 1950s.

The Kardashians, like their ancestors, were Christians. They dutifully attended worship services at the Armenian Apostolic Holy Cross Church in LA. Though she had children ranging in ages from five to nine years old, Helen still managed to donate hours of her time to serve as an officer on the church's Junior Ladies Aid board. While they had regular active roles in their church, Helen and Arthur were not religious zealots who insisted their children adhere to strict old-world traditional rites.

"Helen and Arthur believed in Christianity by behavior, as opposed to practicing religion for the sake of religion," Saroyan said. "It was pure spirituality in the truest sense in the Kardashian household."

Philanthropy and being a part of their community was important to Arthur and Helen. They were involved in a number of high-profile charities in the 1950s and '60s and had their names printed in the society section of *The Los Angeles Times*, alongside big-time fundraisers like John Wayne, Red Skelton, Ann Blyth, and Fred MacMurray. Their favorite charity event was the annual Christmas Tree Ball gala, which raised money for the Daniel Freeman Hospital Auxiliary. The Kardashians chaired bridge game playoffs at the Parkview Women's Club. Their enthusiastic support of luncheons and fashion shows raised proceeds to benefit area children's hospitals and other philanthropic projects.

Arthur was also a faithful member of his local Masonic Lodge. While they were millionaires, they never took for granted the sacrifices their parents made in coming to America so they could have a brighter future. When Robert's grandfather retired, Arthur took over the family.

The Kardashians nurtured relationships with their large extended family of Armenian relatives by attending weddings, parties, and other get-togethers, such as family reunions. However, Helen and Arthur were not clannish.

At the end of summer Helen would take the kids to visit Saroyan's mother on their cozy fifty-acre vineyard farm in Sanger, just outside Fresno, California. She would arrive with bags of gifts for his family. According to Saroyan, as Helen opened the door, she would call out to her cousin Charlotte, "Hello, I'm here!"

"No matter where you were in the house, you knew Helen had arrived," he said. "She had a distinctive, high-pitched voice that you recognized instantly. When she walked in the room, she made a grand entrance, without even trying. She was a powerful force of energy."

From "Kardashian steaks," as they called them—which were prime cuts of meat Arthur had sent along—to clothes and perfume for Charlotte, Helen had something for everyone. Arthur also loved showering his beautiful wife with the latest fashions and jewelry.

"Helen was generous to a fault," Saroyan said. "She and Arthur could be considered millionaires by today's standards, but they were conservative in their spending. Helen was a good money manager."

Helen was not shy about coming into her sister's home or any other relative's house and assuming the role of an organizer and chef. Whether there were ten people or fifty in a home, Helen was prepared to take over the kitchen and cook a hearty meal.

"My mom was used to Helen making herself right at home," Saroyan said.

But some relatives gossiped about Helen's well-meaning takeovers. As Saroyan remembered: "When we had other family in from out of town, they were sometimes taken aback by Helen. They nicknamed her 'The General.'"

As she listened to Robert talk about his family legacy, Kris decided she wanted to meet the endlessly fascinating Kardashians. In fact, she couldn't wait to meet them—especially Helen.

Kardashian's Rising Star

Having grown up in the Baldwin Hills neighborhood in Los Angeles, Robert graduated from Dorsey High, a predominantly black public school in the 1960s. He had a standing offer to join his father's meatpacking business after college, but Robert and his brother and sister were allowed to choose their own careers, even if they diverged from the company the two generations of Kardashian men had built. Since their parents were happy to look after them financially while they pursued academic degrees, none of them had to work their way through college. Barbara became a dentist and Tom joined his father's company in a managerial capacity.

Robert decided on a career in law, living with his parents while he got his undergraduate degree at the University of Southern California (USC) in LA. Tom was also studying at USC. The brothers chased women, played football, and were both senior managers of the school's famous football team, the USC Trojans.

In 1966, Robert graduated with a bachelor's degree in business administration. He got his law degree from the University of San Diego four years later.

Upon graduating, Robert accepted a job at the small Armenian law firm, Eamer Bedrosian. The more civil and criminal cases he handled, the more he discovered that his real passion was entertainment law.

Inheriting his mother's socializing skills, Robert was a natural networker. Under the heading of "potential clients," he racked up numerous bills on the firm's expense accounts as he wined and dined influential leaders of the community and wealthy socialites. They enjoyed Robert's tales and infectious sense of humor as he held court in elegant Beverly Hills and Bel Air restaurants.

Robert blossomed from a preppy, fresh-looking kid into a stylish professional. His lush black hair was set back from the widow's peak in the center of his forehead—a trait he inherited from Arthur. A quirk of nature resulted in a shock of white hair brushed squarely into the widow's peak, which afforded the Beverly Hills attorney a more distinguished look.

The affluent third-generation Armenian American blended in perfectly among the old-money, high-society Beverly Hills citizenry, the *nouveau riche* Hollywood crowd, and the sports celebrities. Robert looked, dressed, and sounded like all of them. And his bosses profited from his pursuit of the Los Angeles elite. Within three years, Robert was made a partner in the firm, which was renamed Eamer, Bedrosian & Kardashian.

Young, good-looking, and successful, Robert and Tommy threw parties at the house they shared in Beverly Hills and drove Rolls-Royces. Yet, even though they were always out at the luxury hotel bars and had been fixtures at expensive restaurants, they weren't attracting the famous, top-tier crowd they wanted. They needed star power, not only as clients at the law firm, but because the Kardashian brothers were hungry for music connections. They were passionate about working in the music industry on an executive level, and it was crucial they break into the "biz" while they were in their prime.

Everything changed in 1970, when Robert met football legend O. J. Simpson during a game of tennis on a client's court in Benedict Canyon. Robert's celebrity appeal quickly climbed the charts. The NFL MVP was also welcomed at any A-list event. Should Robert Kardashian's name not be on a guest list, he could always count on being Simpson's "plus one."

Blood Brothers: Robert and O. J.

As he continued his campaign to seduce Kris, Robert routinely filled her head with stories about his fabulous life. He described the fancy restaurants and the stars he claimed to see nightly, inserting Simpson into the conversation whenever possible, along with the models and starlets that orbited around his famous friend.

When Robert wasn't dining out with friends, he was at some star-studded party, where all the "beautiful people" were in attendance. He dished on all of the good stuff Kris was missing. Robert's goal was to get Kris off the telephone and into his car for a date.

But Robert didn't have to stretch his tales about the depth of his friendship with Simpson. By the mid-1970s, he and Simpson were like brothers.

They were inseparable. They had long lunches at private clubs, played golf and tennis together, and chased women all over Beverly Hills. Rounding out the playboy roster were Robert's brother Tommy and Simpson's friend, A. C. Cowlings.

The four guys were living the high life; however, the Kardashian brothers were mindful of their daily work responsibilities. Tommy's role at the meat-packing business was growing, and as a new and younger partner in his law firm, Robert was expected to bill a certain number of hours for clients. Depositions and trials put a wrinkle in Robert's afternoon playtime.

Simpson was determined to live the good life. By 1979, the thirty-two-year-old running back—affectionately nicknamed "The Juice"—wanted to finish his eleventh NFL season and retire early. Because of his achievement on the football field, the elite athlete was one of the biggest celebrities in the world. He never felt pressured to search for new revenue sources. Business offers came to him.

The Juice Men

Robert had entrepreneurship in his DNA. He was a third-generation idea man.

Though Robert basked in Simpson's celebrity spotlight, he didn't let it blind him from seeing the greater potential He advised Simpson to make a business plan for his future. It had never occurred to Simpson that his gravy train might one day run out. Confident he possessed the business acumen that Simpson was lacking, Robert convinced his friend they would make a winning combination as partners.

Since both men had connections at USC, Robert reasoned that the university campus was the most logical place for their first start-up, Juice Inc. Evoking the image of a trendy cocktail that combined Jägermeister and orange juice, the friends opened Jag O. J., a clothing store that offered high-end jeans and casual apparel. The shop was a hit with the college kids. After the success of their first business venture, they opened Joy, a frozen yogurt shop in Westwood Village, which was heavily populated by University of Southern California students and young professionals.

Robert and Simpson made exceptional profits when they sold both companies a couple of years later. Knowing when to walk away from a company was one of the first rules of business that Robert taught his protégé Simpson. As his business interests grew, Simpson began renting office space from Robert. The attorney even provided his friend with a legal secretary.

Meanwhile, Robert began breaking into the music business. While publishing the weekly music magazine *Radio & Records*, Robert formed a partnership with Robert Wilson, a veteran music scribe who had a wealth of industry contacts. Like his grandfather before him, who started his meatpacking business to capitalize on the demands of the area slaughterhouses, Robert recognized that the music industry needed reports that provided metrics for record company executives to evaluate how their artist's music was faring at radio stations across the nation. *Radio & Records* gained enough credibility to rival *Billboard* magazine, the industry's go-to source for many years.

Kris and Robert: First Date Fiasco

When Kris finally agreed to go out with Robert, she was still living with Cesar, to whom she had become engaged.

"At nineteen, I was too young to be engaged to anyone," Kris reflected years later.

Robert flew to San Diego to pick Kris up for their first real date. He met her at Cesar's condo, they went to the movies, and then they wound up back at the condo. Since Debbie was at work and Cesar was out of town, Kris assumed they would be undisturbed.

Having been phone lovers for over a year, Kris and Robert wasted no time going up to the bedroom Kris shared with Cesar. Their hot and heavy session was thwarted when they heard the front door close. It was Cesar, who had made a surprise visit to the townhouse. He called for Kris as he started up the steps.

The only thing they had going for them in that moment, where speed and quick thinking was everything, was that they still had most of their clothes on. However, they had no escape hatch on the second floor. Robert didn't know his way around the townhouse and couldn't jump from the second-story window. The busted pair decided to blow past Cesar on their way down the stairs and bolt out the front door.

Their plan failed.

Kris recalled Cesar becoming enraged, which prompted her to make a formal introduction.

"Oh, this is my friend Bob," she said, as if one lover meeting another would save the day. Cesar ignored Kris. He just kept screaming at Robert, demanding to know what he was doing in his house. Robert was speechless and frozen. Dressed in Gucci from head to loafers, Cesar went into full attack mode and grabbed Robert. He pulled Robert's sweater off, which gave the attorney a chance to slip away. He and Kris ran out the door to safety.

Kris had grabbed her car keys from a glass dish by the door. Once outside, the two were shaking. While Kris struggled to open the lock of her Mazda, Robert tore down the street. Kris hopped in the car and picked Robert up. She remembers screaming out the passenger window: "Get in the car! Get in the car!"

Kris floored it as soon as Robert got in. In her rearview mirror, she saw Cesar chasing them on foot. After they had driven a few blocks and left Cesar in their dust, Robert's fear turned to anger. He was pissed. As much as he adored Kris, the event was unacceptable. He was a lawyer, not an athlete; a lover, not a fighter.

Kris reiterated that she was all but finished with Cesar, but Robert wasn't interested in her excuses or explanations. That night, he just wanted to remain as far away from her as possible. Robert left her with a parting ultimatum.

"When you get things straightened out with this guy, or decide what you want to do, we'll talk," he said.

For the first time in her adulthood, Kris wasn't in control of the situation. Unsure of how to fix things, she decided to simply bide her time.

Gone for Good

Robert went back to Los Angeles, and Kris went back to Cesar. Soon, all was forgiven. Cesar was crazy about Kris. He gave her a "pass" for being young and immature. Although he was confident that she had learned her lesson, Cesar did keep an invisible leash around Kris's neck. He started staying home a lot more. Kris was no longer a free agent allowed to gallivant around. Word had gotten back to Cesar that Kris had been hanging out with golfers at the country clubs when he was out of town. When asked about these reports, Kris would say she was only being friendly, and the stories were exaggerated. She pointed out that they shared the same friends, and many were men.

Weeks went by with no call from Robert. Cesar kept Kris glued to his side for the next few months. In her private moments, she often thought about Robert. Each time the phone rang, she got butterflies in her stomach hoping it would be him. Kris didn't dare call him. Not out of respect for Cesar, but for her own self-respect. Mary Jo had raised Kris to let the man do the chasing, or rather, to let the man think so. Women didn't call men. Period.

But with nothing going her way, Kris needed a new plan.

Then on Easter Sunday, 1975, Kris answered the phone. It was her grandfather True on the other line.

"I have some really bad news," he told her. "Your dad's been in a terrible accident, and he didn't make it."

Kris listened in suspended disbelief as her grandfather described her father's death. It was a grisly tale. Robert Houghton was killed in Mexico, when the Porsche he was driving on a deserted road crashed as he attempted to avoid a collision with an eighteen-wheeler. Nuns from a nearby convent pulled him out of his car, dragged him into their vehicle, and drove him to the hospital. He died from massive internal injuries. A passenger in the sports car, her dad's fiancée Vicky Thomsen, survived. The couple was to be married the following day. Robert Houghton was only forty-two.

After calling her mother, Kris called Leslie, her dad's ex-girlfriend.

"I picked up the phone and heard Kris crying uncontrollably," Leslie remembered.

"It's Dad," Kris finally managed to say. "He's dead."

Kris reported what she had learned from her grandfather. She could barely talk through the tears.

"I hope he didn't suffer long," Leslie said, grateful that Vicky "made it out alive."

"Leslie, Dad called me a couple of nights before he left and wanted to get together. I just blew him off . . . and now he's dead. How could I be so selfish?"

Leslie comforted Kris as best she could. They suspected alcohol was involved in his fatal car crash, which proved to be accurate. Robert's alcoholism had also destroyed his relationship with Leslie nine months earlier. Leslie vividly remembered the last drunken tirade she witnessed, which was the catalyst for their breakup.

"He was horribly drunk at a Father's Day barbecue at his parents' house. He was just awful to his parents! Just awful. His parents were the nicest people. I thought, 'I can't do this anymore.'"

Leslie broke up with him the following day. Robert had promised to change his ways, but Leslie had heard this line from him too many times before.

"Those were the days that you didn't realize you couldn't cure the person," Leslie later said. "I just thought, 'Oh, all it will take is a lot of love.' Well, it needed a lot more than that, and he did not have the willingness to give up the alcohol."

As Leslie listened to Kris crying, she remembered how good and kind Robert was when he wasn't drinking. "Such a tragic ending for a talented and brilliant man," Leslie later assessed.

"We're trying to get his body back here," Kris informed Leslie.

There were issues retrieving the body from Mexico. Cesar took Kris across the border to claim the body. Kris's grieving was interrupted by further disbelief when she spotted her father's Rolex watch on the wrist of a Mexican police officer.

"That's my dad's watch!" Kris blurted out. "They stole his Rolex! They stole the watch off a dead man's body!"

Cesar did some fast talking in Spanish to smooth over the potential incident that Kris's outburst could have caused. On the way back to San Diego, Cesar noticed Kris was exceptionally quiet.

"Are you okay?" Cesar asked.

"You should have gotten the Rolex back," Kris responded, looking straight ahead, not at Cesar sitting next to her. "My dad would have wanted me to have it. I'm the oldest child. It belongs to me. Why couldn't I have just one thing from him that is all mine? It would be a part of him. It was on his wrist when he took his last breath. That's as close as I would ever get to him again."

Kris looked at Cesar with tear-filled eyes.

"Plus, if I ever got in a jam and needed money I could pawn or sell it. My dad would have wanted me to have some kind of financial security that came from him."

"I can't believe you just said that," Cesar exclaimed. "Are you kidding me?! What was I supposed to do? Beat the officer over the head with my golf club? Really, you tell me what I could have done different."

Kris's rolled her tongue across her front teeth. With her lips shut tight, she turned away from him again.

"I don't know, Cesar," she answered in a sharp, but non-threatening tone. "But I think you generally give up too quickly on things. There's always a way to get what you want. You just have to try. You didn't try."

To get Robert's body back into the US, Robert's brother-in-law, Gaston Lopez, had to sneak the corpse over the border. Once in California, Robert was given a proper burial.

This was the first time Kris had experienced the death of somebody close to her. Her father was gone and there was nothing she could do about it. She would never see him again. She felt the same stinging in the pit of her stomach that she had experienced when her dad first left the family. She hadn't felt it in years, but she instantly recognized the cramping in her gut. Robert's death cheated Kris out of a renewed relationship with her father. That made her mad. Her tears were for missed opportunities to know him better, and to love him more.

Super-Glued to Cesar

In the days after the funeral, Cesar did all he could to comfort Kris, but she didn't want his attention. She wanted Robert Kardashian. When the Los Angeles lawyer heard about her dad, he called Kris and the two picked up their phone affair. Still engaged to Cesar, Kris couldn't commit to spending time with Robert.

"We would make a plan, but every time I would cancel at the last minute before the morning of the planned rendezvous," she revealed. "I came up with the stupidest excuses. I had a toothache or whatever. But how many toothaches can one person have? When I ran out of teeth, I told him I had sprained my ankle or I had the flu. It became ridiculous."

Kris was torn between two lovers. Robert lived 120 miles away in Los Angeles. That was too far, she reasoned. She was only nineteen and the situation was beyond her life experiences. She knew the move was hers to make. She also knew she wanted to leave Cesar but didn't know how to make that happen.

In July 1975, Kris accompanied Cesar to the British Open, where her fiancé was playing alongside golfer Tom Watson. But Kris couldn't stop thinking about Robert. The attorney had phoned her right before she left for Europe. During that conversation, Robert had invited Kris to his housewarming party in Beverly Hills. He insisted on an immediate answer. That was the defining moment, when Kris made the decision to end things with

Cesar while they were overseas. Kris confirmed that she would be Robert's date at his party.

Robert and Tommy were sharing a house together on Deep Canyon Drive in Beverly Hills. Judy Wieder, a popular high-end interior designer during the 1970s, designed the décor in the house. It was the perfect playboy bachelor pad. The requisite tennis court and swimming pool saw plenty of action. Each Kardashian brother had a white Rolls-Royce parked in the garage. Simpson also stayed there on occasion.

The day of Robert's party came and went, and Kris was a no-show. Her departure from Cesar—when she would come back to California alone after telling him they were over—didn't go off as she had choreographed. Kris chickened out. Holding two dozen red roses, Robert had stood at the gate at Los Angeles International Airport. After watching the last person walk off the plane, he threw the roses in the trash and drove home. Once again, Robert was insulted.

"I had made him look like a fool," Kris admitted. "He didn't have a girl-friend, he didn't have a date. This was his big, huge party, and I had blown him off."

She found the courage to pick up the phone and issued another round of apologies to him, but they fell on deaf ears.

After returning from Europe, Kris was filled with fear, angst, and inse-curity about her future. She claimed Cesar wanted to marry her while they were in England. Golfer Tom Watson and his wife Linda reportedly offered to host a cozy wedding ceremony in the backyard of the home they were leasing near the golf course. Feeling backed into a corner, Kris staved off the marriage talk, explaining she couldn't imagine getting married without her mom and the rest of her family in attendance. Cesar accepted her rejection and said nothing more about it. He may well have been testing Kris, to see if she was as serious as he was about getting married. But Kris wasn't the only one with doubts about their future together.

"I never knew them to be engaged," Cesar's friend Jack Spradlin confessed. "I didn't know if he ever asked her to marry him. I would have known. We were that close."

Officially engaged or not, Kris ached for Robert and his freewheeling LA lifestyle. She was very attracted to him, but she also considered him a ticket out of San Diego and into a posh world where she knew she truly belonged. But Kris couldn't bring herself to end it with Cesar. And now she was back in her same rut, in his modest condominium, while Robert Kardashian was living the high life.

After all of their phone conversations, Robert had still been clueless that Kris was engaged to Cesar. It was only after their disastrous first date—when her jealous fiancé almost destroyed Robert—that Kris came clean. Robert chose to let Kris off the hook for failing to mention the true nature of her relationship with Cesar, but her dishonesty was troubling. In essence, Kris had put his life in danger, whether she meant to or not. Granted, she was young, but all the chaos and drama surrounding her life was disconcerting. He had told his buddies all about her and hinted she might be "the" girl for him. They were happy for Robert, but after a couple of these incidents where Kris stood him up, they encouraged him to give up any notion of a future with her.

"Don't be a chump," his pals took turns reminding him.

Tommy was hounding Robert to go out with Priscilla Presley, the ex-wife of the king of rock and roll, Elvis Presley. At the time, Tommy was dating Joan Esposito, a former Miss Missouri, who was divorced from Elvis's road manager and close friend, Joe Esposito. Joanie was a Las Vegas showgirl before marrying Esposito. Joanie and Priscilla bonded as they accompanied their guys on the road during music tours. Joanie was Priscilla's matron of honor, and Joe was Elvis's best man when Priscilla and Elvis wed at the Aladdin Hotel in Las Vegas. The women remained close after they divorced their husbands.

Robert always found himself talking to Priscilla whenever she joined Tommy and Joanie at parties and dinners. He had to admit, the thought of dating Priscilla was tempting. Priscilla was sweet and warm. She even resembled Kris. And unlike Kris, Priscilla was available. She was also famous, which offered many social perks.

The more Tommy talked about Priscilla, the more Robert thought he should take her out. Because the more his mind focused on Kris Houghton, the less he wanted to be with her. She was starting to look like trouble for nothing.

Cesar Tosses Kris

Kris was homesick for her mom while she was in Europe. Her dad's death had hit her hard. His passing was a reminder of the importance of family. She invited Mary Jo and her stepdad Harry to attend Cesar's tournament in Pebble Beach, California. She planned a side trip to tour Hearst Castle, publishing tycoon William Randolph Hearst's sprawling estate on the coast of Central California. Kris was thrilled when Cesar decided to stay behind.

Kris didn't want alone time with Cesar, and her parents created a natural buffer between them. Kris sensed that Cesar was easing up on her, but she was not interested in patching up their relationship. She stopped paying attention to what he did—or didn't do—when they were together.

Although Kris found the relationship tedious, she still didn't have a backup plan. And she wasn't budging from the condo until she had a plan in place. She had no money or way of making a living. She had a glimmer of hope that she would lay her hands on some cash when her dad's estate settled. Technically, Kris was an heiress, but it was yet to be revealed precisely what she was inheriting. Her dad didn't have a will or a trust, but Leslie Johnson knew everything about his financial situation, and she was an honest woman. If there was any cash or valuables that Bob left behind, it all belonged to his two daughters, and Leslie would make sure they received their due.

But Kris learned Bob's only real extravagances were his Rolex watch and his Porsche, the latter his guilty pleasure. And both luxury items were gone.

The only other asset in Bob's estate was a small cottage in San Diego County that he co-owned with Leslie.

"Robert had put a little more into the house than me," Leslie said. "I figured since I was leaving him, I would leave something for him. I knew that when he sold it, I could count on him to pay me."

Leslie wound up with nothing, as the proceeds of the sale of the house went to pay legal fees. There was no question Kris was in a tough spot. Her mother and Harry would have welcomed her anytime, but Kris refused to move back in. She enjoyed her independence and had faith that an opportunity was going to appear.

By this point, Kris was so removed from any kind of emotional or physical intimacy with Cesar that she failed to notice the ambivalent attitude he started showing her. Before she could even worry about what made Cesar change, the answer turned up. When Kris came home from her trip to the coast, she found out that Cesar had slept with a young woman.

It suddenly made sense that Cesar didn't mind staying behind.

That was all Kris needed to know. Fueled by righteous indignation, she packed up her belongings and threw them in her Mazda. But she wasn't going to peel out of the driveway and let Cesar off the hook. She went back inside and waited for her fiancé to come home.

When the golfer returned, he denied any wrongdoing. Kris remained calm, cool, and in control. After she heard what she believed were lies, Kris announced she was leaving him.

"It's over," she said as she walked out the door. Surrounded by everything she owned, Kris let out a sigh of relief as she pulled her little red Miata out of Cesar's driveway.

"She really did a number on my brother," Cesar's brother Rudy said, claiming that Kris was "a gold-digging snake."

Shortly after Kris's departure, Cesar accused his scorned lover of stealing more than his heart.

"Cesar told me that when Kris took off, she stole his collection of gold coins out of his house," Rudy attested. "They were Mexican 50-pesos gold pieces. They were worth $10,000. He never got a penny back."

Spradlin confirmed that Cesar was "devastated" when Kris left, and agreed that Kris was the probable culprit in the coin theft.

"That was the lowest possible blow that could have happened to him because he did adore her," Cesar's friend said.

With nowhere else to turn, Kris went to her mother's house. As Harry helped unpack his stepdaughter's car, Kris updated Robert about her newly single status. The nineteen-year-old hedged all of her bets that she was still the object of Robert Kardashian's adoration.

Robert responded just as Kris had fantasized. He invited her to spend the weekend with him in Los Angeles. He even agreed to buy her a plane ticket for that evening.

Wasting no time, Kris showered and prepped for her getaway. Pulling from her cosmetic bag, Kris carefully chose a soft blush tone for her cheeks and a shiny pastel pink lip gloss to match. She applied her makeup with artistic precision. Several rounds of Maybelline mascara went on her eyelashes before she curled them upward. She sorted through her suitcases for the perfect wardrobe, including sexy negligees, and placed them neatly in an overnight bag. After trying on several outfits, she was dressed and out the door, on her way to the airport, where she boarded the next flight to Los Angeles.

CHAPTER FOUR
FLIGHT RISK

Beckoned by Angeles

Having spent so much time wooing her, Robert was invested in Kris. But he was also a practical man with the mind of a lawyer. He allowed his emotions to overpower the evidence stacked against her. He knew their weekend together would either be the beginning or the end of them.

When Kris arrived at San Diego International Airport, her ticket to Los Angeles was at the counter just as Robert promised. The short flight to Los Angeles gave Kris just enough time to mourn the end of her two-year relationship with Cesar. Her tears were offset by her excitement to see Robert.

Kris took off her sunglasses and looked out her window. She smiled as she gazed into the clouds. Kris wondered what surprises Robert would come up with. She knew he was romantic, and she was desperate for the VIP treatment they often spoke about.

Outside the LAX terminal, Kris saw Robert leaning up against a green Mercedes. Meeting her halfway, Robert pulled Kris close and gave her a passionate kiss, then bent down and grabbed her luggage.

As he pulled the top down on his convertible, Robert introduced Kris to the passenger in his car.

"This is O. J., my best friend," he said.

The magnitude of the occasion overwhelmed Kris. She had barely set her high heels into LA and was already riding in a Mercedes with one of the biggest sports stars in the world.

Kristen Mary Houghton had arrived.

Slice of Heaven

Robert's house was every bit as spectacular as Kris had imagined. As an added bonus, Simpson was crashing at the residence while in another separation from his wife, Marguerite.

After finishing the tour of his bachelor pad, Robert told Kris to freshen up because he was taking her to meet his mother. Kris felt that was a positive sign.

"I rushed into the guest room, closed the door, and called my mother," Kris recalled.

Helen Kardashian's house was full of relatives waiting to meet the woman her son had talked so much about. And Kris was not the least bit daunted by their intense interest. Because of her many phone conversations with Robert, Kris felt like she already knew his family. Helen was exactly as Kris had pictured her: a class act.

Kris followed the matriarch to the kitchen to watch her work. Kris wanted to know about the ingredients, and how to prepare the traditional Armenian fare. The two women charmed each other all evening, which further endeared Kris to Robert.

The rest of Kris's first weekend with Robert was filled with posh meals at Beverly Hills restaurants, where the maître d's welcomed Robert with a friendly embrace before taking the couple to Robert's reserved tables.

Robert was attentive to Kris. She felt like the only woman in the world. They drank martinis and champagne while dining on lobster and caviar and decadent desserts. Kris was in her element, gaily talking to Robert's friends who stopped by his table on the way to their tables or out the door. Kris acted as if she and Robert had been a couple for years.

In between lunches, dinners, and Sunday brunch, Robert and Kris made love. It was the ultimate romantic weekend, and neither wanted Monday to arrive. Kris didn't want to leave, but she also wanted Robert to think she had a life to get back to.

For the next three Fridays, Kris boarded a plane in San Diego and flew to LA to spend the weekend with Robert and his family. And every week, his parade of pals continued. Kris was committed to remembering each person's name and something of mutual interest. She wanted them to feel an instant connection whenever she saw any of them again. Those on their second and third rounds of spending time with Kris found her fascinating. She had a talent for making people feel special. Kris basked in all of the attention, particularly from Simpson. She felt incredibly comfortable around the superstar.

Robert was increasingly mesmerized by Kris. He watched Kris "do her thing" in public, and when they were alone, he saw her vulnerable side. For Robert, it was true love. And the thirty-one-year-old decided to prove it to Kris.

Life in the Fast Lane

After only a few weekends of bliss, Robert was ready to propose to Kris. His friend Joni Migdal was the first to hear his plan.

According to Joni, "He was very serious about her from the beginning. He told me she was the most beautiful girl in the world. He wanted to marry her, and instinctively knew she would make a great mother. He knew she was hungry and eager to do whatever it took to live the way Robert lived. She might have a fashion misstep here and there, but Kris had all the markings of presenting a sophisticated sartorial image for the two. She had the talents and creativity and smarts to flesh out what was missing in his near perfect life."

As Robert told another pal, "Kris has class. I can buy the rest of what she needs."

Robert popped the question on their third weekend. He was stunned by her response. "I don't think I can marry you right now," Kris told him. "I mean, it's kind of too soon."

Once again, Kris had disappointed Robert, but this time it was a bullet to his heart. He believed Kris was the perfect girl for him. He had told his friends and family that she was the one. His mother and father had given their blessings. Everyone knew that he had never come close to proposing to any of the scores of women he had dated over the years. He had plenty of girls who would have jumped at the chance to marry him, but Robert was raised with a deep appreciation and respect for family. Divorce was not an option in his household. He wanted a relationship like his parents had; he wanted a partner in every sense of the word. And Kris's refusal wasn't merely a brush-off to a guy asking her out on a prom date. She was rebuffing the holy union of two souls.

Robert hadn't seen her rejection coming. She was receptive to all of his advances and romantic overtures. They fit together perfectly in bed. He wondered if it was all an act. His embarrassment quickly turned to anger.

But Kris had gone from Cesar to Robert so fast that she had not given herself time to process her situation, which included the death of her father. Lou Ethel and Mary Jo had advised her to maintain her independence, to carve out some kind of career that would give her financial stability. The loss of her father twice—first in life and then in death—showed her that crushing changes could happen at any time. Kris wanted to be ready to deal with them.

Robert had been her backup plan for Cesar, and Kris realized she needed a new one in case her love affair with Robert fell through.

Kris Wants Her Wings

Kris and Robert continued seeing each other, but Robert was not the same enthusiastic suitor.

He could barely contain the sulking between their visits. Kris understood that he was disappointed, and she did her best to avoid discussing it with him unless he brought it up. Because Robert had been interested in her for such a long time, Kris wasn't actually worried about losing him. She wanted to get married, but she knew she had to take care of herself before she could look after someone else. She also believed Robert was the guy for her. He was handsome, successful, and attentive, and he was on board with her dream of being a mother to six kids. Kris hoped he could wait a little longer to settle down. After all, she had plenty of time for marriage and motherhood.

She had been toying with the idea of becoming a flight attendant. Kris was confident her personality was well suited for engaging with passengers. There were so many successful men who would be on the flights, and she would be the object of their attention. She liked the idea of being in control of the passengers in her cabin. She also wanted to see more of the world before settling down. She fantasized about how glamorous it would be to wake up in a big city like New York and to land in Miami by nightfall. She wanted to dine at an expensive oceanfront restaurant with a handsome and successful man sitting next to her. After seeing Robert's place, Kris believed there had to be even better homes in other cities.

While with Cesar, Kris had made a contact with American Airlines, a PGA sponsor. She had kept the airline executive's business card and decided it was time to call in a favor.

Kris easily landed an interview and was accepted into American Airlines' six-week training program in Fort Worth, Texas. As she predicted, Robert Kardashian was not thrilled about Kris jetting off to become a flight attendant. He knew men who had left their wives for the sexy airline hostess they met in transit, and bachelors who played around with stewardesses. Robert cautioned Kris that taking a stewardess to bed was one of the ultimate status symbols for a man. But Kris was undaunted. Her mind was made up. She reminded Robert how young she was, and how she had never really been out on her own. She wanted to feel free, and she didn't see this as them breaking up. Kris promised they would see each other all the time after her six weeks of flight training. She reassured him that he was her future, that she was still his girl.

The King of Rebounds

Kris had no fear of flying. Ironically, it was the turbulence on the ground that nauseated her. During a call to Robert from her dormitory at flight attendant school, Kris learned that Robert had taken Priscilla Presley out on a date.

"Payback is a bitch," Kris quipped years later.

Robert was lonely after Kris left. And he enjoyed being with Priscilla. She had a good sense of humor and was pleasant to be around. They had fun and Priscilla took his mind off Kris. Kris had a healthy self-image and plenty of confidence in her beauty—that is, until she began comparing her attributes to Priscilla. After all, this woman had attracted the king of rock and roll when he was at his most virile and headed toward superstardom. He could have had any woman in the world. Yet he chose Priscilla—and so had Robert.

Kris knew she had to stay in the moment, or she would make herself crazy. Her reality was that she was in Texas, a thousand miles away from Los Angeles. She wasn't about to go running home to California to chase Robert Kardashian back into her arms. She decided to trust that if she and Robert were meant to be, then it would all work out someday.

Flight School Fancy

By the mid-1970s, the word "stewardess" had gotten a facelift. They were now called flight attendants. However, conjuring up a "good time" with images of attractive airline employees was still the underlying theme for advertisers.

The ladies of the jet age had to be pretty and smart. The women had to have a bright smile that lit up the cabin. An attendant should be able to talk about a wide range of subjects to provide interesting and entertaining chit-chat with passengers. Although Kris embodied all of these traits, her flight studies and homework left her exhausted. She attended classes all day, even on the weekends, and nights were needed for studying.

"They introduce you to every single piece of equipment, and you have to know how it functions," revealed Kris's dormitory roommate, Shauna Mayer. "There's a lot of medical stuff. You have to know CPR, what to do if a pregnant woman goes into labor while the plane's in the air. There are certifications you have to pass in order to graduate. A lot of girls quit before it's over."

Despite the rigorous training, Kris found it all stimulating, and she was proud of herself. Keeping busy also kept her mind off Robert.

The girls in Kris's dorm managed to find a small window of time to socialize before lights out, as they removed their makeup and prepared for bed. Kris was popular with her flight school roommates.

"Kris was charming and very likable, so we just became very fast friends, and it was fun," Shauna said. "I loved the fact that she was from California. She loved the fact that I was from Texas."

Their conversations usually revolved around clothes, shoes, and of course men.

"I didn't get the impression Kris was overly crazy about Robert Kardashian at that time," Shauna stated. "She shared that he was a young, driven attorney, and that appealed to her."

Kris had intentionally kept the extent of her feelings for Robert, as well as her wounded pride, a secret from her classmates. She wanted to avoid any humiliation should Robert and Priscilla appear on the cover of a supermarket tabloid. She also kept quiet about her late-night payphone calls to Robert.

Though she quietly seethed, Kris never told Robert she was jealous. Robert even asked Kris's advice on what to buy Priscilla for her birthday. Kris remained cool and collected and chose her words calmly and carefully. She acted as though it was perfectly normal for Robert to be talking about another woman when only a few weeks before he had asked Kris to marry him.

Resisting the temptation to unburden herself with her girlfriends, and not wearing her heart on her sleeve with Robert, could be dismissed as superficially ego-driven, but her behavior in this instance revealed something greater. She had a willingness to only show the world what she wanted it to see, while still seeming completely transparent. Even as a young woman, Kris had the ability to keep her personal life separate from her business affairs. She also exhibited tremendous patience, and an unbridled belief in herself that she would ultimately get what she wanted.

Nothin' but a Hound Dog

Robert was a sensitive and perceptive man who knew how to push Kris's buttons. He had convinced Kris that he and Priscilla had become an A-list couple. And judging from the poses he struck during a professional photo shoot of him and Priscilla, Robert appeared to have fallen for his own PR spin.

"He ain't no Elvis," said a family friend.

Furthermore, Robert bragged to his friend, Lance Robbins, about spending nights at Priscilla's where Elvis would call her. Priscilla would place the receiver on the pillow next to her so Robert could listen in on the King's lengthy calls.

Robert was spending so much time at Priscilla's sprawling Beverly Hills home that he came to believe they were living together.

Priscilla's biographer Suzanne Finstad deemed him a "convenient boyfriend." However, Robert's friend Joni didn't characterize the relationship as being one-sided.

"Priscilla wanted to please Robert," she said. "She made all kinds of food for him. But Robert is a very picky eater. He didn't like her asparagus. He didn't like her meat dishes, or anything else she cooked."

Despite her failure to win him over as a domestic goddess, Joni said Robert's feelings for Priscilla intensified and he wanted to marry her.

"Priscilla was honest with him," Joni recalled. "She told him she would not marry anyone as long as Elvis was alive. That kind of soured the relationship for him."

For Robert, the second woman in a row had rejected his marriage proposal.

Rendezvous in New York

Two weeks shy of Kris's graduation in the summer of 1976, Robert called to tell her he had split with Priscilla. He confessed that he was still in love with Kris. Despite her romantic urges, Kris stayed the course, completed her training, and passed all of her exams.

Mary Jo made the trip to Fort Worth to see her daughter graduate.

"She gave Kris some earrings," Shauna recalled. "They were teeny, tiny stones, but Kris didn't seem to notice. She was over the moon about them, and her mother being there to celebrate her accomplishment."

Kris submitted her preferred home base city choices to the airline, which included three California locations: Los Angeles, San Diego, and San Francisco. Kris was crushed when American Airlines assigned her to New York City. She was homesick for her mother and eager to resume her relationship with Robert. But Robert consoled Kris, calling the arrangement "good news." The attorney was joining Simpson at the 1976 Summer Olympic Games in Montreal, then planned on flying to New York, where Simpson had a sports commentator gig awaiting him at the ABC television network studios.

The news excited Kris, who became eager to pick up her love affair with Robert in New York City.

There were many firsts for Kris when she reunited with Robert in the summer of 1976. She rode in a limousine, stayed at the Plaza Hotel, dined at the 21 Club, and danced at Studio 54—all things that she had only read about in fashion magazines or seen in movies. Kris and Robert also made love again and again.

"I could feel everything around me changing so fast," Kris later confessed. "I knew my life would never be the same again."

It was also Kris's first time seeing Simpson mobbed by fans. As they shopped along Fifth Avenue in Manhattan, people stuck photos and paper in his face to get his autograph.

At the end of the magical week, Robert and Simpson went back to Los Angeles. Kris stayed behind to become an independent career woman.

"Talk about a cold-water moment," Kris reflected years later. "I went from living the high life in the Plaza to sharing an apartment way up on Ninety-Ninth Street and First Avenue with four flight attendants."

In her cramped two-bedroom apartment, two women shared each room, and each slept in a twin bed. The view from her bedroom window was a brick wall and an alley.

But Kris couldn't wait to earn her keep and pay her own way. She was happy to be on her journey and living on her own terms.

Career Gal Kris

Kris was the consummate professional in her cabin on the plane. She loved the interaction with the passengers, with the exception of the drunken salesman types. She quickly adopted a system to thwart the leering gropers.

"I was an airline attendant, not a hooker," she later clarified. "So, I kept my hot, very steamy pot of coffee with me at all times. It's amazing how a guy's attitude would change when I had a hot pot of coffee over his crotch."

But after a few months in the air, Kris grew disenchanted with her flight schedule. She longed to go back and forth from New York to LA. She missed her family, and she craved Robert. The rookie seemed locked into the Midwest routes, which she found tedious. She had somehow missed the memo that only senior attendants got the coastal routes.

That Christmas, Kris was alone in her dreary walk-up apartment. So she made her way to St. Patrick's Cathedral on Fifth Avenue. She lit a candle and prayed for a transfer to Los Angeles. "If somebody tells you no, you're talking to the wrong person," she reminded herself.

At the end of that gnarly holiday season, Kris was granted her west coast transfer.

Back to the Beach

Mary Jo and Harry flew to New York and helped Kris pack up her apartment. The family checked all of her baggage onto the plane, including Kris's television.

Robert was on the receiving end of the move. At Los Angeles International Airport, he loaded Kris's stuff into his new black Rolls-Royce, and they headed for his house in Beverly Hills.

The next morning, Kris didn't even wait to hear Robert's thoughts on whether she should move in with him. His house was full of occupants. Tommy was still living there, and Simpson was renting one of the bedrooms as an office. Kris called Shauna and other local flight attendant girlfriends and they went hunting for a place to share. Making only $500 a month, the women were on a tight budget.

The ladies found a beautiful penthouse apartment in Brentwood, an affluent Los Angeles neighborhood. The location was ideal for Kris, perfectly situated between Robert's house in Beverly Hills and Los Angeles International Airport.

"The leasing agent was eager to tell us that actor Larry Manetti would live next door to us, if we leased the place," one of Kris's flight attendant friends recalled. "He was on the television series *Black Sheep Squadron* before he got the role on *Magnum P.I.* We just all thought it was so funny because Kris jumped up on behalf of the rest of us, when she heard there was a television a star living next door, and said, 'We'll take it!'"

According to Shauna, "It was a fabulous place for the price. It had three bathrooms, which was important for four women living together. Everybody had bits and pieces of furniture. It wasn't overly decorated. Three huge bedrooms. I shared with one of the girls, and Kris and the other girl had their own bedrooms. We did end up becoming friends with Larry."

The women didn't see much of Kris, as she was at Robert's most of the time. Kris would invite her American Airlines coworkers over for parties, where they schmoozed with an eclectic group of stars that were Robert's guests, including Simpson, A. C. Cowlings, Lionel Ritchie, and Sugar Ray Leonard.

"Kris was always cooking up schemes," a close friend revealed. "Kris was dying for a Rolex watch. So she borrowed a silver Rolex watch from another flight attendant and wore it around Robert a few times. Then she gave it back to the girl and cried to Robert that she had lost her precious Rolex, expecting him to replace it. She did several of these shenanigans, and usually got away with them without any repercussions."

Shauna remembered Kris more for her ambition to be a businesswoman, as opposed to a gold digger. "She appreciated beautiful things and wanted a luxury lifestyle," Shauna said. "But all she ever talked about with me was wanting to open up her own clothing store and call it Kris's Kloset."

Born Again, Again

Robert saw Kris when she was between flights. He took her to all of the finest restaurants—Luau, Trader Vic's, and the Polo Lounge at the Beverly Hills Hotel. He ordered the appropriate wines for each dish. He took her shopping on Rodeo Drive in Beverly Hills and bought her clothes, shoes, and handbags. He introduced her to high fashion boutiques like Fred Segal.

Robert was not an extravagant spender, but he purchased a few items that changed Kris's world. He knew she couldn't afford any of these things on her salary. He enjoyed spoiling Kris.

When Simpson moved back in with his pregnant wife, and Tommy bought a house, Kris and Robert finally had privacy at his rambling home on Deep Canyon. Living with Robert gave Kris a different perspective on him, and she was eager to learn about everything that hinted of sophistication and wealth. She looked in his closet and saw his beautiful suits and checked out the toiletries in his bathroom. She smelled his colognes and aftershaves. To Kris, the products in his vanity resembled items belonging to movie star Cary Grant, or at least the class act he conveyed on screen. Robert even had a silk smoking jacket. She surveyed his books, shelf by shelf, for the kinds of subjects that interested him.

There were usually so many people congregating in Robert's kitchen that Kris had never had a proper look at it before. With nobody in the house, Kris was free to turn over the china and see the manufacturers' stamps. She examined his cookware, dishes, glasses, and flatware. She was impressed that Robert had cloth napkins and placemats. His cabinets and pantries were organized, but Kris had ideas about how to improve even the most orderly arrangement. She even inventoried his refrigerator so she would know what kinds of foods he liked. She couldn't afford much, but she bought Robert specialty items from various cities she visited while working.

Kris's eye was drawn to a clay figurine hanging on a rawhide rope in the kitchen. There was writing on it: FOR GOD SO LOVED THE WORLD THAT HE GAVE HIS ONLY BEGOTTEN SON, THAT WHOSOEVER BELIEVES IN HIM SHALL NOT PERISH BUT HAVE EVERLASTING LIFE. JOHN 3:16.

A few mornings later when Kris and Robert were in the kitchen having coffee, she asked him where he got the ornament with the Bible verse. Robert's face lit up.

"It was a gift from my sister, Barbara," he said.

Robert told her that he attended a weekly Bible study at singer Pat Boone's house in Beverly Hills. He asked Kris if she'd like to join him. Besides Pat and his wife Shirley, the regular attendees included Doris Day, Glenn Ford, and Zsa Zsa Gabor. Robert had also introduced Priscilla to the gathering.

"Sure," Kris said with a smile. "Why not?"

At the next meeting, Shirley Boone met Robert and Kris at the door, and Shirley made sure Kris felt comfortable on her first night. She introduced the newcomer to the flock gathered around the family room.

"The minute I walked into Pat's big, beautiful sprawling house in Beverly Hills, I met the most welcoming, wonderful, magical group of people I'd ever known in my whole life," Kris recalled.

Boone was the study leader, but his style was more motivational speaker than fundamental preacher. Members of the study club read from the Bible and shared their personal stories and interpretations of faith and Christian principles. Kris left feeling good about the experience and started going with Robert every week. She learned that Robert was not exactly religious, but more spiritual. Kris, on the other hand, began to understand what it meant to live as a Christian. She accepted Christ and became "born again." Her relationship with Robert deepened as a result of their mutual love for God. Robert was certain that he wanted Kris as his wife. Their union had become sacred.

But the spiritual awakening had unintended consequences.

"We are full-on dating, with full-on sex, and all of a sudden, mid-relationship, he decided that we were not going to sleep together anymore because it was not God's will," Kris confessed, admitting, "I agreed, since that is what the Bible says."

Robert explained they would still date, but they would no longer live together "in sin." Kris packed her bags and Robert's friend A. C. drove her to a small apartment in Sherman Oaks.

Long Live the King

"The King is dead," a somber newscaster announced on television on August 16, 1977. The death of Elvis Presley shocked the nation—and filled Kris with anxiety as Robert checked in with Priscilla. He was concerned about his former flame and her daughter, nine-year-old Lisa Marie.

Kris held her breath as she watched to see what Robert would do. She knew Priscilla said she would never marry as long as Elvis was alive. Now she was freed from that promise. Robert and Priscilla reconnecting would not bode well for Kris.

Kris kept Robert hooked by planning events, always stressing how much fun they would be. She plotted out their Halloween, then her November 5 birthday, then Thanksgiving. He committed to spending Christmas Eve with her folks in San Diego. And for New Year's, Kris and Robert took their first ski trip together.

Upon returning, Kris had made up her mind about their relationship. She was over the apartment. She was through living alone. She gave Robert an ultimatum.

"I felt like I was on the slow boat to China with Robert Kardashian," Kris later opined.

Kris was ready to get married and start a family.

CHAPTER FIVE
MAD DASH

It's About Time

Robert proposed to Kris on the night before Easter Sunday in 1977. The twenty-two-year-old said "Yes!"

"We must go to San Diego and take my parents and Karen out to lunch to celebrate our engagement," Kris told Robert.

"Okay, when?" he asked.

"Today!" she squealed. "If we take a plane instead of driving, we'll be back in time to spend the afternoon with your folks."

Kris enjoyed exercises in time management. And as she sat at the kitchen table making phone calls, she began jotting down tasks associated with her wedding, breaking things down into categories and subcategories. Her pen seemed to have a mind of its own.

"Mom, we're coming down to have lunch with you," she announced. "Pick us up. We're leaving on the next flight out of LAX. Robert and I have something we want to share with you in person."

"I bet I know what this is about," Mary Jo said, revealing that Kris's urgency on Easter Sunday was a dead giveaway.

Unable to contain herself, Kris gave her mother the entire play-by-play of the proposal, which wasn't exactly traditional.

Kris's pre-engagement campaign included bringing fashion magazines like *European Vogue* to Robert's house and leaving them behind when she went back to her tiny apartment in Sherman Oaks. She would read them cover to cover as she sat in a chair next to Robert. She loved the gorgeous layouts and was attentive to every detail of the luxury advertisements. In the weeks leading up to his marriage proposal, she had been studying the most expensive diamond wedding rings. Kris would often call Robert's attention to her picks, and he would smile and nod and go back to his business.

But he heard every word when she ran across an image that excited her. On the night of his proposal, Robert knelt down on one knee. But instead of pulling out a lavish ring, he pulled out a piece of paper and unfolded it to reveal a full-page ad of the exquisite diamond ring in *European Vogue* that Kris had lusted after. Robert told Kris that he was not going to give her this jewel until their wedding day, but that he promised to love her forever. Then Robert asked Kris to marry him. Kris was overjoyed that they were finally getting married, which overshadowed the awkwardness of Robert's ring-less proposal.

Mr. and Mrs. Robert Kardashian

On July 8, 1978, over three hundred guests sat inside the sanctuary of the United Methodist Church on Wilshire Boulevard in Los Angeles, awaiting the entrance of the soon-to-be Mrs. Robert Kardashian.

Kris examined her long satin gown in a full-length mirror. It had embroidered tulle on the square-neck bodice and matching delicate lace on the long, sheer sleeves. Kris dropped her hands after a fretful examination of her chest. Her sister Karen laughed. Kris was always jealous of Karen's much larger bosom.

"Well, you got the itty-bitty waist," Karen told Kris. "Just look at it now in that killer dress."

Kris's bridal party represented every stage of her life. Karen was her maid of honor. Of the bridesmaids, Debbie Mungle had been with Kris at the racetrack the day she first met Robert nearly five years earlier, Cindy Spalloni worked with Kris at American Airlines, and Joyce Kraines—who was nine months pregnant—was married to one of Robert's best friends, Larry.

All the bridesmaids wore white dresses and wide-brimmed hats. They gathered at the altar across from Robert and his groomsmen, who wore white-on-white tuxedos and ties designed by Kris. Simpson was Robert's best man.

Kris and Robert's wedding bands sat on a satin-covered pillow, which had been stitched by Kris's grandmother. Robert had gotten Kris the diamond ring of her dreams.

Robert gasped at how beautiful his bride looked as she walked down the aisle carrying a bouquet of white flowers arranged by Nancy Reagan's florist. It was the fairytale wedding the couple had hoped for.

During the glitzy reception at Hotel Bel-Air, singer Dionne Warwick belted out her hit "I'm Your Puppet." There was an endless supply of Dom Perignon and a professional camera crew to capture the festive event.

Kris and Robert spent their wedding night in a suite at the hotel, then checked out the following day to head to Paris for their honeymoon.

Evenings in Paris

The new Mrs. Kardashian hadn't given her supervisors at American Airlines any notice about her nuptials. At that time, many stewardesses had to wed in secret to avoid automatic termination from the airlines. There were a number of brave women before Kris who challenged this policy, alleging unlawful discrimination based on sex. The commercial airlines industry fought the legal debate all the way to the Supreme Court. Finally, the carriers were forced to allow their employees the right to marry without retribution.

Robert's cousin Cici, who was watching his dogs while they were away, alerted the newlyweds that Kris's supervisors were frantically trying to reach her in California. Explaining why she was not reporting to work was not a high priority for Kris as she blissfully honeymooned with Robert. Ironically, the airline could have easily located her on a recent passenger list. The new Mrs. Robert Kardashian had flown to Paris on one of the airline's international aircrafts. Her wedding present to Robert was two round trip tickets, compliments of her mileage rewards as a flight attendant.

Serving coffee and lining trash cans was the last thing Kris was thinking about as Robert drove a rental car through France toward the pristine beaches of Deauville. Kris's dazzling diamond wedding band looked regal on her finger as Robert squeezed her hand.

"You are my dream come true," he told her. "I'll never forget seeing you at the racetrack on the day we met. I knew then that you were going to be my wife, my future, my love."

Kris was in the altered state that every woman experiences when she's all alone with the man of her dreams. Her heart was filled with such happiness that she had little space for anything other than basking in Robert's adoration and listening to his master plan for their lives.

Kris reluctantly turned her head from the window to ask Robert what she should do about her job. He pulled her soft manicured hand to his lips and kissed it gently.

"Tell them you're retiring," he said with a smile.

Kris and Robert spent hours on the beach kissing, laughing, and talking. Robert made it clear he would not spoil her, but that she would have everything she ever wanted.

"Of course, Robert could have bought me anything he wanted," Kris later said. "But he was a frugal guy. In those days, it was one thing to buy a Rolls-Royce. It was quite another to spend hundreds of thousands of dollars on a diamond."

Kris didn't know it then, but Robert's family fortune was facing financial ruin. The family was under attack from the federal government, and expensive legal battles were ongoing around the time Robert and Kris married. Robert undoubtedly kept the extent of his legal and financial problems away from Kris. She was his young bride and he didn't want to worry her.

After the American Airlines plane from Paris landed at Los Angeles International Airport, Kris Kardashian informed her supervisors that she was not coming back to work, and to keep her final wages.

A Kardashian Baby

When Robert carried Kris over the threshold of Deep Canyon as his wife, it became her home too. It was no longer a flophouse. Robert's roommates would not be returning. His brother Tommy was adjusting to his new life as stepdad to Joan Esposito's children, and O. J. Simpson was juggling his attention between his wife and children and his mistress, a young blonde girl named Nicole Brown.

Part of the blueprint for their lives that Robert shared with Kris in Europe included moving into a new home, one that was large enough to grow their family. She was content with bringing back all of her belongings and weaving them into Robert's world. She appreciated the little things, like a permanent housing for her cosmetics and toiletries, shoes, handbags, and clothes. She had become so tired of living out of overnight bags. Kris was a nesting creature and she was home with Robert at last.

A couple weeks after their honeymoon, Kris learned she was pregnant. Robert loved the idea that they conceived their first child on their honeymoon in Paris or on the beaches of Southern France. The respective in-laws were, of course, delighted to hear the news of the upcoming birth of another generation of Kardashians—but they also had their fears.

"The Armenian women watched and counted the weeks until I gave birth to make sure I wasn't pregnant before I got married," Kris revealed in her autobiography.

Kris and Robert's first baby was a girl. She was born in the early morning hours of April 18, 1979, nine months after her mom and dad married. Simpson was the first family friend Robert allowed into Kris's private room to meet their baby girl.

It was Kris's idea to name their firstborn Kourtney Mary, in honor of Kris's mom, Mary Jo. She was perfect in Kris and Robert's eyes. "I thought I was so much in love with Robert," Kris said, "but I didn't even know what love was until I had Kourtney."

And so Mr. and Mrs. Kardashian's love affair with children began.

Making the Family

As a new mom, Kris treated her first baby the same way many other first-time mothers do: with extreme caution. It took time for Kris to discover that babies are not as fragile as porcelain dolls. She also couldn't bear being away from her daughter. Separation anxiety invaded her soul whenever she trusted anyone to care for Kourtney, including her own mother! Mary Jo happily watched over her granddaughter so Robert and Kris could enjoy celebrating their first wedding anniversary in Hawaii, but Kris confessed to crying herself to sleep because she missed her child so much. Robert understood. He was a doting dad. They came home earlier than planned because Kris was so distraught over being away from their firstborn.

A few months before Kourtney turned a year old, Robert bought Kris her dream house in Beverly Hills. Robert was thriving in 1979. He was happily married and a new father. His *Radio & Records* publication sold for over $12 million. Robert's end of the deal put several million dollars in his pocket. This bought him the freedom to explore projects that satisfied his creative yearnings. He eventually relinquished his license to practice law.

The Kardashians' new two-story manor at 9920 Tower Lane was only four miles from Deep Canyon Drive, but it was a major move up the real estate chain, not only in size, but in social status. For starters, the 7,000-square-foot Cape Cod-style house was one of only three houses on a cul-de-sac. The three properties were protected by enormous wrought iron gates. The privacy factor was a major selling point for realtors eager to attract the upper echelon of the entertainment industry. The property had a swimming pool and cabana, poolside bar, Jacuzzi, and tennis court. In terms of square footage and fancy architectural interiors, it was actually modest with respect to the many more opulent area residences. Yet, for Robert and Kris, the home qualified as a mansion. It was a dream come true for Kris.

A Socialite Is Born

Kris was in her element designing every corner of Tower Lane. Both she and Robert loved Ralph Lauren décor. Fabric swatch books were piled high on her bedside table, and interior design magazines covered every inch of the coffee and end tables in the den. Kris wanted her first home as Mrs. Robert Kardashian to be elegant but comfortable—a plush playground for their friends and business acquaintances who would attend all their fabulous parties, yet a calming sanctuary for their children. It was Kris's quest.

"All the rooms were perfect," said Robert's childhood friend, Joni Migdal. "The dining room had quilted patterned walls. The kitchen was beautiful. Everything was done to perfection."

Kris welcomed Robert's input. After all, their home was a partnership and she saw her older husband as a mentor. "Their goals were similar in that Robert wanted the best for her," Joni said. "He wanted her to be the perfect wife, the perfect entertainer, the perfect mother. He taught her how to bring out the best in who she was then. She was beautiful. He was proud of her."

The Kardashians were not famous when they moved into Tower Lane, but their parties, especially the barbecues, became constant conversation among the citizens of Bel Air.

"Robert always had excellent taste in the way that he dressed, the friends that he had, and the way he thought," Joni added. "He always believed in the goodness of people, and that was infectious. People wanted to be around him."

Kris was already stunning, but now she had Robert's money. She shopped for cosmetics, shoes, and clothes with her girlfriends. Having lost all of her pregnancy weight, she needed a new wardrobe. She was fit and fierce.

With a full-time housekeeper, Kris was free to get manicures, pedicures, and massages and to join her friends and the other ladies who lunched at the most socially accepted restaurants, like La Scala and Spago. She played tennis at the Beverly Hills Country Club and volunteered for seats on committees for charitable organizations. She was meticulous in choosing the highest profile positions in the Beverly Hills community. Robert frequently worked in his home office, so he was available to oversee Kourtney's care while Kris was on the move.

Not everyone in Beverly Hills society accepted Kris. They found her social climbing vulgar. She was faithful to Robert, but she had a way with the men. She was an excellent flirt. Some of the women outside her immediate circle of friends were jealous. The sharp-tongued backstabbers had short memories. Almost all of them were made from the money of rich husbands, but few had the drive and determination to move beyond being a kept woman. Kris was different, and she had a *different* plan than many of the other society matrons. Kris didn't like spending her energy worrying what people thought about her. She was secure in herself before she ever married Robert Kardashian. She chose to remain oblivious to the gossip about her.

Kris was also a sponge for picking up good business tips from men. She enjoyed sharing the ideas with Robert if she thought they would be helpful to his businesses.

Beverly Hills 213 was an upscale glossy magazine that was delivered to homes and businesses in affluent cities in the area. It was filled with photos of all the A-list parties and personalities, and society columns. Almost all of the luxury retailers along Rodeo Drive advertised in the weekly periodical. Kris used the publication to garner press for herself.

"She was always calling up announcing what event she was going to be attending, or afterwards, calling to make sure we had seen the photos of her with the crème de le crème of society and other celebrities," one of the columnists remembered, labeling Kris "annoying."

But Joni defended Robert's wife, claiming that Kris was just having fun. "Kris went from a totally invisible life to being on a pedestal—and she loved that pedestal! She loved every moment of it and did whatever she wanted to do."

Robert's Armenian relatives accepted Kris into the family and embraced her strong and independent nature. She was perceived as adept at balancing the roles of wife, mother, and socialite. "Kris was exciting to be around," recalled Robert's cousin. "It was obvious her first priority was to be a good wife to Robert. We knew she was excited about the opportunities being married to him afforded her, but she made sure to honor traditional holidays and birthdays with thoughtful cards and gifts. She understood the importance of family, above all else."

Robert's mother, Helen, appreciated Kris's dynamic power. Like Helen, Kris was dominant, which could cause competition and jealousies between a mother-in-law and daughter-in-law if they chose to jockey for power. Helen had tremendous influence over Robert, but she never interfered in his relationship with Kris.

"Helen was fond of Kris," Joni admitted. "We all were. Most of us embraced Kris's brilliance. She was a cunning thinker and a hard worker. I will never forget Kris saying, 'Beverly Hills is my town. I'm going to own it one day.'"

Bosom Bunnies

In January 1980, at Kris and Robert's rented townhouse in Aspen, Colorado, the unmistakable voice of pop singer Michael Jackson blasted from the stereo speakers. Robert enjoyed the show Kris put on as she snapped her fingers, clapped, and performed her goofball imitation of the king of pop's dance moves. He found her rendition of the singer's famed moonwalk especially entertaining.

Their daughter Kourtney was nine months old. But they were not alone. Another couple joined them on the trip. Free of his NFL football contract that prohibited players from participating in other potentially dangerous sporting activities, O. J. wanted Robert to teach him how to ski. The superstar brought his girlfriend Nicole.

Kris motioned for the tall, blonde-haired beauty sitting on O. J. Simpson's lap to join her. Nicole turned her head to look at Simpson, who nodded his head in approval for Nicole to get up and perform with Kris Kardashian. The volume rose to a wall-shaking level as Nicole shared the "stage" with Kris.

Robert and O. J. watched their girls sing and laugh. They shook their hips in a sultry manner and pointed fingers at their respective mates, who were smiling from their front-row seats on the couches. The men admired their sexy women, still in their brightly colored, form-fitting ski wear. They were both statuesque beauties with great figures. Nicole resembled the typical Southern California beach girl. She was reserved until she got to know the people around her. But after a few shots of tequila, a party girl emerged.

On this trip, both women were full of life—happy and loud. Whether she was drinking or not, Kris was animated and always kept any gathering moving. She had a propensity for scheduling everyone's time when they were together.

Kris knew that O. J. had cheated on his wife, but Kris preferred to stay out of O. J.'s personal affairs. Several girls had come and gone, but his relationship with Nicole had gotten serious. When Kris and Robert moved out of Deep Canyon Drive, O. J. left his wife Marguerite and leased Robert's house. Nicole moved in with him. Marguerite had been awarded the Simpson family home on Rockingham Drive in Brentwood as part of her divorce settlement. A few months later, their two-year-old daughter drowned in the family swimming pool. The tragedy contributed to O. J. wanting to spend every minute with Nicole.

O. J. constantly talked about Nicole, and Kris found his descriptions of her were not exaggerated.

"Her beauty took my breath away," Kris recalled.

At eighteen years old, Nicole was every bit as stunning as any movie star. When O. J. met Nicole, she was working at a popular nightclub on Rodeo Drive called Daisy. It was a member-only hot spot for the elite showbiz crowd, especially sports celebrities. O. J. even had his own item named for him on the menu—scrambled eggs with sliced orange.

Kris learned a lot about Nicole on that Aspen trip. The friends drank hot toddies in the ski resort lounges while waiting for Robert to return with O. J. from their ski tutoring on the slopes. Kris found Nicole full of vitality, but without much of a plan for her life. Nicole described her short-lived modeling career and her brief stint as a saleswoman in a clothing boutique, where she abruptly quit after two weeks because she hadn't made any sales. She explained that she made great tips at the Daisy and felt it was a stimulating place to work.

Nicole was happy to be O. J.'s pride and joy. He showed her off to friends as proudly as he did his vintage Rolls Silver Cloud. She was his fantasy of a California girl. She dressed how he wanted. He chose the shade of her hair. She was his constant traveling companion during his final year playing professional football. They couldn't keep their hands off one another. As touching as these sights were, Kris also observed another side to O. J.'s relationship with Nicole.

"He was already incredibly possessive of Nicole," she observed. "Even when she would go to the bathroom, O. J. would wonder out loud when she was going to come back."

However, this didn't alarm anyone at the time. In the evenings, Nicole and O. J. went to nightclubs, leaving Kris and Robert alone to make love—and perhaps another baby. They were having such a blast as parents that they couldn't wait to have another child.

More Dashing Babies

Kris and Robert achieved their goal of conceiving a baby during their skiing holiday. The announcement that she had gotten pregnant in Aspen while on a ski trip with O. J. Simpson played into Kris's sense of glamour.

Kimberly Noel Kardashian was born on October 21, 1980. Kris said she named her after a girlfriend and stuck with the "K" for Kardashian. But some argue the "K" is actually for Kris. Either way, the alliteration had officially become a tradition. Years later, Kris claimed that there was no master plan involved in choosing "K" names. "I loved how Kourtney and Kimberly sounded together," she stated.

Kourtney was a pretty child, but the world was awestruck by baby Kimberly's exquisite features. Kris also found herself speechless as she gazed at her newborn daughter. "Absolutely breathtakingly beautiful," she remembered many years later.

Kris and Robert dressed Kim in Baby Dior and crowned their little princess with a pink satin bonnet as they placed her in the bassinet made by Robert's mother. Kris had Mary Jo's keen eye for children's fashion. Kimberly and Kourtney were always dressed like little dolls. Kris dressed the girls exquisitely in matching dresses with big bows in their hair. The junior fashionistas were on display wherever they went. Their nurseries and bedrooms were charming, decorated with details that would capture their individual personalities. Kris was always taking still photographs of the children, and Robert was filming them with his movie camera.

Birthdays, Halloween, Christmas, and Easter were major events, produced by Kris Kardashian. She had the talent and creativity of a seasoned party planner. She called them "Snow White–themed birthday extravaganzas," as she never ran out of Disney characters to wrap a party around. On the night before Easter, Kris stayed up all night painting eggs and decorating ornate baskets for the girls to wake up to. After church services, the Kardashians would drive to Indian Wells, California, to have a wild Easter egg hunt with Robert's parents and the rest of the Armenian clan.

Although Kris had help looking after her kids, she continued to enjoy her own special moments with her little ones. She bathed them in sweet-smelling bubbles. She combed their hair with ornate combs before putting them in their designer satin nightgowns. Robert would read a verse from the Bible to them each night, then Kris would read a children's book. Kris and Robert had created a real fairytale life for them.

Kris volunteered for everything associated with her daughters' early school life, whether it was a school play or coaching their soccer team. Teachers appreciated and publicly recognized Mrs. Kardashian for her devotion to her kids' school life. Kris gained notoriety as the most popular Brownie troop leader when she upgraded the traditional camping experience to a trip to SeaWorld in San Diego.

Kris charmed most of the other mothers, and all of Kourtney's and Kim's friends adored her. She took time to get to know each one of them. She never needed a special occasion to caravan a crew of kids to Disneyland. This was a tradition she fondly remembered Lou Ethel establishing when she and Karen were children. "I was always taking my kids to little kiddie places like Six Flags Magic Mountain or the zoo," Kris said. "We took countless trips to San Diego and the famous zoo there, and to see my mom. Everything about me was all about family."

Several years later, Kim got her first taste of media buzz as a result of one of these outings. In 1988, several photos of the eight-year-old landed her in the "Special California Issue" of *Barbie* magazine. In one image, Kim was wearing the iconic Mickey Mouse ears hat while kneeling beside the animated character's star on the Hollywood Walk of Fame. In another photo on the two-page spread, Kim is pretending to read a map to movie stars' homes. Kris beamed with pride as she showed the magazine to her gal pals. She knew her daughters had star quality.

On their fifth wedding anniversary, Kris and Robert conceived baby number three. Khloé was born on June 27, 1984. Although she was another lovely baby girl Kardashian, she looked different from the rest of her family, and she was definitely not the picture of the traditional Armenian. Instead of dark hair or brown eyes, she had fair skin, blonde hair, and green eyes, like her grandmother Helen.

The Kardashian house was filled with the gaiety of adorable little girls, dancing and singing. They were all outgoing and had a large catalogue of skits to perform for their parents and party guests. With three daughters, Kris was halfway to her goal of six children by the time she was thirty. But with each child's birth, Robert's relatives were expecting a male heir. Kris was determined to do whatever was humanly and scientifically possible to guarantee she bore him a son. She read books on the subject and talked to medical experts. She mixed special drinks and selected specific times of the day and positions for her and Robert to have intercourse.

On March 17, 1987, Kris returned to the delivery room. Family from both sides paced the waiting room while awaiting a birth report. And Kris didn't disappoint. She had a healthy baby boy. Robert named the child after himself, according to Armenian tradition, and gave his son the middle name Arthur in honor of his father.

A new baby meant more photos, more filming, and more pregnancy weight that Kris was determined to shed. And unless she had an outbreak of psoriasis—a rashy skin condition she developed between Kim and Khloé's births—Kris proudly wore bikinis, even playing tennis in them. But the mother of four wasn't completely satisfied with how the top half of her bathing suits were fitting.

Kris and Nicole Get Boobs

In the 1980s, Kris's career was her family. She was fulfilled in that role, and there was no financial need for her to seek employment. Robert, however, pursued many entrepreneurial paths. Some panned out, some didn't, but they never went into debt or suffered from any failed business ventures. Whenever he had a windfall, he invested his profits wisely. He remained a consultant for *Radio & Records* for five years after he sold it. He worked alongside his friend Irving Azoff at MCA and then at Universal, in the music department. Robert earned an entertainment executive's income. Kris had credit cards, including a charge card at the local grocer, but she didn't have a checking account of her own. It was never an issue. Robert was frugal, but not stingy. He took his responsibility as the family patriarch seriously. And he showered the mother of his children with jewelry befitting a Beverly Hills trophy wife, from a diamond bracelet to jewel-encrusted drop earrings and strands of pearls.

"Kris would act surprised when anyone would say she had Robert wrapped around her little finger," revealed an acquaintance from those days. "She wore the pants. He was so in love with her and their children. He adored all of them and wanted to be a family man above all." Kris had influence over Robert's friendships. Most of their friends were other couples, but if she saw a relationship in Robert's life that displeased her, either from a place of possessiveness or jealousy, she persuaded Robert to drop the person from the roster. Joni Migdal was such a casualty.

"When Robert married Kris, Kris wanted to be Robert's best friend," Joni explained. "She was jealous of me to a degree, I guess. So there were years when the kids were growing up that Robert and I didn't talk. I mean, we did, but we were not best friends when they were married."

Days before Christmas 1986, Shauna Mayer stopped by the Kardashian home. It had been nearly a decade since the former roommates had seen each other. A Rolls-Royce and a Mercedes lined the driveway, the Kardashian kids were running around the house, and Kris was effortlessly multitasking. She chatted with Shauna while arranging the flowers her old friend had brought over.

"Our lives were so different by then," reflected Shauna, who had become a Los Angeles Rams cheerleader since living with Kris. "She always wanted the wealthy lifestyle and lots of kids, and that's exactly what Kris had. I was happy for her."

Several of Kris's best girlfriends came from her weekly Bible study group. They lunched and celebrated birthdays, weddings, divorces, anniversaries, concerts, and dinners. They shared tips on where to get the best beauty care and were together at the front doors of Neiman Marcus and Saks Fifth Avenue on shoe sale days. In Beverly Hills, plastic surgery was a constant conversation. These thirty-something women were too young to consider face lifts, but dismay over what breastfeeding had done to their once perky bosoms was of general concern.

By age thirty-two, Kris had birthed four children. She needed a little mental boost, and a new hairstyle was not going to lift her anxiety about approaching middle age. She wanted something to be excited about and talk up with her gaggle of gal pals, but it had to be grand. All her friends were getting boob jobs and she wanted one too. Her B-cup size had annoyed her since she was a teenager. She convinced Robert that it was time for her to go under the knife.

The surgery was a success, medically, but Kris was disappointed with the results. Her expectations were more along the lines of a *Playboy* centerfold. She envisioned her breasts being more taut and perky. She whined to Nicole over her less-than-perfect results. Nicole—who had since married O. J. and given birth to two children—empathized with Kris and shared how she'd like to get breast surgery.

"You should do it!" Kris urged her friend. "After I see how yours look, I'll go in and have mine done all over again!"

Nicole had the operation performed by Dr. Harry Glassman, the premier plastic surgeon of Beverly Hills. His work was exceptional, and he had the added cachet of being married to Victoria Principal, star of the hit television series *Dallas*.

Kris inspected Nicole's new breasts and her "mouth fell open."

"I want two of those, please," Kris gushed.

Dr. Glassman performed Kris's second operation, and she was instantly gratified by her new look.

The Summer of Discontent

The bikini tops were thinner, and the sweaters a size smaller, as Kris and Nicole showed off the fresher versions of themselves during vacations with their husbands. They stayed at the ritziest resorts in Mexico during spring and summer vacations. Winters were spent skiing in Colorado, where they began a tradition of taking all of their children with them during their holiday breaks from school. They were an affluent foursome but enjoyed ordinary fun.

Nicole's former aimlessness had found solid ground in motherhood. By all accounts, she was the ideal mother to her children, Justin and Sydney. Like Kris, she showed a flair for entertaining, often throwing lavish parties at the Simpson house on Rockingham Drive. She sent her rich friends on scavenger hunts, where they scoured the terrain of Beverly Hills for simple objects. The winning prizes were more objets d'art, such as Lalique crystal. The swag at their tennis parties was new tennis racquets.

Kris continued to make a name for herself in the Beverly Hills community. When she was home, she worked in the garden and kept the house fresh with new décor. She baked and cooked for parties, even if they were catered events. She would often look out the window as she stirred cake batter in a bowl and see Robert hit a tennis ball on their court. During those times she would pause and bow her head to thank God for her wonderful life.

"Kris was considered the Donna Reed of our crowd," a friend of Kris's said. "Appropriate, churchgoing, always pregnant, and never did drugs."

Kris and Robert and their four children routinely had dinner together. Prayers of gratitude for their bounty of blessings were always led by Robert. From an early age, the kids found their parents to be interested in their young minds and emotions. Kris would check in with each child and make a mental note of their wants and needs. She treated them like mini adults, never talking down to them in a condescending tone. She and her sister Karen had enjoyed a similar relationship with their parents and grandparents. Robert created a family exercise called "the peak and the pit," where each family member took turns sharing the high and low points of their day.

But the day eventually came where Kris became Robert's "pit."

Party Like It's 1999

At the beginning of 1989, Kris and Robert had been happily married for ten years. Kris was becoming restless. According to those who know her best, her need for attention and admiration is as vital as the air she breathes.

"She is addicted to the release of the chemical oxytocin," revealed a close family friend. "When the praise and accolades soften to a whisper, she has to find new fans to applaud her. Kris likes money, and a lot of it, because it buys her acceptance. But you give her a choice between money and recognition or fame, she'll choose attention. She can always get more money, but she can't get enough adulation."

Young Robert was almost two, and Kim and Khloé were blossoming behind their big sister, Kourtney, who turned ten that year.

While on the surface nothing had changed, a volcano of discontent was bubbling inside of Kris. She would only let her June Cleaver hair all the way down during vacations with Nicole and O. J.

On these adult-only holidays, tequila shots and margaritas in the hotel hot tubs and dancing by the side of the pool and at the nightclubs were acceptable. Sometimes they would bring other friends from the circle, like a friend of Kris's named Faye Resnick. While Nicole had a certain leniency with O. J., Kris could never go all out with her drinking and lose complete control when Robert was nearby. He need only give her a stern nod to let her know she best not cross the invisible line.

Kris had never given Robert any reason to mistrust her, so he gave her freedom to spend time with her girlfriends. It took a while for him to notice that she was coming home later than usual following her frequent dinners with friends at the Hillcrest Country Club. Kris had started taking a detour on her way home from the club. She had a growing network of friends she met at parties and nightclubs. When Robert began hearing Kris walking up the stairs, singing to herself at three in the morning, he knew there was real trouble. He would close his eyes and turn on his side, away from where Kris would lie, before she walked in the room and crawled into bed. He could smell the liquor on her breath when she gave him a quick peck on the cheek. It became increasingly obvious that alcohol had become an important part of her life.

Robert reached out to Joni to talk about this unsettling situation with Kris. He needed a sympathetic and sensible ear, a woman's perspective. He poured his heart out to Joni during the frantic nighttime talks, where he expressed disbelief and shock at Kris's behavior.

"She started off by going out at night and saying, 'I have four kids. I never really had a life. I want to go out with my friends,'" Joni revealed. "She'd go out and drink, and come back late, late, late. He would be home with the kids. She was doing it consistently. She wanted to go out and enjoy herself and have fun. He didn't want her to drink that much. She would go out and stay until three o'clock in the morning. She'd say, 'I drank champagne. I partied with friends. I've had fun.' She wanted to go out and party and recapture the youth she never had because she was home having children."

Robert was concerned for the children and wanted to protect them from their marital problems at all costs. Sometimes his mind raced through crazy thoughts. With Kris's late nights, he couldn't help but wonder if she was cheating on him. That line of thinking brought him back to an old conversation he had with Joni after Khloé was born. He wondered if Khloé was his biological daughter. "He doubted," Joni admitted. "When she was born, Robert kept saying, 'Well, she has blonde hair just like my mom.' I said, 'Robert, why are you making excuses for her? So, if she isn't yours, what would you do? If you learned she wasn't your child, what would you do?' He said, 'I would still love her. I would never, ever give her up! I'm her father.' That's the kind of human being he was."

Reports have surfaced that Kris enjoyed a few flings around the time Khloé was conceived. There's been wide speculation that O. J. Simpson was one of her lovers, and the family has been plagued by years of rumors that O. J. is the biological father of Khloé, with no conclusive results to date. In 2019, O. J. flatly denied any sexual trysts with Kris. "Bob Kardashian was like a brother to me. He was a great guy. He met and married Kris and they really had a great time together when they were together. Unfortunately, that ended. But never—and I want to stress never—in any way, shape, or form had I ever had any interest in Kris, romantically, sexually, and I never got any indication that she had any interest in me. So all of these stories are just bogus. Bad, you know, tasteless."

Kris later admitted that sex with her older husband had become uninteresting. "I was selfish and restless and bored," she said. Kris spent months wondering why she was no longer attracted to Robert, and why she didn't find him as fabulous anymore as everyone else did. She never discussed these feelings with him.

"Kris does not like confrontation," a family member revealed. "She will do anything to avoid it."

Without revealing her inner most doubts as to whether she loved him anymore, Kris mustered up enough courage to ask Robert for a trial separation. Her request knocked the breath out of him.

"Armenians don't get separated," he responded. "It's either marriage or divorce."

When he sensed his bluff might only make things worse, Robert packed a bag and left for his parents' house. But he returned in two days—hardly enough time for Kris to sow her wild oats.

A Tryst for Kris

Kris Kardashian was always the life of every party. She had lost all of her pregnancy weight she gained with Robert Jr., and she was getting plenty of attention from guys.

Things continued to be frosty between Kris and Robert, without either of them discussing any solutions. When Robert went away on a ski vacation with a group of guys, Kris left her kids in the care of her live-in babysitter and joined her friends at a nightclub. One of her best friends was having an affair with a professional soccer player, so there were several guys from the team hanging around. Kris had her eye on the most handsome of the players. He was tall, with thick chocolate hair and intense cocoa eyes. He was also twenty-three years old. His name was Todd Waterman.

The attraction between them was palpable. Kris and Todd danced for hours at a small party at Kris's friend's home. After weeks of giving each other burning glances from across the room, they found themselves passionately kissing the rest of the night. Although Kris contends that she went home before consummating the relationship, Todd recalled their "first time was in her friend's closet."

Kris became obsessed with seeing Todd again.

She couldn't stop thinking about this hunk of burning love and she didn't have long to wage war with her conscience. When Todd called her a few days after their make-out session, Kris hurried over to his North Hollywood apartment.

"This is what I've been missing," Kris said, as she gave in to her insatiable lust and destroyed the sanctity of her marriage.

A one-night-stand turned into a nearly two-year affair.

Kris lied to Robert the entire time. She lied to all her friends. She lied to her mother. She lied to her kids. Whatever she had to say to steal time away from her commitments to be with her lover, she did, regardless of the consequences. Her stories wore thin, and it became increasingly difficult to keep everyone off her tail—and trail. Kris promised herself a million times she was "almost" done, but as her emotional feelings got caught up with her physical pleasure, there was no going back. She was hooked on love.

"We loved each other," Todd recalled. "We were going to get married. That was the plan."

Robert became more like a father to Kris than her husband, as he interrogated her over who she was slipping downstairs to talk to late at night. Kris even brazenly brought Todd onto the tennis courts, as her "coach," in plain view of Robert, who was not fooled by the ruse.

Kris spent thousands of dollars dressing her soccer player lover like a Ken doll. Whether he was dressed up or down, Todd looked like he had just stepped off the cover of a men's fashion magazine. Kris groomed him from head to toe. Her hairstylist in Beverly Hills cut his hair. Kris bought him expensive sports shirts and shorts, blazers, tight-fitting jeans, cashmere cardigan sweaters, socks, and briefs. "There," she would say, obviously pleased with her work and his overall GQ image as it reflected back at them in the mirror. "You look like a bazillion dollars!"

While Robert was a sharp dresser, he preferred to portray a subtler image of wealth. On a date night with Robert, Kris might typically wear a trophy wife's simple black cocktail dress, accessorized with a strand of pearls around her neck. But with Todd, Kris's evening wear was often bold, bright, and bodacious.

Kris took him to star-studded events and private pool parties where he saw an eclectic mix of A-list stars like Magic Johnson, George Michael, and Billy Idol. Todd was happy basking in Kris's dazzling personality as she nimbly worked the room. He was the quieter of the two, and slightly intimidated by the sea of celebrities. His Hollywood good looks and beaming white smile was engaging all on its own. The relative unknowns were swimming upstream with the upper crust of society and Hollywood stars. An endless supply of champagne, caviar, and even cocaine swirled around them nightly. Kris and Todd were privy to the greed and decadence of the decade.

Revenge Sex with Sis?

It was an annual tradition for Kris and Robert to celebrate her birthday with Nicole and O. J. at the Simpsons' spacious New York City apartment overlooking Central Park. Kris felt spending her thirty-fourth birthday away from Todd could save her marriage. Deep down she felt she wanted to rekindle her relationship with Robert.

Todd felt threatened by Kris's trip with Robert to Manhattan. He was fearful it might be the conduit for their reconciliation. Beside himself with angst, Todd showed up at the hotel where Kris's sister Karen worked and insisted she have cocktails with him. He explained that he needed to talk to her about Kris. Karen was shocked but agreed to have a drink with him. It was obvious to Karen that Todd needed to vent. He was filled with anger over what he perceived as Kris abandoning him to go back to Robert. There was no question in Karen's mind that Todd was jealous. Karen listened as her sister's lover shared his fears and doubts over how his relationship with Kris was surely doomed once she came back from New York.

After a couple rounds of drinks, Todd went into full seduction mode with Karen, suggesting they finish talking at her apartment in Brentwood, which was a couple of miles from the bar. "Karen told me she fought off his advances," a friend of Karen's recalled.

"I have a boyfriend, Todd," Karen said. "See that black Mercedes out there that the valet just pulled up? Well, he bought it for me, and I'm leaving in it now . . . alone."

When Todd persisted, Karen got up from the table.

"Todd, my sister, who is also my best friend, is your girlfriend," she said firmly. "How could you disrespect her? You should be ashamed of yourself!"

As Karen drove home, she looked at the clock on her car's dashboard. With the three-hour time difference between New York and LA, it was too late to call Kris. She decided she would call her in the morning.

The next day, as she thought about it more, Karen decided she did not want to ruin Kris's time with Robert, or to spoil her birthday by telling her about Todd's visit. She opted to wait until Kris got home.

Diamonds in the Rough

Kris was not surprised when she discovered a complete lack of intimacy between her and Robert in New York. She revealed later that she realized she was not in love with him. Her feelings had changed. He was more of a friend than a lover. Her fantasy of reigniting the old familiar foursome feeling between the two couples was also shattered, especially when she observed problems percolating between Nicole and O. J.

Kris was troubled by the changes she saw in Nicole.

"She became more withdrawn and private and seemed anxious," Kris recalled. "She was biting her fingernails down to the quick and just seemed to be on edge all the time."

She vividly remembered a two-hour walk in Central Park with her girl-friend. As they strolled along, Nicole slowly opened up to Kris about her "struggling with O. J." and problems between her children with him. Finally, Nicole revealed the deeper, more disconcerting reasons for her unhappiness with her marriage. O. J. was cheating on her with other women.

"She told me about him getting physical and roughing her up," Kris confessed, noting that Nicole found it difficult to talk about. "I so wish I had asked her for specifics, but I didn't want to cross a line if she didn't want to talk about something, which would become one of my biggest regrets. All she told me on our walk was 'I want to leave him, but I don't know how,'" Kris disclosed in her memoir.

While Kris had been a shoulder for Nicole to cry on, Kris had been careful not to share her own marital problems. She didn't want to burden Nicole.

But Nicole knew Kris well, and it was obvious she and Robert were having difficulties.

"I don't feel sexy," Kris generalized.

The next morning was Kris's birthday. While they were shopping at Bloomingdale's department store in Manhattan, Nicole wandered off and came back with a present for Kris: a full set of Christian Dior lingerie. She was hoping it would ramp up Kris and Robert's love life.

"It was just who Nicole was," Kris stated. "She was always thinking about everybody else."

Up until that point, O. J. didn't set off any alarms with Kris. He acted like his old self. But later that night, Kris thought he behaved strangely. The group had reservations at a new restaurant, then planned to go dancing at a nightclub. Kris and Robert had lunched, napped, and were ready to go when O. J. emerged from the bedroom without Nicole. He announced she had the flu and was staying home. Kris was confused because her girlfriend had seemed healthy that morning. O. J. stopped Kris from walking into the bedroom and checking on her.

"She doesn't want to see you," he told Kris.

Kris wrote, "I should have gone into that room to find out what was going on. But you don't imagine in a million years that your friend is in danger or trouble. Not like that. Not back then."

When Kris returned to Beverly Hills, Todd got to Kris with his tell-all before Karen could reach her.

"I slept with Karen while you were in New York with Robert," he reportedly told her.

When Karen joined the party line, an inquisition by Kris ensued. Karen, unaware Todd had already talked to Kris, was clueless about Todd alleging they slept together. So, Karen innocently volunteered how Todd had come by and the two had drinks. Kris was stunned.

"Why would he do that?" Kris pressed. "Why would he go see you without me?"

"I was surprised myself," Karen admitted. "He missed you and as your sister, I was the closest thing to you, and he was scared about you and Robert patching stuff up while you were in New York, and he'd be out in the cold. He just needed to get it all off his chest. He was majorly jealous, Kris."

Kris never came right out and asked Karen whether she had sex with Todd. She didn't have to because Karen was determined to offer full disclosure with her sister, to ensure there would be no understanding.

"He wanted to go to my place and finish talking, and I told him no," Karen said.

"I'll call you back," Kris said and hung up.

Even though Karen hadn't crossed the line with Todd, Kris treated her as if she did.

"Kris flipped out!" a friend of Karen's revealed. "She called Karen repeatedly, telling her to replay the evening with Todd. She wanted to hear the *he said-she said* over and over, so she could compare Todd's story to Karen's. It was awful for Karen. It became obvious Kris didn't believe her. No matter how many times she denied anything sexual happened between them, Kris was not satisfied with her explanation."

Even though she had done nothing wrong, Karen was nervous about facing Kris.

"When Kris perceives she's been wounded, it's a bullet straight to the heart, and she doesn't easily forgive and forget," Karen's friend confided. "There's a punishment period that can last from weeks to months to years."

As Kris continued to be skeptical of Karen's truth, the wedge between the sisters grew wider. Despite the trouble Todd's dastardly plan had caused him with Kris, she continued the affair. But Kris ignored her sister's protests and need to be believed.

Karen was drained from all the telephone calls, which had not gotten her any closer to resolving her conflict with Kris. After a few weeks of awkward conversations, Kris ceased all communications with Karen. When she couldn't get her to return her calls, Karen wrote Kris a letter, passionately declaring her innocence, and letting her know she would never betray her big sister. When Kris didn't respond to her letter, Karen was so miserable that she finally shared her exasperation with her mother.

Karen knew there was nothing she could do but wait it out and hope Kris would come around. Time passed and the matter was never discussed when Kris and Karen were together. "My sister hates confrontation," Karen has stated.

Over the years there have been many estrangements between the two sisters, and all of them at Kris's discretion. Karen is baffled over all the other times Kris has shut her out. The two sisters rely on their mother to relay grievances.

"All these years later, it's not about whether Karen had sex with Todd," a close friend revealed. "It's whether Kris *thinks* they did. All she requires is reasonable doubt. Karen's always the last to know where she stands with her own sister."

An Affair Everybody Remembers

While conducting his own investigation into Kris, Robert also hired a private investigator to follow her. One morning, Kris looked up from canoodling in a restaurant booth with Todd to see her worst fear coming true. There was Robert walking toward them. Terror gripped her as Robert taunted her with his glee of catching her in the act of unfaithfulness to him. Kris assumed it was a freak coincidence.

A chase ensued after Robert peeled out of the parking lot, with Kris following behind. Once they were inside their home there was yelling and shouting, but Kris was undaunted. She went straight to Todd's apartment that afternoon. But when she walked out and ran into Robert, she knew she had been professionally followed.

More vitriolic words were spoken, but Kris continued her affair. Robert kept showing up and catching her with her lover. Kris recalled at least three occasions where Robert confronted her and Todd.

"Do you realize this is my wife?" Robert said during one confrontation. "This is my furniture she is buying for you. Are you prepared to be a father to her four children? Our four children?"

No matter what, Kris seemed incapable of flipping the script, even though it was painfully obvious that this story was not going to end well for her. Her secret was out in a big way. But Kris continued to see Todd while living with Robert.

"I had no idea she was married,' recalled Todd's mother Ilza Waterman. "She told us she was separated. She would always come along with us to events. We even had a neighborhood wedding and she came. They went skiing, went to games. That's why I thought she was separated, because they went everywhere."

In addition to partying with her new set of friends, Kris started parading her boy toy around Robert's friends and business associates. Robert was mortified over Kris's flagrant display of vulgarity. Most of these people were connections she never would have made without him, and that made it all the more insulting and disrespectful.

Robert Kardashian was not a violent man, but he was consumed with rage and jealousy the longer this affair continued, especially when he learned Kris was bringing their children along on her adventures with Todd. They were so familiar with Todd that Khloé talked with her sisters openly about this man their mommy was spending so much time around.

"You don't like him, do you?" five-year-old Khloé asked her sisters.

Of Kris's four children, Khloé was Todd's favorite. It was bittersweet to be around these little ones because he knew, as much as he and Kris loved one another and thought about getting married, that it was only a fantasy.

Robert's a Private Eye

Robert spent much of the Christmas holidays in 1989 spying on his wife and her lover. It wasn't long before he crossed the fine line between tailing Todd and Kris and stalking them. He recorded his disgust over his wife's affair in a private diary, which was made public in 2012, almost ten years after his death.

On December 15, 1989, he wrote: *"Todd drove up to the back gate and parked. He went in the house and slept in my bed . . . Khloé and Robert were in the house. Closer to Christmas Day, she doesn't care!"*

On Christmas, Robert wrote: *"I was home alone with 4 kids."*

He noted that he played with them and tucked them in their beds, while Kris presumably enjoyed Christmas with Todd. Robert graduated from spying on them in the dark of night, to brash confrontations in public, and finally chasing after the illicit lovers in broad daylight with his car.

Todd had a nasty run-in with Robert while he and Kris were pulling out of the garage in his open-top Jeep.

"He comes charging out with a golf club," Todd recounted. "He took a swing and whacked the back of my car. I said, 'Holy shit, Kris, can I pull over and confront him? What do you want me to do?' She screamed out, 'No, keep driving. He might have a gun in the car. I know he keeps a gun.' So we've got this little high-speed chase going on at rush hour and I'm in a Jeep and he's trailing me and he's trying to overtake us. I did a couple of spin out moves and he just kept going, luckily. Maybe he got his composure again or something."

Todd was shaken by the drama, much like Robert had been when Cesar Sanudo came after him in a jealous rage. Todd was new to Hollywood, so fears for his own safety were even more magnified. A wealthy and prominent attorney who had powerful friends like O. J. Simpson wanted him dead.

Todd's mother became increasingly frightened for her son, especially after Robert telephoned her house in the middle of the night asking for Kris. Robert took the opportunity to tattle on Todd.

"She's with your son," Robert told Ilza.

"It's 2:30 in the morning," Ilza responded. "Your wife is thirty-six and my son is twenty-four. I suggest you talk with your wife and I'll talk with my son."

Afterward, Todd's mother pleaded with her son to get out of town until the situation cooled down. He didn't listen.

O. J. Runs with the Ball

While Robert confided in Joni throughout his crisis with Kris, he was reluctant to share his marital strife with any of his buddies. He still hoped that Kris would come to her senses. After Robert caught Kris with Todd multiple times, O. J. got involved. O. J. put aside his own marital infidelity with Nicole long enough to jump on Kris's case.

First, he summoned Kris to his house on Rockingham. When she arrived, he demanded she give him Todd's telephone number. O. J. called Todd in front of her. Although Kris and Todd's versions of O. J.'s call differ slightly, both agree it was basically a one-sided conversation.

According to both of them, O. J. screamed into the phone when Todd answered: *"You just fucked Snow White! You got that? You just fucked Snow White. Do you know what you've done to the entire universe, you asshole? You motherfucker. Now you are going to have to deal with me!"*

O. J. hung up on Todd. He interrupted Kris's justifications for the affair.

"All you had to do is get a vibrator," Kris recalled him telling her. "What'd you need this guy for?"

Robert Ditches Kris

More of Robert's friends and Kris's girlfriends tried to intervene. Some took loving approaches, while others practiced tough-love tactics, but the message was clear: Kris needed to clean up her act. But it all had the opposite effect on her. Kris felt hurt and misunderstood by their well-intentioned attempts to wake her up.

After three months of living in the nightmare of Kris's ongoing affair with Todd, Robert moved out. There was nothing more to say by him or any of their friends and family. As far as anyone could tell, Kris was nowhere near reaching her bottom. She would have to fall further.

Robert wanted a divorce.

Robert's mother was understandably upset by Kris's actions. She and Arthur had rough patches in their fifty years of marriage, but an affair never crossed her mind. Kris had shamed their family. Her unfaithfulness and mistreatment of Robert was incongruent with the Armenian way of life. Family was exalted above everything and everybody else. Still, Helen couldn't give Kris the tongue-lashing she deserved. Her Christian principles would not allow her to. Helen put her grandkids' well-being ahead of her personal feelings. She would not do anything that might jeopardize her ability to spend time with them.

Robert moved into Joni's guest suite in her penthouse apartment, three blocks from the Pacific Ocean in Marina Del Rey. Joni did her best to console her friend. She listened to Robert vent as they took long morning walks along the beach.

"He was devastated," Joni revealed. "He was a changed person. The sweetness and kindness were replaced with anger, frustration, and hostility. I think that he never got over the fact that she cheated on him."

There was a new schedule for the separated Kardashians. Robert looked after the kids on the weekends, while Kris spent the weekends with Todd. With the cat out of the bag, and Robert gone, Kris came down from the clouds and began her descent to bottom on all things Todd.

"He lived in a tiny, dumpy apartment in the Valley, and I had just left my seven-thousand-square-foot mansion with gates and Dobermans and Rolls-Royces," Kris remembered.

When Mondays rolled around, there were no more dreamy love hangovers from time spent with Todd over the weekend. There was only Kris left to look after her kids without Robert. Kris was hurting. The consequences of her actions were heavy on her heart, and her body ached underneath the emotional stress, to the point where she remembers it was "excruciating to even go through the motions of being a mom. It was an effort to tie my shoes."

She confessed to crying uncontrollably all day long. All she wanted to do was sleep.

Kris got more bad news when she learned Mary Jo had breast cancer. Her brave mother had already survived colon cancer. Kris was distressed by the renewed fear of losing her. But she put her pity party on pause when her stepdad Harry reminded her to step up and see her mother through each day of radiation treatment.

Upon hearing her mother's testament of courage and determination, Kris found inspiration for her own life and made a feeble attempt at breaking up with Todd on the day he drove her back from seeing her mom at the hospital. It didn't stick. She continued seeing him even after catching him in bed with another woman at their rendezvous pad. A scene ensued, but it was all much ado about nothing. Within a matter of days Kris took Todd on a ski trip to Deer Valley, Idaho, with her friends Candace and Steve Garvey. Kris and Todd had a series of fights before they got to the airport. She claimed he disrespected her by flirting with Hawaiian Tropic girls. All in all, she was miserable the entire time. Kris was finally done.

Payback's a Bitch

When her head began to clear, Kris found herself ruminating over all the wonderful qualities Robert Kardashian possessed and remembering all the good times. Robert was back on his pedestal. Thinking about how "moody and difficult" Todd could be, the age difference, and his inability to support her and the children undoubtedly helped Kris undergo her love drug detoxification.

While she mourned the collapse of her marriage, Kris made no attempts to restore her relationship with her estranged husband. Robert moved forward as well. He canceled every one of her credit cards. He also denied her charging privileges at their neighborhood supermarket. She was full of anger, angst, and terror. Kris was smart, talented, and creative. There were careers where she could have excelled, but not fast enough to remedy her financial situation. At thirty-four years old, Kris Kardashian had no current job experience or any hope of gainful employment. Her sole occupation for almost eleven years was as a mother and wife. That was not a resume that would afford her immediate currency.

While some might have whispered that Robert was justified in however he chose to punish Kris, considering she destroyed their marriage and happy family, Robert had frequently used his money to control and mold Kris when they were dating.

According to Joni: "She needed tires for her car, and he didn't want to get her tires for the car, and I said, 'Robert, she's your girlfriend. You are supporting her. Why wouldn't you buy her tires?' He said, 'Let her work for it.' So there was an approach that was avoidance and passive aggressive. He was sometimes mean to her. That's why eventually, I believe, she broke loose of that 'power' he had over her. I called it Armenian Housewife Syndrome."

With no credit cards, no cash, no checking account, Kris was down and out in Beverly Hills. Her friend Candace gave her the $10,000 retainer fee she needed to hire a divorce attorney. She was so broke that she was unable to pay the bill for her kids' pizza when they dined at a local pizzeria with Candace.

"If Robert wanted to show me that I was nothing without him, it worked," Kris confessed.

Robert didn't let his children go hungry or want for anything. The roof over their head was still intact. The girls had pool parties and attended summer camps. Kris put on a "mother of the year" face for her kids, but behind the mask she was shattered. She recalled being barely able to function during what she saw as the darkest days of her life that winter and spring. She was consumed with every conceivable negative emotion a mind can access: guilt, shame, self-recrimination, humiliation, regret, and self-hatred. She feared for her future and for her kids. She realized it had been a long time since she had no plan.

Kris thought back to how Robert taught her to be a believer in the power of prayer. Replacing fear with faith became her solution. To get her faith back, she needed to restore her faith in God. She couldn't remember the last time she had prayed or read from the Bible. With constant prayer, she thought less about herself. She focused on her children and began to feel better. The selfless love of a mother replaced Kris's selfishness. Nothing had changed about her circumstances, but her attitude was shifting. She could see the barriers to her progress and began to crawl out of her hole.

Kris had finally picked up a shovel to deal with her life.

Kris Goes Down

Dennis Wasser was building a reputation as a brilliant family lawyer. He was considered America's most feared divorce lawyer. Kris followed his instructions to the letter.

"Let fairness, not resentment, guide you when asking for the deal you want," Wasser advised. "Ask for what you rightly deserve, not just the most money."

Believing she and Robert would be married forever, Kris never saw any need to learn anything about their finances. In general, it was inconceivable she would ever find herself fighting with him about anything too terribly important. She certainly never dreamed she might one day haggle with him over the price of groceries.

Wasser was confident that Kris would maintain her residence, as the court would not disrupt their kids' home life at Tower Lane. She knew next to nothing about the outgoing expenses, like the $15,000 monthly mortgage on their house. She wasn't even aware of how much they owed the bank or the current worth of the house. There was payroll for the maid, housekeeper, and gardener, and she needed Robert to pay off the $21,000 outstanding balances on her credit cards before he canceled them. Robert believed many of the charges were purchases Kris made during her shopping sprees for Todd.

Kris did her homework and quickly got up to speed on her financial portfolio. Her $10,000 legal retainer fee bought more than a divorce. She had purchased an education in finance and artful negotiation.

"Since January 1990, the petitioner has essentially cut me off from all funds," Kris declared in her answer to Robert's petition, explaining what it took to keep up with a Kardashian. "The petitioner and I shared a luxury lifestyle. Nothing was too good for our family. The New Year's Eve party alone cost between $10,000 and $12,000. Even our children's clothing was purchased at exclusive boutiques." Kris's estimates for the Kardashians' monthly wardrobe expenses were specific: $800 a month for the children and $2,000 for her. Additional opulent living budget items included a roundup of swanky dinners and parties and glitzy European getaways.

That June, Wasser petitioned the courts for a monthly allowance for Kris, but Robert pushed back at every turn. Claiming she had been "forced" to quit her job as a flight attendant for American Airlines when she married, Kris contended the only cash she could gather up came from working a small job provided by a friend.

"I am earning less money than our paid household help," she informed the courts.

She requested a total monthly allowance of $37,189 to take care of her household. Robert wasn't willing to meet her even halfway. Declaring himself unemployed as a result of taking time off from his business to look after his personal problems, $2,000 a month was all he could contribute. Kris was incensed. Wasser fired back a demand that Robert get back to work so he could earn the money necessary for Kris to resume her sumptuous lifestyle. Robert made a case for an excess of $35,000 in assets, such as silverware and a gun that he wanted Kris to return, saying they were wedding presents to which he was entitled. Their contentious divorce grew to epic proportions.

It wasn't easy, but Kris refused to let Robert wear her down to a nub. She was patient. She prayed. She read her Bible. She attended church more often. She held onto the advice that Wasser gave her in the beginning.

"Everything's going to be okay," he assured her. "Stick to the plan. Do all you can to keep your divorce peaceful. Make every effort not to say anything negative about your spouse." Kris had shown flagrant bad judgment in allowing the Kardashian children to spend time with Todd, as it gave Robert an immediate advantage in a potential child custody lawsuit.

"Robert contended Kris schooled their children in what to say, or what not to say regarding their field trips with Mommy and her 'friend' Todd," a source close to the drama revealed.

Kris wondered if these kinds of things would be a part of Robert's private investigator's report. She feared what sordid details would surface. What she already knew to be potential evidence was bad enough. Kris could avoid poking that fire by being the good gossip fairy when it came to talking about Robert. But that, too, became almost impossible once the legal proceedings in court got uglier.

Kris and Robert saw separate psychiatrists, but the visits were strictly business-related. Kris wanted "hers" and Robert wanted to keep all of "his," and both wanted their children unscathed. But in reality, it was a nasty split. Robert not only portrayed his wife as an adulteress and absentee mom, but also accused her of physical abuse. It became necessary for both Robert and Kris to submit psychiatric evaluations to the court. Robert extracted notes from the secret diary he kept between 1989 and 1990 to substantiate his claims, including this entry from his diary on March 20, 1990: *"Kourtney started crying . . . She was sad because Mommy wasn't home at all. Kourtney wanted her to cook dinner for them. How sad that a child has to beg her mother to cook her dinner and be home with her."*

Robert continued to log unflattering stories about Kris long after their divorce was finalized, with particular emphasis on any allegations his children made about Kris mistreating them.

On October 20, 1993, he remembered Kourtney on the telephone, "crying and hysterical." Robert said she told him that Kris had twisted her arms and pulled her hair. He claimed Kourtney and her sister Kim "are scared and nervous, have been beat up several times before and are very, very intimidated."

The psychiatrist who interviewed Kris found her to be living in a fairy-tale world with "a Cinderella attitude where situations resulted in everyone living happily ever after." Furthermore, the report stated, "Her sense of self is based much more on fantasy than realistic considerations." She was labeled "manipulative" and "demanding," and she rated high on the narcissistic scale.

Robert was written up as "impulsive and overwhelmed."

No matter what transpired, Wasser was all about staying focused on the big picture. The stakes concerning the kids' welfare were dangerously high. This was definitely a case of the old idiom, "the devil is in the details." Kris's children's lives would be forever affected by the choices she made during her legal separation from Robert. She was not going to lose her children to Robert. She understood what Wasser meant when he insisted, "both parents stay in the picture with visitation rights." She didn't want to keep the kids away from their dad—a game so many women played during and after a divorce. Kris couldn't conceive of behaving this way, no matter what Robert did to her. For one thing, it was not in her nature, and despite any problems between her and Robert, she always wanted him in their lives. Everything was hard enough; splitting the kids' time between parents need not be a complicated affair. If Robert and Kris agreed on nothing else, they were united in their quest to provide their children with as much normalcy as possible.

At first, Kris wasn't willing to make space in her world for much more than her children. She loved being a mom more than ever. She would have plenty of time for a love life after the battle with Robert was over. But for such a passionate woman, Kris's newfound perspective on romance was a short-term proposition.

CHAPTER SIX
BRUCE JENNER

Best Blind Date Ever

"I'm forty years old and I've never been in love," proclaimed the twice-married Bruce Jenner. Upon hearing this line slide off his lips, Kris instantly fell for Bruce.

As best girlfriends, Kris and Candace Garvey had much in common. They were both beautiful Christian wives and career homemakers. They met at Bible study classes. Candace had two daughters from a previous marriage who were close in age to Kourtney and Kim. Candace's long hair was thick and cascaded gracefully around her shoulders. A California blonde with aquamarine eyes, Candace was stunning. Without fail, when she walked in the room, men clocked her as having been a cheerleader in high school. She was, but there was no entitlement about Candace. She was kind, loving, and loyal.

Candace had been married to sports superstar Steve Garvey for a year before Kris's divorce. Candace was always on the go with her husband, but even when they were out of town, she made sure to call Kris to check in. She gave Kris unwavering support.

Garvey proposed marriage to Candace after a one-week courtship, but confessed that two former girlfriends, both accomplished career women, were pregnant with his children. Since Garvey had built his brand as "Mr. Clean," the baseball legend's scandal involving twin paternity cases was a big story. It was still fresh, but Candace was on the other side of the controversy.

Robert wasn't famous, but Kris still endured significant public humiliation and embarrassment. Her entire social circle and family knew about her adulterous affair and subsequent divorce. Candace's experiences inspired Kris to hold onto the dream that she would get past her troubles and enjoy a full life again.

Olympic gold medalist Bruce Jenner and Steve Garvey often ran in the same retired sports heroes circles. They were on the familiar circuit of television shows, fishing and golf tournaments, personal appearances, and other promotional and marketing ventures. Both guys had the acting bug and were milking their connections for film and television roles.

Candace and Steve were both sharp dressers, so she was taken aback by Bruce's unkempt appearance. She got to know the athlete while she and Steve were shooting an outdoor television show in Alaska. To Candace, he looked like a beachcomber, but he was the kindest, sweetest guy. Bruce needed help, the kind only Kris could provide. Candace felt Kris and Bruce might just hit it off. Candace persuaded Kris to go out on a blind date.

In 1990, Kris knew Bruce Jenner's name, but that was about all. She first heard about him in 1976 when Robert was wining and dining her in Manhattan during O. J.'s stint as a sports commentator. Robert and O. J. had just come from the Olympics and as they recapped the highlights of their experience, they were raving about Bruce Jenner winning the gold medal in the decathlon.

Kris didn't care about meeting the "World's Greatest Athlete." She simply agreed because Candace was such a passionate matchmaker. Kris wanted to go to Ivy at the Shore, a swanky restaurant on the beach in Santa Monica. The plan was for Kris to meet up with everyone first at the Riviera Country Club, where Bruce and Steve were playing golf. It was the same country club where, many years before, a lovestruck Robert Kardashian had followed Kris all over the green, hoping she would agree to go out with him.

Kris and Bruce ran into each other at the entrance to the clubhouse before Candace and Steve had a chance to introduce them. Though she wasn't at all famous, Bruce instantly knew who she was.

"He looked adorable," Kris said of the encounter.

She didn't find it odd how this stranger hugged her like a long-lost friend and pulled her up off the ground with his peculiar greeting.

"Finally, I'm in the arms of a real woman!" she recalled him saying.

Cocktails at the country club and dinner at the beach were a success. They all went back to Candace's afterward. The Garveys went to bed, leaving Kris and Bruce to continue their chat on the sofa in their den. They talked until the early morning hours. Kris divulged a brief synopsis about her world, but Bruce did most of the talking. The athlete performed an animated rapid cycling of his life story. Kris found his vulnerability endearing. It was obvious he needed to unburden himself. She was glad this celebrated man felt comfortable enough with her to reveal such personal details about how his life had gone off the rails since his triumphant Olympic win. From two failed marriages to several foundering business deals, Kris was fascinated with hearing it all.

Bringing Up Bruce

While roller-skating with her mother and sisters at a rink in White Plains, New York, Esther McGuire met a dashing young man on the rink. "Bill" Jenner, a Canadian who was raised in upstate New York, was instantly smitten with the beguiling hazel-eyed blonde beauty—particularly her derriere. "He came up from behind me on his roller skates," Esther recalled. "When I turned around, he said, 'You've got the greatest looking rear end!'"

Bill Jenner was three years older than seventeen-year-old Esther McGuire. Their courtship lasted only six months, as they were eager to marry before Bill, who volunteered for the military draft during World War II, was scheduled to ship to Scotland.

William Bruce Jenner was born on October 28, 1949, in Mount Kisco, New York, the second of four children, beginning with an older sister, Pam.

Another boy, Burt, was added to the Jenner family when Bruce was eight years old; daughter Lisa was born eight years after that.

As the grandson and namesake of a Baptist minister, Bruce was practically raised in the senior Jenner's church.

For a time, Bill worked alongside his brother Ted as a tree surgeon. Eventually, Bill established his own arborist business.

Esther enjoyed being a homemaker and mother. Between pregnancies, she sought work outside their home. Once her children were situated in their school lives, Esther assumed an education of her own. Her innate curiosity, intelligence, and outgoing personality landed her the career-making positions of medical transcriptionist and legal secretary. When the claims adjuster for a nationwide insurance agency failed to deliver his quota, Esther picked up the slack. Esther's diligence and talents sped up the closures of stagnant cases. Her hard work in achieving settlements and rejected claims brought her to the attention of her bosses and their bosses. While they enthusiastically applauded her results, they were content to reward her with a promotion and a pat on the back. Instead, Esther requested equal pay for equal work.

"I would like to be paid an insurance agent's salary," she commanded.

It was the era of the Equal Pay Act of 1963, but employers were slow to close wage disparities based on sex, and Esther's brave bidding was denied. While disappointed, she continued to work in the insurance industry. Two incomes afforded Esther and Bill a spacious home at Lake Zoar, a body of water on the Housatonic River. The design and construction of the property was entirely Esther's project. Bill happily gave her carte blanche to supervise every detail. The Jenner lake house became the primary residence, with Bill commuting to his work in Newtown, a half hour away. Every member of the family had at least one trophy to show for their superb water-skiing talents.

"I had so many picnics with our kids and their friends on the beaches at tournaments, my mouth was almost always filled with sand," Esther said with a laugh.

Bruce inherited three generations of athletic talent. While serving in Germany, Bill Jenner competed in the US Army Olympics in Nuremberg. He excelled in pole vault relays and won a silver medal in the 100-yard dash. He was a runner in Boston Marathons. His minister grandfather, "Burt" Jenner, competed in marathon races in New Brunswick, Canada. Bill taught his son Bruce—whom he nicknamed "Bruiser"—to pole vault with poles made out of bamboo bark.

"Bruce was an extremely active boy, full of energy," Bruce's mother recalled.

Young Jenner became known as the fastest runner in elementary school, beating out all his classmates in timed runs. He also developed musical interests and learned to play the accordion.

While Esther was delighted with young Bruce's sports achievements and musical talents, she could not understand why her "easy to raise" son rebelled against reading, writing, and arithmetic. A hatred for classroom studies and homework resulted in Bruce failing the second grade. This was alarming and unacceptable to Esther.

"I used to drill him in homework, relentlessly," she said. "I had numerous meetings with his counselor, the principal, regarding his schoolwork."

Esther had no way of knowing that her bright and otherwise normal son was suffering from a learning disability known as dyslexia. When Bruce was nearing his senior year at Newtown High School in Newtown, Connecticut, Esther discovered the reason behind her son's difficulty. While watching their sons compete on the water, another mother shared that she was a special education teacher, and her son Blake, a friend of Bruce's, was dyslexic. As the schoolteacher described her son's condition, a light bulb went off in Esther's head. She wanted to know more immediately. Once Esther understood the studying challenges Bruce had faced all his life, she went into action and found Bruce solutions. His grades improved and he was awarded a partial football scholarship to Graceland College in Lamoni, Iowa. Attending college would also exclude Bruce from the military draft during the Vietnam War. But when a knee injury halted his football playing, he turned his attention to the decathlon.

Jenner made the dean's list at Graceland College, which later became Graceland University. In 1973, after four years of studies, Bruce graduated with a degree in physical education. Bruce hadn't let dyslexia define him. He had conquered his corner of the academic world by studying harder. Ultimately, his diploma proved to be of very little use to him, but it became a symbol of what dedicating himself to a goal could accomplish.

Solid Gold Hero

In December 1972, several months before his graduation, Bruce married his college sweetheart, Chrystie Crownover, the twenty-two-year-old daughter of a minister. That same year, Chrystie had proudly cheered for Bruce as he competed in the US Olympic trials in Eugene, Oregon, where he placed fifth in the men's decathlon. That victory was a turning point in his athletic career.

After Bruce earned his degree, he and Chrystie—a slender, vivacious, dark-eyed blonde—packed a couple pieces of luggage into their 1963 Volkswagen Beetle and moved to San Jose, California. The Bay Area city in Northern California was known as the "Track Capital of the World." Olympic hopefuls from all over the country trained there: Mac Wilkins, John Powell, Andre Phillips, Millard Hampton, and Al Feuerbach. Working out alongside these high-achievers motivated Bruce in his quest for greatness. *I will outwork you, and I will perform under pressure*, he thought.

As a child, Jenner had demonstrated tremendous resilience in the face of personal obstacles. Outside the classroom, the fifth grader showed the bullies he was boss by outrunning them all.

"On a field of play he would challenge anyone he knew to be a good student, just so he could clobber that kid and then say, 'Read that,'" wrote journalist Mike Downey.

Bruce enjoyed the spotlight that the athletics of his youth provided, but he wanted recognition on a wider playing field. His desire for fame grew stronger during his college years.

"At Graceland, I was a big athlete," he remarked. "Out here [in San Jose], I was a nobody."

Chrystie had entered into a covenant with Bruce that she would support his plan to dedicate the first four years of their marriage to his goals of excelling as a professional decathlon athlete. By day, he trained at the local college and university, and at night he sold life insurance, earning roughly $9,000 a year. The newlyweds could hardly survive on Bruce's monthly salary.

Chrystie searched for a way they could earn more than just rent and grocery money. She found employment as a flight attendant for United Airlines. In addition to providing a second source of income, her mileage bonus as an airline employee enabled Bruce fly free to sporting events.

While Bruce focused intensely on his athletic training, Chrystie took the burdens of everyday life off his broad shoulders. She flew from airport to airport for her job, and when she was at home, she took care of the chores. She didn't complain. She thought of them as equal partners and this was her role.

Sports journalists had started paying attention to Bruce in 1974 when he won the men's decathlon event, and he was gaining media traction when he won a gold medal at the 1975 Pan American Games. The following year, the culmination of Bruce's determination and athletic abilities forever changed the course of sports history. He became an instant international celebrity.

In preparation for the 1976 Olympics in Montreal, Bruce attacked his decathlon training with the discipline of a military soldier. He shut out everything else from his life—including his wife. Chrystie was now his sole financial support and emotionally she was Bruce's rock. When he came home after training six to eight hours a day, he studied performance records of his upcoming opponents. Before bed, Bruce repeated exercises from earlier in the day. His legendary tale is that he was so dedicated to winning that he had a hurdle set up in the living room of their two-bedroom apartment.

But the Jenners' relationship was bruised by Bruce's failure to pay attention to his young wife. "He became so obsessed with the decathlon that it was hard to communicate with him on any other level," Chrystie said.

The distance Bruce put them between them might have been enough to warrant serious examination and therapy, but there were deeper relationship issues, which Chrystie could not possibly have been expected to survive. But to her credit, she certainly tried.

As the wife of the manliest of men, Chrystie Jenner knew she would have to contend with women flirting with her husband. She understood other men would be jealous of her husband's muscular frame and athletic prowess. She accepted this as part of the package, of sharing the same universe with such an exquisite creature. What she hadn't expected was Bruce himself robbing her of their starry-eyed illusions. They had not even celebrated their first wedding anniversary before Bruce told his beloved that she had actually married a "woman." Bruce admitted he had identified as a woman all his life, and desired to be feminine—not masculine—all the way to his core.

"I can't remember the exact words because it was such a shock," Chrystie later revealed.

Chrystie handled it well. In a bizarre way, she was relieved to know what was really going on with him. Instead of anger or betrayal, she felt compassion for her husband.

"Understandably, I was speechless," she admitted. "I was really pleased that he shared that intimacy with me. That he trusted me with his deepest, darkest secret. It didn't threaten me. It didn't destroy our marriage."

Bruce reassured Chrystie that they were his issues.

"This is what I deal with," he said. "I do a little cross-dressing. I do a little of this, a little of that, you know. It's going to be fine. We'll work this stuff out."

Bruce's attitude could be considered cavalier, or even cruel: to expect his wife to accept him as an entirely different person than the guy she believed she married. Undoubtedly, for a man of twenty-six, Bruce was grappling with complex emotions. As a young woman, Chrystie could not have conceived the potential burden she would carry keeping Bruce's secret away from the world. Would she find herself living as a hostage or a heroine when their lives were scrutinized?

Bruce Jenner was not a household name when he stepped into the 1976 Summer Olympics, but a heightened sense of patriotism was circulating in the air for American spectators sitting in the bleachers of the Olympic Stadium. Celebratory themes related to the bicentennial had enveloped America all year. The July 4 commemoration of the 200th anniversary of the signing of the Declaration of Independence had occurred only three weeks before the event. It was also the decade of the Cold War, where the United States and the USSR were locked in a power struggle for world dominance. The 1972 Olympics upset, where three long-standing titles were snapped up by the Soviets, was still an open wound.

Enter Bruce. Under a shaggy mop-top of hair was a golden-tan, clean-cut athlete with bulging biceps. Wearing a red, white, and blue jersey and matching shorts, he was the essence of the all-American boy. Bruce was the biblical David pitted against the Soviet's Goliath, Mykola Avilov, a defending champion. The crowd's roaring support amplified with each event. Jenner heard their screams and they fueled him.

During his victory lap, Bruce traded his vaulting pole for an American flag, which he plucked from a spectator's hand as he continued running to the end of the track.

It was one of those glorious, historic moments that men would relish telling their sons and grandsons about—how they were in the stadium on July 30, 1976, when Bruce Jenner set a new world record for the decathlon.

"I knew he had it in the bag," his mother Esther said afterward, beaming.

Bruce fought his way through the throng of people, searching for his cheerleader Chrystie, who came down from the stands wearing a canary yellow shirt with the words "GO JENNER GO" streaming across it. There was a crushing crowd of hundreds of cheering supporters, reporters, and photographers. Everyone wanted either an autograph or a moment of vicarious glory that standing next to the world's greatest athlete would surely bring.

"Nobody was doing that before," he exclaimed.

As Bruce embraced his partner in love and business, the photographers couldn't get enough of the sports couple. As much as Jenner epitomized America, Chrystie sparked visions of California sunshine. Bruce and Chrystie Jenner became a "celebrity couple." Bruce was applauded as much for his flag-bearing patriotism as he was for his morally upright devotion to his wife. Both assets were bankable. "Jenner is twirling the nation like a baton," Tony Kornheiser of *The New York Times* wrote. "He and wife Chrystie are so high up on the pedestal of American heroism, it would take a crane to get them down."

Bruce didn't bother to go back and pick up his vaulting poles he had tossed, as they were the tools of his past. They had catapulted him into capitalism. The US flag he carried at the end of his run symbolized hope for a bright and profitable future.

"It was a very bittersweet moment because I knew I was going to retire," Bruce said. "I was done. I was missing out on everything in life. It was time to move on. For me, there's more to life than running and jumping."

Since he was the odds-on favorite to win, Bruce looked beyond the competitions in the days leading up to the Olympic Games. In preparation for what he calculated would be an onslaught of financial opportunities, he had discreetly begun positioning himself for marketing manna earlier that year. There were strict Olympic rules banning direct or indirect financial payments prior to competing in the Games. It was illegal to solicit any free products or endorsement deals as an Olympics sports celebrity while still considered an amateur athlete. Bruce risked losing his eligibility to compete if word leaked that he had signed with a sports agent. However, there was nothing in the handbook that precluded him from *listening* when a Hollywood agent called.

* * *

George Wallach was a seasoned sports packager. Over the course of several months, Bruce had a series of conversations with the agent and manager. They mapped out his big picture game plan. Wallach estimated they had a four-year stretch between Olympic Games for capitalizing on Bruce's win.

As he fended off the crush of newfound fans, Bruce gave good television sound bites. Wallach always stood a few feet away, fielding questions from the press about how much gold his hot property client was aiming for.

"I really don't know," Wallach told them. "I can't say how many offers we have. I imagine there will be plenty of telegrams waiting for me when I get back to my hotel room."

Wallach's chest was pushed out in pride as he recognized a few of the hangdog faces in the crowd. They were veteran sports agents who had come ready to pounce on Bruce, only to realize Wallach had beaten them to the gold.

For fear of smelling like a greaseball grafter, no athlete dared to publicly admit the money that could be made. The 1972 public outcry against seven-time gold medalist Mark Spitz for cashing in on his sports triumph was brutal. "If I mention one thing about what I'm considering, everybody will say, 'Hey, the kid's just in it for the money,'" Bruce said.

A few nights later, he kept up the "eager isn't a good look" persona when an ABC executive—the first of many hoping to curry favor over cocktails—sprinted toward him at a post-Olympics party. He was sports royalty now, with no need for an introduction to the strangers representing corporate America who were vying for his attention. With the grace of a seasoned star, Bruce shielded himself from all deal-making conversations with the guys in the monkey suits.

"Good to meet you," he would say. "Let me introduce you to my manager, George Wallach."

Going for the Real Gold

It was late when the Jenners returned from the Olympic Games to their Montreal hotel.

"He didn't sleep all night," Chrystie later revealed. "He would get up and walk around naked with the medal around his neck, beaming and flexing."

The next morning, Chrystie got up and joined Bruce for coffee at the table, which was covered with newspapers. She was so exhausted by the time she was able to finally fall asleep that she didn't hear Bruce when he came back from his trip to the newsstand.

It was his "first day of work" at his new enterprise, which might have been called "The Business of Being Bruce Jenner." Wallach was on the other end of the phone, rattling off the buffet of endorsement deals awaiting Bruce's approval. Bruce's inviting smile energized Chrystie, who was not yet fully awake. He stood up and cradled the phone with his shoulder so he could free his hand to pull a chair out for her to sit. She was further warmed by his mouthing "I love you" as he listened to Wallach.

With his other hand free, Bruce quietly tapped the newspapers. He was grinning from ear-to-ear as he saw Chrystie's still slumbering eyes widen from reading the "BRUCE JENNER" headlines. She was surprised to see the newspapers had chosen to include so many photos of the two of them. As the lights from the cameras flashed on her and Bruce, Chrystie was so genuinely focused on how proud she was of him that she didn't stop to think how she too might now be a celebrity.

"I've got to go meet Wallach to sort out all these deals," he said, hanging up the phone.

"Great! Want me to go with you? What did he say?"

"No, I'll tell you later," he said. "You stay here and get some rest. I'm sure you didn't get much sleep. I'll be back in plenty of time for us to watch the television news coverage. Do you mind if Wallach watches it with us?"

"No, of course not," Chrystie answered.

"Great, I'll tell him, but too bad Bertha's not here right now."

"Bertha?" Chrystie said, puzzled over Bruce's mention of their dog, a Golden Retriever.

"Yeah, so I could be the first one to tell her she's the new face of General Mills."

Chrystie roared at the absurdity, but Bruce wasn't kidding. As of that morning, all of the Jenners, even the four-legged one, were bankable stars.

The book deal Bruce made immediately following his Olympics victory was the launch pad for his motivational speaking gigs, where people paid good money to hear how Bruce triumphed over the adversities in his life to achieve greatness. Publishers also doled out a reported six-figure advance for Mrs. Jenner to pen an upbeat memoir, *I Am Chrystie*. She gave readers an exploration of marital and sexual issues. She shared information about Bruce's sexual experiences before he met her, without telling all about her husband's gender dilemma . . . or how she felt when she discovered they shared a love for the same clothes—*hers*. The truth would have tarnished Bruce's gold-medal win and destroyed his legacy. Being a cross-dresser, wanting to become a woman—none of that was acceptable forty years ago. There was no question that Mr. and Mrs. Jenner had to keep up with the secret.

A Kirkus review gave her book a thumbs-up: "In its own wide-eyed, ingenuous fashion, *I Am Chrystie* delivers the title's promise."

Chrystie's wifely blues, brought on by spousal neglect, disappeared into the ether. Glamour, fame, wealth, and everything else that came with being the world's hottest celebrity couple was a feel-good pill. Bruce had the ultimate press package to make millions of dollars, and the love their adoring fans poured on them was infectious. Bruce showered Chrystie with more attention, praise, and affection. How could the couple not believe their own publicity as the ideal husband and wife? Chrystie felt the exhilaration and comfort of her man needing her again. They were truly a team.

As the "world's greatest athlete," Bruce became the second decathlon winner to grace the iconic Wheaties cereal box. As he munched on milk-drenched flakes, Bruce declared, "Wheaties . . . the breakfast of champions."

From television pitchman to sports commentator, Bruce was on the air. Cable was muscling in on the big three networks—ABC, NBC, and CBS. Promoting the world's greatest athlete was guaranteed to drive viewers to any television channel. ABC got their man. Bruce started off his broadcast career at the top, as a special correspondent for *Good Morning America*. ESPN, then in its infancy, had Jenner as their number one pick for its roster of broadcasters. The cameras loved him, and Bruce loved them in return.

His schedule was insane, prompting *Sports Illustrated* to quip that "they could fill a locksmith shop" with all the keys to the city Bruce had collected. To this day, Bruce's mother Esther marvels at the enormous fees her son commanded for motivational speaking gigs during those halcyon days.

"He would often get something like $20,000 for two days' work," she said.

As Bruce's financial portfolio grew, so did the cynical press, who criticized him for his zealous pursuit of marketing his hero status. Many people found Bruce to be downright greedy. *The Washington Post*'s Kenneth Turan countered, "Is it his fault that he's direct, self-assured, sincere? The type of person we'd all like to be when we grow up?"

His loyal wife opined to *The New York Times*, "After all the work Bruce has put in, he's entitled to make a few bucks."

Despite All Those Powers

Bruce's privileged world stopped its rotation on November 20, 1976. Exactly three months to the day after his record-breaking decathlon, Bruce's spirit was crushed with a phone call. His younger brother Burt had been mangled in a car accident and was clinging to life.

The eighteen-year-old and his high school sweetheart Judith Hutchings were driving Bruce's silver Porsche down a country road in Connecticut when he lost control and slammed into a utility pole. Burt was found on the ground, barely alive, several miles from the accident site. Judith was pronounced dead on arrival at the hospital. Burt was taken to another medical facility where he lived for another five hours. As the Olympic champion and his family kneeled in prayer around the youngest Jenner's hospital deathbed, Bruce was overcome with gut-wrenching grief.

"You never get over something like that," Bruce reflected thirty-five years later.

On September 9, 1978, Bruce honored his late brother's memory by naming his newborn son Burton "Burt" William Jenner.

Lucrative and varied business opportunities continued to come Bruce's way. He stepped into a line of footwear bearing his name for the Buster Brown Company in an advertising print campaign; there were Bruce Jenner "Active Knit" shirts and Bruce Jenner jeans; he sipped orange juice for Tropicana in television commercials. Over the course of a year, he sat on Johnny Carson's couch on *The Tonight Show* and appeared on *The Merv Griffin Show* and *Donahue*, talking about his fabulous life. Being interviewed by the top television chatters was great, but Bruce longed to sign autographs as a movie star.

When Warner Brothers was casting *Superman*, a real-life hero playing the fictional comic book hero Superman seemed a perfect fit for Jenner. The film also had all the potential for a box-office bonanza. Everyone in his life was excited for him. A veteran showbiz star assured Bruce, "The audition is just a formality."

He was flown to Italy to read for the part. The top brass at the studio found Bruce's acting chops too wobbly to merit risking the lead role on the amateur, no matter how seductive the publicity. In the end, the role went to actor Christopher Reeve.

Bruce had his share of rejections, which he usually took in stride. However, he suffered from the devastating blow of losing out on that once-in-a-lifetime role. Many actors have been haunted by such disappointments all the way to the grave.

Nice Knowing You

Being a father was important to Bruce, but he needed to make a living while he was still a hot commodity. Bruce's speaking engagements and public appearances demanded the majority of his time, and he frequently spent several nights away from home while attending to his many business ventures. By his own admission, Bruce was only spending an average of about ten days a month at home.

"Chrystie wants what I want, but the schedule pulls us apart in a lot of ways," he admitted at the time.

Where he once ignored her needs while he trained for the decathlon, he now focused only on acquiring money and fame. Chrystie wondered if she would always rank second as the object of his affection. Bruce was generous; Chrystie wanted for nothing. She was renovating the $200,000 home they bought in Malibu. They had a catamaran and Bruce was driving a Porsche Turbo Carrera.

When his expenses for flight travel exceeded $10,000 in a two-month period, Bruce squeezed pilot lessons into his already backbreaking travel schedule, so he could buy airplanes to fly himself around the country. He could afford the planes and all his other toys, which included three dirt bikes. In 1977, just a year after the Olympics, Bruce's estimated cash haul from all his public appearances, speaking gigs, and endorsements was about $500,000. In addition, he had a lucrative contract as a sports commentator on ABC.

Chrystie had no sooner made her house "home sweet home," and settled into a second property in Tahoe, Nevada, when she realized she was experiencing the familiar pangs of emptiness. The four cars, including two Porsches in the garage, a sailboat, and all the other trappings of a luxury lifestyle wouldn't keep Bruce in her bed.

The couple separated in 1979, just three years after they became overnight multimillionaires. When Bruce rang his mother Esther to tell her he was divorcing Chrystie, Esther was stunned.

"We just don't think alike," he explained.

"But what about your baby boy?" Esther asked.

"I'll make sure he's okay," Bruce said reassuringly.

Esther hung up the phone, puzzled by Bruce's scant explanation for why he was leaving Chrystie and his son, but she was not one to pry.

Esther could never have imagined her daughter-in-law's secret heartbreak. Without question, Bruce was genuinely busy during his marriage, so there never seemed to be any time to have discussions about his gender identity crisis. Perhaps he, along with Chrystie, welcomed all the distractions so they wouldn't have to deal with the perennial elephant in the room. While she desperately loved Bruce, his desire to live life as a woman would have been hard for any twenty-something wife to wrap her head around, especially in the 1970s.

Going All the Way

The eligible bachelors who cruised the plethora of gorgeous, leggy, buxom women at Hugh Hefner's infamous Playboy Mansion in the late 1970s were not shopping for wives. Nor were the married men looking to engage in meaningful conversations with the sexy playmates. It was a social hub of sex, drugs, and rock and roll. It was in this den of iniquity—while still married to the mother of his infant son—that Bruce Jenner met his future wife.

Tall and lithe, with long legs that didn't stop, Linda Thompson could easily have been mistaken for a Playboy bunny. The stunning blonde was just the kind of woman you expect to see gracefully prowling the landscape of powerful men. Thompson was the sexy star of the popular television country music variety series *Hee Haw*. Her looks were disarming. She didn't sleep around and wasn't a party girl. Linda's business at the hip and happening club on that warm spring afternoon in 1979 was as a gorgeous presenter of an award at the conclusion of a tennis tournament.

Linda found Bruce adorably handsome as he chatted her up after the event. Linda's Southern Baptist upbringing in Memphis, Tennessee, dictated that she shun his advances, since she learned from onlookers that he was married. Bruce quickly clarified for her that she was mistaken. He was actually separated, and practically "living at the mansion." As they were still standing on the tennis court, the slightest hint of awkwardness shown by

Bruce in those next few moments could interrupt his flirtation. If so, he might never see her again, and he was smitten with the Southern beauty. Despite his heart racing, Bruce mustered all of the athlete's confidence he could access to score a win. There was no time for fear, just like the seconds passing on a scoreboard. Bruce had to act. What came out of his mouth next could have blown him right out of the game. He hoped his boyish good looks and charm, which had never failed him, would endear him to the former Miss Tennessee. As Bruce ran down an instant intimacy confession, it's a wonder Linda didn't flee for her life.

"Chrystie packed up her things one day while I was away," Bruce explained to his new conquest. "When I got home, I found her closet empty. She had taken our eight-month-old son, Burt, with her to San Jose. I was surprised and devastated by her decision to leave."

It worked. Bruce had hit all the right notes with the young woman, who also happened to be Elvis Presley's former girlfriend. Bruce and Linda went out on their first date the following evening. She claims she insisted they go out as platonic friends, refusing to have sex with him until after he was sure he and his estranged wife were finished.

When Bruce and Chrystie reconciled for a brief period, Linda cut off contact with him out of respect for his marriage.

Several months later, Linda said Bruce called with the news of his pending divorce from his first wife. "She left me again!" he told her.

It was not going to be a clean break, as Chrystie was pregnant. Bruce wanted her to get an abortion, but she refused. Linda thought carefully about this conflict before agreeing to see Bruce again. It was unfortunate for everyone, and sure to be a scandal, but Linda decided to resume their relationship despite Bruce's baggage.

Soon, Bruce and Linda were inseparable. He was rolling in greenbacks with multiple motivational speaking gigs. He was the face of Wheaties cereal and the star in major advertising campaigns for everything from cameras to designer clothing. Linda found Bruce to be an ideal partner, mentally and emotionally, as well as a "perfect physical specimen." When she wasn't taping *Hee Haw* in Nashville, she was staying with Bruce in Malibu or traveling with him on the road.

Meanwhile, Chrystie bore Bruce a daughter, Cassandra Lynn "Casey" Jenner, on June 10, 1980. Bruce did not support Chrystie's decision to have their baby, so he was not present at the hospital when she gave birth to Cassandra, nor did he visit the mother and child afterward. He had moved on.

For Bruce, the king of rock and roll was a hard act to follow when it came to pampering his gorgeous princess. Elvis had bought separate homes for Linda and her parents and covered her lustrous skin with pricey jewelry.

Having competed in no less than ten major beauty pageants, Linda was skilled in the art of adoration. Any man already special enough to be her guy was rewarded with even finer moments when they knew how to shop for her. And Bruce had a knack for turning his perfect presents into major events. From a Porsche 928 with a huge red bow for Christmas, to flying her family and friends in to Malibu for her thirtieth birthday celebration on the beach, Bruce knew the best gift giving was all about the presentation.

After spending time with Bruce, her good friend, country music singer Kenny Rogers, told Linda, "Either Bruce Jenner is the nicest person in the world—or the biggest phony."

"At the time, of course, I just laughed at Kenny, having no way of knowing how true his observation would prove," Linda later admitted.

Bruce wanted to get married the second they learned Linda was pregnant, in the fall of 1980, but they were forced to wait until his divorce from Chrystie was finalized. On January 7, 1981, under coconut and palm trees on the estate of Hollywood film producer Allan Carr, family and friends witnessed Bruce and Linda, who was four months pregnant, take their vows. The ink was barely dry on Bruce and Chrystie's divorce papers—as in, only three days—and Bruce was marrying another woman.

The Bionic Man's Lee Majors picked up the tab in Oahu, Hawaii, for the wedding. Bruce's best man was Burt, his two-year-old son. The nuptials were blanketed with the cachet of celebrity coupledom, including Lee Major's wife Farrah Fawcett, of *Charlie's Angels* fame.

Their first child, Brandon, was born five months later on June 4, 1981. Only a few weeks earlier, the daughter he abandoned had turned a year old.

Linda insisted she and Bruce never argued and defined their marriage as a "picturesque life." They bought a house in Malibu, with a second home in Lake Tahoe, and continued to travel all over the world, with Linda enjoying the fruits of Bruce's acting career. During their marriage he starred on several episodes of *CHiPs* as another amazingly fit, sun-kissed motorcycle cop with great hair. Executive producer Rick Rossner had a penchant for casting to-die-for hunks as cops in the 1980s. His greatest discovery, actor Erik Estrada, had become a superstar as the lead crime-busting biker. When the Latin heartthrob's ego proved too big for his riding boots, Rossner was eager to replace him with Bruce Jenner. Erik decided to behave and came back to the series.

Bruce continued to make guest appearances on a variety of major television shows such as *Murder, She Wrote* and *The Love Boat*. He also consistently worked in films during this time. In *Grambling's White Tiger*, Bruce was the star as well as co-executive producer. He shared the credit with Wallach; the two had formed Jenner/Wallach Productions.

Bruce's foray into feature films was less successful. He played a reluctant music manager of the Village People in *Can't Stop the Music*, alongside actress Valerie Perrine. The critics creamed the movie and Bruce would be plagued by barbs about this acting career misstep for the rest of his professional life.

On August 21, 1983, the Jenners welcomed another son into the world, Sam Brody Jenner. Linda remained in blissful wedded ignorance until 1985, when Bruce sucker-punched her in the stomach with his startling confession.

"I identify as a woman," he revealed.

Stunned, Linda made him repeat himself, and then when she had him qualify this announcement, he repeated it a third time.

"I am a woman trapped in a man's body," he clarified.

In disbelief, she assured him he was the "manliest of men."

As if his revelation weren't enough for one day, Bruce added insult to injury by sharing with Linda his decision to medically transition to being a woman. In her autobiography, which was published in 2016, the year after her ex-husband came out as transgender, Linda maintained she was clueless over Bruce's desire to become a woman during their five-year marriage.

While Linda was initially shaken to her core, once she accepted the gravity of the situation, she was open to exploring it with Bruce in couples therapy. They began seeing a gender dysphoria expert. She learned that her husband was never going to come back into their fairytale marriage as a prince because he had always been a princess. Even colder was the fact that she had two options: she could either stay with him and live with Bruce woman-to-woman—or leave him.

As if all of that were not enough, Bruce offered up a bizarre solution for how everyone could live happily ever after. He would go to Denmark to have his gender reassignment surgery, and when he came back to the United States, he could come back into their children's lives as a female relative, perhaps an aunt. He explained his love for Linda had not changed. He wanted to stay married to her and keep his family intact. But this wasn't going to work for her. For Linda, it was game over.

Linda contends there were never any harsh words spoken between them as she opted to walk away from this person she no longer knew. She loved him enough to end their marriage the way their relationship had begun—as friends. They even continued to see the therapist together.

In what proved to be a last-ditch effort to win Linda's acceptance before she divorced him, Bruce invited her to New York, where he was making a personal appearance. She confessed she went there with the secret hope that maybe Bruce wanted to go back to the way things were between them and forget all about his dreams of becoming a woman. She looked forward to the handsome, virile man she knew answering the door of his hotel room when she knocked. Instead, she found Bruce in full drag from head to toe. She recognized only his smile and his eyes under the wig and makeup. A woman's dress covered his manly muscles and toned legs supported by high heels.

As Linda broke down bawling, Bruce apologized profusely. "I feel bad that I surprised you like that. I just wanted you to see who I really am. It's time you saw me as I truly am. This is me!"

Bruce's revelation could be considered his swan song with Linda. Though she says they shared hotel rooms, they slept in separate beds whenever they traveled together. Six months after Linda learned of her new reality with Bruce, they officially separated. Her public explanation for the split was Bruce's frequent absences from their Malibu home where she was raising their toddler son. Linda summed up their relationship for the world. "We have a great relationship but not a marriage."

"We are living apart and we still have a wonderful relationship," Bruce parroted.

When the Jenners eventually divorced, *People* magazine offered, "Bruce Jenner was a superb athlete, and he's not bad on television either. But as a husband and a father, well, he's not exactly winning medals."

It was time for Bruce to call his mother again. Esther was in disbelief as her son reported the end of his second marriage.

"It's just irreparable," he said.

"But what about your two baby boys?" she asked.

"I'll make sure they're okay," he replied.

This Could Be Love

Kris was fascinated with Bruce's life story as he recreated the pandemonium over his instant stardom.

"There would be so many people lined up on the streets to get a glimpse of me, that it actually caused traffic jams in major cities," Bruce boasted. "My fingers cramped at night from signing autographs. I was traveling to so many cities that I figured I should just take flying lessons, become a pilot, and fly a plane."

"Seriously?" Kris asked. "That's amazing. Do you still have the plane?"

"Oh yeah, sure. I still have it," Bruce told her.

It seemed like only yesterday that Kris had luxuriated in the extravagance of his-and-her black and white Rolls-Royces during her marriage to Robert. The prospect of this hunk of a man flying her to his hideaway in Tahoe was even more glamorous.

With such a captive audience, Bruce could not stop talking about himself. He wanted Kris to hear how he invented "Bruce Jenner."

"I happened to be the right guy at the right time," he said. "Sports marketing has become very big and I would like to think I was one of the guys who kind of got it started. I always say nobody's worked one performance better than I have. I was in the stadium forty-eight hours and now you can't get rid of me!"

He sensed Kris would enjoy his fun anecdotes about toasting Hugh Hefner at his sixtieth birthday party in 1986. The private soiree at the Playboy Mansion in the Holmby Hills of Los Angeles had been a coveted invite, with guests such as Jacqueline Bisset, James Caan, Whoopi Goldberg, and Mel Torme attending.

The following year he was in Nebraska as a celebrity personality for Willie Nelson's annual Farm Aid benefit for America's farmers.

Kris's eyes widened as he told her what a treat it was for him to stand next to his cohost Dennis Hopper as they watched Neil Young, John Mellencamp, John Conlee, John Denver, Rita Coolidge, Steve Earle, Kris Kristofferson, Emmylou Harris, Lou Reed, John Kay, Joe Walsh, and Arlo Guthrie perform.

Bruce had taken Kris on his sentimental journey, the ups and downs, the triumphs and tragedies, which included two failed marriages and four young children. He told her that when he left that night he would be going home to his squalid existence in a "bungalow, with a sink piled high with dirty dishes, and a dried-out Christmas tree in the living room."

Bruce was skilled at seducing a woman's sympathy with his sad story. Whether deliberate emotional manipulation or an overwhelming need to be understood, this was Bruce's method of bonding with the opposite sex. His first wife Chrystie spent the first four years of their marriage in what might be described as selfless servitude. It's safe to say from Linda Thompson's own account that Bruce "had her at hello" as he shared his tales of being a mistreated husband. The common thread was stirring the need-to-be-needed in these bright, intelligent, and capable women, who then rolled up their sleeves and believed they were equal partners in building a future with Bruce. It was the pitch of a lifetime.

Kris was sophisticated, but she was still thirteen years younger than the more worldly Jenner. With the exception of Todd, Kris had always been more interested in older guys. She was stimulated by learning from them and looking after them. However, she was also at the most vulnerable point in her life. She was just coming out of a shattered marriage and concerned over how she was going to raise four children as a single mother with no real job experience.

"The wheels clicked in my mind," Bruce recalled. "She has four children. I have four children. That's eight kids. Kris has the same amount of baggage that I do."

She had been humbled by her life's situation and wasn't ashamed to reveal that she needed rescuing as much as he did. Kris could not help but immediately feel compassion for Bruce. "I might want to be the person to help Bruce find his way again," she recalled thinking. "For all his movie star looks and charisma, super-sweet showbiz connections, it made no sense that he was just scraping by financially. He certainly wasn't living up to his potential, and he was too young to give up on his life."

Kris decided on the spot she was just the person to change the direction of his life. Candace was right: Bruce Jenner did need Kris Kardashian's help.

She held nothing back when it was her turn to talk about what a shamble her life was at the moment. The hours flew by until it was almost dawn. Kris's mascara stained her cheek as she walked Bruce to the door. They stood still and looked into each other's eyes. Bruce squeezed her tightly with his enormous muscled arms before kissing Kris gently on her lips.

"I'll call you tomorrow," he said.

"Sure," she told him as her dark eyes lit up. "Call me when you get home."

Kris woke up at Candace's with Bruce calling her with an offer to buy her an airplane ticket to meet him in Florida. It was to be a jam-packed three or four days, with a boat race, a golf tournament, and a motivational speech. Bruce wanted her to be his date.

"No hanky-panky," Kris remembered him promising. "I'll get you your own room."

Kris didn't hesitate.

The action never stopped as Kris watched Bruce go from speedboat and NASCAR racing, to professional golf, to speaking before a live audience.

"I had finally met my match," Kris admitted.

Kris didn't know how badly Bruce needed a wardrobe and mental make-over until he picked her up to take her to a private cocktail party honoring Ronald and Nancy Reagan. Once she saw the giant hole in his worn jacket, she realized the depths of his depression and self-neglect. It was obvious he spent more time in isolation than he did putting himself out to succeed in the world. It was also the first time he met the Kardashian kids. His charm as he asked permission to take their mom out worked on all but twelve-year-old Kourtney. Kris fondly recalled the bonding moment she experienced as she saw Bruce's easy and natural way with her kids. She later confessed she fell instantly into a relationship.

"I loved everything about Bruce," she said. "I loved his sense of adventure, his spirit, and his love of kids, especially my kids. I loved that he loved me, and he let me be me."

He already knew what to expect when he invited Kris on this getaway. It was a chance to impress her.

Bruce's instant attraction to Kris's panache and fascination with her gregarious personality grew as he spent more time around her. He had not been looking for love, but Kris's powerful persona, which was on display over his meatloaf and her swordfish on their first date at the Ivy at the Shore, was irresistible.

Bruce and Kris had a courtship not only with each other but with the combined eight children they shared as parents. First came Kim's tenth birthday party in October, then Halloween, Thanksgiving, and Christmas. Bruce saw Kris's flair for creating incredible celebrations of holidays. Bruce was adept at delivering magical and memorable moments to any occasion as well. He proved he could not be outdone in the spectacular department when the Teenage Mutant Ninja Turtles dressed as Santa showed up to entertain Kris's children at Christmas 1990. Bruce's brood joined the fun the following month when all eight children, Kris, Bruce, and Candace and Steve went skiing. Bruce was Kris's shadow, accompanying her everywhere she went, from shopping to hair and nail appointments. And Kris loved it. She saw everything happening between her and Bruce as "God's plan."

The devil was still in the details, though. Kris's blissful romance with Bruce was not without conflict. After all, Todd was still in the picture.

"I wouldn't say we were dating, we were still communicating," Todd dished. "She was still coming over to the apartment and we were still sleeping together when she had started dating Bruce."

In the beginning, Todd was unaware Bruce was his new rival. As far as he knew, she was separated and therefore available. It was as if she never left him. Kris was so deliriously happy with Bruce and distracted by her holiday party planning during the winter months of 1990 that she almost completely put Todd out of her mind. Besides, even if Kris wanted to have one last face-to-face conversation with Todd, it would have been impossible. Bruce was joined to her hip. Photos of Kris and Bruce, which appeared in the weekly glossies, rankled Todd and sent him into a drunken rage. He paid her a visit to her house. Bruce wasn't spending the night with her, and the children were asleep. Todd repeatedly rang the bell at the front gate, demanded she let him in, and then climbed over the wall and banged on her door until she let him in. Kris had never seen Todd so angry.

"Bruce Jenner!" he shouted. "Fucking Bruce Jenner?!"

Kris calmed him down enough to persuade him to go home, but she had another messy love triangle on her hands. Todd would join Robert

Kardashian and Cesar Sanudo in the annals of Kris's jilted lovers. Todd was a ticking time bomb. He was not going away gently into the night as she had hoped. Kris was fielding calls on her cell phone while Bruce was riding in her car. When it became clear to Bruce that Kris was unable to get rid of this Todd character, he stepped in and saved his damsel in distress. He snatched the phone out of her hand.

"You're dating my girl," Kris recalled Todd telling Bruce. Bruce was unflappable and direct in his response.

"This is Bruce Jenner. I'm going out with Kris. I would appreciate if you would never dial this number again. You got that? Good."

As far as Bruce was concerned, that was the end of Todd.

* * *

Bruce had yet another male adversary to free Kris from. The ugly legal wrangling between Kris and Robert over money and their children was still a buzzkill for Bruce and Kris's ecstasy. He became an unwitting supporting player in Robert Kardashian's eighteen-month quest to prove Kris was an unfit mother. Amendments to Robert's divorce petition named Bruce as a man who was staying overnight in Robert's home with his estranged wife. He contended Bruce and Kris's relationship was injurious to his children, claiming his three-year-old son Robert Jr. was asleep on the couch in Kris's bedroom while she slept in her bed with Bruce. It was true that Jenner was sharing Kris's house. She never spent nights with him at his teeny one-bedroom bungalow in Malibu. There was no room for her children, and she found the place a depressing reminder that Bruce's finances were in shambles. She and Bruce were already creating a plan to restore his reputation and his finances, but they needed to sort out old business first. They were on a hamster wheel, with both of them strapped for cash.

Bruce decided to step up and take the lead and negotiate closure with Robert, man to man. Bruce wanted to call Robert and ask him to dinner with him and Kris. Kris was all for it. Even though Bruce, by his own recollection, was $300,000 in debt and had only $200 in the bank when he met Kris, he was confident, and so was she, that they could build a magnificent life together.

Kris's faith in God's plan allowed her to trust Bruce when he said, "We don't need his money." Kris was weary of fighting over tomatoes. It was time to take off her boxing gloves. The sooner she conceded to Robert, the sooner she could officially begin her new life with Bruce. She had a newfound belief in herself as she boldly told Bruce, "I came into that marriage with nothing. I'll leave with nothing."

However, there's little doubt Kris knew she wasn't leaving 9920 Tower Lane with just the clothes on her back.

Bruce Gets a Blessing

Bruce and Kris sat next to each other in a circular red booth across the table from Robert Kardashian in the dimly lit Hamburger Hamlet restaurant on Sunset Boulevard. Bruce immediately disarmed Kris's soon-to-be former husband, when he said, "I'm in love with Kris and I'd like to marry her. We'd like your blessing."

Over the course of dinner, Bruce gave up everything of materialistic value that Kris had held as essential to her financial security—much of which her attorney had skillfully waged battle over for almost two years.

"You take your house," Bruce said. "We don't want your money. Pay your child support, because that's fair, and let's call it a day."

Hammering out a property settlement with a Bruce Jenner handshake was not a new concept to Bruce. He had done it to disentangle himself from his second wife, Linda. It's not known whether Kris was fully aware of the fact that when Bruce walked away from his property, he secured another form of currency for himself: silence from Linda. She and Chrystie could be formidable foes, alone and acting together, for they had a devastating weapon they could fire at his golden image. A war with his exes in a divorce courtroom was the last thing Bruce wanted. If they divulged his secret desire to become a woman, and his fetish for dressing as one, he might never be able to recover from the damage.

Had Robert known Bruce's truth, he would most likely have easily been declared the winner and given sole custody of the Kardashian kids. Ignorant of this significant development in his diligent destruction of Kris's character, a stunned Robert was all too pleased to allow Bruce to act as Kris's legal counsel and sort out their settlement. Everything was decided by the time their after-dinner coffee arrived.

The next morning, a shock wave was felt at Wasser's offices when Kris announced to him that she had her divorce all squared away. Wasser couldn't believe his ears, assuring her that she would have received her house in the settlement. Kris didn't care. She was relieved there was an amicable ending to her nightmare. Her new landlord, Robert, agreed she and Bruce could live in his house rent-free for six months, which freed up space in her head that would allow her the luxury of focusing on her new design for living.

Nesting

Kris knew a solid business plan required the establishment of organized and tranquil surroundings. That was the foundation. Her mentors, Lou Ethel and Mary Jo, were entrepreneurs who founded successful businesses. But first and foremost, they were the CEOs of their homes. As a seven-year-old, Kris was devastated when Mary Jo moved her and sister Karen out of their palatial white house after their dad left. In retrospect, Kris could see her mother's wisdom in letting their dream house go. While it seemed purely a financial decision to her at the time, Kris could now look back with a mature appreciation. Her mother had freed up space for something else to come into her life; namely, her stepdad, Harry Shannon.

Kris could no more create a life with Bruce in the house she shared with Robert than she could have settled down at Robert's bachelor digs years previously. Also, between Bruce's brood and the Kardashian kids, the body count was ten. They needed more room for their blended family. Malibu was an expensive community, so finding an affordable home that was spacious enough to meet their needs was challenging. But Kris persevered. She was prepared for the possibility that it might not have all the bells and whistles she enjoyed during her life at Tower Lane. All Kris needed for inspiration was Bruce's love.

After a long financial drought, Kris finally had some money coming in. She decided to use a portion of her divorce settlement—which included $5,000 a month in child support—to rent a property in Malibu. On a Sunday afternoon in March 1991, she and Bruce drove around looking at properties. Kris frequently added items to the notepad of her "to do" list. She had numerous assignments awaiting her execution. As soon as they found a house, she had to move four children and their menagerie of pets. In addition, she needed to organize Bruce's exit from his dreary bungalow. Nothing got Kris Kardashian's juices flowing like a new project. She could hardly wait to dive into all the mess of unlabeled files Bruce had stashed in cardboard boxes. She wondered how much money he had lost by not attending to business.

Bruce never forgot the first time Kris visited his place.

"She stepped inside and saw the dishes in the sink and the old clothes on the rod and the tiny, dried-out Christmas tree beside the front door as my home's only source of decoration. She asked me what I'd done during the holidays. I told her I just stayed home and had a cup of coffee."

"Where's your gold medal?" Kris asked, quietly surveying the living room.

"It's over here," he said, motioning for her to follow him to the set of bureau drawers by his bed.

Kris stopped behind him and cocked her head to peer over his right shoulder as he opened a drawer full of socks. Kris just smiled, making no comments about what an odd burial place it was for such a prestigious award. Bruce reached to the bottom of the pile and pulled out a small, square box. In the center of the dark brown leather sleeve was the distinctive Olympic design, etched in slightly raised gold ink. Bruce took off the sleeve and opened the hinged wooden box. His gold medal was snugly within a hollow pocket cut out of the wood. Kris gently pressed up against him and admired it over his shoulder.

"It's beautiful, Bruce."

"Uh-huh," he said.

She moved around to get a closer look. She reached out her hand; her delicately manicured fingers grazed over the object. It was rough, not smooth and shiny as she had imagined.

"May I hold it?"

Bruce nodded, pulled it out of its resting place, and dangled it by the link chain. She felt the irregular edges. She put one hand over the other, squeezing the medal between her hands. Kris was overcome with the power of the medallion and the moment between them. She unfolded her fingers, glancing at it one more time before she handed it back to Bruce.

"Thank you," she said, as she watched him place it perfectly, right side up, back inside the box.

His eyes lingered on the medal for a few seconds. After closing it and putting the sleeve back on the box, he tucked it underneath his socks. When he turned around, he realized Kris hadn't moved from her spot. She was studying him as she allowed him the space to briefly awaken another time in which he lived. She just looked at him, still silent, waiting for him to speak first.

"What?" Bruce asked, noticing her damp eyes. "What's wrong?"

"We're going to take the moment that you shined brightest in your life and make sure no one will forget it," she said.

She was on a mission to ensure Bruce Jenner never plummeted into such a place of despair ever again.

He may have experienced a long downward slump, but Bruce's chutzpah in obtaining the financing for the home he bought his first wife Chrystie was a testimonial to his resourcefulness.

It was already one of her favorite stories he told: how he walked into the bank and put his gold medal on the loan officer's desk and said, "Here's my collateral. I want to buy a house."

When she relayed this tale to her friends over lunch one day, she noted, "You can't put a price tag on that kind of ingenuity. It turns me on!"

The gold medal was proof of his work ethic, and his transparency in explaining the reasons behind his reversal of fortune evoked trust in Kris. While Kris felt the occasional butterfly of anxiety flit around her stomach over this unexpected new direction her life was taking, she remained hopeful that she was making a good decision.

According to Bruce, "I told her I'd been miserable for umpteen years. That I'd spent the last six years in a Southern California version of solitary confinement."

He also told her he hadn't been on a date in eight years, a claim both Linda and their former live-in nanny disputed in their respective autobiographies. However, both women agree Kris Kardashian was the first and only woman Bruce had taken a serious interest in since his divorce from Linda.

"We hit it off from day one," Bruce reported.

Kris also felt she had found her soulmate in Bruce.

"I had been lacking the self-esteem to just really be myself, in my own skin, in my own home," she confessed. "Bruce had been lacking his own version of the same thing."

But Bruce had a bigger secret to share.

Bruce later claimed that during this time he told Kris his deep and troubling inner conflict over transitioning to a woman. Bruce was tired of hiding his "dirty little secret" with women for fear that they would be scared off by his truth.

"Bruce told me that he was stopping the hormones and that Kris was okay with everything," Linda revealed in her 2016 memoir. "Keep in mind that Bruce had no hair left on his face, neck or chest, and no hope of ever growing hair there again due to the painful electrolysis he had undergone. In addition, he had already had 'feminizing' surgeries to his face."

Bruce had undergone a nose job and a facelift, and had had his eyebrows thinned out. He also had a portion of his Adam's apple surgically shaved. If these were not telling enough to Kris, then Bruce's large breasts had to have been the perennial elephant in the bedroom, which according to Linda were "noticeable even to his four-and six-year-old sons."

"The point is that he would have had a tough time hiding his partial transition from someone with whom he had become intimate," Linda stated.

According to Bruce: "I started on hormones. I was a good 36B. I loved them. I thought this was fabulous. My mission at that point was to transition before I was forty. I got to thirty-nine . . . I just couldn't go any further."

Should Kris have become alarmed, it's likely he told her what he told CNN in 1988: that he had taken muscle-enhancing hormones that made his breasts bigger too. It was a huge step for Kris to uproot her children and move in with a guy she barely knew who had two failed marriages. However, she was not daunted by the facts and was seemingly unfazed by whatever was behind his "man boobs."

Still, Kris had feelings of shame and disgust from her divorce with Robert that were not entirely blotted from her consciousness. Not in a million years did Kris think she would be calling Robert Kardashian her "ex." Nor did she ever dream she would be a divorcee on the other side of a nasty and humiliating split that thrust the innocent Kardashian kids into a battlefield. She had asked God's forgiveness for her sins, especially for the devastating hurt she had caused Robert and their children. Believing God had forgiven her helped Kris keep her cool. She had followed Wasser's advice to stay as calm as possible in front of the children. Despite all the horrific shouting and dramatic scenes that sometimes ensued when Robert came around, Kris controlled her emotions. Robert's angry behavior in front of the kids resulted in the court awarding Kris custody. Kris considered the outcome a miracle only God could have manifested.

It had been difficult but necessary for her to stand up for herself. She needed the judge to hear her plight.

"Every time Robert and I speak, he emotionally abuses me to the point that I am unable to handle the simplest tasks for hours after our conversation," Kris admitted. "In every conversation Robert and I have, he calls me a 'whore,' a 'bitch,' a 'slut,' and other names I cannot repeat."

It had to be heartbreaking for Kris to read the damning psychological and personality profile from the psychiatrist who interviewed her. The analysis, drawn from the Minnesota Multiphasic Personality Inventory, was certainly far from infallible but was devastating just the same. Her behavior with Todd was certainly a major factor when Kris's mental health was evaluated. The psychiatrist found Kris to be "immature, impulsive, a high risk taker who does things others do not approve of just for personal enjoyment of doing so."

But Kris quickly rebounded from the devastating blow to her psyche. Fortunately, she was spared the devastation of more vicious spewing from Robert's personal diary, in which he accused Kris of passing out on the floor drunk and physically abusing their children. Released many years later by Robert's widow, Ellen Pierson, the diary entries painted Kris as a violent "Mommie Dearest." He alleged that she beat, kicked, and threatened to kill Kim. He also contended that Kris yanked Kourtney's hair in a bout of anger. Kris vehemently denied the veracity of these stories after they were leaked to the tabloids years later. Khloé and other members of the Kardashian family went on a vigorous reputation management campaign to clear their mother's name. It's highly unlikely Robert ever meant for the entries to be made public.

As far as thirty-five-year-old Kris was concerned, she knew all she needed to know about Bruce. He loved her. He loved her kids. In addition to cherishing family, they were equally devout Christians. With God guiding them, there was no mountain too big to climb. They were both warriors. They had faith they would overcome their obstacles and emerge as champions.

With a new lease on life, Bruce quietly buried his dream to transition into a woman.

A Winning Formula

Kris was secure as Bruce's "girl." She was not jealous of every event and woman in his past. She mostly retold the celebrity stories while talking to her girlfriends or Mary Jo and Lou Ethel.

"When she told these tales, she gave such vivid details," a lifelong friend of Kris's said. "I never even thought about how she wasn't actually in those scenes with Bruce. She was so at home with celebrity dish. That jet set lifestyle just seemed to belong to her, so it never seemed phony or fake, or boastful. It was just normal, like hearing about the famous people who were at her parties when she was married to Robert. It was just, 'this is my life.'"

While she only shared the most flattering and impressive news regarding Bruce's life, even his failures were fascinating to Kris. As always, she gave her undivided attention to anything and everything that had to do with showbiz and celebrities. She was a sponge, and Bruce loved talking about himself to such a captive audience as Kris. Bruce was needier of women's applause than most. It had been years since anyone had cared enough to listen to him talk.

Kris skillfully nursed Bruce's fragile ego back to health. She told Bruce he needed to "see and be seen" in Los Angeles. No more tossing the party and gala invites in the trash. He brought the unopened envelopes containing invites for Bruce as a "guest, plus one" to Kris, and they decided together which ones they would attend. Bruce found Kris's salesmanship endearing. She pitched him that the events would "not only be fun, but they would be free entertainment for them." Kris also knew they would be a networking nirvana for her.

Bruce didn't need much convincing. He reckoned it might be fun to go back out on the Hollywood party circuit, especially with the gorgeous and entertaining Kris Kardashian on his arm. He had already witnessed her magic when she accompanied him on out-of-town speaking engagements. But that was amateur hour. They planned to hit up the Academy Awards, the Grammys, and the Golden Globes crowd. Bruce knew all he had to do was give Kris a room, any room, and she could suss out the heavy hitters in a matter of minutes.

Kris had always felt she was an equal partner in the Kardashian household. When Robert entertained clients, Kris often went along, but Robert never allowed her on the front lines of executing and implementing business ideas. And she never asked that her role be any different. But as time passed, she realized her entrepreneurial talents and skills were not being utilized.

With Bruce, Kris was on fire. It was impossible not to take notice of the electric sparks radiating from this synergistic coupling. Even people who had known Kris and Robert soon found themselves comfortable fusing Kris Kardashian and Bruce Jenner. Almost overnight, they were simply "Bruce and Kris" or "Kris and Bruce." The new "it" couple didn't care whose name came first, as long as they were being talked about.

Kris and Bruce saw each other as equals. Bruce never minded stepping back whenever it was time for Kris to shine. She was masterful in redirecting a conversation toward her agenda. In those days, Bruce didn't appear to sense that he might just be Kris's warm-up act.

Once again Bruce had played the popular celebrity couple game. The glamorous husband and wife image Bruce enjoyed with both Chrystie and Linda played extremely well with the media. Kris figured this out and was a quick study during her many hours of listening to Bruce babble about his past. She retained the more useful tidbits during her information gathering. These types of details led her to make assessments critical to turning around Bruce's dire financial situation.

As a wife and mother, Kris understood advertising dollars targeted consumers with families. It wasn't rocket science for Kris to assume that when Bruce discarded his families, he fell from grace with corporate sponsors. As Kris connected the dots for him, Bruce undoubtedly drew his own lines of comparison. While the two former Mrs. Jenners had beauty and charisma, they were meek in comparison to Kris Kardashian. She was stunning, stylish, and her vivacious personality was empowering. "When I met her, she was just a little Beverly Hills housewife," Bruce said, "but packed inside her was an entrepreneur."

Let there be no mistake: Kris was a spotlight thief. But she was savvy enough to always have her sights on the bigger picture. As much as she enjoyed the starring role, she could sense when social cues directed her to shut up. Kris was keenly aware of when to let her gold-medal sports hero serve as the main attraction. Bruce Jenner was the brand.

Bruce Puts a Ring on It

Bruce was so in love with Kris that every day was a special occasion. He loved surprising Kris with bouquets of flowers and silly little presents that made her smile. He frequently presented her with touching cards, which brought her to tears.

On a crisp moonlit night in February 1991, Kris and Bruce walked under the lighted trees leading up the flagstone steps to Saddle Peak Lodge. They were meeting Candace, Steve, and their friend Mary Frann—star of *The Bob Newhart Show*—for dinner.

"Hey, let's order a bottle of champagne just for us before Steve and Candace get here," Bruce said, holding the door open for Kris.

Kris remained quiet as they made their way past the Old West paintings hanging on the gold-flocked walls of the fancy-but-rustic restaurant. They were seated next to the stone fireplace, directly underneath one of the beautiful, dimly lit antique chandeliers. The French doors were open, and Kris could see the cascading waterfall surrounded by green gardens and the spectacular view of the Santa Monica Mountains.

The romantic ambience was their way of celebrating the signing of the lease papers for a house in Malibu. It was a stunning home on Malibu Road and the Pacific Coast Highway. Kris had tried to stay within their budget, but this house was too gorgeous to ignore. Bruce would have been content with less, but he wanted Kris to be happy. He was sharing the fees he had earned from his hodgepodge of public appearances during the short time they had been dating, but Kris was going to have to come up with most of the cash for the home.

"The champagne will be here any second, Kris," Bruce said, aware that she was less talkative than usual.

Her dam had burst on the way to the restaurant. Kris bottom-lined for Bruce what had been on her mind all afternoon.

"I'm taking my kids on this journey with me and it scares me a little bit," she said. "We've leased this house together. We're not married, I've got four kids. It's a little bit weird. I love you, but this feels a little crazy. I've got a big responsibility to my kids."

Before Bruce could respond, the server was at their table, placing crystal flutes in front of them. She held the Dom Perignon label out to Bruce. He nodded his approval. As she twisted the wire, it dawned on Kris that it was strange they were drinking champagne together. While she loved bubbly, Bruce was a beer man.

"Look at me," Bruce said, caressing Kris's hand while the champagne was poured. Bruce got out of his chair and knelt down on one knee and took her hand again.

"Kris, will you marry me?"

The dining room was full of people who were immediately intrigued by the obvious proposal of marriage. Some even whispered, "Is that Bruce Jenner over there asking that woman to marry him?"

Kris was not only delirious over his romantic gesture, but also excited by the attention. All eyes were on her. Bruce was confident she would say yes, but Kris kept the remaining audience in suspense.

"Are you serious?" she asked.

While no doubt sincere, Bruce was also aware of his recognition quotient rising the longer he rested on his knee declaring love for his beloved.

"Yes, of course I am serious. I have already told your ex-husband I am going to marry you. I want to marry you. Let's get married. Let's just do it. Why not? What are we waiting for?"

That was Kris's cue to wrap it up.

"Oh my God," she responded, with queenly dramatic elegance, tears rolling down her cheeks. "This is crazy! Yes, okay. Yes!"

The rest of the evening was all about Kris. Candace, Steve, and Mary noticed Kris's gaiety as they approached their table. Kris was clamoring for Candace's attention.

"Bruce has asked me to marry him," Kris announced. "We're getting married, we're getting married!"

Candace and Mary hugged Kris. Steve held his hand out to shake Bruce's. By this time, the other patrons looked like movie extras. Not only did they have the world's greatest athlete to gaze upon, but also the Los Angeles Dodgers' famous first baseman Steve Garvey.

Kris had called Candace earlier in the day to tell her all about her fabulous new house. Candace had filled Steve and Mary in on the way to the restaurant, and Kris described every feature of the property to them over dinner. Bruce and Steve enjoyed digging into their thick steaks as Kris held court.

Over dessert, Kris drank the last drops of the champagne from the celebratory bottle Steve had ordered. She had settled down and was content listening Bruce talk about her as he replayed the proposal for those who had missed it.

There was only one element missing in this romantic scene: the ring. As the evening progressed, Candace's curiosity often prevented her from catching every word of Kris's captivating conversation. As Steve and Bruce fought over the bill, Candace brought her napkin up from her lap, wiped her lips, and motioned for Kris to join her in the ladies' room. Kris went straight for an empty stall.

"I'm dying to pee, Candace! All that champagne we drank!"

Candace checked her hair in the mirror and applied her lipstick while waiting for Kris to emerge. As Kris washed her hands in the sink, Candace exclaimed, "Okay! Where is it?"

"Where's what?" Kris replied.

"Your engagement ring!" Candace said. "I'm dying to see it! Why aren't you wearing it?"

The missing ring had not slipped Kris's mind either, but she would address this with Bruce in private. Even though Candace was a dear friend and had seen her at her lowest, Kris was not going to give any woman the satisfaction of seeing her lacking in this respect. Kris didn't miss a beat as she looked up into the mirror at Candace's reflection staring back at her, waiting for her response.

"It's coming, don't worry," Kris purred. "Bruce and I are going to wait until after we've moved into a new house and we start making millions again. We are going to be spending a fortune on moving out of Beverly Hills and into Malibu, and we'll need new furniture. Will you go furniture shopping with me?"

It was trademark Kris to deflect a potentially embarrassing moment and skillfully divert the dialogue in a different direction without anyone noticing.

"This is all because of you!" Kris gushed. "Five months ago, I had no clue what in the world I was going to do. It was all a hot mess! Here I am tonight with a new love and the promise of a fabulous life. I will always be grateful to you and Steve for introducing me to Bruce—and so will he!"

Malibu's Least Wanted

In addition to the complexities of moving four children and a fiancé to Malibu, Kris Kardashian had a wedding to plan. It would not be the massive church wedding with three hundred guests as when Kris married Robert. Bruce stayed out of the details, allowing Kris autonomy to execute her vision for their wedding. It was indicative of the free rein Bruce would give Kris in handling all of his other affairs.

Before the wedding, Bruce invited Esther to visit him in Malibu so she could get to know Kris. Bruce's mother had divorced his dad after forty years of marriage and had remarried. She and her second husband Sam were living in Northern California. During their two-hour drive down the Pacific coast, Esther shared how much she was looking forward to meeting Bruce's fiancée.

"Maybe I've got a daughter-in-law I can really relate to," she said.

It had been a quick courtship, but Esther was relieved to hear the excitement in Bruce's voice when he talked about Kris. Her son hadn't sounded so positive in years. And from just the few times they talked on the telephone, Esther found Kris enchanting.

"I thought she loved Bruce," Esther remarked. "I was bound and determined I was going to love any woman that loved my son. She convinced me in the beginning she loved my son."

When Esther and Sam arrived at Kris and Bruce's home, nobody was in the house except the housekeeper. "We went out on the patio and sat and read magazines for two or three hours," Esther recalled. "No Bruce. No Kris. No kids. No notes."

When Bruce and Kris finally arrived home, Esther found Kris's behavior strange.

"Kris didn't say hello or look our way, even though she saw us standing there, hugging Bruce," Esther recalled. "Kris headed straight for the telephone. We heard her returning her messages. When we asked Bruce where they had been, he said Kris decided to go to the movies."

This puzzled Esther.

"Knowing we were coming and when we were coming, they just took off and went to the movies," Esther huffed years later. "If that isn't rude!"

Esther decided not to call Kris out on her apparent disregard for Bruce's family. She didn't want to upset Bruce, as she had less than twenty-four hours to visit with her son.

"I was deeply disappointed because I was ready to welcome Kris with open arms, just like I did Linda, and just like I did Chrystie. I loved Chrystie and I loved Linda."

While Kris continued to have a lot of "important things to do" that required Bruce's "immediate attention," Sam took a nap in the guest bedroom and Esther was left sitting on the patio with Kris's sister, who had also been at the cinema.

"I found Karen to be a breath of fresh air," Esther confessed. "She was quietly kicking her feet around in the swimming pool while Bruce and I were talking. She could tell I was out of sorts, so she said, 'Come over here, Mrs. Jenner, and put your feet in the water.'"

Esther obliged and sat next to Karen on the edge of the pool. She smiled for the first time since her arrival.

"Don't let Kris upset you," Karen whispered to Esther. "She can't help it. You're lucky she's ignoring you and not on your ass like she is me! She's been ragging on me all day."

Esther was surprised by Karen's candor, having only just met her. But at the same time, she found it refreshing. She couldn't help but notice how different the two sisters were.

"Karen was a beautiful girl," Esther commented. "She and Kris looked very similar, as they both had striking facial features, but Karen was dressed down and casual, while Kris came back from the movies looking like she had been to a film's premiere."

"Why on earth would Kris take issue with you?" Esther asked.

Karen smiled.

"Kris is so unhappy with me because I won't date the kinds of men she thinks I should date," she responded.

"Well, why does she care who you date, Karen?" Esther wondered.

"First of all, they've got to have money," Karen matter-of-factly explained. "They've got to have a position in life. All Kris really cares about is the money. Money is the most important thing."

"Oh, I see," Esther said, slightly troubled over what her son was getting into by marrying Kris.

"Yeah, my sister was born with a Maserati in her mouth."

Esther mulled that last comment over as Kris called to her through the French doors across the patio.

"Esther, there's plenty of food in the refrigerator. Help yourself. I have some more phone calls to make."

Esther's eyebrows furrowed in disdain. When she turned around to respond, Kris had already vanished from view. Esther turned back around to Karen wearing a saccharine smile.

"I just can't get over how translucent your eyes are," Karen said. "Do you wear contacts?"

Before responding, Esther realized Karen wanted to help her avoid unpleasantness during such a brief visit. Esther appreciated Karen's subtleties in this moment they shared. She noted how Karen could rival her older sister's brand of beauty if she so chose. Karen was indeed much smarter than she let on; maybe Kris didn't even acknowledge just how clever.

"I liked Karen," Esther reflected. "She reminded me of me. I don't pull any punches. I just tell it like it is."

Esther was relieved to know she would have at least one person she could relate to in this new family of Bruce's.

Here Comes the Third

Pam Behan's first day on the job caring for Kris Kardashian's kids was April 21, 1991. The nanny reported to work at the multimillion-dollar Bel Air mansion that Sunday afternoon dressed for a wedding. Pam's new boss was the bride.

The setting for the Kardashian-Jenner nuptials was only a mile from Beverly Hills, where Pam had previously worked as a nanny for Bruce's ex-wife Linda. Her current task was supervising Kris's four children and their soon-to-be stepsiblings. Pam was aware of how any special occasion triples the chances for unpredictable behavior in children. In addition, the new nanny was unfamiliar with their personalities and family rules. The tribe of eight could use this to their supreme advantage.

Nanny Pam's worst fear was realized when saw the girls were all dressed in white dresses and the boys in matching white tuxedo shirts and bowties. But if she successfully prevented stained wardrobe disasters, she hoped to still have her position by the time the wedding cake was sliced.

The wealth and splendor of Kris Kardashian's wedding to Bruce was like nothing she had ever witnessed.

"The event and setting seem like a royal wedding," she said, totally blown away by the "beautiful people and extravagance" of the event.

The elegant affair was held at the magnificent estate of Warner Brothers studio chief Terry Semel. Jane, a former assistant to actress Susan George, married the movie mogul in 1977. Kris had been a friend of Jane's since their twelve-year-old daughters were toddlers.

The lush landscaping provided the backdrop for the ceremony and reception. White and pink rose blooms marked the end of each row of white folding chairs. Across the lawn, where the reception was held, there were arrangements of white roses and hydrangeas as centerpieces. Baccarat crystal flutes and other glassware waiting to be filled with champagne and wine reflected the twinkling of the sun's rays. Bone china and silver flatware rested on the stark white linen coverings.

This was Kris's show. She was the star and was going to make sure her "audience" was left with an affair to remember. By thirty-five, Kris had perfected her studies in chicness and was in her prime as a sophisticated woman.

Kris's dark pixie hair was styled like Princess Diana. Her surgically enhanced bosom was center stage, and her cleavage was exquisitely framed in her form-fitting bodice. She boldly bared her arms, and her skin was exposed from her chest to the simple white choker around her neck. Diamond and pearl earrings dropped just past her earlobes. Her makeup was subtle but sensational, and her false eyelashes had been expertly arranged—a dramatic contrast from the Maybelline spider lashes she sported as the bride of Robert Kardashian.

Bruce's pale pink bowtie atop his white shirt complemented Kris's glamour. He was the essence of handsome masculinity in his black tuxedo. He stood at the altar watching Kris walk down the flower-lined aisle to meet him. As she reached the front row, Kris's moist eyes glanced over at her mother, who was sitting next to Harry, Karen, and Lou Ethel.

Kris winked at Khloé, her flower girl, whose puffy-sleeved dress matched those worn by her sisters, Kim and Kourtney, and Bruce's daughter Casey. The little princesses wore tiaras of baby's breath in their hair. Burt, Brandon, and Brody looked adorable as miniature versions of Bruce, alongside the three-year-old ring bearer, Robert Kardashian Jr. Everyone played their parts to perfection.

The general sentiment was that Mr. and Mrs. Bruce Jenner were Hollywood's new power couple. But Bruce's mom and family were not so impressed with the duo.

"We were seated way, way away from Kris's family and her friends," Esther recalled. "It was pretty obvious where we stood."

Kris eventually made her way over to her new mother-in-law, as Bruce's sister Pam was proudly showing recent Jenner family photos to Esther. Kris put her hands on the backs of their chairs.

"What are you guys looking at?" she asked.

"Pictures of Casey," Pam replied.

Kris gestured for Pam to hand her the small photo album and her eyes moved swiftly over the image of Bruce's only biological daughter. "She's really pale," Kris said. "So much lighter than my three girls." She smiled and snapped the album shut without looking at any other photos. "Well, I've got to get back to my other guests, but there's plenty of champagne and food," Kris stated. "You really must try the wedding cake. It's called a white berry cake and it's from Sweet Lady Jane's, which is a delicious bakery on Melrose Avenue. Make sure you get a slice! It's to die for!"

CHAPTER SEVEN
GETTING DOWN
. . . TO BUSINESS

Under New Management

George Wallach loosened his tie while stopped at a red light on his way home from Bruce's wedding.

It was hard for him to believe the four Jenner kids were now old enough to call him "Uncle" George. The three boys looked just like their dad. He had grown to love Bruce like a son in the fifteen years he'd been his manager. Bruce sought his advice on more than just business issues; he trusted Wallach with his life. After Bruce shared his desperate longing to be a woman, Wallach was fiercely protective of his secret. While he was fairly certain publicity surrounding Bruce's gender transition would jeopardize their joint financial ventures, Wallach never discouraged Bruce from following his heart's desire.

Wallach said nothing to Bruce about his client's changing appearance over the past five years. Wearing shirts a size or two larger generally concealed Bruce's growing breasts, but other feminization procedures were steadily becoming more apparent. A handful of journalists were reporting his changing appearance, which meant corporate sponsors were keeping up with the commentary, and the Jenner brand was in trouble. Wallach was optimistic that Bruce's new wife would change his perspective. His client already seemed happier than he had in a long time. Wallach hoped for the best.

Kris and Bruce postponed their honeymoon in Ireland. Kris wanted the chance to reorganize Bruce's business. They had the rest of their lives for holidays.

Even after the move into their new home, Bruce's gold medal had not been disturbed. It was still with his socks. But it was calling out to Kris. It was not only evidence of past greatness; it was a symbol for moving forward. One evening, she was compelled to get up from her bed and pull the award out of the drawer. Framed and on the wall, it would serve as motivation for them both. Like the medal, which needed to be shined before it was put on display, all Bruce needed was to pick himself up and wipe off the dust.

"So, what's your plan?" Bruce asked.

"Well, there should be Bruce Jenner clothing, Bruce Jenner exercise products, Bruce Jenner endorsement deals, Bruce Jenner vitamin supplements," Kris said. "We'll build this house one speech and one endorsement at a time," she assured her husband.

Bruce liked what he was hearing. He always wanted his partner in marriage to be his partner in business. To a limited degree Chrystie had played agent, but once he won the decathlon neither of them thought any more about it. She most likely would have been in over her head. For a time, Linda thought she wanted to be his representative, and she had the smarts and personality for it, but she admitted later she lacked the necessary ambition. There was no question Kris had the drive and marketing savvy to reignite his career. She never doubted she could go from housewife to Bruce Jenner's new brand builder.

To Kris, it was obvious that Wallach had to go. She broke the news to Bruce.

"We need to write George a letter and give him our new address, so he knows where to send your appearance fees and royalties," Kris said, easing Bruce into the chat.

"Okay, not a big deal," he replied. "I have his address in a book on the desk."

"Secondly," Kris continued. "I need to formally dismiss him as your manager and instruct him to refer all business opportunities to me. This is how this is done, Bruce. I lived with a lawyer, remember?"

"I get it, Kris, and I'm not arguing with you, but George and I go way back. I can't terminate our business relationship with a formal letter. It's cold and it's cruel."

"Agreed," she said. "So, what's your plan?"

"I was thinking I would call him up and ask him to meet us for lunch sometime," Bruce offered.

"If you call him now, maybe he can meet us tomorrow," Kris pressed. "He likes that Italian restaurant on Beverly Boulevard near his office, and there's a slew of stationery shops around there. We can order letterhead and business cards for you and me afterwards."

Bruce consented to the plan.

As Wallach walked the few blocks from his antique store to Il Piccolino, where he was meeting Kris for lunch, he was blissfully unaware that he was going to get the ax. He was ten minutes early, but they were already waiting on him, sitting close to each other in a corner booth.

They exchanged pleasantries as they decided on their lunches. Kris asked Wallach's advice on what she should order. Wallach noticed nothing peculiar about their behavior. Bruce exuded warmth as he and Kris shared their new adventures with the kids living in Malibu.

Wallach was eager to bring Bruce up to speed on the business opportunities he had in mind for him for the rest of the year. It wasn't long before Wallach realized Kris was resisting his ideas.

Kris had no interest in hurting Wallach's feelings. Letting him go was strictly a business decision. She hoped Wallach would take his firing like a professional and not engage in a debate. If he did, he would lose. Kris would inquire why Bruce had been living paycheck to paycheck for the past five years. There could only be two explanations. Either Wallach wasn't hustling, or his client was refusing work. Kris knew Bruce was a hard worker or he would never have accomplished everything he had. If Bruce had turned down some work due to bouts of depression, then a good manager should get the client help for whatever was holding them back from working. Wallach didn't strike Kris as lazy, just perhaps not hungry enough, or maybe he didn't have the creativity Bruce needed at that stage in his life. Whatever the case, out of respect for Bruce, Kris would not point fingers at Wallach unless he laid himself open to criticism. Kris wanted to find solutions, not faults.

"Whatever I wanted to bring in, they weren't interested in," recalled Wallach. "I didn't want to compete. I knew it was over before they even told me. I'm smart enough to know how to handle it. I was used to Chrystie and Linda having their ideas, and I respected them and Bruce enough to listen. And even when he divorced them, there was no animosity between them and me. I was still a part of their lives. Bruce always treated me like family. But this was going to be different, I could just tell. I sensed when lunch was over, Bruce and I would be over, and that made me sad."

Bruce said very little. Kris continued to run the meeting. She wanted all of Bruce's contracts and other files sent to her as soon as possible.

"I felt like she deliberately went out of her way to hurt me," he reflected. "It's one thing that I got fired, but I wasn't given an opportunity in even a small way to continue my relationship with Bruce, not even as friends. She wasn't going to allow the two of us to communicate. Looking back, I don't think I could have done any better than she did, but I could have added stuff. I would have liked to have gone on with my life, made a few extra dollars, and continued the friendship. They took that away from me."

Wallach was offended that neither Kris nor Bruce attempted to validate all the opportunities he had brought to fruition during the fifteen years he worked as Bruce's manager. According to Wallach, "Kris really got my dander up with her smugness. I looked at her, thought plenty, and just kept my mouth shut. I would have liked to have ripped her a new one though. Imagine if I had looked her straight in the eye and said, 'Without me, Bruce Jenner wouldn't have happened. Can you not see that I had a lot to do with Bruce

Jenner's success?'" After she was done with giving Wallach his outgoing "to-do" list, Kris was back to the gaiety they had enjoyed at the beginning of lunch. "Shall we share a dessert, now that I don't have to be concerned with fitting into a wedding gown?"

That evening over supper, while they refereed the kids prattling on about their day, Bruce reviewed Kris's performance with Wallach.

"You did an outstanding job this afternoon on every level," he told her. "After today I hope you never doubt yourself."

"Oh, I don't, but thank you," she said, smiling sweetly.

The Bottom Line

Once she received all of his contracts and files from Wallach, Kris worked around the clock learning everything she could about the business of Bruce Jenner. She was never shy about asking for help from businesspeople in her lives whom she respected. She had Mary Jo, Ethel, and her stepdad's diverse experience, as well as Steve Garvey, whose post-sports ventures were similar to Bruce's brand. By this time, Kris and Robert were on friendly terms and she ran ideas past him. He was knowledgeable regarding the ins and outs of all of O. J. Simpson's endorsement deals and business ventures.

Everybody liked Bruce Jenner. He was an affable guy, in a homespun Andy Griffith way. He didn't need to beat you over the head with his cleverness. He maintained a good relationship with his two ex-wives and believed Kris and Robert, who shared four children together, should be on more friendly terms for their kids' sake. Kris was amicable to seeing Robert socially. When he heard Bruce talk lovingly about his children, and he saw how they were working hard to provide a bright future for his family, Robert began to thaw.

Robert sent his former assistant Lisa Frias to work for Kris. She retired Bruce's decades-old typewriter and replaced it with computers. She also enlisted a posse of gal pals who possessed talents that aligned with Kris's mission, and who were all passionate about helping her.

In the summer of 1991, Kris was sequestered in her office going over figures and reports while Bruce bonded with Kourtney, Kim, Khloé, and Rob Jr. along Malibu's miles of ocean, hills, and trails. Kourtney played along, but it was obvious to everyone that she was not going to roll over and accept Bruce. No man was going to take the place of her dad. Kourtney used fashion to express her displeasure with the new family dynamics. According to Kris, Kourtney "dressed in black during those days whenever Bruce was around."

The Fixer-Upper

Kris hired a production company to compile a promotional reel of Bruce's greatest moments, from the iconic photos of him crossing the finish line at the Olympics to the headlines and magazine covers he dominated. She wanted the video package to include television interviews, clips of him as a speaker, and his pitches for products. It took weeks to organize Bruce's materials, most of which were scattered in boxes.

Before she left each day, Kris's assistant would place a new pile of photos on Kris desk for her to review overnight. Kris was meticulous in her selection of the photos for the press kit she was producing, which she planned to send out to all of the speakers bureaus in the United States. It had to tell a story—Bruce's story. It had to convey the rise of a dyslexic kid from upstate New York who dared to reach for the American dream. Just as everyone remembered where they were when President John F. Kennedy was assassinated, they should wax sentimental over the memory of seeing Bruce Jenner champion the US against their opponent, the USSR, and become an American hero.

Glimpses of Jenner with other celebrities were important for reps of speakers agencies outside of Los Angeles and New York City. However, Kris didn't automatically approve every shot. There was a "keepers" file and a "reject" file. No matter how big the star, if they suggested any negativity or detracted from Bruce's wholesome, fresh-faced image, they were of no use.

The "keepers" shots included Bruce embracing other sports heroes such as Muhammad Ali, or Bruce cohosting alongside the legendary broadcaster Howard Cosell. Meet and greets with major political figures and their wives, like Ethel Kennedy and former President Gerald Ford at the White House, even if his ex-wife Linda Thompson appeared in them, met Kris's criteria.

There was the *Playgirl* magazine for May 1982 with Linda and Bruce on the cover. Kris had long been curious about seeing it. Needing to take a break one day, Kris grabbed a bottle of wine and a glass from the kitchen—plus her professional photographer's loupe—and picked up the issue. The backdrop for the *Playgirl* photo was a white bathroom tile with a wet-headed, shirtless Bruce smiling straight into the camera. Linda's long, curled locks were pulled back from her face and her head was tilted back, eyes closed, giving her hubby a sensual kiss on the cheek. The illusion was that they were in the shower together. It was obvious Bruce had much more hair on his chest. In photos of Bruce standing outside his dressing room trailers, he wore a cut-off shirt and shorts. Kris could not have helped but notice the thick line of hair running down his six-pack abs to his belly button, or the thick hair on his upper thighs and lower legs. Whatever she noticed, she said nothing about it to anyone.

Wallach had been cooperative and compliant in relinquishing his files pertaining to Bruce. He had even turned over more information than Kris had requested. He had done a lot of her homework for her, providing names, telephone numbers, and addresses for people Bruce had worked with in the past. Kris was able to analyze where the fat needed to be trimmed in Bruce's game plan.

"Every time I run across yet another missed opportunity from Bruce's stuff, it makes me sick at my stomach," Kris told her small staff. "Follow-through is critical. I'm really big on the execution of ideas. It doesn't make sense to me for Bruce to have this many people he's needing to pay percentages to, especially right now as we rebuild."

From the stack of press clippings, Kris pulled an interview where Bruce listed his chain of command in his organization to a writer at *Sports*

Illustrated. "This is how the system works," he said. "Number one—George Wallach. George oversees everything. He's my right-hand man, my personal manager. From there, the William Morris Agency. The Wheaties deal . . . they handle all the big stuff."

Going down the list, there was a speakers bureau that handled Bruce's speaking engagements, and the licensing and marketing company for the clothing lines, shirts, shoes, and athletic wear.

At one point, Bruce described Rogers and Cowan, the most powerful public relations firm in Hollywood, to the journalist: "They are the publicity people. They handle all the press. Their main function is to keep me out in the public, in the proper way."

Kris, of course, was familiar with the Beverly Hills PR firm. While on Robert's arm, she had met the owners of the firm at various galas and events, and the Kardashians traveled in the same circle of stars who were represented by the firm. Almost all of the A-list talents from LA to New York were signed to them. Unlike agents and managers who charged commissions for their services, it was standard practice in the industry for publicists to charge a monthly retainer. They had a reputation as the best crisis and reputation management agency in the business. They were powerfully adept at preventing scandals about their famous clients from ever seeing the light of day. All in all, this agency was as pricey as it was quality.

In the notes she retrieved from Wallach pertaining to his conversations with people about Bruce, the name Alan Nierob, from Rogers and Cowan, leapt out at her. Bruce had brought him up a few times to Kris, mentioning how fond he was of the showbiz publicist. He told her how Nierob helped him out a few times without charging him for his services. Bruce didn't give her the particulars as to what the PR professional had done for him. It was not uncommon for public relations firms, no matter how successful they were, to shave off hours off their retainers, especially for elite clients. As a gold-medal sports hero who was popular in the media, it was good business to keep a client like Bruce Jenner happy. She had no way of knowing then

that this Nierob had made a potentially devastating story about Bruce
vanish.

* * *

It was a crisis situation when Wallach reached out to Nierob in the mid-
1980s. A reporter for *The New York Times* was doggedly pursuing a tip that
the world's greatest athlete was a cross-dresser. Bruce was previously represented by a publicist at William Morris, but Wallach trusted only Nierob's
counsel on how to disarm this ticking time bomb. It would take only a single
story about Bruce Jenner dressing up as a woman to destroy his image and
wreck his career. Nierob was a master strategist, and he had nurtured good
relationships with journalists and editors, some of whom owed him favors.
Wallach knew Nierob was an honorable man and would never betray him. If
he was going to help, Bruce was going to have to come clean and tell Nierob
everything.

He revealed to Nierob he had always felt more feminine than masculine.
As far back as a child, he had known he was a girl in a boy's body. His mother
and sister never knew that while they were away from the family's apartment
in Tarrytown, New York, he had dressed in their clothes. He loved both of
his former wives, and wanted the four children they gave birth to, but as
much as it pained him to hurt them, he was unable to deny the woman inside
him. He had explained how he was in therapy with a psychologist who specialized in gender dysphoria and was proceeding with his plan to
transition.

Nierob found Bruce's honesty endearing and had compassion for his
struggle. He agreed to discreetly help Bruce, free of charge, as a friend. If
Bruce didn't pay him, Nierob wouldn't have to turn a timesheet over to the
guys in billing at Rogers and Cowan. The fewer eyes and ears on this, the
better for Bruce. The journalist, his editor, and *The New York Times* management team were no match for Alan Nierob, who tore away at the premise.

They ultimately backed off the news story. While rumors continued to plague Bruce, nothing ever made it into print from that day forward.

It's not known whether Kris was able to connect the dots regarding Alan and Bruce's business together, based purely on seeing his name attached to notes with Wallach's doodling. Even if she did, since Bruce wasn't paying Nierob, there was no need to inquire any further to assess the value of his services. Kris felt if she could handle managing Bruce's business life, she could also look after his public relations.

Kris read the remainder of the *Sports Illustrated* article to finish outlining each of Bruce's business team member's duties. "Then there is the number one boss, Chrystie Jenner. The Boss. She's a very strong, aggressive, determined lady," Bruce reported. The article stated:

> *Chrystie, who also has written a book and is a burgeoning actress, got her nickname last year when she, Wallach, and Jenner's attorney Alan Rothenberg were interviewing potential accountants. One of the applicants was puzzled about her function in the operation and queried her about it. "Well," answered Chrystie, "I guess you could say I'm the boss."*

For Kris, it was yet another position in Bruce's corporate structure that didn't need filling. She had become all the boss lady Bruce would ever need.

Nips and Tucks

Kris's tireless efforts breathed new life into Bruce's business and image. The phones were ringing off the hook. By the fall of 1991, Kris was in a position to increase his speaking fees. Just as she hoped, her gorgeous sales presentation kit opened many doors. Kris dragged Bruce away from his toys—the motorized miniature cars and helicopters—and the two networked tirelessly at every cocktail party, showbiz event, and charity gala.

Bruce and Kris fed off each other's exhilaration over the attention they received when they were out together. They would come home and kick their shoes off and climb into the Jacuzzi on their patio. They were an unstoppable pair. Kris worked closely with a high-end men's clothing designer to outfit Bruce with an executive man's wardrobe. The designer was so stimulated by Mr. and Mrs. Jenner's charisma and passion that he didn't charge them for creating Bruce's new look. They had an "it" factor that was mesmerizing.

When Kris wasn't at an event, she was on the telephone making cold calls. She ignored the well-meaning assistants who attempted to give her the runaround. She politely wore them down by chatting them up and personalizing the call until they put the top influencers and decision-makers on the phone; the more powerful the executive, the more intense the rush for Kris. She loved the masterful feeling of engaging them with her calculating and strategic pitches. She was always prepared with her research on the company and the major players, and she zoomed in on their sweet spot every time. They were compelled to listen.

"Hi, this is Kris Jenner, Bruce Jenner's manager. Are you sitting down? I've got an amazing proposition. Would you like to hear it?"

Kris understood the efficiency and effectiveness a great team afforded them. She never asked anyone on her team, salaried employees or volunteers, to do anything she wasn't doing herself. "She was artful in her ability to listen," an intern from these early days observed. "No matter what the obstacle was, I never saw her act in a reactionary way. She was smooth like that. Disarming."

Kris was generous with praise and presents for jobs well done, but it was sometimes difficult for her office staff to keep up with her, since she was such a fireball. She was aware that no matter how much they cared, the stakes would never be as high for them as they were for her. After all, it was just a job to them. It was her life, her husband's and her children's lives. She could not fail. Whenever she spotted a lull in activity from her worker bees, she could effortlessly, without speaking a word, snap them back into action. Whether she was on the phone or reading at her desk, all she had to do was look up, smile, and nod her head, directing their attention to her inspiration wall to get them back in alignment. Next to Bruce's gold medal on the wall hung Kris's mantra, a framed message penned in green, the color of money: "If somebody tells you no, you're talking to the wrong person."

As Bruce's manager, publicist, and wife, Kris traveled everywhere with him. She relied more and more on her live-in nanny, Pam. The Kardashian children were attending three different private schools.

Despite the assistance of a staff, Kris was understandably under a great deal of stress. She bore the brunt of the responsibility for everyone's well-being. She was fearless because she knew she had to be.

"I have a lot of little mouths to feed, and this is a lot of education to provide," she recalled thinking in those days. "I cannot let them suffer or do without. I can't disappoint them. It's not an option. I must keep going." It was stressful, but Kris's strong will and determination helped her stay with it. Her main objective was to figure out how to make an income happen for her family—no matter what.

"The hard work didn't scare me," she admitted. "Every time I would go to bed at night and put my head on the pillow and thank God for what a great day it had been."

Frenemy First

Upon celebrating a year of marriage, Kris and Bruce packed up their Malibu home in 1992 and moved to a house in Benedict Canyon in Beverly Hills. The new house was closer to where the Kardashian sisters were attending their private Catholic school on Sunset Boulevard. Robert Jr. was also entering elementary school, and all of the children had friends and activities that demanded multiple hours a week in driving time.

It was also more convenient for shuttling the kids back and forth to Robert, who no longer lived in Beverly Hills. The Kardashian kids spent every other weekend with him.

Robert was generous to his children and contributed to their privileged lifestyle, but he was not overly indulgent. He was interested in teaching them the value of money, sharing biblical scriptures and spiritual teachings, as well as helping them with their school studies.

Nanny Pam noted in her diary how Bruce brought "a sense of calm and normalcy" to the Kardashians.

Bruce's biological children were disappearing into the background, despite living nearby with their mom and new stepdad in Malibu. While the Jenner offspring were in close proximity and ages to the Kardashian sisters, they were a country apart in terms of developing close family ties.

Linda had also remarried. A few months after Kris and Bruce's nuptials, Linda wed Grammy-award winning songwriter David Foster. It was David's third marriage.

Unlike Robert and Kris's divorce, where they were temporarily mortal enemies, Linda and Bruce had an amicable divorce and she considered them best friends. She remained his confidant over the several years he was transitioning to being a woman. After marrying David, Linda believed her and Bruce's blended families would provide stability and joy for their boys. But almost immediately after Bruce married Kris, he cut Linda out of his life.

"Of course, I knew Bruce had a new partner," Linda stated. "I had no desire to compete with her."

But Linda was disheartened and disappointed when Bruce turned into an absentee dad with their children. She claims he didn't send cards or call them on their birthdays or Christmas.

"I'm sure Kris was a lifeline for Bruce," she noted. "And having needed my own lifeline in the wake of his revelation to me, I did not fault him for turning to his new marriage as a source of solace. I only wished his distancing himself from his old life had not been so resolute and profound, given the pain it caused our sons. How could a parent not even pick up the phone to call their child on his birthday and say, 'Happy Birthday'?"

This is the same Linda who loved Bruce unconditionally when he withdrew emotional and physical support from his then-pregnant wife Chrystie. Linda loved him no less when he didn't visit the mother and child in the hospital in the days after his daughter's birth. After Linda and Bruce married, his children with Chrystie were always included in Linda and Bruce's family celebrations. But it appears it was Linda, not Bruce, who nurtured these relationships.

"While Kris says, 'family comes first,' she means *her* family," a longtime friend of Kris's revealed. "She's extremely possessive in all of her relationships. She doesn't like attention divided from her. If it's 'her' kids, 'her' mother, it's still all about Kris."

* * *

The hostility and resentments Robert had harbored against Kris were almost nonexistent by the time Robert moved in with his gorgeous blonde fiancée Denice Shakarian Halicki. The couple shared Halicki's fifteen-room house, ten miles away from Beverly Hills in the beautiful suburb of Encino. She was part Norwegian and part Armenian and had her own Rolls-Royce and her own money. The former model and actress had been married to a dynamic multimillionaire film producer, who was also a stuntman with a massive collection of vintage cars he used in movies. A few months after they married, he was killed during a car stunt.

The Kardashian children began spending more time with Robert during the week. The half-hour drive between Kris's house in Beverly Hills, school, and Robert's home was becoming more difficult. They got along well with Denice. Kris liked her as well.

Kris and Bruce were traveling all over the world with his motivational speaking gigs and corporate entertaining for Fortune 500 companies. Kris had built Bruce back to almost-millionaire status within three years, but they were away from their kids more than a hundred nights a year. Kim and Kourtney were more than happy to spend all the time they could with their dad, but Kris and Bruce's travel schedule was taking its toll on the younger Khloé. The innocent nine-year-old dented Kris's carefully crafted image during an interview. Khloé blurted she didn't know where to call Bruce when he and Kris were away, and said she cried when they were gone for long periods of time. She also declared that her teenager sisters "aren't very nice" for spending all their time talking on the phone with friends.

Kris managed to get a polar opposite spin on the sad story a month later. Instead of focusing on the detrimental effects business travel has on kids, the Associated Press wrote that "working vacations/business trips can become fun family adventures."

Bruce was described as "the road-warrior family man." And instead of being chided for leaving their kids home alone for half the year, Kris and Bruce were lauded for often taking "at least one of their eight children" on the road with them.

"It's important for them to see what Dad does on the road," Bruce stated.

Still, despite the retooled image, Khloé didn't quite fit in with the "Brady Bunch" family line. She appeared lonely, braving a closed-mouth half-smile while slumped up against her stepdad's shoulder. However, the older Kardashian girls—dressed in California casual wear—gave off megawatt smiles.

TV Beckons

In the 1980s, when VHS machines moved in to keep color television sets company, celebrity fitness videos became en vogue.

Cable television enabled the transformation of the traditional TV commercial with the introduction of long-form infomercials, half-hour advertisements thinly disguised as entertainment. An eclectic mix of stars capitalized on the new programming.

Both of Bruce's former wives had been willing partners in creating a family fitness empire. They saw the potential. *Bruce and Chrystie Jenner's Guide to Family Fitness* book had been published in 1978. And Linda costarred in the *Bruce Jenner: Winning Workout* video in 1984. Yet neither of these ventures with Bruce's ex-wives progressed any further than the initial splash of publicity.

With Bruce already providing the face for a chain of workout gyms called Bruce Jenner's Westwood Centers, Kris decided they, too, would cash in on the fitness craze. Privately, Bruce detested working out in gyms. He preferred outdoor sports and activities such as golf. He even told his nanny he "would never work out another day in his life, because he was so sick of it." Kris decided Bruce would do an infomercial.

Kris instinctively knew to always go to the top of the food chain when it came to establishing a new business venture. She often resembled an executive headhunter in her strategic pursuit of the most successful direct-to-consumer marketer. So she relied on word-of-mouth advertising. She called everybody she knew with experience and knowledge in this industry and analyzed the leading infomercial celebrities' marketing alliances. She wanted the firms that entertained Fortune 500 status. As usual, Kris found the perfect match on her short list of nominees: Jack Kirby. In fact, Kirby had already worked with Bruce.

Kirby, a pioneer in the industry, was considered one of the leading direct-to-consumer marketers. He loved Kris's idea. He had long wanted to create an infomercial brand around a married couple committed to a healthy lifestyle. Kris began to find that she was instinctively on the cutting edge of the "next big thing" just as it was being introduced.

Kris was always eager to learn the soup-to-nuts principles of any business from a master. Some of these guys could be a little rough around the edges, but they enjoyed mentoring a young woman who was smart and creative. Though these were platonic relationships, it was a plus if she happened to be pretty like Kris.

"I lovingly refer to her as the Velvet Hammer," Kirby said, impressed with Kris's brilliant business acumen from the beginning. "A lot of time women in this business are unfairly categorized as bitchy. Kris was a smart woman, so she would go on a charm offensive and make you love her." Having never appeared on television before, Kris admitted to having a bad case of nerves. For the launch of their first infomercial, she was next to Bruce in her teal spandex shorts and matching sports bra. They were pitching "SuperFit with Bruce Jenner," which involved the SuperStep aerobics machine and Stairclimber Plus fitness equipment.

"With a wife and kid, it's hard to find time to exercise," Jenner explained to their first home fitness infomercial audience. Bruce and Kris's husband and wife workout was an immediate hit with viewers and quickly went to number one. More infomercials followed in rapid succession. Their infomercials were seen over two thousand times a month in over a dozen countries.

To Each Their Own Network

In 1993, Oprah Winfrey and Kris Jenner were living large and dreaming big as they each neared their forties. While their individual backgrounds were as different as night and day, these ambitious and driven women had the same goal: to create a television network. Oprah didn't have the foggiest idea of Kris's existence when she wrote in her journal that she would one day have her own television network. Of course, everyone knew Oprah Winfrey, the multiple Emmy-winning, rich but relatable mogul who had triumphed over adversity and left a past of poverty in Mississippi for a career in broadcast journalism.

However, in 1994, it was Kris Jenner, not Oprah Winfrey, who was poised to launch her own television cable network. Had it not been for a catastrophic unforeseen tragedy of epic proportions, Kris would have gone down in history as the first female to provide empowering health and wellness network cable programming.

Entertainment producers Larry Namer and Alan Mruvka were the founders of E! Entertainment Television. Namer had successfully launched other networks around the world before registering FX television, which gave way to Fitness Interactive Television Inc. (FIT). Namer wanted to partner with Bruce, Kris, and O. J. Simpson to offer 24/7 fitness programming.

Kris was no longer a trophy wife observing from the sidelines. She was taking her own page out of Robert's entrepreneurial digest. Robert's understanding of O. J.'s sports celebrity no doubt inspired Kris to do the same with fallen Olympics star Bruce Jenner. Kris's widespread exposure in the media as the brilliance behind Bruce's millions was limited. Understandable since

"Bruce Jenner" was the brand. But Kris's talents and abilities had garnered attention from powerful industry professionals like Namer and Mruvka. They respected her.

"Kris had this great mind for business," Namer said. "Alan and I were not your normal business guys. Kris was a perfect partner, as she's always thinking out of the box and she had a great mind for pop culture and what the audiences were really interested in."

As Kris told *American Fitness* magazine earlier that year: "My dream is for Bruce and I to host a talk show together, to offer people good information they can trust. Something for people to tune in to and hear about diets, ways to exercise, what you should do, what to avoid. They need a high-quality, consistent message. People recognize we've got this hot thing between us. They enjoy it when we spread that energy and warm feeling around."

Bruce was not only bringing his sports celebrity name, but his role as head of a national fitness council endorsed by the president of the United States gave additional credibility to the Jenners' television network. As part of their networks' programming, Kris and O. J. were slated to cohost a morning talk show. Bruce and O. J. would bring in other famous athletes.

"We were off to a tremendous start," Namer remarked. "You don't get any bigger than one of the greatest football players of all time, and you don't get any better than one of the greatest athletes of all time. We saw it leading into what would eventually become the digital world, where you'd start as television network, but then you'd be on the internet delivering advanced yoga lessons via their computer."

The original launch of FIT was set for summer 1994, but due to some production difficulties, it was rescheduled for the winter. December was an ideal time for capturing the annual New Year's resolution consumers who would be looking for inspiration and solutions to improve their health after the holidays.

As it happened, nothing new on any traditional or cable channel that summer was going to create any buzz. No one could have predicted the dominance of a single story and its impact on mainstream and tabloid media that summer and fall. Neither Namer or Mruvka, nor Kris, Bruce, or O. J. could have known their business venture would be over before it began.

CHAPTER EIGHT
KRIS VS. O. J.

Living the Nightmare

"I went to bed one night and I woke up the next morning and my entire universe had changed," Kris stated.

On June 13, 1994, Kris rushed home after dropping her kids off at their summer schools. She wanted enough time to shower and change before picking Nicole up for the lunch they had scheduled the evening before. When Kris walked in the door, her assistant Lisa told her Nicole's mom was on the phone.

"Tell her I'll call her right back," Kris said.

"You really need to take this call," Lisa said, handing the phone to Kris.

Kris was puzzled over what could be so urgent.

"Nicole's been stabbed!" Judith Brown screamed twice into the phone.

Kris's mind was racing. She wanted to get to her friend and help her immediately.

"Okay, I'm on my way," Kris replied. "Where do I need to go?"

"No," Judy said. "She didn't make it."

At that moment, Kris felt like a bullet had struck *her*. Her whole body went numb with simultaneous disbelief and horror. She turned on her television and watched the bloody images from the crime scene at Nicole's condominium. She learned that at 12:10 a.m., the bodies of thirty-five-year-old Nicole Brown Simpson and her twenty-five-year-old friend Ron Goldman were discovered by a pedestrian who saw Nicole sprawled on the steps of her walkway at 875 South Bundy Drive. Ron was located several feet away, curled up in the bushes. Both victims had been violently, bloodily left for dead about two hours earlier.

Officer Robert Riske, who was first at the crime scene, discovered a bloody glove. Investigators found the matching glove later that night around the perimeter of the home—the former home of Nicole's ex-husband O. J.

Detective Mark Fuhrman—fearing that O. J. might also be in danger—entered the estate without a warrant. O. J. was not home at the time. Subsequent DNA analysis revealed the blood from the second glove belonged to both victims.

Kris's best friend and current business partner, O. J. Simpson, had officially become a murder suspect.

Meanwhile, O. J. had checked into the O'Hare Plaza Hotel in Chicago for a business function. He arrived the morning after the murders at 6:15 a.m. local time (4:15 a.m. PST). The LAPD tracked O. J. down and he flew back to LA that same day. He was cuffed upon arrival and taken to police headquarters.

"We have brought him in to conduct a follow-up investigation and to question him as a potential witness," Officer Rigo Romero stated.

Two hours later, O. J. walked free. But not for long.

The Running Man

When NFL superstar O. J. Simpson was accused of murdering two people, he was offered the chance to turn himself in before 11:00 a.m. on June 17, 1994. By noon, O. J. was still a no-show and the LAPD declared him a fugitive, kicking off one the most sensational manhunts and murder trials in US history.

While the LAPD searched for the forty-six-year-old suspect at his Brentwood home, at approximately 1:00 p.m., O. J. was in the backseat of a white Ford Bronco driven by former NFL teammate Al "A. C." Cowlings. They were riding down the LA freeway toward Orange County, possibly headed for the Mexico border. O. J. knew he was a wanted man. He was traveling with $8,000 in cash, his passport, family photos, fake facial hair, a change of clothes, and a loaded .357 Magnum.

The police got a tip that A. C. had helped O. J. flee. A warrant was also issued for his arrest.

"We will find Mr. Simpson and bring him to justice," District Attorney Gil Garcetti said.

O. J.'s lawyer Robert Shapiro called a press conference at 5:00 p.m., during which Robert Kardashian read O. J.'s alleged suicide note on live television.

Watching from home, Kris's face was filled with horror as she listened to her ex-husband read the handwritten note:

To Whom It May Concern.

First, everyone understand. I have nothing to do with Nicole's murder. I loved her; always have and always will. If we had a problem, it's because I loved her so much.

Recently, we came to the understanding that for now we were not right for each other, at least for now. Despite our love, we were different and that's why we mutually agreed to go our separate ways.

It was tough splitting for a second time, but we both knew it was for the best. Inside, I had no doubt that in the future we would be close friends or more. Unlike what has been written in the press, Nicole and I had a great relationship for most of our lives together. Like all long-term relationships, we had a few downs and ups.

I took the heat New Year's 1989 because that's what I was supposed to do. I did not plead no contest for any other reason but to protect our privacy and was advised it would end the press hype.

I don't want to belabor knocking the press, but I can't believe what is being said. Most of it is totally made up. I know you have a job to do, but as a last wish, please, please, please, leave my children in peace. Their lives will be tough enough.

I want to send my love and thanks to all my friends. I'm sorry I can't name every one of you, especially A. C. Man, thanks for being in my life. *The support and friendship I received from so many: Wayne Hughes, Lewis Marks, Frank Olson, Mark Packer, Bender, Bobby Kardashian. I wish we had spent more time together in recent years. My golfing buddies: Hoss, Alan Austin, Mike, Craig, Bender, Wyler, Sandy, Jay, Donnie, thanks for the fun.*

All my teammates over the years: Reggie, you were the soul of my pro career. Ahmad, I never stopped being proud of you. Marcus, you've got a great lady in Catherine, don't mess it up. Bobby Chandler, thanks for always being there. Skip and Kathy, I love you guys. Without you, I never would have made it through this far.

Marguerite, thanks for the early years. We had some fun. Paula, what can I say? You are special. I'm sorry I'm not going to have, we're not going to have, our chance. God brought you to me, I now see. As I leave, you'll be in my thoughts.

I think of my life and feel I've done most of the right things. So why do I end up like this? I can't go on. No matter what the outcome, people will look and point. I can't take that. I can't subject my children to that. This way, they can move on and go on with their lives.

Please, if I've done anything worthwhile in my life, let my kids live in peace from you, the press.

I've had a good life. I'm proud of how I lived. My mama taught me to do unto others. I treated people the way I wanted to be treated. I've always tried to be up and helpful. So why is this happening?

I'm sorry for the Goldman family. I know how much it hurts.

Nicole and I had a good life together. All this press talk about a rocky relationship was no more than what every long-term relationship experiences. All her friends will confirm that I have been totally loving and understanding of what she's been going through.

At times, I have felt like a battered husband or boyfriend, but I loved her; make that clear to everyone. And I would take whatever it took to make it work.

Don't feel sorry for me. I've had a great life, great friends. Please think of the real O. J. and not this lost person.

Thanks for making my life special. I hope I helped yours. Peace and love, O. J.

A longtime friend of both Kris and Nicole recalled the tense situation. "Though we were watching Robert share O. J.'s edict from our different homes, in front of separate televisions, I felt Kris's anguish at seeing Robert stand up for this man, whom we both thought we knew. O. J. had committed the ultimate betrayal by allegedly killing his ex-wife and leaving their children without a mother. On a whole other level, Kris was looking at a man whom she had shared a bed with for a decade, and suddenly he, too was a stranger to her. We all wished we could turn away from the high-speed chase, but we couldn't, least of all Kris. The two men inside that Bronco were also friends of Kris."

Shapiro implored O. J. to surrender. An hour later, a distraught O. J. phoned police. LAPD traced the call to the I-5 freeway near Lake Forest, ironically where Nicole had been buried the day before. A motorist also called in a tip regarding his whereabouts. Highway patrol units joined the pursuit. The fleeing football player was eventually located on the I-405 at 6:45 p.m. by Officer Ruth Dixon. Dixon kept her distance once it became clear that O. J. had a gun to his head. She was flanked by a dozen police vehicles during the low-speed chase.

The media frenzy began almost immediately. News choppers flooded the sky, spectators crowded the overpasses with supportive signs, and major television shows were interrupted with live footage of O. J. on the run. Almost 100 million people tuned in. Sports announcers begged O. J. to surrender. Radio stations were giving play-by-play coverage. Nearly a thousand reporters gathered at the Parker Center police headquarters in downtown Los Angeles waiting for O. J. to turn himself in. The LAPD didn't think O. J. would survive the hour.

Around 6:00 p.m., LAPD detective Tom Lange called O. J. directly on his cellphone. Incredibly, the suspect picked up.

"I swear to you, I'll give you me, I'll give you my whole body," O. J. asserted to Lange from the back of the Bronco. "I just need to get to my house."

Lange promised he'd let that happen, but begged O. J. several times to "just throw the gun out the window."

"I can't do that," O. J. said apologetically. "This is not to keep you guys away from me. This is for me."

Lange kept O. J. on the phone for almost an hour until O. J. arrived safely in the driveway of his Brentwood home at 7:57 p.m.

The sixty-mile police chase had lasted several hours—nine hours past O. J.'s 11:00 a.m. deadline. Over two dozen SWAT members were in position at 360 N. Rockingham Avenue when O. J. stepped out of the car. First, he apologized to the officers and then sentimentally explained that his first date with Nicole was at this home. Lange was present and persuaded O. J. to hand over his firearm. O. J. was given permission to enter the residence and call his mother. He lingered inside for about an hour, had some orange juice, and surrendered without further incident. Deemed a flight risk, O. J. was kept behind bars without bail.

On July 7, Judge Kathleen Kennedy-Powell decided there was enough solid evidence for O. J. to stand trial for murder. When asked to enter a plea of "guilty" or "not guilty," O. J. unconventionally responded: "Absolutely, one hundred percent not guilty."

Kris felt any remarks she made to the press on behalf of the family, while not officially sanctioned, were hers to make. And she knew how to work the press for the benefit of Nicole's memory. Knowing Kris's love affair with cameras, some people in her inner circle were suspicious of her motives when she inserted herself into the drama, but Kris didn't care. She learned the difference between fame and infamy as she watched Robert get slaughtered in the press. Kris always believed she had a higher calling to help. Whenever she championed for Nicole at a public level, Kris saw herself as her advocate.

"They were two of the best friends I ever had in my entire life," Kris said of O. J. and Nicole. "They were my family. O. J. was like my big brother. I not only mourned the loss of Nicole, but I mourned the loss of O. J. and that relationship."

Indeed, the two families were incredibly close. For nearly two decades the Kardashian and Simpson clans shared vacations with their children, celebrated countless birthdays, and supported each other through good times and bad.

"I have these vivid memories of an amazing friendship and a life that we all had together," Kris later recalled. She credits Nicole for inspiring her love of interior design. "She was funny, she was beautiful and loyal and passionate and the best mom I had ever met."

Third Star to the Right

Selecting an impartial panel of jurors to hear the murder allegations against O. J. Simpson was time-consuming, and prosecutors and defense attorneys were in the thick of it as Kim's fourteenth birthday drew near in mid-October 1994.

The summer had been brutal for the Kardashians and Jenners. It would take a spectacular distraction to divert everyone's attention from the public spectacle of the murder case and the private anguish enveloping them daily. It was just like Kris, known for her epic parties, to flash on the most brilliant birthday celebration ever—a private party at Michael Jackson's 3,000-acre Neverland Ranch near Santa Barbara.

Kim was dating T. J. Jackson, the sixteen-year-old son of Tito Jackson, Michael's brother. Kris had opened her home up to T. J. after the recent death of T. J.'s mother, Delores "Dee Dee" Jackson. Just ten weeks after Nicole's murder, Dee Dee had drowned in a swimming pool. Police suspected foul play.

Even though Kim and T. J. had known each other for years, and had been dating for almost a year, Kris preferred to keep a close eye on them. She thought it best to monitor the couple after both had lost important people in their lives. The same was true for Kourtney and her boyfriend Taryll, T. J.'s older brother. Kris was amazed that these four young people had been united in tragedy that summer.

"We became extra close when my mom passed away," T. J. said of Kim. "She dropped everything to be with me."

Kris was like a second mom to T. J. before his mother's death and her continued support meant everything to him.

All three of Michael's nephews' birthdays fell within weeks of Dee Dee's death. The legendary singer felt sympathy for their loss, but he, too, was in mourning. It didn't matter that Dee Dee had divorced his brother; she was still family. Michael had been only thirteen years old when they had married in the 1970s.

T. J. was no trouble at all to Kris. The young man was a polite and respectful houseguest. She didn't know Michael Jackson personally, but she was sure he appreciated that she shared her home and maternal love with his favorite nephew.

Robert Kardashian had no issue with T. J., either. He was glad his family could offer the Jackson boys comfort. Before all of his time and attention was gutted by O. J.'s criminal troubles, Robert enjoyed when T. J., Taryll, and their brother Taj—who were known as the music group 3T—got together and jammed at his house. Robert was a lifelong lover of R&B and he felt comfortable sharing his knowledge of the industry with them. The boys were signed to their Uncle Michael's fledgling record label MJJ Music, and Tito managed their music careers. Their mom's death came as they were perfecting their debut album.

The only reservation Robert had about Kourtney and Kim dating the Jackson brothers was the negativity they might experience from those who looked upon interracial relationships unfavorably. As "colorblind" teens in Beverly Hills, it was nothing out of the ordinary for Kim and Kourtney to date black guys. It was duty, not racial discrimination, that Robert expressed when he pulled Kim aside for a talk about her love life.

"He said I should prepare myself for people to say things to me," Kim recalled. "He explained to me that he'd had a lot of interracial friends and it might not be the easiest relationship."

According to Joni, "Robert was always good friends with black women growing up. Robert loved black women. He had a relationship with a female attorney who worked for Johnnie Cochran during the O. J. Simpson trial. This affair resulted in the end of his engagement to Denice Halicki. It was a good relationship between them, but when push came to shove, she wanted to get married. He couldn't do it because his parents didn't like the idea of him marrying a black woman."

But Kris's concerns had nothing to do with race. She wanted the girls to avoid an unwanted teen pregnancy. Kim told Kris she had decided T. J. was going to be the one she gave her virginity to. Kris put Kim on birth control before her first act of sexual intercourse, which Kim later told Oprah happened when she was "almost fifteen."

Since T. J. and Taryll loved their Kardashian girlfriends and adored Kris, it would have taken very little hinting to get them to call in a birthday favor from Uncle Michael. It's doubtful Michael would have refused any request from the Jackson boys. If Kris had pulled the puppet strings for this stunning invite, she's never confessed. She's stuck to her story that Michael "invited all of us up to the Neverland Ranch for Kim's birthday party."

Nothing gets Kris's juices flowing like a party for one of her kids.

It all but took her mind off the gut-wrenching sadness she had felt all summer. Kris and Bruce rented a Mercedes bus to haul Kim's friends and the Jackson brothers the hundred miles from LA to Neverland. Despite the tension between Kris and Robert over his defense of O. J., Kim's dad was invited to her birthday party. His gift to his daughter was makeup lessons—a suggestion made by his glamorous girlfriend Denice.

Everyone was in heaven at Neverland. The bright red narrow-gauge steam locomotive transported guests from the main house to the amusement park for turns on the Ferris wheel, carousel, roller coaster, bumper cars, and swinging pirate ship. There was a zoo on the premises which delighted ten-year-old Khloé, who aspired to be a veterinarian. Kris and Bruce went horseback riding and go-karting. That night they watched films in Michael's fifty-seat movie theater.

"We never saw Michael," Kris revealed. "I was told he was there that night, but he never came out to say hello."

Michael was infamous for his reclusiveness, but even more so since battling sexual abuse allegations a year earlier. Kris was undoubtedly disappointed that she also didn't get to lay eyes on Michael's bride of five months, Lisa Marie Presley, daughter of her old nemesis Priscilla. She would have wasted no time letting Lisa Marie know about the decades-old connections between the families.

Marcia's Secret Weapon

"A collect call from O. J. Simpson," the jail operator announced.

Other than calls to his family and attorneys, O. J. called no one else from jail except Kris Jenner. The networks' star interviewers—Diane Sawyer, Barbara Walters, Katie Couric—were tripping over themselves to get an interview with O. J. Simpson. Friends, enemies, fans, and strangers would have given anything to hear his voice on the other end of the line. Anyone connected to Simpson was potentially a hot interview.

While Robert was tirelessly devoted to overseeing O. J.'s legal team, O. J. was closer with Kris. Kris said he broke into a self-pitying tirade during which he claimed he was framed by the police.

"I wish they would have put that glove in your backyard," he snapped, referring to the notorious bloody glove discovered on his property in Brentwood.

As he wept into the phone, O. J. thought he was talking to a friend of twenty years—and his business partner—but Kris was on a mission to avenge her friend's death. Also, she knew the value of jailhouse chats. Kris Jenner had the scoop the world wanted.

One way or another, Kris was determined to make O. J. pay for Nicole's death. Whatever degradation or dissing he received by the media was nothing compared to the open wounds Kris and Nicole's other friends and family felt. So when he called her from his jail cell, Kris was in super-sleuth mode. No matter what O. J. blabbered, it would make Kris the center of attention the second she hung up. She hoped for an admission of guilt that she could turn over to the cops and Marcia Clark immediately. She would just let him get it all out, whatever he had to say. She listened intently.

According to Kris, they talked for about an hour. Kris contends O. J. was out of his mind over the revelation by Nicole's friend, Faye Resnick, that she had a lesbian tryst with his ex-wife a month before her death. A publisher had swooped Resnick up and attached her to a writer to knock out a book about her friendship with Nicole and O. J.

"He just said, 'Did you know about the alleged affair?'" Kris later told the authorities. "I said, 'No.'"

O. J. called Kris again later in the day. He wanted to talk about the whole scenario between Nicole and Resnick again. He was still beside himself with angst over the thought of Nicole and Resnick having a "night of girlish passion."

Around the same time, Kris received another phone call. Nicole's mother rang and asked Kris to go over to the condo and pack stuff up for Nicole's children, eight-year-old Sydney and five-year-old Justin. The kids were going to live with their grandmother.

Kris was happy to do anything to help Nicole's family.

She had no idea what she was in for as she walked into the house. It was eerie. Her emotions took over when she walked through the door.

"I almost fainted, because the whole house was black," Kris recalled.

While inside, she kept an eye out for any clues that could help the prosecution. Since Kris knew Nicole so well, she hoped to be able to shine some light on something of value to law enforcement. While she was in Sydney's room, Kris recoiled from her bed when she thought she had discovered a bloody handprint. Kris immediately phoned Marcia Clark, the lead prosecutor charged with avenging Nicole's murder. Within a half hour, a forensic team was at the door to lift the substance for prints. Kris just knew she had stumbled onto something. It turned out to be Jell-O. The scenario was not funny but was just the kind of awkward situation Kris was prone to falling into.

But Kris did recall something that Nicole had said to her months earlier, words that still haunted her.

"He's going to kill me," Nicole had confessed to her friend. "And he's going to get away with it."

Kris has only publicly revealed two regrets that continue to plague her. She saw herself as failing both Robert Kardashian and Nicole Brown Simpson during their lifetimes. Admissions of her selfishness toward two people she loved were not easy confessions for Kris to make, but it was necessary and somehow comforting to hold herself accountable to them. Although she hadn't responded in time to save Nicole, Kris was prepared to share her friend's scared confession with those who could keep Nicole's killer behind bars.

Life and Death Struggle

O. J.'s trial began on January 24, 1995. It was held at the C. S. Foltz Criminal Courts Building in downtown Los Angeles. Judge Lance Ito presided over the murder case. There were twelve jurors and twelve backup jurors.

O. J.'s defense team was helmed by Shapiro and included F. Lee Bailey, Alan Dershowitz, Robert Kardashian, Shawn Holley, Carl E. Douglas, and Gerald Uelmen. At O. J.'s request, Shapiro hired former assistant DA Johnnie Cochran. Cochran quickly took control of O. J.'s defense. O. J.'s so-called "dream team" cost $50,000 a day.

The prosecution was led by deputy district attorneys Marcia Clark and Christopher Darden. The dynamic duo didn't believe they could convince a jury the beloved athlete deserved to die—so the prosecutors fought to put O. J. behind bars for life.

During the course of the trial, the prosecution would attempt to show that O. J. and Nicole had a history of violence that culminated in a double murder.

During the seven-year marriage, O. J. had been accused of spousal abuse several times. The prosecution played a recording of a 911 call from 1989 in which O. J. was heard screaming while Nicole told the operator that she was in danger.

Nicole filed for divorce on February 25, 1992, but that didn't stop the abuse.

"My ex-husband has just broken into my house and he's ranting and raving outside in the front yard," Nicole told another 911 operator on October 25, 1993. O. J. "was still at large" when police arrived at the scene.

Los Angeles coroner Dr. Lakshmanan Sathyavagiswaran testified during the trial that Nicole was likely unconscious and facedown on the ground when her right-handed attacker grabbed her by the hair and stabbed her exposed neck four times before slicing her throat and severing her carotid artery. Her larynx could be seen through the wound and her C3 vertebra was incised—meaning, her head was barely attached to her neck.

Nicole's eyes were open.

A bruise on the right side of her head, likely from a fist or knife-handle strike, indicated that she was unconscious. Her blood had collected on the ground, instead of in her throat and lungs, which suggested that she was facedown before dying.

"She was alive at least a minute or more before the last wound was inflicted," the doctor said, believing that the killer may have gone after Ron before ending Nicole's life.

Lakshmanan then explained how "abrasions and contusions" on Ron's knuckles did not come from hitting the killer, but rather when Ron—cornered between two trees and a fence—fell back and scraped them against the bark and metal. His palms had several knife wounds that came from facing the slasher with his hands raised in defense.

Forensic pathologist Dr. Michael Baden—a witness for the defense—stated that Ron had been stabbed twenty-two times on his face, neck, chest, and torso. His shoe was also sliced after he apparently kicked the killer. The doctor said his jugular vein had been opened.

The wounds on both bodies indicated that the blade was approximately six inches long and single-edged—just one sharpened side—which pointed to a lone killer.

Testimony revealed that the couple's children were asleep inside the Mediterranean-style residence during the murders. There was no indication that the home had been entered or robbed.

Family friends testified that O. J. had been trying to rekindle his relationship with Nicole. They had been sleeping together, the court was told, but had called it quits again weeks before her murder. Darden did not dispute that and charged that Simpson had killed Nicole in a jealous rage.

One of the last people to see O. J. before the murders was his houseguest, aspiring actor Kato Kaelin, at 9:36 p.m. O. J. was next seen at 10:54 p.m.—an hour and eighteen minutes later—when he entered a limo to go to LAX. The killings took place during that period and gave O. J. plenty of time to pull it off. The residences were only two miles apart.

A witness stated they saw a white Bronco leaving the crime scene at 10:35 p.m. Limo driver Allan Park testified that he arrived early at O. J.'s home, at around 10:24, and didn't see O. J.'s vehicle. He claimed he rang the buzzer at the front gate at 10:40 and got no response. At around 10:50, Kato heard several thumps against his guest house. At the same time, Park saw O. J. enter the main house. O. J. told Park he'd overslept and would be out soon. Kato helped his host put his bags in the car.

Dozens of special forensic witnesses placed O. J. at the scene. Blood was discovered on O. J.'s socks and in his Bronco. Both specimens matched Nicole's DNA. A bloody shoe print was found at the crime and was identified as a size-12 pair of Bruno Magli shoes. Only twenty-nine pairs were sold in the US and O. J. had one of them. Several pieces of O. J.'s hair were removed from Ron's shirt and from a knit cap that was found at the scene. Dark blue clothing fibers were also found on Ron that matched the sweat suit O. J. wore that night.

To the prosecution, the case against O. J. seemed open and shut.

After sitting in the crowded courtroom hearing testimony each day, Bruce and Kris would come home exhausted. There were no after-hours during the trial. If they attended a gala or dinner party, or even sat quietly having dinner, people approached them wanting to know their opinions about the case, and even offering their own obscure theories. Everyone seemed to feel connected to the case. Even at home, there was no respite from the drama. There was little else on television, so they watched the day's news coverage as they ate their evening meal on trays in front of the television. Tears rolled down Kris's cheeks every time she heard the 911 tape of Nicole crying to the police for help.

After the news segments, while Bruce was watching sports coverage, Kris would prop her feet up on a pillow on Bruce's lap. She would lean back into the couch to ease the discomfort in her back from sitting on the hard court benches all day.

She was several months pregnant.

Their phones rang all evening. The messages piled up on her answering machine. If it wasn't calls from the media requesting interviews, it was close friends of Nicole's. They would call either Kris or Bruce, or sometimes both, to rehash the day or gossip about what all the other girls were wearing or saying. It was an addiction that played out despite the best intentions by some of the principals to ignore it.

Kris always called her mom back first, then, one by one, she would ring her girlfriends back. It was usually the same refrains: "I knew it!" or "What did you think?" and "That's what I thought? Can you believe it?" and "Did you see O. J. rolling his eyes again today? What's up with that?" and always "What's going on with Robert?"

Bruce had his own list of calls to return from his buddies. Sometimes he would be on the phone with Steve Garvey while Kris was on with Candace. Everyone's lives were meshed. It was like an ongoing giant slumber party. Then it would be time to get ready to fall into bed for the night, only to rise the next morning to start all over again. This routine went on for the eight-month duration of the trial. It was a sentencing all on its own.

The O. J. Simpson case so dominated the news in 1994 and 1995 that even a complete stranger was like a moth to the flame. With so many of their close friends connected to the case, and considering their own relationship to the victim and the accused, there was nowhere for Kris and Bruce to escape.

Day after day, the prosecution kept squaring off against the slick super-stars on the defense's dream team, lawyers who spent their evenings preparing for the next day in court and talking to their agents about possible book deals and talk show hosting opportunities once the trial of the century was over.

Robert Shapiro was the most polished of all the attorneys who sat at O. J. Simpson's table. He carried himself like a 1940s movie star, and he became every bit as famous. The media knew it, and the jury quickly learned it.

Johnnie Cochran was equally charismatic and had the celebrity cachet of having represented Michael Jackson. During breaks from the testimony, Shapiro and Cochran could be found affably chatting up news reporters and producers in the hallway outside the ninth floor of the Los Angeles court-house, as Marcia Clark and the prosecutors walked past wearing icy half-smiles.

Kris Is Marcia Clark's Ally

Marcia was the first and only woman in the LA special trials unit when she took the O. J. case. She was twice divorced and a single mother of two young sons. It was a demanding and powerful role as the lead prosecutor in the "trial of the century."

As Marcia navigated Nicole's myriad friends, she settled on Kris as the go-to girl.

"She was very helpful," Marcia said. "She was the one who kind of mar-shaled the forces and got the women who knew about him abusing Nicole, witnesses to his abuse, and brought them forward."

Kris did tell Marcia about Nicole's fears that O. J. was going to kill her.

"I wanted to put it on a testimony," Marcia admitted, but couldn't because it was hearsay. "In order to get a statement like that in there, Nicole would have to be saying, 'He's coming for me! He's coming to kill me now!' It can't just be we're having wine, 'Hey, I know he's going to kill me,' unfortunately."

As the case progressed, Marcia also witnessed Robert lose faith in O. J.'s innocence.

"I could see the change," the prosecutor stated. "I could see him having more and more trouble as the case wore on, as more evidence came out. I think he started out a true believer. 'My friend couldn't do it.' I could see the shift. I could see the trouble in his eyes. And I think by the end of it he certainly knew."

The prosecution's mountain of evidence seemed insurmountable. And yet, on June 15, 1995, Darden made the fatal mistake of asking O. J. to try on one of the bloody gloves. The prosecution had already decided against it since the leather gloves had been in cold storage and were likely to have shrunk. Because the gloves were evidence, O. J. was required to wear a pair of latex gloves underneath, making the bloody glove an even tighter squeeze.

The glove looked two sizes too small for the six foot one inch athlete with big, pigskin-grabbing hands.

"If it doesn't fit, you must acquit," Cochran famously said.

The prosecution presented an old photo of O. J. wearing the same gloves, but it was too late to change the jury's minds. It was later revealed that O. J. took the precaution of skipping his anti-inflammatory arthritis medication, which further swelled his joints.

Johnnie Cochran continued to add more "reasonable doubt." The seasoned lawyer claimed that the LAPD framed O. J. for murder. Cochran accused lead witness Fuhrman of using racial slurs and caught him lying about that on the stand. Fuhrman was subsequently charged with perjury. The detective was also accused of planting the second glove at O. J.'s place. When originally asked if he tampered with the evidence, Fuhrman said, "no." When asked again during a second round of testimony he took the fifth. The jurors interpreted that as a "yes."

The jury had seen enough.

"Live" with Kris and Kathie Lee

Kris had endured a lot leading into the fall of 1995. She lost two close friends and had experienced further strain in her relationship with Robert during the O. J. Simpson debacle. She struggled to accept that Nicole was dead. And if Simpson was acquitted, she might never have the closure that justice could provide for her murder.

Simpson was also dead to her. She wanted nothing to do with him, whether he went to prison or walked out of the courtroom a free man. As for Robert, while they had bitterly disagreed over his role as O. J.'s staunchest defender in public and private, she had to concede they would agree to disagree.

By this stage, Kourtney, Kim, Khloé, and Rob were living half of the week at Robert's and the rest of the time with Bruce and Kris. They were all old enough to choose where they wanted to live, and it would have killed Kris if they chose to live full-time with their father. But to be fair, Kris also missed Robert's presence in her life. She was grateful for his friendship and their four children.

Despite all of the stress she had endured, Kris managed her pregnancy in a healthy way. She was seven months pregnant by September, when Bruce was tapped to judge the Miss America pageant in Atlantic City. They both needed a break from the insanity of the trial. Talk show hosts Kathie Lee Gifford and Regis Philbin were cohosting the event. In advance of the telecast, Kris and Bruce visited Kathie Lee and her husband, New York Giants football legend and television sportscaster Frank Gifford, at their sprawling Connecticut estate.

Bruce knew Frank from the retired athlete circuit and both were television commentators. Over the years, Bruce had appeared as a celebrity guest on Kathie Lee and Regis's hugely popular syndicated morning television gabfest, *Live with Regis and Kathie Lee*.

Kris and Kathie Lee had been friends since the early 1980s. They met in Bible study classes in Los Angeles as young twenty-something born-again Christian women.

The two women's lives had changed drastically since they sat in a circle with their Bibles in their laps, interpreting scriptures and comparing notes about their boob jobs. When Kathie Lee divorced her first husband (Christian composer Paul Johnson) in 1983, she moved to New York City, where she thrived as a morning talk show personality. When Kathie Lee married Gifford, Kris was having her extramarital affair, so the girlfriends drifted apart.

Kris was awestruck by the sheer beauty of Kathie Lee's Riverside, Connecticut, home. The mansion sat atop a stretch of land surrounded by the Atlantic Ocean, giving it the appearance of a private island. In the mornings, Kris and Kathie Lee would sit on lounge chairs and gaze out at the water. They were surrounded by the peaceful calm of nature. Kris took off her large black sunglasses and held her hand over her eyes. In the distance was a shadowy skyline of Manhattan. It was just far away enough for Kris. She welcomed the slower pace for a few days, and the beauty of colorful leaves sliding off the old trees. And, of course, the charming company of her dear old friend.

While Bruce and Frank played golf and talked sports, Kris and Kathie Lee drank fresh brewed coffee and read a devotional from the Bible. While always on the go, it was difficult for Kris to maintain a consistent church home to attend worship services and Bible studies, so spending this time with God and another believer was precious. The two took turns reading aloud. As Kathie Lee closed her Bible, she turned into Kris and reached for her hands to lead them in prayer.

"Kathie, I would love for you to be our baby's godmother," Kris told her. "Bruce feels the same and he's asking Frank to be godfather today. There's no woman I trust more to help raise my child spiritually than you, my friend."

Kathie Lee was silent. She closed her eyes and took in a deep breath. The scent of salty, warm air brushed over them gently. A spark from the sun's rays bounced off Kathie's sunglasses, which rested on her head. As she exhaled and opened her eyelids, her solemn expression shifted as a smile moved across her face.

"Kris, it is my honor to serve you and your child in this role. Let us pray."

The Gifford house was the essence of spacious luxury. There was even a separate parking lot for Kathie Lee's household and office staff. Kathie Lee made sure Kris was pampered like a princess during her visit. It was a joy to talk about everything but O. J. Simpson. It didn't interest Kathie Lee. The best girlfriends had so much catching up to do about their lives. They had almost everything two women could have in common. They had triumphed over the adversities of broken marriages. Kathie Lee was forty-two, with two young children, and Kris was soon to be a new mother again in her early forties. Both had suffered the heartbreak of miscarriages. Fulfilling a legacy of love by giving their husbands children and establishing a Christ-centered family was a shared value.

They were married to men who understood and appreciated their vibrant, take-charge personalities. They were free to be themselves with their second husbands. Neither Bruce nor Frank penalized their wives for their ambitions.

In just five years cohosting her syndicated show, Kathie Lee had amassed a fortune. Using her television platform, which grew to eight million viewers, she created a base for building an empire. Kris greatly admired Kathie Lee's success. She had always wanted to be a talk show host. Kathie Lee was living Kris's dream. They may have had little contact over the past few years, but Kris had been taking notes. Kathie Lee interjected her personal life on television, incessantly talking about her husband and their young children, Cody and Cassidy, which made her relatable to the everyday woman. Social media had yet to be invented, but Kathie Lee managed to be everywhere all the time.

She was a tireless self-promoter. With her multiple lucrative endorsement deals, she was shoulder-to-shoulder with former athletes, without catching a football or jumping over a hurdle in the Olympics. She had a line of cosmetics, nail polish, and diet products, and had just launched her own clothing line at Walmart. Popular television stars and models like Jaclyn Smith, Connie Sellecca, Delta Burke, and Kathy Ireland were lending their names to fashion designs that were more affordable than Calvin Klein and Ralph Lauren. Middle-class women in middle America could wear clothes with celebrity tags, and Kathie Lee Gifford was outselling them all.

In the afternoons, Kris sat in the peach-and-cream living room of Kathie Lee's renovated farmhouse sipping iced tea. The ladies talked about furnishings and interior design. As Kris breathed in the grandness of Kathie Lee's life, Kathie Lee acknowledged Kris's achievements. In six short years, Kris had repackaged and remarketed Bruce Jenner. He had a full schedule of motivational speaking engagements and maintained lucrative relationships with major corporate sponsors. The exercise infomercials costarring Kris and Bruce were airing in thirty-five countries, with sales of fitness equipment that generated an estimated $300 million in 1995. She had successfully branded them as a celebrity couple passionate about family fitness. The messaging was to trade up from the coldness of the gym and its fees and become part of the Jenners' celebritydom with a membership in their "SuperFit Club." They were rich, but they were real.

Recipes for Kris's swordfish steaks and healthy pasta were featured in Robin Leach's *Kitchen of the Stars* cookbook. As guests on talk shows, the Jenners juiced oranges and prepared healthy salads. When asked to feature a room in their house for a book that looked inside celebrity homes, naturally they chose their equipment-filled exercise den. In truth, this was a room they rarely saw since they were away from home most of the year, and videos and photographs of them were shot elsewhere. But Kris understood it was the image that was important, not the reality.

All of the fitness-related publicity was carefully orchestrated by Kris to sell the hell out of exercise equipment for the masses and to pick the pockets of corporate executives. She and Bruce had paid their dues and wanted to expand their messaging for bigger profits. Kris was in final negotiations for a full partnership with a major corporation on a line of vitamins and other nutritional supplements.

Kris smiled as Kathie Lee gushed over her savvy smarts. Although Kris didn't reveal her secret longing to eclipse Bruce and become a star in her own right, Kathie Lee would not have been surprised. They were cut from the same cloth. As they walked arm in arm through the enormous, chicly designed rooms of Kathie Lee's mansion to meet their guys on the veranda for dinner, Kris mentioned how much she wanted a similar home of their own. They were financially stable enough to buy a property, and it was time. Kathie pulled her close to her for a hug.

"Kris, you know my mantra. Trust God with your life and He'll make something beautiful out of it. It may take a long time, but *He* will."

"Thank you, Kathie Lee. Hopefully, we'll get back here before too long. I need you in my life."

"I've got a great idea," Kathie Lee said, unlocking her embrace with Kris. "Why don't the four of us cruise the Mediterranean in March. I assume you have a nanny for my goddaughter and the rest of the kids?"

"I think that would be an amazing trip," Kris replied. "I'll talk to Bruce and clear our schedules."

She paused. "Oh, of course, he'll say yes! OK! Let's do it!"

As they dined by candlelight, the two couples were served elegant cuisine prepared by the Giffords' chef. The wives smiled adoringly at their husbands while they told their athletic "war stories." Every so often, Kris and Kathie Lee could be caught giving one another a conspiratorial wink across the table, which did not go unnoticed by Bruce. He knew Kris's cues.

He stood up and lifted his crystal champagne flute to his wife. "This past year, with so many losses, makes me even more appreciative of my family, especially this incredible woman I proudly call my wife. Kris, you are my lover, best friend, mother of our children, partner in life, and a great businesswoman all rolled into one. I owe you what I am today. You've remade me from head to toe. I love you."

Tears rolled down Kathie Lee's cheeks as she patted her chest over her heart. Kris's eyes were moist as well. Kris tapped her water glass and began humming the familiar tune from Kathie Lee's Carnival Cruise Line commercial. The two women busted out the lyrics in a rousing rendition of "If My Friends Could See Me Now."

Born and Bred to Get Ahead

While both Kourtney and Kim shared Kris's expensive tastes in clothing and furnishings, Kim was more like Kris when it came to thinking about how to monetize a lifestyle.

Kris was impressed with how centered Kim was, how wise beyond her years. She could share her dreams and visions with Kim, and she just "got it." Kim was quiet and observant. As her mother turned their lives around financially, she became increasingly interested in watching Kris in action. But she was also still a teenager with schoolgirl interests, so while Kris prattled on about courting fashion designer Vera Wang at the Miss America pageant, and all the ins and outs of Kathie Lee's clothing empire, Kim wanted to know what Kris had gleaned about the Spice Girls, who had been guests on Kathie Lee's show.

Kim was nuts about the Spice Girls. She had instructed her mom to find out every detail from Kathie Lee about their appearances on her show. No nugget was too small. Kris had not forgotten to make good on her assignment and told her all that she had learned—which took about two minutes.

Kris had missed all of her children while she was on the east coast, and the one-on-one time with Kim felt good. They were as much best girlfriends as they were mother and daughter. They were confidants. While other young girls kept their sexual lives a secret from their moms, the Kardashian kids knew that they could tell Kris *anything*—and Kim was approaching an age where Kris could confide in her as a young woman.

Kris checked in with Kourtney, who continued her love affair with her new car. For her sixteenth birthday earlier that year, Robert and Kris bought her a black BMW. Like most teenagers in Beverly Hills, she was on the road, traveling between friends' homes and the shopping malls, usually with Kim in the passenger seat.

"She was obsessed with Jennifer Lopez," revealed fashion designer Nikki Lund, Kim's childhood friend. "She would sing 'If You Had My Love' all of the time."

Meanwhile, Khloé was diligently attending her horseback riding lessons, which had replaced her previous ice-skating tutelage. The eleven-year-old shared her aunt Karen's passion for horses. Khloé was also the unofficial custodian of the family dog, Harley.

Kris didn't have much to report back to eight-year-old Robert. He was a homebody whose main chore was to keep his room clean, which he took pride in doing.

As their nanny for five years, Pam had a deep connection with the children. She also had a front-row seat to their chaotic formative years. "In my opinion, because of how I grew up in the Midwest, the kids seem spoiled in terms of material possessions," she wrote in her diary. "That doesn't mean they are naughty, but they do think they deserve the best of everything. Despite this, they are sweet, loving, well-behaved (for the most part), and respectful children."

Kourtney and fifteen-year-old Kim were close and shared a passion for fashion and beauty products. Kim had braces on her teeth and spent a lot of time studying herself in the mirror. But nanny Pam didn't find Kim's obsession with her looks to be unusual, as most girls her age were self-conscious. She never found Kim to be self-centered or egotistical. "I catch myself sometimes staring at her natural beauty," Pam admitted at the time. "Of course, she knows she is beautiful. Yet, she maintains her sweetness. I'm glad she hasn't allowed beauty to go to her head."

Even Kris was constantly in awe of Kim's gorgeous looks.

While she felt blessed to have four children with striking good looks, Kim was an extraordinary creature. Kris couldn't help but bond deeply with Kim. They were tuned to one another.

While catching up with her kids and going through her pile of mail, Kris received a call from Marcia Clark's office. The O. J. Simpson jury had reached a verdict. Kris and Bruce raced to the courthouse, where Marcia had arranged for them and Nicole's sisters to watch the reading of the verdict on a television in her office. Marcia was keen on protecting Kris's health. She worried that if the verdict went sideways and O. J. was found innocent, the stress might adversely affect Kris and her unborn baby.

Given that she was eight months pregnant, it was a valid concern.

The jury had heard from 126 witnesses throughout 133 days of testimony. They'd seen 857 exhibits presented by twenty attorneys. There were over 50,000 pages of court transcripts and four days of closing arguments. After spending 266 days sequestered, the jury needed less than four hours to deliberate. It was reasonable to assume it would be a guilty verdict, since the deliberation time was so short. Only four of the original twelve jury members still remained when the verdict was read on October 3, 1995. At 10:07 a.m., with 100 million people watching on television, O. J. was found "not guilty" on both murder charges.

"After the verdict was read in the Simpson case, as the jury was leaving," an exasperated Clark stated, "one of them, I was later told, said, 'We think he probably did it. We just didn't think they proved it beyond a reasonable doubt.'"

Like the rest of the world, Kris and Bruce were shocked. They also blamed themselves for not saving Nicole when they had the chance.

"I beat myself up because I felt like I wasn't paying attention," Kris later admitted, claiming she first learned of Nicole's secret domestic abuse during the trial. "I saw all the pictures and the police reports, and I heard tapes of Nicole calling 911. That was stuff I didn't know anything about. But that's typical in an abusive relationship—that the woman doesn't speak out about how she's being treated.

"Domestic violence is a real tragedy in our lives," she continued. "Nicole's death could have been prevented. I want women everywhere, especially women of this new generation, to know the story. They need to realize that they have a voice and they need to tell somebody if someone has hurt them. And if Nicole's legacy can be protecting other women, then that would be a really positive thing."

"My heart breaks because of all the pain and suffering she went through," Bruce added. "I wish I had noticed the signs. She was fighting for her life many days, I'm sure. I try to pay attention to things more now. I follow my intuition."

O. J. ultimately spent 474 days in jail and the cost of his defense was in the $3 to $6 million range, which O. J. paid for by signing massive amounts of memorabilia while incarcerated. A subsequent civil trial in 1996 found O. J. "responsible" for the murders. Jail time was not an option, but he was ordered to pay over $33.5 million to the victims' families.

Another Girl for Kris and Bruce

Aware that the victory party celebrating O. J. Simpson's acquittal would undoubtedly go into the wee morning hours, Robert decided instead to get home to his kids.

He wanted to make sure he checked in on their feelings about everything that had happened, so they did not go to bed with any unresolved concerns. He cared what they thought about it all. They had an open dialogue between them throughout the trial. It had been difficult on the kids that their parents were divided on whether their Uncle Juice was innocent. Robert didn't like it either. He knew Kris was hurt that all the children supported his defense of O. J., and it must have embarrassed her for courtroom observers to see them sitting behind the defense table, and not with her on the prosecution's side.

He wanted a truce with Kris, and he would not wait until it was a convenient time These kinds of discussions have a way of being postponed, especially since Kris was always going a million miles an hour. In a few weeks it would be Kim's birthday, and Kris would have her baby, then Kris's birth-day—and he did not want the kids uncomfortable during the holidays. There was no reason to put off having a conversation with her. If she had learned anything from Nicole's death and O. J.'s criminal battle, it was that every day is precious. There was no way of knowing what tomorrow would bring.

He looked at his watch as he walked out of O. J.'s house in Brentwood. It was still early. He called Kris and asked if he could come over for a few min-utes. He promised not to stay long, assuring her that he wanted to get back home to the kids. Kris had seen the television coverage of Robert and O. J. pulling up to his house and was surprised to hear from him. She was curious what was so important that he needed to stop by that night but refrained from asking him on the phone. She and Bruce were tired. She imagined Robert was as well.

Bruce was cordial to Robert but had little to say to him. Kris and Robert went out on her patio to talk. He told her that he wanted to move forward peacefully for the children, and for them. He reminded her that family came above all else, and Kris agreed. They embraced and both of them wept. Their feud had prevented them from sharing their mutual grief over losing Nicole until that very moment.

"Our future memories were gone, and our former memories were destroyed," she later revealed.

Kris's protruding belly provided more evidence of how much their lives had changed over the past few years. It was the first time the ex-husband and wife had been civil long enough in each other's presence to absorb that Kris was about to give birth to another man's baby. While they had both moved on with other partners, it was only natural for Kris and Robert to reflect on the times when Kris was pregnant with their four children. Kris was in the final weeks of her pregnancy with Bruce's baby, and she was coming up on five years of marriage to Bruce. For Robert, that meant he and Kris had been divorced nearly as long.

With their line of communication open again, they launched into a brief chat about the kids. Even though the girls were living with Robert most of the time, Kris wanted Robert to know she kept tabs on them. Robert talked mostly about helping them with their homework and church, and Kris filled him in on more of the fun stuff. An emotional day for them both ended on a good note. Neither would wake up in the morning dreading how they were going to face each other.

Bruce heard the door close and Robert's car pull away. He caught up with Kris as she walked toward the bedroom. Following behind her, he was unable to see the tears gently rolling down her cheeks.

"What did he want?" he asked.

"It's all good," Kris answered softly. "I'm so tired. I'm sure you are too. I'll tell you all about it in the morning."

CHAPTER NINE
NEW BEGINNINGS AND ENDINGS

The Jim J. and Kris Show

On November 3, 1995, two days shy of her fortieth birthday, Kris and Bruce became parents of a baby girl. She was born exactly thirty days after O. J.'s acquittal. They named the newborn Kendall Nicole Jenner, in honor of Kris's slain friend.

Kourtney was in the delivery room to greet her new sister.

Robert stopped by the Jenner home on Kris's birthday. She asked her private nurse, Jackie, to leave the nursery so she and Robert could have privacy. It was a tender moment as Robert picked up and held Kris's fifth child. Tears welled up in both their eyes.

"Oh Kris, she's so beautiful, it makes me cry," he said, handing Kendall back to his ex-wife.

After he left, Kris reflected on all the wonderful memories she and Robert had shared with the births of their children, and her mind went back to his vigilance in photographing and videotaping all their family's special moments. Kendall's birth was a fresh chapter for her family, and it deserved to be celebrated.

Seeing Robert so happy for her was a cathartic experience for Kris. Robert had seemingly forgiven her for breaking up their family, and Kris hoped she could begin to forgive herself. She also wished Nicole were there to hold her newborn baby girl.

As she changed clothes that afternoon, Kris looked at the maternity clothes Nicole had given her once upon a time. They transcended her passing and became deeply satisfying and symbolic to Kris in the moment. Nicole's parting gift to Kris was her faith that she would have the baby with Bruce that she so desperately wanted. Kris stepped back and realized she needed to step into the present for her five children and Bruce, as well as herself. She called to her nurse.

"Jackie. Come in here, please. I need your help in packing up my maternity clothes."

Immediately following Kendall's birth came Thanksgiving, Christmas, and New Year's Day. There was no such thing as maternity leave for Kris Jenner. She was strategizing Bruce's appearances at the 1996 Olympic Games. It was of major financial importance to them. Not only was it the Centennial Games, but it was the twentieth anniversary of Bruce winning his gold medal. In addition, the corporate sponsor of the Games was Coca-Cola, one of Bruce and Kris's major clients.

She was fulfilled as a wife and mother and she was proud of what she had achieved for Bruce as his manager. But the old familiar yearning to be a celebrity in her own right still gnawed at her. After watching Kathie Lee and Regis Philbin cohost the Miss America pageant, Kris's fantasies about hosting her own television show were more powerful than ever. As a result of Bruce's appearances, she was friendly with all the top television bookers and she kept up with them by sending notes and cards and calling them to catch up on their lives. She had a few who consistently campaigned for Kris to become a regular special correspondent.

Kris's chance at the big time came in 1996, when television personality Jim J. Bullock sought a replacement cohost for his syndicated talk show *The Jim J. and Tammy Faye Show*. Only a few months after the debut of the show, Tammy Faye exited the program following a cancer diagnosis.

Kris pulled some strings and landed an audition for the top slot.

"When I heard Bruce Jenner's wife was auditioning as my new host, I was excited," Bullock recalled. "She did well. She was bubbly and we definitely had chemistry."

Kris was still high from the exhilaration of the audition when she came home. She told Bruce every detail. She just knew she had knocked it out of the park. Bruce was happy for her but was concerned about how the rigors of a national daytime talk show would affect their lives. He knew Kris had the managerial aspects of his career running so smoothly that she could stay on top of their business matters without any difficulty, but Kendall was an infant.

"I'll take her to work with me, and Jackie can come along too," Kris assured him. "While I'm working on the set, they can sit in my dressing room. I will have that as a part of my contract. It might even cover Jackie's salary. Don't you worry about a thing, Bruce. I've already thought it all out."

But in the end, they replaced Tammy Faye with actress Ann Abernathy.

"She was their first choice all along," Bullock confirmed.

Although she had been beaten, Kris didn't stay down for long. She never did.

Unfortunately, the opposite was true for Robert Kardashian. His fame was more accurately described as infamy. It cost him his reputation and his emotional and physical health. While O. J. Simpson was again a free man, roaming the world, playing golf with beautiful models on his arm, Robert lived in something of an invisible prison. After all of his public displays of defending O. J., the two were no longer friends. Robert had contributed to friend and author Lawrence Schiller's book *I Want to Tell You*, where he dished about the nightmares associated with the "dream team." Robert had appeared on Barbara Walters's *20/20*, discrediting his own staunch defense of O. J. when he told her he seriously doubted Simpson's innocence. Celebrity criminal defense attorney Leslie Abramson dismissed her colleague as a "fake lawyer." After O. J.'s acquittal, Robert spent thousands of dollars on his own legal counsel. He spent hours of his time in briefings and depositions associated with a multimillion-dollar civil lawsuit brought against O. J. by the families of Nicole and Goldman. Allegations that he was in collusion with O. J. haunted him for the remainder of his life. He was forever the topic of conspiracy theories. After years of living in O. J.'s shadow, Robert always believed he would emerge as a popular celebrity in his own right, but instead, he suffered humiliation and brought shame on his Armenian family.

"He thought he would come off as the best friend," Joni revealed. "He was going to parlay it into speaking tours, as a pedestal upon which to speak from."

Kris was still affected personally by the trials and tribulations of the O. J. Simpson case, but in the eyes of the public she had been on the right side of it, and she thrived from an image standpoint. She had achieved her own notoriety as the best friend of the murder victim. She was respected for refusing to sell out Nicole's memory for personal gain during the trial. The full-page advertisements featuring photos of Kris and Bruce on their exercise equipment, which ran in newspapers across the country, and the frequent airing of their infomercials were never seen as anything but business as usual. They were produced before the murders, and since the Jenners were viewed as merely the faces of the fitness machines, they were far enough away from the advertiser's decisions to ramp up production of the ads without it tainting Kris. Bruce and Kris profited greatly from the increase in sales during this time.

Kris's interviews on the topic were never viewed as wanting her fifteen minutes of fame, but merely as her way of helping move justice forward for her girlfriend and to bring closure for Nicole's family. Bruce consistently reminded everyone they were only at the trial at the invitation of the Browns. Without being a principal to the most gruesome criminal proceedings of the twentieth century, Kris might never have fulfilled one of her secret fantasies—to be interviewed by Barbara Walters. With no journalism, acting, or other formal on-camera training, she managed to secure television correspondent gigs during the trial for shows like *The Insider*—a spin-off of the hugely popular *Entertainment Tonight*. Kris never exaggerated her friendship with Nicole or O. J. She didn't have to. She truly was the ultimate insider, feeding the world's insatiable hunger for every morsel of this drama. It was a statement on where our celebrity culture was headed, and Kris was in many ways a pioneer.

Even the most cynical investigative reporter would have been hard pressed to make any legitimate dents in the family's coat of honor. Bruce had fathered six children. The rumors about his cross-dressing that popped up in the 1980s and early '90s continued to fade as he produced two beautiful babies with his vivacious wife Kris. Obviously, Bruce was having fulfilling sex as a married man. His gender dysphoria closet remained locked, and other doors revealing Bruce as a virile—but vulnerable—man were opened.

Kris Celebrates Her Hero

Kris and Bruce celebrated their fifth wedding anniversary in April 1996, just a few months before the entire Kardashian-Jenner clan had to relocate for six weeks to Atlanta for the 1996 Olympic Games. Kris was preoccupied with organizing her family's living arrangements and attendance schedule for the Olympic events. It was a major business networking opportunity for her, and as Bruce's manager, Kris wanted to stroke the egos of their major clients.

There had been a plethora of news articles and interviews with Bruce and Kris leading up to the historic event. Incredibly, the decathlon world record Bruce had set 1976 remained unbeaten. Additionally, publicity for the September publication of his motivational book *Finding the Champion Within* was strategically planned to coincide with the hoopla surrounding the Games. Even Oprah featured Bruce on a show devoted to former Olympic winners.

To celebrate the anniversary of his athletic heroism, Kris organized a surprise party for Bruce. She and Bruce were almost always together, so keeping his event a secret from him was a job in itself. Kris was a perfection-ist as a party planner, so she saw to every detail with exacting precision. She invited many of his Olympic pals and their mutual friends. She flew Bruce's dad there as the biggest surprise, as well as Mary Jo and Harry. But Bruce's four children from his two prior marriages were not included. Nor was his mother, Esther.

Despite all of the major planning and execution involved in the Atlanta trip, Kris remained undaunted. And instead of waiting until they were past such a monumental task, she decided to find their new dream home, because when Kris makes up her mind about a new plan, she's incapable of procrastination, even if there are the best reasons to delay acting on a decision. She wanted to have a new house to call home upon their return.

Since Kris was extremely organized, as were all her children, she wasn't worried about the actual moving of seven people. She was always energized by the thought of any new project, but creating and breathing life into a house was the ultimate high for her.

The neighboring cities of Hidden Hills and Calabasas were not on the tip of Kris Jenner's tongue. She had never even heard of this area or Los Angeles County. It might as well have been on another planet. She came to discover it through her friend Lisa Miles, who had moved there a few years before. Kris thought nothing of accepting Lisa's invitation to join her for a long overdue lunch until she was well into the forty-five-minute drive down the Ventura Freeway to Lisa's home.

Whatever reservations Kris may have had about the journey to the other side of her world were quashed once she saw the massive acres of land and huge properties. She loved the magnificent gates she drove through and the sounds of birds chirping. There were horses and llamas roaming in lush green fields. She was blown away by Lisa's grand residence, her tennis and basketball courts, and her menagerie of farm animals. Kris instinctively knew this was her new nest and she would get a lot more for her money in this area.

Kris wanted a house with at least six bedrooms. They had looked at similar homes that met her criteria in Beverly Hills, and they all priced around $10 million. Bruce's meager protests were quickly put to rest as Kris decided to move her family to Hidden Hills.

She went on an intensive search with a realtor, and after looking at scores of homes, she settled on an enormous Spanish-style house that needed some repairs and was in foreclosure. It had all of the features she envisioned.

A few days before she left for Atlanta, the deal fell through when another buyer stole it out from under her. Kris cried herself to sleep over the news. She didn't have time to look at other houses before leaving for the Olympic Games.

The Return of the World's Greatest

It was a Kardashian-Jenner convoy to Atlanta. Kris's private nurse, Jackie, accompanied Kendall with Bruce and Kris, and Robert and Khloé flew on a separate plane with Mary Jo and Harry.

A few days before Kourtney and Kim's flight, the girls got spooked by news of a bomb exploding at a rock concert in Centennial Olympic Park. The explosion killed two people and injured hundreds of others. As the plane was taking off, Kourtney and Kim convinced themselves a terrorist was on board. They were hysterically crying and screaming, "That guy has a bomb! We want to get off this plane!" They were bumped off the plane before it took off. An angry flight supervisor called Bruce in Atlanta. They were not allowed to fly that day and were sent home.

The next day they flew to Atlanta without a hitch.

The rest of the trip was a major success, especially Bruce's surprise party at Planet Hollywood, which was covered by *Access Hollywood* and NBC Sports. Kris, the adoring wife behind the gold-medal star, was center stage. She had spent months producing a video of Bruce's friends telling the story of his life and career. The retrospective even included an interview with President Gerald Ford. Chocolate gold medals and Dom Perignon champagne further elevated the festive event. The top of the cake had an image of Bruce's historic finish in 1976. It was designed by Hansen's Cakes in Los Angeles and was flown in its own seat on a commercial plane. Bruce was moved to tears. Kris had outdone herself as the ultimate gift giver. Her penchant for creating spectacular surprise events was becoming legendary.

Bruce recounted how Kris had his favorite plane restored and repainted red, white, and blue. She received accolades and applause from not only Bruce, but the rest of her audience.

For this magnanimous gesture, and many other reasons, Bruce discounted his two previous wives.

"I've had one marriage, and I'm married to her right now," he told members of the press.

The father of nine—who only six years earlier had been secretly transitioning to a woman—also revealed he wanted a second biological child with Kris.

"I do things in multiples of ten," he said, poking fun at his decathlon win.

Although Bruce's appearance at the Olympic Games was well received, reviews of his book were mediocre. It didn't score points for originality in the self-help genre, but Bruce's ebullience and charm distracted harsh reporting. He fielded the occasional good-humored ribbing from reporters who couldn't resist gouging Bruce about his film flop, *Can't Stop the Music*. While he laughed at himself along with the reporter, there was a trace of egotism in one interview that pointed out that his film had gone down in the annals of Hollywood history as the worst movie of all time.

"Well, it was," Bruce responded.

One brave journalist shot past the uber protection of publisher Simon and Schuster's publicity team and went for the blunt questioning about plastic surgery. Images of a twenty-something Bruce were all over Atlanta during the Centennial Olympics. He was turning forty-seven in a couple of months and not expected to look eternally young, but the mug on the Wheaties cereal boxes was definitely different from the face on view during Jenner's press junkets.

Fortunately, not enough of his Adam's apple had been shaved for anyone to notice the lump that must have risen in Bruce's throat.

"It was a stupid thing to do," he admitted. "I didn't like the hook of my nose, so I had it fixed."

Bruce was lucky to field only a nose job query, for even the laziest reporter could easily have noticed the feminization of his physique. Wearing polo shirts and khaki shorts revealed less facial hair and a different body tone than the taut, athletic figure of his past. If they had looked closely enough, they could have even discovered his enlarged breasts, which were the result of taking hormones during his early days of gender transitioning, prior to meeting Kris. Even with weekly tabloids and television shows like *A Current Affair* and *Hard Copy* at their height of popularity, nobody speculated how the champion within Bruce Jenner was actually a woman. Nor did anyone bother to check in with Bruce about his admission on CNN in 1988 that "a few years before" he competed in the Montreal Games, he had experimented with banned steroids substances "to see what the benefits were, or were not."

"Honestly, I got too big," Jenner said, noting that he also stopped because "it wasn't worth the possibility of getting caught."

The media had plenty to report without added sensationalism. Bruce Jenner was a terrific human interest story without any frills, so most of the coverage was positive. Journalists bought the three-act script Bruce and Kris carefully devised, which was the core of the branding messaging of all things Bruce Jenner. Yes, he was rich and famous, but he had known adversity and pain. He was still the perfect example of the anything-is-possible-if-you-work-hard-enough idea. He emphasized his dramatic fall from grace, when he was near homeless, practically living in squalor in his one-room shanty. How he was $500,000 in debt and had been rescued from his lonely existence by his glamorous wife, Kris. Everybody loves a comeback kid, so people applauded his incredible financial success.

Sure, he was making millions, but he had nine children to support, he reasoned. What better way to help himself than by helping others? He was being of service to the people who paid to hear him talk about greater mental and emotional health. His fitness machines and nutritional health products were essential to increasing physical health, which meant living more productive and longer lives. He charmed female journalists with his tales of changing diapers and carpooling teenaged children with raging hormones in between his demanding business travel. Of course, he was talking about Kris's kids and not his own four, but journalists always seemed to overlook the facts. They avoided speculating why it was only the four Kardashian children and Kendall who were photographed for features.

However, there was one book reviewer who took Bruce's "Frank Capra" tales to task.

"He's willing to pull at the reader's heartstrings describing his loneliness, and lack of love post-1976, but he conveniently glosses over the fact that he embarked on two marriages, and sired four children," the *Philadelphia Daily News* wrote. "Obviously, they didn't quite fit the storyline."

A Home of Their Own

While Bruce got the surprise of his life on the east coast, Kris got exactly what she wanted on the west: a 9,000-square-foot house in Hidden Hills.

Her realtor called her during the Games to tell her about a property she had passed on early in her real estate quest. Kris remembered the one. She tagged it "borderline ugly" and referred to it as "the monstrosity." It had purple carpet, black marble floors, extensive earthquake damage, no trees in sight, and a less-than-appealing pool trim. However, the realtor assured Kris there was another buyer on her heels, so she needed to decide quickly. The steep price drop on the six-bedroom, nine-bathroom property helped Kris convince herself and persuade Bruce that it was still a good investment. They agreed to approach it the same way they handled their business—one day at a time.

Escrow had closed by the time they touched down in Los Angeles.

Bruce Jenner's twentieth Olympic Games anniversary production was child's play compared to the massive work involved in turning their dreary fixer-upper into a dream palace. While Kris possibly sighed "hoo-boy!" in her private moments, such as when she was alone on the half-broken toilet in a downstairs bathroom, she never let the rest of the Kardashian-Jenners see her cry or whine. She was the team captain and the cheerleader.

Bruce and her stepdad Harry helped out in a number of handyman roles. Kris worked right alongside Bruce pulling up carpet and changing out the black marble flooring. After applying cheery yellow paint to the exterior, their new home began looking like it might one day be something special.

They were all moved in the week of August 16, 1996, barely a month after the Olympic Games. Bruce painted each bedroom himself, beginning with Kendall's. He also chose all of the colors. Every bedroom had its own patio. While they hired construction workers to lay tile, Kris decided she wanted to lay out Kendall's floor herself. It was hard work, but blissfully satisfying.

One of Kris's fondest memories was of Bruce planting all three hundred of the white iceberg rosebushes she bought to fulfill her fantasy of them surrounding the picket fence they had erected. His reward was getting a golf putting green in the backyard.

Their new home was a work in progress, but it was their sanctuary.

They named it the Haven.

The entire family was thrilled with the small-town vibe in the community, which included bake sales, parades, carnivals, fairs, and horse shows. They were living real-life versions of Aaron Spelling's prime-time television shows. This *Dallas* ranch-style living was still close enough to Los Angeles for everyone to continue keeping up with their hectic *Beverly Hills 90210* socialite lifestyles.

As Bruce went back out on the road to fulfill his promotional responsibilities, the fall season once again brought multiple birthdays and holiday celebrations. As this was their first home, and baby Kendall's first Christmas, Kris had set an even higher bar for herself than usual. Her neighbors would soon discover the Kardashian-Jenners knew how to throw a party. Lacking trees on which to string classic white lights, Kris improvised with elegant tall bushes, Christmas-themed statues, and a tasteful blow-up Santa and reindeer. When all was done, the outside looked every bit as magical as any star's home in a magazine layout.

Kris's Beverly Hills posse of gal pals hadn't a clue what to expect from her new home as they confirmed attendance at her annual Christmas Eve bash.

One girlfriend quipped, "Kris! I still can't believe you moved to Pluto! I'm fairly certain we will all need our passports for the trek."

Kris just smiled and said, "Oh, I'm sure you'll have an amazing time, and we'll have a car service pick you up, if you like."

Rolling down the windows of their blacked-out Mercedes to take in the majesty of the exclusive suburb put the brakes on any sneers. This was a Kris Jenner production in all of its traditional Christmas glory. Even the snarkiest of the socialites curbed their claws in appreciation of the beautiful environment Kris had created. It was a new beginning not only for Kris and Bruce but for many of their friends. The change of scene was a surreal experience for those guests who had shared memories of singing carols with Nicole and O. J. around Kris's tree. The previous two Christmases had been tainted by the horrors of Nicole's murder, the trial, and its aftermath. Most everyone had just gone through the motions for the sake of their children, but they found no authentic joy in those holidays. This year's vibe was different.

Making the holiday that much sweeter, Kris and Bruce announced to their dearest best friends they were pregnant with a second child. Nicole's namesake, one-year-old Kendall Nicole Jenner, toddled around the room generating smiles and warming hearts. It was as if a collective "pause" button of sadness had been released in their lives. It truly was a magical Christmas.

Inner Valley Girl

A few months shy of forty-two, Kris was living her dream: she was married with six children. Her second child with Bruce was born on August 10, 1997. Continuing the "K" tradition, they named her Kylie Kristen Jenner.

Understated but never underrated in her life's blueprint, Kris was also wealthy and almost famous. She had achieved every single bullet point of her plan and undoubtedly exceeded her own expectations. Yet there was always more fleshing out of Kristen Mary Houghton-Kardashian-Jenner's master to-do list. For other women Kris's age who were married to uber-successful men, with children entering adulthood, a comfortable retirement consisted of a safety deposit box full of financial security and dazzling jewelry. These hard-earned acquisitions as supporting players to their husbands' ambitions were enough to make them smile. This scenario never satisfied Kris.

Kris cut back on her travels with Bruce but remained as involved as ever in his business affairs. Taking time off from traveling to different cities and living out of hotel rooms was a welcome retreat. In the six years Kris had been Bruce's manager, she had not stopped to have any sort of real vacation time.

Even if only for a few hours a week, Kris captured precious bonding moments with each of her children. But having everything from toddlers to teenagers was a bittersweet package.

"Every day's a decathlon at our house," she reported. "We have ten different activities going at once. With kids ranging from a seventeen-year-old teenager to a seven-month-old infant, life can be crazy. My friends ask what I'm doing, and I say, 'I'm waxing one and diapering the other.'"

With two baby sisters at their mom's house, cell phones, fax machines ringing, and a constant flow of people coming in and out, Kim and Kourtney continually sought the solace of living with their doting dad. With Robert, they received more individual attention. They were the two most important people in his life. They also believed their fifty-three-year-old father needed them. The "trial of the century" was over, but Robert was still negatively affected and embroiled in the controversial aftermath. His high-society fiancée Denice had broken their engagement and moved out of their home, leaving him without a stick of furniture. She handled the breakup discreetly, but sources close to her say she was done with Robert's involvement in all things O. J. Simpson. Robert's cheating on her with a young attorney associated with O. J.'s legal team also remained a private matter. However, it was a huge event in Robert's personal life. It contributed to his depression and signaled the finale for his relationship with Denice.

Robert moved to a smaller home in Ventura and began dating his neighbor, Jan Ashley, the widow of a Hollywood actor and producer. It was a brief courtship before they married on Thanksgiving Day in 1998. He took his kids on their ski trip honeymoon in Vail Colorado. Thirty days later, the new Mrs. Kardashian annulled the marriage. She blamed her unhappiness in her marriage on Robert and Kris's children.

Kris was grateful Robert had relieved her of the more arduous and tedious aspects of parenting. She had neither the interest nor the inclination to stay on top of their school studies and welcomed Robert as the stricter disciplinarian of the two. The Kardashians' dad wasn't always the somber, strict father figure. He could also be playful and amusing, but Kris would never let him get a leg up on her when it came to entertaining. She exclusively owned the rights to being the most popular and lively, entertaining, and sometimes zany parent. But to avoid any disparaging favoritism between parents, she made sure they took equal credit with the kids for all major purchases, such as Kim's car.

No matter what age her children were, Kris was always relevant. They were always proud to show off their hip and worldly mom. A sophisticated and savvy mother increased their own social standing and image.

Kris's stunning eldest daughters were establishing their own business identities and independence during this time. Kourtney was no doubt greatly influenced by her adoration and respect for her father when she decided to study law. Kris cried for days upon her return from Dallas, where she and Robert helped Kourtney settle in at Southern Methodist University.

"It became time to say goodbye and a pit began growing in my stomach, probably the biggest pit I've ever had," Kris said. "I just didn't know how to say goodbye."

Kourtney switched her major when she failed classes that required public speaking. She continued her education at the University of Arizona and graduated with a degree in Spanish and theater.

Being at the center of twin scandals surrounding a fallen sports hero and a pop music idol increased Kim Kardashian's popularity in high school.

Scores of classmates wanted to boost their own profiles for being in the inner circle of the goddaughter of O. J. Simpson and girlfriend of Michael Jackson's nephew. Kim received accolades right alongside T. J. Jackson for his successful debut album, which sold over three million copies. In 1996, his group 3T was the second biggest-selling group in Europe, ranked behind the Spice Girls.

Kim and T. J. continued to date until shortly after her senior prom. As the relationship fizzled, Kim was establishing herself as a fashion stylist. To pay for repairs on her BMW, Kim began working in a clothing store in Encino. She also had her own "kimsaprincess" online store, where she bought and sold high-end clothing, shoes, and handbags. Kim earned the nickname Queen of the Closet Scene by reorganizing the closets of her wealthy girlfriends and their mothers.

With Kim and Kourtney out of high school, Khloé was lonely at Marymount. She started struggling with her weight. "All of Kris's children were born beautiful," a friend of Kris's said before accusing her of "fat-shaming" Khloé. "She had an image she wanted to portray. Everybody and everything had to be a reflection of her perfection."

But Khloé had other plans. She claimed her mother taught her to drive at thirteen so she could take her younger sisters to the hospital in the event of an emergency. But instead, Khloé snuck out of the house and drove the car to clubs to meet guys. She usually flanked Paris Hilton, who was three years older. Khloé admits to losing her virginity to an older man when she was fourteen.

From Kris's Mercedes catching on fire, to crashing head-first through the front windshield during a major car accident, Khloé's escapades were concerning. Kris was beside herself and out of solutions. Khloé suggested homeschooling. Kris and Robert agreed to let her drop out of her traditional classroom education and be homeschooled, but that didn't mean Kris was going to tutor Khloé. Robert hired a private teacher to assist Khloé with her lesson plans and she excelled at her studies. This was an ideal situation for Kris as well. Not only could she keep a closer eye on her middle daughter, but

Khloé became a surrogate mom to Kendall and Kylie. She relieved Kris of being tied to their house. She was able to shop and see her friends.

Although Bruce's mom Esther didn't spend much time in Kris's home, when she was there, she observed Kris's interactions with Kendall and Kylie. "I never saw her pick either one of those girls up to play with them," Esther revealed. "She always had to go someplace to 'meet the girls' for lunch. She had a lot of friends she liked to run all over with." Esther wasn't surprised Kris didn't take time away from her busy social schedule. "She didn't want to be bothered. She's going to do her 'thing' regardless of anybody else's feelings, or what normal people do. She would tell me on her way out, 'Oh, there's all kinds of food in the refrigerator. You just fix what you want.' When someone comes to my house, I entertain them. I cook ahead for them . . . I understand they were running a home business, and she might be too tired to make dinner."

According to another family member, sitting around at home with extended family made Kris uncomfortable. "She can't sit down and just be still and visit," the source said. "She needs a crowd, or a mirror. I'm not kidding. Some of our best conversations have been when we are sitting around her makeup tables in her dressing room."

Kris kept busy with several philanthropic groups and attended high-profile charity fashion events at famous residences of other socialites, such as the palatial home of Sugar Ray Leonard. She talked about fashion and babies alongside other young mothers like Sylvester Stallone's wife, model Jennifer Flavin.

A Hole in Two

Bruce played golf at the ritzy Sherwood Country Club in Thousand Oaks, a half-hour drive north of their house.

Sherwood became like a new home for Bruce, and when Khloé announced that she was leaving the Haven as soon as she graduated from high school, Kris and Bruce bought an undeveloped property within the gates of Sherwood. The Haven had been an incredible home for the Jenners, but it no longer suited their needs. Once Kris purchased the Sherwood land, she was already living there in her head. She convinced Bruce they needed to downsize and buy a townhome there while they waited on their new house to be built. Kris rented storage rooms for her Hidden Hills furnishings.

Bruce had only to step a few feet out his front door to play golf, and Sherwood certainly had the A-list star factor Kris enjoyed. The weekend they moved in, superstar golfer Tiger Woods was hosting a tournament there, so the place was crawling with celebrities. The new happening home brought the Kardashian kids back around from spending more time with their dad, and Kris and Bruce's cadre of friends came in droves to glimpse Kris's latest adventure. Her exotic Halloween party productions became legendary. Kris's costumes ranged from a sexy Alice in Wonderland to borrowing the actual Cruella De Vil costume worn by actress Glenn Close in the film *101 Dalmatians*. She dressed all the kids as "white fluffy Dalmatians."

"If you pressed their hands, the costumes would bark," Kris recalled.

Even Robert Kardashian dressed up as the Cowardly Lion to Kris's Wicked Witch when *The Wizard of Oz* was the theme.

Still, the new life at Sherwood had its drawbacks. In her haste to establish a residence, Kris had to forgo her usual meticulous attention to detail. Besides being a smaller residence, there was very little public parking on the cul-de-sac. It only took a couple of weeks for her to realize the stream of visitors, which included her children, was dwindling. She was further north from Hidden Hills, and thirty miles from Los Angeles, and nobody cared to make the drive. Kris began to doubt her impulsive decision. She couldn't get anyone but her mom and stepdad to visit when she was laid out on her back for two weeks due to bunion surgery on her toe. Kris sensed she was living her own version of the role Bruce was playing as one of the stars trapped in a jungle on the television show *I'm a Celebrity . . . Get Me Out of Here!*

"I felt I was marooned in my own reality," she later claimed. "I had disrupted my mojo with that move."

Kris braced herself for an exhaustive and expensive retooling of her plan. By the time Bruce returned from taping his three weeks in the jungle, Kris was able to summarize her misgivings about their move. She wanted her familiar life in Hidden Hills back. She wanted her friends over for pasta dinners followed by sipping wine on the floor in front of the fireplace as they played board games like Scattergories and Scrabble. Usually not one to wallow in self-recrimination, Kris had to admit to everyone she had made a huge mistake. She knew she should have thought it through more carefully. Though she and Bruce made the decision together, Bruce had blinders on when it came to pursuing his hobbies and activities. Kris needed to convince him to go in the opposite direction and lead him back to the area they had called home for almost a decade.

The Greatest Guy in the World

Moving back to Hidden Hills was not as easy as Kris thought. She had always bought and sold her homes at the right times, but the prices of homes that met her criteria in her former neighborhood started at $15 million. She realized that even when the children didn't live with her, she wanted plenty of room for them to visit.

Kris searched for properties in Calabasas, which was as close to Hidden Hills as she was going to get. She found a turnkey property while Bruce was out of town on a business trip, and negotiated with the seller and signed a contract without discussing it with him. Bruce returned to Los Angeles the proud owner of a new home he had never seen. Kris waited until the next morning, after he was fully rested, to spring the news on him that she bought a house without his knowledge. People have divorced for less, but Bruce kept his cool until after he saw the house. When he did, Kris was in the clear, as he announced, "I love it!"

"That is when I knew I had married the absolute greatest guy in the world," Kris reflected.

* * *

In the spring of 2003, Kris had only been back in Hidden Hills a few days when she received an emergency call from Mary Jo. Her husband Harry's health was declining due to a myriad of issues associated with diabetes.

Harry had been chipper and in fine form in April around Easter, when Kris and Kourtney visited him at his home in Clairemont. But while driving his Mercedes, the seventy-eight-year-old blacked out from an unknown cause and crashed. He was experiencing severe chest pains from the impact of the car's airbags. By the time Kris arrived at Scripps Hospital in La Jolla, he was breathing under an oxygen tent in the intensive care unit with a crushed sternum. Complications from the accident continued to mount. The most serious, especially for the elderly diabetic, was a staph infection.

Mary Jo stayed by his side day and night. Everyone prayed he would recover, but there was no indication of how long Harry would be hospitalized, or what he kind of care he would need after he returned to their home, so Mary Jo told Kris she would close her children's clothing boutique, Shannon & Co.

Kris refused to allow her mom to turn off the lights on her business of thirty-five years. It was a popular shop in the coastal community, as well as for tourists visiting La Jolla.

"You can't close your store," Kris told her. "You just bought all your stuff for spring and Easter. I'll come down and run the store for you while Dad's in the hospital."

Kris did not see this as a sacrifice. She was only doing what was expected of a daughter. Harry's wreck reminded her how her selfishness had kept her from seeing her biological father Robert Houghton before a fiery car crash ended his life. Nor would she forget how she chose her sexcapades with Todd Waterman over time spent with Mary Jo when she needed her. No matter what, she was going to fully support her mom during this difficult period. Bruce stepped up to assure Kris he would look after Kendall and Kylie while she tended to her parents.

Kris had no idea of what this act of generosity would entail, but whenever she gave her word, especially to family—and above all, to her mother—she kept it.

Besides, Harry had always been there for Kris. She called him Dad and her kids called him Papa. Mary Jo had been married to him for over three decades. He was always a generous, caring, and consistent stepfather to her and Karen. Kris had learned a great many lessons about life and business from him. He showed up for holidays and births and attended Grandparent's Day at the Kardashian kids' schools. And whenever Kris needed help, Harry would drop whatever he was doing and drive hundreds of miles to help.

Kris started commuting the hundred-plus miles to La Jolla each day and back to her home every evening. She would spend time with Bruce and the girls for five or six hours, and then she was back on the freeway to open the doors to her mom's shop, which was open on weekends. This exhausting schedule continued through May and June. She made sure Mary Jo had a good breakfast every morning before she left for the hospital, where she would sit by Harry's bedside until he had fallen asleep for the night. She would get up and do it again the next day. Kris also visited Harry, who was still under an oxygen tent in the morning. Karen usually came by in the late afternoon.

For several weeks, Kris looked after Mary Jo's business as if it were her own. She went through every drawer, nook, and cranny looking for anything she could find to clean and straighten. This had always been good therapy for her. But Mary Jo was quite the organizer, so Kris had her work cut out for her to find anything out of place.

Harry's health continued to worsen. He died in late June, with Mary Jo, Kris, and Karen by his side.

As Kris grieved the passing of her stepdad, she learned that another man whom she loved greatly was also on the verge of death.

Stage Four

Robert Kardashian attended Harry's memorial with Bruce and the kids.

Despite his and Kris's divorce, Robert was always considered family. He and Harry had a special rapport. As he comforted his ex-wife, fifty-nine-year-old Robert was facing his own mortality. As Kris cared for her parents, she was coping with Robert's announcement that he had been diagnosed with esophageal cancer. There had been some false hope over a potentially faulty diagnosis and a planned trek to China for a cure, giving Kris and Robert cause to cry and pray together. It wasn't long before their hopes were crushed as they learned his cancer had progressed to stage four, which was a death sentence.

Kris never forgot where she was standing when she got the devastating news from Robert.

"Are you sitting down?" he asked when she picked up the phone.

Kris didn't even articulate her worst fear before putting up the CLOSED sign in the window of Mary Jo's boutique and locking the door. Alone in the shop, Kris was filled with anxiety. She paced around the tiny store as she listened to Robert. She sensed the room was spinning around her and her ears were ringing. She couldn't believe what he told her. This was one of the most important people in her life, a man whom she loved dearly. He was the father of her children and it was fairly obvious he was soon going to leave her—this time permanently.

With her eyes swollen from crying, it was impossible to hide the news of Robert's cancer from her mother. She needed to tell somebody, and despite what Mary Jo was going through, Kris needed her mom. They cradled each other in their arms. Kris explained that she needed to go back to Los Angeles for a day.

Kris cried all the way to Calabasas. She realized that summer would have marked their twenty-fifth wedding anniversary.

Robert had told their children about his cancer after hanging up with Kris. Despite desperately wanting to surround herself with her four Kardashian children, Kris had to return to her mother, who needed to tend to her dying husband. It was important that after a draining day at the hospital, Mary Jo didn't walk into an empty house. After Kris closed the shop and visited Harry, she would take Mary Jo out to dinner. The two even got into somewhat of a routine watching the television program *American Idol.* If only for a moment, it took their minds off their shared overwhelming sadness.

Kris stayed with her mom a few days after Harry's service before going home.

Robert didn't look well at the funeral and left the gathering early. By the time Kris had returned to Los Angeles, he was bedridden. Kim and Kourtney were with him around the clock, taking turns caring for him and feeding him. She shared her children's heartbreak watching their dad get weaker and weaker, slipping away. She had gone through the very same thing with her mom during Harry's decline. Kris was so proud of how her kids were looking after Robert. Kourtney read to him while Kim made him Cream of Wheat cereal.

But Kris was worried about nineteen-year-old Khloé. She was staying away and kept her feelings bottled up. She wasn't coping well with her grandfather's death, and the prospect of losing her father too was too much for her

One of the last times Kris saw Robert alive was when she walked into his home with his sister Barbara, who kept Robert's wife Ellen occupied while Kris and Robert sat outside, just the two of them.

Kris held back her tears over her heartbreak of seeing Robert so frail and weak. Her mind flashed back to when she was seventeen. Robert was an older man, strong, powerful, and successful. He was the patriarch of their family. She looked up to him, and now he was a shell of his old self.

Priscilla Presley heard the news of Robert's terminal illness from Kris. While neither Kris nor Robert had spoken to her in decades, Kris decided Priscilla deserved to say goodbye to him. She called her ex-husband's former flame and held the receiver up to Robert's ear. The call was brief, but long enough to incense Ellen, Robert's bride. The two had barely returned from their honeymoon in Italy when Robert discovered he had cancer. Friends of Robert's soon-to-be widow believed Kris was meddling for the sheer purpose of making Ellen unhappy, while appearing to be executing a good deed.

But for Kris, it was the last big surprise she could arrange for her former husband. He did not live to see another holiday or birthday.

Another voice from the past reached out to Robert: O. J. Simpson. Kris claimed Ellen refused to let O. J. speak to his old friend before he died. Kris thought it was horrible of Ellen to prevent their farewell. But it never occurred to Kris that Robert, knowing he was dying, had given Ellen instructions to keep O. J. away.

"Believe me when I tell you that if it had been up to Kris, she would have delighted in being the guard at the gate, and taken great pleasure in telling O. J. to either bugger off, or facilitate them," observed a friend of Robert's. "Ellen could do nothing right where Kris was concerned. I think she was jealous that Ellen was the 'Widow Kardashian,' and not her."

However, any sympathy Ellen received as a result of Kris orchestrating the call to Priscilla was overshadowed by critical disbelief when Ellen refused entry to Robert's lifelong friends, Larry Kraines and Randy Kolker. Many of Robert's relationships had been strained due to his involvement in the O. J. Simpson case and had not been mended eight years later, when Robert was dying.

Kris said her final goodbyes to Robert the day he died, on September 30, 2003. Robert was heavily medicated and unable to speak, but Kris believed he heard and understood everything she said. Even decades after their divorce, some of Robert's friends still viewed Kris as Robert's beloved.

At the funeral, the kids sat in the front row with Robert's parents. Kris sat next to music mogul Irving Azoff, a lifelong friend and business associate of Robert's, and his wife Shelli Irving. Azoff told Kris she should be in the front row next to their children,

"Oh, no, no, that's not my place," Kris responded.

"No, actually, it is," Irving replied. He stood, picked up an empty chair, and placed it at the end of the front row next to the four Kardashian children.

Immediately after his burial at the family cemetery in Inglewood, relations between Ellen and the Kardashian gang were frosty. Friends and family members gathered together at the Bel-Air Country Club, where Kris and Robert's wedding reception had been held in 1978. Kris graciously held court, welcoming all of Robert's ex-girlfriends, including his former fiancée Denice. Robert's official widow was largely ignored.

"No one spoke to Ellen," Joni recalled. "She was by herself. She wasn't well liked."

It would seem Ellen was apparently disliked second only to O. J. Simpson. Even after being told Robert would not talk to him, O. J. continued reaching out to members of the Kardashian family after his death. In an interview, Robert told Barbara Walters that he doubted O. J.'s innocence. Robert was still conflicted inside. About a year before he died, Robert gave his sister Barbara a book that laid out a compelling argument for O. J.'s innocence. It was written by a private investigator who contended that O. J. Simpson did not kill his ex-wife Nicole and her friend. The central theme of the investigative story is that the real killer was not O. J., but a blood relative of Simpson's. Apparently, Robert even gave a copy to Barbara and asked for her feedback.

Despite their bad blood, O. J. will always remain a central character in Robert and Kris's private lives and public biographies.

CHAPTER TEN
THEIR SHOW
MUST GO ON

A New Chapter for Kris and Ko.

The deaths of two of the most influential and important people in Kris's life occurred just a few months before her forty-eighth birthday. It was a holiday season filled with deep reflection.

Every child from a broken home carries scars into adulthood, and Kris Jenner was no exception. But she looked back on her past only long enough to revise her future by creating new goals in the present. Kris's modus operandi in business was a solid formula for success. She simply expanded on what was directly in front of her at the time. She always built on a foundation that others had laid and perfected it as she executed her own vision. Over a decade earlier, she had picked up all of the elements that had once made Bruce Jenner great and retooled them. She had learned about obtaining endorsements and the world of public speaking from friends like O. J. Simpson and Steve Garvey. Costarring with Bruce in their fitness videos was nothing new—Bruce and his second wife Linda Thompson had released an exercise tape during their marriage—but Kris took that idea and turned it into a million-dollar enterprise. Nor did people remember Linda and Bruce baking protein chip cookies with Regis and Kathie Lee. Once Kris took control of an idea, she was unstoppable.

While she had marvelous mentors, going all the way back to her mother and grandmother, Kris instinctively understood marketing with publicity. Whatever strategies she and Bruce cooked up, they never deviated from their blended family brand. They were making plenty of money with a handsome financial portfolio, which included savings, investment and retirement funds, and life insurance policies, as well as money earmarked for college educations for their children. However, Bruce, the Olympic gold medalist, was at the top of the pyramid. All future income began with Bruce. He had just turned fifty-four, and while it was never openly discussed, Bruce's mortality crept into Kris's thoughts as she grieved the deaths of Harry and Robert.

Kris held onto the dream of starring in a television show. She knew she would never be content going into a workplace as an employee, even if she was a powerful CEO of a major corporation. Entrepreneurship was in her blood and she had tasted the sweet success of an unlimited earning capacity. Salaried and commission positions were dead ends by comparison, no matter how attractive. Also, she would never want to be away from the beautiful home she created, or to become unavailable to her children and Bruce, as she toiled at a nine-to-five job. There was no question that she wanted to work for herself. She knew she had to choose a business that interested her, or else she would lose her joy for it, grow restless, and eventually become discontented. Her work ethic was such that she would be fully committed, so she could not afford an error in judgment where something so important was concerned.

As she listed her passions, they included shopping and owning beautiful things, such as clothes, shoes, handbags, luxury cars, and homes. Shopping for anything that added beauty to her environment, and the money to buy all these things for her family and friends, brought Kris great pleasure. A common thread emerged: fashion, shopping, and family. A chic clothing boutique was a no-brainer.

She remembered her idea from the 1970s about opening a fashion store called Kris's Kloset. She had been so busy as a wife, mother, and manager that she had forgotten her dream of owning her own clothing boutique. Running Mary Jo's store while Harry was sick had reawakened these desires. She had styled all six of her children in the finest children's clothing. Each of them looked good enough to grace the cover of a magazine.

Kris hoped Kourtney, who had studied fashion at the University of Arizona, would want to become her business partner. Kourtney was already designing and selling a line of T-shirts to area stores, so a solid expansion would prove a valuable foundation for gaining experience in retail sales. It might also be a way to rein in nineteen-year-old Khloé, who needed some direction and motivation. Kris had worried about Khloé's difficulty in coming to terms with her dad's death. As major clumps of Khloé's thick hair fell out, it was obvious she was internalizing her grief.

As for Kim, Kris secretly hoped she would come into the partnership. She saw how much fun Kim was having running her eBay business, and the attention she was getting as a fashion stylist. But Kris would wait and let Kim come around to her. When it came to proposing change to her children, Kris knew the importance of timing. She knew when and how to get them fired up so they'd do whatever she wanted. Kris's real skill was getting them to a place where they started believing it was their own idea.

Kris was very much aware of the potential for her three young daughters to gravitate to career interests that might result in her seeing less of them. This was perfectly natural, but not acceptable to her. Even though everyone remained close, Kourtney, Kim, and Khloé were forging their individual identities. Kris craved more frequent moments with her girls. She decided to focus on how to weave everyone into their familiar family formation.

Before speaking to Bruce or the kids, Kris ran her idea past Mary Jo, who immediately gave her blessing.

"Just go out there, Kris, and do it," Mary Jo said, offering her thirty years of experience.

That was all Kris needed to hear to get out and hunt for retail space in Calabasas. She would sort out how to pay the rent after she found the perfect location. It was the exact opposite of how traditional businesspeople operated, but Kris got a rush out of achieving impressive results without conforming to convention. It also made for a much better story when she recounted how she went from nothing to something with only a mind's eye picture of what it would be like. Anyone who knew Kris well understood that while she may not have put pen to paper, she had plenty of calculating methodology swirling around in that brilliant business brain of hers. She showed her usual resourcefulness as she pulled Kendall and Kylie's high-end baby furniture out of storage. The decorative pieces added panache as store fixtures to display the adorable clothing and accessories she sold.

Within a matter of weeks, Kourtney was installed as part-owner and operator of her children's fashion business in a shopping district in the heart of Calabasas. A girlfriend of Kris's came up with the name: Smooch.

When the doors opened in January 2004, a little over four months had passed since Robert's death. Kris was proud to keep the Kardashian legacy alive. The store was also a physical manifestation of the promise she had made to the father of her children: to look after them emotionally, mentally, and financially.

Preparing for the launch of Smooch was a marvelous way for the Kardashians to distract themselves from the pain surrounding those first winter holidays without their father. While she was busy opening the store, Kris also decided to move into a new home. A few days into the new year, she signed a $1.7 million contract to purchase a five-bedroom, five-bath French Colonial house in the exclusive gated community of Calabasas Park Estates.

Kris finally had all the space she needed for her family and friends.

Bruce, We Hardly Knew Ya

By 2004, Bruce was looking less and less like a formidable sports figure. The once-revered Olympic hero was getting creamed in the media for his plastic surgeries. *The Orlando Sentinel* called him "the unrecognizable Bruce Jenner."

In a picture distributed to the Associated Press for his Olympics-related profile, Bruce's eyebrows were noticeably tweezed thinner than his wife's.

The banter became more aggressive and brutal when Bruce's name started appearing on the "worst plastic surgery" lists. Occasionally Bruce would kick back.

"Yeah, there's a lot of ugly stuff on the internet. The media today is tough, to say the least. It's ridiculous. Yeah, I had the hook taken out of my nose twenty years ago, and they're still talking about it."

Public figures are expected to be good sports about criticism. In Bruce's case, the spotlight's glare was more severe. He changed the playing field by going from a macho hunk to a more feminized version of himself, which was not what he had sold the world on. Of course, the public's disdain when their favorite stars age like ordinary people has always been a cruel and unfortunate cross for celebrities to bear, but photojournalists who captured Bruce's image in later years sensed there was more to his changing looks than vanity. Bruce's masculine physique and chiseled face had been his calling card in the late 1970s. Back then, Man Watchers Inc.—a San Diego women's organization—declared Bruce was in the same league of desirability as film stars Sylvester Stallone, John Travolta, and Sean Connery and NFL great Joe Namath. The group unanimously voted Bruce as "the most watchable man in the world," due to his "fantastic body, rhythmic movements, and animal magnetism."

Almost thirty years later, Bruce naturally preferred reporters to highlight his staying power as an in-demand motivational speaker for IBM, Coca-Cola, and Visa. He highlighted his smarts for jumping in on the latest technology when he entered into a venture with Grand Prix Auto Racing.

"I'm producing a virtual online racing show," he boasted.

The jabs at her husband's appearance were no doubt hurtful to Kris, but as his manager and publicist she could be counted on to trot out photographs that anchored Bruce's wholesome father image.

"I've got ten kids," he reminded members of the press. "Want one?"

Although Bruce's family continually ran interference for him, the next generation of Jenners started catching the public's eye. Young and adorable, Kendall and Kylie were frequently paraded in front of the media wearing matching dresses, often sitting on their parents' laps. When he wasn't fielding questions about his changing looks, Bruce was responding to queries about his less-than-stellar acting career. He revised the history of why he never made it to the big screen in the iconic role of *Superman*. Bruce recalled the Warner Brothers honchos asking him if he wanted to "test" for the role of Superman.

"Knowing nothing about the movie industry, I asked, 'Will it be a true-false, multiple-choice, or essay? I usually choke on tests.'"

Bruce was a pro at winning over the snidest journalist with his disarming, self-deprecating humor.

But Bruce wasn't the only family member repeatedly going under the knife. Kris had her share of plastic surgery in a relentless quest to look as youthful as her bombshell daughters. "Kris is obsessed with looking like she's still in her thirties or forties," a concerned pal said.

Based on photo evidence, a reputable cosmetic surgeon believes Kris "most likely first went under the knife in 2000 for a face and neck lift." "It also appears she had a chin implant and nose shaping to thin and lift her nose tip and slim down the top," according to a prominent Beverly Hills plastic surgeon. "The cost is staggering. Some experts charge upward of $35,000 to $50,000 for one procedure."

Primed for TV

Kris was never satisfied until she got her way, and living in Calabasas—as opposed to Hidden Hills—bothered her. She grew restless after the first year of holidays and birthday celebrations and once again scouted for a new home in her old neighborhood.

In November 2005, the Jenners' quest for a new house became headline news.

"More Room to Store the Javelins," spun real estate columnist Ruth Ryon.

"Bruce Jenner and his wife Kris have ten children. Need a bigger house," *Florida Today* newspaper claimed.

After only having lived at their Calabasas residence for a little over a year, Kris listed the French Country–style manor for $2.7 million.

"It's a great house," she told a reporter. "It's just not big enough."

The big news was how the Jenners were moving up to a 10,000-square foot, equestrian-zoned property in the San Fernando Valley. Kris must have been pointing to Kylie, Kendall, Robert, and Khloé when she listed her kids' ages as ranging from eight to twenty-one.

She certainly wasn't referring to Bruce's other four children, who factored into the equation as part of the legend of the real-life Brady Bunch. It had slipped under the radar of the media how their stepmother never mentioned Bruce's brood or included them in family photo shoots for the better part of a decade. Kris never corrected the faulty assumption that Bruce's biological children were always underfoot, as presumably it was part of their shtick. The son and daughter from Bruce's first marriage—Burt, who was nearing thirty, and twenty-five-year-old Cassandra—were content living their lives away from Kris and the spotlight. However, Brody, twenty-four, and Brandon, twenty-two, were getting an enormous amount of media attention during the summer of 2005. They were the stars and producers of their reality show on Fox, *The Princes of Malibu*. The cameras followed Brandon and Brody as they lived out their pampered, ambitionless lifestyle. They were college dropout slackers surfing the high tides of the Pacific Ocean. They lived on a twenty-two-acre Malibu estate belonging to their composer stepdad David Foster. Linda costarred in her sons' television series.

It would never have occurred to Kris during all those years she kept her stepsons at a safe distance, rarely including them in the inner circle of her family, that they would end up with a show. They were suddenly everywhere—online, television, radio, newspapers, and even in the sanctuary of Kris's home, where she had to hear about it all again from Bruce, who was the last person on earth Kris could enlist as a coconspirator in scoffing about this turn of events. He was, after all, the proud papa, and relished seeing his name in print alongside his sons' on an almost daily basis.

Brody had made it into the tabloids and weekly glossy magazines as the bad-boy stud sleeping around with some of the famous girls in Kim's circle, including Nicole Richie, Kristin Cavallari from *Laguna Beach*, and Lauren Conrad of *The Hills*. To their credit, Brody and Brandon initially never talked badly about their dad, nor did they bring up their stepmother Kris in their many interviews. Kris was confident that their public theatrics would be short-lived. She also had faith in Kim, who was gaining attention as she moved in on Paris Hilton's action. Kim had wrangled guest spots on Paris's show *The Simple Life* as her closet consultant.

But privately it was hard for Kris to wrap her head around how Bruce's kids were now celebrities in their own right, getting more attention than Kris and all of her kids. Few people have witnessed what a prideful and competitive creature Kris can be.

"She would rather be tarred and feathered with chewing gum and dog shit than let anybody see she's jealous of anybody," revealed a family member who has known her since childhood. "You have to know Kris like I do to understand how she operates. She's not going to let on to anyone how she's burning up on the inside. Not even her kids get to see much of that, except Kim. She's always been her confidant, and back then, they were coconspirators, because Kim was her real partner, as the heiress apparent to Paris Hilton. Lots of plotting and planning went on between Kimmy and Kris over this."

The combination of Paris raking in millions from her throne as the princess of reality television, plus Brody, Brandon, and Linda's fame slapping Kris in the face every day was especially unnerving. She knew she possessed the superior product. Kris was determined to do all of what Paris and Linda and her sons were doing, only better. The recent hype surrounding her real estate listing was evidence of how Kris could command attention without much of a hook. Bruce's brand had survived almost thirty years. Kris imagined what would happen when the Kardashians and *her* Jenners got into the reality show arena.

Kourtney Cracks the Code

As a top-tier networker and the most beautiful and outgoing of Kris's six children, Kim was the obvious choice to star in a television series. However, it was Kourtney who roped in the first big role on a reality show in 2005.

Courtenay Semel had been cast in a new show produced by the E! network called *Filthy Rich: Cattle Drive*, and she wanted Kourtney, her best friend since childhood, to be her costar.

"What's the show about?" Kris asked Kourtney over the phone.

"Me and Courtenay would ride horses and rope cattle on a ranch in Steamboat Springs, Colorado," Kourtney explained as she folded her new shipment of clothes at Smooch. "I'm not sure I want to do it. It's far away, and it's going to be like camping out in the sticks for six weeks. Who's going to open and close the shop?"

"I'm happy to cover for you, Kourtney. Don't worry about that. How much are they paying you?"

"All the money goes to charity."

"I see," Kris said. "Honey, think it over. It might be terrific exposure. Who else is on the show?"

Kourtney didn't have all of the particulars, but she knew her nine castmates would all be kids of celebrities who leave behind the luxurious comfort of their lives in LA for the Wild West. Kourtney was already dreading the unyielding smell of cow dung. Kris listened quietly before interjecting any thoughts.

"Sounds a lot like Paris's show *The Simple Life*," Kris commented. "Or that movie *City Slickers*."

Kourtney referred to her notes as she read the names of the crew producing and directing the series.

"Have you told Kimmy?" Kris asked.

"No, I called you first," Kourtney said. "Mom? Should I do it?"

"Let me think about it, honey. I will call you back."

Kris rang Kim and told her the news.

"Jessica Simpson's dad is the creator and one of the executive producers, along with that kid from *Malcolm in the Middle*, Justin Berfield," Kris told her.

"You're kidding!" Kim exclaimed. "Joe Simpson?! Why aren't Jessica and Ashlee on the show then?"

"Exactly!" Kris said. "That was my first thought."

It was a legitimate question since Joe was the manager of his two famous actress-singer daughters. He also starred in and produced episodes of Jessica and her husband Nick Lachey's wildly popular MTV television reality series *Newlyweds: Nick and Jessica*. The Simpson girls would have been an enchanting draw. Joe later clarified why his girls didn't participate in his series: "They weren't given the option because they didn't have wealthy parents," he said.

NFL player Mark Gastineau's daughter, Brittny, was a casting coup since she was already popular on another E! reality soap, *The Gastineau Girls*. Kim was stunned.

"But Brittny already has a show, Mom," Kim balked.

After socialite Fabian Basabe, the roster for *Filthy Rich Cattle Drive* went downhill regarding public recognition and star power. In addition to Courtenay, who was the daughter of Terry Semel, the chairman of Yahoo! and former head honcho of Warner Brothers, there was Kourtney. As a "nobody," she would have no real claim to fame. Her debut to a worldwide television audience was as "the daughter of Robert Kardashian, O. J. Simpson's friend."

Other fish out of the water included bodybuilder Lou Ferrigno's daughter Shanna, retired boxer George Foreman's son George III, singer Pat Benatar's daughter Haley Giraldo, movie idol Anthony Quinn's kid, Alex, and actor Robert Blake's son Noah.

It was an expensive three-month proposition for the cable channel, but the president of E!, Ted Harbert, had confidence that young audiences would get tremendous satisfaction out of watching the rich and privileged trudge miserably through the literal and metaphorical manure like ordinary folks.

Despite the fact that a majority of the cast were no-names with practically no previous on-camera experience, Harbert felt his talented production team could deliver a ratings winner. As the former head of NBC and ABC Entertainment, he had culled from a talented pool of independent producers, such as James A. Jusko and Brady Connell, whose credits in the adventure-reality genre included *The Amazing Race* and *Survivor*.

Kourtney was anything but a lazy, spoiled, trust-fund brat. She ran her own business. She was a college graduate. Sure, her birthright was that of a Beverly Hills socialite, raised with the best of everything. Yes, she dressed the part, and had been given the prerequisite brand-new car for her sixteenth birthday, but that was where her high living stopped. Unlike her friends, Kourtney and her siblings did not possess an accordion file of plastic credit cards with which they could run up endless bills. Nor was she an heiress to a fortune left by her dad. While it was the perception held by many, Robert Kardashian was not wealthy when he died. Except for money he had squirreled away for her Robert Jr.'s college education, the remainder of his estate went to his widow. Kourtney did not need humility branded into her. It would seem the premise for this cattle call went against the fabric of Kris's design for the family's carefully crafted image of nothing being handed freely to any of them. They worked hard for their money. Entitlement was a harsh word for deserving all the finest creature comforts they earned from the sweat of their perfectly arched brown brows.

Kris tried to ignore the potential downside of Kourtney's television offer. The bigger picture was exposure and future television opportunities for the entire Kardashian-Jenner family. As always, it was up to the individual to shine and gain respect for her discipline and hard work. Even in a desolate cow pasture, Kourtney was a Kardashian and would rise above her adversities. Regardless of whether the networks were feeding the public's insatiable and joyous appetite for seeing the fabulous famous fail, Kourtney could still entertain while staying true to the Kardashian brand. Kris knew that her daughter could get down and dirty with the best of them.

But Kris couldn't help but wonder why Kim wasn't in the running. She started daydreaming that maybe there was room for two Kardashians in that covered wagon. Kourtney liked the idea of her sister riding shotgun. Courtenay Semel agreed it would be great fun. In no time, Kim was introduced to the casting agents, and the producers put her on tape. Kris even managed to squeeze into the audition. Her inclusion was an asset to E!'s sales presentation tape, which went out to all of the programming decision-makers at individual stations all over the world. It was an easy sell to Australian broadcasters. The masses "down under" had a reputation for "taking the piss" out of Hollywood. Australian natives Peter Brennan, Steve Dunleavy, and Wayne Darwen were the creative geniuses behind the celebrity-driven tabloid television shows *A Current Affair* and *Hard Copy*, which gained prominence in the US in the 1980s and '90s. It was big news when Bruce Jenner toiled in the Outback as part of the B-list cast of *I'm a Celebrity . . . Get Me Out of Here!* Aussie network honchos eagerly picked up the series but renamed it *Rich Kids: Cattle Drive*.

Everyone was all too happy to have Kim's beauty and demurely unscripted whining seduce the buyers. In less than a minute and a half, she had three sound bites in the teaser that suitably conveyed the chaos of clueless deprivation viewers could expect.

"Are there showers there?" Kim said in the audition footage. "I need my tweezers."

Seated in a nondescript production office, Kim wore a crisp white blazer with a soft gold tank top underneath. Her French manicured nails pointed to her long dark hair. "I don't know what I'm going to do if I don't have a blow dryer," she announced.

This 2005 rough presentation tape was the first professional video of Kim as a future reality star.

Ultimately, Kim did not appear on the show, and there has never been any mention of her consideration for the role by her or anyone in her family. The tape popped up online in 2013. Executive producer Connell was unaware of the video four years later. He had almost forgotten Kim was even in the running for a role in the eight-episode series. "It was early on when the show's producers offered the part to her, but she backed out, saying she had a scheduling conflict," said Connell. "We were disappointed because Kim was fantastic."

Considering how much she wanted to be on television, it's surprising that Kim passed on her first television opportunity. Rumors hint that Kim's "scheduling conflict" was her unwillingness to leave her boyfriend, R&B singer William "Ray J" Norwood Jr., for three months. Their relationship was troubled, with both parties accusing the other of having other lovers. It was a well-known fact in the Kardashian household that Kim possessed a superior talent for snooping. "She's so good at breaking into people's voice-mail and has all sorts of other little espionage tricks up her sleeve," Khloé revealed.

It certainly would have been difficult for Kim to spy on Ray J from a remote area. Perhaps Kim saw the writing on the wall that there might not be room for more than one Kardashian on the cattle range, and as a loyal sister she didn't want to jeopardize Kourtney's chances.

"That's possible," confirmed Connell, "but we didn't get that far. Certainly, the network wanted Kim, but I didn't hear whether it was one or the other of the girls, but I also didn't hear they would take the two of them. Kourtney did an outstanding job. It proved emotionally exhausting for the cast, and Kourtney not only endured, but excelled."

Whatever Kim's reasons for rejecting the show, Kris signed off on it. Everyone supported Kourtney as she packed her faded blue jeans, cowboy boots, and hat and headed for the boonies. Bruce gave her on-camera professional pointers, and Khloé, as the official equestrienne in the family, gave her big sister riding tips. Kourtney, who had never mounted a horse, was expected to ride a horse for a hundred miles while driving a herd of cattle.

A few days before Kourtney's show premiered in August 2005, Kris, Bruce, Kim, and Kourtney were photographed on the red carpet at E!'s Summer Splash event at the Tropicana in Hollywood's Roosevelt Hotel. Kris and her girls showed off their ample cleavage in spaghetti strap dresses.

Both daughters wore white—their traditional show of sibling solidarity. Kourtney stood in between Kris and Kim, and Bruce was on the end. Kris and Kim pointedly aimed their faces in the same direction for every shot, without fail, but it was evident Kourtney had much to learn about posing on the red carpet. Kris buzzed around, networking on behalf of her girls for the rest of the night. It was the first time in almost fourteen years that Bruce wasn't the golden goose in her pitch.

In some television markets, Kourtney's show aired opposite her step-brothers Brody and Brandon's series, an irony that has never been noted by the media, though at the time, it was probably a non-story. Kourtney was still an unknown; Kim Kardashian was hardly relevant herself. Her identity remained handcuffed to Paris Hilton, as her constant wing woman.

Filthy Rich: Cattle Drive—as it was ultimately titled—resonated with its young demographic, earning over a million household viewers during its first season, which led the production team to believe there would be a second season. They were already bouncing around ideas for the next location and whether they would bring in an entirely new cast or keep their current crop of characters.

But the planning was over before it even began. Despite a winning four seasons, Fox pulled the plug on *The Simple Life*, saying their programming plate for mid-season shows was full. The story had a funny smell since Paris's series was already contracted for two additional years and plans to tape the show on the island of Maui in Hawaii were underway. Rumors swirled that Fox was fearful that they were not going to be able to control the two stars of the show. Paris eventually revealed that she and costar Nicole Richie were no longer friends. As if that wasn't enough of an implosion, Paris boldly announced that Nicole would no longer be needed on her show. Furthermore, she claimed her replacement would be Kimberly Stewart, her other longtime best friend. Paris provided reporters with the backstory of how singer Rod Stewart's daughter was her original first pick.

Kris's mouth fell open in stunned disbelief as Kim read her the article about Paris.

"This can't be good," Kris remarked.

"No, it can't," said Kim, as she locked eyes with her mother as if to say, "Are you thinking what I'm thinking?"

After assuring the world that Kimberly was not the new girl on the show, Fox promptly pulled the plug. It was exactly what Kris predicted would happen when Paris backed the mighty network into a corner.

Enter the fearless and ferocious Ted Harbert. He proved his television mogul chops as he brilliantly outbid his former bosses at NBC, as well as VH1, MTV, and the WB Network. He not only snapped up the pending two seasons of *The Simple Life* that his competitors wanted, but he also snagged the rights to rebroadcast the previous seasons. The bold move made good on Harbert's vow to "spend as much money as necessary to find hits."

"No one show is more important than the brand," he stated.

In the end, *Filthy Rich: Cattle Drive* was sacrificed to make room for *The Simple Life*. Harbert no longer needed a show bearing the likeness of the real McCoy.

Kris watched and learned and realized Ted Harbert was the kind of guy she needed to make her new best friend.

Shopping the Kardashian Show

While it's true that Kim's allure, ambition, and expert schmoozing skills were key elements in the Kardashians' rise, Kourtney also did her part.

She was always viewed as the daughter least interested in starring on a show, the one who reluctantly followed the herd and made the best of the situation. But Kourtney assumed the lead in moving the family's show business plans along with producers at E! well over a year before Kris courted the network.

"Shortly after the show was canceled, Kourtney called me and asked for a meeting to pitch a show," producer Connell revealed. Connell confirmed she arrived at the meeting without her mother or Kim. Instead, she brought her former costar and friend Courtenay. They did not have a pilot tape to present, as most likely they assumed the producers already knew what they were like on camera.

As Connell listened to Kourtney's pitch, he realized it was not a good fit for his production company. "My partner and I were more interested in outdoor transformational reality shows," Connell later admitted.

"What Kourtney pitched was a docu-soap show about following her and Courtenay around. An up-close, personal look at their lives, which would have included their families, I'm sure. And, yes, I do recall Kourtney telling us she owned a clothing store, which would have been an aspect of the show."

Celebutante television shows, such as the one Kourtney was proposing, had been dominating the airwaves for a few years. They revolved around those wealthy young socialites who were capable of getting media attention: the "famous for being famous" genre.

Kopy Kat

Kris was vague, almost secretive about the content of the reality show she shopped around to networks the following year. She has never disclosed the identity of the producer she paid to shoot and package it. The video of Kim, Khloé, and Kourtney as young Beverly Hills socialites running their high-end clothing boutique has never surfaced, with only a handful of industry insiders recalling seeing it.

Kris wants history to remember her soup-to-nuts version of how she engineered the creation of *Keeping Up With the Kardashians*.

Meanwhile, shortly after *The Princes of Malibu* aired, Linda filed for divorce from David Foster. Brody Jenner picked up gigs on other reality shows, including MTV's *The Hills*.

While Brody's love life with starlets continued to make the gossip columns, his stepsister Kim Kardashian was gaining the lead on him, and on her girlfriend Paris as Hollywood's new "It" girl. Kim moved in on her stepbrother Brody's action and even had a cameo with him on *The Hills*. When Kim's appearance ended up on the cutting room floor, it was no doubt viewed by Kris as another missed opportunity for Kim's discovery as television's next superstar.

But Kris was still just getting started with her foxy family's foray into television. She marked the spot where she left off networking, scheming, and dreaming for a show only long enough to buy her next home. It could not have escaped Kris's savvy business mind that whatever home she chose would become an integral part of her future series. A novice observer of television programming had only to channel surf to see wrapping houses around storylines was thematic and en vogue, as was the case with singer Ozzy Osbourne's reality show, *The Osbournes.*

When a home that Kris had previously desired in Hidden Hills went on the market, Kris told her realtor to make an offer on it before they even went inside. She wasn't about to let it slip through her hands. She had not seen the property since her first house hunt in 1996, but she had never forgotten the place and had often driven by it, wishing it was available.

Kris admired the beauty and graceful elegance of the property. The long winding driveway was surrounded by lush green lawn and pink roses. There was a covered veranda with rocking chairs. It didn't have Kathie Lee Gifford's waterfront view, but it was similar to the grand but cozy feel of her friend's home on the east coast. Just shy of 4,000 square feet, it was roomy. Kris inspected the four bedrooms and the decadent walnut floors. There were three fireplaces and skylights overhead in the open and coffered beam ceilings. The property boasted a pool and a spa. Flagstone flooring on the deck added to the picture-perfect outdoors.

For a second time, she made the decision to buy a house without consulting Bruce. And again, she got away with it. It was their third move in four years.

Soon after the Jenners settled into their new home, Esther Jenner visited her son. After divorcing Bruce's dad later in life, Esther was planning to marry another man, Frank Avery. They were visiting Frank's twin brother in a nursing home near Hidden Hills, so Bruce invited Esther to bring her beau over to meet the family. Frank sat on the other side of the living room to allow Esther space to have her reunion with Bruce, Kendall, Kylie, and Brandon, who had come over to see his grandmother. Esther didn't notice when Kris came in the room. Eventually, she saw her chatting up Frank.

"We hadn't seen one another in years, but Kris didn't get up to greet me," Esther recalled. "She didn't make any effort to talk to me. Not even a hug, and of course, I didn't expect her to invite us to dinner. She would never have put herself out this way."

Back at the nearby hotel where they were staying, Frank told Esther about their bizarre exchange. According to Esther, "She sat down next to Frank. He said, 'I don't think we've been introduced,' and Kris said, 'I am Bruce's manager.' Most of the evening, Frank thought she was only Bruce's manager. She didn't correct herself. Can you believe that? Frank told me he was confused because she talked business to him, but then he said, 'I could tell as the conversation was going on with all of you that she was his wife!'"

Kim Swipes Right on Paris

It is standard practice for paparazzi and entertainment news reporters to court members of a celebrity's entourage for insider tidbits. By analyzing photos, editors profile the virtual "nobodies" who most frequently pop up alongside the most marketable stars. They write down license plate numbers and track down friends and associates of their famous prey and pay private investigators to obtain the identities and phone numbers of potential sources.

In the mid-2000s, the internet changed the gossip game. As celebrity publications like *The National Enquirer* and *Star* were losing readers, competition for celebrity scoops was fierce. The new breed of poison pens were bloggers. Perez Hilton (no relation to Paris) was the premier source for news about celebutantes, but Harvey Levin—a former criminal attorney who went from courtside reporting for local LA network television news affiliates to prominence as a celebrity crime expert for slickly produced syndicated shows—was gaining ground. Levin was in the right place at the right time covering murder cases involving the rich and famous, like Lyle and Erik Menendez, the brothers who were convicted of slaughtering their parents. Harvey launched the celebrity online news site TMZ. He had incredible law enforcement contacts that ran license plates and passed tips along to him when stars went sideways and ended up in the slammer.

In May 2006, Kim stuck the sweet spot of media coverage when she was caught walking out of an afternoon showing of *The Da Vinci Code* at a Brentwood movie theater with reality show hunk Nick Lachey. She was the first girl to be seen on a date with Nick since his split from Jessica Simpson. Kim became fresh meat for the paparazzi and her public persona immediately skyrocketed.

Nick later said, "We went into a movie. No one followed us there. Somehow, mysteriously, when we left, there were thirty photographers waiting outside. There are certain ways to play this game, and some people play it well."

Kim's attorney, infamous legal eagle Marty Singer, denied that his client ever tipped the paparazzi to her movements—or leaked any stories.

The following night while making the rounds with Paris on Sunset Strip, Kim realized the swarm of photographers were screaming to *her* instead of Paris. "Whatever you do, just smile," Paris advised her former shadow. "Don't say anything under your breath because they now have video cameras, too." It didn't take long for Paris to realize Kim was a quick study.

Over in Hidden Hills, Kris was content.

"This house was more than a house," she remarked later. "This house was a stage. This was the house that everybody would fall in love with. This was a home dying for an audience. I could never have dreamed of how large that audience would become."

There was a synergistic vibe as her kids once again marked their own territories in the house. They came and went, swam in her pool, and stayed on weekends, even when they were paying rent on their own places. Kris Jenner's chicks with Robert Kardashian had come home to roost, and it filled Kris's heart with happiness. She loved being needed and watching her children interact with one another.

When a store space opened around the corner from Smooch, Kourtney decided to expand her clothing line to include teenagers and young adults. Khloé became an official partner in the new venture. As Kris had predicted, Kim wanted to join in on the fun. They named the new store D-A-S-H—short for Kardashian—in honor of their dad's nickname.

As their business partner, Kris talked shop with her daughters over pasta. They talked profits and projections for opening more apparel boutiques. Ideas for a family reality show continued to pop up in conversation. They all agreed that a television series would catapult their stores to greater success.

Seeds of a Sex Tape

Kourtney threw her entire being into running her new boutique. Kim admired her older sister's dedication, especially since she knew Kourtney secretly couldn't stand kids.

"She hated when the kids came in," Kim later revealed.

Meanwhile Khloé, who was wearing wigs to hide bald spots from picking hair from her scalp, continued to seek refuge in the nightclub scene. She was still struggling to mourn the death of her father properly. Khloé's emotional eating had racked up almost thirty extra pounds on her frame. When it became apparent that fat-shaming her daughter was counter-productive, Kris led by example and enrolled the two of them in a Tae Bo exercise class.

Kris never had to worry about Kim. She was always the "good girl." Kris approved of her daughter's romance with Ray J. He was a good-looking, successful rapper, and the brother of pop singer Brandy, who was a stylist client of Kim's. Of all her children, she knew Kim best—or so she thought.

Kim also had a secretive side. Shortly after her dad died, Kim planned a trip with Ray J for her twenty-third birthday. Ray J brought along a camcorder. The night before heading to the Esperanza resort in Cabo, Mexico, Ray J filmed everything from the mundane to an explicit sex romp. Later, they shot more sex scenes in a hotel room in Santa Barbara, California.

Home movies of young couples baring it all and having sex were not unusual in the emerging age of video, especially in Kim's circle of liberal friends who were always tirelessly pursuing relief from the boredom of too much time and money to burn. Fast cars and the party life could become as dull a routine as working a nine-to-five.

Kim had undoubtedly been influenced by Paris Hilton's foray into the forbidden world of porn. The diminutive, blonde, blue-eyed hotel heiress already had untold millions in trust funds as she embarked on her television career in 2003. The sex tape Paris made with her former boyfriend Rick Salomon was an open secret in Paris's camp of confidantes. But publicly, Paris contended she was unaware that a camera was on her while she had sex with Salomon.

News of Paris's boudoir video hit the gossip columns and was in circulation for the world to see. Kim watched from the sidelines as Salomon's tape went from his personal website to making millions of dollars in distribution as the raunchily titled *1 Night in Paris*. Kim saw Paris through the exhaustive drama of legal proceedings against Salomon and the production house. Kim and Kris observed how the scandal contributed to the surge in ratings for Paris's *The Simple Life*. Ordinarily, a good girl like Kim, who was still relatively unknown to the world, would shy away from such scandal, but Kim continued to see and be seen with her famous friend, who became ultra-famous.

Paris was more accessible than ever. She signed a music contract with Warner Brothers and immediately landed a book deal. *Confessions of an Heiress: A Tongue-in-Chic Peek Behind the Pose* was an instant bestseller.

Kris's Mad Men

Ryan Seacrest, the E! network, and Bunim/Murray Productions are the names most commonly associated with the development and execution of Kris Jenner's vision for a television show featuring her family.

Yet the contributions of Seacrest's agent John Ferriter and Seacrest's producing partner Eliot Goldberg are essential for accurately reporting how it all began. Everyone was talented and driven to succeed, but without the combination of luck, opportunity, timing, and of course Kris Jenner, any number of scenarios could have transpired. They are all equal partners in revolutionizing the face of television, breeding a new pop culture, and ushering in social media as the lollapalooza of marketing tools.

In addition, Goldberg and Ferriter are credible sources who can put the infamous Kim Kardashian sex tape in perspective. For years the traditional party line for explaining the Kardashians' rise to power goes as follows: desperate for fame and fortune, the wildly ambitious Kris Jenner birthed a television show on the back of her daughter Kim Kardashian's porno flick.

As Kim's individual brand grew, she was reputed to be equally as hungry as her mom for notoriety and money. She has repeatedly denied she was complicit in unleashing her sexual adventures on the world in February 2007 in order to land a television show—one of those true Hollywood mysteries that has never been proven but is widely accepted as fact.

It's worth noting that no one quoted here, either on or off the record, came looking for attention. They are all successfully employed with nothing to gain from telling how the then-untitled television series was developed in 2006. Nor did a single one of them express any bitterness or jealousies toward either Kris or Seacrest. This makes the re-creation of events, from their viewpoint, all the more credible and compelling. Their unanimous confirmation that Kris drove her dream to reality further validates her significance to the show becoming the wild success it became and remains to this day. None of them ever dreamed they were making history.

"It's a phenomenon. What can I say?" Goldberg said in 2016, a decade after he was introduced to Kris and her family.

In 2006, Goldberg and Seacrest were hungry producers. Both men were in their late twenties and had a lot riding on their production deal with E!. The network was the source of their seed money to grow Ryan Seacrest Productions. As a radio and television personality, Seacrest wanted to be the next Casey Kasem or Rick Dees. After working with Merv Griffin, Seacrest realized producing television shows was a more lucrative and lasting pursuit than being a television host.

Enter Seacrest's agent, John Ferriter. As the senior vice president of programming for William Morris, Ferriter was known as a star maker, and has even been referred to as the "real deal Jerry Maguire" for his tenacity and persistence in promoting his talent to the top of the showbiz pinnacle. Ferriter believed in Seacrest's dream to be the next Dick Clark and tapped into his potential. He took him from a Los Angeles radio DJ from Georgia to a major media figure. He was responsible for passionately pushing him in front of the decision-makers to host *American Idol*. The move immediately transformed the *American Top 40* morning radio personality's career. In addition to Seacrest, Ferriter represented Larry King, Donny and Marie Osmond, and the Osbourne family.

In his mid-forties, Ferriter still had the look of a fresh-faced kid. His laid-back surfer-in-a-suit look was disarming. He was a powerfully persistent and tenacious agent. While he shared the representation of Seacrest with fellow agent Andrew Scher, it was Ferriter who was the driving force behind securing an unprecedented development deal and talent contract with E! in 2006. The cable channel reportedly spent $21 million on the three-year package. Under E!'s umbrella, they had a shoestring staff search for the next hit television series that would rocket E! into orbit. But Seacrest couldn't do it alone. He needed a strong right hand.

Ferriter and Seacrest knew Goldberg was their guy. They tapped the thirty-something whiz kid, who looked like a young Michael Douglas, to lead the development team. Goldberg had been a part of the reality genre explosion. He had studio, syndication, and cable experience. He could fuse celebrity pop culture with soap opera dynamics. His task was to create and execute a reality television series that complemented the network's entertainment-centered programming

But a year later, Goldberg and Seacrest were coming up short, despite having sold a few shows. Nothing was screaming super hit.

"We have to get something for E!" Goldberg told Seacrest. "What's the fastest way to get a show on E!?"

"A family show," they said in unison.

"A wild Hollywood family, for sure," Goldberg said. "But that's hard to find."

"I loved the Osbournes," Seacrest said. "Why can't we find something like that?"

The men agreed if could find another wacky showbiz family, they would have a chance at creating a dynamite series. They put the word out to several casting directors in LA to search for "families who want to be on a series."

Deena Katz was one of the talent executives Goldberg approached. She immediately thought of Kris Jenner. When Deena was a talent executive on *Pet Star*, a series devoted to deciding the most talented pet in America, she booked Bruce as a celebrity judge. Over the past few years Bruce had appeared on *The Weakest Link* and *Hollywood Squares*. Deena and her husband made a beeline to Kris's house for dinner. As she remembered it, their house was a zoo of activity. She told Kris the time was right for her family to make their mark in television. Of course, Kris said, "I'm in!"

Since Kris and her kids were a largely unknown entity, Deena heavily dropped Bruce Jenner's name into her conversation with Goldberg. The world's greatest athlete was the best starting place of recognition.

Goldberg knew of Bruce Jenner, the sports hero. A memory of the orange Wheaties cereal box bearing Bruce's image popped into his head for a quick second.

"Bruce Jenner was the big thing," Goldberg recalled ten years later. "He was an Olympic athlete. He'd been on some other reality shows. They were known because of O. J. . . . There were little bits of the story you knew, but I didn't know them at all."

Deena connected the dots for Goldberg as she ran down Bruce's credits on celebrity reality shows.

"You should meet them," she coaxed. "Trust me. My husband and I just had dinner in their home. Complete chaos swirls around this family constantly. It's exactly what you told me you are looking for."

Eliot respected Deena, who went on to become the top talent executive and producer for *Dancing with the Stars*.

"Okay," he said. "I don't really know how I can sell them. I don't know what the story is. I'm looking for something special. Bring them in. I'll see them."

Goldberg called Seacrest to give his partner the update.

"Don't get excited. It may turn out to be nothing, but Deena Katz just turned us onto a potential family for a series."

"Who are they?" Ryan asked.

"I'll tell you what I know, which isn't much, but I trust Deena. Bruce Jenner—"

"Yeah, the Olympic champion sports celebrity," Ryan interrupted. "I know him."

"Yeah, well, it was described to me as a mother and her three daughters, and they embody every bit of the craziness and mad mayhem of the Osbournes. That's all I know. May be something, may be nothing, but I'm open to taking a meeting with them. What do we have to lose?"

"Well, you are right," said Seacrest. "Let's see what they're about. You know my thoughts about the Osbournes."

The following day, Kris, Bruce, Kim, Kourtney, and Khloé were sitting in the waiting area of E!'s high-rise office suites on Wilshire Boulevard in the Miracle Mile district of Los Angeles. Kris smiled as she glanced over the framed photos of the E! stars like Paris Hilton and Nicole Richie. She had known them since they were babies. Her daughters' photos would soon be hanging alongside theirs; Kris was sure of it. While Kris recalled she was all on her own at Seacrest Productions, Goldberg remembers the first meeting somewhat differently, with Bruce and the eldest Kardashian girls with her.

Once everyone was settled in Goldberg's office, Kris just riffed. She told him it would be a "blow-by-blow look at our crazy, loving, fun, and incredibly close family."

He understood the nucleus of the show would revolve around the five people in the room: Kris, Bruce, Kim, Kourtney and Khloé.

"The family dynamic is what would make this a special show, and that is what we need to focus on," Kris said just before her daughters got in on helping with the pitch.

That's when Goldberg saw the magic of the chaos that is the Kardashians. "Within five minutes, I watched a show performed in front of my eyes," he said "It was the yelling, the bitching. I'd never seen anything like it in my life! I was like—is this real? This is insane! This is how they talk to each other? *You fucking bitch?!*"

Goldberg looked over at Bruce, who was sitting in the corner, shaking his head.

"We start talking about sports," Goldberg recalled. "I'm thinking, *Oh, my God! It's Bruce Jenner, the American athlete!*"

Kris was positive that Goldberg was on the hook by the time she concluded her presentation.

"The girls would be the stars of the show, but all of us around the girls will also be the ones that people can relate to. We will be able to broaden our demographic and our audience because, together, we span all kinds of age groups. We could cover ten to one hundred."

Goldberg stood up and thanked the family for coming. He said he would be in touch shortly. Kris stepped back just long enough for Bruce to lead the girls out ahead of her. She was the last one to walk out of the producer's office for a reason. As Goldberg held the door open for Kris, she stopped and placed her hand on his arm. Eliot never forgot Kris's enthusiasm and confidence when she said, "Let's do this show together. Listen, Eliot. Shit always happens to our family. I can tell you and promise you—if we do the show, shit will happen to us!"

As he walked back to his desk, Goldberg thought, "I don't know what that was, but there's something there."

Yet, he admitted, "I had no idea how to sell it because nobody really knew what 'this' was, or who they were."

After what he had just witnessed, Goldberg was confident Kris and her daughters could create a compelling pitch meeting with E! executives, but he wanted to call around and check on them before he ran the idea up the flagpole.

Ferriter ensured that everyone stayed on point. He was eager for Seacrest and Goldberg to find the hit the network needed, and quickly, and it was his job to keep the fire underneath them hot. There was a lot riding on this production deal.

Ferriter, Seacrest, and Goldberg all found themselves in awe of Kris Jenner. With each meeting they got to watch her in action, and it was always a powerful experience. She had a family full of "K" names, but "S" words were her essence. By being self-assured, substance savvy, solid, sharp, sensational, stunning, and a survivor, she seduced these guys into trusting her with the fate of their production company. She was just doing her thing with no real understanding of how it all worked behind the scenes. She just knew the synergy was there and that's all she needed. "Ryan is one of those guys who gets very excited and animated," Kris said. "He has great energy and I could tell he 'got' it. He had a vision."

Kris recalled the moment she knew she Seacrest and Goldberg were the guys. "When you are pitching a show to someone, you want them to get on your bandwagon and see the same thing you are seeing in your head. It's organic. And Ryan and Eliot got it. They just did. It was one of those magical moments where everything clicked."

Seacrest remembered only one meeting, followed by a home video of a family barbecue shot by his team, and then the show was instantly on the air. In the first scene, Kris was discussing Kim's butt. Yet Kris insisted that the show was anything but exploitative: "My family could have said, 'Are you out of your mind?' But everyone was excited!"

Everyone except for E!'s vice president of programming, Lisa Berger, who candidly relayed her initial reluctance about the concept.

"When we got a call from Ryan Seacrest Productions asking if we had met the Kardashian sisters, I said, 'Honest to God, I'm not sure if there's a show there,'" Lisa recalled.

"Bruce Jenner was the big thing," Goldberg recalled. "He was *the* Olympic athlete. The Kardashians were known because of O. J. The Kardashian sisters had been making the rounds about the store, so they were on E!'s radar. There was a little bubbling about the [sex] tape, but . . . nobody really knew who Kim Kardashian was."

Ferriter agreed that the sex tape was of little significance to making the show happen.

"It was of zero importance to getting the show on the air," he said. "How the video was utilized after the fact, I have no idea."

Seacrest persisted and Berger agreed to take a meeting with the mother, sisters, and stepfather. Berger was blown away once she saw the family dynamics and gave her approval for a pilot to be shot.

"The addition of Kris and Bruce made the show what it is," Berger later declared.

With a sizzle reel in the works, it was time for Kris to make her play as executive producer before the cameras rolled.

"I need to have my hands in this," she told Seacrest and Goldberg. "I need to have some control."

Both men unanimously agreed.

In Kris's mind, it was a done deal. She gathered everyone around the table and made the announcement over dinner.

"You're not going to believe this, but we got our own reality show," she told her family. "It's going to be on E!"

While Kim and Khloé jumped for joy, Kourtney and Bruce had their reservations. Kourtney was in a serious relationship with her new boyfriend, Scott Disick, and wasn't sure she wanted cameras invading their privacy. Bruce later revealed that he was pressured by Kris to participate. But his reality television history suggested that he was easily persuaded.

A Show of Her Own

Kris was most excited about performing on camera.

It was her dream come true. However, she was far too disciplined to get swept away by the thrill of it all. Being on television was going to be fun and glamorous, but Kris took her role as executive producer seriously. While it may have been casually thrown her way as a means of network executives keeping the "talent" happy, it was more than a vanity title to her.

As executive producer, she had control of her dynasty's destiny. That was of singular importance to Kris. She need not remind anyone. It was enough that she knew.

Officially, Kris's producer title meant she had a say in the show. The only person who could limit Kris was Kris. She was going to outthink and work harder than anybody else. She would earn everyone's respect.

As Kris told a friend of Mary Jo: "Of course, I have a bit of the jitters sometimes, but I'm actually not scared. I'm surrounded by an incredible team! Ryan and Eliot's passion and commitment makes my heart sing, but God knows it's really all up to me. Bruce and every one of the kids are so supportive and have so much faith in me. I can't let them down . . . I can't let myself down. I've got to stay a step ahead of everyone for my show to take off. Listen, tell my mom when you see her Kris said, 'Nobody looks after my money like me.'"

"I know exactly where that came from," her mom's friend said with a laugh. "Harry Shannon!"

Kris's voice suddenly dropped to almost a whisper.

"I so wish my dad—both my dads—and of course my dear sweet Robert were alive to see this."

Kris was determined to give E! executives the hit they wanted. That was a no-brainer, but she also knew how to knock it out of the park in terms of what they needed. Going the extra step in thinking about longevity for not only her show, but the network's bigger picture agenda would endear them to Kris. This meant praise, which she craved more than money.

As she studied the *Real Housewives* franchise, Kris saw a trend that was disturbing. Sure, the Bravo network was reaping huge benefits, but the people on the show had a short shelf life. How would they survive beyond the end of their usefulness to the series? Reality stars for the sake of being reality stars was too limited. Few were going to become legitimate actresses, and even then, the instability of an actor's life, going from job to job, was a difficult struggle. So, if they had any aspirations for businesses beyond the show, how would they attract attention for their products on their own power, without a show behind them? Kris knew she had to think in reverse in order for her children to have a future. She was already in her fifties; an opportunity like this was probably not going to come along again. *Keeping Up With the Kardashians* would serve her kids and not the other way around. By the time E! figured this out, the momager's machine would be too far out of the station to pull back.

The scenario she proposed for the first episode of *Keeping Up With the Kardashians* was the epitome of Kris Jenner: calculated risk-taking.

"Sex sells," Kris declared to her kids as she sold them on what was about to happen.

To date there is no evidence that Kris leaked Kim's sex tape in 2006 for the purposes of launching a show, but since it was out there anyway, it was hay for the horses.

Cooking Up a Hit

According to Goldberg, the sizzle reel of the Kardashians being themselves around the pool of their home in Hidden Hills during a barbecue was "gold."

"As I watched it in the edit bay, I thought, *I'm not crazy!* But, still, how are you going to market a show about a family that nobody really knows?"

When Goldberg showed it to Lisa, she fell in love with it too.

"This is great," she reported to Ferriter. "There's something here. We've got to give this a shot. Like I told Eliot and Ryan, we want this. We need this, and now that we want it, I need it fast!"

It was music to Ferriter's ears. He knew E! had a specific need, and this show's concept was right up their alley. Lisa had a condition, which Ferriter deemed more than reasonable and a great idea. She wanted to combine Ryan Seacrest Productions with Bunim/Murray Productions.

Mary-Ellis Bunim and her husband Jonathan Murray defined reality television when they merged the elements of soap opera and documentary together with *The Real World* in 1992. It remains MTV's longest-running non-scripted television show. Ferriter could see potential for a great relationship for many more projects with Bunim/Murray, and Seacrest could only grow as a producer working with them. They had a number of projects ongoing at all times. The bottom line was Ryan Seacrest Productions needed Murray's experience of producing on the fly with people who had never been on camera before.

When Ferriter wanted a quick rundown of the series he called Seacrest, but when he wanted down-and-dirty specifics he rang Goldberg. He needed to hear Goldberg's take on the show following the sizzle reel, before they got into bed with Bunim/Murray.

"Talk to me," Ferriter told Goldberg. "What are we doing here? So, we're doing a show on a bunch of these girls? What are the beats? What's going on? I need answers."

"Well, the show's Kris," Goldberg said.

"The show's the mother?" Ferriter asked, wanting to make sure he heard Goldberg clearly. "You're telling me this show is wrapped around the mother?"

"Yes. Kris has this unbelievable vision for her daughters. It's almost like she's the quarterback of how to run the plays with everybody. And she knows the daughters so well and they respect and respond to her in such a compelling way. Kris is constantly moving the chess pieces around on the board. Yet she loves the daughters and doesn't want to put them in harm's way, but she knows what she has to do to look out for their best interest, without flinching."

Ferriter heard the commitment in Goldberg's voice as he described each of the characters to him.

"Eliot figured out the basic template after he saw the sizzle reel they shot," Ferriter said. "Kris figured out where to put the pieces, and Bunim/Murray figured out how they would make it work."

Seacrest's memories of producing the initial episodes of *Keeping Up With the Kardashians* now blend into the charmed path of his career, but Ferriter recalled there were many tense moments.

"He was a busy entrepreneur and personality, figuring out what his place was in this entire universe. Ryan didn't really know whether it was going to work or not. Because I don't think he was hands on. I don't think he had the vision. Ryan was being Ryan. He's doing a radio show. He's doing the E! show. We had endorsements for him at that time, and there were other specials coming in."

Seacrest relied heavily on Goldberg to lead the development team, but just as the *Keeping Up With the Kardashians* was about to launch, he was having conflicting thoughts about whether the return on this new show was going to be worth the effort. Seacrest complained to Ferriter.

"You know, Eliot's spending all of his time on this, to the point where he's not really doing anything else."

Ferriter called up Goldberg.

"Is there a problem? I'm hearing from Ryan that certain things are not getting done."

Goldberg was calm but firm: "No. What's getting done is we're making a show that's going to be a hit. And it's this show that will enable everything else to get done."

No Stopping Kris

The series got the green light from E! for four episodes and debuted on October 14, 2007. While, according to Ferriter, Kim's sex tape had little to do with launching the show, Kris seized a golden opportunity under the age-old theory that sex sells. The first season was all about the sex tape. Kris explained on camera, "When I first heard about Kim's tape, as her mother, I wanted to kill her, but as her manager, I knew that I had a job to do, and I really just wanted to move past it." Such contradictions are consistent with Kris's nature. Ellen DeGeneres once called Kris out: "Do you ever confuse your lies . . . like to me? Cause you lie to me all the time." Kris remained cool and just laughed it off.

During the first season Kim also posed nude for *Playboy* with her mother in attendance. Khloé got arrested for a DUI, and ten-year-old Kylie slithered up and down on a stripper pole. The series had established itself as no-holds-barred intimate entertainment for drama, scandal, and chaos within this family. It was an instant hit with audiences who were hooked on this guilty pleasure escapism. Over the ensuing seasons there was no shortage of conflicts between siblings, marriages, babies, divorces, spin-off series, and all forms of delicious decadence. Kris had established herself as her six children's "momager." There was no stopping her.

By 2011, when Barbara Walters told the clan in a television special they were all void of talent—"You don't really act, you don't sing, you don't dance"—the Kardashians were laughing all the way to the bank. They had reportedly made $65 million the previous year through clothing lines, cosmetics and perfume, magazine covers, mobile games, and all kinds of product endorsements.

But it was Kris and Kim's mastery of social media—Twitter and later Instagram—that took the reality stars to another level of fame and fortune and allowed them to connect with fans directly.

Kris's Top Influencers: Kim and Kanye

Kim dating rapper Kanye West in 2012 and ultimately marrying him in 2014 afforded Kris a whole new playbook. Kim received a makeover by Kanye, and the notoriety of their coupledom landed them covers on respected fashion magazines such as *Vogue*, forcing Anna Wintour, *Vogue*'s editor-in-chief, to acknowledge them as fashion powerhouses. This meant inclusion to— *after* exclusion from—the famous *Vogue*-sponsored Met Ball, a fundraiser that is regarded as one of the most prestigious and exclusive social events in the world, held each year in New York City.

Kris's invites were not far behind. The connections and new friendships Kris made as a result of being introduced to Kanye's fashion world was a dream come true for Kris, who fantasized in her youth of opening Kris's Kloset. Posing on the red carpet at the Met sent her into another universe. She was accepted in the fashion industry as a major player.

While he originally declined to appear on *Keeping Up With the Kardashians*, after four children with Kim, Kanye can now be seen on episodes, which is a plus for Kris.

The Gift of Gab?

By the summer of 2013, Kris's lifelong dream of hosting a talk show was finally a reality. While her marriage to Bruce was in peril, as he had moved out and taken a place in Malibu the year before, Kris was not going to ruminate over the two-decade marriage as a new TV opportunity presented itself.

She was a few months shy of fifty-eight when *Kris* debuted on a limited run of Fox television stations. The show's title attempted to put the television personality in the same league as first-name-only icons Oprah and Kathie Lee.

For many years, showbiz types were refused entry to television journalism. Even those who were raised in the major television markets such as Los Angeles, Manhattan, and Chicago had to go to smaller markets to gain experience after college. The prestigious jobs were scarce.

But being a television newswoman or a daytime talk show host never looked too complicated to Kris, who studied pros like Joan Lunden, Diane Sawyer, and Katie Couric. She undoubtedly had all the qualifications. In addition to a pretty face and winning personality, she was intelligent and possessed the charisma to engage viewers. She was always confident she would eventually get to the soundstage where she stood in July 2013, in front of a live television audience—an audience that was there to see *her*.

"I love the whole talk show world," Kris gushed to *Rolling Stone* magazine. "If I could dream as big as I want, I would dream to be able to get up and do this every single day."

Kris was aware that being relevant was the key to talk show success. It's about the here and the now. She understood that even though she and her family were the biggest stars on television, she needed a reel of clips that demonstrated her ability to carry off interviewing guests outside the weekly episodic format.

Kris proved she had the chops and paid her dues as a supporting player on the daytime discussion series *The Talk*. For two years, she had been a frequent guest host on the CBS-produced syndicated show. With the prerequisite coffee mug in front of her, she sat around a table kibitzing. She often cohosted with Sharon Osbourne, her former—but friendly—reality show rival. Then–CBS president Les Moonves must have approved of Kris's talent or she would not have appeared alongside Les's wife, cohost Julie Chen. After all, Kris was warm, bright, personable, and popular. Judging by how often she was called to substitute for an absent cohost, she was an obvious fit for her show.

That no one had brought her talk show out of development—where it had been stuck for years—and into syndication was an open wound for Kris. It was a secret pain she shared with few people. It was beyond her comprehension that it could take six long years for her to have a show she didn't have to share.

A construction crew built a set that resembled her real-life opulent home, with custom ceiling-to-floor drapes that framed arched windows and pillars. Guests sat on plush armless chairs. Bouquets of fresh-cut calla lilies and roses in her favorite color, white, were staged about. Everything was designed to accurately represent the elegance of Kris Kardashian. Kris was unfazed by the six-week run that the Fox network required before committing to producing a full season. She didn't even mind that she was required to have a cohost.

The show premiered on July 15, a month after Kim and husband Kanye West gave birth to their first child, North. There were lots of oohs and ahhs when Kris came out holding a baby, believing it was her new granddaughter. In reality, the child belonged to one of her staffers. Kim and Kanye were adamant that they didn't want Kris to monetize the baby.

"He's made it clear to Kim that he won't let Kris run their life," a close friend said, explaining that Kanye prevented a $5 million sale of Kim's "pregnancy diary."

Whenever guests went silent on the short-lived talk show, Kris filled uncomfortable seconds of dead air with her gift of gab, offering up unsolicited revelations. One of her "truth talk" segments had her sharing a story where she and Bruce had airplane sex. Adding to the awkwardness of the story was the fact that Kris was, at the time, estranged from her husband of over twenty years. She was simultaneously telling the media that while they were living separately, she and Bruce still slept together.

"I think she was pretty uninteresting," confessed Frank Cicha, a senior VP of programming for Fox. "When the camera was on she looked not just like a deer in the headlights, but like a deer that already got hit."

Cuttin' Bruce

Almost immediately after the sixteenth and final episode of her talk show aired, Kris confirmed she and Bruce were officially separated.

She said they were "happier" living apart. When pressed for the reason for her breakup after two decades of marriage, Kris pondered the same question. "I don't think it was the pace of life. We've always gone 150 miles per hour, and Bruce has more energy than anybody. I just think it evolved. I really can't put my finger on it."

But according to insiders, Kris continually made Bruce feel unwelcome in his own home, and even his own skin.

"She constantly yells at him," an insider said at the time. "She calls him terrible names and makes jokes about how ugly she thinks he is."

The separation was the latest in a long line of failed Kardashian marriages in the twenty-first century. Kim had already racked up two. Back in 2000, Kim eloped with music producer Damon Thomas. Kim blamed their 2003 divorce on physical and emotional abuse. She tried marriage again in 2011, this time with NBA player Kris Humphries. After making $1.5 million on a wedding photo deal, the pair split after only seventy-two days of marriage.

Meanwhile, Khloé married basketball star Lamar Odom in 2009. Believing it to be true love, she even took her husband's surname. But after months of separation speculation, the couple filed for divorce in 2013, allegedly due to Lamar's infidelity and rampant drug use.

To fans and the media who kept up with the Kardashians, Bruce seemed like the clan's latest casualty, appearing distant and detached for several seasons.

Stunts like bringing her ex-boyfriend Todd Waterman on the show for a reunion was no doubt a sign of disrespect. While the show is plagued with accusations that storylines are manufactured, Bruce's disgust and anger over Todd's appearance back in their lives seemed authentic and palpable. Todd's popping up at Kris's request also traumatized the Kardashian children, who saw his affair with their mother as the catalyst for their parents divorcing. Kourtney sought therapy soon after the show's airing.

And there were plenty of other issues. "Bruce and Kris have reached the biggest impasse in their marriage yet," an insider revealed. "He loved being a team with her in the early days of the marriage, but there seems little hope for reviving that between his outside interests and her managing and running the Kardashian-Jenner empire 24/7."

Bruce's mom had a slightly different take on her son's home life. "The last four years were living hell," Esther Jenner claimed her son told her. "'And that's long enough to live in a living hell,' he told me."

Kris did not seem to be losing any sleep over her beloved Bruce's absence, but rather was pining away for her first husband.

"The only regret, if I had to do it over, would be divorcing Robert Kardashian," she confessed at the time. "But then there wouldn't have been Kendall and Kylie, so that's the way I look at it."

Kris and her four children with Robert had mourned the tenth anniversary of his passing just the month before, so it's natural that her ex-husband's memory was still on her mind. But it seemed odd to some to be discussing Robert so intimately when Bruce was barely out the door.

As time went on, Kris attempted to dig deeper for the answers the prying public wanted. "There was definitely a shift in the way we treated each other," she reflected. "We will always be the best of friends because that's the dynamic of our relationship. We definitely get along as a family and with the kids. We're so connected in that way. We love each other."

A month later, the separation from Kris appeared to be a good look on Bruce, who had just turned sixty-four. He was all smiles for the cameras as his soon-to-be ex-wife presented him with an athletic award at the All Sports Film Festival.

"She supports me," Bruce told reporters who asked him about their strained relationship. "I see her every day. We're doing absolutely great."

But privately, Bruce was tremendously embarrassed. "He hates it when cronies at the country club jokingly call him Bruce Kardashian," divulged an insider. "Kris is continually perceived as the money maker and the one who wears the pants in the family, and he's sick and tired of the humiliation."

He first confessed to his mother that he and Kris needed a break. "We're going to live separately for a while," he told Esther.

A few months later, Bruce was back at the beach, living on his own. Esther noticed a different tone in her son's voice. "We didn't talk long when he called, but he seemed unhappy and very lonely," she recalled.

As Bruce ventured out from his bachelor's pad in Malibu, photo editors carefully scrutinized every photo of him, searching for the latest changes in his looks, hoping to confirm rumors that he'd had feminization surgeries. During the last few years of his marriage to Kris, he wore his long hair in a ponytail and was spotted with painted nails. Just before Christmas in 2013, *TMZ* reported that Bruce consulted a Beverly Hills plastic surgeon about flattening his Adam's apple. It was the tip the media had been waiting for, but Bruce still denied he was, again, in the first stages of a sex change.

Bruce explained he initially saw the surgeon about removing a large scar on his nose, which was the result of the removal of a cancerous growth. He explained talk between doctor and patient proceeded to a discussion about his Adam's apple. "I just never liked my trachea," Bruce noted.

Suddenly, his sixty-three-year-old ex-wife Chrystie emerged from the shadows to attack Kris, accusing her of leaking a photo to cause Bruce grief.

"You're crazy," Kris said when she was ambushed by a *TMZ* reporter wanting to know whether she whether she was aware of Bruce's transitioning and if she supported this decision.

"Ninety-nine percent of the rumor is made up."

But Chrystie wouldn't let Kris off the hook that easy. "This is a plan by Kris to destroy his life," the mother of his oldest two children told the press. "She's not a pleasant woman. She's out to get him. She doesn't want him to be happy."

Bruce had been married to Chrystie for nine years. She vehemently denied he was anything other than a "manly man." But Bruce later revealed that Chrystie was the first person he told about his desire to become a woman. He even fathered his two kids with her after his revelation.

Exactly one year after they announced their separation, in September 2014, Kris filed for divorce from Bruce, citing irreconcilable differences. She continued to deny rumors that Bruce was transitioning.

"They've been saying that since 1976," Kris told *Entertainment Tonight*. "For me, that's not my experience with Bruce. He's a great guy. I love him. I don't know what he's going through right now. I think he's just very happy and I think every time he makes a change in his life, whether it's emotional or physical or whatever he's doing, somebody's going to comment on whatever look you have going on for the day."

* * *

Not surprisingly, Esther breathed a big sigh of relief when Bruce called and told her about the divorce. "They weren't living together, but she was butting in on everything he did," she said. "They used an accountant instead of a lawyer, and I'm sure she came out with the bigger end of the stick. But money isn't everything."

According to court documents, the Jenner divorce settlement was reportedly a split of $60 million. Kris also paid out an additional $2.5 million to her ex-husband. Their assets, which were profits from their television shows, Bruce's speaking engagements, and their co-owned businesses, were reportedly placed in a joint account. Kris kept her Hidden Hills compound and Bruce retained his Sherwood Country Club membership. One of Bruce's first purchases was an eleven-acre property in Malibu. The $3.5 million, four-bedroom home featured 360-degree canyon, mountain, and ocean views. He bought a Porsche, a motorcycle, terrain vehicles, and other toys. He also underwent breast augmentation surgery, where he had silicone breasts implanted in his chest.

In April 2015, he came out as a trans woman during a prime-time interview with Diane Sawyer.

"For all intents and purposes, I'm a woman," Bruce confessed, clarifying that he had no attraction to men.

The following month, in an emotional two-part special of *Keeping Up With the Kardashians*, Bruce discussed his personal agenda about his transition and answered his family's questions.

"Are you planning on not being Bruce anytime soon?" Khloé asked on the episode.

"That's quite possible, yeah," Bruce told her. "I got everybody out of the nest, everybody's doing great. I've got to deal with myself. The last thing in the world I want to do is hurt any one of you. Maybe if I'm not honest, it's because I'm afraid to talk to you about this subject because I know it hurts. I understand that. Am I doing it right, Khloé? You can never do this right. There is no right way to do this."

In June, Bruce revealed his new name and new look to the world. He had officially become Caitlyn Marie Jenner.

"If I was lying on my deathbed and I had kept this secret and never ever did anything about it, I would be lying there saying, 'You just blew your entire life,'" she confessed.

CHAPTER ELEVEN
TRANSITIONS

Kris Gambles on a New Love

Kris wasted no time fueling the media's unquenchable thirst for her to date again. She was linked to several eligible Hollywood hunks, including Britney Spears's former fiancé Jason Trawick and *The Bachelor*'s Ben Flajnik.

"My mom is living the good life right now," Khloé said at the time, keeping up the party line of Kris as a highly sought after single woman: "When I found out she was dating, or even texting back and forth, it was so weird to see her giggly."

Kris continued to surprise her children when she became romantically involved with thirty-two-year-old Corey Gamble, whom she met in Spain at designer Riccardo Tisci's fortieth birthday party in 2014. The much younger man was listed as an employee of Justin Bieber's manager, Scooter Braun. The story over the years has been elevated to Corey having been Bieber's tour manager, thus explaining Corey's estimated net worth of $2.5 million.

He emerged from the shadows of obscurity to instant fame as Kris's lover. Nobody, especially Kris's children, expected the romance with a guy twenty-five years younger than her was going to last. Corey never gives interviews, despite being a recurring character on the show. Little is known about his family in Georgia. Being free of familial ties suits Kris just fine. It's a bonus because she only has room for her own immediate family.

Corey's ex-wife, *Atlanta Exes* star Sheree Buchanan, talked about her relationship with Kris's beau in an issue of *In Touch* magazine. She advised

Kris to beware. "I know Corey. He's all about power and money and will do whatever it takes to get it."

Kris paid no attention to the warning, and while many believe Corey is little more than a traveling companion and bodyguard for Kris, the relationship suits Kris just fine. They are still going strong six years later, whatever they are, with Kris repeatedly stating she has no plans to marry.

The Woman Within

In April 2017, two weeks before Caitlyn Jenner began promoting her autobiography *The Secrets of My Life*, she announced she had undergone genital surgery.

"I am telling you because I believe in candor. So all of you can stop staring," she said about her penis extraction. "You want to know so now you know, which is why this is the first time, and the last time, I will ever speak of it."

Undoubtedly, her six children—especially twenty-one-year-old Kendall and nineteen-year-old Kylie—were relieved. Surely they could do without hearing news broadcasts about their dad's sexual organs.

Caitlyn's third memoir was one of the most highly anticipated books of the year, since she was expected to reveal scandalous tales about her ex-wife. Her body parts may have changed following gender reassignment surgery, but Caitlyn's brain-for-blame remained the same. The book was a litany of episodes where she perceived that Kris had castrated her mentally and emotionally when Caitlyn was Bruce.

Readers were eager for examples of what Caitlyn meant when she confided that Kris was "mean to me."

However, days before the book's publication, these attacks on Kris were already ricocheting back on Caitlyn. Even Kris's harshest online critics reproached Caitlyn as "ungrateful" and "a narcissist incapable of taking responsibility for her actions."

At the beginning of her tour, Caitlyn also shared that she never felt comfortable having sex with Kris Jenner, though she also admitted they enjoyed many happy years as husband and wife. Caitlyn dissed Kris for forcing her to repress her outer woman for two decades. She admitted stifling her true identity was not the real reason their marriage ended.

"It only began to implode when *Keeping Up With the Kardashians* became a runaway success, and Kris was at the helm of a multimillion-dollar family franchise in which she controlled all the purse strings, including mine," Caitlyn divulged. "I have a credit card but purchases are carefully pored over."

What she didn't explore was how the Jenners' bookkeeping methods were a mutual decision, made when Caitlyn appointed her ex-wife as her manager. In countless interviews over many years, Caitlyn publicly credited Kris for bringing her back from financial ruin. Back in the day, Caitlyn blamed her money woes on her previous management and complained she was relegated to a meager allowance. As a result of Kris's shrewd handling of the former Olympic gold medalist's business, Caitlyn is a multimillionaire today. Caitlyn did not contest the terms of their out-of-court divorce settlement the year before, where she walked away from the marriage with over $30 million, so the financial split was obviously satisfactory to the former athlete then.

Even as she was appearing on the 2017 episodes of *Keeping Up With the Kardashians*, Caitlyn maintained Kris was a Svengali. The sixty-seven-year-old entrepreneur alleged that Kris pushed her into appearing on the hit television series, where she remained a fixture for almost a decade and was still starring on episodes the week her book went on sale.

While she dismissed the television series, Caitlyn claimed the concept for the show was her idea.

"I don't remember any involvement other than this very awkward guy who was uncomfortable in his own skin showing up on camera," *Kardashians* producer Ferriter said, weighing in. "I just looked at Bruce as somebody who I thought had way too much facial surgery, and seemed to be completely, you know, pussy-whipped."

The more salacious details about the inside of their marriage were omitted from Caitlyn's manuscript after her E! show *I Am Cait* was canceled. While she was in the process of dictating her story, it had become essential that she curry Kris's favor for her inevitable return to *Keeping Up With the Kardashians*. However, Caitlyn claimed the manuscript was censored because she didn't want to "hurt the kids."

According to Caitlyn, the pain her other four biological children felt as they grappled with the effects of an absentee father was Kris's fault. By all other accounts, it is true Kris showed little to no interest in uniting the families, but it was Caitlyn's decision to stay away from her kids.

"Kris wasn't comfortable with her spending time with her four older children, so I think she threw a monkey wrench into it, but he allowed it," admitted Esther, who was by far the saddest casualty on Caitlyn's list of alienated Jenners.

There's no better example of Caitlyn's selective memory in her tell-all than her failure to fully share the blame for abandoning her mother. Following years of neglect, the ninety-year-old Jenner had nothing good to say about her ex-daughter-in-law. She will never understand why Kris didn't show her the respect due to a mother-in-law or keep her looped into their family. As she nears the end of her life, Esther's heart aches over how she missed out on enjoying relationships with her grandchildren Kendall and Kylie.

"I would ask Bruce repeatedly, 'Get those girls to me in the summertime,'" she said. "They were still in grammar school. They were free for the summer."

But Esther contends that she is not bitter. Nor does she point to the irony of how total strangers shared the majority of these momentous family events as they unfolded on television. All the while, Caitlyn's kids with Kris were practically strangers to her.

"When I would see Kris on television talking about how important family is, it would just make me cringe inside," Esther admitted.

Since 1990, not a day has passed where Esther didn't wish her son was on the other end of the phone when it rang. Now, atoning for her decades of abandonment, Caitlyn calls her mom every night, like clockwork. On any given evening, as Esther sits alone at her Iowa home, sipping the occasional whiskey highball as she talks to a friend on her telephone, when Caitlyn's number appears on her cell phone, Esther immediately hangs up on the other caller. "I've got take this. It's Cait," she'll say.

The conversations are mostly about Caitlyn's day. The dutiful daughter pilots her private plane from Malibu to show up at Esther's door for impromptu visits. This newfound attention thrills Esther. Unlike Caitlyn, Esther refuses to allow the hurt caused by years of unexplained absences to rob her of whatever time she has left with her daughter. She harbors no bitterness, not even for Kris. However, she's glad she "never has to see her again in this life.

"I know I must forgive her," Esther concluded. "I have to."

* * *

Wholeheartedly, without any reservations, Esther embraced Caitlyn's gender transition with enthusiasm and verve. But there was one memory of mistreatment that continued to haunt her. It pained Esther to concede Kris did not act alone in the instance. She couldn't ignore Caitlyn's complicity in this deeply hurtful betrayal.

As the story goes, Bruce had flown Esther to LA for her eighty-seventh birthday. He secured Esther's permission to tape her birthday celebration for *Keeping Up With the Kardashians*. As they rode to the Jenner home from the airport, Bruce led Esther into what she believed was a private conversation between a mother and son about Kris. She was unaware that she was secretly being taped.

The cameras caught a choked-up Esther agreeing to Bruce's suggestion to take Kris aside and "tell her, 'I love you'" to "make everybody feel better." After blowing out the candles on her birthday cake following a celebratory dinner at the family table, Esther kept her promise. She and Kris had a heart-to-heart chat in the kitchen with cameras hidden from view. Though Esther poignantly apologized to Kris, Kris made no amends of her own.

Esther was humiliated and hurt when she saw the episode. It featured a variety of snarky comments and backstories from individual perspectives, which included Kris and other family members. Esther was not privy to their statements as fact and was deprived of any opportunity to share her truths on camera as part of the show. She was stunned to watch Kendall and Kylie call her their "invisible grandma" to millions of television viewers. Esther was also seen telling Bruce that he was her "favorite child." This no doubt created an awkwardness between Esther and her other two children.

"How could you do this?" Esther sputtered during her next conversation with Bruce. "I could have said all kinds of awful things about Kris, which I would never have intended for anyone to hear but you! What if something horrible had happened between us when she and I talked?"

But Bruce downplayed the sticky situation. "You were great," he told her. "Don't worry about it."

The moment serves a prime example of the partnership between Kris and Caitlyn—personally and professionally. They sacrificed the elderly matriarch of the Jenner family for the sake of the show.

I Am Woman, Hear Me

Caitlyn wisely believed she should quietly offer up the final draft of her manuscript to Kris before she handed it over to her publisher.

After poring over Caitlyn's memoir, Kris's critique was pointedly brief. She chose her words carefully. "That's not the way I remember it," Kris said. "You know this didn't happen this way, but do whatever you want. You're going to anyway."

"Kris, this is my book," Caitlyn shot back indignantly. "This is my perspective. This is how I see it. People can have the same experiences and perceive [them] differently."

What was not brought to the forefront by the media who fanned the feud between Kris and Caitlyn was that when Caitlyn's book was released, Kris had already taped her reaction episode two months beforehand. Of course, she would choose to air the segment to coincide with the week Caitlyn's memoir hit the shelves. And Caitlyn should have expected just such a scenario. What Kris said was nothing more than what she had always stated: that she was not aware of Caitlyn's transition plans when they married and he fathered two children with her.

It all seemed like fuel to drive Caitlyn's book up the bestseller list.

What few compliments Caitlyn did pay her ex-wife and manager were ambiguous.

"Basically, the only nice thing Caitlyn could say was that I was great socially at a party one time," Kris said.

"I really tried hard to improve the relationship," Kris stated. "I've done nothing but open up my home and heart to a person who doesn't give a shit. So I'm done."

Caitlyn blamed Kris for bringing O. J. into their lives, which put the Jenners in the center of a maelstrom of media coverage. But she glossed over her own relationship with O. J. that began years before she met Kris. The Olympic gold medalist gushed in public about O. J. and sought his advice as a mentor on how to play the endorsements game. Are we also to believe Kris forced Bruce to be a partner with O. J. and her in the fitness network they were creating at the time of Nicole's death? That is a secret that both aren't keen on sharing with the world.

Caitlyn can be sure Kris will have the last word on many of the memories when she writes her next autobiography. When the fury dies down, they will most likely be cordial, if only for the sake of their children. Kris does not like to hold onto resentments. Her divorce from Robert was a nasty, gnarly mess, but they moved past it. They were at odds during the O. J. Simpson trial, but again made peace with their opposing viewpoints. When Robert died in 2003, they were loving friends. Kris can be expected to forgive Caitlyn, but it might take her a while to get past it all.

Caitlyn clarified why she didn't involve the Kardashian kids, including Kendall and Kylie, in her original announcement about being transgender. "They were slighted on purpose because of research showing that anytime a Kardashian is on television, many in the public tend to think it is a publicity stunt to make money," Caitlyn admitted. "I love my kids and the last thing on earth I ever want to do is somehow think I am rejecting them. But because of research, I needed to build a wall and distance myself for this interview. It was too important."

None of the children came out in public support of Caitlyn's book.

Kim was the only one to talk in depth about the betrayal Kris experienced. "My heart breaks for my mom, you know, because I feel like she's been through so much," Kim shared with talkmeister Ellen DeGeneres. "She's promoting this book and she's saying all these things. I don't think it's necessary and I just feel like it's unfair. Things aren't truthful. I feel like it's taken a really long time for her to be honest with herself, so I don't expect her to be honest about my mom now. Tell your story, but just don't bash other people."

A few weeks later, Caitlyn would say Kim was her "greatest ally."

Cait's Out of the Bag

After she stood her ground on the episode of *Keeping Up With the Kardashians* and challenged Caitlyn's recollection of events, Kris refrained from catfighting with her ex over her memoir.

In a word, she was "done."

"None of it makes sense," Kris grumbled. "Everything she says is all made up. Why does everything have to be that Kris is such a bitch and an asshole."

Caitlyn did appear to step down from her strident accusations that Kris was lying when she appeared on British morning talk shows in mid-May 2017. Perhaps her righteous indignation was relaxed once her book was in the bestselling category. She is, after all, an athlete and a performer who admits to being intensely competitive.

"I was honest with her, but did I downplay it? Absolutely," Caitlyn remarked. "At that time, I had been taking hormones for four-and-a-half years. I had been in therapy. I was developing breasts and I had been having electrolysis to get rid of my beard. I was getting ready to transition and I wanted to do it before I was forty. But I got to the age of thirty-nine and I just couldn't take it any further because of society."

By week five of her book tour, Caitlyn was sounding like she was agreeing with Kris, though nobody seemed to be listening for the similarities. "When we met, I had been going through years of hell, so I decided to invest in our marriage and having children," Caitlyn confessed. "It was a distraction. I got into trouble with my kids for saying that before, so let me clear that up—they weren't a distraction, I was just distracted from who I really was."

Yet in all the conversations about the deceptions and betrayals one or both of the marriage partners endured, neither has ever been taken to task over why they didn't explore the issue on their reality show. Kris has not veered from her position that she did not know her husband desired to transition to being a woman. However, at the very least, Kris thought her man had a fetish for cross-dressing. Most of the children have talked about their awareness of the locked closets that contained women's clothes belonging to Jenner. Some of the kids have revealed they caught their dad dressed up in drag. Khloé once called her father Robert in tears after she found women's clothing, including size-thirteen shoes, in a separate closet in Kris and Bruce's bedroom.

"Kris threw that back in Bruce's face," a source divulged. "She hissed, 'How'd you like to be me? If I'm known as the slut, you're my cross-dressing husband!'"

When daughters Kendall and Kylie were still living at home, they used to steal each other's clothes, so they set up security systems in their rooms to secretly alert them if anyone entered. "One day, everyone had gone out, so I thought, 'Great, I can be myself for a few hours,'" Caitlyn recounted. "Kylie had a full-length mirror in her room, so I went in to use it. About two hours later, I could hear her screaming. I'd been caught on her security system and she saw everything. Technology got me. And that's how Kylie found out."

The children went screaming to Kris.

"Everyone brushed it off," Caitlyn maintains. "We never spoke about it again. Everyone stayed quiet."

But that was not the first or the last instance where Caitlyn was caught coming out of one of the girls' closets. She gleefully shared multiple examples of taking off with cosmetics, handbags, and clothes. The deceit and the betrayal of her family for over twenty years is mind-boggling for most people. Perhaps it's as simple as Kris—like Caitlyn's other two wives—was keeping her husband's secret because he asked her to. Kris would have done that for Kylie and Kendall's benefit.

"We did not separate for me to transition," Caitlyn stated. "I never thought I'd have the guts to do it. But then a year out, I was getting hammered by the paparazzi following me wherever I went. I didn't have the privacy to do this quietly."

Prior to Caitlyn's comments, John Ferriter expressed a similar sentiment as an impartial insider. "I don't know if Caitlyn knew she was going to be a Caitlyn at some point," he said. "So how was anyone else in his life supposed to know what he was going to do?"

Over-Extended Family

Kris Jenner is a girl gone wild when it comes to observing national holidays with her famous family.

As always, she was eager to see her mother's face light up in approval at her extravaganzas. But for Easter 2017, Kim telephoned her grandmother to invite her to come to the celebration that she and her husband Kanye West were hosting at their mansion.

"MJ, I want you to come," Kim exclaimed. "It's going to be so much fun! All of your great-grandkids will be hunting Easter eggs, just like I did with Kourtney, Khloé, and Rob. We're posting our Easter photos of us and Dad when we were younger. You remember Kourt and I are wearing adorable little dresses, holding our Easter baskets."

"I'm afraid I can't make it, dear," Mary Jo responded. "I'm sorry."

Kim's excitement turned to concern.

"Are you okay? Is everything alright, MJ?"

"Yes, I'm fine, dear."

"Well, then why aren't you coming? Mom is going to be so disappointed! Does she know? It's a family tradition for us all to go to church, and then have brunch. Tell me, what's wrong?"

"I've decided to stay here in La Jolla and spend Easter with Karen and Natalie at their house. I was at your mom's house for Christmas and I want to be with Karen for this holiday. But I love you and all my grandchildren and great-grandchildren, and of course, your mother."

By Kris's decree, her younger sister was persona non grata from her immediate family gatherings. Karen and her nineteen-year-old daughter Natalie lived in a lakefront home in San Marcos, California, a two-hour drive from Kris's mansion in Calabasas. The last time Karen was invited to a family gathering was during the summer of 2013. It was a baby shower for her niece Kim, who was expecting her second child with Kanye West. Kris barely spoke to her only sibling at the party. As Karen stepped out of the private home in Beverly Hills, she was bombarded by photographers and a barrage of shouted questions by a hungry pool of reporters.

"Sorry, I can't help you, I signed a confidentiality agreement," Karen explained.

The journalists were relentless, so Karen had a good time with them, teasing that the party favors and swag included the Rolex wristwatch on her arm. When they asked for details about the kinds of food served, Karen rattled off a menu she concocted on the spot as a jocular attempt to throw them off the scent of the actual affair.

Karen is fun, loyal to fault, and loves her sister with all her heart. But like Kris, she knows who she is, and she can't be censored. The divorced single mother is every bit as beautiful as Kris, but unlike her sophisticated and media-savvy sister—who calculates and measures every word before it rolls off her perfectly painted lips—Karen is unfiltered. As a result, she's frequently portrayed by the press as a madwoman and the black sheep of the family.

Her candor when talking about her famous sister is often taken out of context by the time it's available online for public consumption.

"I don't care what anyone thinks of me," Karen said. "I'm the character of the family. But it does hurt me that Kris doesn't want me in her life. I'm her only sister. We were so close."

Kris rarely mentions her sister in public, but whenever Karen steps over the Kardashian brand line, Kris retaliates.

"Unfortunately, my sister has been dealing with demons for years," Kris shared shortly after the baby shower incident.

Besides her dialogue with the media, Kris has other issues with Karen that mostly revolve around her refusal to live her life in the reflection of Kris's carefully constructed image. Karen's choice to live a simpler, less luxurious existence than her wealthy sister has always been a source of contention.

Karen is never seen on *Keeping Up With the Kardashians*. That's fine with Karen, who has no desire to be on the show.

Mary Jo's greatest wish, to see a lasting reconciliation between her daughters, will probably not come to pass. However, a health scare for Mary Jo a few years ago had Kris bringing her sister to the house to see her. While she's a vibrant eighty-five-year-old, Mary Jo, or "MJ" as she is called by her grandchildren, decided to close down Shannon & Co., her clothing boutique. She accepted Kris's offer to move into a condominium near her in Calabasas but keeps her residence in La Jolla. She is appearing on the show regularly.

Mary Jo insists that Karen and her daughter Natalie be welcome to visit her in LA and when she's visiting Kris's home in Palm Springs. Kris, however, continues to keep her distance from Karen. To please her mother, she paid off Karen's house and bought Natalie a luxury car.

"Mary Jo was materialistic too when she was young," recalled a family friend, who consistently tries to keep the peace. "Karen has never understood it's not personal, the way Kris treats her. I've told her over and over, 'Don't you get it? When Kris left for LA she was gone!'"

The strife on the other side of the family between Kris and her stepchildren—the four biological children of Kris's ex, Caitlyn Jenner—has been widely reported over the years. All six Jenners are in agreement regarding their beef with Kris: that she kept them away from their dad for the two decades they were married.

Many families have frayed relationships for a variety of reasons, but this reality television family's brand is rooted in family unity, which provides a glaring contradiction in the terms they have made with the public. It would seem this is another example of how much is too much to reveal.

Spiritually Speaking

The Kardashian matriarch and her six children publicly identify as born-again Christians.

"On This Good Friday may we never forget the true meaning of Easter," Khloé tweeted in April 2017. "For when He was on the Cross, I was on His mind!"

Other than to poke fun at it, the public isn't interested in keeping up with the Kardashians' and Jenners' spiritual life. On the surface, it would seem a contradiction. It's hard to reconcile that Kris is scripturally correct when she's seen on her television show hurling four-letter expletives at her daughters during alcohol-fueled catfights. She doesn't apologize for the exploitation of her children, who drop their clothes to pose nude—or, in Kim's case, star in a sex tape—as casually as they would pour themselves a glass of water.

Yet Kris is an ordained minister. As a woman of the cloth, she has officiated at wedding ceremonies for her friends. From the public wedding of *The Real Housewives of Beverly Hills'* Faye Resnick, to the private ceremony of her own pastor, Dr. Brad Johnson, Kris has been the presiding preacher.

There's no question that the past few years have been doubly difficult for Kris Jenner. She not only dealt with the aftereffects of a failed marriage, but was forced to accept that the man she was married to for over twenty years is a woman. She had not only her own feelings to consider, but those of her six children.

"She's not perfect, she knows that," Kanye West said of his mother-in-law. But, he noted, "her mistakes never come from a bad place."

* * *

In early 2016, Kris had to relive the horror and sorrow of her best girlfriend Nicole Brown Simpson's brutal murder when it played out before her eyes in the FX television series *The People v. O. J. Simpson: American Crime Story*. As always, Kris made the best of it all. She courted actress Selma Blair to portray her on the show. *Friends* actor David Schwimmer sought Kris's counsel as he prepared to step into the role of Robert Kardashian. And Kris was back in the news telling the same stories about her friendships with O. J. and Nicole. It didn't matter that Kris had nothing new to say. She was still a part of the conversation and even stole the show. By the time the ten-week series was over, Kris had managed to attract more attention for herself than Schwimmer, Blair, Cuba Gooding Jr. (O. J. Simpson), Sarah Paulson (Marcia Clark), and even John Travolta (Robert Shapiro).

For her part in achieving major publicity for herself and *Keeping Up With the Kardashians*, Kris merely said she was fortunate to be able to bring awareness to domestic abuse. Case closed.

Later that year, the nightmare of Kim's robbery and heist in a Paris hotel room brought the entire family to its knees. It's impossible to understand the horror any mother experiences as she ponders how close her child came to death. On the night of October 3, Kim was bound and gagged in her suite with a gun pointed at her. The thieves made off with over $11 million in jewels and other valuables. Kim's life was spared. "We've changed the way we live our lives and the way we take care of our kids, and my grandchildren," Kris told Ellen DeGeneres. "It's been a process."

Kris beefed up security for all of her children. But even with these extra precautions, Kendall was the victim of thieves who took off with $200,000 worth of jewelry during a party in her home in March 2017. The girls have all had their share of stalkers over the years. Kris even had a former security guard arrested and charged for breaking into her compound. It was his third attempt to "get at" the television star. Security for all of her family members has become a top priority.

The birth of Kris's sixth grandchild was a bittersweet bundle of joy. Dream Renée Kardashian is the daughter of her only son, Robert. But the baby was born out of wedlock to his former girlfriend, Blac Chyna. Kris is mindful that their shared custody might become precarious. Robert suffers from depression, obesity, and diabetes. They are not life threatening when treated, but Rob has often neglected consistent treatment of his illness.

EPILOGUE

E! president Adam Stotsky stated he doesn't see an end in sight for the Kardashians. He feels the public still has a "real insatiable interest" in them.

But television can be a precarious employer when ratings continue to slide. In April 2020, the show was moved from Sunday nights to Thursdays. Even though people were sequestered in their homes during the COVID-19 pandemic, there was still a resistance to continue keeping up with the Kardashians. E! decided to pull the show and bring it back in September. Meanwhile, the first two seasons became available on Netflix, to hopefully generate a whole new audience and remind once loyal fans what they loved about the series.

Oddsmakers should know by now to never doubt Kris's ability to pull her family back from the brink of disaster, as she has successfully done time after time.

In 2017, she re-upped her contract with E! and secured $150 million for five more seasons of *Keeping Up With the Kardashians*. It's believed she's angling for double that amount to $300 million for future seasons. "Kris knows at the end of the day she is going to get what she wants because they are the Kardashians and no one will come to take their place right now," an insider revealed.

Kardashian haters wish the end of the show on Kris, as if it will be the end of her money-making machinery. There are those who insist that her children are hostages to her exploitation, and once the show's over they will flee from her as their former patriarch, Caitlyn Jenner, did with her exit. This could not be further from the truth.

While the show has arguably been a thirteen-year-long infomercial for all of Kris's schemes and designs, she's already begun planting her feet on other television platforms, and as always, she's envisioned how she can involve her children and a few of her ten grandchildren. Kris will continue to expand her children's fashion and product lines and secure them lucrative endorsements, earning her 10 percent momager fee.

As wealthy businesswomen in their own right, each Kardashian-Jenner woman has parlayed profitable entrepreneurial ventures into lucrative Instagram cash. All totaled, the "famous for being famous" family members have over 750 million Instagram followers, which means unlimited earnings for posts. Kris reportedly receives $188,800 per post. A single Instagram post for Kim is in the neighborhood of $954,200—nearly a million dollars. All of the other kids make hundreds of thousands of dollars for every post. Nobody's left behind in this cash game.

The all-time leader of the family, though, is the youngest member, Kylie Jenner. Her beauty and clothing line profits have exceeded all records, attracting the attention of *Forbes* magazine as the world's youngest self-made billionaire. Kylie is twenty-three years old.

Since the eldest Kardashians were young adults, Kris has always sought to anchor her maternal bond with her children in business ventures. Family defines her dynasty. She needs their love, respect, and adoration. She needs them to need her. She has made them millionaires and billionaire in careers specific to their individual talents and passions.

But privately, Kris's ever-expanding family may be moving beyond her reach, causing the proverbial empty-nest syndrome. It wasn't just that Kendall and Kylie were officially moved out of Kris's mansion into their own multimillion-dollar estates. Kris has always been thrilled for her kids to buy homes of their own. Each purchase is rewarding, as it is proof she has done her job as a manager and a mother, helping them to achieve their independence and validating the entire family's incredible successes. They also all have homes within minutes of Kris, in the cozy bedroom community of Calabasas. Any new home is a great excuse to shop for housewarming gifts or furnish the entire home and redesign it from top to bottom, if she's allowed.

"I feel guilty all the time because I can't be everywhere at once," Kris admitted. "I feel like I want to be there for everybody, whoever needs me. I just worry about them all."

All of the Kardashians and Jenners continue to give hundreds of thousands of dollars to various charitable organizations. Typically, they prefer that the media not keep up with their philanthropic activities, but that policy has changed in recent years. While promoting their Smile lip kit, Kylie and Kris made a detour to Lima, Peru. There, they visited a clinic that treats babies born with cleft palates. Before Kylie and her mom left the country, they gave a million dollars to a charity that provides surgeries to repair children's mouths.

While exploring—on camera—how President Trump's administration was affecting health care for women, Kim, Khloé, and Kourtney stepped inside their local Planned Parenthood to ask how they could help raise awareness. Although they've represented social issues of importance to everyday people in the past, there appears to be a more strategic planning of shows that present the family as more socially conscious.

Naturally, there have been a few Kardashian gambles over the years that haven't paid off. For Kris, managing other people's children was a no-brainer. In 2009, she briefly oversaw the BG5 (Beach Girl5), an all-girl band that she envisioned to be the next Destiny's Child. Despite an appearance on *Keeping Up With the Kardashians*, the group quickly fizzled.

In 2011, Kim attempted a music career with the release of her single "Jam (Turn It Up)." Even Kim hated the track, citing it as the "one thing in life that I wish I didn't do."

"I don't like it when people kind of dabble into things they shouldn't be," she said. "And that I don't think I should have. Like, what gave me the right to think I could be a singer? I don't have a good voice!" She donated the proceeds from the record sales to a cancer organization.

And in 2018, the Kardashians announced that, after twelve years, they were closing all of their D-A-S-H storefronts, which had locations in Los Angeles, Miami, and New York.

"We've loved running D-A-S-H, but in the last few years we've all grown so much individually," Kim announced. "We've been busy running our own brands, as well as being moms and balancing work with our families."

Despite the occasional setback, Kris has proven there's really nothing she can't do if she sets her mind to it.

"Ambition is what drives us," Kris said, summing up her legacy. "Passion is what keeps us up at night. The impact we want to make. Now that's what guides us to our success."

Living such an intensely public life doesn't give her the option of crawling into bed and pulling the covers over her head. She's secured great wealth for herself, her children, and her grandchildren. The Kardashians' seemingly overnight stardom was actually born from years of painstaking grooming and plotting by Kris.

As she approaches sixty-five, Kris seems perfectly content with her life's quid pro quo, and wishes the rest of us wouldn't lose any sleep over her choices.

"I think there's definitely an attitude when a woman accomplishes anything, but I also think people are very jealous," she said. "So maybe they don't have anything else to do but be nasty and criticize someone else. That sounds like a simple answer, but I don't think it's much deeper than that. And there are so many millions of people who are great to us that I can't worry about some idiot in Oklahoma. You just have to have a thick skin and say, 'That poor person, I feel sorry for you.'"

Kris and her kids have perfected the legend that will be passed along to her grandchildren when they are older. One day they will learn about how the matriarch of their dynasty created an empire for them. Objective reporting does not negate the seeds of Kris's truth. Nor does it marginalize her brilliant business acumen and Herculean accomplishments that forever changed the face of television and pop culture. The very fact that *Keeping Up with the Kardashians* resonated with audiences enough to be viewed in over a million households during the debut season in 2007 is due to Kris's fearless and uncompromising showbiz savvy.

If she had left the fate of her family's show in the hands of her harshest critics, who were the industry's most esteemed judges, the Kardashians and Jenners might never have become the household names they are today. What she managed to do in less than a year to ensure her show's high ratings, and propel her family to fame and fortune, is what made *Keeping Up With the Kardashians* an overnight sensation. How she sustains this platform from which all good things come to her and her kids is the real Kris Jenner story.

People often ponder how this socialite trophy wife created a megamil-lion-dollar business. The easiest answer for many is to dismiss Kris as a greedy stage mother who exploited her children. But the truth is, Kris is "guilty" of exploiting everything in her world, not just her kids. As an astronomer studies the alignment of celestial bodies in the cosmos, Kris studies her universe of people, places, and things, and her killer instincts help her align many components at any given moment.

If radio personality Howard Stern was the "King of All Media" for the twentieth century, then Kris Jenner deserves to be crowned the "Mother of All Media" in the current century. Her tiara is timing and her scepter is patience.

Whether you love or hate Kris Jenner, all she asks is that we keep on watching her. "My fantasy is to have *Keeping Up With the Kardashians*, Season 26," Kris once said. "My job was trying to take my kids' fifteen min-utes and turn it into thirty . . . I should have had more kids."

AFTERWORD

No More Keeping Up With The Kardashians

On September 8, 2020, after twenty seasons, the Kardashians announced their show was over.

Depending on who you believe, the decision to end the show was made by the Kardashian-Jenner family, or E!'s top brass, the victim of a changing culture and the protracted death of legacy cable television.

"This show made us who we are and I will be forever in debt to everyone who played a role in shaping our careers and changing our lives forever," Kim said in bidding farewell to E!.

What wasn't announced was that the Kardashian clan could not keep up with the ratings.

When the first episode of the final season premiered in September, it brought in just 677,000 total viewers, the lowest number ever in the history of *Keeping Up With the Kardashians*. When the show stopped earlier that year in April, the final episode then was at 810,000—a near 17% drop.

Rewind to August 2015, and the fifth season premiere debuted with nearly 4.7 million total viewers, which ranked as the highest-rated season premiere of the franchise.

But members of the Kardashian family have been on our televisions since 1994, when Robert, the late patriarch of the family, represented OJ Simpson in his defense trial for allegedly murdering Nicole Brown Simpson and Ronald Goldman.

So, therefore, It's unlikely we have given up keeping up with the Kardashians or Jenner on the small screen.

ABOUT THE AUTHORS

Cathy Griffin and Dylan Howard have reigned supreme over Hollywood reporting for more than a combined five decades. As two of the world's best-known Tinseltown journalists and leading authorities on modern celebrity, the pair have written extensively for major newspapers and magazines. For fifteen years, Cathy was the West Coast editor for syndicated entertainment columnist Liz Smith, and her own bylined column, "Society Bytes," appeared for many years in *Los Angeles Confidential* and *Beverly Hills 213* magazines. She was the Los Angeles bureau chief for the Australian publication *New Idea* for almost a decade and was editor-at-large of Bauer Publications' *Life and Style* magazine.

As a man with unprecedented access to the facts and a reporter who is one of the most feared journalists in Hollywood, Dylan has brought down the careers of Mel Gibson, Charlie Sheen, Hulk Hogan, and Paula Dean via explosive scandals. Dylan's sense for news saw him rise to become undisputedly the most powerful gossip editor in the world—publishing dozens of salacious tabloid magazines each week. Described by *The New Yorker*'s Jeffrey Toobin as "a tabloid prodigy" and *AdWeek* as "the king of Hollywood scoops," Dylan brought to light the hate-fueled audiotapes of Oscar-winning actor/director Gibson blasting former girlfriend Oksana Grigorieva; the scandal-plagued death of screen darling Farrah Fawcett; the naming of the mother of Arnold Schwarzenegger's love child; the demise of star-on-the-rise politician Anthony Weiner; the Tiger Woods sex scandal; and broke open the A-list high-stakes poker scam that was later made into the Oscar-nominated film *Molly's Game*. Most recently, Dylan made a name for himself with a stunning expose into Charlie Sheen that revealed Hollywood's most unapologetic hedonist was HIV-positive. In 2011, Howard was named Entertainment Journalist of the Year at the National Entertainment Journalism Awards, where the judges labeled him the "go-to guy for authoritative showbiz news and analysis on cable and over-the-air television."

Cathy lives in Los Angeles, while Dylan resides in Manhattan. Both traveled extensively in the United States in their research for this biography.